MW00736298

A Systematic Approach
to Neuroscience

A Systematic Approach to Neuroscience

Formerly
A Functional Approach to Neuroanatomy

Third Edition

E. Lawrence House, Ph.D.
Professor Emeritus of Anatomy
Formerly, College of Medicine and Dentistry of New Jersey

Ben Pansky, M.D., Ph.D.
Professor of Anatomy
Medical College of Ohio

Allan Siegel, Ph.D.
Professor of Neuroscience
College of Medicine and Dentistry of New Jersey

McGraw-Hill Book Company

New York St. Louis San Francisco Auckland Bogotá Düsseldorf
Johannesburg London Madrid Mexico Montreal New Delhi Panama
Paris São Paulo Singapore Sydney Tokyo Toronto

NOTICE

Medicine is an ever-changing science. As new research and clinical experience broaden our knowledge, changes in treatment and drug therapy are required. The editors and the publisher of the work have made every effort to ensure that the drug dosage schedules herein are accurate and in accord with the standards accepted at the time of publication. Readers are advised, however, to check the product information sheet included in the package of each drug they plan to administer to be certain that changes have not been made in the recommended dose or in the contraindications for administration. This recommendation is of particular importance in regard to new or infrequently used drugs.

A SYSTEMATIC APPROACH TO NEUROSCIENCE

Copyright © 1979 by McGraw-Hill, Inc. All rights reserved. Formerly published under the title of A FUNCTIONAL APPROACH TO NEUROANATOMY, copyright © 1967, 1960 by McGraw-Hill, Inc. All rights reserved. Printed in the United States of America. No part of this publication may be reproduced, stored in a retrieval system, or transmitted, in any form or by any means, electronic, mechanical, photocopying, recording, or otherwise, without prior written permission of the publisher.

1 2 3 4 6 7 8 9 0 D O D O 7 8 3 2 1 0 9 8

This book was set in Times Roman by Black Dot, Inc. (ECU).
The editors were Alice Macnow and Henry C. De Leo;
the cover was designed by Charles A. Carson;
the production supervisor was Robert C. Pederson.
The drawings were done by Tek/Nek Inc.
R. R. Donnelley & Sons Company was printer and binder.

Library of Congress Cataloging in Publication Data

House, Earl Lawrence.

    A systematic approach to neuroscience-formerly
    A functional approach to neuroanatomy

    Bibliography: p.
    Includes index.
    1. Neuroanatomy. I. Pansky, Ben, joint
author. II. Siegel, Allan, joint author.
III. Title. [DNLM: 1. Nervous system—Anatomy
and histology. 2. Nervous system—Physiology.
WL101.3 H842]
QM451.H68   1978   611'.8   78-2477
ISBN 0-07-030468-8

To Grace, Julie, and Carla
our devoted wives,
whose patience, understanding, and encouragement
made this book possible

Contents

2

THE AFFERENT OR SENSORY SYSTEMS

3

THE EFFERENT OR MOTOR SYSTEMS WITH A SUMMARY OF THE FUNCTIONAL COMPONENTS OF PERIPHERAL NERVES

4

THE INTEGRATING AND COORDINATING MECHANISMS

5
ATLAS

6
CLINICAL CORRELATIONS

7
APPENDIXES

Preface

This book was written primarily with the medical student in mind; it is designed to meet the needs of basic courses in neuroscience at a time when time itself has become a great factor in medical education. So overwhelming is the material confronting the medical student that a clear, concise textbook, systematically organized, is almost a necessity if he or she is to achieve any semblance of comprehension and understanding in the limited time afforded each subject.

Our approach is functional, to be sure, but above all it is systematic, strictly adhering to the systems once the basic considerations of development, physiology, and anatomy have been covered. The early chapters dealing with the fundamentals of the nervous system are comprehensive and thoroughly illustrated, since we have always felt that a solid, basic comprehension is a prerequisite for an understanding of the intricacies of both the normal and the abnormal functions of the nervous system. To us, a strong foundation and systematic method seem to be the most logical, the most interesting, and at the same time, the most utilitarian approach to a subject whose name itself somehow seems to imply complexity.

It might be argued that too great stress is placed on reflex activity and the descriptions of the reflex pathways in each of the system chapters. However, one must admit that though the conscious pathways are those most likely to be described in many courses or discussions of human neuroanatomy, it is the reflex mechanisms that are the foundation upon which the more complex nervous system is built.

To further our aim, illustrations are presented not only to clarify but to amplify the text. They have been simplified into concise black and white line drawings or schematics, all with a minimum of labeling. In many instances numerous small illustrations are used in lieu of one or two large overwhelming drawings in order to eliminate some of the involved complications which often defeat the purpose of illustrations. It is our hope that students will be able to direct their efforts toward learning from the illustrations rather than being forced to decipher them.

In common with other teachers in all fields, it has been our observation that repetition is an essential of the learning process. Thus, every chapter is followed by a summary of all parts and connections which should enable, perhaps even encourage, the student to work frequent reviews into an already overcrowded schedule.

Considerable emphasis is placed on clinical conderations. This, we feel, is important, since it strengthens motivation not only by demonstrating a reason for learning the material as it is presented, but it also assuages the appetite of the neophyte doctor for all things directly pertaining to the practice of medicine. This is a spark lodged in the hearts of all beginners which should be fanned at the outset of their young careers.

It should be obvious that a book of this kind could not be written without the published findings of many individuals and teams of investigators from all over the world. However, the list of contributors is now becoming so vast that to be completely impartial a distractingly large, overwhelming list of references would be a necessity. We have, therefore, omitted from the text proper all specific bibliographic references, not because the authors have failed to appreciate the importance of the contributors in this field, but for the sake of smoother reading. Thus, at the risk of offending countless individuals whose works are worthy of note, we thought it preferable to place a modest, general bibliography at the end of the book.

We are indebted to McGraw-Hill Book Company, Williams and Wilkins Company, W. B. Saunders Company, Oxford University Press, J. B. Lippincott Company, Cambridge University Press, C. V. Mosby Company, and Little, Brown Company for permission to use or modify illustrations from several of their publications, which, in each case, have been duly credited.

We are grateful to J. Harold Walton, M.D., editor of *Ciba Clinical Symposium*, for permission to modify figures 21-2 and 21-10 through 21-18, inclusive, based upon original paintings of Dr. Frank Netter from the article, "The Hypothalamus," *Ciba Clinical Symposia*, Vol. 8, No. 4, by W. R. Ingram, Ph.D.: Mr. Joseph Kerrigan, General Publicity and Projects Supervisor of the Schering Corporation, for permission to use or modify material from certain of their publications; Drs. Alfred Ebel, Nicholas Panin, Milton Holtzman, Jose

Cibeira, and Andor Weiss for the use of their outline on Common Vascular Brain Syndromes; and to Dr. S. L. Palay of the Harvard Medical School who provided us with excellent electron micrographs.

The authors wish to express their appreciation to: the Research Committee of the New York Medical College for their original support for the project; to our students, especially Drs. Gustave Mork, Charles Burton, and Harvey Cooper for making suggestions concerning the manuscript; to the Research Committee of the College of Medicine and Dentistry of New Jersey for their financial assistance in preparing this third edition; and to Geraldine B. House for her efforts in preparing the manuscript. A word of special thanks must go to Dr. Henry Edinger for his outstanding contribution as coauthor of Chapter 5. Finally, we must thank Dr. Iris F. Nostrand of Kings County Hospital and Dr. William K. Jordan of the University of Arkansas for their careful review of the clinical aspects, especially the material on clinical-neurological testing techniques.

We also deeply appreciate the guidance, advice, and generosity of the publisher McGraw-Hill Book Company, without which the book could not have been prepared.

E. Lawrence House
Ben Pansky
Allan Siegel

A Systematic Approach
to Neuroscience

Anatomy of the Brain

TELENCEPHALON

General Topography of the Cerebral Hemispheres

The cerebral hemisphere consists of three parts: the pallium, or cortex, the rhinencephalon, and the basal nuclei. Each hemisphere has three poles: frontal, occipital, and temporal; four lobes: frontal, occipital, parietal, and temporal; and three surfaces: dorsolateral, medial, and basal. To the lobes should be added the central lobe, or insula (island of Reil, Fig. 1-1), which lies at the bottom of the lateral fissure, obscured by overlying parts of the frontal and temporal lobes.

Pallium, or Cortex

Dorsolateral Surface (Figs. 1-2, 1-3) Each hemisphere is divided into lobes by distinct fissures, or sulci, and by arbitrary lines. The central sulcus, the lateral fissure, the preoccipital notch, and the parietooccipital fissure serve as landmarks by which the frontal, parietal, occipital, and temporal lobes are set apart.

Frontal Lobe This is bounded posteriorly by the central sulcus (fissure of Rolando) and inferiorly by the lateral cerebral fissure (fissure of Sylvius). The lateral cerebral fissure consists of two portions: a short stem which divides into two anterior rami—the anterior horizontal and the anterior ascending—and a long posterior ramus. The central sulcus is situated about the middle of the lateral surface of the hemisphere. Running parallel to the central sulcus is the precentral, usually divided into an upper and lower part. From the precentral sulcus, the superior and inferior frontal sulci run rostrally. These sulci divide

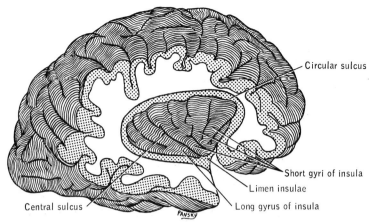

Figure 1-1 Lateral view of the human cerebral hemisphere with the operculum removed to expose the insula, or central lobe (island of Reil).

the frontal lobe into the following gyri: precentral and superior, middle, and inferior frontal, the latter being further subdivided into the orbital, triangular, and opercular (Broca's area) portions.

Temporal Lobe The temporal lobe is separated superiorly from the frontal by the lateral cerebral fissure and from the parietal lobe by an arbitrary line drawn between the angle of the posterior ramus of the lateral fissure and

the occipital pole; posteriorly, it is separated from the occipital lobe by a line connecting the superior end of the parietooccipital fissure and the preoccipital notch. The superior temporal sulcus begins near the temporal pole and runs parallel to the lateral fissure. Ventral to it is a less distinct and disconnected sulcus, the middle temporal, most of which lies on the basal surface of the hemisphere. These sulci limit the superior and middle temporal gyri.

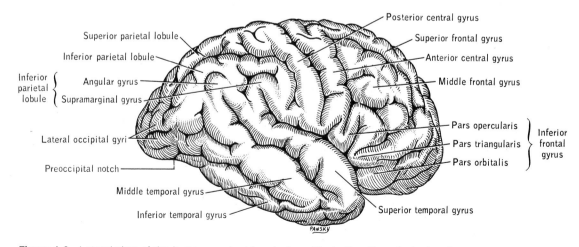

Figure 1-2 Lateral view of the human cerebral hemisphere illustrating the principal gyri.

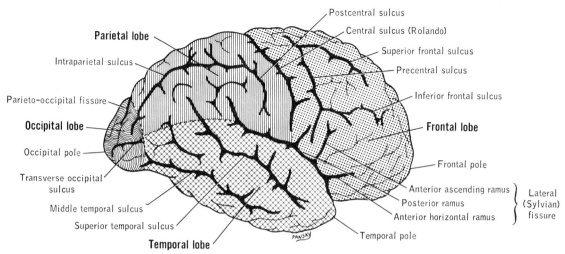

Figure 1-3 Lateral view of the human cerebral hemisphere illustrating the principal sulci and lobes.

On the dorsal surface of the superior temporal gyrus, lying in the lateral fissure, are the transverse temporal gyri.

Parietal Lobe This lobe lies posterior to the central sulcus which separates it from the frontal lobe. It is separated inferiorly from the temporal lobe by the lateral fissure and a line extending from the angle of the posterior ramus of the lateral fissure to the occipital pole. Parallel to the central sulcus is the postcentral sulcus, which may consist of two disconnected parts—a superior and an inferior. The intraparietal sulcus, extending dorsocaudally from the postcentral, runs in a course roughly paralleling the dorsal border of the hemisphere but some distance ventral to it. Between the central and postcentral sulci lies the postcentral gyrus. The cortical area dorsal to the intraparietal sulcus is referred to as the superior parietal lobule; that portion ventral to it is the inferior parietal lobule.

Related to extensions of the lateral cerebral fissure and the superior temporal sulcus, but lying in the inferior parietal lobule, are the supramarginal and angular gyri, respectively.

Occipital Lobe Only a small portion of this lobe is seen from the lateral side. It is separated anteriorly from the parietal and temporal lobes by a line extending from the superior end of the parietooccipital fissure to the preoccipital notch.

The Insula (Island of Reil) (Fig. 1-1) After removing the overhanging operculum and parts of the frontal, parietal, and temporal lobes, the insula is seen to be somewhat conical in shape, surrounded at its base by the circular sulcus. The apex of the cone is directed rostrocaudally. Extending medially from the apex to the basal surface of the hemisphere is the limen insulae. On its lateral aspect a fairly prominent sulcus, the central sulcus of the insula, can be seen. Caudal to the central sulcus is the long gyrus; rostral to it are several "short gyri" of the insula.

Medial Surface (Figs. 1-4 through 1-6) Since the medial surface merges gradually with the basal, it is almost impossible to describe either without overlap. Further, portions of the lobes described with the dorsolateral surface are also represented here.

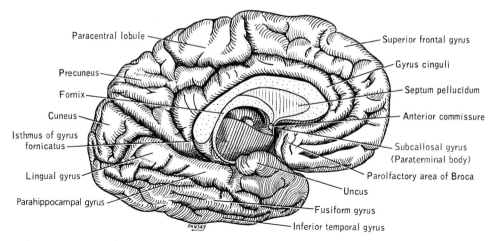

Figure 1-4 Human cerebral hemisphere as seen from the medial side, showing the principal gyri.

Among the most obvious features seen on the medial aspect of the brain is the corpus callosum, which consists of the rostrum, genu, body, and splenium. The corpus callosum is separated from the adjoining cortex by the sulcus of the corpus callosum, which begins just ventral to the rostrum and curves dorsally and posteriorly around the corpus, becoming confluent with the hippocampal fissure along the basomedial surface. The cortex which parallels the corpus callosum and its sulcus is the gyrus cinguli. Along the outer periphery of this gyrus is the sulcus cinguli (callosomarginal fissure). This begins a short distance ventral to the rostrum of the corpus callosum and runs dorsally around the gyrus cinguli, terminating in the formation of two branches. The longer branch appears to be a posterior con-

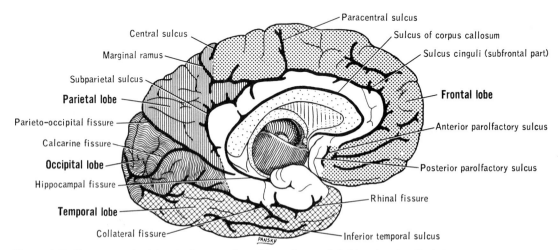

Figure 1-5 Human cerebral hemisphere as viewed from the medial side, showing the lobes together with the principal sulci.

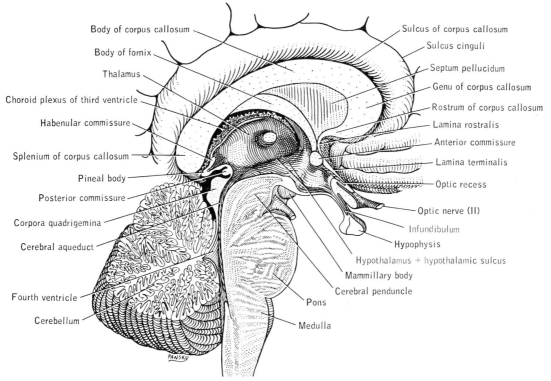

Body of corpus callosum
Body of fornix
Thalamus
Choroid plexus of third ventricle
Habenular commissure
Splenium of corpus callosum
Pineal body
Posterior commissure
Corpora quadrigemina
Cerebral aqueduct
Fourth ventricle
Cerebellum
PANSKY

Sulcus of corpus callosum
Sulcus cinguli
Septum pellucidum
Genu of corpus callosum
Rostrum of corpus callosum
Lamina rostralis
Anterior commissure
Lamina terminalis
Optic recess
Optic nerve (II)
Infundibulum
Hypophysis
Hypothalamus + hypothalamic sulcus
Mammillary body
Cerebral penduncle
Pons
Medulla

Figure 1-6 Median sagittal section through the human brainstem.

tinuation of the sulcus, ending just behind the splenium of the corpus callosum. This branch is the subparietal sulcus. The shorter branch, known as the marginal ramus, curves superiorly to reach the border of the hemisphere. A very short continuation of the central sulcus can be traced from the dorsolateral surface to the medial surface. A short ascending branch from the sulcus cinguli, lying anterior to the central sulcus, extends almost to the superior border of the hemisphere. This is the paracentral sulcus. An arbitrary line drawn from the central sulcus to the sulcus cinguli serves as a boundary line between the frontal and parietal lobes on the medial surface.

There are several other important fissures. The calcarine fissure consists of two parts. The rostral, deeper portion begins behind the splenium of the corpus callosum and extends to the parietooccipital fissure. The second part continues from this point posteriorly to the dorsal surface of the hemisphere just above the occipital pole. The parietooccipital fissure angles dorsally from the high point of the arch of the calcarine fissure to the dorsal border of the hemisphere. The hippocampal fissure is a continuation of the sulcus of the corpus callosum. It curves around inferior to the splenium of the corpus callosum and continues anteriorly toward, but not to, the temporal pole. The collateral fissure begins near the occipital pole and runs rostrally, parallel to the inferior temporal sulcus and separated from the latter by the fusiform gyrus. Occasionally, in its rostral course, the collateral fissure passes without interruption into the rhinal fissure. An arbitrary line drawn downward from the rostral end of the calcarine fissure to the collateral fissure serves as the anterior boundary of the occipital lobe.

Frontal Lobe The chief representation of this lobe on the medial surface is the superior frontal gyrus which continues over the border of the hemisphere from the dorsolateral surface. Its inferior border is the cingular sulcus. Its posterior boundary is a line drawn from the central sulcus to the cingular sulcus.

Parietal Lobe This is represented by a continuation, over the dorsal border of the hemisphere, of the superior parietal lobule. It is limited inferiorly by the subparietal sulcus. That portion of the parietal lobe lying between the marginal ramus of the sulcus cinguli and the parietooccipital fissure is the precuneus.

Paracentral Lobule This is the term applied to the cortex surrounding the dorsomedial end of the central sulcus, bounded rostrally by the paracentral sulcus and posteriorly by the marginal ramus of the sulcus cinguli.

Occipital Lobe This consists of two portions, the cuneus and a part of the lingual gyrus. The former is a wedge-shaped area lying between the parietooccipital fissure superiorly and the calcarine fissure inferiorly. That part of the lingual gyrus which contributes to the occipital lobe lies posterior to an arbitrary line drawn vertically downward from the inferior end of the subparietal sulcus to the collateral fissure. It may be seen bulging superiorly within the arch of the posterior part of the calcarine fissure.

Basal Surface (Figs. 1-7, 1-8) This consists of the territory lying in a horizontal plane rostral to the temporal poles.

A distinct groove that begins near the frontal pole, lateral to the longitudinal fissure and diverging slightly from the midline in its posterior course, is the olfactory sulcus, occupied by the olfactory bulb and tract. Between this sulcus and the longitudinal fissure is the gyrus rectus. Lateral to the olfactory sulcus is a variable number of irregular orbital sulci and gyri.

Rhinencephalon

This is the most ancient portion of the hemisphere and has no representation on the dorsolateral surface, being predominantly situated on the basal and medial surfaces.

The olfactory bulb and tract occupy the olfactory sulcus on the basal surface of the frontal lobe. The olfactory tract runs posteriorly into the olfactory trigone. From the trigone, diverging toward the medial side of the hemisphere, is the *medial olfactory stria*. Also from the trigone, the *lateral olfactory striae* course laterally and posteriorly, becoming continuous with the hippocampal gyrus. The anterior part of the hippocampal gyrus plus the lateral olfactory stria are often referred to collectively as the pyriform lobe (area). Behind the olfactory trigone, bounded posteriorly by the optic tract, is the *anterior perforated substance*. The posterior part of the anterior perforated substance is known as the *diagonal gyrus* (diagonal band of Broca), which can be traced to the medial side of the hemispheres just ventral to the rostrum of the corpus callosum. This area is called the *paraterminal body* (subcallosal gyrus). In front of the paraterminal body, a very narrow band, the *hippocampal rudiment*, extends from the rostrum of the corpus callosum toward the medial olfactory stria and then continues completely around the outer surface of the corpus callosum. In some brains a swelling occurs in the anterior perforated substance. This is the *olfactory tubercle* (tuberculum olfactorum).

The position of the gyrus cinguli has already been noted. Posteriorly, this gyrus is continuous with a narrow cortical band which runs ventral to the splenium of the corpus callosum. This band is the *isthmus* (Fig. 1-4). It

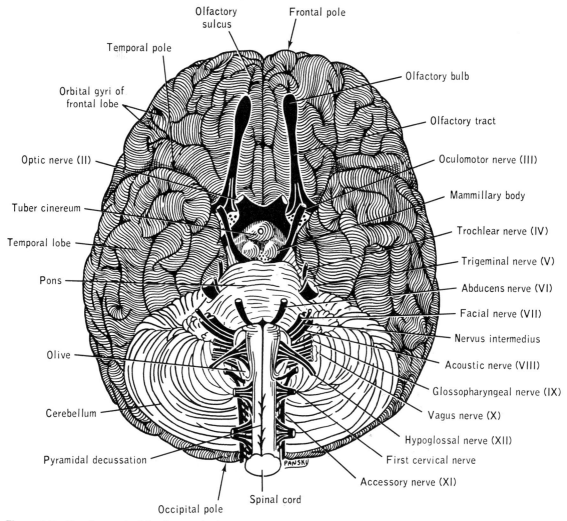

Figure 1-7 Basal aspect of the human brain.

extends rostrally to merge with the parahippocampal gyrus, which is a thick convolution lying between the hippocampal fissure dorsally and the collateral and rhinal fissures ventrally. The parahippocampal gyrus bends sharply around the rostral end of the hippocampal fissure to form the *uncus* (Fig. 1-4). In the older terminology, the gyrus cinguli, isthmus, parahippocampal gyrus, and uncus are grouped together as the *gyrus fornicatus*, or *limbic lobe* (Fig. 1-4). This designation was based upon the belief that the limbic lobe belongs exclusively to the rhinencephalon. More recent evidence indicates that it might be preferable to consider the parahippocampal gyrus and uncus as a part of the temporal lobe rather than part of the rhinencephalon. Similarly, that part of the gyrus cinguli which lies

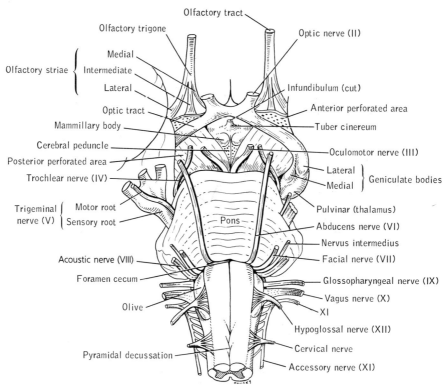

Figure 1-8 Central portion of the basal aspect of the human brainstem, enlarged.

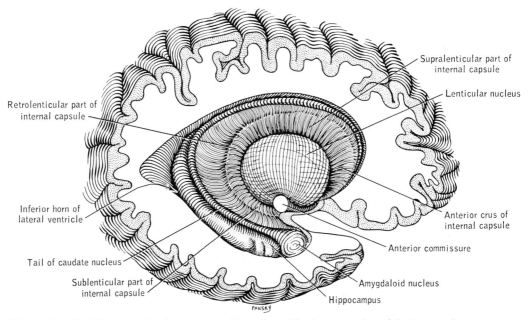

Figure 1-9 All of the insula has been removed, together with a larger portion of the temporal lobe, exposing the lenticular nucleus and inferior horn of the lateral ventricle.

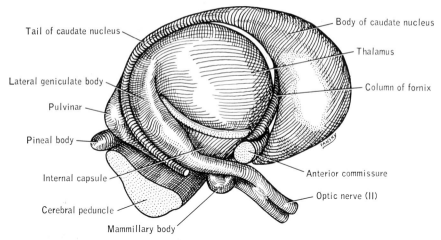

Figure 1-10 Cortical parts, as well as internal capsule and lenticular nucleus, have been removed.

rostral to the line of division between the frontal and parietal lobes may be said to belong to the frontal lobe, while that portion posterior to it, including the isthmus, belongs to the parietal lobe.

Basal Ganglia (Figs. 1-9 through 1-14)

Four nuclear masses comprise the basal ganglia (nuclei): the caudate, lenticular (lentiform), amygdaloid, and claustrum. When the

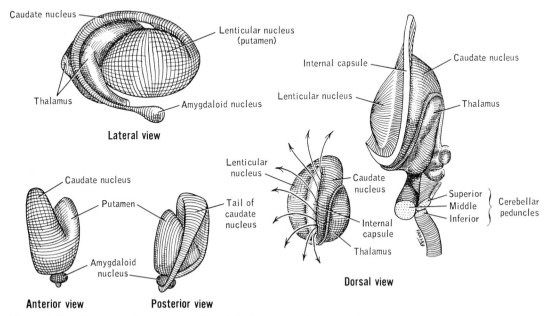

Figure 1-11 Diagrammatic representation of the basal ganglia as seen from various aspects. (*Adapted from Krieg, Functional Neuroanatomy, 2d ed., McGraw-Hill Book Company, New York, 1953.*)

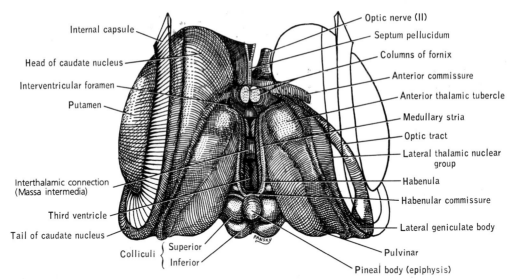

Figure 1-12   Basal ganglia, diencephalon, and a portion of the mesencephalon as seen from the dorsal side.

internal capsule and the adjacent caudate and lenticular nuclei are considered together, the term *corpus striatum* is applied.

Caudate Nucleus   (Figs. 1-9 through 1-14) The pear-shaped head of this nucleus is large, and its rostral extremity lies just dorsal to the anterior perforated substance. As the nucleus curves posteriorly, it tapers down into a slender tail, which extends almost to the temporal pole, ending at the amygdaloid nucleus. Anteriorly, rostral to the internal capsule, the head of the caudate is fused with the lenticular nucleus.

Lenticular Nucleus   (Figs. 1-9, 1-11 through 1-14)   This gray mass is buried deeply in the white core of the hemisphere. It is shaped somewhat like a biconvex lens, the convexity of which is directed laterally. Where it is fused with the caudate nucleus, it lies just above the anterior perforated substance. The ventral surface is closely related to the roof of the inferior horn of the lateral ventricle. The

lateral surface underlies the insula, from which it is separated by the external capsule and claustrum. The medial surface lies against the internal capsule. This nucleus appears to be subdivided by two thin fibrous layers. The most lateral, the *external medullary lamina,* divides the nucleus into a lateral, cell-rich zone known as the *putamen.* Medial to this lamina lies the *globus pallidus.* The latter is further divided into an internal and external zone by the *internal medullary lamina.*

Claustrum   This is a thin gray mass embedded in the white substance of the hemisphere between the lateral side of the lenticular nucleus and the insula. It is separated from the lenticular nucleus by a thin white lamina of nerve fibers, the external capsule. (Fig. 1-14)

Amygdaloid   Nucleus   (Figs.   1-9,   1-11) This is a small, round aggregate of nuclear masses lying far forward in the temporal lobe.

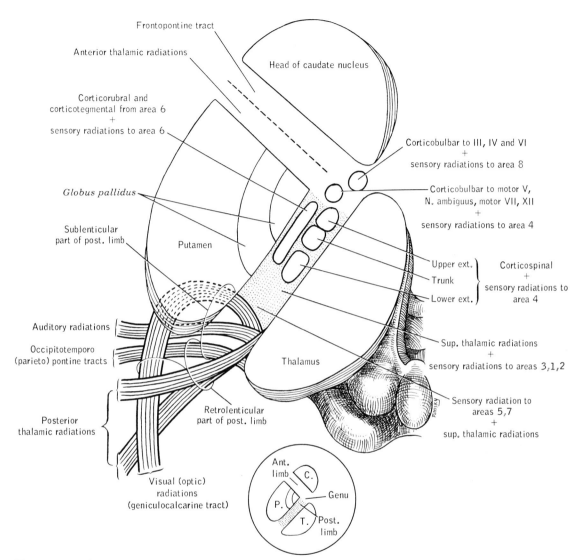

Figure 1-13 Diagrammatic representation of the left internal capsule showing its relations and major components.

It merges with the cerebral cortex lateral to the anterior perforated substance.

Medullary Substance of the Cerebral Hemispheres

The medullary substance underlies the cortex. It varies greatly in thickness in different areas and consists of myelinated fibers. Generally, these fibers are classified as *projection, association,* and *commissural.*

Projection Fibers

These are of two types: afferent (corticipetal) or efferent (corticofugal), depending upon the

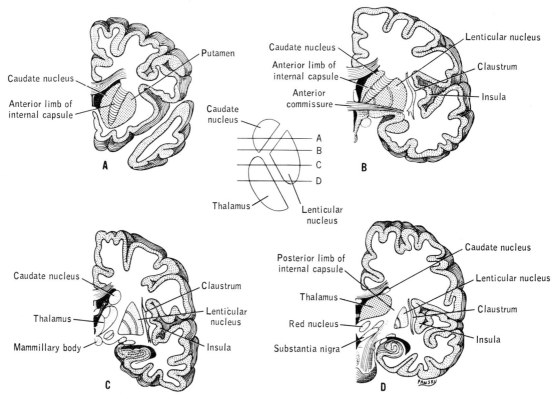

Figure 1-14 Series of vertical (coronal) sections through several levels of the basal ganglia and internal capsule, arranged in a rostral-caudal sequence.

direction of the impulse toward or away from the cortex, respectively. Many of the projection fibers are grouped together in named bundles: the internal capsule and the fornix.

Internal Capsule (Figs. 1-9 through 1-15) This is the great fiber mass containing both afferent and efferent fibers of the neopallium. In a horizontal section, it has the form of an obtuse angle with its apex pointing medially. The fact that it more nearly resembles a fan can be appreciated only in a gross dissection. That portion of the capsule which lies between the head of the caudate and the rostral end of the lenticular nucleus is called the *anterior*

limb. The fibers here tend to be directed rostrally and dorsally. The region of the angle is known as the *genu*. The remainder is called the *posterior limb*. The latter part is applied to the medial surface of the lenticular nucleus, wrapping around its posterior aspect as well as its posteroventral surface. The posterior limb consists of three parts: the *lenticulothalamic*, between the thalamus and the lenticular nucleus, in which the fibers are directed approximately vertically; the *retrolenticular*, behind the lenticular nucleus, in which the fibers run posteriorly; and the *sublenticular*, beneath the posterior half of the lenticular nucleus, in which the fibers are directed laterally. The efferent fibers of the capsule converge inferi-

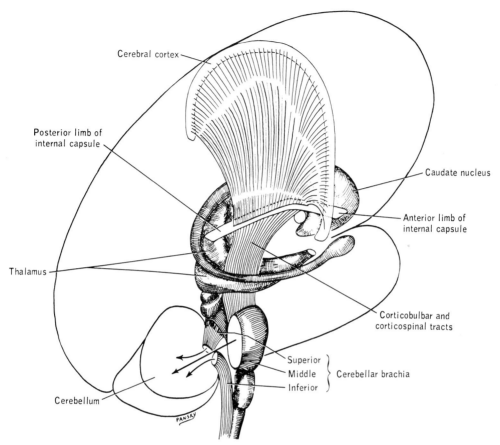

Figure 1-15 Diagrammatic illustration of a portion of the internal capsule and the brachia of the cerebellum.

orly into the *cerebral peduncles* of the mesencephalon. Dorsal to the lenticular nucleus the fibers of the capsule spread out to form the *corona radiata.*

Fornix (Fig. 1-16) These are projection fibers of the archipallium. They originate in the hippocampus, which they leave via the *fimbria.* The fibers curving upward from each fimbria form the *crus* of the fornix. The crura pass medially and dorsally, approaching each other beneath the splenium of the corpus callosum. Here the fibers run rostrally, direct-

ly beneath the corpus callosum, as the *bodies of the fornix.* Anteriorly, the fibers arch to form the *columns of the fornix,* which terminate in the mammillary bodies and other parts of the hypothalamus.

Association Fibers (Figs. 1-17, 1-18)

These are also divided into two groups. The first are short, running in the deeper parts of the cortex, interconnecting closely adjoining areas (intracortical), or they may run just below the cortex (subcortical), uniting neighboring gyri. Many of the subcortical fibers

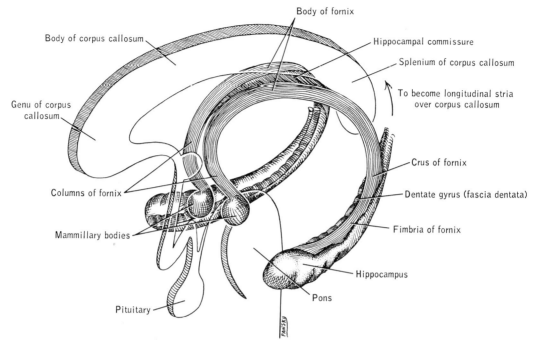

Figure 1-16 Diagrammatic representation of a reconstruction of the fornix.

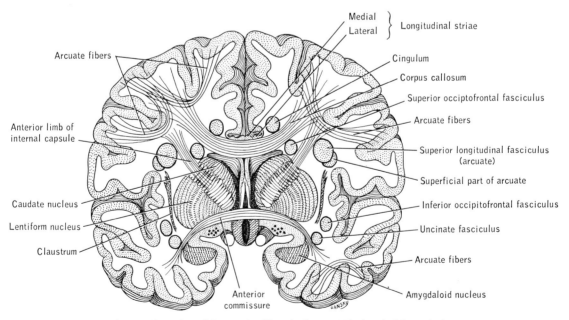

Figure 1-17 Vertical (coronal) section of the cerebral hemispheres at the level of the anterior commissure, showing the locations of the association bundles.

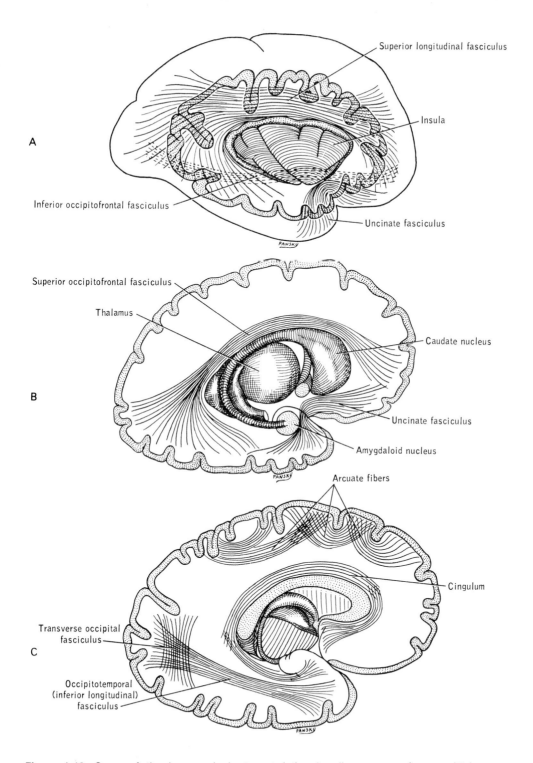

Figure 1-18 Some of the long and short association bundles as seen from sagittal dissections through the cerebral hemisphere.

Labels in figure:

A
- Superior longitudinal fasciculus
- Insula
- Inferior occipitofrontal fasciculus
- Uncinate fasciculus

B
- Superior occipitofrontal fasciculus
- Thalamus
- Caudate nucleus
- Uncinate fasciculus
- Amygdaloid nucleus

C
- Arcuate fibers
- Cingulum
- Transverse occipital fasciculus
- Occipitotemporal (inferior longitudinal) fasciculus

appear U-shaped and are designated as arcuate. The second type are long, running deep in the medullary centers and uniting widely separated cortical regions in the same hemisphere. Most of the convolutions contain numerous intracortical and subcortical fibers which are not specifically named. There are, however, some fairly distinct sets belonging to the long type.

Cingulum (Figs. 1-17, 1-18) These fibers lie in the white substance of the gyrus cinguli, close to the corpus callosum. They begin in the parolfactory area of the cortex, caudal to the rostrum of the corpus callosum. They swing dorsally, following the gyrus until they reach the level of the splenium, at which point they curve caudally, then rostrally, into the hippocampus and uncus.

This bundle helps interconnect parts of the frontal, parietal, and temporal lobes.

Superior Longitudinal Fasciculus (Figs. 1-17, 1-18) This begins in the frontal lobe and passes through the frontal and parietal opercula, with some fibers terminating posteriorly in the occipital lobe and others ventrally in the temporal lobe.

Superior Occipitofrontal Fasciculus (Figs. 1-17, 1-18) This bundle passes posteriorly from the frontal lobe along the dorsal border of the caudate nucleus and beneath the corpus callosum. In many places, it parallels the

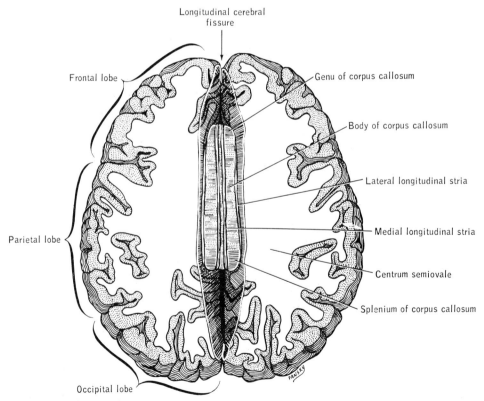

Figure 1-19 Horizontal section of the human telencephalon taken just above the dorsal surface of the corpus callosum.

superior longitudinal fasciculus, but it is separated from the latter by the corona radiata.

Inferior Occipitofrontal Fasciculus (Figs. 1-17, 1-18) These fibers extend from frontal to occipital lobes but are in a more ventral plane than the superior occipitofrontal fasciculus. They run along the ventrolateral edge of the lenticular nucleus. In the frontal lobe, they adjoin the uncinate fasciculus.

Uncinate Fasciculus (Figs. 1-17, 1-18) These fibers begin in the orbital gyri of the frontal lobe, arch over the lateral fissure, and end in the rostral part of the temporal lobe.

Inferior Longitudinal Fasciculus (Figs. 1-17, 1-18) These fibers extend from the temporal pole, pass through the length of the temporal lobe, and terminate in the occipital lobe.

Commissural Fibers (Figs. 1-6, 1-16, 1-17)

These are fibers from an area of the cortex of one hemisphere which cross the midline to areas of the opposite hemisphere. The hemispheres are joined by three such fiber groups: the corpus callosum and the anterior and hippocampal commissures.

Corpus Callosum (Figs. 1-6, 1-19, 1-20) This massive accumulation of fibers is one of the most obvious structures on the medial surface of the hemisphere. Most of the fibers connect corresponding areas of cortex of the neopallial portions of the two hemispheres. Fibers of the corpus callosum intermingle with those of the corona radiata of the internal capsule as the latter fan out toward the cortex. The fibers which pass by way of the genu of the corpus callosum to the frontal lobes form

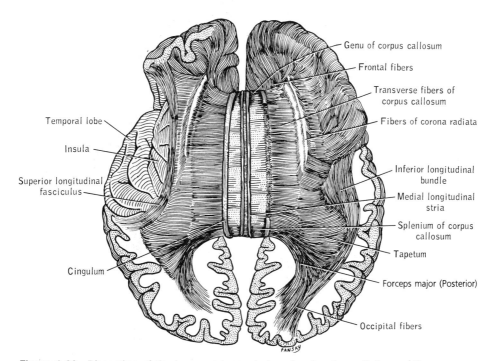

Figure 1-20 Dissection of the human telencephalon showing the radiations of the corpus callosum as seen from the dorsal aspect.

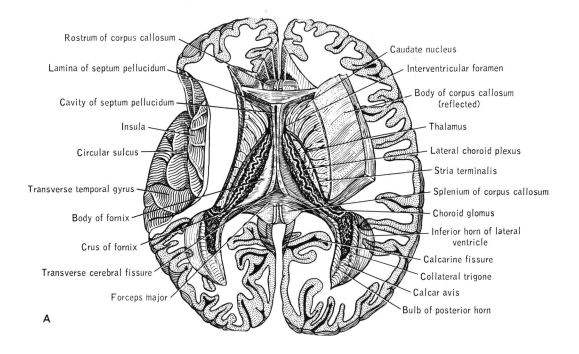

Rostrum of corpus callosum

Lamina of septum pellucidum

Cavity of septum pellucidum

Insula

Circular sulcus

Transverse temporal gyrus

Body of fornix

Crus of fornix

Transverse cerebral fissure

Forceps major

Caudate nucleus

Interventricular foramen

Body of corpus callosum (reflected)

Thalamus

Lateral choroid plexus

Stria terminalis

Splenium of corpus callosum

Choroid glomus

Inferior horn of lateral ventricle

Calcarine fissure

Collateral trigone

Calcar avis

Bulb of posterior horn

A

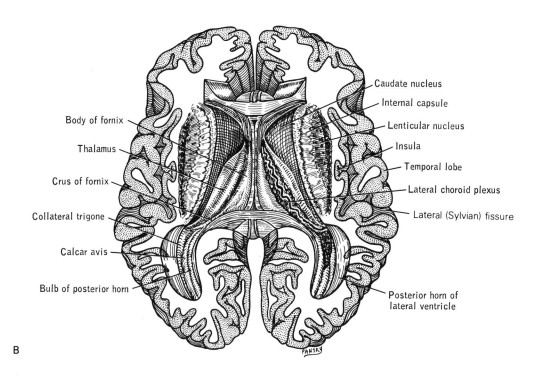

Body of fornix

Thalamus

Crus of fornix

Collateral trigone

Calcar avis

Bulb of posterior horn

Caudate nucleus

Internal capsule

Lenticular nucleus

Insula

Temporal lobe

Lateral choroid plexus

Lateral (Sylvian) fissure

Posterior horn of lateral ventricle

B

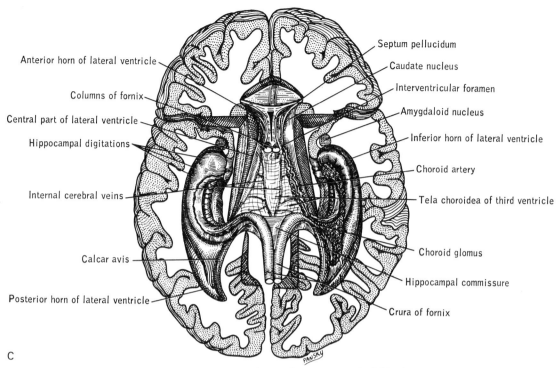

Anterior horn of lateral ventricle

Columns of fornix

Central part of lateral ventricle

Hippocampal digitations

Internal cerebral veins

Calcar avis

Posterior horn of lateral ventricle

Septum pellucidum

Caudate nucleus

Interventricular foramen

Amygdaloid nucleus

Inferior horn of lateral ventricle

Choroid artery

Tela choroidea of third ventricle

Choroid glomus

Hippocampal commissure

Crura of fornix

C

Figure 1-21 Dissections of the telencephalon viewed from above. *A.* With the corpus callosum reflected on the right and removed on the left to show the lateral ventricles. *B.* With the temporal lobe partially removed to show the relation of the basal ganglia to the ventricle. *C.* With the fornix reflected to expose the choroid tela of the third ventricle and the hippocampal commissure.

the so-called forceps anterior (forceps minor) while those traversing the splenium of the corpus callosum to the occipital lobes form the forceps posterior (forceps major). The tapetum of the corpus callosum is composed of fibers passing through the body of that structure.

Anterior Commissure This is a bundle of fibers which crosses through the lamina terminalis. The majority of fibers interconnect portions of the rhinencephalon (archipallium). The anterior fibers of the commissure unite the olfactory tubercle, anterior olfactory nucleus, and olfactory bulb. The posterior fibers terminate in the middle temporal gyrus. (Fig. 1-17)

Hippocampal Commissure (Fig. 1-16) These fibers, which unite the two hippocampi, cross through the bodies of the fornices, where the fornices diverge from the midline.

Septum Pellucidum (Figs. 1-6, 1-21)

This is a thin-walled septum which fills the interval between the corpus callosum and the columns of the fornix and separates the two lateral ventricles. It consists of two vertically placed sheets, separated by a narrow cleft, the cavity of the septum.

Cavity (Ventricle) of the Telencephalon (Figs. 1-21 through 1-27)

Within each hemisphere is an ependyma-lined cavity called the *lateral ventricle*, consisting of

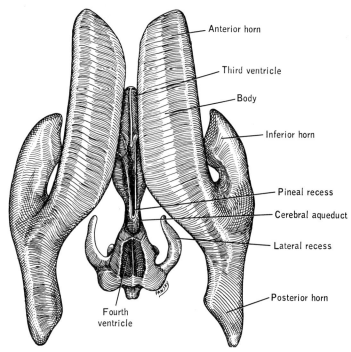

Figure 1-22 Cast of the ventricular system of the brain, viewed from above. (*Adapted from Woerdeman, Atlas of Human Anatomy, McGraw-Hill Book Company, New York, 1950.*)

several parts: anterior horn, body, collateral trigone, posterior horn, and inferior horn.

Anterior Horn

This is the portion extending rostrally from the interventricular foramen. It is triangular in outline, the sloping floor also serving as the lateral side. Medially, the wall is vertical and is composed of the septum pellucidum. The head of the caudate nucleus forms the floor and lateral wall. The roof and rostral end are formed by the fibers of the corpus callosum.

Body

This extends posteriorly from the interventricular foramen to the splenium of the corpus callosum. The medial wall is again vertical and is composed of the septum pellucidum. The roof is formed by the corpus callosum. The lateral wall, which slopes gradually to meet the roof at an acute angle, is formed from below upward, by the fornix, the choroid plexus, dorsal surface of the thalamus, stria, and vena terminalis, and the caudate nucleus.

Collateral Trigone

This is a region at the posterior end of the body, from which the posterior and inferior horns diverge.

Posterior Horn

This portion extends into the occipital lobe. Here, the roof and lateral wall form an arch composed chiefly of the tapetum of the corpus callosum. On the medial wall, two swellings

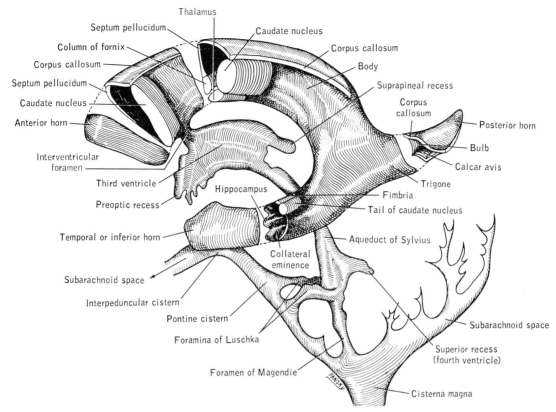

Figure 1-23 Diagrammatic representation of the ventricular system of the human brain, showing the relations of various structures to the walls of the ventricles.

are evident. The more dorsal is called the bulb of the posterior horn, caused by the occipital portion of the radiations of the corpus callosum. The larger, more ventral one, known as the calcar avis, is caused by the deep indentation of the calcarine fissure.

Inferior Horn

This curves ventrally and then rostrally from the collateral trigone. It extends through the medial part of the temporal lobe almost to the temporal pole. The roof is composed chiefly of the white substance of the lobe, the stria terminalis, and tail of the caudate nucleus.

Rostral to the end of the caudate nucleus lies the amygdaloid nucleus, which bulges into the end of the ventricle. The medial wall and floor, in order from medial to lateral, are formed by the fimbria, choroid plexus, hippocampus, and collateral eminence.

DIENCEPHALON

The diencephalon (Figs. 1-6, 1-25) is almost completely hidden when the hemispheres are in place. Several parts are described, namely, epithalamus, thalamus, subthalamus, and hypothalamus.

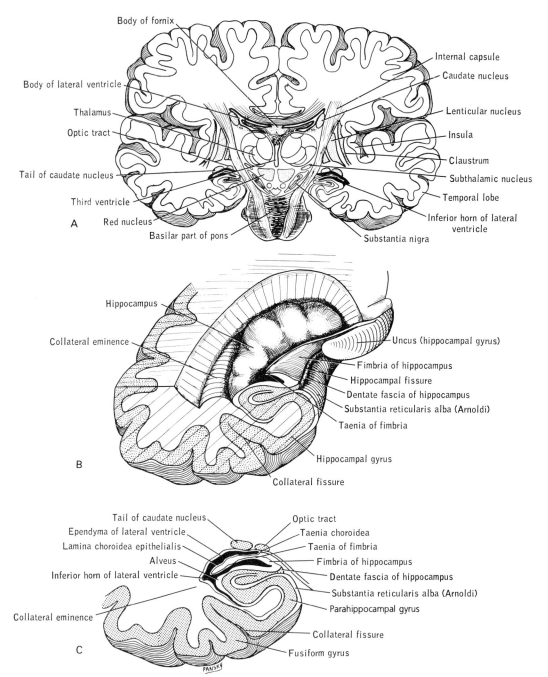

Figure 1-24 *A*. Vertical section through the human brain at the level of the third ventricle. (*Adapted from Woerdeman, Atlas of Human Anatomy, McGraw-Hill Book Company, New York, 1950.*) *B*. Dissection of the inferior horn of the lateral ventricle. *C*. Enlargement of a part of *A* to show the hippocampus, the choroid plexus, and inferior horn of the lateral ventricle (left side).

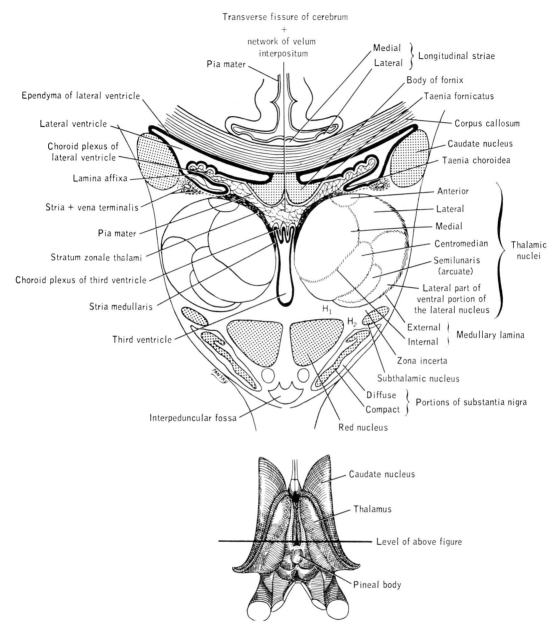

Figure 1-25 Diagrammatic representation of a vertical section through the diencephalon, illustrating the thalamus and its adjoining structures.

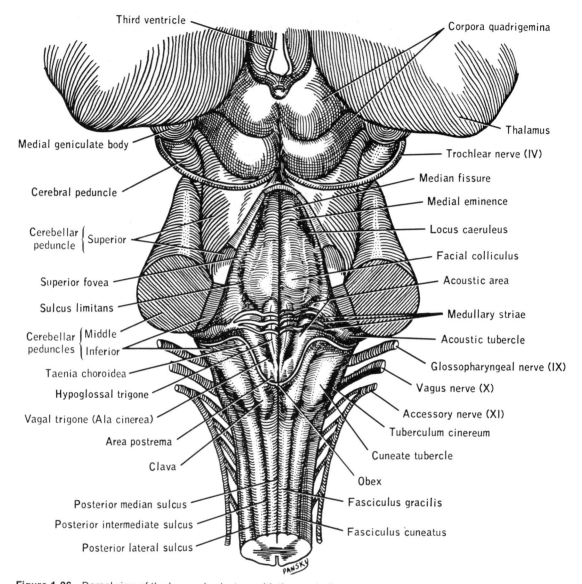

Figure 1-26 Dorsal view of the human brainstem with the cerebellum removed to expose the rhomboid fossa.

Epithalamus (Figs. 1-6, 1-25)

This consists of the *pineal body* (epiphysis), *habenular trigone, stria medullaris*, and *habenular commissure*. The last lies just rostral to the pineal body and serves to connect the nuclei in the habenular trigone. The posterior commissure, which lies just behind the attach-

ment of the pineal body, is sometimes described as part of this region.

Thalamus

External Morphology

This is the largest portion of the diencephalon. It is bounded ventrally by the hypothalamic

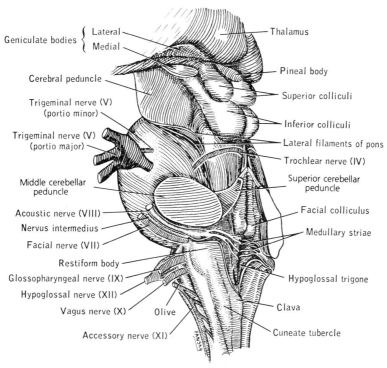

Figure 1-27 Human brainstem viewed from the side.

sulcus, its caudal limit is at the level of the posterior commissure and cerebral aqueduct, its rostral limit is at the interventricular foramen, and dorsally it is related to the stria medullaris and the roof of the third ventricle. The two halves of the thalamus are frequently joined across the midline by a bridge of gray substance known as the interthalamic connection (*massa intermedia*).

The *lateral surface* (Figs. 1-10, 1-11, 1-12) is intimately applied to the posterior limb of the internal capsule.

The *dorsal surface* (Figs. 1-12, 1-25) is free and slightly convex. The thalamus appears as two obliquely placed oval masses, the long axis of each extending from the anterior tubercle caudally through the pulvinar. This posterior part of the thalamus overlaps the rostral mesencephalon. The stria and vena terminalis lie in a groove which separates the lateral edge of the dorsal surface from the caudate nucleus. Medially, the dorsal surface is separated from the medial surface by the *tenia thalami*, the edge of the ependymal roof of the third ventricle. This dividing line is usually made more prominent by the stria medullaris thalami. The dorsal surface is further divided into a lateral and medial portion by a slight, oblique groove, the choroid sulcus. The area lateral to this groove is covered by the *lamina affixa*, the ependyma lying in the floor of the lateral ventricle which became secondarily fused to the thalamus during development. The area medial to the groove is covered by the pia in the floor of the transverse fissure of the cerebrum.

The *ventral surface* (Figs. 1-6, 1-25) adjoins the subthalamus. Caudally it is continuous with the tegmental region of the mesencephalon, through which most ascending fibers enter the thalamus. The caudal region (Fig. 1-28), sometimes called the *metathalamus*, contains

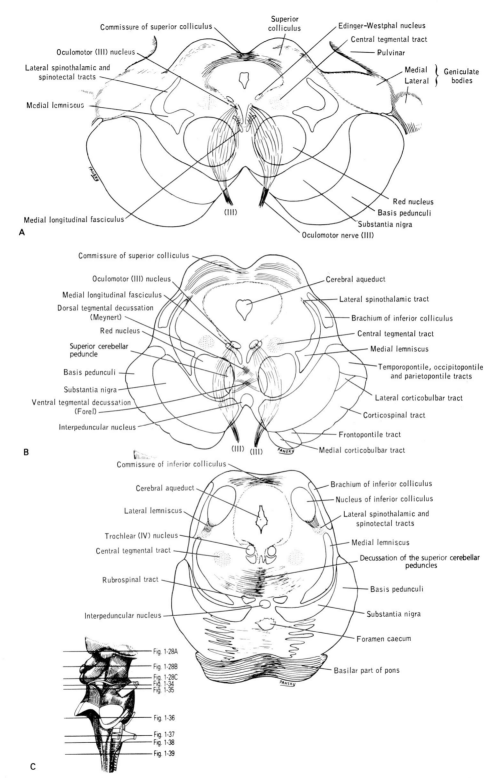

Figure 1-28 Sections through the mesencephalon. *A.* At the rostral end of the midbrain showing the pulvinar of the thalamus. *B.* Through the caudal level of the superior colliculus. *C.* Through the inferior colliculus.

two swellings, the *medial* and *lateral genicu-late bodies.*

Internal Morphology (Figs. 1-24, 1-25)

The thalamus is a large mass of gray matter divided into a number of nuclear groups. No attempt will be made here to describe each of these nuclei (Chap. 23). However, some of the more gross aspects will be considered.

The dorsal surface of the thalamus has a thin covering of fibers called the *stratum zonale.* Along the lateral surface is the external medullary lamina. Medially, beneath the ependymal lining of the third ventricle, lies a homogeneous zone of gray substance called the *central gray* (matter). This area is lacking in myelinated fibers and is occupied by several nuclear groups. The stratum zonale sends fibers ventrally into the substance of the thalamus, forming the *internal medullary lamina.* This divides the thalamus into a medial and a lateral portion. Rostrally, in the region of the anterior tubercle, the internal lamina splits, partially separating the anterior thalamus from the medial and lateral.

The Subthalamus (Figs. 1-24, 1-25)

This is a transition zone between the thalamus and tegmental portion of the mesencephalon. Both the *red nucleus* and the *substantia nigra* of the mesencephalon protrude into the caudal portion of the subthalamus. Lateral to it is the region where the internal capsule joins the cerebral peduncles. The hypothalamus lies medially and rostrally.

Hypothalamus

External Morphology (Figs. 1-6 through 1-8)

This region lies ventral to the hypothalamic sulcus. It consists of several parts, including the lamina terminalis, optic recess, optic chiasma, infundibulum, tuber cinereum, and mammillary bodies. The optic chiasma, infundibulum, tuber cinereum, posterior perforated substance, and mammillary bodies lie between the cerebral peduncles in the interpeduncular fossa. The enlarged upper end of the infundibulum is called the *median eminence* and is part of the tuber cinereum. Its inferior end is the posterior lobe (neural lobe) of the hypophysis.

Internal Morphology

The medial portion of the hypothalamus is predominantly cellular, containing many nuclear groups (Chap. 21). The lateral portion of the hypothalamus contains scattered nerve cells and many longitudinally running myelinated fibers. The hypothalamus may also be subdivided transversely into a supraoptic area, overlying the chiasma; a tuberal or central portion, containing the median eminence and the infundibulum; and the posterior, mammillary region, containing the mammillary bodies.

Cavity of the Diencephalon (Figs. 1-12, 1-22 through 1-25)

This is a narrow, perpendicular cavity called the third ventricle. Its lateral walls are formed by the thalamus dorsally and the hypothalamus ventrally. On the lateral wall, the hypothalamic sulcus extends from the cerebral aqueduct caudally to the interventricular foramen (of Monro). In most cases, the third ventricle is traversed by a bridge of gray substance, the *interthalamic connection* (*massa intermedia*).

At the anterior end of the ventricle, the lamina terminalis extends upward from the region of the optic chiasma to the anterior commissure. Between the chiasma and the ventral edge of the lamina lies the optic recess.

In the floor of the ventricle are the optic chiasma, infundibulum, tuber cinereum, mammillary bodies, and subthalamus.

The roof is narrow, a thin lamina of ependyma stretching between the medullary striae. To this is added the vascular pia, forming the choroid tela, the folds of which invaginate into the ventricle as the choroid plexus.

Three foramina are associated with the ventricle: one for each of the lateral ventricles (interventricular foramina, or foramina of Monro) and an opening for the cerebral aqueduct.

MESENCEPHALON

External Structure (Figs. 1-6, 1-12, 1-25 through 1-27)

Dorsal Surface

When cerebrum and cerebellum have been removed, it is seen that the dorsal surface of the mesencephalon consists of four rounded swellings, the *quadrigeminal bodies*, or *colliculi*. Two furrows, in the form of a cross (cruciate sulcus) divide the four into paired superior and inferior colliculi. The pineal body overlaps the rostral end of the longitudinal groove. From the caudal end of this same groove is a band of fibers, the *frenulum veli*, which ends in the anterior medullary velum of the metencephalon (cerebellum). The rootlets of the fourth nerve (IV) emerge from the brain on either side of the midline just caudal to the inferior colliculus.

Lateral Surface

Laterally (Figs. 1-26, 1-27), two fiber bands, associated with each colliculus, are represented by elevations. One band, the brachium of the inferior colliculus, joins the inferior colliculus to the medial geniculate body of the thalamus. The other, the brachium of the superior colliculus, connects the superior colliculus to the lateral geniculate body of the thalamus.

Basal Surface

On this side (Figs. 1-7, 1-8), the cerebral peduncles diverge laterally from the rostral edge of the pons, leaving a triangular depression, the *interpeduncular fossa*, between them. Within the fossa, there is a groove on the medial side of each peduncle, the sulcus of the

oculomotor nerve (III), through which the rootlets of that nerve emerge from the brain. On the lateral aspect of the peduncle, there is also a longitudinal groove, called the lateral sulcus of the mesencephalon. Just above this sulcus is a faint indication of fibers curving dorsally toward the inferior colliculus. These represent the *lateral lemniscus*.

Cavity of the Mesencephalon (Figs. 1-6, 1-22, 1-23, 1-28)

The cavity of the mesencephalon, the *cerebral aqueduct* (of Sylvius), is a small canal usually triangular in shape with the apex directed ventrally. It is surrounded by a thick zone of gray matter, the central gray stratum, which is continuous with a similar zone along the third ventricle of the diencephalon.

Internal Structure (Figs. 1-28, 1-34)

Dorsal to the aqueduct is the tectum, or lamina quadrigemina, made up of both white and gray substance. Ventral to the aqueduct, the mesencephalon can be divided into two parts: the basis pedunculi and the tegmentum. The former is the most ventral part and consists of a large area of longitudinally running fibers. The tegmentum is an area of reticular formation composed of both nuclear gray masses and fibers continuous with the tegmentum of the pons. A large area of pigmented nerve cells, the *substantia nigra*, lies between the tegmentum and the peduncle. Among the fiber groups located in the tegmentum are the lemniscus system, the dorsal and medial longitudinal fasciculi, the superior cerebellar peduncle and its decussation, the brachium of the inferior colliculus, and fibers of the third and fourth cranial nerves. The dorsal and ventral tegmental decussations are associated with the tecto-spinal and rubrospinal tracts. Certain cell groups are also located here: the dorsal and ventral tegmental nuclei, the interpeduncular nucleus, the red nucleus, the nuclei of the third and fourth cranial nerves, and the

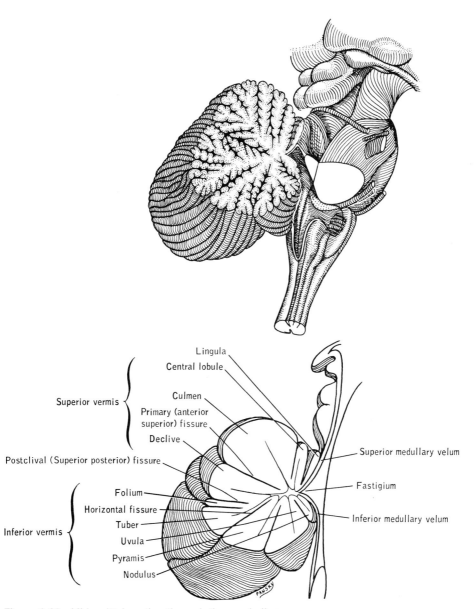

Figure 1-29 Midsagittal section through the cerebellum.

mesencephalic nucleus of the fifth cranial nerve.

METENCEPHALON

This consists of two parts, the cerebellum and pons.

Cerebellum

External Morphology (Figs. 1-6, 1-7, 1-29 through 1-33)

The surface of the cerebellum, the cortex, is thrown into folds, called folia, the long axis of which runs transversely across the cerebel-

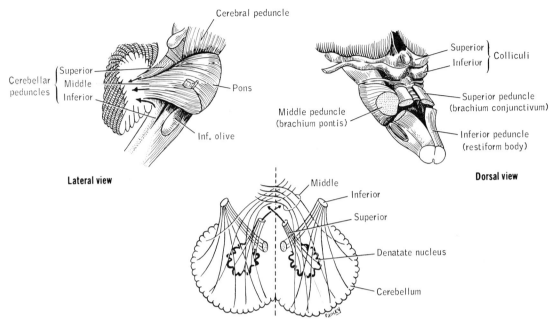

Figure 1-30 Diagrams of the brainstem to show the three cerebellar peduncles.

lum. This portion of the brain consists of three parts: a single central portion, the *vermis*; and two *hemispheres* located on either side. Dorsally, the vermis forms a median elevation not clearly separated from the hemispheres. This is the superior vermis. Ventrally, the vermis lies at the bottom of a deep fissure (cerebellar notch) and is here referred to as the inferior vermis.

A deep groove, the *primary fissure*, divides the cerebellum into lobes—*anterior* and *posterior*. The anterior lobe is the area rostral to the fissure and includes a major portion of the superior vermis and a portion of the hemispheres. From front to back the vermis consists of the *lingula*, the *central lobule*, and the *culmen monticuli*. The regions of the hemispheres included in the anterior lobe are called the ala centralis and the anterior quadrangular lobule.

The posterior lobe lies behind the primary fissure and includes the caudal portion of the superior vermis, all of the inferior vermis, and the major portion of the hemispheres. That portion of the superior vermis included in the posterior lobe is the *declive* (of Monticulus). From front to back, the inferior vermis consists of *the folium, tuber, pyramis,* and *uvula.* The most rostral part of the hemisphere found in the posterior lobe is the posterior quadrangular (simple) lobule. It is bounded posteriorly by the *postclival sulcus.* Behind this sulcus lies the *ansiform lobule,* sometimes divided by the *horizontal cerebellar sulcus* into the *superior* and *inferior semilunar lobule* which sometimes shows a partial division in its caudal portion. This is the gracile lobule (Chap. 17). A small lateral projection between the tonsil and the flocculus, the paraflocculus, is also described (Chap. 17). On the ventral surface of the posterior lobe, the ansiform lobule is not sharply delimited from the more anterior *bi-*

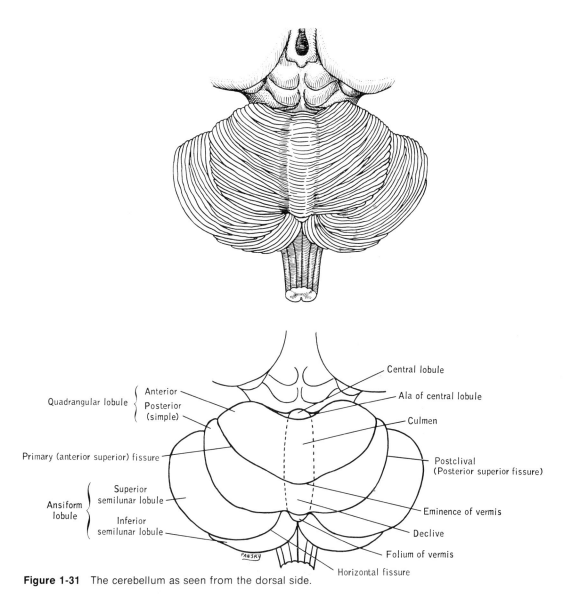

Central lobule

Ala of central lobule

Quadrangular lobule { Anterior / Posterior (simple) }

Culmen

Primary (anterior superior) fissure

Postclival (Posterior superior fissure)

Ansiform lobule { Superior semilunar lobule / Inferior semilunar lobule }

Eminence of vermis

Declive

PANSKY

Folium of vermis

Horizontal fissure

Figure 1-31 The cerebellum as seen from the dorsal side.

venter lobule; by many neuroanatomists, the biventer lobule is considered to be a part of the ansiform lobule. Two small rounded areas, lying on either side of the vermis, are called the *paramedian lobules* (tonsils).

Along the most caudal border of the ansi-

form, or biventral, lobule, lies the *posterolateral fissure*, which separates this lobule from the small, almost vestigial *flocculonodular* lobe. The latter includes the most inferior portion of the vermis, the *nodulus*, and two small portions on either side associated with

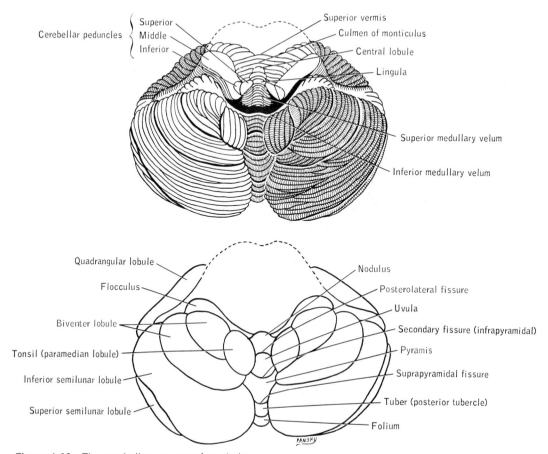

Cerebellar peduncles { Superior / Middle / Inferior

Superior vermis
Culmen of monticulus
Central lobule
Lingula
Superior medullary velum
Inferior medullary velum

Quadrangular lobule
Flocculus
Biventer lobule
Tonsil (paramedian lobule)
Inferior semilunar lobule
Superior semilunar lobule

Nodulus
Posterolateral fissure
Uvula
Secondary fissure (infrapyramidal)
Pyramis
Suprapyramidal fissure
Tuber (posterior tubercle)
Folium

PANSKY

Figure 1-32   The cerebellum as seen from below.

the hemispheres, the *flocculus* and a connecting band, the *peduncle of the flocculus.*

Internal Structure   (Figs. 1-30, 1-33)

The details of cortical structure will be given elsewhere (Chap. 17). Long, narrow folds of cortex, called folia, cover a central core of white substance which is continuous from one hemisphere to the other through the vermis. Embedded in the medullary core are groups of gray substance, the cerebellar nuclei. The largest and most lateral is an irregular lamina of gray substance which resembles a crumpled sac with an open mouth, the hilus, directed medially. This is the *dentate nucleus.* Close to

the hilus lies a narrow, vertical plate of cells called the *emboliform nucleus.* Medial to the inferior portion of the latter lie one or more rounded gray areas called the *globose nuclei.* Closely adjoining the midline, in the core of the vermis, are the *fastigial nuclei.*

Cerebellar Connections   (Figs. 1-11, 1-15, 1-26, 1-30)

The cerebellum is connected with the brain stem by large fiber bundles called the cerebellar peduncles or cerebellar brachii. The lowest, or *inferior peduncle(restiform body),* runs rostrally along the lateral wall of the fourth ventricle, bending sharply to enter the cere-

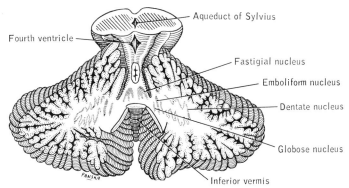

Figure 1-33 Horizontal section through the cerebellum, illustrating its central nuclei.

bellum. The largest and most lateral of the brachii is the *middle peduncle (brachium pontis)*, the fibers of which ascend dorsally from the lateral aspect of the pons. The *superior peduncle (brachium conjunctivum)*, runs ventrally and rostrally along the lateral wall of the superior part of the fourth ventricle.

Pons

External Structure (Figs. 1-6 through 1-8, 1-26, 1-27)

The dorsal surface of the pons is completely obscured by the cerebellum, where it forms the floor of the fourth ventricle. The ventral

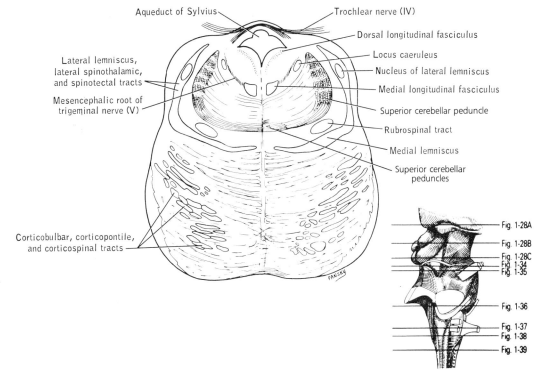

Figure 1-34 Section through the upper pons at the level of the decussation of the emerging fibers of the trochlear nerve (IV).

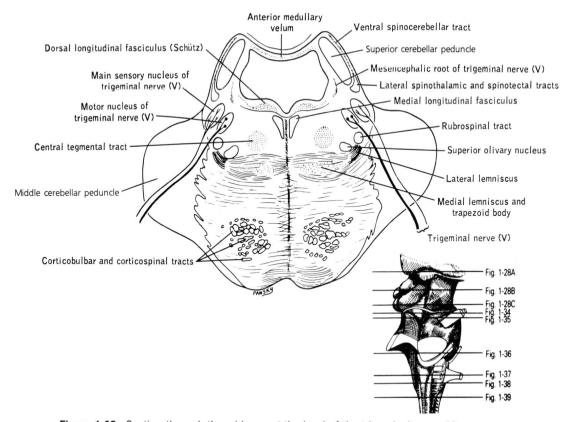

Figure 1-35 Section through the midpons at the level of the trigeminal nerve (V).

surface is convex, both longitudinally and transversely. A median groove, called the *basilar sulcus,* extends the full length of the ventral surface of the pons. The trigeminal nerve roots emerge from the ventrolateral aspect of the pons near the point where pons and brachium pontis become confluent.

Internal Structure (Figs. 1-34 through 1-36)

The pons is composed of two parts which are structurally different: the *dorsal,* or *tegmental, region,* which is similar to and continuous with the medulla; and the *ventral,* or *basal,* portion.

The basilar portion of the pons is the largest. It is composed of scattered, longitudinally running fiber bundles, irregular in size and shape. There are also groups of fibers passing laterally from the pons to the brachium pontis. Interspersed among all the bundles are gray masses, the *nuclei pontis.*

The smaller tegmental portion contains several gray masses, among which are the dorsal and ventral cochlear nuclei; certain of the vestibular nuclei; the superior olivary nucleus; the nuclei of the abducens (VI) and facial (VII) cranial nerves; and the spinal, main sensory, and motor nuclei of the trigeminal (V) cranial nerve. There are also important fiber groups here: trapezoid body; fibers of the abducens, facial, and trigeminal nerves, including the mesencephalic root of the latter; the medial longitudinal fasciculus; the medial lemniscus; the inferior, middle, and superior cerebellar peduncles.

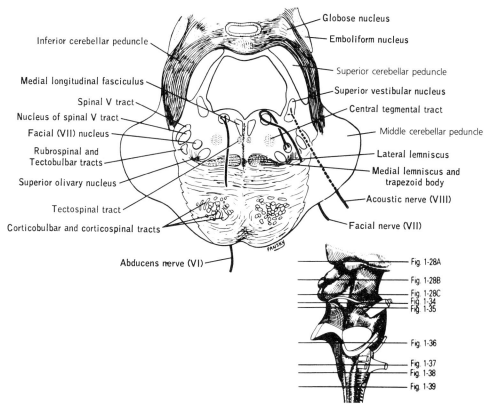

Inferior cerebellar peduncle
Medial longitudinal fasciculus
Spinal V tract
Nucleus of spinal V tract
Facial (VII) nucleus
Rubrospinal and Tectobulbar tracts
Superior olivary nucleus
Tectospinal tract
Corticobulbar and corticospinal tracts
Abducens nerve (VI)

Globose nucleus
Emboliform nucleus
Superior cerebellar peduncle
Superior vestibular nucleus
Central tegmental tract
Middle cerebellar peduncle
Lateral lemniscus
Medial lemniscus and trapezoid body
Acoustic nerve (VIII)
Facial nerve (VII)

Fig. 1-28A
Fig. 1-28B
Fig. 1-28C
Fig. 1-34
Fig. 1-35
Fig. 1-36
Fig. 1-37
Fig. 1-38
Fig. 1-39

Figure 1-36 Section through the lower pons at the level of the nuclei of cranial nerves VI and VIII.

MYELENCEPHALON

Medulla Oblongata

External Structure   (Figs. 1-6 through 1-8, 1-26, 1-27, 1-30)

A line just rostral to the highest rootlet of the first cervical nerve represents the caudal boundary of the medulla. It is separated from the pons by a transverse sulcus. In shape, it resembles a truncated cone with apex pointed toward the spinal cord.

The surface of the medulla is traversed by several longitudinal fissures and sulci, which serve to divide it into several areas. On the dorsal surface of the caudal part of the medulla is the *dorsal* (posterior) *median fissure*, which is continued caudally onto the spinal cord. Lateral to this is the *dorsal lateral sulcus*, made outstanding by rootlets of the glossopharyngeal (IX), vagus (X), and accessory (XI) cranial nerves. Between the dorsal median and dorsal lateral fissures lies the *dorsal intermediate sulcus*. On the ventral midline is the *ventral* (anterior) *median fissure*, which continues downward onto the cord and ends rostrally at the caudal border of the pons as the *foramen cecum*. Lateral to the ventral median fissure is a less distinct groove called the *ventral lateral sulcus*. Along this line emerge fibers of the hypoglossal (XII) nerve. This groove also continues onto the cord.

Between the dorsal median fissure and the dorsal intermediate sulcus is the *fasciculus gracilis,* the direct continuation of the same bundle from the cord. Lateral to the dorsal intermediate sulcus is the *fasciculus cuneatus.* Rostrally these fasciculi end in swellings because of the presence of their nuclei of termination. The nucleus gracilis lies in the region called the *clava,* while the nucleus cuneatus lies in the *cuneate tubercle.* Just above the middle of the medulla, the clava and cuneate tubercle are shifted far laterally and are replaced by the inferior cerebellar peduncle. Running parallel to the cuneate fasciculus, between the latter and the roots of the ninth, tenth, and eleventh cranial nerves, is another longitudinal ridge called the *tuberculum cinereum.*

The lateral area of the medulla, between the dorsal lateral and ventral lateral sulci, is a continuation of the corresponding lateral funiculus of the cord. However, in the rostral end of this funiculus is a prominent oval swelling, the *olive.* Fibers running dorsally either from the ventral median fissure or from the groove between the pyramid and olive are called the *ventral external arcuate fibers.* They join the inferior cerebellar penduncle.

The ventral area, between the ventral median fissure and the ventral lateral sulcus, consists mainly of an elongated swelling, the *pyramid.* Each tapers toward the spinal cord, and at the caudal end of the medulla, the pyramids undergo nearly complete decussa-

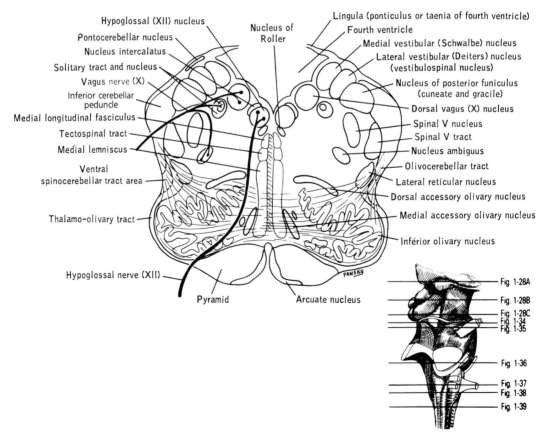

Figure 1-37   Section through the medulla in the lower third of the fourth ventricle.

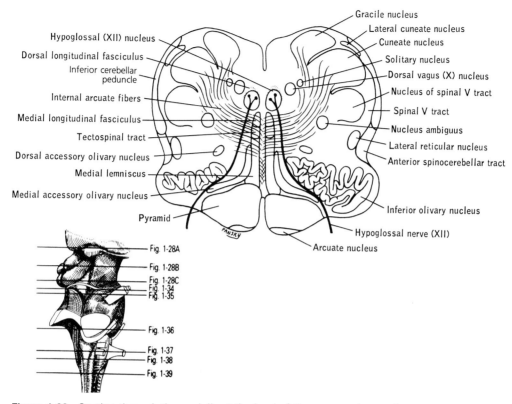

Figure 1-38 Section through the medulla at the level of the sensory decussation.

tion, in which region the median fissure is almost obliterated.

Internal Structure (Figs. 1-37 through 1-39)

It is a mixture of gray and white substance. Among the tracts and fiber bundles are the following: the pyramids and their decussation, the fasciculus gracilis and cuneatus, the medial longitudinal fasciculus (MLF), the spinal tract of the trigeminal nerve, the internal arcuate fibers, the restiform body, tractus solitarius, the spinal vertibular tract, and the medial lemniscus. Emerging fibers of the hypoglossal, vagus, acoustic, and abducens nerves are also seen. The nuclei located here are nucleus gracilis and cuneatus; nucleus of the spinal tract of the trigeminal nerve; spinal

vestibular nucleus; dorsal motor nucleus of the vagus; nucleus of the hypoglossal; nucleus ambiguus; the inferior olivary nucleus; the dorsal and ventral cochlear nuclei; the accessory cuneate and accessory olivary nuclei. In addition to these special circumscribed fiber bundles and nuclei, there are the dorsal and ventral spinocerebellar fibers, the tectospinal tract, and the olivocerebellar fibers. Also scattered among the fibers in the region dorsal to the olive are nests of cells, the *reticular nuclei.*

Cavity of the Hindbrain (Figs. 1-22, 1-23, 1-29, 1-35 through 1-38)

The cavity of the hindbrain is the *fourth ventricle.* It lies between the cerebellum dorsally and the tegmentum of the pons and

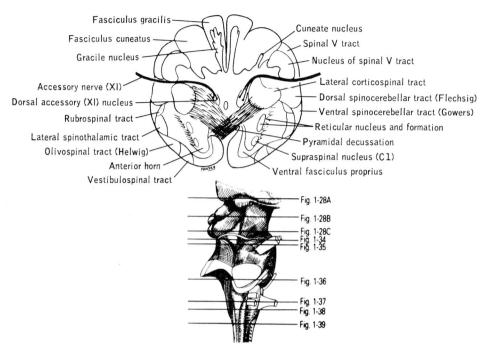

Figure 1-39 Section through the lower medulla at the level of the pyramidal decussation.

medulla ventrally. Rostrally, it is continuous with the cerebral aqueduct, while caudally, through the canal of the closed portion of the medulla, it is confluent with the central canal of the spinal cord. In the broadest portion of the ventricle, the *lateral recess* extends to the surface of the restiform body. Each recess opens laterally into the subarachnoid space through a foramen of Luschka.

Because of its shape, the floor of the ventricle (Fig. 1-26) is called the *rhomboid fossa*. The boundaries, from rostral to caudal, are superior and inferior cerebellar peduncles, cuneate tubercles, and clavae. The median sulcus divides the fossa into right and left halves. The fossa is usually divided transversely into three parts: inferior, superior, and intermediate.

The inferior part has the shape of an inverted triangle, the base being represented by an arbitrary line joining the horizontal part of the *tenia* on either side. The tenia is a band

through which the ependymal roof is attached to the boundary of the ventricle. The apex, the *calamus scriptorius*, is directed caudally. Lateral and parallel to the median sulcus is the *sulcus limitans*. In the latter is a small depression, the *inferior fovea*. From the fovea, a groove extends caudally and medially to form the inferolateral boundary of the *hypoglossal trigone*. Caudal to the hypoglossal trigone is another triangular area, the *ala cinerea*, separated from the former by an obliquely placed band of thickened ependyma called the *funiculus separans*. The elevated zone lying between the sulcus limitans and the median sulcus is the *median eminence*, found throughout the length of the rhomboid fossa.

The superior part is also triangular in shape, with the apex directed rostrally. Its base is formed by a line drawn transversely through the upper ends of the *superior fovea*. The superior fovea are depressions in the sulcus limitans lying rostral to the inferior fovea.

Medial to the superior fovea, the median eminence enlarges to become the *facial colliculus.* The region lateral to the sulcus limitans in the superior part of the rhomboid fossa is the *locus caeruleus.*

The intermediate part is that portion of the fossa which lies between the parallel bases of the superior and inferior zones. Horizontal ridges, the *medullary striae,* cross this region.

In addition to the three zones just mentioned, the *area acoustica* is also described. It includes a portion of the superior, intermediate, and inferior parts of the fossa. It is triangular in outline, the base being the sulcus limitans while its laterally directed apex points toward the end of the lateral recess of the fourth ventricle.

The roof of the fourth ventricle (Figs. 1-29, 1-35) is formed by three structures: the anterior medullary velum, the white substance of the cerebellum, and the choroid tela. Rostrally, the white substance of the cerebellum is stretched thin between the dorsal borders of the superior cerebellar penduncles as far as the caudal border of the tectum of the mesencephalon. This thin area is the *anterior medullary velum.* Near the midline, the lingula of the cerebellar vermis adheres to it. In a narrow zone near the middle of the ventricle, the roof is formed by the white core of the cerebellum. Caudal to the latter lies the choroid tela, composed of ependyma to which the vascular pia has been fused. The vessels of the tela invaginate into the fourth ventricle along two lines, one vertical, the other horizontal. This is the choroid plexus of the fourth ventricle. There is a median opening in the roof into the subarachnoid space, called the foramen of Magendie.

CLINICAL CONSIDERATIONS

Craniocerebral Topography (Fig. 1-40)

It is essential for the clinical neurologist interested in the localization of cerebral lesions, and for the neurosurgeon who may be called upon to investigate such pathologic change, to have an understanding of the relationships between the bones of the skull and the brain. A general review of the *skull* will be of considerable assistance in fully appreciating this relationship.

The position of the cerebral landmarks var-

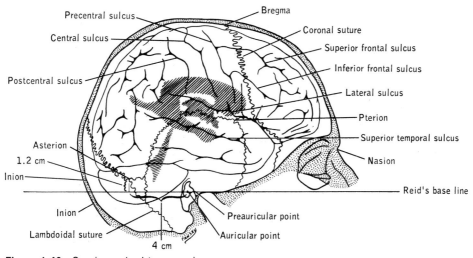

Figure 1-40 Craniocerebral topography.

ies within normal limits, and it is therefore possible to locate them in a general way only.

Dorsolateral Surface Relations (Fig. 1-40)

Base of Cerebrum This is indicated by a line (Reid's line) drawn from the inferior margin of the orbit through the upper margin of the external auditory meatus.

Longitudinal Fissure This corresponds to the midline or sagittal line of the scalp between the external occipital protuberance (inion) and the midpoint of the frontonasal suture (nasion).

Lateral Cerebral Fissure (Sylvian) The pterion (Sylvian point), 3.5 cm behind and 1.2 cm above the frontozygomatic suture, corresponds to the point where the lateral cerebral fissure divides into its ascending and posterior rami. A line drawn from the pterion to a point 2 cm below the parietal eminence overlies the posterior ramus. Another 2-cm line, perpendicular to the previous line, also originating from the pterion, overlies the ascending ramus. A third line, drawn 2 cm rostrally from the pterion, corresponds to the anterior horizontal ramus of the fissure.

Central Sulcus This is determined by a line joining two points: the superior, 1.25 cm behind the center of the sagittal line; the inferior, determined by the intersection of a line perpendicular to Reid's base line, originating at the preauricular point, and the line outlined for the posterior ramus of the Sylvian fissure.

Pre- and Postcentral Sulci These are parallel to the line of the central sulcus, lying 1.5 cm in front of or behind it, respectively.

Superior Frontal Sulcus This is indicated by a line drawn rostrally, parallel to the longitudinal fissure and about 3 cm lateral to it.

Parietooccipital Fissure This is a posterior continuation of the line drawn from the posterior ramus of the Sylvian fissure to the sagittal line. The last 2.5 cm of this continuation overlie the fissure.

Interparietal Sulcus This can be best represented by a curved line running from a point on the central sulcus, 3 cm above the Sylvian point. It parallels the longitudinal fissure located halfway between the latter and the parietal eminence. It then turns downward, ending about midway between the lambda and the parietal eminence.

Basal Surface Relations

This aspect of the brain is related to the anterior, middle, and posterior cranial fossae located in the floor of the cranial cavity.

Anterior The basal surface of the frontal lobe occupies this fossa, resting upon the orbital plates of the frontal bone. The olfactory bulb and tracts lie in the olfactory grooves of the ethmoid bone, with the olfactory nerve fibers entering the skull through the cribriform plates.

Middle This is occupied predominantly by the temporal lobe laterally and the hypothalamus medially. Associated with the latter are the optic chiasma, resting in the chiasmatic groove, and the pituitary gland, lying in the sella turcica of the sphenoid bone. Certain of the cranial nerves exit from the skull through this fossa: the optic through the optic foramen; oculomotor, trochlear, and abducens, plus the ophthalmic division of the trigeminal, through the superior orbital fissure; the maxillary division of the trigeminal through the foramen rotundum; and the mandibular division of the trigeminal through the foramen ovale. A small branch, the great superficial petrosal of the seventh cranial nerve, enters the fossa through the hiatus of the facial canal.

The carotid artery lies in the carotid groove, entering the fossa through the foramen lacerum, while the middle meningeal artery enters through the foramen spinosum, occupying grooves in the lateral aspect of the fossa. Medially, above the carotid groove on the petrous temporal bone, lies the shallow trigeminal impression. Still other small vessels and nerves associated with this fossa are too numerous to mention here.

Posterior Fossa This houses the cerebellum, pons, and medulla oblongata. The pons and the medulla rest upon the dorsum sellae and basilar portion of the occipital bone. The junction between the cord and medulla lies in the foramen magnum, through which also pass the vertebral arteries and the spinal portion of the accessory nerve. The remainder of the cranial nerves leave the skull through the foramina of this fossa: the facial and acoustic, through the internal auditory meatus; the glossopharyngeal, vagus, and accessory, through the jugular foramen; and the hypoglossal, through the hypoglossal canal (anterior condyloid foramen).

Summary

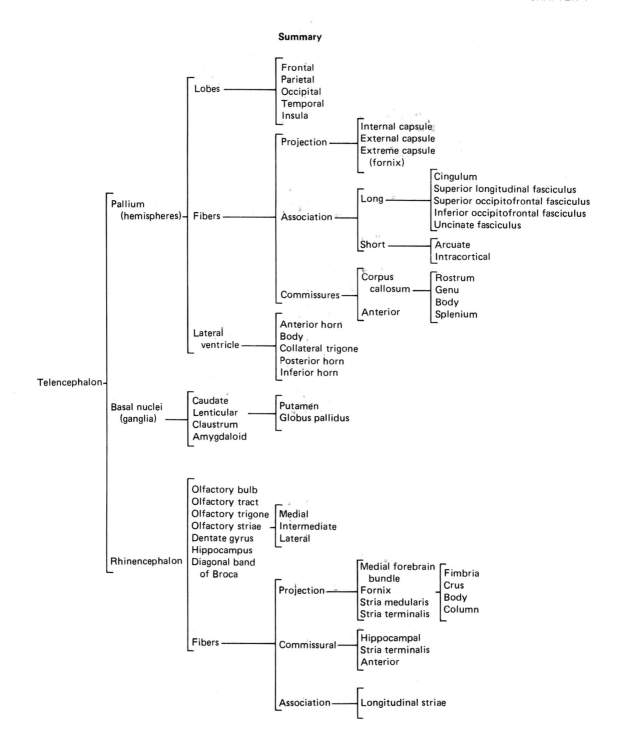

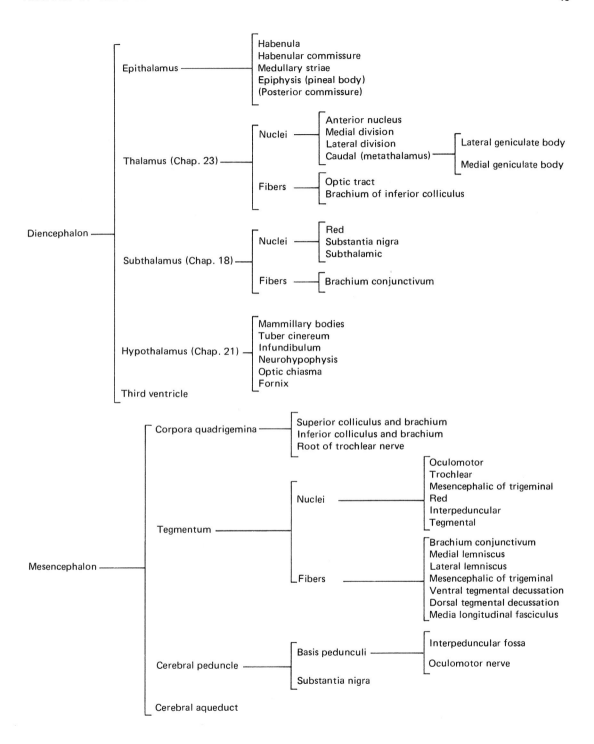

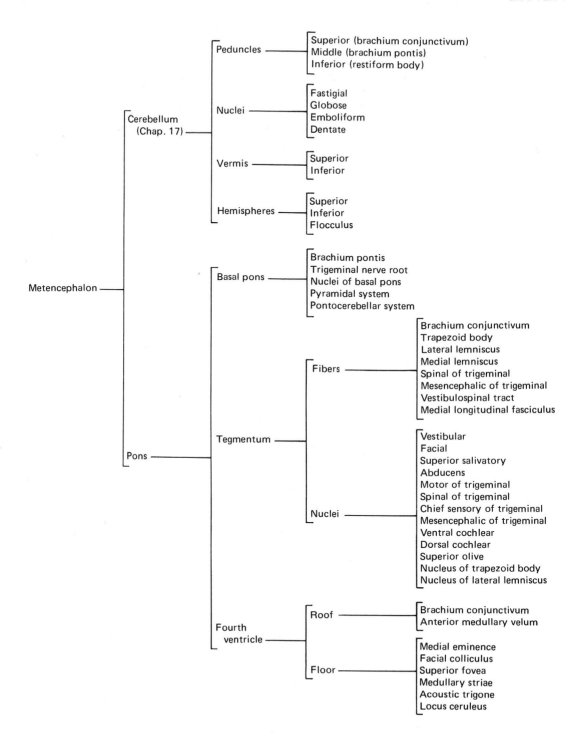

Metencephalon

Cerebellum (Chap. 17)

Peduncles
- Superior (brachium conjunctivum)
- Middle (brachium pontis)
- Inferior (restiform body)

Nuclei
- Fastigial
- Globose
- Emboliform
- Dentate

Vermis
- Superior
- Inferior

Hemispheres
- Superior
- Inferior
- Flocculus

Pons

Basal pons
- Brachium pontis
- Trigeminal nerve root
- Nuclei of basal pons
- Pyramidal system
- Pontocerebellar system

Tegmentum

Fibers
- Brachium conjunctivum
- Trapezoid body
- Lateral lemniscus
- Medial lemniscus
- Spinal of trigeminal
- Mesencephalic of trigeminal
- Vestibulospinal tract
- Medial longitudinal fasciculus

Nuclei
- Vestibular
- Facial
- Superior salivatory
- Abducens
- Motor of trigeminal
- Spinal of trigeminal
- Chief sensory of trigeminal
- Mesencephalic of trigeminal
- Ventral cochlear
- Dorsal cochlear
- Superior olive
- Nucleus of trapezoid body
- Nucleus of lateral lemniscus

Fourth ventricle

Roof
- Brachium conjunctivum
- Anterior medullary velum

Floor
- Medial eminence
- Facial colliculus
- Superior fovea
- Medullary striae
- Acoustic trigone
- Locus ceruleus

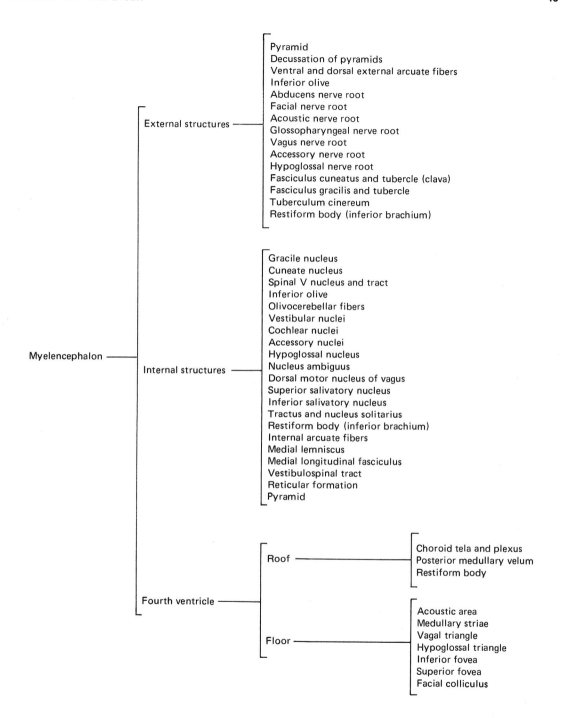

Myelencephalon

External structures
- Pyramid
- Decussation of pyramids
- Ventral and dorsal external arcuate fibers
- Inferior olive
- Abducens nerve root
- Facial nerve root
- Acoustic nerve root
- Glossopharyngeal nerve root
- Vagus nerve root
- Accessory nerve root
- Hypoglossal nerve root
- Fasciculus cuneatus and tubercle (clava)
- Fasciculus gracilis and tubercle
- Tuberculum cinereum
- Restiform body (inferior brachium)

Internal structures
- Gracile nucleus
- Cuneate nucleus
- Spinal V nucleus and tract
- Inferior olive
- Olivocerebellar fibers
- Vestibular nuclei
- Cochlear nuclei
- Accessory nuclei
- Hypoglossal nucleus
- Nucleus ambiguus
- Dorsal motor nucleus of vagus
- Superior salivatory nucleus
- Inferior salivatory nucleus
- Tractus and nucleus solitarius
- Restiform body (inferior brachium)
- Internal arcuate fibers
- Medial lemniscus
- Medial longitudinal fasciculus
- Vestibulospinal tract
- Reticular formation
- Pyramid

Fourth ventricle

Roof
- Choroid tela and plexus
- Posterior medullary velum
- Restiform body

Floor
- Acoustic area
- Medullary striae
- Vagal triangle
- Hypoglossal triangle
- Inferior fovea
- Superior fovea
- Facial colliculus

Anatomy of the Spinal Cord

EXTERNAL STRUCTURE (Figs. 2-1, 2-2)

The spinal cord averages 40 to 45 cm (16 to 18 in) in length. It is nearly oval in cross section, with the longer diameter in the transverse plane. The diameter is not uniform throughout its length. There are cervical and lumbar enlargements to accommodate the nerve supply to the upper and lower extremities. Caudal to the lumbar enlargement, the cord diminishes rapidly, having a cone-shaped termination called the *conus medullaris,* from the apex of which extends the *filum terminale internum,* which descends to be attached to the coccyx.

The cord is divided into areas by several longitudinal grooves (Fig. 2-2). In the midventral line is the deep *ventral median fissure,* which indents the cord to at least one-third of its dorsoventral diameter. Opposite this, on the dorsal surface, is the shallow *dorsal median sulcus.* A median septum extends inward from this sulcus, helping to divide the cord into symmetric halves. Lateral to the ventral median fissure are the *ventral lateral sulci.* Along these grooves emerge the ventral rootlets of the 31 pairs of spinal nerves. Parallel, but some distance lateral to the dorsal median sulcus, are the *dorsal lateral sulci,* along which the dorsal rootlets of the spinal nerves enter the cord. Beginning in the upper thoracic region and becoming quite definite on the cervical cord is another sulcus, lying between the dorsal median and dorsal lateral sulci. This is the *dorsal intermediate sulcus.*

Each half of the cord is divided into columns called funiculi. The *anterior funiculus* is found between the ventral median and ventral lateral sulci; the *lateral funiculus* lies between

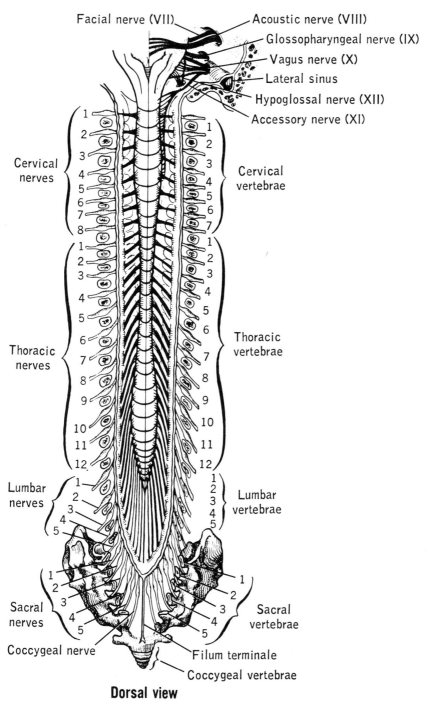

Dorsal view

Figure 2-1 Gross aspects of the spinal cord and lower brainstem viewed from the dorsal side with bone and meninges removed.

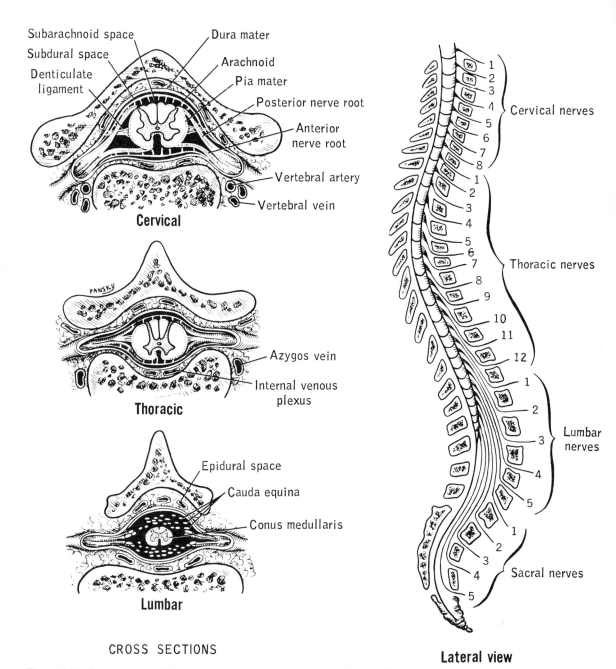

Figure 2-2 Gross aspects of the spinal cord and nerves as related to vertebral levels seen in the sagittal plane. The relations of the cord and nerves to the meninges together with variations in size and shape of the cord at different levels is shown in a series of three cross sections.

the ventral lateral and dorsal lateral sulci; the *posterior funiculus* is situated between the dorsal median and dorsal lateral sulci. In the cervical region, the posterior funiculus is subdivided by the dorsal intermediate sulcus into a medial *fasciculus gracilis* and a lateral *fasciculus cuneatus*. In the region of the upper five or six cervical nerves, rootlets of the accessory nerve (XI) emerge from the lateral funiculus.

The cord is a segmented structure, and it gives rise to 31 pairs of nerves. Arbitrary lines drawn through the most rostral root filaments of each pair serve as demarcation between the segments. The highest of these lines is the boundary between the cervical cord and the medulla.

INTERNAL STRUCTURE (Fig. 2-3)

The cord is composed of two fundamentally different materials. In fresh specimens the

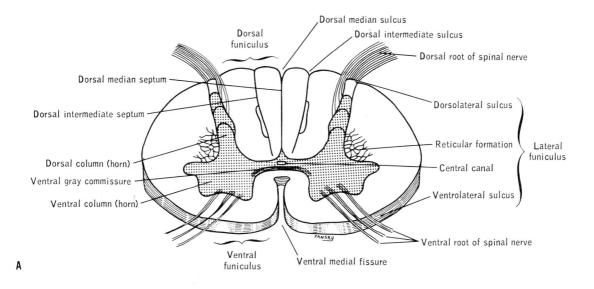

A

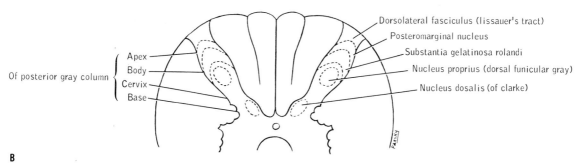

B

Figure 2-3 *A.* Transverse section of the spinal cord at the level of C5 to indicate the general arrangements of its parts. *B.* Diagram of the dorsal gray columns of the spinal cord showing the divisions and principal nuclei.

more peripheral part appears glistening white, because of the fatty myelin sheaths covering the longitudinally running fibers contained in the area. This region is called the *white matter*. Internal to the white substance lies an H-shaped mass which appears less white, since it contains fine, nonmyelinated fibers together with all the neuron cell bodies of the spinal cord. This is the *gray matter*, which, like the white, extends through the length of the cord as columns.

Gray Substance   (Figs. 2-3 through 2-5)

Although the shape of the gray mass varies from level to level, the *posterior gray column* tends to be relatively narrow and in some places nearly reaches the bottom of the dorsal lateral sulcus. The posterior gray column con-

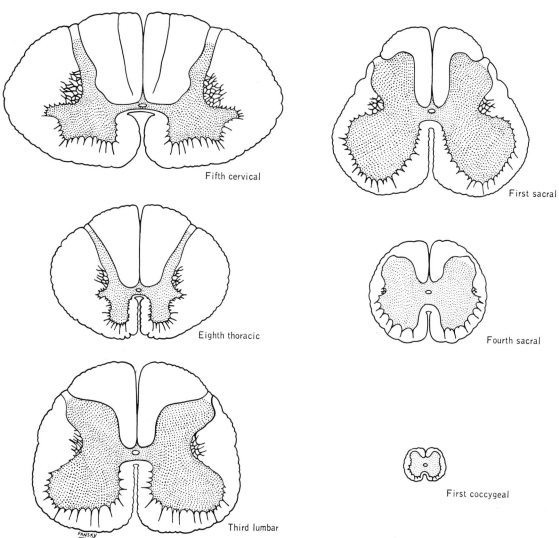

Fifth cervical

First sacral

Eighth thoracic

Fourth sacral

Third lumbar

First coccygeal

Figure 2-4   Transverse sections of the spinal cord at different levels to show the variations in amount and configuration of the white and gray matter.

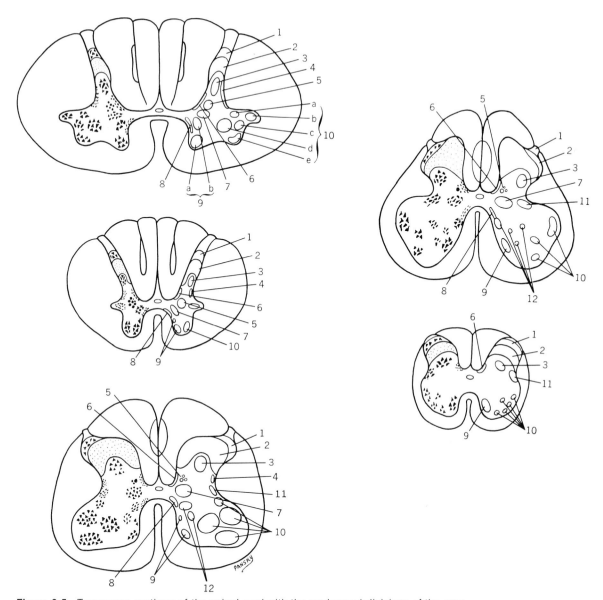

Figure 2-5 Transverse sections of the spinal cord with the nuclear subdivisions of the gray matter indicated. (1) Posteromarginal cells (nucleus magnocellularis pericornualis); (2) substantia gelatinosa of Rolando (nucleus sensibilis proprius); (3) nucleus proprius cornu dorsalis (nucleus magnocellularis centralis; nucleus spinothalamicus; nucleus centrodorsalis); (4) nucleus reticularis; (5) Clarke's column (nucleus dorsalis; nucleus magnocellularis basalis; nucleus spinocerebellaris); (6) nucleus commissuralis posterior (dorsomedial diffuse cell group of Jacobsohn); (7) nucleus intermediomedialis; (8) nucleus commissuralis anterior (ventromedial diffuse cell group of Jacobsohn); (9) nucleus medialis: (a) anteromedial, (b) posteromedial (medial motor); (10) nucleus lateralis: (a) posterolateral, (b) mediolateral, (c) anterolateral, (d) central, (e) anterior; (11) intermediolateral column (nucleus sympatheticus lateralis); (12) nucleus myoleioticus (nucleus sympatheticus medialis).

sists of three parts, namely: apex, caput, and cervix. At the apex, the gray matter is of a consistency different from that found in other parts of the column and is known as the *substantia gelatinosa* (Rolando).

Just lateral to the cervix of the posterior column is an area of mixed white and gray. This is the *reticular substance* of the cord and is most prominent in the cervical region.

The *anterior columns* are shorter and broader than the posterior, directed toward but not approaching the ventral lateral sulcus.

In the thoracic and upper lumbar levels, a lateral protrusion of gray matter appears. This is the *lateral* or *intermediolateral column*.

The strip of gray matter connecting the limbs of the H is the *gray commissure*, near the middle of which lies the *central canal*. The position of this canal divides the commissure into an *anterior* and *posterior* gray commissure. Ventral to the former is a narrow band of myelinated fibers referred to as the *anterior white commissure*.

The gray substance contains all the nerve cell bodies of the cord as well as many glial supporting elements. In the posterior columns, afferent neurons terminate, while association neurons of the reflex arcs and secondary neurons to higher levels arise. In the intermediolateral columns, present throughout thoracic and upper lumbar cord segments, are found the cell bodies of the preganglionic neurons of the autonomic system. The ventral columns contain cells of neurons supplying skeletal muscle.

Within the gray substance, the neuron cell bodies tend to be assembled in groups. In the posterior gray columns, the aggregation of cells at the apex is known as the *posteromarginal nucleus*, ventral to which lies a much larger cell mass, the *substantia gelatinosa* (Rolando). At thoracic levels, a group of cells collected on the medial side of the base of the dorsal column forms the nucleus dorsalis (Clarke's column). In the ventral column, the cells are generally divided into lateral and medial groups, each of which is again subdivided (Fig. 2-5). In the midcervical region, a central group is also found. Generally, it is believed that the cells in the medial group give rise to axons destined for the axial musculature, while the lateral, which are more marked in the cervical and lumbar enlargements, are concerned with the muscles of the girdles and extremities.

In order to simplify some of the confusion concerning the names and locations of the nuclear groups in the spinal gray matter, a description based on laminae has been tried and found useful (Fig. 2-6). No attempt will be made here to detail the cytoarchitecture of any of these layers. However, at this point the old nuclear designations will be related to the appropriate lamina: 1 is the posteromarginal nucleus; 2 is the substantia gelatinosa; 3 is the outer and smaller part of the proper sensory nucleus (nucleus proprius); 4 is the major portion of the proper sensory nucleus; 5 is a band across the neck of the posterior horn, the lateral part of which contains the reticular nucleus; 6 is at the base of posterior horn, is best defined in the cervical and lumbar enlargements, and may be absent between T4 and L2; 7 includes most of the intermediate zone of gray matter, the extent being variable at different levels—the nucleus dorsalis (of Clarke), the intermediolateral nucleus, and the sacral autonomic nucleus belong in this lamina; 8 is a variable zone mainly on the medial side of the ventral horn in the cervical and lumbosacral enlargements and may contain some of the motor neurons for the axial musculature; 9 is the lateral part of the ventral horn containing the largest neurons of the cord, especially those concerned with the appendicular musculature; 10 is a small area of gray around the central canal.

White Substance (Figs. 2-3, 2-7)

The ratio of white substance to gray varies

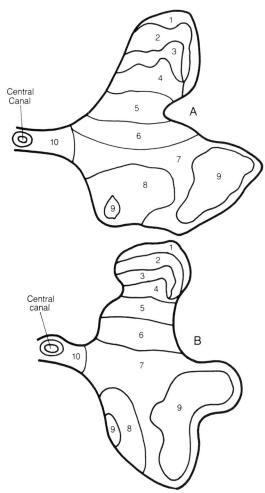

Figure 2-6 Lamination of gray matter. Thick sections of spinal cord. *A.* Lower cervical level. *B.* Lower lumbar level. (*Modified after Carpenter, Core Text of Neuroanatomy, The Williams & Wilkins Company, Baltimore, 1972.*)

from level to level in the cord, the amount of white being greatest in the cervical region.

Although most of the bundles of fibers in the white matter are not clearly defined, the area overlying the apex of the dorsal gray column is pale by comparison with other white areas. This is called the *dorsal lateral fasciculus* (Lissauer's tract).

The white matter, like the gray, is supported and held together by numerous glial elements.

CLINICAL CONSIDERATIONS

An understanding of the relationships between the spinal cord, the vertebral column, and the body surface is important not only to the neurosurgeon but to the diagnostician and anesthetist as well.

Spinovertebral Topography   (Figs. 2-8, 2-9)

Fourth Lumbar Interspace

This is used both for spinal anesthesia and for withdrawal of cerebrospinal fluid. It may be located by a line drawn across the dorsum at the level of the iliac crests.

Sacral Hiatus

This is important in sacral block. The articulation between sacrum and coccyx must be located by palpation. The needle is inserted into the gap between the bones and then directed upward along the axis of the sacrum for a distance of 2.5 to 4.0 cm.

Posterior Sacral Foramina

These may be used for transsacral anesthesia.

First Foramen   This lies about opposite the tip of the transverse process of the fifth lumbar vertebra.

Second Foramen   This lies about 1 cm medial and slightly below the posterior superior iliac spine.

Third, Fourth, and Fifth Foramina   These are approximately in a line drawn caudally from the point of the second foramen, separated from each other by a distance of about 2.5 cm

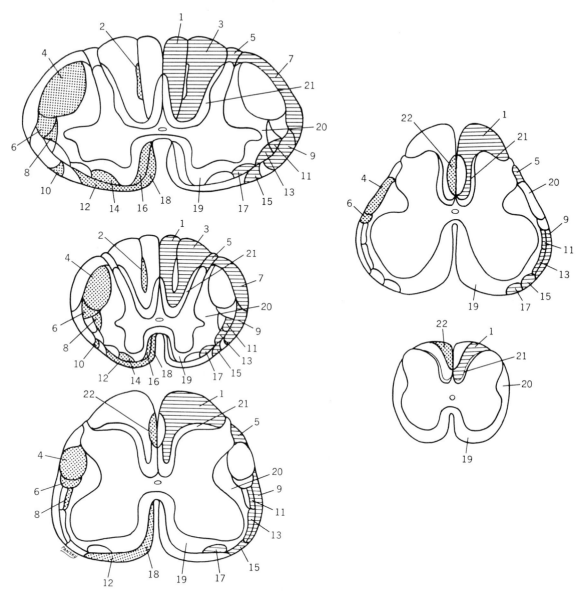

Figure 2-7 Transverse sections of the spinal cord. Ascending tracts in the white matter are on the right, descending on the left. The tracts indicated by numbers 19, 20, and 21 are mixed. (1) Fasciculus gracilis, (2) comma tract (interfascicular fasciculus), (3) fasciculus cuneatus, (4) lateral corticospinal tract, (5) dorsal lateral tract, (6) rubrospinal tract, (7) dorsal spinocerebellar tract, (8) vestibulospinal tract (lateral), (9) ventral spinocerebellar tract, (10) olivospinal tract (tract of Helwig), (11) lateral spinothalamic tract, (12) anterior vestibulospinal tract, (13) spinotectal tract, (14) tectospinal tract (colliculospinal tract), (15) spinoolivary tract, (16) ventral corticospinal tract, (17) ventral spinothalamic tract, (18) sulcomarginal tract, (19) fasciculus proprius anterior (ground bundle), (20) fasciculus proprius lateralis (ground bundle), (21) fasciculus proprius posterior (ground bundle), (22) septomarginal tract.

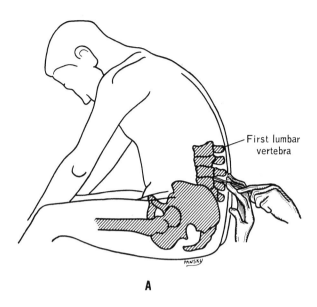

First lumbar
vertebra

A

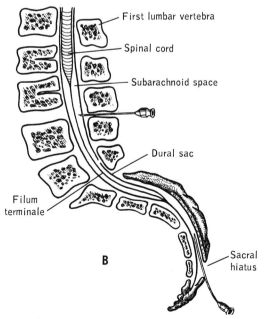

First lumbar vertebra

Spinal cord

Subarachnoid space

Dural sac

Filum
terminale

Sacral
hiatus

B

Figure 2-8   *A*. Lumbar (spinal) anesthesia. *B*. Spinal and caudal anesthesia.

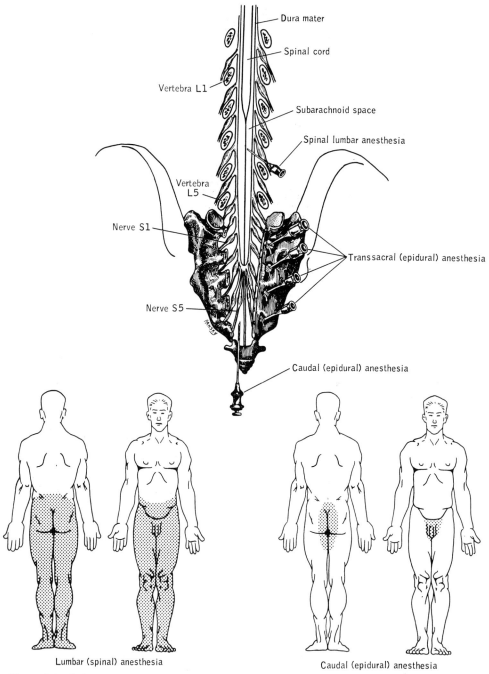

Figure 2-9 Spinal, caudal, and transsacral anesthesia. Areas of anesthesia are also indicated.

Summary

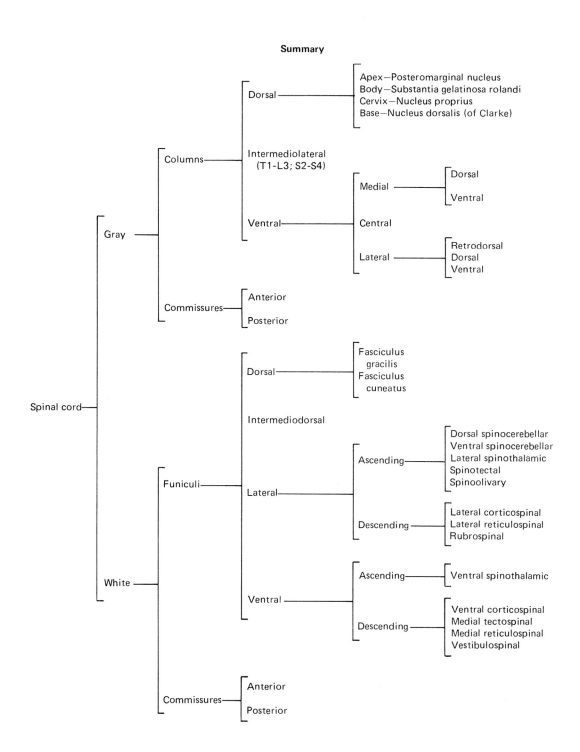

Coverings and Vascularization of the Central Nervous System

MENINGES

The fibrous coverings of the CNS are of great importance in support, protection, and nourishment. They consist of three major layers, from without inward: the dura mater, the arachnoid, and the pia mater. Associated with these layers are three spaces: a potential epidural space, external to the dura; a subdural space, between the dura and the arachnoid; and a subarachnoid space, between the arachnoid and the pia.

Coverings of the Brain

Dura Mater   (Figs. 3-1; E, back endpaper)

This is the outermost covering. It is a thick, tough membrane which serves as both the internal periosteum for the cranial bones and a support for the brain. It consists, therefore, of two layers: an external, endosteal layer and an inner, meningeal layer. The former is intimately attached to the bones and is closely applied to the meningeal layer except in the areas of the venous sinuses. The meningeal layer is smooth and is lined, on its inner surface, by mesothelium. At the foramina in the base of the skull, the dura joins the epineurium of the exiting cranial nerves and also becomes continuous with the external periosteum (pericranium). At the foramen magnum it joins the spinal dura. The meningeal layer also sends four major processes deep into the cranium, forming compartments for portions of the brain. These are the falx cerebri, the tentorium

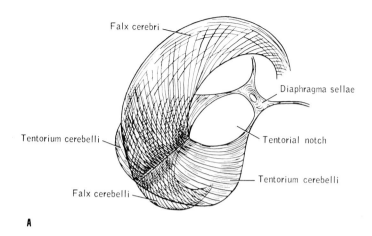

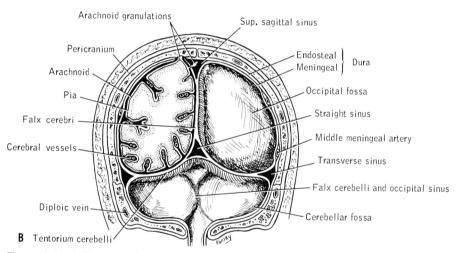

Figure 3-1 *A.* Diagram of the reflections of the dura mater as seen from the right lateral aspect. *B.* Coronal section of the head at the level of the foramen magnum illustrating the relationships of the meninges, the venous sinuses, and the blood vessels.

cerebelli, the falx cerebelli, and the diaphragma sellae.

Falx Cerebri This descends into the longitudinal fissure between the cerebral hemispheres. Anteriorly, it is attached to the crista galli of the ethmoid. Posteriorly, it becomes continuous with the tentorium cerebelli. Its superior convex border is attached to the skull on either side of the midline as far posteriorly as the internal occipital protuberance. The *superior sagittal sinus* is lodged in it. The inferior margin is concave and free and contains the *inferior sagittal sinus.*

Tentorium Cerebelli This forms a tentlike roof for the posterior cranial fossa, sloping downward from its median attachment to the falx cerebri toward its lateral attachments on the petrous temporal bone. It separates the occipital lobes of the cerebral hemispheres and the superior surface of the cerebellum. Its rostral border is free and bounds the incisure (opening) of the tentorium. The cerebral peduncles descend through this gap. The tentorium is attached to the ridges of the occipital bone posteriorly. The *transverse sinuses* are enclosed along this attachment. Laterally and rostrally, the edges are attached along a groove on the superior angle of the petrous temporal bone. The *superior petrosal sinus* runs along this attached border. Anteriorly, the tentorium continues to the clinoid processes of the sphenoid bone. In the midline, along its attachment to the falx cerebri, is the *straight sinus.*

Falx Cerebelli This is a small triangular projection which dips into the posterior cerebellar notch. Above, it is attached to the most posterior part of the inferior surface of the tentorium and posteriorly to the internal occipital crest.

Diaphragma Sellae This is a small sheet which overlies the sella turcica, forming a covering for the hypophysis. In its center is a small opening for the pituitary stalk (infundibular stem).

Arachnoid (Figs. 3-2 through 3-5)

This is a delicate membrane lying internal to the dura mater. It surrounds the brain rather loosely and does not dip into the sulci or fissures, except the longitudinal fissure. Projections of arachnoid invaginate the overlying dura, particularly in the region of the superior sagittal sinus and the *venous lacunae,* which adjoin the sinus. These are the *arachnoid villi* (granulations, Pacchionian bodies). Where the arachnoid lies close to the brain, delicate trabeculae of connective tissue traverse the subarachnoid space to join the pia mater. In certain regions around the base of the brain, the arachnoid and the pia are separated by considerable intervals, called cisterns. The major cisterns are the *cerebellomedullaris, (cisterna magna);* the *interpeduncular;* the *pontine;* and the *chiasmatic.*

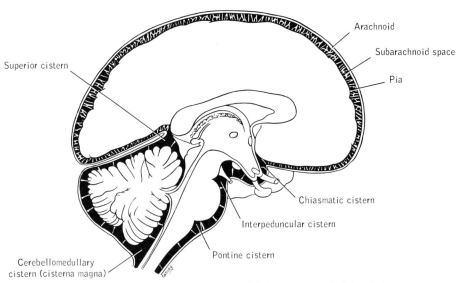

Figure 3-2 Diagram of the principal subarachnoid cisterns seen in lateral view.

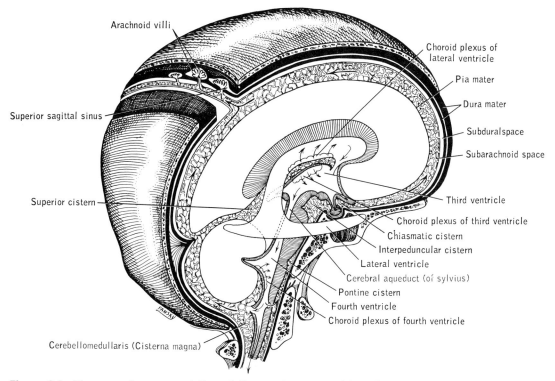

Arachnoid villi

Choroid plexus of lateral ventricle

Pia mater

Dura mater

Superior sagittal sinus

Subdural space

Subarachnoid space

Superior cistern

Third ventricle

Choroid plexus of third ventricle

Chiasmatic cistern

Interpeduncular cistern

Lateral ventricle

Cerebral aqueduct (of sylvius)

Pontine cistern

Fourth ventricle

Choroid plexus of fourth ventricle

Cerebellomedullaris (Cisterna magna)

Figure 3-3 Diagrammatic representation of the meninges, ventricles of the brain, and subarachnoid space. The direction of flow of the cerebrospinal fluid is indicated by arrows.

Cisterna Cerebellomedullaris (Magna)   This is a region where the arachnoid is reflected from the inferior surface of the cerebellar hemispheres and the dorsum of the medulla. It is continuous with the subarachnoid space of the vertebral column through the foramen magnum.

Cisterna Interpeduncularis   This is the space where the arachnoid crosses between the two temporal lobes, enclosing the cerebral peduncles and the interpeduncular fossa. It is continuous rostrally with the chiasmatic cistern and caudally with the pontine cisterna.

Three other cisterns are also recognized: the bilateral *cisterna fossae cerebri lateralis*, where the arachnoid bridges the lateral fissures; and the *cisterna venae magnae cerebri*,

a single space lying between the splenium of the corpus callosum and the superior surface of the cerebellum.

Pia Mater   (Figs. 3-2 through 3-5)

This layer, deep to the arachnoid, is a vascular membrane composed of very small plexuses of blood vessels held together by delicate connective tissue fibers and covered externally by mesothelial cells. The pia, especially the mesothelial component, dips into the substance of the brain along the penetrating blood vessels, forming a lining for the perivascular spaces. Thus, it intimately invests the entire surface of the brain, extending into the depths of the cerebral sulci and the cerebellar folia. In certain regions, it joins the ependymal tissue of the brain to form the tela choroidea.

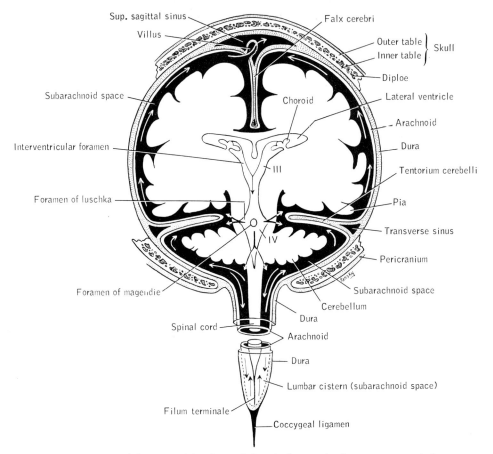

Figure 3-4 Diagram of the essential points relating to the production, course, and absorption of cerebrospinal fluid. Meningeal layers are also shown.

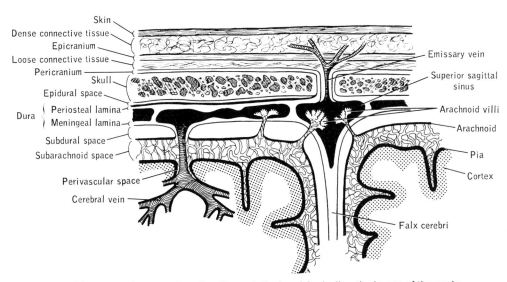

Figure 3-5 Diagrammatic coronal section through the head, including the layers of the scalp and the superficial cerebral cortex. This shows the emissary veins and the relations of the arachnoid villi to the dural sinuses.

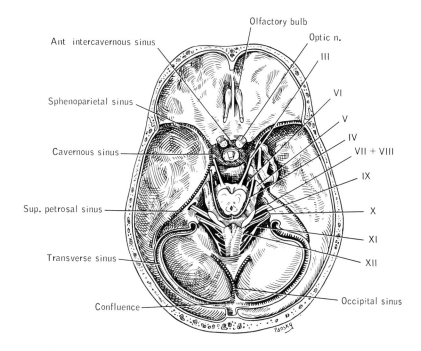

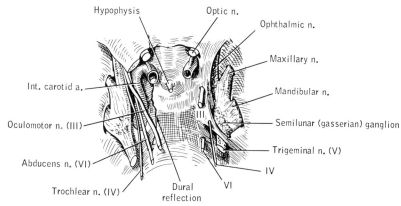

Figure 3-6 Brainstem and base of skull viewed from above. The relations of the cranial nerves and internal carotid artery to the cavernous sinus are shown. The dura has been reflected on the left to better demonstrate the nerves and arteries.

Coverings of the Spinal Cord

Dura Mater   (Figs. 3-7, 3-8)

In the vertebral canal, the dura consists only of the meningeal layer, since each of the vertebrae has its own periosteal covering. Areolar connective tissue and a plexus of veins fill the epidural space. The subdural space contains a minute amount of fluid. The dura is attached firmly to the borders of the foramen magnum and also to the second and third cervical vertebrae. Below this level it sends fibrous slips to the posterior longitudinal ligament. At the level of the second sacral vertebra, the dura ends except for a rudimentary prolongation, the *filum terminale exter-*

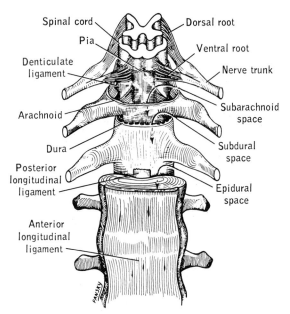

Figure 3-7 The meninges and their associated spaces as shown through a longitudinal reconstruction of the spinal cord.

num, which ensheaths the filum terminale internum to form the coccygeal ligament. This ligament continues caudalward to be attached to the coccyx. The spinal dura forms tubular prolongations along the spinal nerves where the latter pierce the dura. These sheaths pass with the nerves through the intervertebral foramina.

Arachnoid   (Figs. 3-7, 3-8)

The arachnoid is a thin, delicate, tubular membrane forming a loose investment for the cord, joined to the dura by connective tissue trabeculae. Through the foramen magnum, it is continuous with the cranial arachnoid, while inferiorly, it expands to surround the cauda equina. It forms tubular prolongations on the nerve roots, extending with each to their foramina of exit.

The subarachnoid space is widest caudally in the region of the cauda equina, ending at the level of the second sacral segment in the adult.

The space is incompletely divided by a longitudinal, cribriform partition, the subarachnoid septum, which joins arachnoid and pia along the line of the posterior median sulcus of the cord. Laterally, it is also subdivided by the denticulate ligament. In addition, the space is traversed by a meshwork of delicate connective tissue trabeculae.

Pia   (Figs. 3-7, 3-8)

Along the cord, the pia is thicker, stronger, and less vascular than in the cranium. Ventrally, it is reflected into the ventral median fissure. In the midventral region it is a thickened, longitudinal band called the *linea splendens.* On either side, between the dorsal and ventral nerve roots is another band of longitudinal fibers, the *dentate ligament.* At intervals, the lateral aspect of the dentate ligament becomes attached to the dura. Below the conus medullaris of the cord, the pia continues as a slender filament along the filum terminale. At the level of the second sacral segment, it blends with the dura and continues caudally to insert into the dorsum of the coccyx.

CEREBROSPINAL FLUID   (Figs. 3-3 through 3-5)

This fluid is found within the ventricular system of the brain, the central canal of the spinal cord, and the subarachnoid space. Since it surrounds both the brain and cord, it helps to support the weight of the former and acts as a fluid cushion for the protection of both. This fluid may be formed in three ways: under hydrostatic pressure in the thin-walled, highly convoluted vessels of the choroid plexus; by a secretory mechanism inherent in the epithelial cells overlying the vessels of the plexus; or by a combination of both. The total amount has been estimated to be between 90 and 150 ml in adults. That formed in the lateral ventricles passes through the interventricular foramina (of Monro) into the third ventricle, where it is

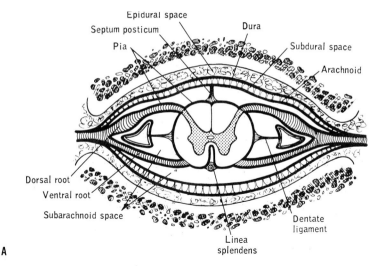

A

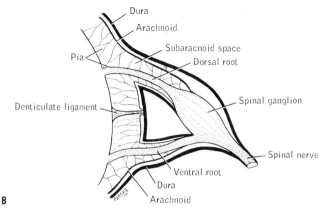

B

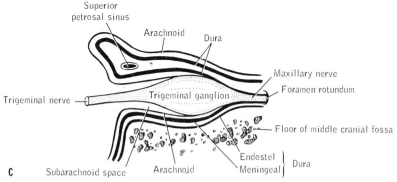

C

Figure 3-8 *A.* Transverse section of the spinal cord showing the meninges and their associated spaces. *B.* The meningeal relations of a spinal nerve. *C.* Meningeal relations of the trigeminal ganglion in the cavum trigeminale. The dura is folded over the ganglion forming the floor of the middle cranial fossa. The cavum trigeminale has two layers of dura superior to it, but otherwise the dural relations are the same as that in the dorsal root ganglion.

added to by the plexus of the latter. From here, the fluid courses caudally through the cerebral aqueduct into the fourth ventricle. Augmented by more fluid produced by the plexus in this cavity and by fluid ascending from the central canal of the cord, in which place it is formed by ependymal secretion, it finally leaves the ventricular system to enter the subarachnoid space through the foramen of Magendie and the foramina of Luschka. In the subarachnoid space, the fluid flows down and around the cord and up its ventral side to the basal part of the brain and then dorsally over the hemispheres, where it enters the arachnoid villi and is discharged through them into the venous system of the superior sagittal sinus or its lacunae. There is also evidence that at least a small amount of fluid is derived from the nervous tissue of the brain itself, passing outward into the subarachnoid space

through the perivascular channels which occur along the penetrating blood vessels.

BLOOD SUPPLY

Arterial Blood

Brain[1]

Arterial blood is supplied to the brain through four main channels, namely, the two internal carotid and two vertebral arteries.

Internal Carotid Arteries These channels (Figs. 3-9 through 3-12; A, front endpaper) enter the skull via the carotid canal, cross the foramen lacerum, pass into the middle cranial fossa, and ascend in the carotid grooves on the sides of the sphenoid bone. At the level of the

[1]In this section, only those major branches giving direct blood supply to the brain will be included.

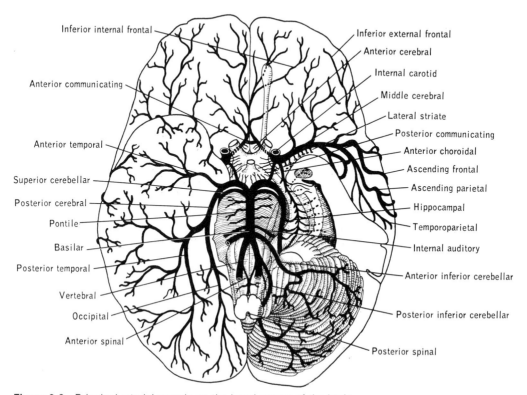

Figure 3-9 Principal arterial vessels on the basal aspect of the brain.

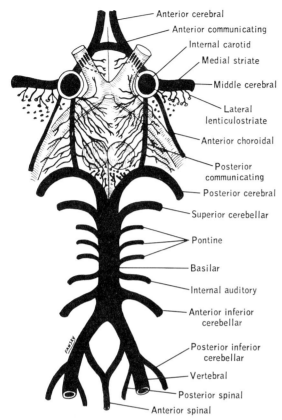

- Anterior cerebral
- Anterior communicating
- Internal carotid
- Medial striate
- Middle cerebral
- Lateral lenticulostriate
- Anterior choroidal
- Posterior communicating
- Posterior cerebral
- Superior cerebellar
- Pontine
- Basilar
- Internal auditory
- Anterior inferior cerebellar
- Posterior inferior cerebellar
- Vertebral
- Posterior spinal
- Anterior spinal

Figure 3-10 Enlargement of the central portion of Fig. 3-9 showing some of the smaller branches in greater detail.

lateral cerebral fissure, they branch into several important divisions.

Anterior Cerebral Arteries (Figs. 3-9 through 3-11, 3-13 through 3-16; A, front endpaper) These arteries course rostrally and medially across the anterior perforated substance and superior to optic tract to the beginning of the longitudinal fissure. Here, as the vessels from the two sides lie close together, an anastomotic branch called the *anterior communicating artery* is formed (Figs. 3-9 through 3-11). Then each vessel continues upward through the fissure, around the genu of the corpus callosum, and posteriorly along the dorsum of the latter, to terminate by joining branches of the posterior cerebral ar-

teries. In its course, the anterior cerebral artery sends branches to the medial surfaces of the frontal and parietal lobes, the anterior perforated substance, the rostrum and the body of the corpus callosum, and the septum pellucidum. Frequently, a large recurrent branch, the *medial striate artery* (Heubner) is seen (Figs. 3-10, 3-12). It supplies the lower and rostral part of the caudate nucleus, the lower part of the rostral end of the putamen, and the anterior limb and genu of the internal capsule.

Middle Cerebral Arteries (Figs. 3-10, 3-12, 3-15, 3-16, 3-17) These are the largest branches of the internal carotid arteries. They run in the lateral cerebral fissure, then curve posteriorly over the insula, where they are distributed to the lateral portion of the hemispheres. Near their origin, two sets of small vessels are given off which penetrate the anterior perforated substance. These are the *medial striate arteries,* which may also arise from the anterior cerebral (see above); and the *lateral striate* which supply a large part of the putamen, the lateral area of the globus pallidus and adjacent parts of the internal capsule. Since the latter vessels, especially the so-called lenticulostriate, are frequently disrupted in cerebrovascular accidents, the group is often referred to as the artery of cerebral hemorrhage.

Posterior Communicating Arteries (Figs. 3-9, 3-10, 3-12; A, front endpaper) These run posteriorly to join the posterior cerebral branches of the vertebrobasilar artery. Their branches run medially and enter the brain between the infundibulum and the optic tract. They supply the genu and anterior third of the posterior limb of the internal capsule, the rostral portion of the thalamus, and the walls of the third ventricle.

Anterior Choroidal Arteries (Figs. 3-9, 3-11, 3-12) These usually arise from the internal carotid arteries just before their bifurcation. They pass backward along the optic tract and around the cerebral peduncle as far

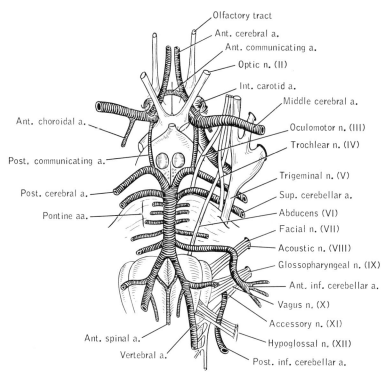

Figure 3-11 Arteries at the base of the brain showing their relations to the cranial nerves.

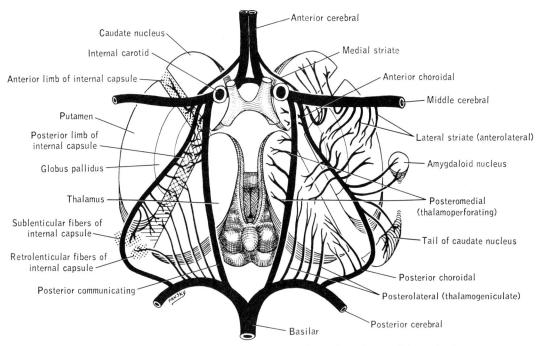

Figure 3-12 Diagram of a horizontal section through the brain to show the arterial supply of the thalamus, internal capsule, and basal ganglia.

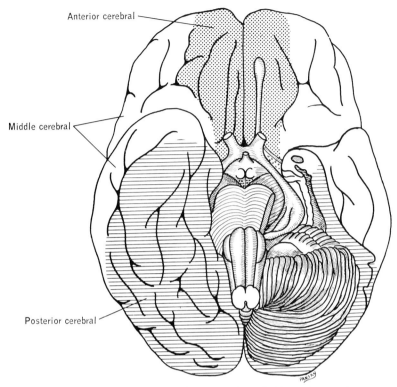

Figure 3-13 Areas of distribution of the anterior, middle, and posterior cerebral arteries on the base of the brain.

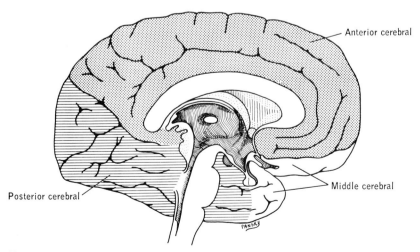

Figure 3-14 Areas of distribution of the anterior, middle, and posterior cerebral arteries on the medial side of the brain.

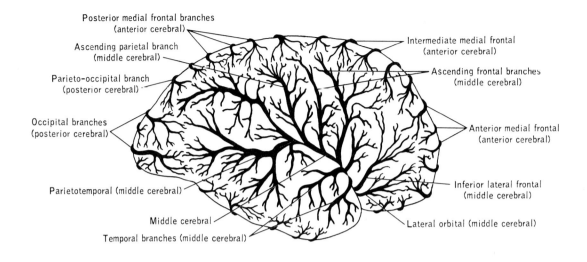

Posterior medial frontal branches
(anterior cerebral)

Ascending parietal branch
(middle cerebral)

Parieto-occipital branch
(posterior cerebral)

Occipital branches
(posterior cerebral)

Parietotemporal (middle cerebral)

Middle cerebral

Temporal branches (middle cerebral)

Intermediate medial frontal
(anterior cerebral)

Ascending frontal branches
(middle cerebral)

Anterior medial frontal
(anterior cerebral)

Inferior lateral frontal
(middle cerebral)

Lateral orbital (middle cerebral)

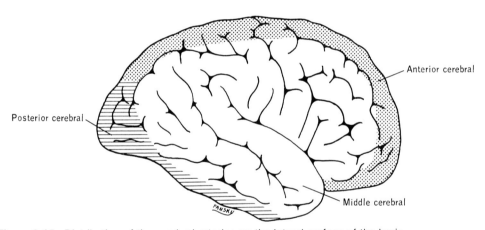

Anterior cerebral

Posterior cerebral

Middle cerebral

Figure 3-15 Distribution of the cerebral arteries on the lateral surface of the brain.

as the lateral geniculate body, where their main branches turn to enter the inferior border of the lateral ventricle. They supply the choroid plexus of that ventricle. In their course, branches are given to the optic tract, hippocampus, tail of the caudate nucleus, medial and intermediate portions of the globus pallidus; posterior two-thirds of the posterior limb of the internal capsule including its retro- and sublenticular portions; the middle third of the cerebral peduncle; and the external part of the lateral geniculate body.

Vertebral Arteries (Figs. 3-9, 3-10, 3-18; A, front endpaper) These vessels enter the skull through the foramen magnum and ascend along the lateral ventral side of the medulla. Near the rostral end of the medulla, the two arteries join to form the *basilar artery.* In their intracranial course, the vertebral arteries give off several branches: the *anterior spinal* artery, which joins its fellow to form a single median vessel along the ventral side of the medulla and spinal cord; the *posterior spinal* artery, which descends onto the cord along the

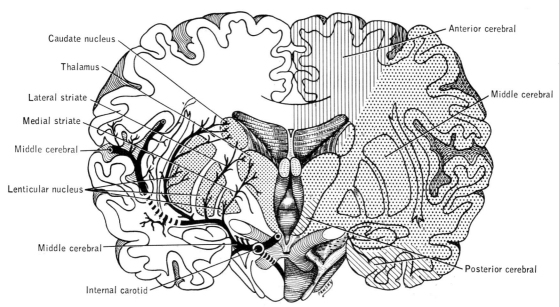

Figure 3-16 Vertical section through the hemispheres and diencephalon. *Left,* distribution of branches of the middle cerebral artery to the basal ganglia, internal capsule, and thalamus. *Right,* the areas of distribution of the anterior, middle, and posterior cerebral arteries are indicated.

dorsal roots of the spinal nerves; the *posterior inferior cerebellar* artery, which usually comes off just below the union of the two vertebral arteries to form the basilar artery (occasionally, it is a branch of the basilar artery).

Basilar Artery (Figs. 3-9, 3-10, 3-12, 3-19; A, front endpaper)   This ascends on the ventral surface of the pons to terminate by dividing into the *posterior cerebral arteries.* Along its course the basilar artery gives several *pontine* arteries, to supply the pons; *internal auditory* artery, to the inner ear; *anterior inferior cerebellar* artery, to the rostral portion of the inferior surface of the cerebellum; *superior cerebellar* artery, to the upper surface of the cerebellum, where it branches to supply this region, as well as the corpora quadrigemina, pineal body, and choroid plexus of the third ventricle.

Posterior Cerebral Artery (Figs. 3-9 through 3-17; A, front endpaper)   This vessel passes lateralward, receives the posterior communicating artery from the internal carot-

id artery, and bends around the cerebral peduncle to reach the inferior surface of the occipital lobe, where it branches out to supply both the inferior and medial surfaces of both

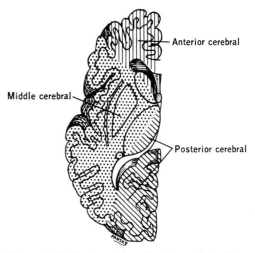

Figure 3-17 Horizontal section through the left cerebral hemisphere, showing distribution of the anterior, middle, and posterior cerebral arteries.

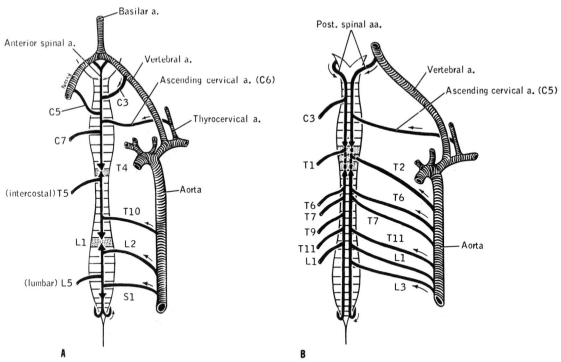

Figure 3-18 Diagrams of the arterial vessels to the spinal cord. *A.* Anterior surface. Note that the chief sources are through radicular arteries of segments C6, T10, and L2. The arterial bed at T4 and L1 (stippled) are said to be the weak points in the circulation since blood pressure is lowest there. Direction of flow is shown. *B.* Posterior surface. The region of poorest circulation (stippled) is thought to be from T1 to T3. Direction of flow is indicated. *(Modified after Bolton, 1939, and Zülch, 1954.)*

temporal and occipital lobes. Posterior choroid branches of the posterior cerebral artery pass to the choroid plexuses of the third ventricle and the lateral ventricle.

Circle of Willis (Figs. 3-9 through 3-12) The anastomosis of the internal carotid and vertebral circulation forms a circular pattern known as the circle of Willis. This anastomosis makes possible an adequate blood supply to the brain in case of occlusion of either the carotid or vertebral arteries.

Spinal Cord

Posterior Spinal Arteries (Figs. 3-10, 3-18; C and D, front endpaper) These arise from

the vertebral artery and run caudally either just medial or lateral to the dorsal roots of the spinal nerves. In their course, they are joined by small spinal branches of the vertebral, intercostal, lumbar, and sacral arteries.

Anterior Spinal Arteries (Figs. 3-9 through 3-11, 3-18; C and D, front endpaper) These begin as medial branches from the vertebral arteries near their terminations and unite into a single trunk in front of the medulla at the level of the foramen magnum. This trunk descends to the lower end of the spinal cord, receiving contributions from spinal branches of the same vessels which contribute to the posterior spinal arteries.

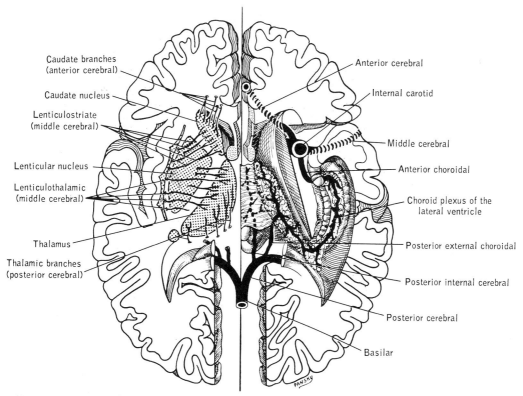

Figure 3-19 Horizontal sections through the cerebrum. *Right,* the lateral ventricle has been exposed to show the arteries supplying the choroid plexus. *Left,* distribution of vessels to the basal ganglia and thalamus.

Meningeal Arteries

Cranial (Fig. B, front endpaper) The meninges in the posterior cranial fossa are supplied by the posterior meningeal arteries, which are branches of the ascending pharyngeal arteries; and by posterior meningeal branches of the vertebral and occipital arteries.

The meninges in the middle cranial fossa are supplied by the middle meningeal and the accessory meningeal arteries, both branches of the maxillary arteries (branches of the external carotid arteries) and by the ethmoid arteries from the ophthalmic branches of the internal carotid arteries.

Spinal The spinal branches that supply the cord also supply its meninges.

Venous Drainage

Since the venous blood from both brain and meninges drains into the venous sinuses of the dura, a description of the latter, which are endothelium-lined spaces between the two layers of the dura, is essential.

Venous Sinuses of the Dura

Superior Sagittal Sinus (Figs. 3-1, 3-5, 3-13; F, back endpaper) It begins at the foramen cecum, where it receives a vein from the nasal cavity, and courses dorsally and posteriorly in the attached border of the falx cerebri. Just above the internal occipital protuberance, in the majority of cases, it passes to the right, to enter the transverse sinus on that side. In its course, it receives the superior cerebral veins and cerebrospinal fluid from the arachnoid villi and the venous lacunae. The superior part of the dura also drains into this sinus.

Inferior Sagittal Sinus (Figs. 3-4; E and F, back endpaper) This occupies the posterior half or two-thirds of the free margin of the falx cerebri. It receives a few veins from the medial surface of the cerebrum and ends in the straight sinus.

Straight Sinus (Figs. 3-1, 3-19; E and F, back endpaper) This lies along the line of attachment of the falx cerebri to the tentorium cerebelli. As it nears the internal occipital protuberance it deviates into the left transverse sinus. The great cerebral vein (of Galen) and the superior cerebellar veins also terminate in the straight sinus.

Transverse Sinuses (Lateral Sinus) (Figs. 3-1, 3-4, 3-6; E and F, back endpaper) These run laterally from the region of the internal occipital protuberance. The first part of their

course lies in the attached border of the tentorium cerebelli. When they reach the base of the petrous temporal bone, they leave the tentorium and curve downward and forward, to enter the jugular foramen, where they end in the internal jugular vein. The portion of the sinus which courses caudally to the foramen is sometimes called the sigmoid sinus. These sinuses receive the inferior cerebral and the inferior cerebellar veins as well as the superior petrosal sinuses.

Occipital Sinus (E and F, back endpaper) This is the smallest of the sinuses. It begins near the margin of the foramen magnum by the union of two tributaries, through which it may communicate with the sigmoid sinuses. It ascends in the attached margin of the falx cerebelli and ends at the confluence of the sinuses, a region overlying the internal occipital protuberance where the superior sagittal, straight, transverse, and occipital sinuses join. It also receives the inferior cerebellar veins.

Cavernous Sinuses (Figs. 3-6, 3-20; E and F, endpaper) These lie on either side of the body of the sphenoid bone between the superior orbital fissure and the apex of the petrous temporal bone. Their chief afferent vessels are

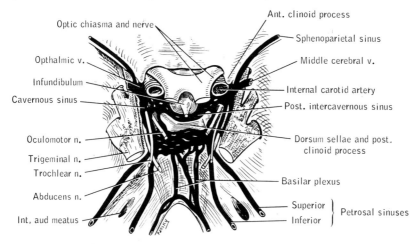

Figure 3-20 Detailed diagram of the cavernous sinus showing its relations to the pituitary gland, the internal carotid artery, and cranial nerves II, III, IV, V, and VI.

the superior ophthalmic and the cerebral veins. Sometimes a division of the inferior ophthalmic vein also opens into the sinus. Blood leaves the cavernous sinuses by way of the intercavernous sinuses and the superior and inferior petrosal sinuses. Although separated from the blood of the sinus by an endothelial lining, the internal carotid artery, the ophthalmic and maxillary divisions of the trigeminal nerve, the oculomotor, trochlear, and abducens nerves are all intimately related to the cavernous sinuses.

Superior Petrosal Sinuses (Figs. 3-6, 3-20; E and F, back endpaper) These leave the cavernous sinuses and pass posteriorly in the tentorium cerebelli along the superior angle of the petrous temporal bone to join the transverse sinuses. They receive blood from the cerebellum and cerebrum as well as the tympanic cavity.

Inferior Petrosal Sinuses (Figs. 3-20; E and F, back endpaper) These begin in the cavernous sinuses and course caudally between the petrous temporal and the basilar part of the occipital bones, to terminate directly into

the superior jugular bulb at the jugular foramen. They receive veins from the medulla, pons, inferior portion of the cerebellum, and inner ear.

Veins of the Brain (Figs. 3-19, 3-21, 3-22; G, back endpaper)

The veins of the brain all terminate in the dural sinuses described above. They are classified as external and internal cerebral and cerebellar veins.

The *external cerebral veins* are usually described as (1) *superior cerebral veins,* 8 to 12 of which drain the superior, lateral, and medial surfaces of the hemisphere and terminate in the superior sagittal sinus; (2) *middle cerebral veins,* beginning on the lateral surface of the hemispheres and ending directly or indirectly in the cavernous sinus (there are also intercommunications with the superior and transverse sinuses); (3) *medial cerebral veins* which drain part of the medial surface of the hemispheres and terminate in the inferior sagittal sinus; (4) *inferior cerebral veins,* which are small and drain the inferior surfaces of the hemispheres, those on the frontal lobe connecting via superior cerebral tributaries with

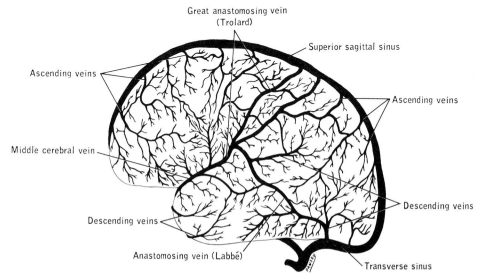

Figure 3-21 Venous drainage of the external surface of the brain as seen from the left side.

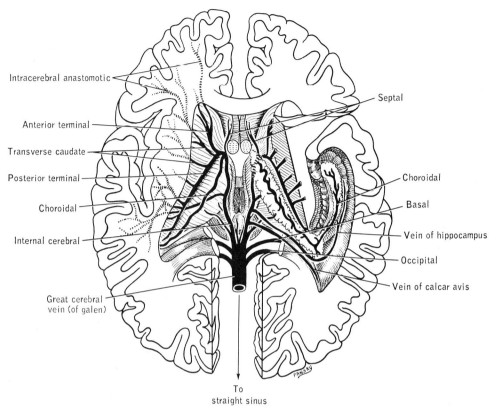

Intracerebral anastomotic

Anterior terminal

Transverse caudate

Posterior terminal

Choroidal

Internal cerebral

Great cerebral
vein (of galen)

Septal

Choroidal

Basal

Vein of hippocampus

Occipital

Vein of calcar avis

To
straight sinus

Figure 3-22 Internal venous channels of the cerebrum showing the vein of Galen and its tributaries.

the superior sagittal sinus, those on the temporal lobe joining either the middle cerebral or the basal venous system and terminating in the cavernous or superior petrosal sinuses; (5) *basal veins,* formed by the confluence of three small veins: the anterior cerebral vein, draining the frontal lobe; the deep middle cerebral vein, draining the insula and adjoining gyri; and the inferior striate veins, draining the corpus striatum. The basal vein receives tributaries from the interpeduncular fossa, the parahippocampal gyrus, the inferior horn of the lateral ventricle, and the mesencephalon. It terminates in the great cerebral vein.

There are two *internal cerebral veins,* each in turn formed by the confluence of two veins: (1) the *terminal vein,* lying in the groove between the thalamus and the corpus striatum and

receiving tributaries from both; and (2) the *choroid vein,* which runs the entire length of the choroid plexus and drains the hippocampus, fornix, and corpus callosum. When the internal cerebral veins reach the splenium of the corpus callosum, they are joined by the basal veins to form the great cerebral vein (of Galen).

The *cerebellar veins* are divided into two groups: (1) the *superior,* which passes rostrally and medially to end in the straight sinus, internal cerebral veins, transverse sinus, and superior petrosal sinus; and (2) the *inferior,* which ends in the transverse, superior petrosal, and occipital sinuses.

Emissary and Diploic Veins

The emissary veins (Figs. 3-5; E and F, back endpaper) connect the intra- and extracranial veins. Since blood can flow in either direction in these veins, the venous pressure in both the sinuses and the superficial veins can be equalized. The more important emissary veins are (1) the parietal, (2) the emissary veins of the foramen cecum, (3) the mastoid, and (4) the ophthalmic.

The diploic veins (Figs. E and F, back endpaper) form venous plexuses between the inner and outer tables of the skull. The veins form a plexus drained by four major venous trunks on each side: the frontal, anterior parietal (temporal), posterior parietal (temporal), and occipital. These trunks then drain into the sinuses of the cranium.

Veins of the Spinal Cord (Figs. 3-23; H, back endpaper)

The pia of the cord contains a minute and tortuous venous plexus, within which are found six or seven longitudinal channels. When six are present, one lies over the posterior sulcus, one in front of the anterior fissure, while the remaining four are laterally disposed along the anterior and posterior surfaces of the cord. When seven are found, one vein overlies the posterior sulcus with one channel on either side just medial to the dorsal root fibers; those on the anterior side are arranged in pairs, lying between the anterior fissure and the anterolateral sulcus. In the upper cervical region near the skull, these units unite to form two or three small vessels which communicate with the vertebral veins and end either in the inferior cerebellar veins or in the inferior petrosal sinus. Below the cervical region, the

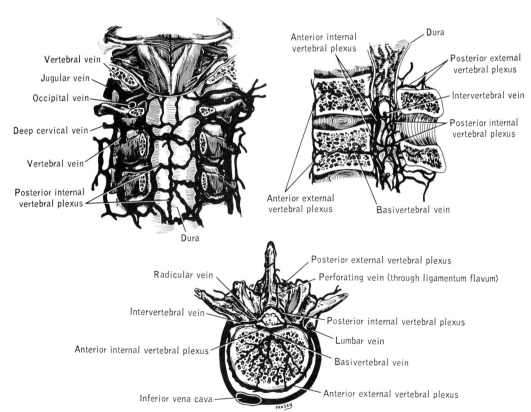

Figure 3-23 Venous drainage of the vertebral column, spinal meninges, and cord. *Upper,* longitudinal arrangement. *Lower,* transverse section.

veins communicate laterally with the intervertebral veins, which exit through the intervertebral foramina as tributaries of the vertebral, intercostal, lumbar, and lateral sacral veins.

In addition to the veins associated with the surface of the cord, there is a complex arrangement in the epidural space. This is the internal vertebral venous plexus, which communicates with veins about the exterior of the vertebral column. Around the foramen magnum, they communicate with the vertebral veins, and superiorly there are connections with the occipital sinus and the basilar plexus of veins.

CLINICAL CONSIDERATIONS

Surface Topography

Because of the frequency of injury to the vessels following fracture of the skull, it is essential to have an understanding of their relationships and to be able to delineate their position on the surfaces.

Arteriocranial Topography

Middle Meningeal Artery (B, front endpaper) The trunk of the vessel and its bifurcation can be found directly above the middle of the zygomatic arch. The *anterior branch* is located at a point about 3.75 cm behind the zygomatic process of the frontal bone and 4.5 cm above the zygoma. This locates the vessel as it crosses the pterion. The *posterior branch* is located 2.5 cm above the highest point of the external auditory meatus as it passes backward toward the lambda.

Sinocranial Topography

The *superior sagittal sinus* is indicated by a line in the median plane joining the nasion and inion.

The *transverse sinus* can be located by a line drawn slightly convexly upward, from a point just above the inion to the top of the root of the auricle.

The *sigmoid sinus* is indicated by a line beginning at the top of the auricular root and extending downward behind the auricle toward the tip of the mastoid process. At the level of the lower border of the external meatus, the line turns rostrally to the margin of the meatus.

Cisternal Puncture   (Figs. 3-2, 3-24)

The spine of the second cervical vertebra is identified, and a point in the midline is taken immediately above it. The needle is then inserted forward and upward, paralleling an imaginary line joining the nasion and the external auditory meatus. The needle penetrates to a depth of about 4 to 5 cm to reach the posterior atlantooccipital ligament. The cistern lies just in front of this ligament, with the medulla about 2.5 cm anterior to the ligament.

Pneumoencephalography   (Fig. 3-25)

This is also important, particularly in the localization of brain tumors. Following the technique for lumbar puncture described in the chapter on the spinal cord (Chap. 2), cerebrospinal fluid is removed in the lumbar region and replaced by up to 200 ml air or oxygen. At the outset, the cerebrospinal pressure is measured, since this procedure must never be used when there is an increase in intracranial pressure.

Ventriculography   (Figs. 3-25, 3-26)

This is important in diagnosis, particularly in the localization of tumors and obstruction of the ventricular system. This procedure is used in patients in whom pneumoencephalography is contraindicated, especially if there is evidence of increased intracranial pressure or suspicion of an expanding lesion in the posterior fossa.

The technique consists of making two small incisions in the scalp, approximately 2.5 cm (1 in.) on either side of the midline and approximately 5 cm (2 in.) above the lambdoid suture. Two small holes are drilled through the skull,

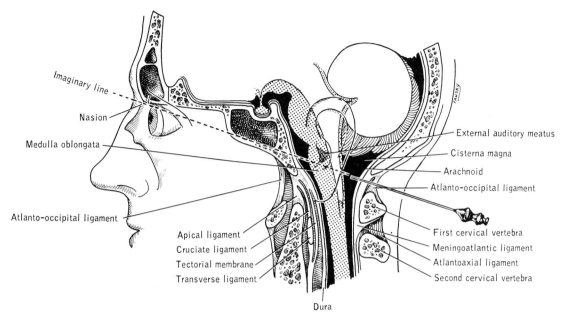

Figure 3-24 Cisternal puncture, showing surface markings and structural relationships.

and a small incision is made in the dura. A ventricular needle is introduced through the incision, passing downward, forward, and inward to enter the lateral ventricle in the region of its collateral trigone. Fluid is removed and replaced by 50 to 120 ml of air or oxygen. Lateral and anteroposterior roentgenograms are taken.

Specific Pathology

Meningitis

The meninges may be the seat of infection, hemorrhage, and tumor formation. Infection of the meninges is called meningitis; it may involve the dura (pachymeningitis) or the piarachnoid (leptomeningitis). Headache; neck stiffness; flexion at ankle, knee, and hip, when the neck is bent (Brudzinski's sign); inability to extend the leg completely when in the sitting position or when lying with the thigh flexed upon the abdomen (Kernig's sign); fever; mental confusion—all are indications of meningeal infection. Furthermore there is usually an increase of cells in the spinal fluid.

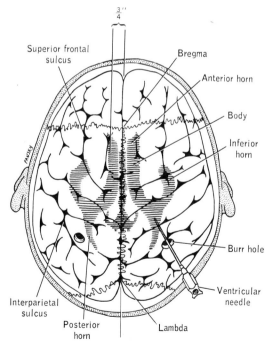

Figure 3-25 Surface projection of the ventricular system of the brain related to the bones and sutures of the skull. The approach to the lateral ventricle is shown.

Meningeal Hemorrhages

These are more frequent as a result of causes not primarily vascular.

Extradural This bleeding occurs between the dura and the skull. It is almost always *arterial* in origin, caused by trauma, and is usually due to a rupture of the *middle meningeal artery.*

Subdural This is bleeding between the dura and arachnoid. It is predominantly *venous* in origin and may or may not be due to *trauma.*

Subarachnoid This is bleeding between the arachnoid and pia and is usually *arterial*, involving the cerebral vessels. It may be *spontaneous* or *traumatic.*

Cerebral Vascular Pathology

Both hemorrhage and occlusion of the vessels in the central nervous system are of frequent occurrence. However, the symptoms presented involve many higher centers whose functions are, as yet, unknown to the beginning student. Therefore, the detailed account of pathology in specific vessels has been deferred until the study of the entire system has been completed. (See Appendixes I and II.)

Cerebral Hemorrhage

This occurs within the brain substance, is arterial in nature, and is usually spontaneous (non-traumatic).

Ventricular Hemorrhage

This may be primary or secondary and usually results from the rupture of a cerebral hemorrhage into the adjacent ventricle.

Cerebral Embolism and Thrombosis

These conditions lead to vascular occlusions of the cerebral arteries (sometimes even of the internal carotid or vertebral arteries), resulting in symptoms or signs that depend upon the area involved.

Hydrocephalus (Fig. 3-26)

These cases may be placed in two general categories, communicating and noncommunicating. The former is the result of obstruction of the arachnoid villi and perivascular spaces by blood, serum, or an inflammatory process. The latter is caused by blocking of various portions of the ventricular system by tumors or other growths. If the block is located at the interventricular foramen, distention of the

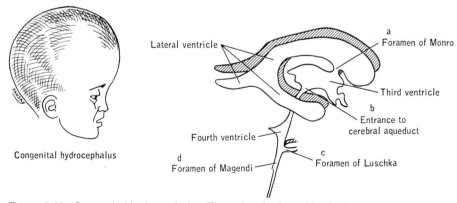

Lateral ventricle

a
Foramen of Monro

Third ventricle

b
Entrance to cerebral aqueduct

Fourth ventricle

c
Foramen of Luschka

Congenital hydrocephalus

d
Foramen of Magendi

Figure 3-26 Congenital hydrocephalus. The points indicated by the letters a to d represent locations at which the ventricular system may be blocked to create this condition.

ventricle on the side of the block occurs: if the block is in the cerebral aqueduct, there is distention of both the lateral and third ventricles; if the block occurs near the opening of the fourth ventricle, all the ventricles are distended.

Intracranial Tumors   (Fig. 3-25)

Unless they contain calcium, intracranial tumors are difficult to localize by roentgenography. However, using either pneumoencephalography or ventriculography, the position of a

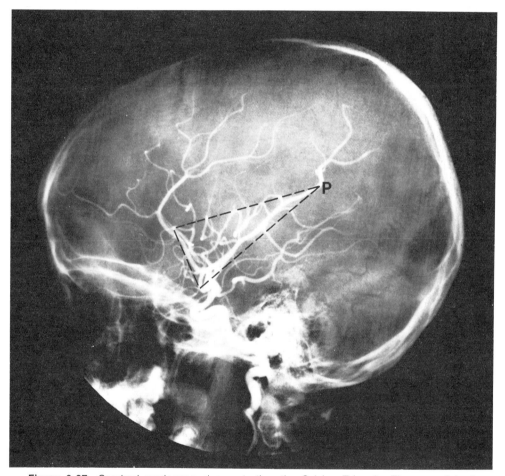

Figure 3-27 Cerebral angiogram demonstrating the Sylvian Triangle. There are 5 to 8 branches of the middle cerebral artery on the surface of the insula. As they course upward, they reach the deepest portion of the sulcus formed by the junction of the insula and the frontoparietal operculum. Upon reaching this point, the middle cerebral branches change direction and proceed downward a short distance to emerge from the laterial sulcus (Sylvian fissure). The points of reversal can be identified in the angiogram and a line is drawn from the most anterior to the most posterior point (P) forming the upper margin of the Sylvian triangle. The inferior margin of the triangle is a line from the most posterior point (the angiographic Sylvian point, P) to the anterior extremity of the middle cerebral artery. The anterior aspect is drawn from the rostral extremity of the middle cerebral artery up to the turn of the first opercular branch. The triangle contains the middle cerebral vessels as they are disposed on the insula. (*From Malcolm B. Carpenter,* Human Neuroanatomy, *7th ed., Williams and Wilkins Baltimore Md., 1976*)

tumor (and some conception of its size) can be visualized.

Another tool that sometimes proves useful in diagnosing and localizing tumors is arteriography (angiography) (Fig. 3-27). In this procedure a radiopaque substance such as thorium dioxide is injected into the internal carotid artery which is usually exposed just above the clavicle. Two or three x-rays are made as quickly as possible as the injection is being made. If the normal and abnormal arteriograms are compared a shift in pattern can be observed in the area of the growth.

Another method also making use of the high vascularity of tumors consists of the use of radioisotopes. After injection, the head is "scanned" both photographically and mechanically. The soft parts surrounding the cranium show up as heavy shadings due to heavier uptake while the brain remains relatively clear in the normal condition. A tumor will appear as a dark area against the pale, normal background. (The use of the EEG and the echogram will be discussed in Chap. 24.)

Summary

Venous Sinus Drainage

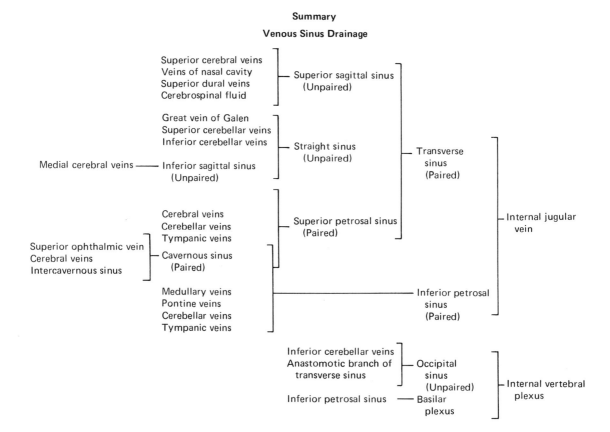

Area Drained	Initial Venous Channels	Second Venous Channels	Main Venous Channel	Dural Sinus
External cerebral veins				
Dorsal and medial cerebrum	Superior cerebral veins			Superior sagittal
Medial cerebrum	Medial cerebral veins			Inferior sagittal
Lateral cerebrum	Middle cerebral veins			Cavernous
Inferior cerebrum	Inferior cerebral veins			
Frontal lobe				Superior sagittal
Temporal lobe				Cavernous and superior petrosal
Frontal lobe	Anterior cerebral	Basal vein	Great cerebral vein	Straight
Insula	Deep middle cerebral			
Corpus striatum	Inferior striate			
Hippocampal gyrus				
Lateral ventricle				
Mesencephalon				
Internal cerebral veins				
Thalamus	Terminal vein	Internal cerebral vein	Great cerebral vein	Straight
Corpus striatum	Terminal vein			
Fornix				
Hippocampus	Choroid vein			
Corpus callosum				
Cerebellum				
Superior area	Superior cerebellar			Straight, transverse and superior petrosal
Inferior area	Inferior cerebellar			Transverse, superior petrosal, occipital

83

Summary
Arterial Supply

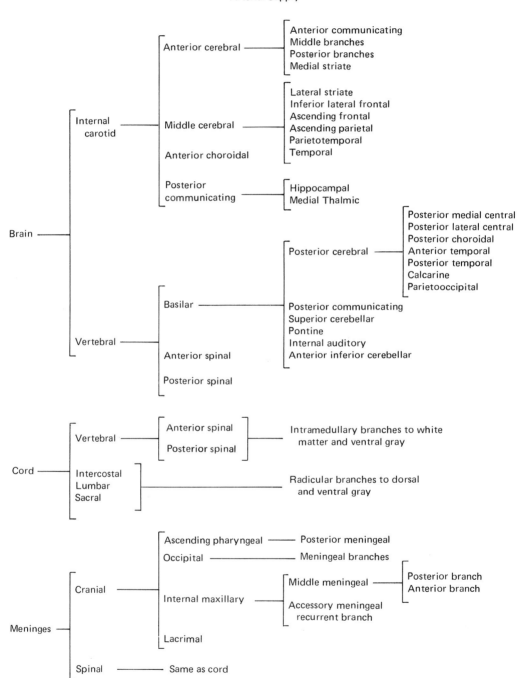

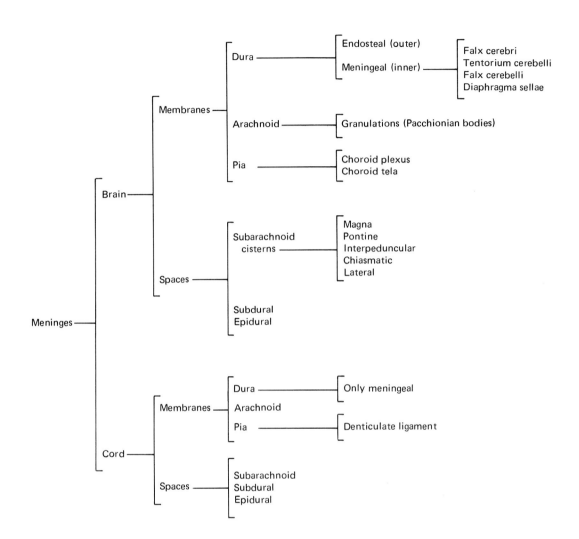

Development of the Nervous System

GERM LAYER ORIGIN

Both central and peripheral nervous systems arise from the *ectoderm* of the embryo.

Neural Plate (Fig. 4-1)

By the nineteenth day of embryonic life, the ectoderm has begun to thicken dorsally. This is the neural plate, which even at this stage shows a longitudinal groove along the middorsal line—the *neural groove*. The anterior end of the plate is much broader. This portion becomes the brain, while the narrower, caudal part forms the spinal cord. From the beginning, the prospective brain region shows subdivisions suggestive of the three primary brain vesicles (Fig. 4-2). The most rostral gives rise to the *forebrain* (prosencephalon); the middle and smallest represents the *midbrain* (mesencephalon); the most caudal becomes the *hindbrain* (rhombencephalon).

As the neural plate thickens and expands, its lateral edges are carried dorsally. These are the *neural folds*. During the third week the neural folds begin to meet and fuse along the middorsal line, forming the *neural tube* (Fig. 4-1). For a time, the neural tube is open at both extremities. However, by the end of the fourth week, the tube is completely sealed.

Neural Crest (Fig. 4-1)

During the time that the neural folds are fusing, a proliferation of cells occurs along the boundary between the neural and general surface ectoderm. This is the *neural crest*, which forms two longitudinal bands on either side of the line of fusion of the neural folds.

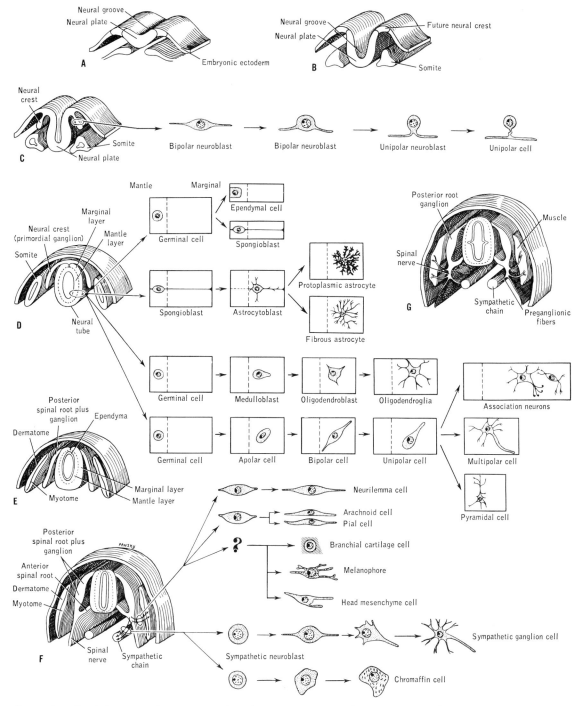

Figure 4-1 Semidiagrammatic representation of the development of the neural tube from the neural plate, showing the histogenesis of the CNS as well as the differentiation of the neural crest.

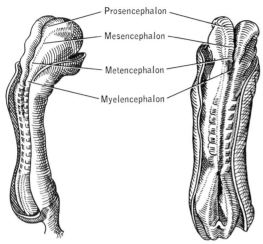

Figure 4-2 Human embryos, 3 to 3½ weeks of age, showing the development of the neural tube and the establishment of body segments.

EXTERNAL MORPHOGENESIS OF THE SPINAL CORD

For a time, the spinal cord is a simple, thick-walled tube completely filling the neural canal.

Very early, before definite skeletal parts are formed, spinal nerves become associated with each of the adjacent mesodermal segments (somites). In this way, all the skeletal muscle derived from this mesoderm will be supplied by these nerves.

In the first 3 months of development, the spinal cord and the vertebral column grow at the same rate. Shortly thereafter, body growth exceeds that of the CNS, particularly in the caudal half of the fetus. Thus, at birth, the cord no longer fills the canal but ends near the lower border of the third lumbar vertebra (Fig. 4-3).

This growth phenomenon also has a profound effect upon the direction of spinal nerve fibers. Originally, nerve fibers leave at right angles to the cord. With the formation of the vertebrae, these nerves exit from the neural canal firmly held between the edges of adjoining vertebrae. Therefore, as the body grows caudally, the foramina containing the nerves are carried along (Fig. 4-3). As a consequence,

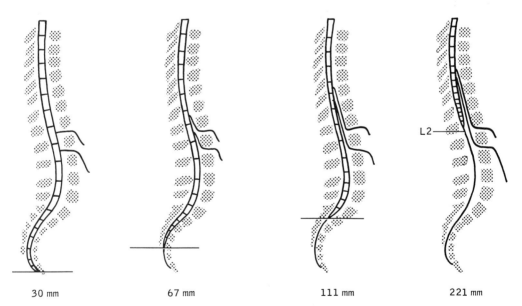

| 30 mm | 67 mm | 111 mm | 221 mm |

Figure 4-3 Diagram showing the relation of growth of the spinal cord to that of the vertebral column. Stages represent embryos from 30 to 221 mm in length.

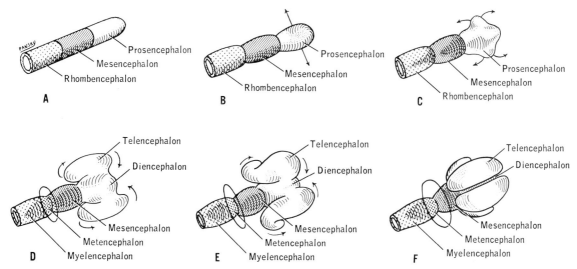

Figure 4-4 Development of the brain, with special emphasis on the prosencephalon, as seen from the dorsal aspect.

the roots of the nerves, especially those derived from the lower third of the cord, become greatly elongated and may extend considerable distances within the vertebral canal before exiting through the proper intervertebral foramina. In this way, the *cauda equina* is formed.

In addition to changes in length, the cord shows regional increases in diameter to accommodate the large nerves passing to the extremities. In the fourth fetal month, a cervi-

cal enlargement for the brachial plexus and a lumbosacral enlargement for the plexus to the lower extremity appear.

EXTERNAL MORPHOGENESIS OF THE BRAIN (Figs. 4-4 through 4-6)

In the fourth and fifth weeks, changes occur in the primary brain vesicles. From the prosencephalon appear two lateral evaginations. These are the *telencephalon,* later to become

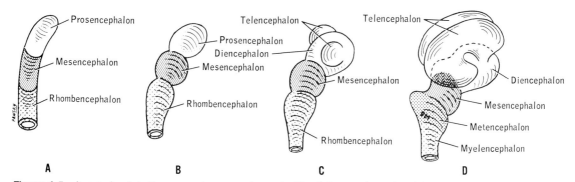

Figure 4-5 Approximately the same stages as shown in Fig. 4-4, seen from the side.

the cerebral hemispheres. That portion of the forebrain which remains medial is now called the *diencephalon.* The mesencephalon undergoes no radical changes. The rhombencephalon, however, subdivides. The rostral part becomes the *metencephalon,* the more caudal part the *myelencephalon.* Later, the metencephalon differentiates into the dorsal *cerebellum* and the ventral *pons.* The myelencephalon becomes the medulla oblongata.

During the third week, the growth rate of the neural tube is so much more rapid rostrally and dorsally that a ventral bend occurs, first in the region of the midbrain. This is the *cephalic,* or *midbrain, flexure.* At about the same time, the *cervical flexure* forms at the junction of the hindbrain and spinal cord. Between 5 and 6 weeks, a third flexure appears in the region of the metencephalon. This is the *pontine flexure.* Eventually, both pontine and cervical flexures tend to straighten out. However, evidence of the cephalic bend remains.

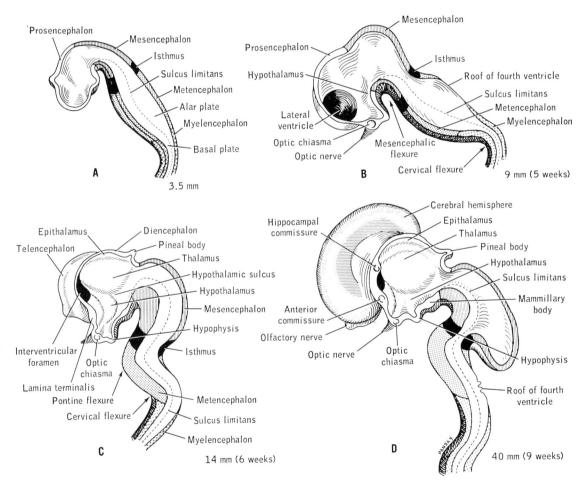

Figure 4-6 Sagittal reconstructions of the brain, including the cerebellum, in embryos ranging in age from 3 to 4 weeks to fetuses of 5 months (3.5 to 150 mm).

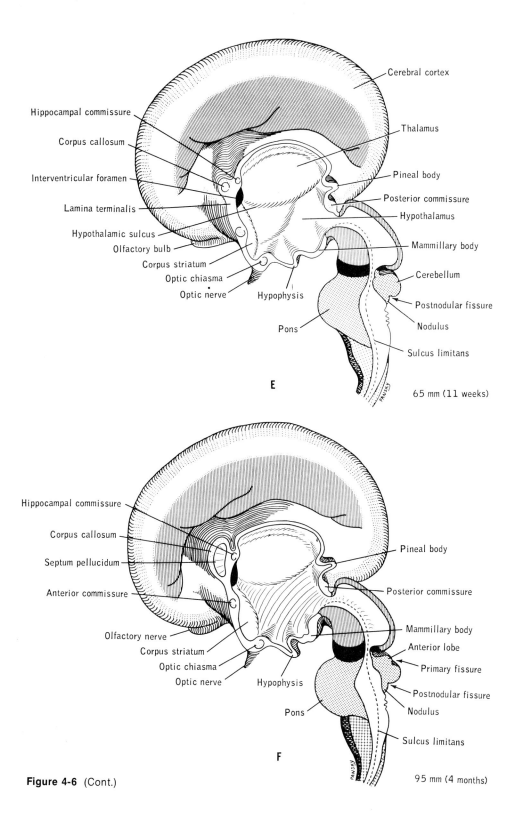

Labels for figure E (65 mm, 11 weeks):

Cerebral cortex
Hippocampal commissure
Corpus callosum
Interventricular foramen
Lamina terminalis
Hypothalamic sulcus
Olfactory bulb
Corpus striatum
Optic chiasma
Optic nerve
Hypophysis
Pons
Thalamus
Pineal body
Posterior commissure
Hypothalamus
Mammillary body
Cerebellum
Postnodular fissure
Nodulus
Sulcus limitans

E

65 mm (11 weeks)

Labels for figure F (95 mm, 4 months):

Hippocampal commissure
Corpus callosum
Septum pellucidum
Anterior commissure
Olfactory nerve
Corpus striatum
Optic chiasma
Optic nerve
Hypophysis
Pons
Pineal body
Posterior commissure
Mammillary body
Anterior lobe
Primary fissure
Postnodular fissure
Nodulus
Sulcus limitans

F

Figure 4-6 (Cont.)

95 mm (4 months)

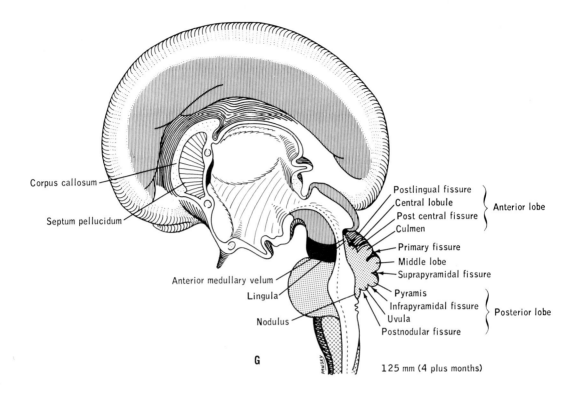

Corpus callosum

Septum pellucidum

Postlingual fissure
Central lobule   } Anterior lobe
Post central fissure
Culmen

Primary fissure
Middle lobe
Suprapyramidal fissure

Anterior medullary velum

Lingula

Pyramis
Infrapyramidal fissure } Posterior lobe
Uvula
Postnodular fissure

Nodulus

G

125 mm (4 plus months)

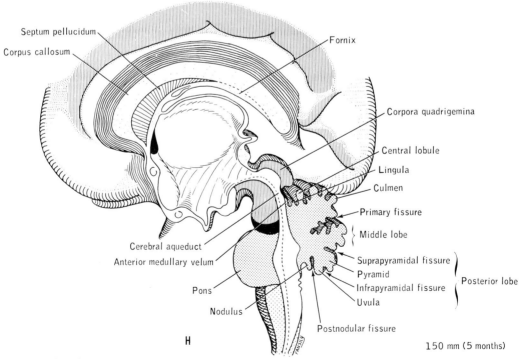

Septum pellucidum

Corpus callosum

Fornix

Corpora quadrigemina

Central lobule

Lingula

Culmen

Primary fissure

Middle lobe

Cerebral aqueduct

Anterior medullary velum

Suprapyramidal fissure
Pyramid
Infrapyramidal fissure   } Posterior lobe
Uvula

Pons

Nodulus

Postnodular fissure

H

150 mm (5 months)

Figure 4-6 (Cont.)

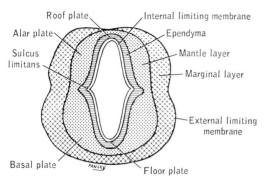

Figure 4-7 Schematic cross section of the spinal cord showing its primitive divisions and layers.

STRUCTURE OF THE NEURAL TUBE

Macroscopic (Fig. 4-7)

In cross section of the tube, certain portions are clearly indicated. In the dorsal midline is the thin *roof plate.* In the ventral midline lies the *floor plate.* Both roof and floor plates are continuous with the thickened lateral walls. Near the midpoint of each lateral wall is a shallow, longitudinal groove, the *sulcus limitans.* The latter serves as a boundary between the dorsal part of the wall, called the *alar plate*, and the ventral part, the *basal plate.*

Microscopic (Fig. 4-7)

Although originally the ectoderm is but one cell layer in thickness, rapid proliferation produces many layers by the time the neural tube has formed. Soon, two limiting membranes are

discernible, an internal one, which lines the cavity of the neural tube (neurocele), and an external one, lying at the periphery.

The cells adjoining the neurocele are at first most active in proliferation. Eventually, the mitotic activity among them becomes greatly reduced and the cells next to the lumen elongate, giving the appearance of a columnar epithelium. This layer is the *ependyma.* Surrounding the ependyma is a very cell-rich, heavily nucleated zone, the *mantle layer.* External to the mantle layer, a narrow, pale, almost cell-free area called the *marginal layer* can be seen. All these layers are present by the end of the fourth embryonic week.

DIFFERENTIATION OF THE SPINAL CORD (Fig. 4-8)

The ependyma remains as the lining epithelium for all the cavities of the CNS and is an important component of both the roof and floor plates.

The marginal layers of the lateral walls increase in size by the accumulation of processes of nerve cells. Some supporting cells also migrate here. The marginal layer is destined to become the white matter of the cord.

One must not lose sight of the fact that the mantle layer, like the other two, is continuous in its longitudinal extent from one end of the primitive neural tube to the other. In that part

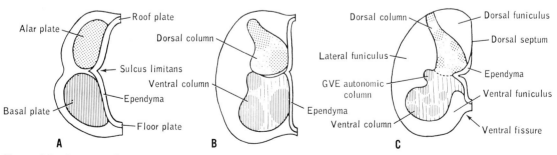

Figure 4-8 Cross sections of the spinal cord at different stages of development, showing the differentiation of the alar and basal plates.

of the lateral wall dorsal to the sulcus limitans, the mantle layer gives rise to the cell bodies which are functionally associated with the sensory mechanism. Thus arise the *dorsal gray columns* (horns). The mantle layer of the basal plate also gives rise to gray matter. Here, however, are found the cell bodies of motor neurons. Thus, the mantle layer of the basal plate forms the *ventral gray columns* (horns).

DIFFERENTIATION OF THE BRAIN

Myelencephalon (Figs. 4-6, 4-9)

There are differences between the differentiation of the brain and the cord even though they both develop from the same basic layers. This is probably because of several factors. First, in the cord, there is a definite relationship between neural and body segments. In the brain, existence of such a definite segmental arrangement is controversial. Therefore, since there is no need for a continuous chain of dorsal and ventral roots attaching to the myelencephalon, breaks in the continuity of the dorsal and ventral gray substance occur here. A second difference is related to the branchial arches. Since these differentiate into striated muscle related to viscera, new motor centers to supply these arches develop. The appearance of organs of special sense found in

the head also results in structural differences and is associated with the formation of still other new cell masses. Further, the appearance of higher brain centers, which provide for better integration of sensory impulses and improved control of motor function, leads to structural changes in the medulla because of the establishment of long fiber bundles to and from these new centers.

One of the most striking events in the development of the myelencephalon is the tremendous enlargement of the neural tube cavity. This expansion does not involve all the walls equally. The floor plate remains fixed. The two lateral walls migrate laterally and ventrally, stretching the roof plate between them. The latter forms the thin roof, composed chiefly of ependyma, for the fourth ventricle. Thus, the two lateral walls are now in a nearly horizontal plane, the median sulcus indicating the region of the primitive floor plate. In this position, the lateral walls of the tube now form the floor of the fourth ventricle.

Surrounding the brain wall at this time mesenchymal tissue is becoming highly vascularized, giving rise to the *pia mater.* The latter becomes intimately related to the ependymal roof of the fourth ventricle. The two tissues combined are known collectively as the *cho-*

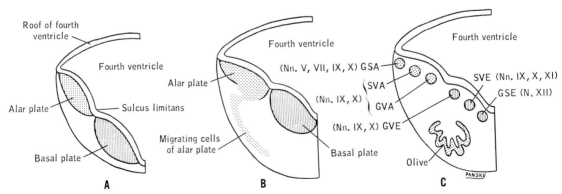

Figure 4-9 Same as Fig. 4-8 except that these sections are through the myelencephalon.

roid tela (tela choroidea). Near the center, where the ventricle is broadest, vessels in the tela invaginate into the ventricle. This vascular mass is the *choroid plexus.*

Although the plane of the lateral walls has changed, the primitive sulcus limitans is still evident and acts as a boundary between alar and basal plates.

The marginal layer forms white matter here also, but its appearance has altered because it is now interspersed with gray substance and contains fibers running in many planes.

The important consideration here is the fate of the mantle layer. As in the cord, the alar plate is sensory, but here in the myelencephalon, it lies lateral, rather than dorsal, to the motor area. In the medulla, the sensory zone is usually subdivided, although not by any visible, anatomic structures. Investigation has proved that the most medial part, next to the sulcus limitans, is concerned with visceral sense, while more laterally lies the area for the reception of somatic impulses. The extreme lateral portion is devoted to special somatic sense (Fig. 4-9).

The basal plate gives rise to efferent neurons. In the cord, the ventral gray columns supply skeletal muscle while the intermediolateral columns, when present, lie more laterally and supply smooth and cardiac muscle

and glands. Similarly, in the medulla, the most medial portion of the basal plate differentiates into nuclei supplying skeletal muscle of somite origin, including the muscles of the tongue and eyes. Lateral to the somatic column lies the visceral area, the neurons of which pass to autonomic ganglia. Because of the addition of skeletal muscle derived from the branchial arches, a portion of the basal plate lying intermediate between the somatic and visceral columns differentiates to supply this.

Metencephalon (Figs. 4-6, 4-10)

This region has three zones. The first, and oldest, is the axial portion, or *tegmentum,* which is merely the rostral continuation of the myelencephalon. The second, and largest, is the *cerebellum,* while the third is the *basal portion of the pons.*

The roof plate here, although thin, acquires some neurons and is known as the *anterior medullary velum.* The ependymal layer is present but inconspicuous.

Cerebellum (Figs. 4-6, 4-10)

Viewed from above, the fourth ventricle is seen to be lozenge-shaped. When the pontine flexure occurs, its transverse plane is through the broadest portion of the ventricle. Here, at the zone of transition between the thick-

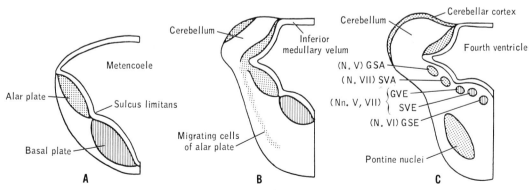

Figure 4-10 Same as Fig. 4-8 but here the sections are through the metencephalon.

walled alar plate and the thin roof, lies the so-called rhombic lip. It is from a proliferation of this lip, just caudal to the lateral recess, that the oldest part of the cerebellum, the flocculo-nodular lobe, arises.

Rostral to the lateral recess, the rhomboid fossa is narrower, so that the alar plates of the lateral walls approach each other. The most dorsal parts of these plates begin to enlarge, at first inward toward the ventricle. In the third fetal month, these paired enlargements become obvious. Soon these swellings fuse in the midline. The medial portions, in the region of fusion, do not grow so markedly as the areas on either side. Thus, the central portion, or *vermis*, of the cerebellum is overshadowed by the expanding cerebellar hemispheres.

Subsequently, fissures and other local differentiations occur. The primary fissure appears in the fourth fetal month. By the end of the seventh month, all parts are recognizable.

Basal Pons

This is a much later development, serving to connect the cerebral and cerebellar hemispheres. The massive bundles of fibers which account for the bulk of this region have been secondarily wrapped about the ventral and lateral aspects of the original tegmentum.

Mesencephalon   (Figs. 4-6, 4-11)

The mesencephalon shows the least specialized differentiation of any part of the brain. It consists of three major zones: The dorsal portion is the *tectum*, the intermediate part is the *tegmentum*, the ventral portion is the *peduncular area*. Primitively, roof, alar, and basal plates are present. The floor plate is said to be missing, having terminated in the metencephalon.

The cavity of the mesencephalon remains narrow and is known as the *cerebral aqueduct* (aqueduct of Sylvius), for which the ependyma forms a lining.

The roof plate is a narrow band joining the two alar plates, through which commissural fibers pass.

A major portion of the alar plates thicken to form the *tectum*. This consists of four paired swellings, the *corpora quadrigemina*. A small, ventral portion of the alar plate gives rise to at least one sensory nucleus, the *mesencephalic* of the *trigeminal* nerve. Some cells of the alar plate migrate ventrally to become the *red nucleus* and *substantia nigra.*

The basal plate differentiates into the remainder of the tegmental area. This includes the rostral continuation of the motor cell columns begun at lower levels.

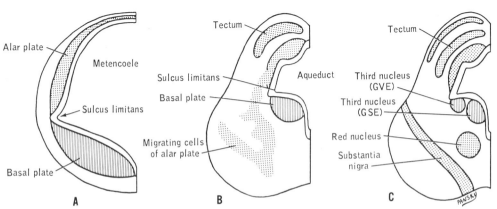

Figure 4-11   Same as Fig. 4-8 but here the sections are through the mesencephalon.

The peduncular region is a recent acquisition laid down on the ventral surface of the midbrain as the long fiber tracts descend from the forebrain to lower levels of the brainstem and spinal cord.

Diencephalon (Figs. 4-4 through 4-6)

The diencephalon is that portion of the prosencephalon which remains medial after the telencephalon has evaginated. Certain peculiarities set this portion of the brain apart from the caudal levels thus far studied: First, there are no typical nerves attached to it. Second, not only is the embryonic floor plate missing, but the basal plates are also absent.[1] Thus, only the roof and alar plates remain; the former is composed chiefly of ependyma, while the latter has the three typical layers.

At first, the diocoele, or cavity, of the tube, is broad. However, with the enlargement of the two alar plates, the cavity becomes the slitlike *third ventricle.*

The roof plate becomes intimately associated with the pia mater, forming a *choroid tela.* This, with the enlargement of some of its vessels, invaginates into the third ventricle, forming the choroid plexus.

The remainder of the diencephalon develops from a differentiation of the alar plates. By the tenth fetal week, three main regions can be distinguished: the epithalamus, dorsally; the thalamus laterally; and the hypothalamus ventrally.

Epithalamus (Fig. 4-6)

This lies at the junction between roof and alar plates. Near its inferior border adjoining the midbrain, the roof plate develops a caudal evagination called the *epiphysis,* or *pineal body.* A small thickening of the alar plates lateral to the pineal body represents the chief epithalamic differentiation, the *habenula.*

Thalamus (Fig. 4-6)

The walls of the third ventricle undergo such extensive growth that in most brains the two sides meet and form a bridge, the *interthalamic connection (massa intermedia),* across the ventricle. A sulcus, the hypothalamic sulcus, appears as a longitudinal groove separating the thalamus from the ventral hypothalamic region.

Hypothalamus (Fig. 4-6)

The lateral walls of the hypothalamic region thicken, but not to the degree seen in the thalamus. In addition to the nuclei, the optic chiasma is found associated with its rostral end. Other parts of the hypothalamus which arise ventrally include the tuber cinereum; the infundibulum, which gives rise to the neural hypophysis; and the mammillary bodies.

Telencephalon (Figs. 4-4 through 4-6, 4-12)

The telencephalon begins as a pair of lateral evaginations just behind the rostral limit of the forebrain. At first, the cavities (telencoele) open widely into the third ventricle, but later they become reduced in diameter. These are the *interventricular foramina* (of Monro).

As the hemispheres expand rostrally and then dorsally, to rise above the diencephalon, the roof plate of each side is stretched vertically and fuses with the pia, forming the *choroid tela* of the lateral ventricles. This invaginates into the ventricles to create the *choroid plexus.* Later, as the hemispheres increase in mass, the region through which the blood vessels enter the plexus becomes very narrow but persists as the *choroid fissure.*

The telencephalon has three principal parts: the neopallium, the rhinencephalon, and the corpus striatum.

[1] Some investigators feel that the hypothalamic sulcus is a continuation of the sulcus limitans and therefore the hypothalamus would differentiate from the basal plate.

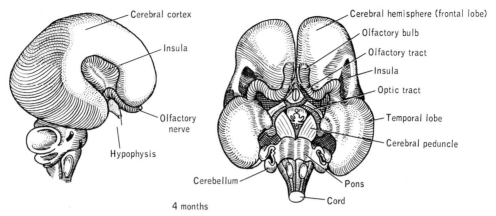

Figure 4-12 Human brain at 4 months. *Left,* seen from the right side. *Right,* from below, showing the development of the insula and parts of the rhinencephalon. *(Adapted from H. K. Corning.)*

Corpus Striatum

This begins as an enlargement of the floor of the telencephalon just lateral to and below the interventricular foramina, in direct line with the thalamic portion of the diencephalon. In each of these masses, two major nuclei, the *caudate* and *lenticular,* differentiate. The largest portions of these nuclei remain fixed. However, the caudal part of the caudate nucleus, the tail, is caught up in the growth and migration of the hemisphere, accounting for its adult shape and position.

Because of the extensive development of fibers to distant parts of the hemispheres, in particular those ascending from the thalamus, the internal capsule appears between the thalamus and the lenticular nucleus. Descending fibers from the hemispheres follow the same path, accompanying the ascending groups. Later, a portion of the internal capsule, created by descending fibers (but later acquiring some ascending fibers), appears anteriorly, between the caudate and lenticular nuclei. This is the *anterior limb of the capsule.*

Rhinencephalon   (Fig. 4-12)

This begins as paired swellings on the ventral surface of each hemisphere which enlarge to become the *olfactory lobes.* These have two divisions: the more rostral becomes the *olfactory bulb* and *tract;* the more caudal differentiates into the *anterior perforated substance* and the *parolfactory area.*

Because of growth, posterior migration, and lateral expansion, the olfactory lobe becomes bent and partially obscured. Further, two pallial areas differentiate, the *archipallium* and *paleopallium* (the *hippocampal formation*).

Neopallium

During the first 4 months, the outer surface of the hemisphere is smooth. At about this time, the external gray substance begins to grow faster than the underlying white. This results in the throwing of the cortex at the surface into folds or convolutions *(gyri)* separated by furrows *(fissures and sulci).*

The largest fissures appear first, the region for the *sagittal fissure* being indicated almost from the beginning, when the telencephalon first evaginated. The *rhinal* and *hippocampal fissures* appear in the fourth month. About the same time, a suggestion of the *lateral (sylvian) fissure* may be found, but this is not complete until after birth. This fissure is due, at least in part, to the fact that the cortex overlying the striatum, the *insula* (island of Reil), grows more slowly than surrounding regions (Fig.

4-12). Thus, opercular coverings from frontal, parietal, and temporal lobes begin to overgrow it. The continued rostral advance of the temporal lobe serves to elongate this fissure still more. The *central fissure* (of Rolando) is evident at 6 to 7 months. The parietooccipital, calcarine, and collateral fissures come into being at about the same time.

A word should be added here concerning the inversion of the layers of the cortex. In its original condition, the alar plate consists of the three typical layers. In the hemispheres, there is little change in the ependyma. However, there occurs a mass migration of cells outward from the mantle layer into the relatively cell-free marginal zone. Thus, the cortical gray substance comes to lie on the outside, while fibers going to or coming from it form the underlying white matter.[2]

COMMISSURES   (Fig. 4-6)

From the beginning, the lamina terminalis, representing the most rostral end of the prosencephalon at the time the hemispheres first appear, serves as a bridge, linking the two sides. It is natural, then, that commissural fibers, subsequently developed, would utilize this bridge. The commissures to be discussed here are the anterior and hippocampal, associated with the archipallium, and the corpus callosum, belonging to the neopallium.

Anterior Commissure

This is the most rostral and ventral of the commissures. Its fibers pass through the lamina terminalis, uniting the anterior portions of the olfactory apparatus.

Hippocampal Commissure

This also has its origin in the lamina terminalis, but with the subsequent development of the corpus callosum and the caudal migration of the hippocampi, it comes to lie a consider-

able distance behind its site of inception, now being associated with the crura of the fornix.

Corpus Callosum

It begins in the roof region of the lamina terminalis rostral and dorsal to the hippocampal commissure and almost directly dorsal to the anterior commissure. This area is extended caudally and is further enlarged by the growth and fusion of the medial walls of the hemispheres.

HISTOGENESIS

Myelination in the CNS

The deposition of myelin sheaths is of physiologic importance, for it appears that fiber tracts in the CNS begin to function at about the time they acquire myelin. Myelination begins in the spinal cord at cervical levels during the middle fetal months but is not completed until the first and second years after birth with the myelination of the corticospinal[3] and tectospinal tracts.

In the brain, myelination begins about the sixth fetal month and is not actually completed until adolescence. Only the fibers in the corpus striatum and the tracts ascending from lower levels are myelinated at birth. Among the last fibers to become ensheathed are the commissures.

Peripheral Nervous System (PNS)   (Fig. 4-1)

Afferent Fiber

In the region of the cord, each of the columns of the neural crest breaks up into small, spherical masses corresponding to each pair of somites, beginning with the first cervical and extending to the first coccygeal. They lose their longitudinal interconnections and slip down along the cord so that their position is

---

[2]The same inversion is also seen in the cerebellum.

[3]It is possible that at least some of the fibers of the corticospinal tracts are not completely myelinated until the twenty-first year.

more lateral than dorsal. These are the primordia of the spinal ganglia.

In the cranial region, the crest also breaks up but the arrangement is irregular.

Within these primordia, two types of cells differentiate. One of these is the *neuroblast,* the other is the *spongioblast.*

The neuroblast elongates, forming a spindle-shaped cell, which sprouts a process at either end. This is the bipolar neuron. The central process of this cell grows toward the neural tube and enters the marginal layer of the spinal cord, terminating about a cell in the dorsal part of the mantle layer. The peripheral process of the bipolar neuron grows ventrally and aligns itself with the efferent fibers of the ventral root to form the spinal nerve trunk. Later, the original bipolar cell undergoes a series of transformations to become a unipolar (monopolar) cell. These morphologic changes are underway in some ganglia by the tenth fetal week.

At first, the spongioblasts in the ganglia form a syncytial net around the ganglion cells. Some of the spongioblasts remain close to the neuron cell body to become *capsule cells.* Others migrate along both central and peripheral processes, giving rise to the *sheath cells of Schwann.*

Efferent Fiber

Within the mantle layer of the basal plate two types of cells differentiate, *neuroblasts* and *spongioblasts.*

The neuroblasts multiply by typical mitosis, the rate of which gradually slows down until, during the first postnatal year, the ability to reproduce is lost entirely. At first the neuroblast is spindle-shaped. Gradually, it becomes more pear-shaped, with a thin process growing out of its more slender end. This is the axon, which elongates, penetrates the marginal layer, and leaves the spinal cord to become a part of the ventral root. The details of development are the same whether these fibers terminate in

skeletal muscle or in autonomic ganglia. After the axon is well established, many shorter processes, the dendrites, sprout from the broader portion of the neuroblast. Thus, the typical multipolar neuron develops.

Many of the spongioblasts remain within the CNS to form *neuroglia* (Fig. 4-1), both *astrocytes* and *oligodendroglia.* Others migrate outside the CNS to become *Schwann's sheath* for efferent fibers.

Myelination in PNS

Myelin begins to be deposited on many afferent fibers in the fourth fetal month and continues for 3 months after birth. On efferent fibers, myelination begins slightly earlier.

DISTRIBUTION OF PERIPHERAL NEURONS

Afferent Fibers (Fig. 4-13)

There is one pair of spinal nerves to each pair of somites. As growth continues, bringing sensory fibers to the surface, a nerve-to-skin relation is established. This is the *dermatome.* In certain body areas, where there has been little shifting or migration during development, this relation is easy to follow, e.g., in the upper portion of the thorax. However, the evolution of the limbs and their subsequent rotation have complicated the picture.

The development of sensory neurons from cranial ganglionic masses is essentially the same.

Efferent Fibers (Figs. 4-13, 4-14)

Very early, efferent nerve rootlets become intimately associated with the myoblasts (of the somites), which become skeletal muscle. This basic relationship is maintained regardless of the size of the muscle or the distance it may have migrated from the original site of formation. This same general principle holds true for efferent fibers of the cranial nerves.

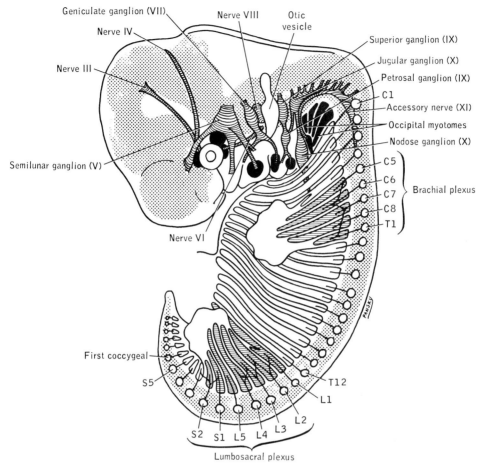

Figure 4-13 Relation between the body musculature and the nerves. *(Adapted from Patten, Human Embryology, 3d ed., McGraw-Hill Book Company, New York, 1968.)*

GANGLIA

Sensory

See Afferent Fiber, under Peripheral Nervous System, above (Fig. 4-1).

Motor (Figs. 4-13, 4-14)

It was originally believed that neuroblasts which give rise to all postganglionic neurons of the autonomic nervous system arose from migrations of the neural crest. More recently, the evidence indicates that at least some of the autonomic ganglion cells arise through a mi-

gration from the basal plate of the neural tube. In the thoracic and lumbar regions, the migration is regular and on a segmental basis, groups of crest cells accumulating in series along the lateral aspects of the vertebral column. These represent the chain ganglia. Here, neuroblasts become the multipolar *postganglionic* neurons of the *thoracolumbar outflow*. Spongioblasts give rise to the *Schwann sheath* for these fibers. Here, myelin fails to appear.

There is still further ventral migration of the crest cells, some of which become localized anterior to the aorta, becoming closely associ-

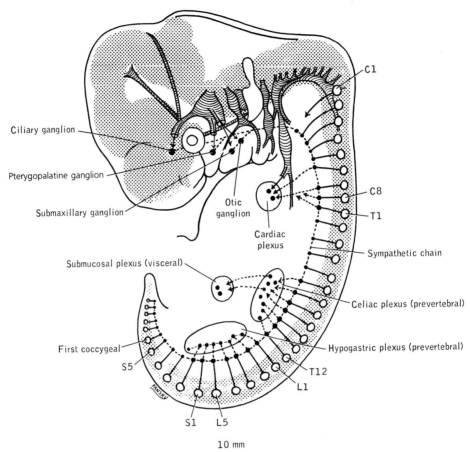

Ciliary ganglion

Pterygopalatine ganglion

Submaxillary ganglion

Otic ganglion

Cardiac plexus

Submucosal plexus (visceral)

First coccygeal

S5

S1   L5

C1

C8

T1

Sympathetic chain

Celiac plexus (prevertebral)

Hypogastric plexus (prevertebral)

T12

L1

10 mm

Figure 4-14 Sagittal reconstruction showing the migration of autonomic cells, the primary migration being linked together longitudinally in the neck and trunk to form the sympathetic chain, while the second and third migration give the prevertebral and visceral plexuses, respectively.

ated with the origins of arteries arising from the aorta. These are the *collateral autonomic ganglia,* i.e., the *celiac* and *superior mesenteric.* Some of the migratory cells differentiate into the *adrenal medulla.*

A scattering of crest neuroblasts migrates still further toward the viscera, forming ganglia in or near the walls of individual organs. These are the *terminal ganglia,* the cell bodies of which may be arranged in the *intermuscular plexus (Auerbach's)* or *submucosal plexus (Meissner's).*

Terminal ganglia also develop from the

neural crest in the sacral and cranial areas for the craniosacral outflow of the autonomic system, i.e., the ganglia of the prostatic and vesical plexuses of the pelvis, and the otic, ciliary, pterygopalatine, and submandibular ganglia of the head.

CLINICAL CONSIDERATIONS

General

In addition to the obvious conditions to be discussed below, there are many factors in the development and histogenesis of the nervous system of which a thorough understanding is of great value to the clinician. Among these are the following:

1 The difference in growth rate between the spinal cord and body length, which accounts for the fact that during the third fetal month the cord completely fills the vertebral canal; at birth the cord terminates at the lower border of the third lumbar vertebra, while in adults the caudal end of the cord lies near the upper border of the second lumbar vertebra. This is likewise why cord segments, particularly in the lower half of the body, do not lie adjacent to vertebral segments of the corresponding number.

2 The constant relation between the nerve and the mesoderm giving rise to muscle, whether somite or branchial arch, is maintained. Hence, knowing the embryonic origin of a muscle, it can be assumed that the nerve supply will be the same as that established in the embryo.

3 The early nerve-to-surface relation, with the establishment of the dermatomes, is an invaluable aid in localizing the level of a lesion in the CNS. Even on the appendages, the development of which interrupted the trunk dermatomal segmentation, this primitive relationship still can be seen.

Specific Pathology

Congenital Deficiencies

A partial or complete agenesis or hypoplasia is not a problem peculiar to the nervous system but is encountered throughout the development of all viscera. One of the most common manifestations, *microcephalus,* is a condition in which there is defective development of the whole brain and premature ossification of the skull. Whether cerebral maldevelopment is due to the premature ossification, or vice versa, or to pre- or postnatal meningeal involvement is not known. Microcephalic persons are usually idiots or imbeciles and are often epileptic. *Cerebral palsy* may also result

from a hypoplastic condition involving certain motor centers of the brain.

Cranioschisis

This is caused by the failure of the neural tube to close in the brain region. This defect further results in a massive deficiency of the skull, thus leaving the inside of the CNS exposed to the exterior. In most cases, the remainder of the brain does not develop to even close-to-normal proportions, and for this reason the term *anencephaly* is often applied. Because of the combination of little development and exposure to infection, death usually ensues shortly after birth.

Myeloschisis (Fig. 4-15)

In such cases, the neural tube fails to close at spinal cord levels. This, too, is associated with a secondary condition in which the neural arch of the vertebra also fails to form, again leaving the inside of the CNS exteriorized. The defect in the spine is called *spina bifida.* The latter condition can also occur without abnormalities of the spinal cord and is primarily a skeletal abnormality.

Spinal Bifida (Fig. 4-15)

Unlike myeloschisis, this condition is not an inherent defect in the development of the cord. Fundamentally, it involves a failure on the part of the surrounding mesoderm to form normal or complete neural arches on one or more of the adjacent vertebrae. Thus, the spinal cord may become secondarily involved. In its simplest form, *spina bifida occulta,* the neural arch is missing, but there is no protrusion of either meninges or spinal cord through the hiatus. Thus, the skin lies flat over the surface, and, except for a lack of a protective lamina of bone, the cord and spinal nerves are normal. When the bony deficiency is greater, the pressure of the cerebrospinal fluid in the subarachnoid space may cause a visible herniation of a meningeal sac filled with fluid. This is called *spina bifida with meningocele.* In this

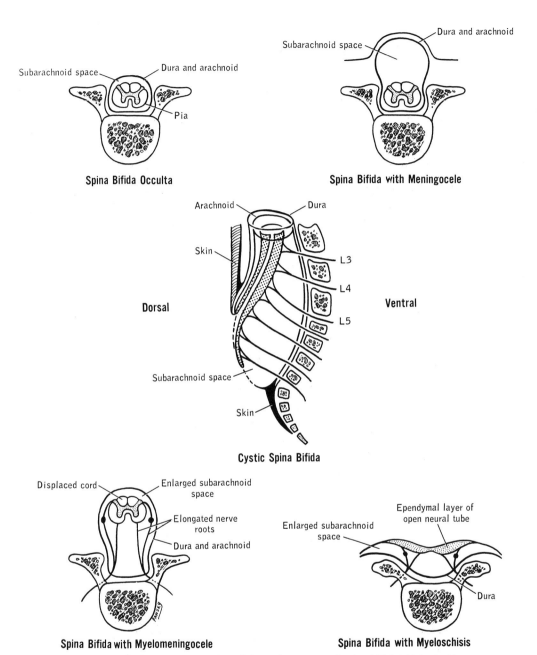

Figure 4-15 Diagrammatic representation of the various types of spina bifida. *(Adapted from Patten, Human Embryology, 3d ed., McGraw-Hill Book Company, New York, 1968.)*

case the spinal cord and its attached nerves are also normal, but the cord is left without the protection usually afforded by hard tissue. Again, when the bony deficiency is great, fluid pressure building up ventral to the cord may also cause it to protrude dorsally through the hiatus. In such cases, a variable extent of the cord has been distorted, and the spinal nerves in the area are greatly stretched. Furthermore, the cord is now in a superficial position, making it extremely vulnerable to trauma. This condition is *spina bifida with myelome-ningocele.* A final anomaly belonging in this category is *cystic spina bifida.* In this type, it appears that the caudal end of the neural tube does not quite close off from the skin, leaving an opening from the central canal of the cord to the body surface. At the same time, the subarachnoid space fills up with fluid forming a kind of cyst anterior and caudal to the lower portion of the spinal cord, putting consider-able stress on the spinal nerves in this area.

In this instance, the cord has an abnormal curvature, and even the normal portions are vulnerable. Perhaps the most serious conse-quence is that the cord is open to bacterial invasion.

Hydrocephalus (Fig. 3-27)

In the course of development, an occlusion may form in the ventricular system, especially the interventricular foramina or cerebral aq-ueduct. This leads to the expansion of the brain and cranium under pressure from cere-brospinal fluid. This pressure causes poor development of other portions of the brain, the cortex in particular.

Arnold-Chiari Deformity

This condition is characterized by elongation of the cerebellar tonsils; a small and deformed medulla; a small pons with degeneration of its transverse fibers; and herniation of the cere-bellum into the vertebral canal.

Summary
General Development

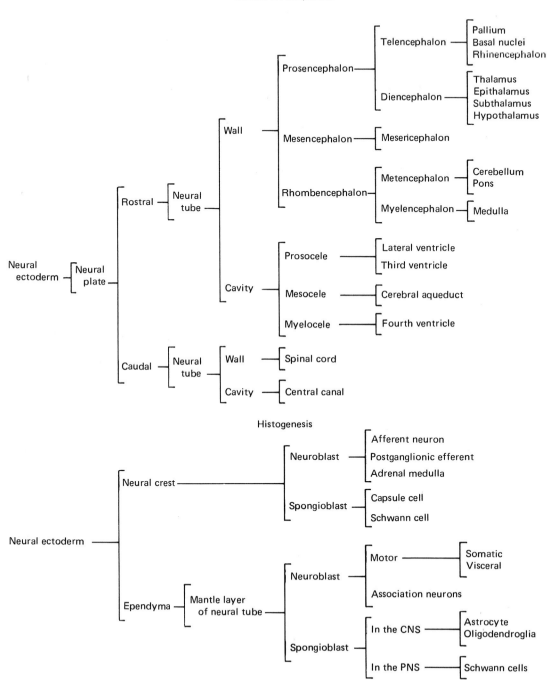

Histogenesis

Differentiation of Neural Tube

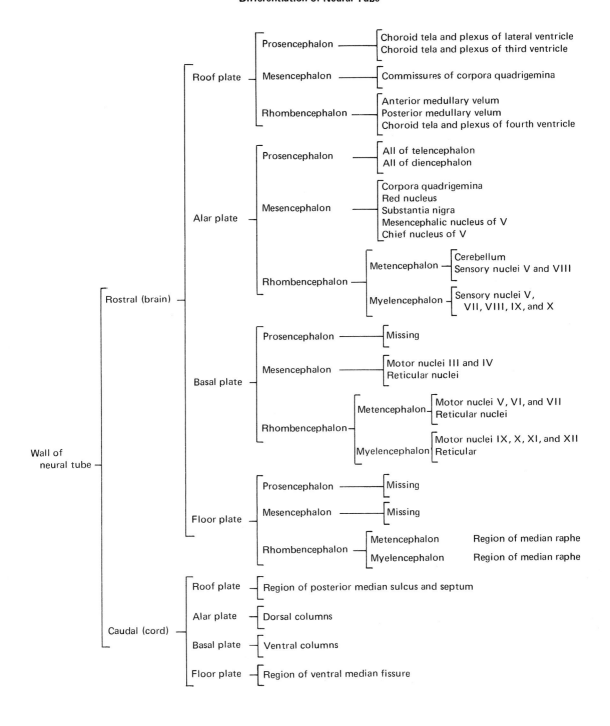

Basic Structure and Function of the Nervous System

STRUCTURE
The Neuron in the CNS

Definition

A neuron is the unit of structure and function of the nervous system, composed of a cell body and one or more processes.

Classification of the Neuron Processes

From a functional standpoint, *axons* conduct impulses *away* from the cell body and *dendrites* conduct impulses *toward* the cell body.

Morphologic Classification of Neurons

Neurons are classified on a morphologic basis according to the number of their processes or upon the length and disposition of the axons.

Classifications According to Number of Processes *Unipolar (Monopolar)* (Figs. 5-1, 5-2) The cell is spherical and has a single process. A short distance from the cell, the process splits into two branches which travel in opposite directions. Most authorities agree that the single-stem process and its branches are structurally similar to axons. However, it is preferable to speak of a peripheral process leading toward the stem of the cell and a central branch leading impulses away from the stem toward the CNS. Neurons of this type are afferent (sensory) and are found almost exclusively in the peripheral system.

Bipolar (Fig. 5-2) Neurons of this type have two processes, a dendrite and an axon attached to opposite ends of a fusiform cell

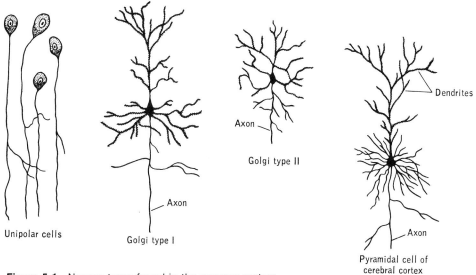

Figure 5-1 Neuron types found in the nervous system.

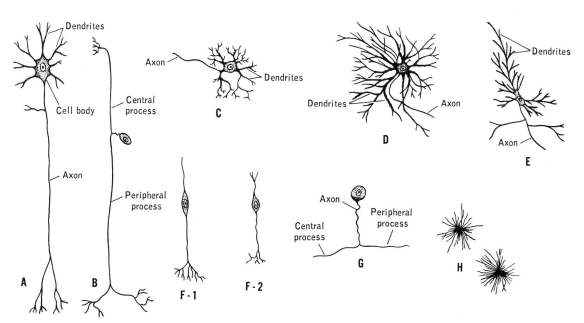

Figure 5-2 Varieties of cells of the human nervous system illustrating cell bodies, axons, and dendrites of the neurons. *A.* Motor neuron. *B.* Sensory neuron. *C.* Sympathetic ganglion cell. *D.* Ventral horn cell. *E.* Fusiform cell of the cerebral cortex. *F.* (1) Olfactory bipolar cell. (2) Retinal bipolar cell. *G.* Spinal ganglion cell. *H.* Neuroglia cells of the cerebral cortex.

body. Bipolar elements are found in the retina, in cochlear and vestibular ganglia, and in certain places in the CNS.

Multipolar (Figs. 5-1 through 5-3) The cell has several poles, each representing the point of attachment of a process. Although occasionally a cell may have only one dendrite, there are usually several, each of which may give off secondary branches. The dendritic network makes contact with the terminations of other neurons possible. Each neuron has only one axon (axis cylinder). This arises from a small conical elevation of the cell body, the *axon hillock,* or *initial segment.* The axon may travel considerable distances [from 1 mm to 1 m (a fraction of an inch to several feet)] and may give off branches. However, near its termination, a considerable arborization occurs. These branches, the *telodendrons,* vary greatly in number, shape, and distribution.

Multipolar neurons comprise the bulk of the neurons whose cell bodies lie within the CNS. They are also typical of the autonomic division of the peripheral nervous system.

Classification on the Basis of Axon Length *(Golgi Classification)* Morphologically, these neurons are all of the multipolar type.

Golgi Type I (Fig. 5-1) These neurons have long axons, most of which leave the CNS through the ventral roots of spinal nerves or through the main trunks of the cranial nerves.

Golgi Type II (Fig. 5-1) These are neurons having short axons, all of which stay within the CNS. The majority of association neurons (interneurons) are of this type.

Classification According to Fiber Size and Electrophysiology This material is presented in Chaps. 7 and 13.

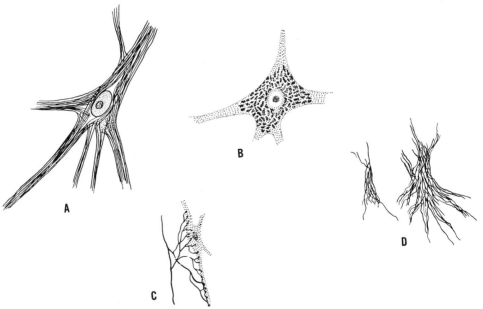

Figure 5-3 Diagrammatic representation of structural details of several nerve cells. *A.* Neurofibrillar network of a pyramidal cell of the human motor cortex. *B.* Nissl bodies of an anterior horn cell from the human spinal cord. *C.* Nerve fiber endings on a nerve cell. *D.* Golgi network (pericellular). *(After Cajal.)*

Microscopic Structure of the Neurons

The Cell Body

This is the portion of the neuron which contains the nucleus and is frequently called the *perikaryon*. These cells assume different shapes (round, oval, fusiform, and pyramidal) and vary in size from 4 to 120 μm.

The Cytoplasm This is differentiated into several components: neurofibrils, neuroplasm, Nissl bodies, mitochondria, Golgi apparatus, and centrosome.

Neurofibrils (Fig. 5-3) These are fine cytoplasmic fibrils distributed in a complex network throughout the cell body. Electron microscopy indicates that they consist of aggregates of minute filaments 60 to 100 Å thick which extend into all the cell processes. Those found in dendrites are finer than those in axons. They may represent an internal supporting structure.

Neuroplasm This is the semiliquid, undifferentiated cytoplasm surrounding neurofibrils; in axons it is sometimes referred to as *axoplasm.*

Nissl Substance (Figs. 5-3, 5-4) This substance, also called Nissl bodies, chromophil, chromidial substance, and tigroid bodies, is the most conspicuous element in the cytoplasm when sections are stained with basic aniline dyes. It takes the form of irregular clumps or finely granular particles. Although these blocks (or particles) may vary in size from cell to cell, they tend to have the same appearance in cells which have similar functions, for example—in large motor neurons, the blocks are of considerable size, while in large sensory neurons they are fine and dustlike. Electron microscope studies reveal that these bodies are composed of parallel cytoplasmic lamellae, possibly vesicular in nature, among which are scattered numerous granules, thought to be ribonucleic acid (RNA). It

has been shown that the ratio of lamellae to granules varies considerably. No evidence for a limiting membrane has been found. Generally, Nissl bodies lie in the interstices between neurofibrils. They are absent beneath the cell membrane and immediately surrounding the nucleus. They extend into the dendrites but not into the axon hillock or axons. It is believed that Nissl bodies are directly concerned in the continuous synthesis of new cytoplasm which flows continuously down the axon (axoplasmic flow). They change in appearance under different physiologic conditions: in extreme fatigue, or in pathologic conditions where there is injury (either trauma or disease) to the cell body or axon, they disappear almost completely (chromatolysis). Temporary chromatolysis, together with a shift of the nucleus to one side, is noted when an axon is cut. These phenomena constitute the *axon reaction.*

Microtubules Seen only under the electron microscope, these appear as hollow, unbranched cylinders which average 225 Å in diameter and are said to be many micrometers in length. They frequently occur in groups of 30 or more. They are important both in intracellular support and for transport of substances within the cell.

Pigments In some nerve cells pigments such as lipochrome and melanin also appear.

Golgi Net and Mitochondria Both these organelles are found in neurons. The Golgi apparatus (or net) is a network of irregular threads or bands, heavier than the neurofibrils. It varies morphologically in neurons of different types. Filamentous mitochondria are scattered freely between the Nissl bodies and the neurofibrils. Their function here is probably similar to that in other body cells; i.e., they act in protein synthesis, in respiration, and in the production of secretions. There is evidence for the presence of a continuous distal

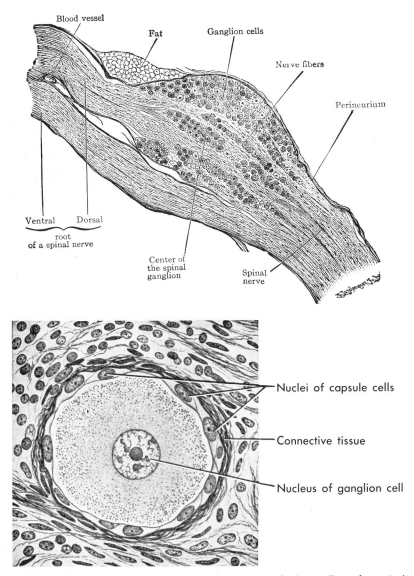

Figure 5-4 *Upper,* longitudinal section through a spinal ganglion of a cat showing the relation of the ganglion to the dorsal and ventral roots. *(From Greep and Weiss, Histology, 3d ed., McGraw-Hill Book Company, New York, 1973, p. 256.) Lower,* cell body and surrounding sheaths and connective tissue in semilunar human ganglion. × 600. *(From Greep and Weiss, Histology, 3d ed., McGraw-Hill Book Company, New York, 1973, p. 267.)*

flow from the region of the perikaryon. This flow not only is responsible for the maintenance of the ultimate branches of the cell but also brings to their terminations the sub-

stances required for the chemical transmission of nerve impulses. Thus, the neuron can perform as a type of gland cell in which the axon serves as a duct and which releases secretions in small quantities to come into contact with the tissue to be affected.

The Cell Membrane The thin membrane (80 Å) that separates the neuroplasm from the external medium is known as the *plasmalemma* or *axolemma*. Under the electron microscope it has a sandwichlike appearance with two dense bands on either side of a clear center (Fig. 5-5). The matrix of the membrane is made up largely of phospholipid molecules. Each molecule consists of two long fatty acid chains which are hydrophobic (nonpolar) joined together by a "head" which is hydrophilic (polar). The molecules (Fig. 5-6) line up in a double layer so that the hydrophilic ends are in contact with the watery solutions on the outside and inside of the cell and the hydrophobic ends are sequestered in the center of the membrane. Embedded within this phospholipid matrix are protein molecules, such as enzymes. This "unit membrane" structure is common to all cell membranes including those surrounding subcellular organelles.

The function of the cell membrane is to act as a barrier against the diffusion of harmful materials into the interior of the cell and against the loss of useful substances into the

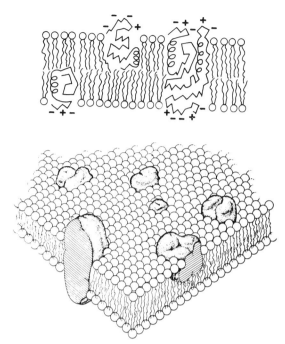

Figure 5-6 Diagram of the molecular structure of the unit membrane indicating the two fatty acid chains joined to a spherical head. Protein molecules are also shown. *(From Singer and Nicolson, Science 175:720–731, copyright 1972 by the American Association for the Advancement of Science.)*

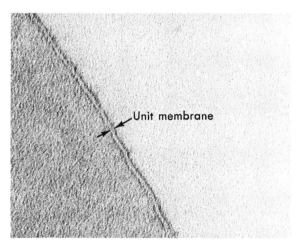

Figure 5-5 Electron micrograph of the unit membrane (× 280,000). Note the trilaminar character of the cell membrane showing two dark laminae separated by a light one. *(From Weiss and Greep, Histology, 4th ed., McGraw-Hill Book Company, New York, 1977.)*

extracellular environment. Thus, the membrane is a relatively impermeable structure and acts to retard the diffusion of chemicals into or out of the cell.

Lipid-soluble molecules introduced into the extracellular fluid penetrate into the cell much more easily than molecules that are not lipid-soluble. This can be understood in terms of the high lipid content of the matrix of the cell membrane. In addition, small particles—such as sodium, potassium, or chloride ions—can pass through the membrane much more easily than can large organic molecules. This "sieving" of the particles is thought to occur because of the presence of pores (Fig. 5-6) which perforate the cell membrane. These pores may have a fixed chemical structure.

The Nucleus (Figs. 5-1, 5-2, 5-4) This is relatively large, generally round, and centrally placed. Both relative size and position may appear to vary considerably when seen in different parts of the nervous system, because of the great irregularity and size of the many cells. There is a definite nuclear membrane which is not often outstanding in ordinary preparations. The nucleus is predominantly made up of pale-staining nucleoplasm. The linin framework is prominent but sparse. The basichromatin granules are fine and greatly dispersed. There is usually one large, very distinct, oxyphilic nucleolus in each nucleus. A smaller, round basophilic body lies so close to the nucleolus that it is referred to as a nucleolar satellite (sex chromatin). This is said to be present in the nuclei of females but not in males.

Support

Ependyma This is a term applied to the epithelial cells lining the ventricles of the brain and the central canal of the spinal cord. In the latter location and over the choroid plexuses, these cells are important for reasons other than lining or support, for there they may play a role in the production of cerebrospinal fluid.

Neuroglia (Fig. 5-7)
Astrocytes These are found throughout the CNS. Their nuclei are oval and contain little chromatin. Nucleoli are usually absent. In general, astrocytes may be divided into two classes, *protoplasmic* and *fibrous.* Both types have many processes, one of which is larger than the others. This process extends to adjacent blood vessels, terminating there in an *end foot.* The protoplasmic astrocytes with their numerous and relatively heavy branches predominate in the gray matter. The fibrous astrocytes are found in the white matter. Their longer, thin, and less numerous branches are seen to contain minute fibrillae. These cells tend to be arranged in rows parallel to the nerve fibers among which they lie. Their end feet form a complete layer outside the endothelium of the capillaries within the CNS and, together with the endothelium, are responsible for the "blood-brain barrier" which may serve to prevent certain substances from passing from the blood to the nervous tissue. At the surface of the CNS is found a layer of small astrocytes which is adherent to the overlying pia. Internally, the processes of these cells join the processes of other astrocytes lying deeper in the tissue. The external membrane is continued as a sleeve around the blood vessels entering the CNS from the pia and there becomes continuous with the layer of end feet around the intraneural capillaries. After injury to the nervous tissue, astrocytes are capable of rapid proliferation, forming a kind of "scar tissue" which interferes with the regeneration of neurons by blocking the path of growing cell processes.

Oligodendroglia These cells are smaller than astrocytes, and their nuclei contain more chromatin. Their nuclei also lack nucleoli. Oligodendroglia may be found in both gray

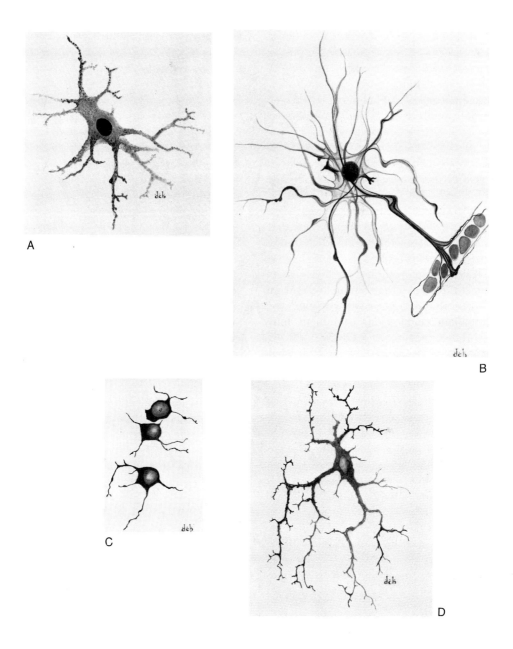

Figure 5-7 Neuroglia. *A.* Protoplasmic astrocyte showing gliosomes, in the human cerebral cortex. *B.* Fibrous astrocyte with a vascular foot process. Several fibrils are seen crossing the cell. Human cerebral cortex. *C.* Oligodendrocytes from a silver carbonate preparation. Monkey thalamus. *D.* Microglia from a silver carbonate preparation. Rabbit cerebral cortex. All × 975. *(From Peele, The Neuroanatomic Basis for Neurology, McGraw-Hill Book Company, New York, 1976.)*

and white matter of the CNS. They appear to help hold the gray matter together, but they are not so important in this respect as are the astrocytes. Since they are often seen closely surrounding neuron cell bodies, they are sometimes spoken of as *perineural satellites.* In the white matter they tend to align themselves between the axis cylinders of neuron, their processes forming incomplete sheaths for the nerve fiber. They appear to be the counterparts of the Schwann cells of the peripheral nerves and, like them, are responsible for the formation of myelin in the white matter (Fig. 5-8). Unlike the Schwann cells, each oligodendrocyte forms myelin segments on several different axons rather than on one, as is the case in the peripheral system.

Microglia   These are the smallest of the neuroglia. Their nuclei are also smaller than those of other types; they stain more darkly and may be irregular in shape. They are only moderately branched. Unlike the other glia, they are highly mobile, as can easily be demonstrated under pathologic conditions. Thus, they may serve as macrophages. Microglia are more common in gray than in white matter. In the former, they also appear in limited numbers as perineural satellites but are more often arranged along blood vessels as *perivascular satellites.* In the white matter they are distributed among the nerve fibers.

Insulation   (Figs. 5-8 through 5-10)

Myelin   During the fourth fetal month, an insulating substance begins to be laid down in the white matter of the cervical spinal cord. It is, however, absent or scarce around the cell bodies and dendrites. This material is known as myelin. Since myelin, when seen grossly in the CNS, appears a glistening white, the regions occupied by these fibers are called *white matter.* Myelin is a fatty substance containing cholesterol, cerebrosides, and certain phospholipids, the most important of which is sphingomyelin. The lipid is said to be in the

form of a lipid-protein complex. Apparently, myelin develops under the influence of nerve fibers in collaboration with neuroglia. The persistence of myelin, however, is dependent upon the integrity of the axis cylinder. Although myelin is not essential for the conduction of nerve impulses, it does seem to be required if impulses are to be conducted to such a degree that delicate and precise movements may result. It also influences the speed of conduction.

The Neuron in the Peripheral Nervous System

In the peripheral nervous system (PNS), axons carrying impulses away from the CNS are mingled with the peripheral processes of neurons carrying impulses toward the CNS. This combination of fibers is called a *nerve.* Each nerve contains a variable number of fibers, together with their supporting elements.

Components of a Nerve

Axis Cylinder   (Figs. 5-8 through 5-12) This consists of bundles of neurofibrils set in axoplasm. There is no Nissl substance, but mitochondria have been demonstrated. The diameters of the axis cylinders are subject to much variation (from one to several micrometers).

Myelin   (Figs. 5-8 through 5-13)   The vast majority of the peripheral nerve fibers are myelinated, at least to a small but demonstrable degree. However, a certain group of fibers, belonging to the autonomic portion of the peripheral nervous system, their cells of origin lying in ganglia, show no myelin and are referred to as nonmyelinated or nonmedullated fibers. The peripheral myelin is of the same general composition as that found in the CNS. It is apparently supported by a protoplasmic neurokeratin net, which, in part, may be intrinsic to the myelin or may represent trabeculae penetrating from the overlying lay-

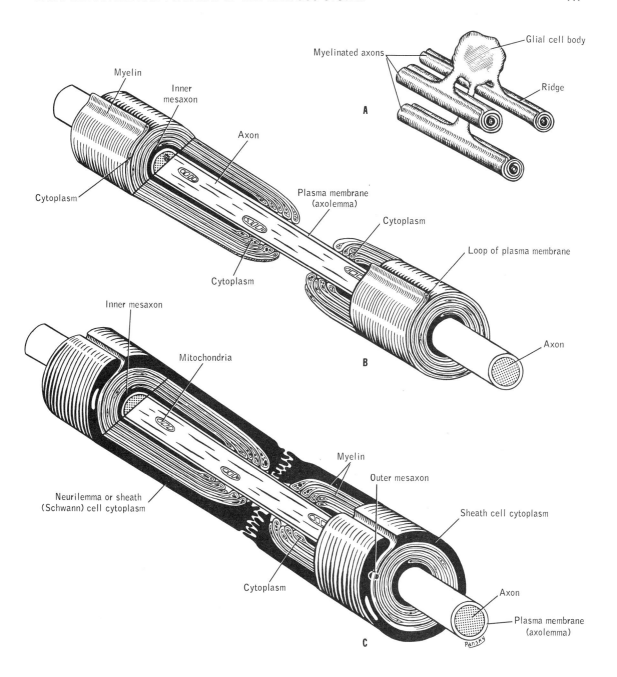

Figure 5-8 *A.* Myelin-glial relation in the CNS. *B.* Myelinated fiber in the CNS. The inner mesaxon completes its initial turn around the axon. Small regions of cytoplasm are occasionally trapped in the layers of laminated myelin. *C.* Myelinated fiber in the peripheral nervous system.

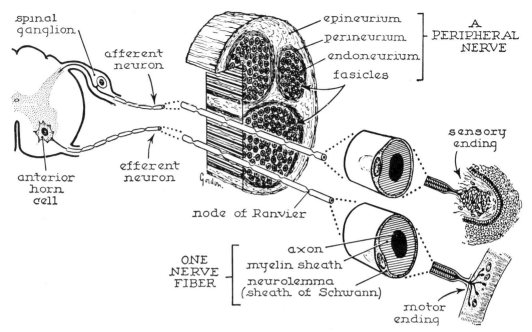

Figure 5-9 Diagram showing the parts of a peripheral nerve. *(From Ham, Histology, 3d ed., J. B. Lippincott Company, Philadelphia, 1957.)*

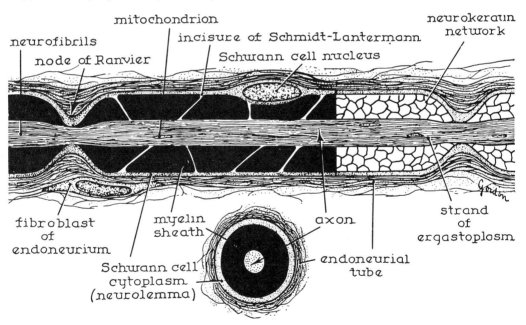

Figure 5-10 Semidiagrammatic drawing of a longitudinal and cross section of a myelinated nerve fiber and its endoneureal sheath. *Upper left*, the myelin has been preserved and blackened by osmium tetroxide. *Right*, the fatty portion of the myelin has been dissolved away. *(From Ham, Histology, 3d ed., J. B. Lippincott Company, Philadelphia, 1957.)*

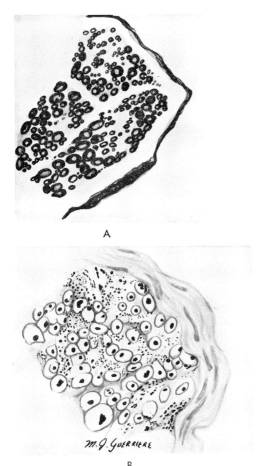

A

B

Figure 5-11 Cross section of a nerve. *Upper,* after fixation in osmic acid, which stains myelin black. *Lower,* stained according to the Cajal silver technique. In this case the axis cylinders are black.

er. However, the myelin sheath is not continuous but is interrupted at intervals by constrictions, or *nodes of Ranvier.* The internode, or the distance between nodes, varies in different fibers from 50 to 1,000 μm. The greater the diameter of the fiber, the longer the internode. In addition, certain preparations show that the myelin is broken up by little oblique clefts known as the *incisures of Schmidt-Lantermann.* The existence of the latter as real structures and not artifacts has been confirmed by electron microscopy.

Neurilemma (Figs. 5-8 through 5-11) Although some authorities prefer to separate the sheath external to the myelin into two layers, the *sheath of Schwann* and the *neurilemma* (also spelled *neurolemma),* the terms will be used synonymously in this book. This covering is found on all peripheral nerves, whether myelinated or not. It is a delicate, transparent membrane composed of Schwann cells. Each of the latter contains a flattened, oval nucleus surrounded by protoplasm in which a Golgi net and mitochondria are found. The remainder of the cytoplasm extends in both directions along the fiber. In myelinated nerves, the edges of these cells dip into the nodes, there joining the edge of another Schwann cell (Figs. 5-8, 5-10). Thus, there is one such cell per segment, the nucleus lying near the center of the internode. In nonmyelinated fibers, from one to a dozen axis cylinders may invaginate the surfaces of Schwann cells (Figs. 5-12, 5-14). This sheath not only is important for support but apparently is essential to the normal metabolism of the axon.

The descriptions of the myelin and neurilemma given above follow the established classic line. However, more recent evidence indicates that these two sheaths must be considered together, as a single unit. It is now clear that the myelin sheath (myelin lamella) is formed by the plasma membrane of the Schwann cells. In the process of myelination, the first step appears to be the settling of a naked axon into a groove on the Schwann cell surface. Gradually, the cytoplasm and plasma membranes of the latter completely envelop the axon. Where the two enveloping cell ends meet along the opposite side of the axon, a double-layered membrane, the mesaxon, is formed. If the fiber is to remain unmyelinated, several axons may thus "invaginate" a single Schwann cell (Fig. 5-14). If myelination is to occur, there is a 1:1 relation between axon and Schwann cell. After the stage of envelopment,

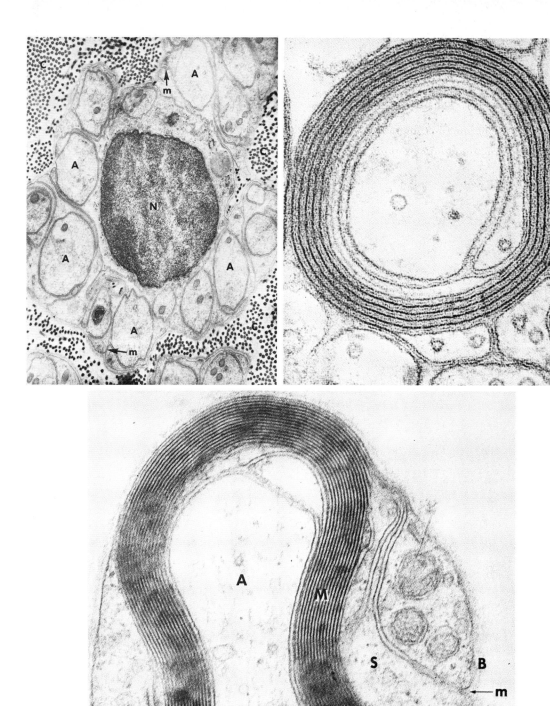

Figure 5-12 Electron micrographs of nerve fibers. *Upper left,* nonmyelinated nerve fibers in cat splenic nerve. Several fibers share the same Schwann cell. A, axon; m, mesaxon; N, nucleus of Schwann cell; C, collagen. Approximately × 25,600. *(Courtesy of L. G. Elfvin, J. Ultrastruct. Res., 7:5, 1962.) Upper Right,* myelinated axon from central white matter of the rat. Note the adaxonal cytoplasm, inner mesaxon, intermediate dense line of wrappings, and outer oligodendroglial processes. A single continuous spiral can be traced from the inner to the outermost layer. × 166,000. *(Courtesy of A. Hirano and H. M. Dembitzer, J. Cell Biol., 34:555, 1967.) Lower,* myelinated nerve fiber from the acoustic ganglion of the rat. A, axis cylinder; M, myelin; S, Schwann cell; B, basement membrane; m, external mesaxon. Approximately × 64,000. *(Courtesy of J. Rosenbluth, J. Biophys. Biochem. Cytol., 12:351, 1962.)*

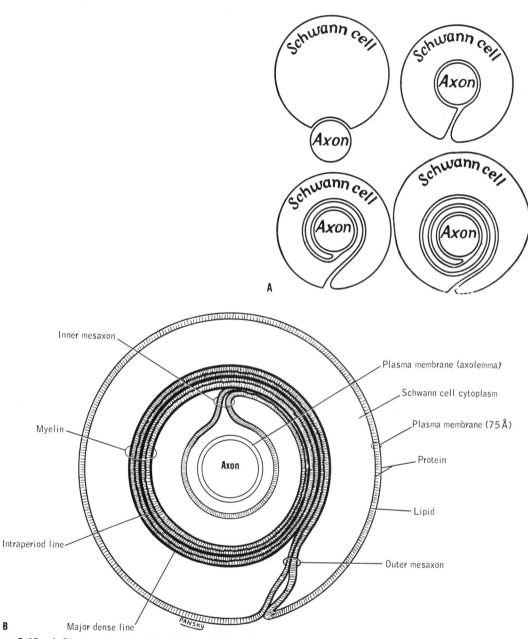

Figure 5-13 *A.* Diagram to show the "jelly roll" hypothesis of myelination. *(Courtesy of B. Geren-Uzman in Maximow and Bloom, A Textbook of Histology, 7th ed., W. B. Saunders Company, Philadelphia, 1957.) B.* Diagram of an electron micrograph showing the relations of myelin to the Schwann cell. The plasma membrane (unit membrane) of the Schwann cell consists of outer and inner layers of protein separated by lipids. The major dense lines are formed by the fusion of the inner layers of the plasma membrane after the cytoplasm is squeezed out of the cell during rotation about the axon.

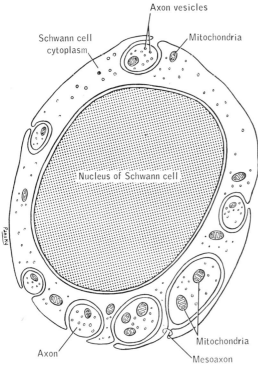

Figure 5-14 Diagrammatic representation of an electron micrograph illustrating the relations of unmyelinated fibers to a single Schwann cell.

there follows a growth and elongation of the mesaxon which spirals around the axon—the "jelly roll" effect (Fig. 5-13). At first the coils of the mesaxon are separated from each other by neurolemma cytoplasm. However, in time, this layer is almost completely obliterated, so that the inner surfaces of the Schwann cell membrane are in close contact. The fusion of these membranes becomes the dense line of the definitive myelin sheath. Where the outer, or contact, surfaces fuse is represented by the intermediate (intraperiod) line of mature myelin. Since the unit membrane of the Schwann cell consists of a bimolecular layer of lipids, this would account for the fact that adult myelin is seen to consist of many lamellae (Fig. 5-12) made up of two bimolecular leaves of lipid.

Endoneurium (Figs. 5-9, 5-10) This consists of fine strands of connective tissue which extend inward to fill the spaces between individual nerve fibers.

Perineurium (Fig. 5-9) This is a connective tissue sheath located external to the endoneurium which surrounds groups of nerve fibers, thus dividing the entire nerve into bundles, or fascicles. In the course of a given nerve there apparently is much communication between fascicles where nerve fibers pass from one to another. It also appears that individual nerve fibers may branch within fascicles.

Epineurium (Fig. 5-9) The entire nerve trunk is surrounded by this covering of dense connective tissue.

The Ganglia

Definition

A ganglion is an aggregation of neuron cell bodies outside the CNS.

Classification

Ganglia are divided into two major classes, sensory and motor.

Sensory Ganglia (Fig. 5-4) These are described as belonging to two groups: spinal or cranial. The spinal ganglia, also called dorsal or posterior root ganglia, are found on the posterior roots of the spinal nerves. Certain of the cranial nerves—V, VII, VIII, IX, and X—have cell bodies in cranial ganglia located near the attachment of the nerves to the brainstem.

Motor Ganglia These are part of the autonomic nervous system. Here originate all the fibers which terminate in the heart, glands, or smooth muscle (Chap. 14).

Structure of the Ganglia

Sensory The cell bodies in such ganglia, except those in cranial nerve VIII, which are bipolar, are all of the monopolar type. The nucleus is round and large with a distinct nucleolus. The cytoplasm contains finely granular Nissl substance. The cells themselves tend to be peripherally placed in the ganglion. Each nerve cell is surrounded by a single layer of flattened cells which form a capsule (Fig. 5-4). Because of this arrangement, the term *satellite* is sometimes applied to them. Actually, the capsule cells become continuous with the sheath of Schwann down along the single process of the nerve cell body. The internal (central) portion of the ganglion is occupied by myelinated fibers. The fibrous coverings of the peripheral nerve are continued to the ganglion. The epineurium, in particular, forms a dense connective tissue capsule for the ganglion.

Motor The cell bodies are multipolar. When compared with dorsal root ganglia, the cells look smaller, with nuclei which "seem" eccentric and are more scattered throughout the ganglion. Because these cells have many dendrites, their capsules may appear to be incomplete or lacking. Both myelinated and nonmyelinated fibers are present.

ELECTROPHYSIOLOGY OF NEURONS

Resting Membrane Potential

Neurons, along with all other living cells, are electrically polarized in the resting state. The interior of the cell is electrically negative in relation to the external environment; in the quiescent neuron this potential difference is about 70 mV. Intracellular potentials are measured by means of microelectrodes—glass pipettes drawn out to very fine tips and filled with concentrated salt solution—which are inserted into the cell. A second electrode is placed in the extracellular fluid, and a voltage-measuring device, such as an oscilloscope, is used to measure the potential difference between the cell and the extracellular fluid. The biophysical mechanisms responsible for this *resting potential* are explained in the following paragraphs.

Concentration Gradients

Ions and molecules in solution are constantly in random thermal motion. Therefore, if some soluble material is placed on one side of a chamber filled with water, particles (molecules or ions) will move randomly and, given sufficient time, will eventually be distributed uniformly throughout the entire chamber. Another way of expressing this is to say that substances tend to move down their concentration gradients. The molecules will not remain in an area of high concentration but, because of the randomness of thermal movement, will tend to pass into areas of low concentration until a uniform concentration is achieved throughout the chamber.

Separation of Charge

If some anions and cations in solution can be spatially separated across a boundary or membrane, then a potential difference (PD) will be established between the two sides of the boundary. In the resting cell a spatial separation of charge of a small number of anions and cations is produced across the cell membrane. This charge separation results from the selective permeability of the cell membrane to small ions.

Selective Permeability

In order to illustrate the importance of selective permeability in the generation of the membrane potential, one should examine the results of some idealized experiments with artificial (collodion) membranes whose permeability to various ions can be manipulated by appropriate chemical treatment. In the example shown in Fig. 5-15, the membrane separating the two compartments of the chamber is selectively permeable to cations such as K^+ but is impermeable to anions such as Cl^-. Consequently, K^+ ions will tend to move from compartment I, which contains a concentrated KCl solution, to compartment II which contains a lesser concentration of KCl. This ionic movement through the membrane pores results from the random thermal motion of particles in solution; the number of random collisions of K^+ ions with the left face of the membrane greatly exceeds the number of collisions with the right face resulting in a net passage of K^+ ions into compartment II. Since Cl^- anions cannot penetrate the barrier, the negative ions remain in compartment I. This results in a gradually increasing buildup of negative charge on the left side. This, in turn, causes K^+ ions to be attracted back into the left compartment I. Thus two tendencies are apparent: (1) the tendency of the K^+ ions to cross over into compartment II as a result of the concentration gradient and (2) the tendency of the K^+ ions to pass back into compartment I as a result of the electrostatic attraction of K^+ for the Cl^- ions trapped on that side.

The net result of the conflict of these two tendencies is a dynamic equilibrium, in which a small number of positive charges pass across the membrane and a certain PD is built up (the equilibrium potential). At this equilibrium point, the force of the concentration gradient in one direction equals the force of the electric gradient in the opposite direction.

In this way a selectively permeable membrane produces a spatial separation of positive and negative ions and generates a potential difference across a membrane.

It should be pointed out that the separation of a relatively small number of ion pairs can give rise to large voltages. Thus, the excess number of K^+ ions on side II and the excess number of Cl^- ions on side I is far too small to change the chemically measured concentra-

tions of K^+ or Cl^-. Therefore, distinction should be made between macroscopic concentrations in solutions and charge separations occurring at the microscopic level at the membrane boundary.

Gibbs-Donnan Equilibrium

A somewhat more complex situation, approximating the situation in the living cell more closely than the previous example, is the Gibbs-Donnan equilibrium. In this instance, the properties of the membrane are such that anions and cations of small diameter can penetrate the membrane. However, the membrane is not permeable to large protein anions (Fig. 5-16).

To calculate the concentrations of the solutions at equilibrium the Gibbs-Donnan equation is used:

$$\frac{[K^+]_I}{[K^+]_{II}} = \frac{[Cl^-]_{II}}{[Cl^-]_I}$$

This formula states that the concentration ratio of monovalent cations equals the reciprocal of the monovalent anion ratio. This allows calculation of the concentrations in the bulk solutions on either side of the membrane at equilibrium.

At the microscopic level K^+ ions will tend to cross from the side of higher concentration to the side of lower K concentration. This crossing will leave an unneutralized protein anion behind and thus build up an electrostatic force.

The PD developed across the membrane can be calculated by the Nernst equation which applies to systems such as these:

$$E = -\frac{RT}{F} \ln \frac{[K^+]_I}{[K^+]_{II}}$$

where E is the potential in volts, R is the universal gas constant 8.31 J/mol. °C, T is the absolute temperature which is 310 at 37°C, and F is the faraday constant of 96,500 C/mol.

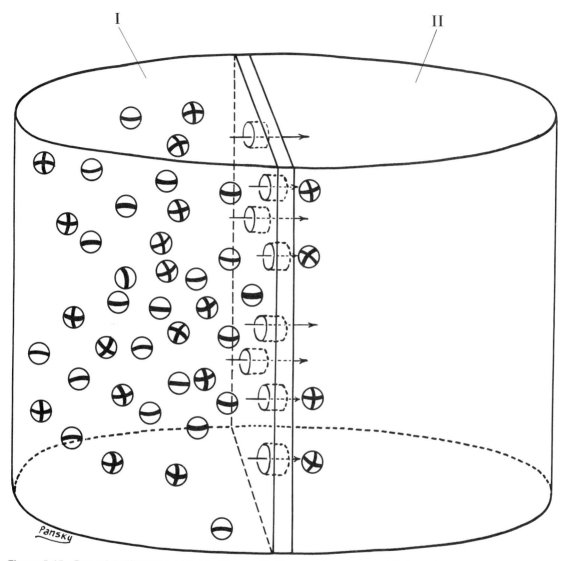

Figure 5-15 Potential difference generated by a collodion membrane permeable to cations only. The positively charged ions will pass through from side I to side II through selective membrane pores. The result is a potential difference with side I electrically negative to side II.

Converting to logarithms with base 10 and inserting the values of these constants yields

$$E = -61 \log \frac{[K^+]_I}{[K^+]_{II}}$$

if E is expressed in millivolts.

This potential represents the equilibrium potential for potassium (K), i.e., the potential calculated for a situation in which the voltage is determined solely by the differences in potassium ion concentrations.

It should be noted that increasing $[K^+]_{II}$ by the addition of KCl to side II will result in a decrease in the membrane potential because

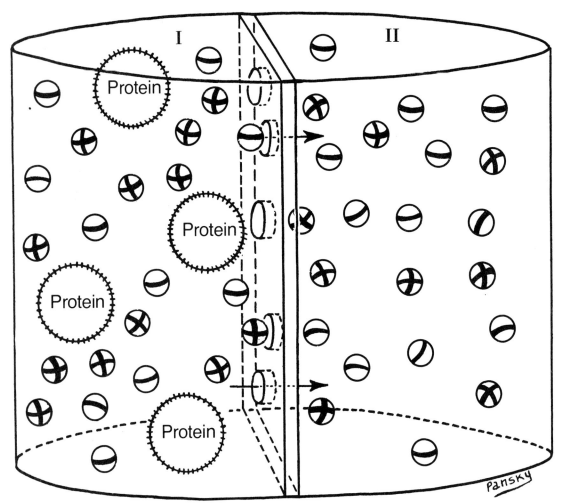

Figure 5-16 Gibbs-Donnan equilibrium. In this case the membrane is permeable to small cations and anions but not to large protein anions. The higher concentration of K+ on side I will result in the passage of K+ down the concentration gradient to side II. This transfer will build up an opposing electrostatic force (side I negative) which can be measured as the membrane potential.

of a reduction in the concentration gradient and a matching reduction in the electrical force (the membrane potential).

That the Gibbs-Donnan equilibrium is a useful model for understanding the genesis of transmembrane potentials is indicated by the following observations concerning glial cells: In these cells [K+] of the intracellular fluid is 105 meq/L and [K+] of the extracellular fluid is 3.4 meq/L. The calculated membrane potential is − 91 mV, which is the value found experimentally. Furthermore, altering the concentration of K+ in the extracellular medium bathing the glial cells shows that increasing extracellular [K+] in logarithmic steps will reduce the measured transmembrane potential (Fig. 5-17).

The Na+ ion makes no contribution to the

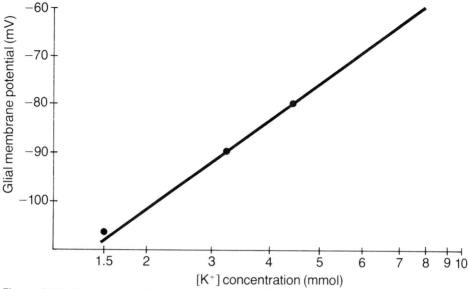

Figure 5-17 Dependence of transmembrane potential of glial cells on the extracellular concentration of K⁺. As the extracellular K⁺ is increased logarithmically, membrane potential falls. Normally, extracellular K⁺ is about 3.4 meq/L. *(From Aidley, The Physiology of Excitable Cells, Cambridge University Press, London, 1971.)*

membrane potential, because the membrane of the glia cell is impermeable to this cation.

Neuronal Resting Membrane Potentials

In neurons, the observed resting membrane potential is usually about −70 mV, with the intracellular compartment negative in relation to the extracellular. The estimated ionic concentrations of the intracellular *(i)* and extracellular *(e)* fluids of vertebrate nerve tissue are presented in Table 5-1.

If the membrane potential resulted entirely from the effect of K⁺ concentration differences across the membrane, then the resting potential would equal the K equilibrium po-

tential as calculated by the Nernst equation. However, the measured resting potential is actually −70 mV.

The explanation of this discrepancy is that the Nernst equation does not hold precisely in a situation in which the membrane is also permeable to ions other than K⁺, e.g., Na⁺. The equation to be used in this circumstance is the Goldman equation:

$$E = -\frac{RT}{F} \ln \frac{P_K \, K^+_i + P_{Na} \, Na^+_i}{P_K \, K^+_e + P_{Na} \, Na^+_e}$$

where K^+_i and Na^+_i represent the intracellular concentrations of K and Na; K^+_e and Na^+_e represent the concentrations of these ions in

Table 5-1   Ionic Concentrations of Fluids of Vertebrate Nerve Tissue

Ions	Intracellular fluid, mmol/L	Extracellular fluid, mmol/L
Na⁺	12	145
K⁺	155	5
Cl⁻	8	110

the extracellular fluid; and P_K and P_{Na} represent permeability, or the ease with which molecules pass through the membrane and which, in the case of the ions under discussion, may be thought of as related to pore size. In resting neurons P_{Na} is 1 percent of P_K. Consequently it is the K terms in both the numerator and denominator which contribute most to the value of E. However, the Na terms do contribute something and thus decrease the magnitude of the membrane potential from the K^+ equilibrium potential to about -70 mV. It can be seen that, as P_{Na} approaches zero, the Goldman equation reduces to the Nernst equation, and this obtains for glial cells. In neurons, however, P_{Na} has to be considered.

The graph shown in Fig. 5-18 compares the results to be expected from an experiment in which the extracellular $[K^+]$ is varied.

One can observe that at low extracellular K^+ levels the results expected from the Goldman equation differ significantly from the results predicted by use of the Nernst equation alone. The importance of this discrepancy is the fact that in the normal organism the value of $[K^+]$ in the extracellular fluid is only about 5 meq/L.

The equilibrium potential for each ion present in the cell can be calculated by finding the value of the potential if this ion only were considered to the exclusion of the other ions in the system. This is done using the Nernst equation.
Consequently

$$E_K = -61 \log 155/5 = -91 \text{ mV}$$
$$E_{Cl} = -61 \log 110/8 = -70 \text{ mV}$$
$$E_{Na} = -61 \log 12/145 = +66 \text{ mV}$$

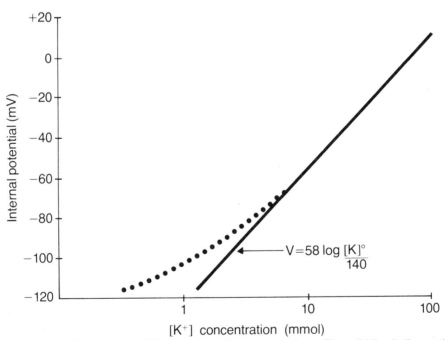

Figure 5-18 Comparison of the Nernst and Goldman equations. The solid line indicates the expected effect of variations in extracellular K^+ concentrations on transmembrane potential utilizing the Nernst equation. The actual data fall on the interrupted line at low extracellular K^+ concentrations. This curve is described by the Goldman equation. *(From Aidley, The Physiology of Excitable Cells, Cambridge University Press, London, 1971.)*

Since the true resting membrane potential is −70 mV, it can be seen that Cl⁻ is distributed according to the membrane potential. The Cl⁻ ion is distributed passively, depending entirely on the PD as generated by the other ions involved. The K⁺ ion, if it alone generated the PD, would produce a potential of −91 mV. This degree of negativity is not quite achieved because of the small but definite contribution of the Na⁺ ion. The most drastic discrepancy between equilibrium conditions and the reality is the Na⁺ ion. If it alone generated the membrane potential, the PD would be in the opposite direction; that is to say, it would cause the cell to be *positive* in relation to the extracellular fluid. It is the relatively low membrane permeability to Na⁺ which keeps the membrane nearer the K⁺ equilibrium.

The Sodium Pump (Fig. 5-19)

The true membrane potential is so different from the Na equilibrium potential that both the concentration gradient and the electric gradient tend to bring Na⁺ into the cell. To prevent swamping the cell with Na⁺ ions, an enzymatic pump mechanism exists in the membrane which picks up Na⁺ ions from the intracellular fluid and extrudes them into the extracellular space. The same mechanism also picks up K⁺ ions from the extracellular fluid and transports them into the interior of the cell, thus maintaining the high internal K concentration. This *active transport* system requires metabolic energy from the breakdown of ATP to ADP.

The Action Potential

The action potential (nerve impulse, spike) is the unit of response of the neuron. When a neuron is stimulated, the membrane becomes momentarily depolarized from its internal negativity for a brief time. In fact the transmembrane potential overshoots zero and becomes internally positive (Fig. 5-20).

Ionic Basis of the Action Potential

The ionic basis of the action potential can be understood in terms of the Goldman equation. When a nerve is stimulated, molecular alterations occur which cause the membrane to become enormously more permeable to Na⁺ ions for a brief moment. In fact, the membrane permeability to Na⁺ increases 2000 times over its value in the resting state. As can be seen from the Goldman equation, the Na terms in both the numerator and denominator

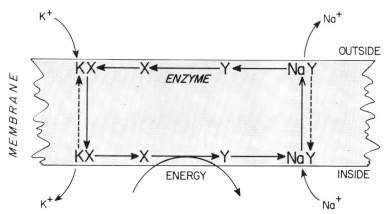

Figure 5-19 Hypothetical scheme of an Na⁺–K⁺ exchange pump. The substances X and Y are assumed to be confined to the membrane. X has a high affinity for K⁺; Y has a high affinity for Na⁺. X and Y move through the membrane only when in combination with an ion. *(From Ruch and Patton, Physiology and Biophysics, W. B. Saunders Company, Philadelphia, 1976.)*

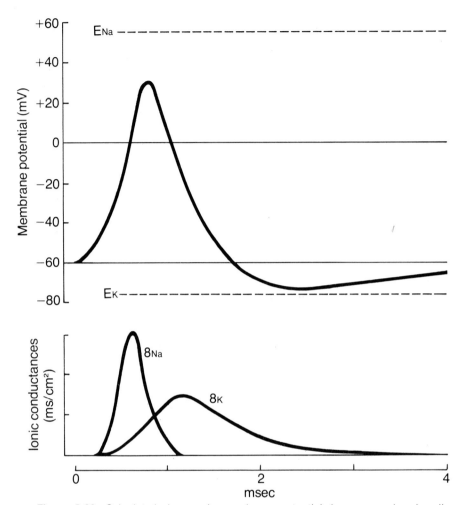

Figure 5-20 Calculated changes in membrane potential *(upper curve)* and sodium and potassium conductances *(lower curves)* during a propagated action potential in a squid giant axon. The scale of the vertical axis is correct, but its position may be slightly inaccurate—a resting potential of −60 mV has been assumed. The position of E_{Na} and E_K are correct with respect to the resting potential. *(From Aidley, The Physiology of Excitable Cells, Cambridge University Press, London, 1971.)*

become much more important in determining the transmembrane potential than was the case in the resting state. In fact, there is now a tendency for the membrane potential to approach the Na equilibrium potential making the intracellular compartment *positive* in relation to the extracellular fluid. This explains the overshoot in the positive direction. Although the precise configurational changes in the membrane pores or channels are unknown, it is clear that the amplitude of the action potential depends on the ratio of the concentrations of Na^+ in the extracellular and intracellular fluids.

The time course of the permeability change to sodium during the brief instant of the action potential is shown in Fig. 5-20. The sodium conductance of the membrane shoots up in a process labeled *sodium activation.* This represents a sudden alteration of the configuration of the membrane pores or channels allowing sodium to rush into the cell. It is followed by a decline in the membrane conductance to sodium in a process dubbed *sodium inactivation.* This is thought to be the result of a sudden closing down of the sodium channels.

It should also be noted that there is a delayed and small increase in K^+ permeability as well. This increase in P_K which occurs during the declining phase of the action potential represents a reassertion of the importance of the K contribution to the transmembrane potential. The rising phase of the spike, then, is clearly the result of Na activation, or an increase in the conductance of the Na channels. The declining phase of the spike is caused by (1) Na^+ inactivation (closing of the

Na channels) and (2) increased K^+ permeability which tends to bring the PD closer to the K equilibrium potential.

The persistence of the latter effect is responsible for slight hyperpolarization noted immediately following a spike (afterhyperpolarization). The membrane potential in this period approaches the K equilibrium potential before returning to the resting condition (Fig. 5-21).

Excitability Properties of Neurons

Excitation of nerve or muscle occurs when a negative charge delivered to the surface of the axon depolarizes the transmembrane potential. When the transmembrane potential is reduced from 70 to 60 mV, threshold is reached, the configurational changes of the membrane channels which allow Na^+ to penetrate the membrane are unleashed, and the action potential proceeds to completion.

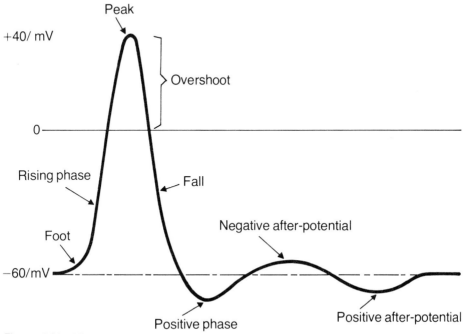

Figure 5-21 Diagram to show the nomenclature applied to an action potential and the afterpotentials which follow it. *(From Aidley, The Physiology of Excitable Cells, Cambridge University Press, London, 1971.)*

Subthreshold stimuli can produce passive *electrotonic potentials* in the nerve axon membrane. These potentials represent charge redistributions along the resting membrane which are, however, insufficient to cause the configurational changes in the Na channels characteristic of an action potential. The electrotonic potentials are due to the capacitance and resistance properties of the membrane. There are time and space decrements in these potentials, and they are not propagated as are the action potentials. They are graded in amplitude in contrast to action potentials, which are an *all-or-none* phenomenon.

Conduction of the Action Potential

The *local circuit theory* explains how the action potential can propagate down a long axon (which may reach several meters in length) and yet reach the axon terminal undiminished in amplitude.

As can be seen in Fig. 5-22, the nerve axon may be conceptually divided into a series of patches. Depolarization of one patch will cause a flow of ions to the adjacent patch. If this flow is sufficient to depolarize the adjacent patch to threshold level, a full-fledged action potential will be generated in this patch as well. The reversed charges in this patch may then depolarize the next adjacent patch in a similar manner, and thus the action potential can be propagated undiminished over long stretches of nerve. It is obvious from this explanation that a stimulus applied somewhere along the course of an axon will be propagated in both directions away from the point of stimulus. Propagation in the direction normally taken by action potentials along this axon in the intact organism is called the *orthodromic* direction. Propagation in the opposite direction is named *antidromic* conduction.

Conduction Velocity The velocity with which an action potential is propagated down a nerve axon is in fact quite slow when

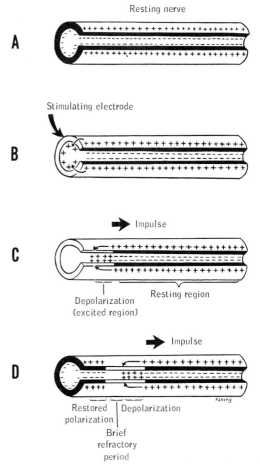

Figure 5-22 Diagram to illustrate the membrane theory of nerve conduction.

compared with the speed of electric currents. Several factors influence the conduction velocity of a nerve axon. The larger the diameter of an axon, the greater is the conduction velocity. The myelin sheath found around axons greatly increases the conduction velocity. Myelin has a high resistance to current flow and acts as an insulator. Thus, the ionic movements of the action potential will not occur at the internodes but only at the nodes where the neural membrane is directly exposed to the extracellular fluid. Depolarization occurs, not between adjacent patches of axolemma, but between adjacent nodes, which may be separated by up to a millimeter. The action potential therefore jumps from node to node, the mode of conduction known as *saltatory conduction* (Fig. 5-23). It has been discovered that different functional classes of neurons differ in their conduction velocities. Thus, for example, fibers of the autonomic system innervating the viscera are unmyelinated and have a very slow conduction velocity, while motor and certain afferent neurons have fast conduction velocities (Chaps. 7, 13).

Refractory Periods Using a test stimulus delivered shortly after a suprathreshold stimulus applied to a nerve, it can be demonstrated that a nerve has a refractory period following a stimulus during which it is not activated by a second stimulus. The *absolute refractory period* represents the period during which a test stimulus, no matter how intense, will be unable to elicit a second action potential. This period lasts from the time that the Na channels have opened until inactivation, or the closing of the Na channels, has been completed. During the period when the channels are returning to their resting condition, a second stimulus may produce a spike if it is sufficiently intense to reopen the Na channels and overcome the elevated K permeability. This period is called the *relative refractory period*, since to evoke a second spike the test stimulus must be of considerable intensity.

Influence of Environment on Excitability The properties of excitability and conductivity of a nerve can be greatly altered by the chemical

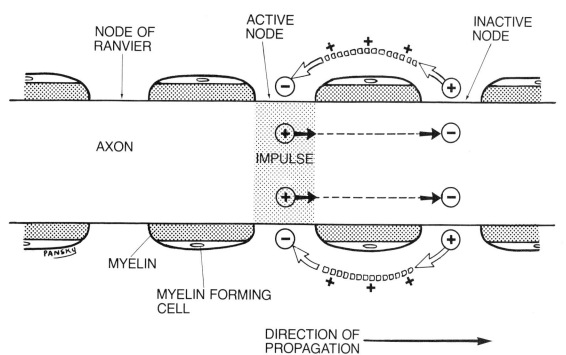

Figure 5-23 Saltatory conduction. A diagrammatic representation of conduction in a myelinated nerve fiber where depolarization leaps (the Latin *saltare*-to leap) from one node to the next, thus accounting for the greater velocity of the nerve impulse in myelinated fibers than that observed in nonmyelinated nerves, where there are no nodes.

composition of the surrounding fluid. This is particularly true of the concentrations of sodium and calcium. For example, a calcium-free solution increases excitability, while increased calcium reduces excitability. Prolonged treatment in low-calcium or calcium-free solution actually leads to spontaneous neuron activity. Clinically, increased nervous excitability, called *tetany*, is observed in cases of calcium deficiency.

Synaptic Transmission The conduction of the neural message in the form of spikes from the cell body along the axon has been covered in a previous section. However, information must be passed from one nerve cell to another (synapse) in order to effect even the simplest of behaviors (i.e., the two-neuron reflex arc). The passage of information from the axon terminals of one neuron to the dendrites of a second is usually accomplished by chemical means. The action potential, upon reaching the terminal boutons of the presynaptic neuron, causes the release of packets of neurotransmitter substances into the synaptic cleft (Figs. 5-24, 5-25). The molecules of transmitter

diffuse across the gap separating the two neurons and combine with sites on the postsynaptic membrane. This combination causes a change in the permeability characteristics of the postsynaptic membrane to small ions and thus changes the transmembrane potential. Should the membrane be depolarized sufficiently to reach threshold, an action potential will be generated and then propagated down the axon to the terminals of the second neuron as well.

In the nervous system several different types of neurotransmitter substances have been identified, although each neuron possesses only one transmitter (Fig. 13-3). The known transmitter substances are (1) acetylcholine (ACh) (Chap. 13), (2) the catecholamines—dopamine (Chap. 18) and norepinephrine (Chap. 14), (3) the indolamine serotonin (Chap. 19), (4) certain amino acids such as glycine (Chap. 13), and (5) γ-aminobutyric acid (GABA) (Chap. 13), and perhaps other substances which may be specific to certain regions of the brain. These substances are synthesized by the metabolic machinery of the neuron and packaged in small vesicles (Figs.

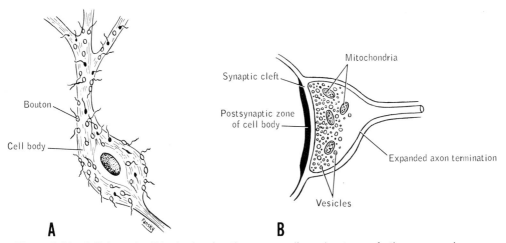

Figure 5-24 *A.* Enlarged cell body showing the neuropodia, or boutons, of other neurons in a typical synaptic relationship. *B.* Diagram of an electron micrograph through a bouton showing the expanded axon terminal with its mitochondria and vesicles. The postsynaptic zone of the cell is also shown.

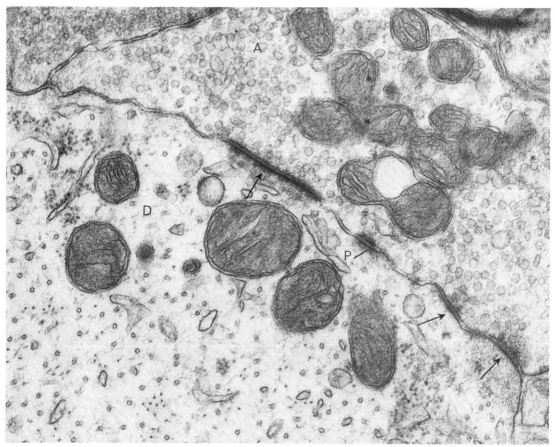

Figure 5-25 Electron micrograph through an axodendritic synapse. In the large axon, terminal A consists of spherical synaptic vesicles and many large mitochondria. At the junction between pre- and postsynaptic membranes are four dense patches associated with a widening of the intercellular gap. Three of these patches *(arrows)* represent synaptic complexes, for the dense material is asymmetrically disposed and there is an accumulation of synaptic vesicles. The fourth and smaller dense patch P is a punctum adhaerens. The dendrite is indicated by D. × 46,000. *(Courtesy of Dr. Sanford Palay from Peters, Palay, and Webster, The Fine Structure of the Nervous System, W. B. Saunders Company, Philadelphia, 1976.)*

5-24, 5-25) which are released into the synaptic cleft by the transmembrane potential changes induced in the terminal endings by the arrival of the action potential. Following release of the transmitter, enzymes present in the synaptic cleft may cause degradation of the released transmitter (Fig. 14-8) and thereby limit the duration of action of substance to a short interval of time. Transmitter material may also be removed from the synaptic receptor sites

by reuptake mechanisms. There are active transport pumps which move transmitter substance from the synaptic cleft back into the presynaptic terminal ending.[1]

Postsynaptic Potentials Stimulation of a presynaptic neuron can produce two types of potential effects on the postsynaptic

[1]Neuropharmacologic agents which interfere with the synthesis, release, degradation, reuptake, or postsynaptic effects of the transmitters are available.

neuron—excitatory or inhibitory. In both cases the effect is usually a local subthreshold, decrementing and nonpropagated potential change. The excitatory postsynaptic potential (EPSP) is a small depolarization (on the order of several millivolts) which is localized to the dendrites and adjacent soma membrane. The transmitter substance increases the membrane permeability to all small ions (Na^+, K^+, Cl_∇), and the membrane potential therefore tends to go toward an equilibrium potential of 0 mV. If a sufficiently large number of terminal boutons produce local depolarizations (Fig. 5-24), a sufficiently large area of the soma-dendritic membrane surface will be depolarized. Should this depolarization be large enough, the membrane potential will be brought to the threshold level, and a full-fledged action potential will occur. This action potential will then be propagated in normal fashion down the length of the axon. Clearly, whether or not an action potential occurs in response to any particular pattern of presynaptic inputs will depend on the threshold level of the postsynaptic membrane. The area of lowest threshold is the initial segment, mentioned early in this chapter. Thus, if the depolarization produced at the initial segment by the action of the EPSPs generated at distant dendritic or nearby somatic sites exceeds threshold value, an action potential will occur. If they do not achieve threshold, the EPSPs will decrease in time, and no action potential will occur.

Inhibitory effects induced by the release of inhibitory transmitter substances produce hyperpolarizations of the soma-dendritic membrane known as inhibitory postsynaptic potentials (IPSPs). These substances produce a selective increase in membrane permeability to K^+ ions which causes the membrane potential to shift in the direction of the K equilibrium potential of -90 mV. This can be deduced from the Goldman equation, where it may be seen that an increase in P_K will mean that the resulting potential will be less influenced by the Na and more by the K terms in the equation.

The effect of an IPSP is to stabilize the membrane and take the potential farther away from the threshold level.

The logical system used by the neuron should now be clear. A neuron, such as a motorneuron, transmits information solely in the form of action potentials. Whether or not an action potential is propagated at any instant in time depends on the sum total of the inhibitory and excitatory influences that are playing on the neuron. If the sum total of EPSPs is sufficiently large, threshold will be exceeded and an action potential generated. If the IPSPs are sufficiently large to counteract the effects of the EPSPs, no action potential occurs.

The effect of subthreshold EPSPs on the postsynaptic neuron can be enhanced if they are delivered closely spaced in time so that a second EPSP occurs before the effect of the first has completely decreased. This is termed *temporal facilitation.* The effect of EPSPs can also be enhanced if a larger area of the postsynaptic membrane is depolarized—a process known as *spatial facilitation.* This can be accomplished by activation of a larger number of inputs to the postsynaptic neuron.

Thus, synapses have the logical function of adding up all the excitatory and inhibitory inputs until a decision level is reached. Synapses produce a noticeable delay in the passage of impulses, since the entire process of neurotransmitter release and action may take about 0.5 ms.

Myoneural Junction The motorneuron terminates in a long and complex troughlike junction on the surface of the muscle fiber (Fig. 13-1). The transmitter released here is acetylcholine, which has a depolarizing effect on the muscle membrane. The potential produced at the muscle end plate is called the end plate potential (EPP). The ionic mechanisms of the EPP are similar to those of the EPSP in that the transmitter causes the membrane permeability to small ions to increase and the membrane potential to depolarize. When threshold for the muscle membrane is reached, an action potential is propagated along the muscle surface which initiates the contractile process. In mammalian forms no inhibitory potentials are generated on skeletal muscle, although they are found in smooth and cardiac muscle. It has been demonstrated, furthermore, that there is a continual release of small quantities of acetylcholine even when no action potentials are occurring on the motorneuron. This induces miniature EPPs which can be detected as small fluctuations in membrane potential of the end plate region.

Unusual Synapses Recent evidence indicates that synaptic mechanisms in various regions of the CNS may have certain distinct features. In certain areas of the brain, presumably where simultaneous or rapid activation of neurons is required, synapses may be electric rather than chemical. In such synapses, the close apposition of pre- and postsynaptic membranes *(gap junctions)* permits the electrical event in the presynaptic neuron to be transmitted electrotonically to the postsynaptic neuron.

Another unusual synapse is the axo-axonic synapse which is responsible for *presynaptic inhibition.* In this case a depolarizing transmitter is released on the presynaptic axon terminal and reduces the total amplitude of the spike in the presynaptic fiber. This results in a reduction in the amount of transmitter liberated by the presynaptic neuron and a reduction in the effectiveness (i.e., an inhibition) of its action on the postsynaptic cell.

CLINICAL CONSIDERATIONS

Since both central and peripheral neurons are frequently interrupted through trauma, the problems of degeneration and regeneration are important to the clinician.

Degeneration and Regeneration of Neurons in the CNS

It is well-established that as long as the neuron cell body is alive, all the processes still attached to it will also live. Further, since protoplasmic synthesis is continually going on, such processes are capable of growth. Thus, axis cylinders interrupted through trauma should theoretically once more reach the destination formerly attained by the damaged axon. However, certain difficulties arise which, as yet, have proved insurmountable. First, when the axis cylinder is cut, the myelin insulation surrounding that portion of the axon lying distal to the point of interruption disintegrates along with the axon itself. Secondly, the processes of the supporting neuroglia soon fill the space once occupied by the fiber and its sheath, becoming such a dense tangle that it is impossible for new growth to get through.

Degeneration of Neurons in the PNS

Nerve Damage

In nerve damage, certain points of reference are important. First, the location of the site where the nerve is interrupted must be determined; second, the location of the cell bodies of the damaged neurons should be established. Two terms are used in connection with nerve interruption. The first of these is *proximal portion,* used when speaking of that portion of the nerve still attached to the cell body between the CNS and the site of the trauma. The second is *distal* or *peripheral,* referring to that portion of the severed nerve which is no longer attached to the cell body, lying between the cut and the peripheral termination of the nerve. With these concepts in mind, it is now possible to classify degeneration into two types: retrograde and Wallerian.

Retrograde Degeneration (Fig. 5-26) This usually involves the proximal few millimeters of a severed nerve closely adjoining the site of trauma. The extent of degeneration toward the

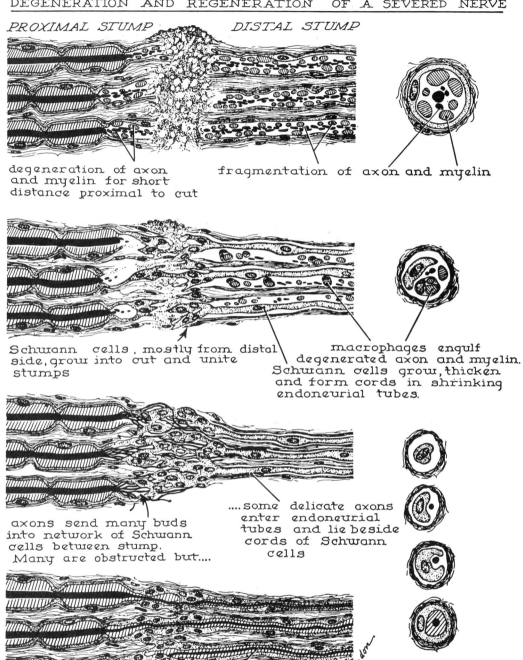

PROXIMAL STUMP   DISTAL STUMP

degeneration of axon
and myelin for short
distance proximal to cut

fragmentation of axon and myelin

Schwann cells, mostly from distal
side, grow into cut and unite
stumps

macrophages engulf
degenerated axon and myelin.
Schwann cells grow, thicken
and form cords in shrinking
endoneurial tubes.

axons send many buds
into network of Schwann
cells between stump.
Many are obstructed but....

....some delicate axons
enter endoneurial
tubes and lie beside
cords of Schwann
cells

axons continue to push along
endoneurial tubes of distal stump and are
enfolded by Schwann cells after which new myelin is formed

Figure 5-26 Diagram showing the changes that occur in a nerve when it is severed:
degeneration followed by regeneration *(From Ham, Histology, 3d ed., J. B. Lippincott
Company, Philadelphia, 1957.)*

CNS is to some degree determined by the nature of the wound. When the site of trauma lies close to the cell body, the latter may also become involved in degenerative changes which eventually result in death of the cell. In any event, one should recall the axon reaction which occurs when nerve fibers are damaged, the degree of reaction diminishing as the injury site approaches the periphery. At any time, there is a small amount of breakdown in both axis cylinder and myelin. The Schwann cells constituting the neurilemma remain alive and may actually proliferate.

Wallerian Degeneration (Fig. 5-26) This involves the entire length of the distal portion of the severed nerve. The axis cylinder, cut off from its metabolic center, soon dies. Actually, within a few days, the axon consists merely of scattered debris. Furthermore, it is equally certain that disintegration of the axon will lead to the disappearance of myelin. This disappearance occurs a little more slowly, although changes have been observed within 24 h after injury. The Schwann cells remain viable and even proliferate, forming a syncytium with longitudinally disposed slits. Phagocytes formed in the surrounding connective tissue pass through the spaces in the mesh to clean up fragments of disintegrated myelin and axons, after which they disappear. Thus, if the two ends of the severed nerve are close enough together, the neurilemma soon becomes once more continuous. Degeneration of the axis cylinders often has profound effects upon the end organs supplied by them. In the case of somatic motor fibers to skeletal muscle, nerve death leads to complete atrophy of the muscle fibers. Certain sensory receptors are also affected. This is especially true of the taste buds on the tongue, which degenerate almost immediately after denervation.

Degrees of Nerve Injury

Although nerve injuries have been classified according to the severity of the damage, only a brief and general discussion will be attempted here.

First Degree This is usually due to pressure strong enough to prevent action currents from passing into the part of the nerve fiber distal to the point of applied pressure. There is no degeneration.

Second Degree This is also usually due to pressure, but here the axon has been destroyed at the point of pressure and all the axons distal to that point degenerate. All the supporting structures remain intact. The term *axonotmesis* is applied to this phenomenon.

Third, Fourth, or Fifth Degrees In each of these degrees of injury, the axon is completely severed, together with variable amounts of its supporting structure. For this type of injury the general term *neurotmesis* is often used. In third-degree cases, the injury involves not only the axon but also the endoneurium, the fascicles of the nerve being still intact. In fourth-degree injuries, the fascicles are also severed. In fifth-degree injuries, the entire nerve trunk, including the epineurium, has been cut through.

Any of these injuries will lead to at least a temporary loss of sensation in the area of distribution of the involved nerve and to paralysis of the muscles supplied by it.

Regeneration of Neurons in the PNS

Axons still attached to their cell bodies are viable and capable of growth. Unlike the discouraging situation encountered in the CNS, the possibility of restoring function to the peripheral nerve is greater for several reasons. First, the presence of significant connective tissue sheaths makes it possible to bring together and hold in approximation the cut ends of the nerve. Next, the fact that debris from degeneration has been cleared away leaves a relatively open field. Further, the living, proliferating neurilemma has left channels through which growth of axons from the proximal portion can pass toward the end organ (Fig. 5-26). Under good conditions, growth is said to occur at the rate of 1 to 4 mm/day. The rate of growth of the regenerating fiber, directly related to axoplasmic flow, is influenced by many factors, including the above-mentioned degrees of injury.

One should not be misled into believing that regeneration described above will eventually result in 100 percent return of normal function. Such is not the case, since even when severed nerve ends are carefully joined, it cannot be expected that each axon will find its own proper path. Thus, many may be wasted by going to the wrong type of end organ. Fortunately, this waste may be to some extent circumvented by the fact that growing axis cylinders tend to form many branches as they pass through the maze of slits in the neurilemma. Another disadvantage is the tendency of connective tissue to overproliferate when damaged. Thus, there is the ever-present possibility that fibroblasts which produce collagenous fibers will create a scar between the severed ends. Scar formation can be minimized by close, firm union of the severed ends and the use of measures to combat possible infection.

Nerve Grafts

The nature of the damaging agent and the longitudinal extent of the traumatized area influence regeneration. Occasionally, an area of a nerve is damaged to such an extent that the two ends cannot be joined. An area of a nerve may even be deleted completely. In such cases, a piece of nerve taken from a storage bank or removed from the body of someone who died recently is sutured in to close the gap. It should be understood that this is a "scaffold graft" which will act as a bridge over which axons may pass to reach the neurilemma in its own distal portion. Gradually, the graft will be replaced by the host's own tissue.

Axonal Transport

Axonal transport, or axoplasmic flow, is important for reasons other than regeneration. It is essential for the life of the axon and for the delivery of transmitter substances (or their basic ingredients) to axon terminals. There is a fast transport component with a rate of about 400 mm/day and a slow component.[2] The fast component requires energy which depends upon cellular oxidative metabolism and ATP. Apparently, microtubules are also important. Sugar and phospholipids are said to be transported rapidly. The slow component requires no energy. Certain soluble proteins and some particulate matter are among the slower-moving substances.

[2]Depending on the investigator, the fast component ranges from 100 to 400 mm/day, while the slow ranges from 2 or 3 to 200 m/day.

Summary

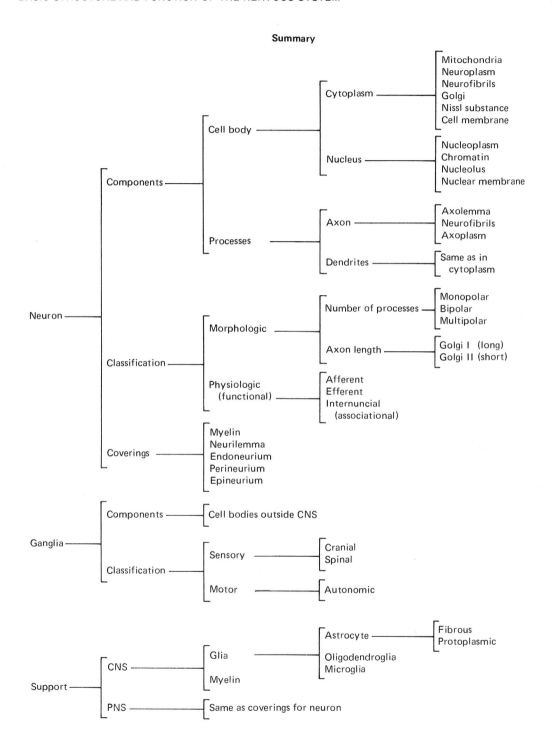

Chapter 6

Functional Classification of Systems

It is essential to have a definite understanding of the descriptive terms used in connection with the functional components of the nerves and the systems to which they belong.

SYSTEMS

Afferent (A)

Afferent means that the conduction current is traveling toward the brain or spinal cord. The terms *afferent* and *sensory* are often used synonymously. However, in the strict sense of the word, sensory implies consciousness. Thus, not all afferent impulses can be classed as sensory, since many of them never reach the level of consciousness. The letter A will be used to designate afferent.

Afferent fibers are placed in three major categories, depending upon the region where the impulse originates: somatic, visceral, or proprioceptive.

Somatic (S)

This term can be thought of as pertaining to the framework of the body as distinguished from the viscera or organs. Embryologically, it is concerned with those parts derived from the somatopleure. Thus, somatic afferents carry information concerning changes in the external environment. The letter S will be used for somatic.

The somatic afferent fibers are of two principal classes, general and special.

General (G) This refers to those impulses which begin at or near the body surface. The letter G will be used for general.

Within the *GSA* system are three sensory modalities, or types of sensation. In other words, three different environmental changes can be detected by receptors: *pain; temperature,* both warm and cold; and *touch.* The latter is often regarded as being of two sorts: *light touch,* requiring stimulation by very slight surface changes, and *deep touch,* which is synonymous with pressure. This requires stronger stimulation to activate the receptors, most of which lie in the deeper tissues below the surface.

Special (S)   The receptors in this case are highly specialized. Instead of having the widespread distribution of the general receptors, they are concentrated in relatively small areas or organs, no longer located directly on the surface. They are usually contained within a framework of nonnervous tissue and are often associated with accessory structures (as in the eye and ear) which may enhance or modify the stimulation. Another characteristic of the organs of special sense is that they are activated by environmental changes which may occur at some distance from the receptor. The letter S will serve as an abbreviation for special.

Within the *SSA* system are two modalities: *vision,* the stimuli for which are short, high-frequency waves called light; *hearing,* for which the stimuli are long, low-frequency waves known as sound.

Visceral (V)

This term implies afferent impulses arising in or around the viscera. These impulses are essential in the reflex regulation of all visceral activity. The letter V is used for visceral afferents, which are also described as being of two sorts, general and special.

General (G)   These receptors are found in or on mucous membranes and in the walls of most organs.

The *GVA* system carries impulses which arise as a result of physical or chemical composition of the substances contained within the organ and the amount of distention of their walls.

Special (S)   There is no general agreement among neuroanatomists as to the existence of this category. However, the receptors for this system do answer, at least in part, the structural and functional requirements of organs of special sense. The stimuli are chemical in nature, and the impulses initiated by these substances have profound effects upon the activity of certain organs.

The *SVA* category also includes two modalities: *taste,* whose receptors are taste buds located chiefly on the dorsum of the tongue and inside the cheeks and lips, as well as on the palate and pharynx; *smell,* the olfactory receptors being found in the roof of the nasal cavity.

Proprioception (P)[1]

The division of the afferent system designated as proprioceptive is peculiar in many respects. Although its receptors often lie deep in the body tissue and, in this respect, are similar to visceral receptors, this system is concerned not with the internal adjustment of viscera but with the position and movement of the body. The letter P will symbolize this system.

General (G)   The receptors for this system are widely dispersed throughout the body: in muscles, together with their fasciae; in tendons; and in or around articular capsules.

The *GP* system possesses receptors of the pressure or tension type, activated by changes in tension of muscles or tendons and by movements at joints. In general, the activity of

[1]This category is included in most books under the somatic afferent system—both general and special.

this system takes place outside consciousness, the impulses making possible normal walking, balancing (in part), regulation of head position, and the adjustment of the proper amount of muscle contraction to perform a specific act.

Special (S) The receptors for this system are in the inner ear, particularly in the ampullae of the semicircular canals, the utricle, and the saccule.

The *SP* system consists of a group of cells related to a fluid medium in such a way that the slightest movement of the head will cause a current to flow, thus stimulating the receptors. Impulses beginning here carry information concerning the position of the head at rest, any changes in position of the head, and the plane in which movement occurs.

Efferent (E)

Efferent impulses originate in the CNS and flow outward, away from the brain or spinal cord. The term *motor* can justly be applied to this system, since its conduction currents result in activity.

Somatic (S)

The tissue activated through these motor fibers is skeletal muscle which traces its origin to the embryonic somites. As in the afferent systems, the letter S will be used as a symbol for somatic.

General (G) Since there is no "special" category, the use of the term "general" in this connection is almost superfluous. However, since the terminations of all these fibers lie in the motor end plates of skeletal muscle derived from somites, and since they have a very general distribution, the term is not inappropriate.

In the *GSE* system, most of the efferent fibers originate in the ventral gray columns of the spinal cord, pass through the ventral roots, join the spinal nerve trunks, and run directly to the myoneural junction (motor end plate) of skeletal muscle. Fibers of this system also originate in the nuclei of cranial nerves III, IV, VI, and XII, the first three supplying the extrinsic muscles of the eye, the last innervating the muscles of the tongue.

Visceral (V)

This is a system of efferent fibers the conduction current of which activates organs. The letter V will be used to designate visceral.

The visceral motor division consists of two parts, a general and special.

General (G) The distribution of these fibers is widespread; they pass to all smooth muscle, to cardiac muscle, and to all glands.

The *GVE* system is concerned with the maintenance of body homeostasis, including the regulation of heart rate and blood pressure, temperature, glandular secretion, peristalsis, sphincter tension, and pupil size.

Special (S) This group of fibers has a relatively small distribution. Peculiarly enough, the tissue activated is, histologically, typical striated muscle. However, this muscle is not derived from somites but from the embryonic branchial arches.

The muscles innervated by the *SVE* system include those of facial expression, of mastication, of the pharynx and larynx. Since these muscles are actually related to the rostral end of certain visceral systems, the digestive and respiratory, and to such organs of special sense as the eye and ear, the term visceral is applicable to them. The cells of origin for these efferent fibers lie in groups or nuclei in the special visceral efferent column limited to the brainstem and send their impulses out over certain of the cranial nerves (V, VII, IX, X, XI).

SUMMARY

I Neurons
  A Afferent
    1 Somatic
      a General—pain, temperature, touch
      b Special—hearing, vision
    2 Visceral
      a General—organ content and distention
      b Special—taste, smell
    3 Proprioception
      a General—muscle, tendon, joint capsule
      b Special—equilibrium
  B Efferent
    1 Somatic
      a General—to skeletal muscle of somite origin
      b Special—none
    2 Visceral
      a General—smooth muscle, heart, glands
      b Special—to muscles of branchiomeric origin

General Somatic Afferent System (GSA)

Portions of the GSA system are phylogenetically very old. Originally its prime purpose was to transmit information concerning environmental changes to deeper and more remote parts of the body, namely, the CNS. Within the CNS this information was disseminated in such a way as to make possible immediate and automatic adjustments to alterations in surroundings. In other words, this system began as the afferent limbs of reflex arcs upon which the animal depends for survival. This is true whether the change consists of extreme alterations in temperature which might lead to the destruction of living matter or whether it consists of a light touch which might indicate the presence of small, particulate food material.

Later on in evolution, higher CNS centers developed at the rostral end of the reflex-oriented spinal cord and hindbrain. The acquisition of these so-called conscious levels made it possible for an animal to make voluntary adjustments to at least some changes in its surroundings, while at the same time it provided a mechanism for learning, the latter being dependent upon sensory (afferent) experiences. Consequently, conscious and/or ascending pathways were built onto the preexisting reflex system. Since there are differences in both reflex and conscious routes depending on whether the environmental change, the *stimulus,* is detected along the trunk (including the extremities) or on the head, these regions are discussed separately. Likewise, since there are differences related to the nature of the stimulus—pain and temperature on the one hand or touch on the other—these are considered individually.

PAIN AND TEMPERATURE

Trunk

Conscious Pathway (Fig. 7-1)

Receptors Pain receptors are the most primitive, being naked, free, unembellished terminations of the peripheral nerve fibers which have sprayed out among the epithelial cells of the epidermis and are distributed uniformly over the body surface, including the orifices (mouth, anal canal, etc.).

Temperature mechanisms also differentiate early. The receptors, the bulbs of Krause for cold and the organs of Ruffini for warmth, consist of nerve endings covered with a capsule of some complexity. These are located at various distances from the body surface, in the dermis.

Neuron I Nerve fibers for both pain and temperature are small in caliber (Table 7-1). Their cell bodies, lying in dorsal root ganglia, are small and unipolar. As the central processes of these neurons approach the spinal cord, they join others belonging to the same system along the lateral side of the dorsal root of the spinal nerve and enter the *dorsolateral fasciculus (Lissauer's tract).* Within this fasciculus, each fiber bifurcates into an ascending and descending branch. Unlike the fibers belonging to other systems, these branches are very short, the longest probably extending no more than two (or three) segments. Each branch gives off collaterals which terminate, together with their parent fiber, in that portion of the dorsal horn nearest the fasciculus, the *substantia gelatinosa* (Fig. 2-5). It is now believed that short interneurons extend from the substantia to other, more ventrally placed areas (laminae) of the gray matter (Chap. 2). Here are located the cells of origin of associa-

tion fibers for the reflex arcs and the secondary fibers in the pathway to consciousness.

Neuron II These neurons arise in the dorsal horn very close to the level at which the primary fiber enters the cord. Each secondary fiber tends to cross the cord immediately. The crossing occurs just ventral and in close proximity to the central canal. After reaching the periphery of the lateral funiculus of the opposite side, these fibers bend rostrally in the *lateral spinothalamic tract* to terminate in the *ventral posterolateral (VPL) nucleus* of the thalamus (Chap. 23). Within the tract there is a definite layering of fibers, those representing the most caudal regions of the body lying most lateral while those from more cephalic levels are more medial (Figs. 7-1, 7-2). It is also held that pain fibers are more ventral and somewhat medial to those fibers mediating temperature. In addition, some fibers of the spinothalamic tracts either terminate in or send collaterals into the reticular formation of the brainstem in both the medulla and pons (Chap. 19). Farther rostrally, before these tracts terminate in specific thalamic nuclei (VPL), some of their fibers enter such nuclei as the medial intralaminar nucleus of the thalamus (Chap. 23). In any event, whether ascending all the way to the cortex in the reticular system through some as yet undetermined route or passing through the *diffuse thalamic system (thalamic reticular system)* (Chap. 23), they form an integral part of the so-called reticular activating mechanism (Chap. 19) of the cerebrum. Throughout its extent in both spinal cord and brainstem, the lateral spinothalamic tract lies close to the lateral surface of the CNS, those fibers arising from more caudal levels lying more superficially (Fig. 7-2).

Neuron III From the VPL nucleus of the thalamus, a third neuron arises which passes through the posterior limb of the internal capsule (Chap. 1) to end in the postcentral gyrus.

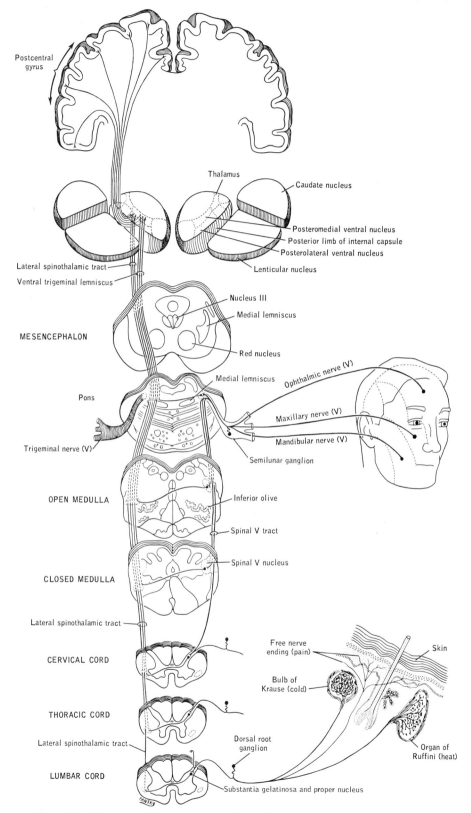

Figure 7-1 Diagram of the conscious pathway for pain and temperature, including the types of receptors.

Table 7-1 Classification of Afferent Fibers

Type	Diameter, μm	Conduction, m/s	System
A alpha*(α)	12.0–22.0	70.0–120.0	GP
A beta * (β)	5.0–12.0	30.0–70.0	GP, GSA, touch, pressure
A delta (δ)	2.0–5.0	12.0–30.0	GSA, pain, temperature
C	0.1–1.3	0.4–1.2	GSA, pain

*Some writers use the designation Ia and Ib for fibers associated with the annulospiral endings in muscle and the Golgi tendon organs, respectively, rather than A α and A β.

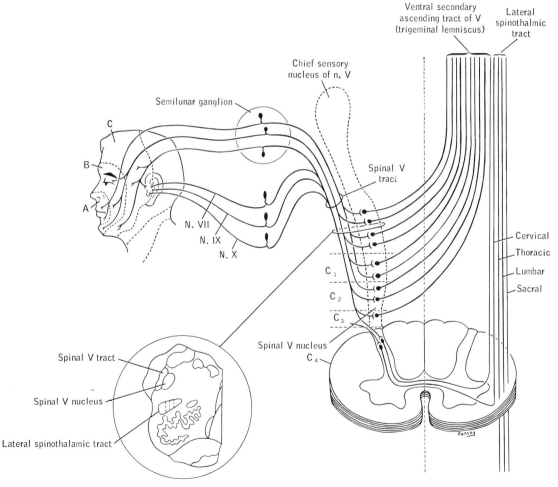

Figure 7-2 Diagram showing the distribution of pain fibers from the cranial nerves to the nucleus of the spinal V tract; the origin of the ventral secondary ascending V tract (trigeminal lemniscus) mediated from the caudal part of this nucleus.

Reflex Pathways   (Fig. 7-3)

Receptors and Afferent Neurons   These are identical with those of the conscious pathway.

Association Neurons[1]   These neurons must be numerous. Their cell bodies are in the same location as neuron II, above. Their axons have a variety of courses: (1) they may pass to the

---

[1]Because of their diverse courses, the existence of these neurons, let alone their exact positions, has rarely been proved experimentally. Therefore, the reflexes indicated are purely hypothetical, based almost exclusively on observed reactions.

ventral and intermediolateral cell columns of the same side, traveling up or down the cord via the fasciculus proprius, or (2) they may cross to the opposite side and terminate in the same gray areas of the contralateral side. In addition to these strictly intersegmental connections, some axons cross to the opposite side and bend rostrally to form a part of the *spinotectal tract* (Fig. 2-7) and ascend to the roof of the mesencephalon. From this region fibers descend in the *tectospinal tract* (Fig. 2-7) to synapse around small interneurons in the ventral gray columns of the spinal cord.

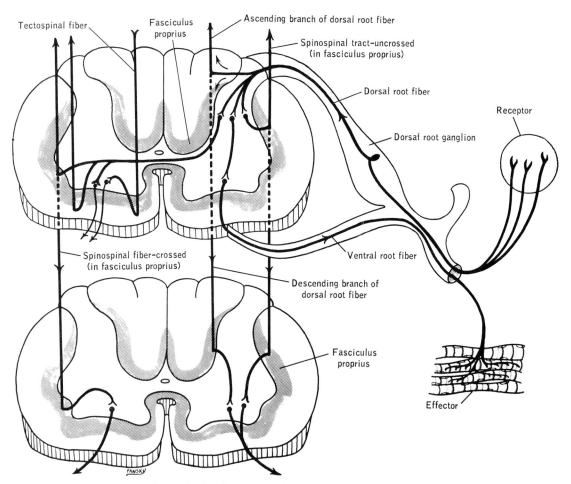

Figure 7-3   Intersegmental (intraspinal) reflex connections.

These, in turn, terminate around the large somatic motor neurons (Chap. 13).

Efferent Neurons Those neurons whose cell bodies lie in the ventral horns control skeletal muscle and result in such reactions as withdrawal, as from a hot object. Those neurons which arise in the intermediolateral cell column are preganglionic autonomic fibers (Chap. 14) and are responsible for such reactions as dilation of the pupil due to pain or sweating due to high temperature.

Head

Conscious Pathway (Figs. 7-1, 7-2, 7-4)

Receptors (Fig. 7-1) These are identical with those described with the spinal mechanism.

Neuron I[2] These occur in all divisions of the trigeminal nerve, their typical monopolar cells lying in the semilunar (Gasserian) ganglion. The central processes of these cells form a large part of the sensory root (portio major) of the nerve. After entering the brainstem, the primary pain and temperature fibers bend caudally to form a distinct bundle known as the spinal trigeminal (spinal V) tract (Figs. 7-2, 25-1 through 25-8). The latter extends from midpons as far caudally as the third or fourth cervical segment, there merging with the dorsolateral fasciculus of the cord. Regardless of root of entry, pain fibers lie more medially than do those for temperature. Within the spinal trigeminal tract, many collaterals arise; together with the terminals of all primary neurons, they enter the elongated nuclear mass which adjoins the tract on its medial

---

[2]Other cranial nerves—VII, IX, and X (Fig. 7-2)—have some GSA fibers. The facial nerve, with receptors in the deep face and cells in the geniculate ganglion; the glossopharyngeal, from the middle ear and pharynx with cells in its superior ganglion; and the vagus, from the external auditory meatus with cells in its superior ganglion also send primary neurons into the spinal trigeminal tract to end in its nucleus.

side. This nucleus, known as the *spinal,* or *descending,* nucleus, is continuous with the substantia gelatinosa of the cord and contains the cell bodies of both the associational neurons of the reflex circuit and the secondary neurons in the pathway to consciousness (Fig. 7-2).

Neuron II These fibers are given off along the length of the spinal trigeminal nucleus. They pass ventromedially across the midline at about their level of origin in the nucleus and approach the lateral spinothalamic tract of the opposite side. Here, they turn rostrally along the medial border of the latter as the *ventral trigeminal lemniscus* (ventral secondary ascending V) (Fig. 7-2). Thus, these two functionally similar bundles accompany each other to the thalamus. In the thalamus, the trigeminal lemniscus enters the *ventral posteromedial (VPM) nucleus* (Chap. 23). There are also contributions from the trigeminal lemniscus to the reticular system.

Neuron III These fibers, arising from cells in the VPM nucleus, pass through the posterior limb of the internal capsule to terminate in the inferior portion of the postcentral gyrus.

Reflex Pathways

Receptors and Afferent Neurons These are the same as those discussed in the conscious pathway.

Associational Neuron These are given off along the entire medial and ventromedial borders of the spinal trigeminal nucleus. They pass into the surrounding reticular formation, where some of them aggregate into longitudinal bundles, passing cranially and caudally to synapse directly in the cranial motor nuclei. Others pass into the cord through the reticulospinal tract to end around cells of the anterior and intermediolateral columns. It is also believed that chains of associational neurons are formed from a series of synapses among the cells of the reticular formation.

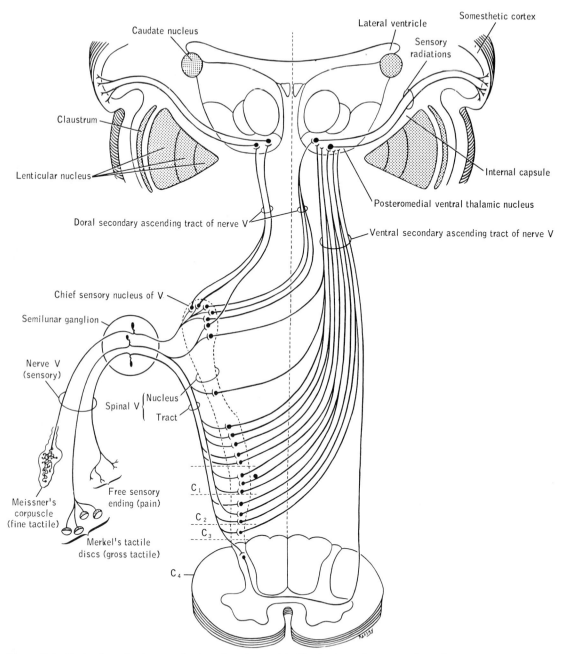

Figure 7-4 Projection of exteroceptive impulses transmitted by the somatic sensory branches of the trigeminal nerve. *Note:* The chief sensory nucleus transmits only impulses of gross and fine tactile stimuli; pain is transmitted only via the caudal part of the spinal nucleus. Gross tactile impulses are transmitted throughout all parts of the nuclear complex. *(Modified after Crosby, Humphrey, and Lauer, Correlative Anatomy of the Nervous System, The Macmillan Company, New York, 1962.)*

Efferent Neuron The efferent limbs of reflexes involving the trunk musculature are the same as those described earlier and in Chap. 13. An example of such a reflex response is striking at an insect that has stung the face. There are also reflexes which involve skeletal muscle of somite origin innervated by certain cranial nerves. In these cases the efferent neuron leaves the brainstem by way of cranial nerves III, IV, VI, and XII. Such a reaction could be exemplified by the retraction of the tongue from a hot object or the movement of the eyes toward a site of stimulation on the face. The efferent limbs of reflex arcs involving either branchiomeric muscle (Chap. 15) or the viscera (smooth muscle, heart, or glands) supplied by autonomic fibers (Chap. 14) consist of neurons whose axons travel via cranial nerves V, VII, IX, X, and XI. Examples of these kinds of responses would be the blinking of the eye (branchiomeric) resulting from irritation of the cornea or the dilation of the pupil (autonomic) due to a severe toothache.

Special Considerations Regarding Pain

Since pain is the cardinal symptom of disease and is indicative of tissue destruction, it has vast clinical significance. Thus, it was felt that some additional material should be presented for this important sensory modality.

Not only does pain, unlike other sensations, have a strong emotional component, but its affect quality is universally unpleasant. It is also unique among afferent systems in that pain can be perceived at subcortical levels (thalamus). Lastly, it has relatively little adaptability.

The receptors are classified as nociceptors, a type of chemoreceptor, responsive to noxious substances. The adequate stimulus depends upon the rate of tissue destruction. Apparently, cell injury leads to the release of proteolytic enzymes. These react with the gamma globulins of blood and tissue fluid. The product of this reaction is a series of polypeptides or a substance referred to as *bradykinin* which stimulates the nerve endings.

Although there seems to be but one kind of receptor, two types of superficial pain have been described, both related to the properties of the fibers which serve as the primary neuron.

The first type of pain is sharp, bright, pricking, and accurately localized. This is often referred to as *fast pain* whose duration is short and related closely to the duration of the stimulus. This type is carried by A delta fibers (Table 7-1).

The second type is the so-called *slow pain.* This is a burning kind of sensation, slower in onset than the first type. It is diffuse and is poorly localized. It may persist for some time after the removal of the stimulus. This sort is related to unpleasant feeling together with emotional involvement. This type is carried by C fibers (Table 7-1).

A third type of pain has also been described. This arises from deeper structures such as muscles or internal organs. It may be called deep somatic, or visceral, pain. Like the second type above, it may have a burning quality but most frequently is said to be "aching." It too is an unpleasant feeling with emotional sequelae. It appears that the C fiber is involved.

Visceral pain is briefly considered later and in Chap. 9. For pain arising from muscle, another humoral mechanism seems to be involved. During muscle contraction, a P factor is said to be formed. This could be lactic acid or a derivative thereof which is normally carried away in the circulation. However, during periods of absolute or relative vascular insufficiency, this factor builds up in the tissues and acts as a stimulus for pain fibers—in angina pectoris, for example, resulting from the ischemia of coronary occlusion.

Control of Pain

Because of its clinical importance, knowledge of the control of pain is essential.

Medicaments   First, there is a class of *narcotic analgesics.* These merely block out the emotional response to pain. Pain is still felt, but it does not bother the patient. The *general anesthetics,* of course, block out consciousness with the loss of all sensation. *Local anesthetics* apparently close the Na and K pores in the neuronal membrane, which prevents the buildup of an action potential (Chap.5).

Surgical   Several techniques have been developed: *denervation,* in which the nerves from a painful area are removed; *posterior rhizotomy,* in which the dorsal roots of spinal nerves are transected between the spinal cord and ganglion; *cordotomy (tractotomy),* in which the lateral spinothalamic tract is cut (page 157) and which has also proved effective.

Neuronal   This is dependent upon the connections of the fiber complexes within the CNS and is part of the normal physiology of this system in the control and/or modulation of pain. As described here, it includes the *gate theory of pain control.*

For a better understanding of these phenomena, examine Fig. 7-5. The spinal cord normally receives a stream of afferent impulses even in the absence of any frank stimulation. This stream utilizes the small (C) fibers which seem to be tonically active without noticeable adaptation. On the other hand, the large (L) fibers are inactive without stimulation. From the figure, it is seen that the C fiber not only excites (+) the transmitter cell (Tr) but at the same time sends a collateral into the substantia gelatinosa which inhibits (−) the interneuron (G), there. With this inhibitory influence, the interneuron cannot reduce the activity in the transmitter neuron. Therefore, the gate to higher brain centers is relatively open. Now, if a pain ending (P) is stimulated, a great flood of afferent impulses will pass

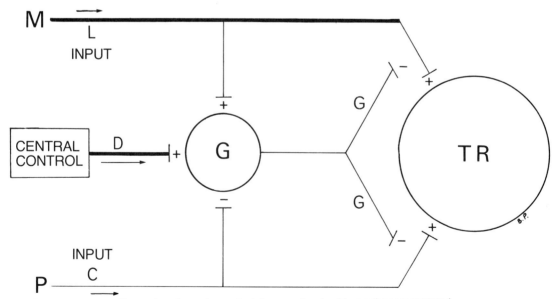

Figure 7-5 Diagram illustrating the gate control theory of pain. M, mechanoreceptor; L, large myelinated fiber; G, interneuron of the substantia gelatinosa; Tr, transmitter neuron (neuron I in the pathway to consciousness) to higher brain centers; P, pain receptors; C, small, lightly myelinated fiber; D, cortifugal fiber descending from higher levels; +, excitation; −, inhibition. *(Modified from Melzack and Wall, 1965, Science 150:971, copyright 1965 by the American Association for the Advancement of Science.)*

through the C fibers, which will open the gate still wider with the generation of many impulses in the ascending transmitter system. At this time, if the mechanoreceptors M associated with the large fiber L are strongly stimulated, as by rubbing, collaterals from this fiber will activate (+) the interneuron G of the substantia gelatinosa. When these interneurons are active, they place presynaptic inhibition on the terminals of the C fibers. This closes the gate before the Tr cells can be stimulated. With the diminution of ascending impulses in the transmitter system, pain sensation is reduced.

Under certain conditions, numbers of the large L fibers may be destroyed. With the loss of these, there is a proportional loss of fibers capable of stimulating the interneurons of the substantia gelatinosa. The resulting loss of inhibitory influences on the transmitter system leads to a greater sensation of pain.

Descending fibers D from the cortex may also send their excitation (+) into the gelatinosa, as might occur in fixed attention or concentration. Such excitation would also stimulate the G neurons to produce their presynaptic inhibitory influences of the transmitter system and thereby reduce the consciousness of pain by cutting down on the number of impulses reaching the cortex. It should be noted here that the descending fibers do not necessarily need to reach all the way down to the nuclei of the spinal cord. They may exert their influence at any point in the ascending transmission system in either brainstem or diencephalon.

Clinical Considerations

Testing

Pain   The integrity of the pain pathway is determined by pricking the skin with a pin, pinching a fold of skin, or applying a faradic current. The sensibility is described as analgesia (absence), hypalgesia (diminution), hyperalgesia (exaggeration).

Temperature   The integrity of this system is determined by having the patient distinguish between cold or warm objects, e.g., tap water with ice or water warmed to 50°C placed in separate test tubes and applied to various areas of the skin. The sensibility is described as thermoanesthesia (absence), thermohypesthesia (diminution), and thermohyperesthesia (exaggeration).

Specific Pathology

Referred Pain   (Fig. 7-6)   Technically, the consideration of sensory phenomena associated with internal organs belongs in another chapter (Chap. 9). However, since pathologic conditions in many organs exhibit symptoms in the form of pain directly related to specific skin areas and are so characteristic that they are useful in clinical diagnosis, an account of referred pain seems justified at this point.

Viscera are supplied with nerve endings of variable complexity (Chap. 9), distributed particularly among the smooth muscle cells of the muscularis. These are stimulated by overdistention (as stones in the ureter or biliary ducts), abnormal contraction (spasm), inflammation (as in appendicitis), or impaired blood supply (ischemia). Peripheral fibers from these visceral receptors usually accompany the visceral motor system all the way to the spinal nerve trunk. This occurs particularly in the thoracic, upper lumbar, and midsacral levels.[3] Visceral afferent fibers follow the dorsal roots of spinal nerves having their cell bodies in the dorsal root ganglia. After entry into the cord, their disposition is identical with that of afferent fibers arising from receptors on the body surface. Potentially, too, the sensory neurons are similar. The chief difference may lie in the fact that there are no specific thalamic nuclei or cortical areas for individual organs. Therefore, the brain is only able to interpret the

[3]Heart, T1 to T5; liver, gallbladder, and stomach, T6 to T9; small intestine, T9 to T11; colon, T11 and T12, L1, S2, and S3; ureter, L1 and L2; bladder and uterus, T11, T12, L1, S2, and S3.

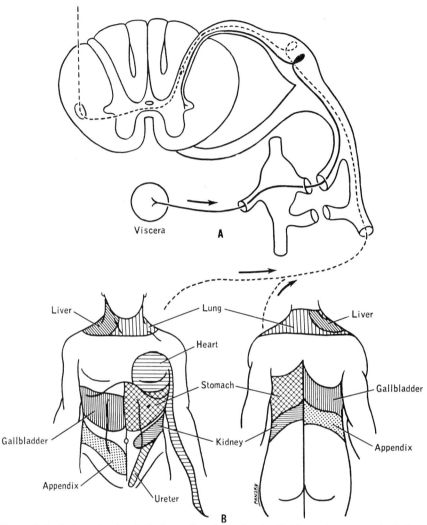

Viscera   A

Liver   Lung   Liver

Heart

Stomach   Gallbladder

Gallblader

Appendix

Kidney   Appendix

Appendix

Ureter

B

Figure 7-6 Referred pain. *A.* Pathway for visceral pain. *B.* Visceral areas projected on the body surface.

stimulus as occurring in the neighborhood of the receptors belonging to those nerve trunks which the visceral fibers join and in the dorsal roots of which they pass.

Another explanation is also given. Here, of course, the impulse from an organ follows the same path as that described above, but in this case, the emphasis is placed upon the fact that the visceral fibers terminate in the same region of the substantia gelatinosa and proper sensory nucleus as do the fibers from the surface area of the nerve trunks which the visceral fibers join. Thus, when there is disease in a particular organ, so many impulses pass into the substantia gelatinosa that its threshold for painful impulses from that particular surface territory is so greatly reduced that even light touch at the periphery may seem painful.

A third explanation may be that some neurons in the posterior or sensory root of the spinal nerve may bifurcate, one branch arising in receptors in the skin, the other having its terminals in the walls of viscera.

One of the best-known and most specific examples of referred pain is angina pectoris, in which the pathologic condition is in the heart but the pain radiates from the upper part of the chest down the medial side of the arm, forearm, and hand. This is because the visceral afferents carrying pain fibers from the heart join the upper thoracic nerves, which carry somatic sensory fibers from the chest and the medial aspect of the upper extremity.

Trigeminal Neuralgia (Tic Douloureux, Facial Neuralgia) This is a severe neuralgia of the trigeminal nerve associated with intense pain along one or more of its divisions. The ophthalmic division is rarely at fault, but involvement of the maxillary and mandibular portions is common. This disease is of unknown cause; it is localized in or near the semilunar ganglion. Certain surgical measures have been adopted to alleviate the symptoms, among them the injection of alcohol into peripheral parts of the nerve or the ganglion. If this fails, section of the sensory root (portio major) near its attachment to the pons may be resorted to.

Occasionally, pain may arise from blood vessels of the face and may be confused with trigeminal neuralgia.

Syringomyelia (Fig. 7-7) This is a chronic, slowly progressive disease, mainly of the cord but sometimes seen in the brainstem. The essential pathologic change consists in the formation of a cavity (or cavities) around the central canal of the cord. Whether the lesion is primarily a gliosis, i.e., a tumorlike proliferation of glia with secondary cavity formation, or a primary cavitation, the clinical findings are generally the same.

To understand the clinical findings, one must recall that secondary pain fibers arise and pass across the cord close to the level of entry of the primary fibers and that, in crossing, the secondary fibers are in the anterior white commissure which lies just ventral to the central canal. Thus, in overdistention of the central canal, the secondary neurons from both sides, on their way to the lateral spinothalamic tracts, are broken. The number thus interrupted will depend upon the longitudinal extent of the enlarged canal. As a result, there will be analgesia and thermoanesthesia on both sides of the body in the areas supplied by the spinal nerves in the territory of the lesion. The amount of the sensory disturbance will be proportional to the size of the lesion. When this condition occurs in the low cervical or upper thoracic region, the area of anesthesia will cover the shoulders and arms and is referred to as *jacket-type anesthesia.*

Cordotomy (Fig. 7-8) This is a surgical procedure which makes use of the knowledge of the location and function of the lateral spinothalamic tract. It is used in cases where some pathologic condition (e.g., cancer) has progressed to such a stage that the control of pain with drugs is difficult or impossible. If the lesion is peripheral, as in the skin or connective tissue, a unilateral section of the lateral spinothalamic tract, at a level about two segments above the entrance of the highest spinal nerve involved in the area and on the side opposite to the lesion, is performed. If the disease involves an organ, bilateral section of the tract must be made.

It has been noted, however, that, if a patient lives long enough after tract section, a return of the sensation of pain may occur. This is doubtless owing to those long chains of associational neurons passing into the dorsal gray columns at levels well above the cordotomy site where contact is eventually made with a secondary neuron of the conscious pathway.

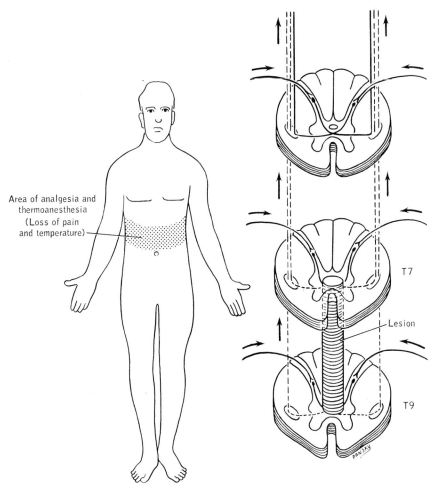

Figure 7-7 Syringomyelia (dissociated type of anesthesia), showing the location of the lesion and the areas from which pain and temperature have been lost.

Area of analgesia and thermoanesthesia (Loss of pain and temperature)

T7

Lesion

T9

Since this course would involve such a large number of synapses, long exposure to a constant flow of impulses is required to open it up, for under normal conditions impulses would follow the course of least resistance and bypass the more complex fiber system.

Phantom Limb   Although the authors have tried to point out that each fiber belonging to the sensory component of every nerve has a receptor at its peripheral end while its central process is followed by a series of fibers which

lead to consciousness, it should be understood that if some physical shock or chemical substance were applied anywhere along this chain of conduction, the brain would interpret the point of stimulation as being at the skin surface where the receptors belonging to the stimulated fibers are located. Thus, a patient who has had an amputation of one of his extremities may state that he feels pain from a particular area on a limb he no longer possesses. This is possibly because some of the pain fibers have been pinched in the scar tissue of

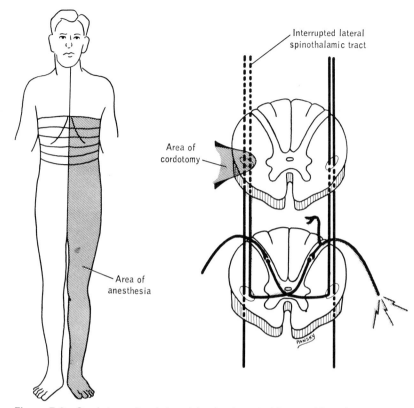

Figure 7-8 Cordotomy (tractotomy) for treatment of intractable pain.

the limb stump. It is immaterial that the portion of the fiber attached to the receptor is missing, for there is still a region in the cerebral cortex particularly for that portion of the extremity. All that is required is that an impulse reach the cortex for that area.

LIGHT (CRUDE) TOUCH AND PRESSURE

Trunk

Conscious Pathway (Fig. 7-10)

Receptors (Fig. 7-10) The receptors belonging to this system are of several types. *Merkel's disks* are platelike expansions of nerve fibers associated with specialized epithelial cells in the epidermis. Over most of the body surfaces, fine nerve fibrils entwine themselves around hair follicles, the *peritrichial arborizations.* These are sensitive to the slightest movements of the hair. In the dermal papillae, particularly over the volar surface of the fingers and hand, as well as on the soles of the feet, are the encapsulated tactile *corpuscles of Meissner.* Lying deep in the dermis, around tendons and joints and in the mesenteries and walls of the body cavities, are nerve terminals enclosed within numerous lamellae of connective tissue, the *Pacinian corpuscles. Genital corpuscles,* also encapsulated, are found in the connective tissue portions of the external genitalia.

Neuron I The peripheral process leading from the receptor is large and well myelinated. The cell body, located in the dorsal root ganglia of the spinal nerves, is of considerable

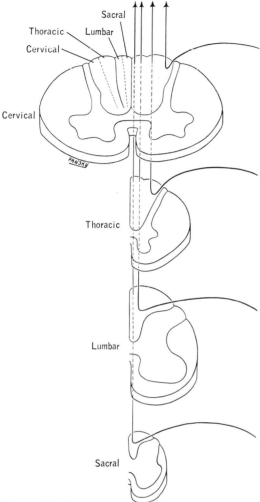

Figure 7-9 Arrangement of ascending tactile fibers according to the level of entry of the primary neurons into the cord.

branch, both of which give off collaterals to the gray matter. Fibers in the posterior funiculus have a definite orientation, those entering from caudal levels lying most medially, while those added from more cranial segments take a progressively more lateral position (Figs. 7-9, 7-11). This tendency toward regional separation becomes grossly visible above the midthoracic cord when a thin septum appears running obliquely ventromedially from the dorsal intermediate sulcus. The division of the posterior funiculus medial to this sulcus and septum is the *fasciculus gracilis* (Goll's column) and contains fibers from the lower half of the body. The more lateral portion of the dorsal funiculus is made up of fibers from the upper half of the body and is known as the *fasciculus cuneatus* (Burdach's column). All the descending branches, all the collaterals, and some of the ascending branches of the primary afferent neuron end in the dorsal gray column around cells of the proper sensory nucleus. Many of the ascending fibers continue upward into the lower medulla, where they terminate in the *nucleus gracilis* and *cuneatus*.

Neuron II   The cells of this second neuron, like those of the association fibers, are located in the body of the dorsal column. From here, their axons pass across to the opposite side of the cord through the anterior white commissure into the anterior funiculus. As they approach the ventral margin of the cord, they bend sharply rostrally as the *ventral spinothalamic tract* (Fig. 2-7). Fibers added to the latter at successively higher levels would occupy more dorsal positions within the tract. There is a general feeling that few of these secondary neurons go all the way to the thalamus without interruption. Many terminate among cells adjoining the tract, particularly in the medulla and pons. These in turn give rise to other fibers which reenter the tract. Since such synapses may occur repeatedly, the entire tract is actually composed of a

size and unipolar in type. The central processes of the primary tactile fibers tend to aggregate into the medial division of the dorsal root as the latter joins the spinal cord along the dorsolateral sulcus. After entry, all fibers of this medial division become a part of the posterior funiculus of the same side. In the funiculus, each fiber divides into a very long ascending portion and a short descending

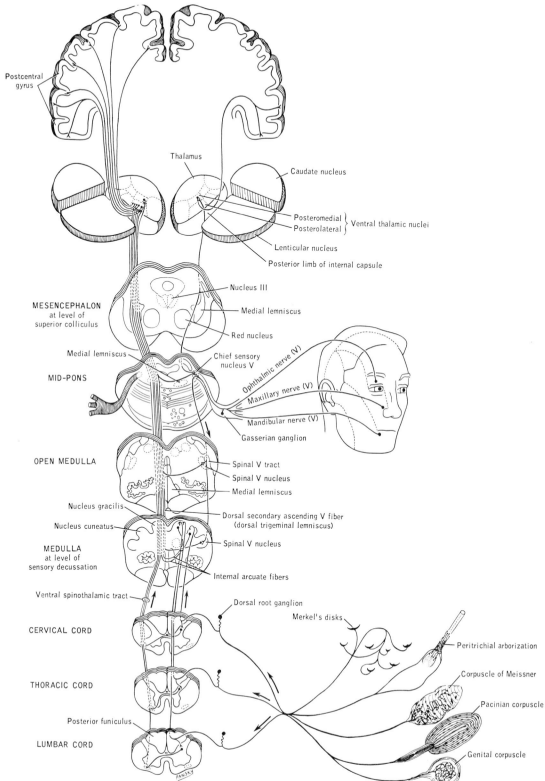

Figure 7-10 Diagram of the conscious pathway for light (crude) touch.

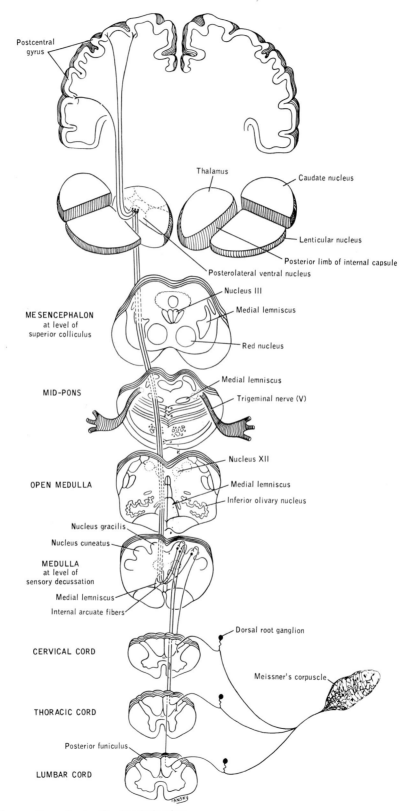

Figure 7-11 Conscious pathway for tactile discrimination.

series of short relays. Eventually, all the fibers end in the VPL *nucleus of the thalamus* (Chap. 23). In its course, the ventral spinothalamic tract may give off collaterals which are involved both in reflex activity and in the reticular activating mechanism.

The course of the ventral spinothalamic tract, particularly in the medulla and pons, has not been definitely established. Some investigators believe that it joins the lateral spinothalamic tract to form a single spinothalamic lemniscus. Others feel that it becomes associated with the medial lemniscus, and still others place it in a position intermediate between the two.

Neuron III This originates in cells of the VPL nucleus of the thalamus, from which axons pass laterally into the posterior limb of the internal capsule to terminate in the postcentral gyrus.

Reflex Pathways (Fig. 7-3)

Certain reflexes are particularly associated with light touch, e.g., scratching; blinking and lacrimation at the slightest touch on the cornea; and sneezing, after the inhalation of small, irritating particles which come in contact with the nasal mucosa.

Receptors and Afferent Neurons These are the same as in the conscious pathway.

Association Neuron From cells in the dorsal horns, axons of these neurons have a wide distribution similar to that described under Pain and Temperature. The spinotectal-tectospinal tracts may also assist in spreading reflex activity over the entire body.

Efferent Neuron Axons from cells in the anterior horns of the spinal cord leave the CNS through the ventral roots of spinal nerves to be distributed to the skeletal muscles of the trunk and extremities. Visceral efferent fibers arise from the intermediolateral

cell column and pass through ventral roots and white rami communicantes to reach autonomic ganglia.

Head

Conscious Pathway (Fig. 7-9)

Consciousness of even the slightest touch upon the facial area, particularly about the eyes, lips, and nasal mucous membrane, is extremely acute.

Receptors Reflexes activated by appropriate stimuli applied to the facial area, including the cornea, conjunctival sac, and mucous membranes of the nose and mouth, begin with receptors of the same type described for the trunk.

Neuron I The peripheral processes follow all the divisions of the trigeminal nerve and have their cell bodies in the semilunar (Gasserian) ganglion, while the central processes make up a part of the sensory root (portio major) of that nerve. The sensory root joins the lateral aspect of the pons where the tactile fibers pass obliquely dorsomedially across the middle cerebellar peduncle into the ventrolateral portion of the tegmentum. Here, these fibers bifurcate into short ascending and longer descending branches. The former end in the chief (main) sensory nucleus of the trigeminal nerve (Figs. 7-2, 7-4, 7-10, 7-12, 25-9), while the latter enter the descending (spinal) V tract to end around cells lying in the medial portion of the descending (spinal) V nucleus. Tactile fibers are apparently not well localized in the spinal V tract and probably do not extend as far caudally as do the pain and temperature fibers.

Neuron II The cell bodies of secondary neurons lie in the medial aspect of the descending (spinal) V nucleus and in the chief sensory nucleus (Figs. 7-4, 7-10, 7-12, 25-9). From the former, fibers stream ventromedially toward the midline. Beyond this

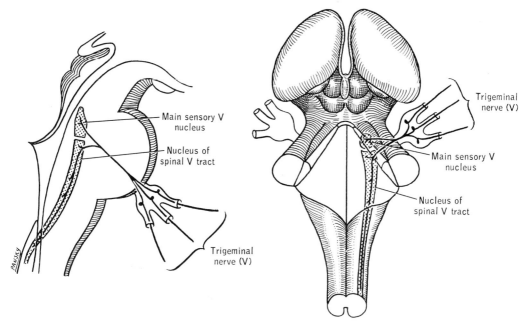

Figure 7-12 The spinal (descending) and chief sensory nuclei of the trigeminal nerve. *Left,* lateral view; *right,* dorsal view.

point, the exact distribution of these fibers is in dispute. Some may join the opposite medial lemniscus, while others may accompany the ventral spinothalamic tract in whatever location the latter may be.

The majority of secondary neurons in the conscious pathway arise in the chief sensory nucleus. From here, part of the fibers run medially across the midline directly below the hypoglossal nucleus and turn rostrally in the dorsolateral portion of the tegmentum just beneath the side of the fourth ventricle. This is the dorsal secondary ascending V, or the dorsal trigeminal lemniscus (Figs. 25-10 through 25-12). Other fibers ascend ipsilaterally in the same tract. Throughout the pons and midbrain, the dorsal trigeminal lemniscus remains in the dorsal position, staying medial to the superior cerebellar peduncle proper and dorsal to the decussation of the latter. Near the caudal end of the diencephalon, however, this lemniscus slopes ventrally to approach

the ventral trigeminal and medial lemnisci, with which it enters the thalamus, terminating in the ventral posteromedial (VPM) nucleus.

Neuron III From the VPM nucleus, tertiary neurons pass laterally into the posterior limb of the internal capsule to reach the postcentral gyrus.

Reflex Pathway

Receptors and Afferent Neuron These are the same as for the conscious pathway.

Association Neuron These originate in either the spinal V or main sensory nucleus of the trigeminal nerve and pass almost immediately into the adjacent reticular formation. Through the latter they extend in any direction to end in any of the cranial motor nuclei (somatic or special or general visceral) and also in the ventral column of the spinal cord, which is reached by way of trigeminospinal fibers in the reticulospinal tract.

Efferent Neuron Efferent neurons may originate in such cranial motor nuclei as III, IV, VI, or XII, or in the anterior gray columns of the cord. Thus, tongue movements in response to touch, or eye movements toward the side of the face that has been stroked are examples of this mechanism. Another familiar reaction is sneezing. This is initiated by irritation of the nasal mucosa. The excitation spreads over the reticulospinal tract to the phrenic nucleus (diaphragm) in the midcervical cord and to the anterior horn cells at other cervical and thoracic levels. Some efferent neurons originate in branchiomeric nuclei and pass via cranial nerves V, VII, IX, X, and XI. Others supply glands and smooth muscle through nerves III, VII, IX, or X. Twitching of the face as it is lightly stroked or closing of the eye as the cornea is touched are both examples of a branchiomeric reflex. Salivation resulting from the presence of an object in the mouth (not tastes) and lacrimation resulting from irritation of the conjunctiva are examples of visceral (autonomic) reflexes.

TACTILE DISCRIMINATION—STEREOGNOSIS

Tactile discrimination is the ability of the individual to recognize separately two distinct points of contact and to identify an object by its size, shape, weight, and texture. Although tactile localization is primarily a function of the cortex, tactile discrimination requires much greater cortical involvement. The latter is not solely a function of the tactile system alone, since the judgment of size and shape depends on movements at joints, while judgment of weight depends upon tension in muscles and tendons. Such discrimination requires the function of the proprioceptive system.

Similarly, *pallesthesia (vibratory sense)*, the perception of repetitive mechanical stimuli, goes beyond simple touch or pressure, since the element of time must be taken into account. Thus, it is not possible to complete the entire picture of the stereognostic mechanism at this time.

Since tactile discrimination is primarily a cortical problem, reflexes need not be considered. Furthermore, since the primary function of this system is associated with the extremities, only passing attention will be given to pathways beginning in facial receptors. Although the ability to recognize as distinct entities two contact points separated from each other by variable distances is a function of the tactile apparatus, it should again be emphasized that much of discrimination involves more than simple touch. This, unfortunately, may be misleading when the term *two-point touch* is used to include all of discrimination. At this point, only the data pertinent to the tactile system will be considered. (For additional material, see Chap. 11).

Trunk

Conscious Pathway (Fig. 7-11)

Receptors (Fig. 7-11) The receptors, *Meissner's corpuscles*, are located in dermal papillae closely applied to the surface epithelium. They are placed close together on the volar areas of the fingers and hands and on the plantar surface of the feet. Elsewhere, they tend to be much farther apart.

Neuron I The peripheral process of the primary neuron, running centrally from the receptors, is heavily myelinated. The cell bodies are large and unipolar, located in the dorsal root ganglion. The central process joins others belonging to the same system in the medial division of the dorsal root and enters the cord along the dorsolateral sulcus.

Within the cord, these fibers enter the posterior funiculus and are oriented in a manner similar to that of the fibers of light touch (Fig. 7-9). Likewise, each fiber bifurcates, the long ascending branches being most essential to the system. The latter continue rostrally in the posterior funiculus of the same side of the cord, enter the lower medulla, and terminate in the nucleus gracilis or nucleus cuneatus (Figs. 1-38, 25-3).

Neuron II The secondary neurons have their cell bodies in the nuclei mentioned above. From the ventral aspects of both, axons sweep ventrally and medially, forming an inverted arc around the central gray matter. As a result of this course and their depth within the medulla, they are called the *internal arcuate fibers* (Figs. 1-38, 7-11, 25-2, 25-3). All these arcuate fibers cross the midline, the fibers of the two sides interlacing as they cross. This is the *sensory decussation* (Figs. 25-2, 25-3). Almost immediately after reaching the contralateral side, all fibers turn rostrally, forming the *medial lemniscus* (Figs. 1-38, 7-11, 25-3 through 25-13).

Within the lemniscus there is a definite anatomic lamination. Fibers representing lower levels of the body lie more ventrolaterally, while those from successively higher regions are piled on dorsally. Throughout the medulla, the medial lemniscus is seen to be compressed from side to side, its long axis being in the dorsoventral plane. In the pons, the configuration changes so that its long axis lies in the horizontal plane. With this shift, fibers from the lowest body levels come to occupy the most lateral position, while those from the neck region, for example, are most medial. In the mesencephalon, the lemniscus moves outward toward the surface of the brainstem. Here, the lateral extremity of the lemniscus joins the lateral spinothalamic tract, which, in this part of the brainstem, lies quite superficially. All secondary neurons terminate in the VPL nucleus of the thalamus but at a level more rostral and dorsal than that which receives the endings for crude touch, pain, and temperature (Figs. 1-31 through 1-38).

Neuron III These begin with cells in the VPL nucleus of the thalamus, pass laterally into the posterior limb of the internal capsule,

and terminate in the postcentral gyrus and the adjacent parietal cortex.

Head

Conscious Pathway (Fig. 7-10)

It is well-established that Meissner's corpuscles are abundant at the tip of the tongue, where two points are distinguishable as close together as 1.1 mm. Meissner's corpuscles are associated with the mandibular division of the trigeminal nerve. Such receptors are also common on the lips, related to both the maxillary and mandibular divisions of nerve V. Impulses originating here would follow the same peripheral course and have the same terminations as those for crude touch in the corresponding area. The course of secondary neurons in the path to the thalamus is not clear, but it would not be illogical to speculate that they might lie close to similar neurons arising in the cord for the same purpose—in other words, near the medial lemniscus.

Clinical Considerations

Testing

Crude or Light Touch The integrity of this system may be tested with a fine, soft paint brush, a wisp of wool, or even a piece of paper. The sensibility is described as tactile anesthesia (absence), tactile hypesthesia (diminution), tactile hyperesthesia (exaggeration).

Tactile Localization Using the same materials, the patient must close his eyes and then indicate the exact spot that the examiner has touched.

Tactile Discrimination This may be tested in several ways. An area of skin is touched simultaneously with two points of a compass or calipers. The minimum distance between the points when felt separately, as two points, is noted. This may vary from 3 to 8 mm on the fingers to as much as 75 mm on the upper arm or thigh. Further, the patient is asked to discriminate between materials of different texture, such as silk, wool, linen, or emery cloth. The disturbance of sensibility may be described as *allocheiria* or *astereognosis*. The former concerns false localization; i.e., if one extremity is stimulated, the sensation is referred to the other side. The latter is a disturbance of discrimination in which the patient is unable to recognize, by feel, familiar objects when the eyes are covered.

Specific Pathology

Syringomyelia   This condition has been described previously. It is mentioned again here, since in these cases, the patient experiences *sensory dissociation.* In other words, sense of pain and temperature may be completely lost on both sides of the body in areas corresponding and in proportion to the lesion, while crude touch is not clinically diminished. The latter phenomenon is due to the fact that primary tactile fibers pass long distances before synapsing with secondary fibers. Actually, many of these primary fibers pass all the way into the medulla before making synapse with the second neuron.

Tabes Dorsalis   This lesion is of neurosyphilitic origin and leads to the destruction of primary neurons in the dorsal roots of spinal nerves. Although the filaments of the medial divisions are apparently destroyed first, leading to the degeneration of the posterior funiculi, all sensory fibers of the dorsal root may eventually become involved. In the tabetic patient, there is loss of position and vibratory sense below the lesion on the same side of the body. However, the disease may spread to the other side. With destruction of the entire root, loss of pain and temperature perception will also be noted.

Traumatic Lesions of the Cord   In the cord, most tactile loss which is clinically detectable is that of discrimination which occurs on the same side of the body below the level of the lesion.

Traumatic Lesions of the Medulla   When the medial lemniscus of one side is involved, there results a complete loss of position, vibratory sense, two-point discrimination, and pressure sense over the entire contralateral side of the body. Because of the proximity of the two lemnisci, it is quite possible for a single lesion to involve both of them. Since the ventral spinothalamic tract also lies close to the medial lemniscus in the brainstem, this too is frequently involved in the same lesion. Because by this time the secondary neurons in the conscious pathway for light touch are grouped within this tract, a destruction of the ventral spinothalamic tract here would result in a noticeably diminished crude touch on the contralateral side.

Phantom Limb   After limb amputations, this phenomenon is also common, expressing itself as itching or tickling. The explanation is the same as that given under Phantom Limb (see Pain and Temperature, above).

Summary of Conscious Pathways

Pain and Temperature

Trunk		Head
Trunk	Pain and Temperature	**Head**

1. Free endings (pain)
   Bulbs of Krause (cold)
   Organs of Ruffini (warmth)

   Receptor

   1. Same as trunk

   Somatic
2. Through all spinal nerves with cells in dorsal root ganglia, into dorsolateral fasciculus, ending in substantia gelatinosa of dorsal gray column

   Neuron I

   2. Through all roots of trigeminal nerve with cell bodies in the semilunar ganglion, into the brainstem via the portion major to end in the spinal V (descending) nucleus

   Visceral
   From viscera through white rami to spinal nerves with cells in dorsal root ganglia; end as above

   Somatic and visceral
3. Same; from cells in more anterior parts of dorsal gray column to contralateral side through anterior white commissure to lateral spinothalamic tract, thence rostrally to end in the ventral posterolateral (VPL) nucleus of the thalamus

   Neuron II

   3. From cells in spinal V nucleus to opposite side to enter the ventral trigeminal lemniscus (ventral 2^0 ascending V), thence rostrally to end in the ventral posteromedial (VPM) nucleus of the thalamus

   Somatic and visceral
4. Same except that there is no definitive cortex for organs

   Neuron III

   4. From VPM through posterior limb of the internal capsule to the postcentral gyrus

   From VPL through posterior limb of internal capsule to the postcentral gyrus

Crude Touch

Trunk		**Head**

1. Merkel's disks
   Meissner's corpuscles
   Pacinian corpuscles
   Peritrichial arborizations

   Receptor

   1. Same as trunk

2. Through all spinal nerves with cell in dorsal root ganglion; enters the posterior funiculus to end in the nucleus proprius of the dorsal gray column

   Neuron I

   2. Same as for pain and temperature up to the brainstem. Here the fibers end in the chief (main) sensory nucleus

3. From nucleus proprius or more anterior areas of the dorsal horn across the cord in the anterior white commissure to end in the ventral posterolateral (VPL) nucleus of the thalamus via the anterior spinothalamic tract

   Neuron II

   3. From the chief sensory nucleus fibers may (1) stay on same side or cross to the opposite side and ascend in the dorsal trigeminal lemniscus (dorsal 2^0 ascending V); (2) may cross to the opposite side and ascend in the medial lemniscus. In either case the termination is the VPM nucleus of the thalamus

4. From VPL through the posterior limb of the internal capsule to the postcentral gyrus

   Neuron III

   4. From VPM through the posterior limb of the internal capsule to the postcentral gyrus

Tactile Discrimination

Trunk	Receptor / Neuron	Head
1. Meissner's corpuscles	Receptor	1. Same as trunk
2. Through spinal nerves with cells in dorsal root ganglia into posterior funiculus (fasciculus gracilis and cuneatus), running rostrally to terminate in either nucleus gracilis or nucleus cuneatus	Neuron I	2. Essentially the same as neuron I in conscious pathway for crude touch in the head
3. From cells in either nucleus gracilis or nucleus cuneatus, through internal arcuate fibers, across to the opposite side in the sensory decussation, then rostrally in the medial lemniscus to the VPL nucleus of the thalamus	Neuron II	3. About the same as neuron II in the conscious pathway for crude touch in the head but the termination may be farther dorsally and rostrally in the ventral posteromedial nucleus
4. From cells in the VPL nucleus of the thalamus through the posterior limb of the internal capsule to the postcentral gyrus and adjoining parietal cortex	Neuron III	4. Same as neuron III in the conscious pathway for crude touch in the head

Special Somatic Afferent System (SSA)

VISUAL SYSTEM

Development (Fig. 8-1)

The first trace of photoreceptors in the evolutionary process is found on the skin, particularly on the dorsal side of the trunk. In time, these receptors become concentrated near the rostral end of the animal and are enclosed within the developing neural tube. With further development, these receptors can be traced to the lateral evaginations of the neural tube called the *optic vesicles*. These appear in the human embryo between the third and fourth weeks and later lie in the *optic cup*, which develops from the vesicles. Essentially, at 7 months of development, the neural elements which lie in the retina of the eyeball are complete and perceptive of light.

Although the emphasis will be placed on the neural structure, it is essential to have an understanding of the anatomy of the eyeball, including the cornea, lens, iris, and ciliary body, since these are important for normal vision under changing conditions (Fig. 8-2). Although, the extrinsic muscles of the eye also play a part in vision, their specific anatomy will be dealt with in a later chapter (Chap. 13). Since the neural mechanism lies in the retina of the eyeball, a knowledge of the finer structure of this layer will help in comprehending its function (Fig. 8-3).

General Definitions

Before going into a detailed study of the nervous pathways, it is necessary to understand what is meant by optic axis, visual fields, retinal fields, retinal quadrants, and macular vision.

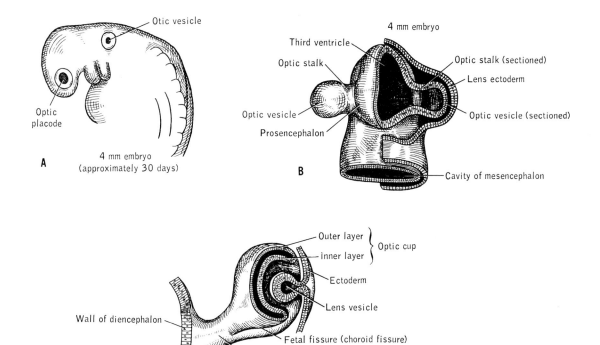

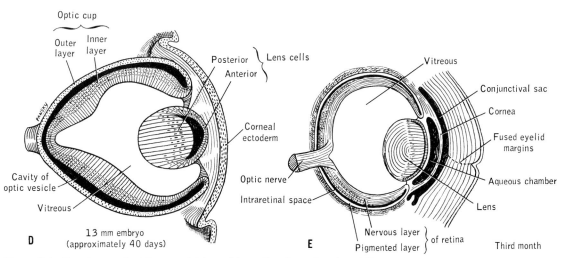

Figure 8-1 Development of the eye. (*Adapted from Hamilton, Boyd, and Mossman, Human Embryology, 4th ed., The Williams & Wilkins Company, Baltimore, 1972.*)

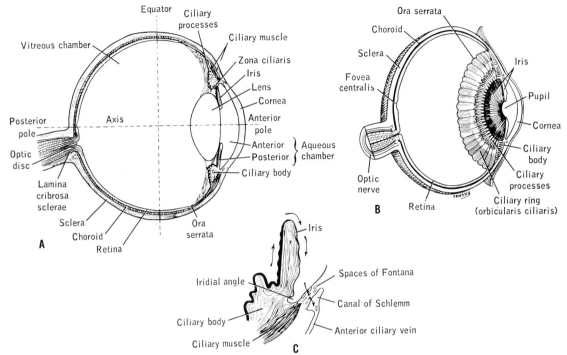

Figure 8-2 Structure of the eye. *A.* Horizontal section of the left eyeball seen from above. *B.* Hemisection of the right eyeball seen from above and behind. *C.* Illustration of the filtration angle showing the path of flow of the aqueous humor. (*Adapted from Schaeffer (ed.), Morris' Human Anatomy, 11th ed., McGraw-Hill Book Company, New York, 1953.*)

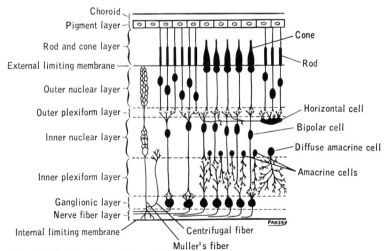

Figure 8-3 Structure of the retina.

The central points of the anterior and posterior surfaces of the eyeball are its anterior and posterior poles (Fig. 8-2). A straight line connecting the two poles is called the *optic axis*. The optic axis can be considered a sagittal plane of cleavage which divides each eyeball into a medial, or nasal, half and a lateral, or temporal, half. Thus, the retina is divided into a nasal and temporal *retina field*. A horizontal cleavage plane through the middle of the eyeball, at right angles to the sagittal plane, further subdivides the retina into upper and lower nasal and temporal *retinal quadrants* (Fig. 8-4).

The term *visual field* refers to that part of space seen by a specific area of the retina; e.g., the nasal half of the retina of each eye receives light impulses from the temporal area in space, and the temporal halves from the nasal area in space (Figs. 8-4, 8-5).

The center of best vision is at the macula lutea of the retina, which is a little to the temporal side of the posterior pole of the eyeball. Vision here is called *central*, or *macular*, *vision* (Figs. 8-2, 8-4).

Pathways

Conscious   (Figs. 8-3 through 8-5)

Receptors[1]   (Fig. 8-3) Within the retina are two types of receptors, the *rods* and *cones*.

The rods are the most numerous (estimates range from 100 to 130 million). They are absent from the fovea centralis but gradually increase in number in areas of the retina farther removed from that point. The rods react to low-intensity illumination and are said to subserve twilight and night vision. The rod cell is capable of changing length. In strong light, the cell lengthens and is pushed deep into the pigment layer which lies superficial to it. In dim light, it contracts, drawing away

[1]There is a belief, held by some, that the rod and cone cells not only are receptors but also are the primary afferent neurons, as well.

from the pigment, thus exposing a greater portion of the rod to what little light may be available.

The cones number 6 or 7 million. Except at the fovea, where they are the only cells found, their distribution is fairly even among the predominant rods. The cones have a higher threshold of excitability than the rods and are stimulated by light of relatively high intensity. They are important for clear vision and for color determination, adequate light being required for both. Cones are also thought to have the ability to extend or contract, perhaps to a greater degree than the rods.

Both rods and cones are absent from the optic disk, or blind spot, the point where the optic nerve fibers converge to leave the retina (Fig. 8-5). The nuclei of the rods and cones lie in the outer nuclear layer of the retina, those of the cones being located next to the outer limiting membrane. Each also has a fibrous process which extends into the outer plexiform layer of the retina (Fig. 8-3). Here the terminals of these fibers contact the peripheral process of the afferent neurons and the dendrites of the association cells (horizontal cells), the latter interconnecting groups of cone cells in one area with both rods and cones of another.

Neuron I   (Fig. 8-3) The primary neurons of this system are the shortest encountered anywhere, their entire extent lying within the retina. They are of the bipolar type. Their nuclei, covered by a thin layer of cytoplasm, are found in the *inner nuclear layer*. The peripheral process (functionally the dendrite) of each bipolar cell lies in the outer plexiform layer. They branch to receive the endings of several rod fibers. Cones more generally have a 1:1 relation to the bipolar elements. The central process (axon) of the first-order neuron lies within the inner plexiform layer, where it synapses with the dendrites of the ganglion cells (Fig. 8-3).

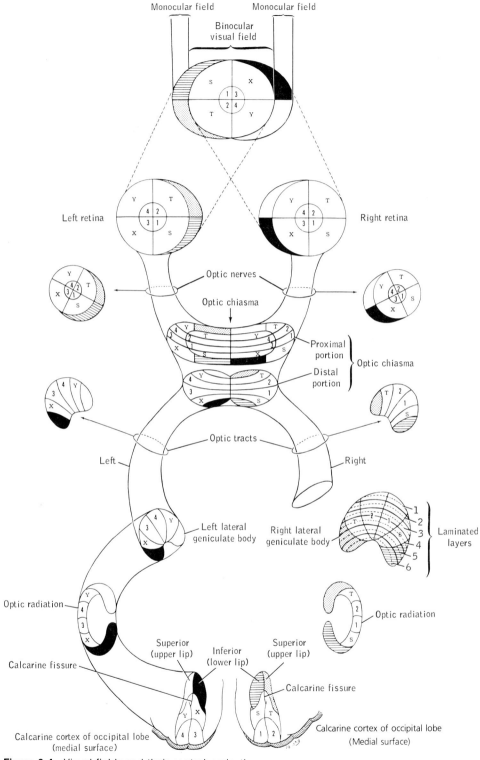

Figure 8-4 Visual fields and their central projections.

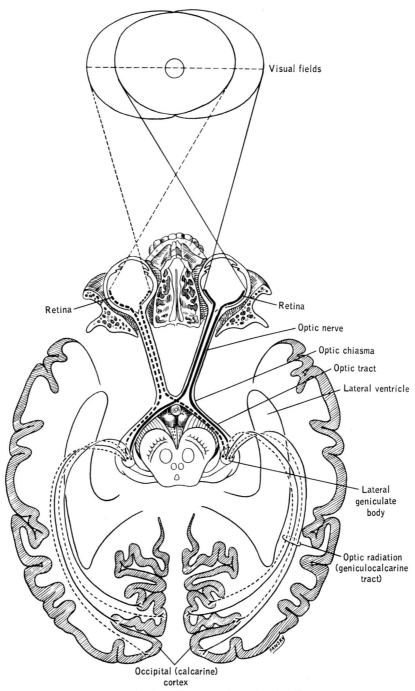

Figure 8-5 Visual mechanism. The conscious visual pathway.

Neuron II The ganglion cell layer may be thought of as a nucleus of termination for the afferent neurons, a feature common to all afferent mechanisms. This layer is composed of from one to several strata of large, multipolar cells. The dendrites of these cells spread out in the inner plexiform layer, where they synapse with the axons of the afferent neuron. Bipolar and ganglion cells are further interconnected by the processes of amacrine cells which spray out in the inner plexiform layer (Fig. 8-3). The axons of the ganglion cells accumulate in the nerve fiber layer of the retina (Fig. 8-3). This layer is separated from the vitreous body by the inner limiting membrane. The axons of the ganglion cells then pass around the inside of the retina to approach the papilla, or optic disk. At the disk, these fibers bend sharply to penetrate the outer coats of the eyeball. In order to permit passage of these fibers, the heavy scleral coat of the eye is perforated with many small holes. This region is known as the lamina cribrosa (Fig. 8-2), the weakest point in the ocular bulb. When the axons of the association neuron emerge from the sclera, they form the optic nerve. However, if one recalls the connections made within the retina, it will be seen that this "nerve" more nearly fits the description of a fiber tract of the CNS.[2]

Within the nerve, the axons are arranged on the basis of origin (Figs. 8-4, 8-5). Fibers arising from the cells in the temporal side lie in the lateral portion of the optic nerve, while those from the nasal retina occupy the medial part.

The optic nerves pass dorsally through the orbit, exit through the optic foramina, and enter the middle cranial fossa. Here, they approach each other and enter the *optic chiasma* (Figs. 8-4, 8-5, 8-6, 25-19, 25-20). In the

chiasma the fibers from the nasal retinae undergo complete decussation. Those which arise in the lower nasal quadrant form short loops in the medial part of the opposite optic nerve before becoming a part of the optic tract. At the same time, fibers from the superior nasal segment send loops into the rostral end of the optic tract on the same side before they enter the contralateral optic tract. Fibers from the temporal halves do not cross at all (Figs. 8-4, 8-5). Dorsal to the chiasma, the large fiber bundles running along the lateral aspect of the diencephalon are known as the *optic tracts* (Figs. 8-4, 8-5, 25-15 through 25-18). These contain the fibers from the temporal retina of the same side (homolateral or ipsilateral) and the fibers of the opposite (contralateral) nasal retina. Thus it should be understood that the entire left field of vision is being projected centrally by the right optic tract.

The fibers of the optic tract sweep backward around the hypothalamus, cross the rostral portion of the cerebral peduncles, and curve upward to reach the thalamus. Here, the fibers to consciousness terminate in the *lateral geniculate nucleus (body)*.

In the optic tract, fibers arising from the macular region of the retina occupy an intermediate position between those arising from the upper quadrants which lie in the anteromedial area of the tract and those originating in the lower quadrants which run in the posterolateral part. There is also apparently a very exact relation between points in the retina and specific parts of the lateral geniculate nucleus. Fibers arising in the upper quadrants of the retina terminate in the medial part of the nucleus, while those from the lower quadrants end in the lateral portion. The macular area of the retina is represented by a relatively large central area of this nucleus. As noted in Figs. 8-4, 8-6, the lateral geniculate nucleus shows six fairly distinct layers. It has been established that those fibers arising in the contralat-

---

[2]The fact that there is myelin without neurilemma, neuroglia rather than endoneurium, and dura in place a typical epineural sheath lends further support for the tract concept.

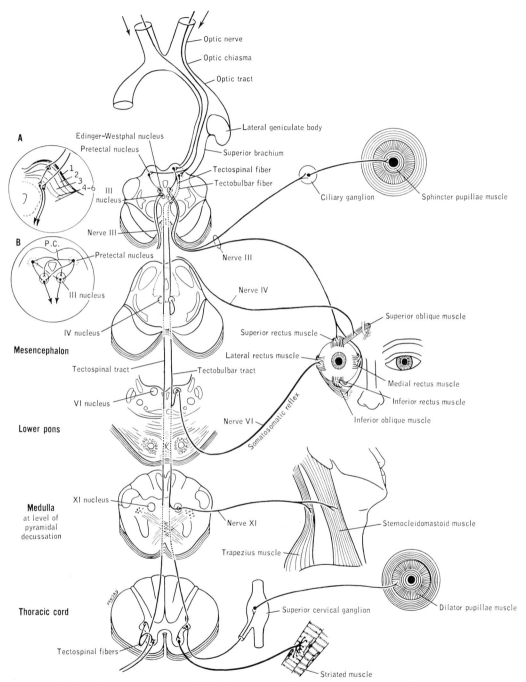

Figure 8-6 Visual reflex pathways. *A.* Chief laminae of the superior colliculus: (1) stratum zonale; (2) stratum cinereum (griseum); (3) stratum opticum; (4 through 6) strata lemnisci. *B.* Connections of the pretectal zone to the oculomotor complex.

eral retina end around cells in layers 1, 4, and 6 while the ipsilateral retina sends its impulses to layers 2, 3, and 5.

Neuron III   The cell bodies of these neurons lie in various portions of the lateral geniculate body. Their axons make up the *geniculocalcarine tract* (Figs. 8-5, 8-7). The most dorsal of these fibers pass almost directly backward to the cerebral cortex located along the calcarine fissure on the medial surface of the occipital lobe. The more ventrally placed fibers first run forward and downward into the temporal lobe, spread over the tip of the inferior horn of the lateral ventricle, and then loop backward, close to the lateral ventricular wall, to reach the calcarine cortex. Within the geniculocalcarine tract (optic radiations), which passes chiefly through the retrolenticular part of the internal capsule, the relation between retinal areas and tract fibers is also evident (Fig. 8-4). Diagrammatically, the geniculocalcarine tract can be represented as being crescent-shaped with its concavity directed medially. The macular region of the retina occupies the entire body of the crescent and is most lateral in position. The fibers

representing the upper quadrant of the retina lie along the superior arch, while the inferior retinal quadrant pathway is on the inferior arch. The relation between the areas of the lateral geniculate nucleus and the optic cortex is also very precise. From the medial half of the nucleus (upper retinal quadrants), third-order neurons pass to the upper (superior) lip of the calcarine fissure, while the lateral half of the nucleus (lower retinal quadrants) projects to the lower (inferior) lip of this fissure. The intermediate part of the nucleus, related to the macular retina, sending its fibers through the middle portion of the optic radiations, is projected to a large cortical area along both sides of the posterior third of the calcarine fissure.[3]

Reflex   (Figs. 8-6, 8-8)

Receptors and Afferent Neurons   (Figs. 8-3, 8-5, 8-6) These are the same as the receptors and neuron I in the conscious pathway.

[3]There is some controversy over the possibility that the maculae retinae have a bilateral cortical representation. If such pathways exist, they may account for the fact that, in large cortical lesions involving the occipital cortex, the macular region is often spared.

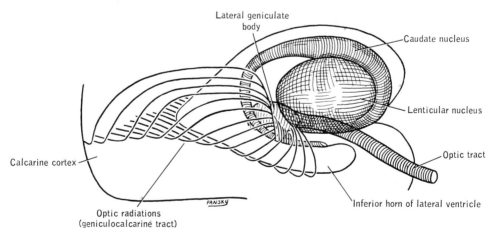

Figure 8-7   Lateral view of the visual radiations showing the formation and course of the geniculocalcarine tract.

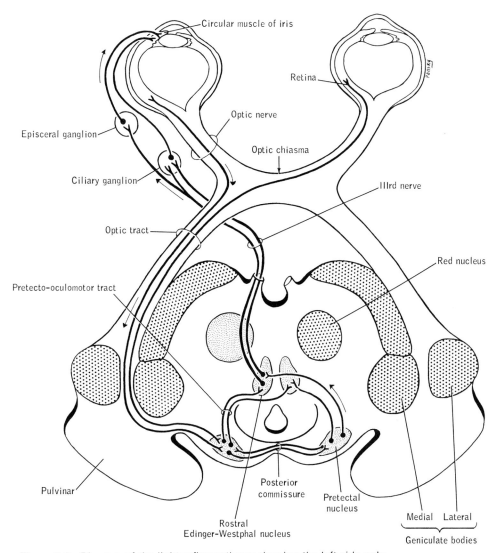

Figure 8-8 Diagram of the light reflex pathway showing the left side only.

First Association Neuron These are like neuron II in the conscious pathway except that they do not reach the lateral geniculate nucleus. They have a variety of terminations. Some of these fibers pass dorsally and medially over the lateral geniculate body and approach the rostral end of the mesencephalon to synapse either in the *superior colliculus* or the *pretectal zone* (Figs. 8-6, 8-8). The latter is a small gray area lying between the anterior border of the mesencephalon and the caudal margin of the epithalamus. Some fibers also pass into the hypothalamus to terminate both in the supraoptic nucleus and among the cells in the medial portion of the tuber cinereum. By way of fibers descending through the infundibulum, the pituitary is reflexively related to the retina. In lower forms, this may be part of the mechanism involved in pigment distribution. In human beings, the function of this pathway is not clearly understood.

Second Association Neuron (Fig. 8-6) These neurons have a variety of terminations, depending upon the final distribution of the efferent limbs of the reflex arcs.

From some cells in the superior colliculus, axons pass ventrally and caudally, undergoing partial decussation. They then descend as the *tectospinal tract* (Figs. 25-1 through 25-11) near the midline throughout the brainstem and continue into the cord in the anterior funiculus. These fibers terminate in either the anterior or intermediolateral cell column.

From other cells in the superior colliculus, fibers pass ventrally and caudally but *do not* decussate. They descend in the reticular formation of the brainstem as the *tectobulbar tract*[4] and enter the cervical cord as a part of the *reticulospinal system*. These fibers terminate in the cranial motor nuclei of nerves III, IV, VI, and XI (Figs. 1-28, 1-36, 1-38) and in the anterior gray columns of the cervical cord.

From cells in the pretectal zone, axons pass ventrally and caudally around the cerebral aqueduct to terminate in the *Edinger-Westphal (EW) nucleus*. This nucleus lies in the mesencephalon surrounding the rostral end of the oculomotor nucleus.

Efferent Neuron (Figs. 8-6, 8-8) From cells in the anterior gray column of the entire cord, axons leave through the ventral roots of the spinal nerves to reach the skeletal musculature of the trunk and extremities.

From cells in the cranial motor nuclei of nerves III, IV, VI, and XI, axons pass by way of the roots of these nerves to certain muscles of the neck and eyes. This enables the coordinated movement of head, neck, and eyes.

From cells in the intermediolateral cell column, axons pass from the cord through the ventral roots of appropriate spinal nerves. These diverge from the nerve trunk as white rami communicantes, pass through the thoracic sympathetic chain, and terminate in the superior cervical sympathetic ganglia. These fibers are referred to as preganglionic fibers (Chap. 14). Postganglionic fibers from the superior cervical ganglia are then distributed to the dilator pupillae muscle of the eye.

From the *Edinger-Westphal nucleus* in the mesencephalon, the axons pass ventrally and accompany the fibers of the oculomotor (III) nerve. After the oculomotor nerve reaches the orbit, these fibers diverge to enter the ciliary ganglion, in which they synapse. Thus, these fibers are also referred to as preganglionic fibers. From the ciliary ganglion, postganglionic fibers pass by way of the short ciliary nerves to the sphincter pupillae muscle. This constricts the pupil in the presence of strong light (Fig. 8-8).

Activation of the Retina

The outer segment of the rod (Fig. 8-3) contains *visual purple*, or *rhodopsin*, which is vitamin A aldehyde, *retinene*, bound to a protein, *scotopsin*. This photopigment is contained in closely stacked membranous disks or sacs. When exposed to light, rhodopsin is bleached, breaking the bond between aldehyde and protein, leaving retinene and scotopsin. The retinene is reduced by alcohol dehydrogenase, working with reduced NAD, to vitamin A.[5]

---

[4]Some fibers which technically should be classified as tectobulbar, since they terminate around nuclei of the brainstem, apparently cross with the tectospinal fibers and descend in this tract.

[5]The resynthesis of rhodopsin following breakdown is responsible for dark adaptation. In the absence of light some of the retinene and scotopsin join to form new rhodopsin. However, any extensive new synthesis depends upon fresh supplies of vitamin A from the bloodstream. Absence of vitamin A results in "night blindness."

During the bleaching out of the visual purple, which actually is said to be an isomerization process, transitory intermediate products are formed, and light energy is transduced to chemical energy (action potential) according to the following theory.

Before discussing the total process, however, certain basic principles should be understood: First, the ganglion cells of the retina have an intrinsic capacity to fire spontaneously unless some outside factor inhibits their activity. Therefore, it must be assumed that, in the absence of light, some inhibiting force must be applied to them. Second, this inhibiting force originates in the bipolar cells.

When light impinges upon the rod, Ca^{2+} ions are liberated from the stacked disks. These cations diffuse through the rod cytoplasm to the cell membrane, where they block the Na channels (which are normally open in the absence of light). As a result, the K channels in the basal part of the rod hyperpolarize the rod membrane potential. This light-induced hyperpolarization of the rod reduces the release of an excitatory transmitter substance at the axon terminal where synapse with bipolar cell occurs. Because of this diminution in excitatory substance, the bipolar cell also becomes hyperpolarized. As a consequence of this, the bipolar cell reduces its release of an inhibitory substance (which is normally released in the dark) at its synapse with the ganglion cell. Because of diminished amounts of the inhibitor substance, the ganglion cell is no longer held in check and thus will fire an impulse along the optic pathway to the cortex, where it will be recorded as light.

Unlike the rods, all of which contain the same pigment, the cones are of three types, each containing a different pigment. One contains *cyanolabe*, which reacts to blue light. The second contains *erythrolabe*, which absorbs light in the red range of the spectrum. The third contains *chlorolabe*, which reacts to the green portion of the spectrum. As far as is known, these substances perform in a manner similar to rhodopsin.

Accommodation   (Fig. 8-9)

The process by which an image is kept in sharp focus when the gaze is shifted from a far object (beyond approximately 40 cm, or 16 in) to a near object (less than 40 cm, or 16 in) is called *accommodation*. Several reflex activities are involved in this, including thickening of the lens, constriction of the pupil, and convergence of the eyes.

The reason for discussing this phenomenon at this point, rather than with other reflexes, lies in the fact that for the complete act of accommodation, it is necessary for the visual impulses to reach the cortex. This they do by way of the conscious pathways. Thus, when such impulses reach the cortical visual area, it is here that the reflex is initiated by associational neurons which pass forward to the motor centers of the frontal lobe. Secondary association neurons arising from such motor areas, then descend through the internal capsule, and diverge into the brachium of the superior colliculus to synapse there in the gray substance. From cells in the superior colliculus, fibers descend to the posterior portion of the Edinger-Westphal nucleus and the nucleus of Perlia (medial part of the third nucleus), where they synapse.

Efferent Limbs   Some fibers from the Edinger-Westphal nucleus pass ventrally as preganglionic fibers to join the oculomotor nerve, with which they enter the orbit. They then diverge from this nerve to pass through the ciliary ganglion *without* synapse, terminating about the cells of the *episcleral ganglia* on the sclera of the eyeball. The short axons of the postganglionic fibers terminate in the ciliary muscle. Thus, this reflex results in an increase in thickness of the lens in its antero-posterior diameter.

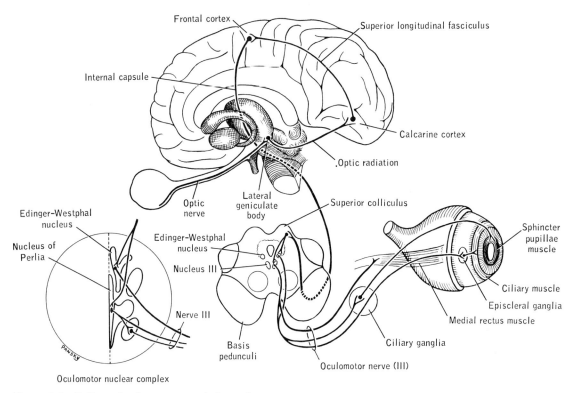

Figure 8-9 Pathway for the accommodation reflex.

Other fibers from the Edinger-Westphal nucleus pass by way of the third cranial nerve to the *ciliary ganglion*, where the preganglionic fibers terminate. From here, postganglionic fibers pass to the sphincter pupillae muscle of the iris, enabling *constriction of the pupil.*

From the *nucleus of Perlia*, fibers pass either directly to the medial rectus muscles of the eyes or by way of short axons into the main third nucleus itself and then to the muscles. This reflex enables the eyes to *converge.*

Clinical Considerations

Many clinical conditions, both congenital and acquired, lead to impairment of vision. Among them are coloboma, albinism, cataract, opaque cornea, and retinal separation. Furthermore, certain systemic conditions, not primarily concerned with vision but often affecting it adversely, such as severe diabetes, could be mentioned. However, these, together with the general ophthalmologic problems of astigmatism, myopia, and hyperopia, cannot be considered here. Only the purely neurologic conditions will be discussed.

Further, visible signs about the eyes, such as drooping of the eyelids (ptosis) and constriction of the pupils (myosis), as seen in connection with Horner's syndrome, are closely associated with defects of the autonomic nervous system. Therefore, a discussion of this condition will be delayed until the study of the GVE system is undertaken (Chap. 14). Defects involving position and movement of the eye will also be considered under the GSE system (Chap. 13).

The terms *visual axis*, *visual fields*, *retinal fields*, and *macular vision*, discussed early in this chapter under General Definitions, should be reviewed. Other terms frequently encountered in reference to the visual system are *anopsia* (without vision); *hemianopsia* (blindness, unilateral or bilateral, in one-half of the visual field); *heteronymous hemianopsia* (bitemporal or binasal loss of vision); *homonymous hemianopsia* (loss of vision in the nasal half of one eye and the temporal half of the other).

Testing

Visual Fields (Figs. 8-4, 8-5) The examination of the visual fields is of great clinical importance in localizing lesions involving the visual pathways. The fields may be mapped by the use of a perimeter or tangent screen. However, a fairly accurate picture may be produced by having the patient gaze directly ahead, on a dark field several feet away, with one eye covered. The examiner then moves a small, silvered sphere on the end of a wand, from the periphery toward the central fixation zone. The patient is required to tell when there is failure to see the sphere. This process is carried through to cover the four quadrants of the field, and is then repeated for the other eye.

Convergence and Reflex Pupillary Constriction (Fig. 8-10) With the examiner standing directly in front of the patient, the finger, wand, or comparable object is held some distance (more than 40 cm, or 16 in) from the patient's nose. It is then moved rapidly in toward the nose. It should be noted whether the eyes converge and the pupils constrict.

Light Reflex A small beam of light is directed into one eye; it should be noted whether the pupil of the eye into which the light is shining shows constriction (*direct light response*), and then it should be noted whether the pupil in the other eye constricts simultaneously (*consensual light response*).

Ophthalmoscopic In the sense used here, the examination of the retina through the ophthalmoscope is to search the retina for defects primarily located there.

Specific Pathology

Lesions Involving Optic Nerve, Optic Chiasma, or Optic Tract (Fig. 8-11) Figures indicate the location of possible lesions, fibers destroyed or damaged, and the resulting visual field defects. Thus, complete anopsia in one eye may result from loss of blood supply to the retina or optic nerve. Compression of the optic nerve in the orbit may also lead to variable degrees of blindness. Tumors, expanding forward from the pituitary gland or hypothalamus, may impinge upon the optic chiasma to such an extent that decussating fibers of the nasal retinae will be disrupted, thus leading to *bitemporal hemianopsia. Binasal hemianopsia*, in which the uncrossed fibers from the temporal retina of both eyes are interrupted with the consequent loss of both nasal visual fields, is theoretically possible, but rare. Bilateral aneurysms of the internal carotid arteries have been observed to cause binasal hemianopsia. Unilateral compression of one side of the chiasma due to this arterial defect, destroying the fibers from the temporal retina of the same side with the loss of the nasal visual field for that eye, is more common (*nasal hemianopsia*). Injuries or tumors may also involve the optic tracts, thus producing *homonymous hemianopsia*. However, the destruction of these tracts is often only partial. This is also true of the geniculocalcarine tract and the visual cortex. So many variations are possible that a complete description of all of them is too complex for this book.

Lesions of the Pretectal Zone It has been pointed out that the reflex pathways for pupillary constriction and for accommodation are not the same. Thus, if a disease such as tabes dorsalis spreads to the pretectal zone, an important link in the light reflex circuit is broken and *no pupillary constriction in response to light is elicited*. On the other hand,

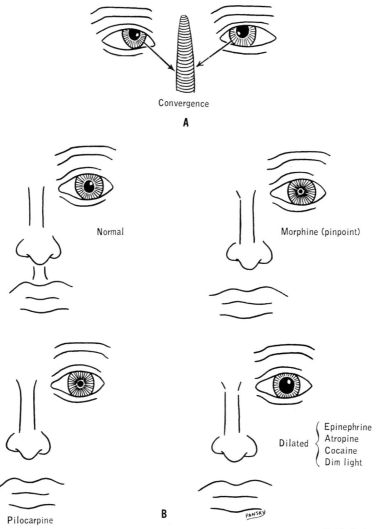

Convergence

A

Normal   Morphine (pinpoint)

Dilated {
Epinephrine
Atropine
Cocaine
Dim light

Pilocarpine   **B**   PANSKY

Figure 8-10 Eye movement and pupil changes. *A.* Convergence. *B.* Variations in pupillary size due to various causes, especially the use of certain drugs.

the *pupil does constrict for near vision.* This is the so-called *Argyll Robertson pupil.*

AUDITORY SYSTEM

Development (Fig. 8-12)

Unlike the eye, the essential structure for hearing, lying within the inner ear, develops from a thickening of the surface ectoderm along the dorsolateral aspect of the hindbrain. This essential structure first appears as a definite placode in embryos between 2.5 and 3.5 weeks. The series of changes which occurs during the next weeks of development is best described through illustration. The ear grossly approaches typical adult structure at 16 weeks, although hearing does not occur until some time after birth.

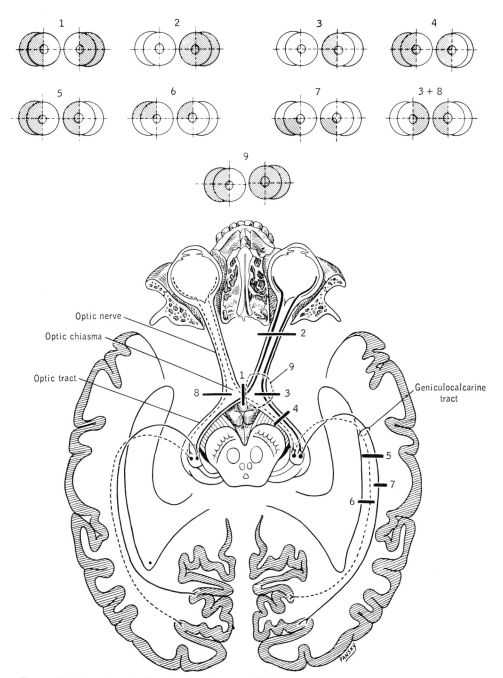

Figure 8-11 Lesions in the visual pathways. (1) Bitemporal heteronymous hemianopsia; (2) homolateral blindness; (3) right nasal hemianopsia; (4) lateral homonymous hemianopsia; (5) homonymous hemianopsia; (6) homonymous partial quadrantanopsia; (7) same as (6); (8) plus (3) nasal heteronymous hemianopsia; (9) homolateral blindness plus contralateral temporal hemianopsia. *Note*: Lesions shown at (6) and (7) would involve more than those fibers indicated, thus accounting for loss of visual fields for both eyes.

185

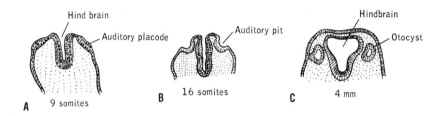

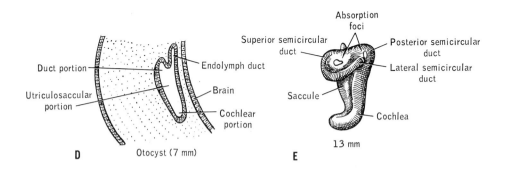

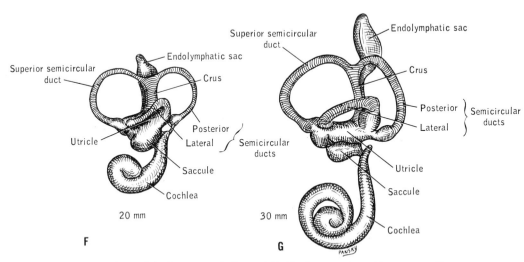

Figure 8-12 Embryology of the inner ear. *A. through D.* The human otocyst in cross section. (*Adapted from His, in Arey, Developmental Anatomy, 7th ed., W. B. Saunders Company, Philadelphia, 1974.*) *E through G.* Development of the left membranous labyrinth. (*Adapted from Streeter, in Arey, Developmental Anatomy, 7th ed., W. B. Saunders Company, Philadelphia, 1974.*)

Sound Transmission and Cochlear Activity

In order to understand how the energy of the sound waves in the air is transformed into nervous energy, it is necessary to visualize not only the inner ear but also the middle and external ears as well (Fig. 8-13). With these gross relationships in mind, the orientation of the parts of the inner ear should next be studied by examining a section through the cochlea, including the endolymph and perilymph (Figs. 8-14, 8-15). Thus, sound waves pass through the external auditory meatus, where they impinge upon the tympanic membrane. The membrane is set into motion with the same frequency as the incident waves and in relatively the same amplitude. Since the ansa (handle) of the malleus, the first of the auditory ossicles, is fixed to the membrane, it transmits the motion to the incus and finally to the stapes. The foot plate of the stapes lies in an oval aperture (oval window) in the wall of the bony labyrinth. Thus, the motion of the stapes sets up waves in the perilymph. In their passage through the scalae, the waves of perilymph result in vibrations of the basilar membrane. The undulations of the latter produce an up-and-down movement of the hair cells which rest upon it.

Hair cells are mechanoreceptors. The so-called hairs are stereocilia which have the structure of microvilli. These are embedded in, and firmly bound to, the overlying tectorial membrane. As seen in Fig. 8-15, the basilar and tectorial membranes are attached (hinged) at different points. Thus, movements of the hair cells result in a shearing action on the hairs. The net result is the transduction of wave energy to generator potential.

It appears that the ionic composition of endolymph and perilymph is important in the creation of both receptor and action potential. Endolymph is similar to intracellular fluid with a 50 to 100 mV potential, positive to the fluid in the scalae, while perilymph resembles extracellular fluid with high Na^+ and low K^+ ions. These fluids are separated by two membranes, the vestibular, which is impermeable to Na^+ and K^+, and the basilar, which is permeable to both. As the basilar membrane

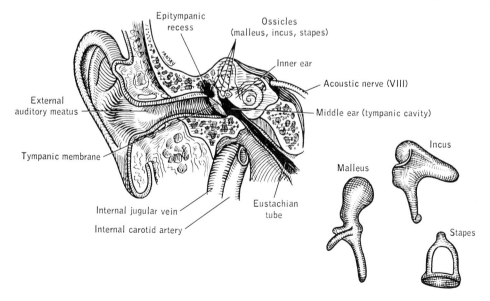

Figure 8-13 Anatomy of the external, middle, and inner ear.

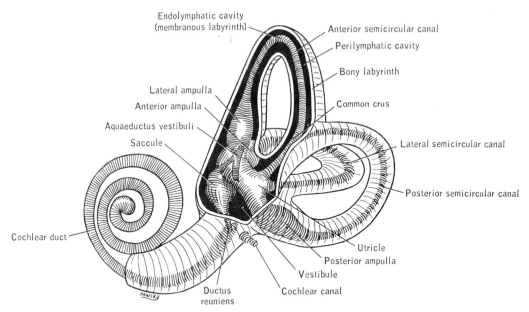

Anterior semicircular canal
Perilymphatic cavity
Bony labyrinth
Common crus
Lateral semicircular canal
Posterior semicircular canal
Utricle
Posterior ampulla
Vestibule
Cochlear canal
Ductus reuniens

Endolymphatic cavity (membranous labyrinth)
Lateral ampulla
Anterior ampulla
Aquaeductus vestibuli
Saccule
Cochlear duct

Figure 8-14 Relationships of the parts of the inner ear with special emphasis on the endolymph and perilymph.

rises and falls, there is an alternating reduction and increase in endolymph potential.

The potential in the hair cells is transmitted to the naked nerve terminals which end synaptically at the base of the cells, and action potential is set up along the afferent neuron.

Although the entire basilar membrane vibrates for all notes, it has been shown that certain parts of the cochlea vibrate maximally to one frequency while other parts are more sympathetic to other frequencies. Thus, tones of low pitch are received in the apical coil while high pitch is maximal in the basal coil. This phenomenon is related to the length of, and tension on, the fibers in the membrane. At the base the fibers are short and stiff, while at the apex they are 5 times longer and are more flabby.

Pathways

Conscious   (Fig. 8-16)

Receptors   These are the *hair cells* which lie along the entire length of the organ of Corti, in the cochlear duct (Figs. 8-15, 8-16).

Neuron I   A group of neurons end synaptically at the base of each hair cell. These nerve fibers pass down the cochlea in a small space just beneath the receptor cells, enter the basilar membrane, and turn medially in the latter toward the lip of the bony modiolus, which forms the core of the cochlea. Here, the fibers become myelinated. After a short course in this thin shelf of bone, the peripheral process joins its cell body. These bipolar cells lie in the bone, arranged along the inner edge of the spiral bony shelf. This aggregation of cells is the *spiral ganglion*. From the ganglion cells, processes are directed centrally, accumulating in the center of the modiolus. There, they turn downward toward the base of the cochlea, where they enter the internal acoustic meatus to be joined by the fibers from the vestibular division of the eighth nerve. They traverse the entire length of the meatus and enter the posterior cranial fossa, where they immediately enter the brain in the cerebellopontine angle (Figs. 1-7, 1-8).

After entering the substance of the brain,

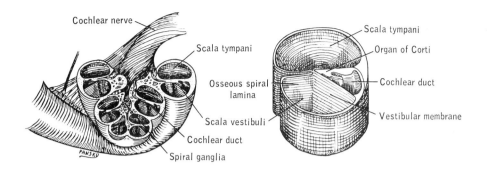

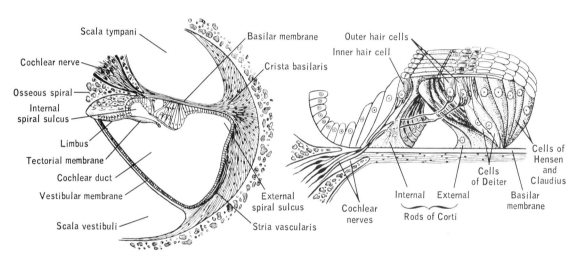

Figure 8-15 Auditory receptive mechanism showing the cochlear duct and the organ of Corti.

the cochlear fibers segregate into two main bundles. One group passes lateral and dorsal to the inferior cerebellar peduncle to terminate in the *dorsal cochlear nucleus* (Figs. 8-17, 8-18). The other group remains slightly ventral and medial to the inferior cerebellar peduncle and ends in the *ventral cochlear nucleus* (Figs. 8-17, 8-18, 25-6).

Neuron II The cell bodies of this neuron lie in either the dorsal or the ventral cochlear nuclei.

Fibers from the *ventral nucleus* pass medially with a slight rostral inclination and are collectively known as the *ventral trapezoid body* (Figs. 8-17, 8-18, 25-9). These fibers lie

between the basilar and tegmental areas of the pons. The fibers of the trapezoid body cross the midline and, on reaching the level of the superior olivary nucleus, bend around the lateral side of this nucleus and turn rostrally, forming a band called the *lateral lemniscus* (Figs. 25-9 through 25-11). In its ascent, this becomes the most lateral part of the lemniscus system and can be traced into the caudal part of the mesencephalon.

Fibers arising from the *dorsal cochlear nucleus* follow a variety of courses. Some remain on the same side, running rostrally to join the lateral lemniscus. Others travel medially, lying a little below the floor of the fourth ventricle. Reaching the raphe they cross to the opposite

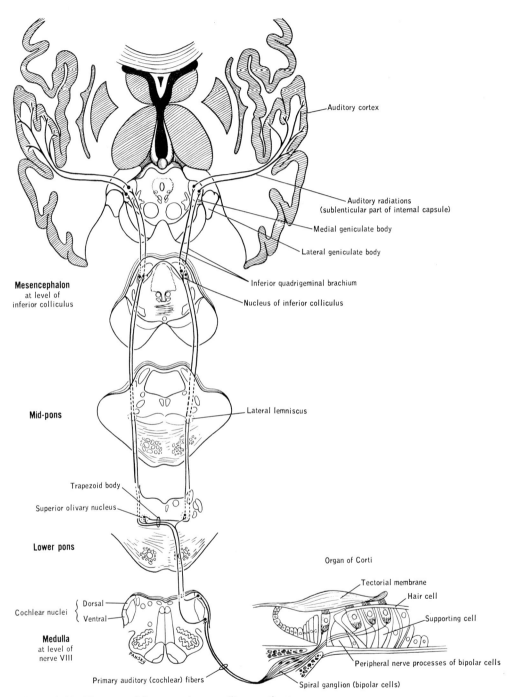

Figure 8-16 Diagram of the conscious auditory pathway.

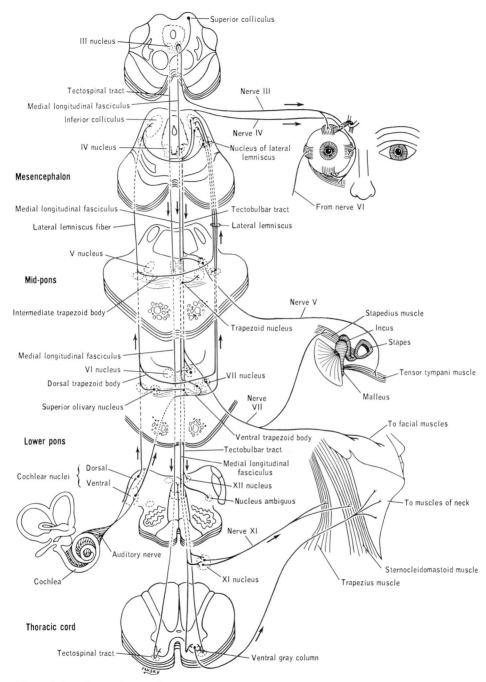

Figure 8-17 The auditory reflex pathway.

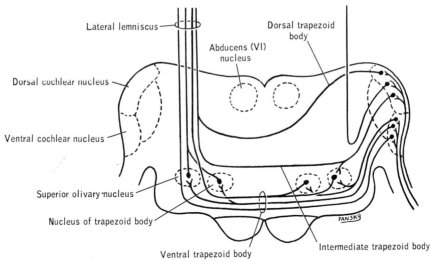

Figure 8-18 Enlargement of the auditory pathway in the region of the medulla to illustrate the trapezoid bodies and the formation of the lateral lemniscus.

side and then run ventrolaterally to join the lateral lemniscus. Fibers following the latter course are said to form the *dorsal trapezoid body.* Other axons from the dorsal nucleus sink more deeply into the tegmentum, passing medially to cross the midline about halfway between the dorsal and ventral trapezoid bodies. After crossing, these fibers join the contralateral lateral lemniscus. These fibers comprise the *intermediate trapezoid body.*

After leaving the cochlear nuclei, impulses may reach the forebrain by two divergent routes: direct and indirect.

Direct Route Some of the fibers from the ventral cochlear nucleus and perhaps most of the fibers from the dorsal nucleus that cross through the dorsal and intermediate trapezoid bodies bend rostrally and continue forward in the lateral lemniscus of the other side. When they reach the mesencephalon, near the caudal border of the inferior colliculus, they diverge more laterally, to bypass the colliculus (collaterals may be given off to the latter). This bundle is then known as the *brachium of the inferior colliculus* (Fig. 25-11). Its termination is the *medial geniculate nucleus (body)* (Fig.

25-12) of the thalamus. It is believed that the uncrossed fibers from the dorsal nucleus which travel in the ipsilateral lateral lemniscus also go directly to the medial geniculate body via the brachium of the inferior colliculus (Fig. 1-28).

Indirect (Relay) Circuit This route consists of a number of short relays and may include synapses in one or more of the following nuclei: superior olive, nucleus of the trapezoid body, nucleus of the lateral lemniscus, or nucleus of the inferior colliculus. Ultimately, the last neuron of the series passes through the brachium of the inferior colliculus to reach the thalamus. Thus, whether direct or relayed, all impulses reach the medial geniculate body. This nucleus is divided into a small ventral and large dorsal portion. It is the latter that receives most of the auditory impulses directed toward conscious levels.

Neuron III The cell bodies of these neurons are located in the dorsal part of medial geniculate nucleus. Their axons, called *auditory radiations* or *the geniculotemporal tract,* pass laterally, mainly through the sublenticular part of the internal capsule, to terminate in the transverse temporal gyri. Tones of different frequencies have specific reception areas on the auditory cortex.[6] High tones are localized in the medial portion while low tones are perceived in the anterior and lateral portions.

Reflex (Fig. 8-17)

Receptors and Afferent Neurons These are the same as receptors and neuron I of the conscious pathway.

First Association Neuron These have the same origin as neuron II to consciousness, but they terminate in such gray areas as the nucleus of the trapezoid body, superior olive, nucleus of the lateral lemniscus, and inferior colliculus.

Second Association Neuron The cell bodies of such neurons are located in four nuclear masses: nucleus of the trapezoid body, nucleus of the superior olive, nucleus of the lateral lemniscus, and inferior colliculus.

From the nucleus of the trapezoid body, some fibers cross to the superior olive of the opposite side; others enter the reticular formation of either side.

From the superior olive, some axons enter the adjacent lateral lemniscus of the same side to continue rostrally either to the nucleus of the lateral lemniscus or to the inferior colliculus. Some fibers may enter the neighboring reticular formation[7]; still another group stream dorsomedially in the peduncle of the superior olive to join the medial longitudinal fasciculus (MLF) of either side. Among those fibers in the peduncle are some that arise

---

[6]There is also experimental evidence to indicate that there are descending fibers from the auditory cortex to the sensory receptors in the organ of Corti.

[7]Additional association neurons may be involved where fibers entering the tegmental reticular formation may make scattered synapses.

either in the superior olive proper or in the medial accessory olive (or in the adjoining tegmentum). This group is known as the *efferent cochlear bundle.* The latter cross inferior to the genu of the seventh nerve and leave the brain in company with the vestibular nerve of the opposite side. These may be joined by fibers originating in the principal cell mass of the superior olive of that side. Ultimately, both crossed and uncrossed fibers leave the vestibular nerve and join the cochlear with which they travel until they terminate on hair cells of the organ of Corti (Fig. 8-19). Stimulation of this bundle leads to suppression of activity in the cochlear nerve. This is basically a feedback mechanism from the primary auditory receptors. There is a possibility that other relay nuclei may also contribute to this system.

From the nucleus of the lateral lemniscus, some of the fibers merely continue upward in the lemniscus of the same side; others enter the tegmental reticular formation[7] of the opposite side; and a last group apparently reaches the lateral lemniscus of the opposite side to ascend to the inferior colliculus.

From the superior olive, axons may ascend or descend in the medial longitudinal fasciculus (Figs. 25-2 through 25-12) to reach cranial motor nuclei, particularly III, IV, VI (possibly V, VII, and XI), and the ventral columns of the cervical spinal cord. It is likely that the fibers from the superior olive, nucleus of the trapezoid body, and perhaps the lateral lemniscus reach these same motor regions through the reticular formation.

Third Association Neuron Axons arising in the inferior colliculus pass ventromedially, cross the midline, and join fibers descending from the superior colliculus in the *tectospinal tract* (Figs. 25-1 through 25-11). In the higher mammals and human beings the number of descending fibers which actually take origin in the nucleus of the inferior colliculus is uncer-

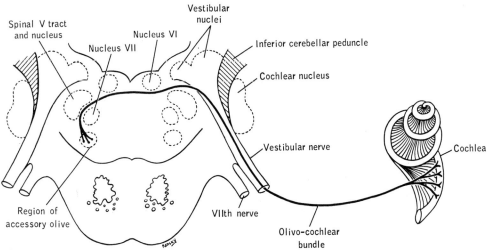

Figure 8-19 Diagram showing the pathway by which activity of the auditory nerve is suppressed by the efferent fibers to the cochlea.

tain. It appears that most of the fibers arising here ascend by way of the central gray column or through capsular connections to the superior colliculus where they synapse. Cells in the latter then send their axons into the tectospinal and tectobulbar tracts. This tract sends its terminals into the ventral gray column of almost the entire cord. Some fibers apparently remain on the same side, traveling in the ipsilateral *tectobulbar tract* (see fn. 4) to terminate among the cranial motor nuclei (Fig. 8-17). Furthermore, connections from the inferior colliculus to the hypothalamus have been reported. Although the exact location is vague and their functions are not clear, it appears that sound does have effects upon visceral activity. The latter phenomenon might be explained on the basis of such connections.

Efferent Neuron From cells in the anterior column of the cervical cord, fibers leave by way of the ventral roots of the cervical nerves to be distributed to muscles in the neck. Thus, a reflex enables the head to react to sound by turning toward the direction of the sound. This reflex is further augmented by fibers leaving the nucleus of cranial nerve XI to the sternocleidomastoid and trapezius muscles. Fibers leaving the nuclei of cranial nerves III, IV, and VI to the muscles of the eye enable the use of the eyes for sound locations. It should be understood that the reactions mentioned are in relation to ordinary sounds. However, the entire body may react to loud and unexpected sounds, since the tectospinal tract involves the entire extent of the cord.

Fibers arising from the motor nucleus of cranial nerves V and VII pass to the accessory muscles of the middle ear (tensor tympani and stapedius, respectively). This sets up a reflex which protects the delicate membranes of the middle ear against rupture. Incidental to loud and sudden noises, blinking of the eyelids and grimacing facial expression are produced by efferent neurons in these same two cranial nerves.

Clinical Considerations

Testing

Two types of test are generally used, those designed to test auditory acuity and those used to differentiate between central and peripheral deafness.

Acuity These are relatively simple and consist merely of noting the distance from either ear at which a patient can hear the ticking of an ordinary watch, one ear being tested at a time.

Differentiation One of the more common tests used to differentiate between lesions of the nerve and disease in or around the transmitting mechanism (external meatus and middle ear, including ossicles) is the Rinne method. In it, a tuning fork is placed against the mastoid bone, and the patient is instructed to state immediately when the sound is no longer heard. The interval is timed. Ordinarily, the patient can still hear the sound if the fork is removed and held behind the ear. The time at which nothing is heard is noted. The test result is said to be positive, or normal, when the tuning fork is heard about twice as long by air conduction as by bone conduction. An abnormal Rinne test result is a sign of middle ear or external meatus defect. When the nerve is involved, both air and bone conduction are reduced but the Rinne test result is normal. The Weber test is preferred by some examiners. In it, the base of a tuning fork is placed on the vertex of the skull. If hearing is normal, the sound will be heard by both ears. When there is disease of the middle ear or stoppage of the external meatus, the sound will be heard best on the diseased side. If the nerve is damaged, the sound will be stronger on the normal side.

Because some of the central auditory fibers cross[8] while others remain on the same side, a unilateral lesion with the CNS, unless large enough to destroy both cochlear nuclei or entering fibers of the acoustic nerve, would not cause total deafness. This holds true whether involvements include the lateral lemniscus, brachium of the inferior colliculus, geniculotemporal tract, or auditory cortex. Even total ablation of the auditory cortex will not cause deafness, although hearing in the opposite ear will be diminished.

Therefore, to localize exactly a lesion involving this system, it is often necessary to note how its parts are related to portions of other systems and to observe the various signs and symptoms of lesions in neighboring pathways. For example, a lesion along the course of the nerve may easily involve the vestibular portion of the nerve, whereas a lesion in the posterior part of the internal capsule might interfere with the visual system.

[8]These crossings may occur at several points: at the level of the cochlear nuclei by way of the trapezoid bodies; at the level of the nuclei of the lateral lemniscus where fibers arising may pass to the opposite side; in the lower mesencephalon by way of the commissure of the inferior colliculus.

**Summary
Vision**

Conscious

1. Rods and cones — Receptors

2. Bipolar cells with bodies in inner nuclear layer of retina, terminating on ganglion cells of retina — Neuron I

3. From ganglion cells in nasal half of retina into optic nerve, across to the opposite side through the optic chiasma into optic tract to end in the lateral geniculate body — Neuron II

   From ganglion cells in the temporal half of the retina into optic nerve and through the optic tract of the same side to the lateral geniculate body

4. From cells in the lateral geniculate body through the geniculocalcarine tract passing by way of the sublenticular and retrolenticular parts of the internal capsule to reach the cortex along the banks of the calcarine fissure — Neuron III

**Summary
Vision**

Reflex

Skeletal musculature
1. Same as conscious — Receptors — *Branchiomeric musculature* 1. Same

2. Same as conscious — Afferent Neuron — 2. Same

3. Origin and course through optic nerve and tract same as conscious but these fibers pass via the brachium of the superior colliculus to end in the superior colliculus — Association neuron(1) — 3. Same

4. From cells in the superior colliculus fibers descend via the tectobulbar tract to end in nuclei III, IV, VI, and XII — Association neuron(2) — 4. Same as for skeletal except that the tectobulbar fibers terminate in nuclei of nerves V, VII, and XI (also IX and X)

   From cells in the superior colliculus fibers descend in the tectospinal tract to end in the ventral horns of the spinal cord

5. From nuclei III, IV, VI, XII fibers pass via the corresponding cranial nerves to the extrinsic ocular muscles and muscles of the tongue — Efferent neuron — 5. From nucleus V to muscles of mastication

   From nucleus VII to facial muscles

   From nucleus XI to sternocleid-mastoid and trapezius muscles

   From nuclei of IX and X to muscles of pharynx and larynx

Reflex

Light response

6. Same as 1, above	Receptors	6. Cortical reflex (see conscious path)
7. Same as 2, above	Afferent neuron	7. Cortical reflex (see conscious path)
8. Same as 3, above, except that fibers end in both the superior colliculus and in the pretectal zone	Association neuron(1)	8. From cortex through the internal capsule and brachium of the superior colliculus to end in that nucleus
9. From the superior colliculus through the tectospinal tract to end in the intermediolateral cell column of the spinal cord (dim light) From the pretectal zone to the Edinger-Westphal (EW) nucleus (bright light)	Association neuron(2)	9. From the superior colliculus fibers descend to synapse in the EW nucleus and medial part of nucleus of nerve III
10. From the intermediolateral column through pregnaglionic fibers ascending in the cervical sympathetic trunk to synapse in the superior cervical ganglion. Postganglionics ascend through the carotid plexus to reach the dilator pupillae muscle of the iris (dim light) From the EW nucleus through preganglionics in nerve III to synapse in the ciliary ganglion from which postganglionics pass to the sphincter pupillae muscle of the iris (bright light)	Efferent neuron	10. From the EW nucleus preganglionics pass through nerve III to terminate in the ciliary ganglion with postganglionics going to the sphincter pupillae Some fibers from EW bypass the ciliary ganglion to synapse in the episcleral ganglion with postganglionics going to the ciliary muscle From the oculomotor nucleus (III) fibers pass via nerve III to the medial recti muscles —for convergence

Summary
Hearing
Conscious

Direct

1. Hair cells in organ of Corti	Receptors	1. Same as in direct path
2. Through nerve VIII with cells in spiral ganglion, ending in dorsal or ventral cochlear nuclei	Neuron I	2. Same as in direct path
3. Fibers from ventral cochlear nucleus and many from dorsal cochlear nucleus cross to the opposite side via the trapezoid bodies, enter the lateral lemniscus into the mesencephalon, thence pass through the brachium of the inferior colliculus to end in the medial geniculate body From cells in the dorsal cochlear nucleus, some fibers ascend in the lateral lemniscus, pass through the brachium of the inferior colliculus, and terminate in the medial geniculate body of the same side	Neuron II	3. This is represented by a chain of neurons beginning in either cochlear nucleus using the nucleus of the trapezoid body, superior olive, nucleus of the lateral lemniscus, and the inferior colliculus as relay stations and finally entering the medial geniculate body via the brachium of the inferior colliculus. The ipsilateral chain from the dorsal cochlear nucleus would probably use the same relays with the possible exception of the nucleus of the trapezoid body
4. From cells in the medial geniculate body through the geniculotemporal fibers in the sublenticular part of the internal capsule to end on the superior temporal gyrus	Neuron III	4. Same as in direct path

Indirect

Reflex

Skeletal musculature		*Branchiomeric musculature*

1. Same as conscious path

<u>Receptors</u>

1. Same as for skeletal

2. Same as conscious path

<u>Afferent neuron</u>

2. Same as for skeletal

3. Generally, they have the same origin as neuron II in the conscious pathway, but they send collaterals or terminals into the nucleus of the trapezoid body, superior olive, nucleus of the lateral lemniscus, and the inferior colliculus

<u>Association neuron (1)</u>

3. Same as for skeletal

4. From cells in the nucleus of the trapezoid body to the superior olive or to the reticular formation

   From cells in the superior olive to the nucleus of the lateral lemniscus or the inferior colliculus

   From cells in the superior olive by way of the MLF to nuclei III, IV, VI

   From cells in the nucleus of the lateral lemniscus to the inferior colliculus

<u>Association neuron (2)</u>

4. Same as skeletal except fibers from MLF may go to nuclei V, VII, XI (also IX and X)

5. From cells in the reticular formation to any somatic motor nucleus of the brainstem

   From cells in the inferior colliculus through the tectobulbar tract to somatic motor nuclei of the brainstem

   From cells in the inferior colliculus via the tectospinal tract to the ventral horn of the spinal cord

<u>Association neuron (3)</u>

5. Same as skeletal except terminations would be in nuclei V, VII, and XI (also IX and X)

6. From cells in nuclei III, IV, and VI to extrinsic ocular muscles

   From cells in ventral horns to skeletal muscles of trunk and extremities

<u>Efferent neuron</u>

6. From nucleus V to muscles of mastication and tensor tympani muscle

   From nucleus VII to muscles of facial expression and stapedius muscle

   From nucleus XI to sternocleidomastoid and trapezius muscles

   From nuclei IX and X to muscles of pharynx and larynx

Chapter 9

General Visceral Afferent System (GVA)

This system is predominantly concerned with the initiation of reflexes which control the activity of the viscera by way of the autonomic system. The sensations from the viscera at conscious levels are much less specific and are very poorly localized. They may, however, have great intensity, e.g., intestinal colic, labor pains, or injuries in the celiac plexus or testicles. Other forms of visceral sensibility include nausea, thirst, hunger, sexual feelings, and the sense of well-being or malaise. Since the question of visceral pain is often related to surface areas and is thus somatic in character, *referred pain* has been discussed in connection with the GSA system (Chap 7).

TRUNK

Reflex Pathways (Fig. 9-1)

Receptors

There are three major types of receptors: the many-branched *free* endings devoid of any coverings; the complex *tangle* of nerve fibers with or without a light capsule; and the heavily encapsulated and laminated *Pacinian corpuscles*. The free endings are usually found on mucous surfaces associated with the lining epithelial cells. The tangles are found both on serous surfaces and in the muscular coats of the viscera. They are adapted to register pressure changes. The Pacinian corpuscles are located in the mesenteries, in the supporting tissue of the viscera, and in the body wall.

Afferent Neuron

From the receptors in the walls of the viscera, the peripheral process of the afferent neurons accompanies efferent fibers to reach the cord. Thus, on the way to the cord, afferent fibers may pass through one or more autonomic ganglia, but they do not synapse in any of them. They enter the main spinal nerve trunk by way of the white rami communicantes and pass into either the lateral or medial division of the dorsal root, where their unipolar cells lie in the ganglia. The central process enters

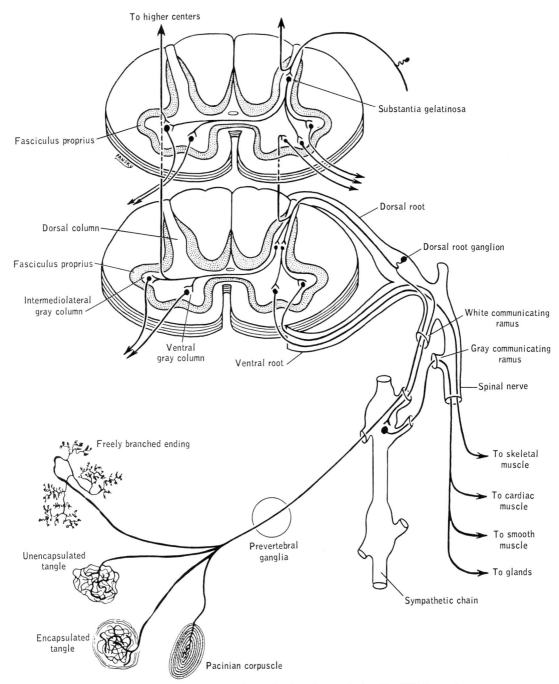

To higher centers

Substantia gelatinosa

Fasciculus proprius

PANSKY

Dorsal root

Dorsal column

Dorsal root ganglion

Fasciculus proprius

Intermediolateral
gray column

White communicating
ramus

Gray communicating
ramus

Spinal nerve

Ventral
gray column

Ventral root

To skeletal
muscle

To cardiac
muscle

Freely branched ending

To smooth
muscle

To glands

Unencapsulated
tangle

Prevertebral
ganglia

Sympathetic chain

Encapsulated
tangle

Pacinian corpuscle

Figure 9-1   General visceral afferent reflex pathway for impulses entering the CNS through
spinal nerves.

the cord along the dorsolateral sulcus in the thoracic, upper lumbar, and midsacral regions. Within the cord, these fibers undergo a typical bifurcation into long ascending and short descending branches. The collaterals and terminals of these branches end in the dorsal gray column of the cord.

Those fibers particularly concerned with *visceral pain* accompany the somatic pain fibers in the lateral division of the dorsal root to enter Lissauer's tract and terminate in the substantia gelatinosa. Those fibers particularly concerned with pressure go through the medial division of the dorsal root and end in the dorsal column just ventral to the substantia gelatinosa.

Association Neuron

Since the important part of this system lies in the reflexes which it initiates, it is of more than passing interest to show how impulses entering via visceral afferents are distributed to the efferent limbs of the reflex arcs.

Associational neurons in the cord have their origins either in the substantia gelatinosa or in the more ventral portions of the dorsal gray column. Their distribution is variable. Some may run directly to the intermediolateral or ventral gray columns of the same side or may cross over to comparable regions of the other side through commissural fibers. Other associational fibers spread out through the fasciculus proprius of the same and opposite sides to reach the intermediolateral and ventral columns of other levels of the cord. It is likely that some of these fibers continue to ascend through either the fasciculus proprius or the reticular formation to influence the cranial motor mechanism.

Efferent Neuron

The efferent neurons innervating skeletal muscle will be discussed in Chap. 13. Those neurons involved with visceral reflexes, having their origin either in the intermediolateral cell column of the spinal cord or in certain brain stem nuclei and their terminations in smooth muscle, cardiac muscle or glands, comprise the autonomic nervous system (Chap. 14). Thus, through these efferents, the reflex mechanisms are completed which cause the secretion of glands and speed up peristalsis in response to the presence of food in the digestive tract; slow the heart and reduce blood pressure when pressure becomes too high in the vascular system; initiate exhalation when the air cells of the lungs are distended. Other examples will be cited in subsequent chapters (Chaps. 13, 14).

Conscious Pathways　(Fig. 9-2)

Receptors

These are the same as described under Reflex Pathways, above.

Neuron I　These are identical with the afferent neuron described under Reflex Pathways, above. However, some of the central processes may ascend in the dorsal funiculus (particularly in the fasciculus gracilis) to terminate in the nuclei of the dorsal funiculus.

Neuron II　These have their origins either from cells of the substantia gelatinosa or from more ventral portions of the dorsal gray columns, cross the cord in the anterior white commissure, and join the lateral spinothalamic tract of the opposite side. Within this tract they bend rostrally and ascend to the ventral posterolateral (VPL) nucleus of the thalamus, where they synapse. It has also been demonstrated that some of the fibers arising in the dorsal gray column do not ascend directly but do so through short, ascending relays in the fasciculus proprius, often remaining for some distance on the same side, and ascend through the brainstem reticular formation.

Neuron III　From cells in the VPL nucleus of the thalamus, a small number of fibers ascend through the posterior limb of the inter-

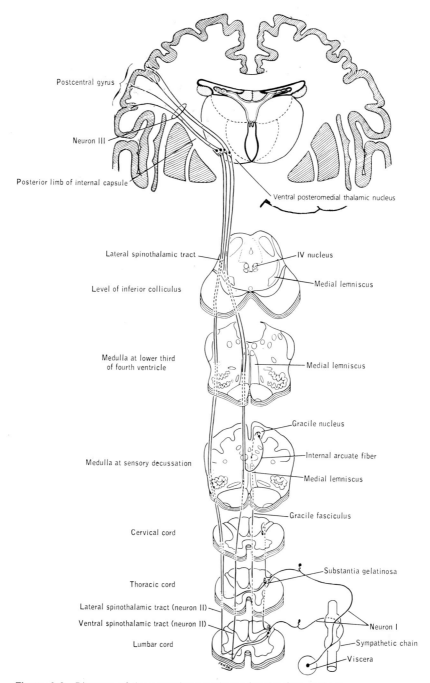

Figure 9-2 Diagram of the conscious pathway for the GVA system.

nal capsule to be distributed to the postcentral gyrus according to the segmental arrangement of somatic afferent systems in which they run.

HEAD

Reflex Pathways   (Fig. 9-3)

Receptors

These are the same type as those described for the reflex pathways of the trunk, above. In addition, however, special receptors are associated with cranial nerves IX and X. These are the carotid body and aortic bodies, respectively. They are small structures, somewhat glandlike in appearance, of the chemoreceptor type. They are sensitive to changes in concentration of carbon dioxide (and oxygen?) in the blood.

Afferent Neuron   From the receptors, the afferent neurons make up a portion of cranial nerves VII, IX, and X and pass with these nerves into the CNS.

Facial Nerve (VII)   The distribution and course of the GVA system in this nerve are controversial, because so many of the impulses carried by this nerve remain below conscious levels. However, it is believed that the facial nerve is associated with receptors deep in the face, middle ear, auditory tube, and adjoining pharyngeal wall.

From these areas, the peripheral processes of all the afferent neurons become segregated in the sensory root of the facial nerve (VII), the *nervus intermedius*. The cell bodies for these neurons lie in the *geniculate ganglion* (Fig. 9-3). The central processes continue toward the brain, forming a distinct bundle which runs between the motor root of the facial nerve (VII) and the acoustic nerve (VIII) and joins the brainstem at the cerebellopontine angle (Figs. 1-7, 1-8, 25-7).

After entry into the brain, the central processes run dorsomedially and approach the lateral aspect of the fourth ventricle, where they turn caudally in a bundle called the *tractus solitarius* (Fig. 9-3 and Chap. 10). After running caudally for variable distances, all these fibers terminate in the *nucleus of the tractus solitarius*, which nearly completely surrounds the tract (Figs. 9-3, 9-4, 25-2 through 25-5).

Glossopharyngeal Nerve (IX)   From the receptors in the posterior tongue, tonsil, and auditory tube, the peripheral processes of the afferent neurons pass through the pharyngeal, lingual, and tympanic branches and enter the main trunk. Their cell bodies are found in the *inferior (petrosal) ganglion* (Fig. 9-3). The central processes join the medulla along the posterolateral sulcus dorsal to the rostral end of the inferior olive (Figs. 1-7, 1-8, 25-5). After entry, the central processes course dorsomedially until they reach the *tractus solitarius* (Fig. 9-3). Here they bend caudally to become a part of that tract. They also synapse on the *nucleus of the tractus solitarius* (Figs. 9-3, 9-4, 25-2 through 25-5).

Of special interest is the small *carotid sinus branch* of this nerve (Fig. 9-3). In this branch, afferent neurons run from the special chemoreceptors of the carotid body and from pressure receptors in the walls of the carotid sinus to join the main trunk nerve.[1] From here their course is similar to that just described.

Vagus Nerve (X)   These afferent neurons originate in receptors in the walls of the viscera, including the entire digestive system, from the root of the tongue to the middle of the transverse colon; the respiratory system, from the larynx to the pulmonary air sacs of the lung; and the arch of the aorta and the walls of the right atrium of the heart. The peripheral processes join the main trunk of the vagus at various points along its course. The cell bodies lie in the *nodose ganglion* (Fig. 9-3). The central processes pass upward to join the

---

[1]There is some disagreement as to whether the pressure endings are associated with the sinus branch of cranial nerve IX or with a small sinus branch of nerve X.

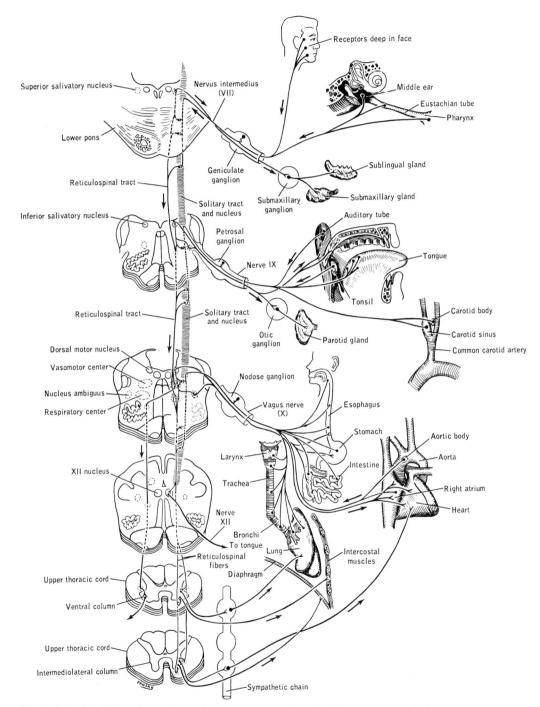

Figure 9-3   The GVA reflex pathway for impulses entering the CNS through cranial nerves.

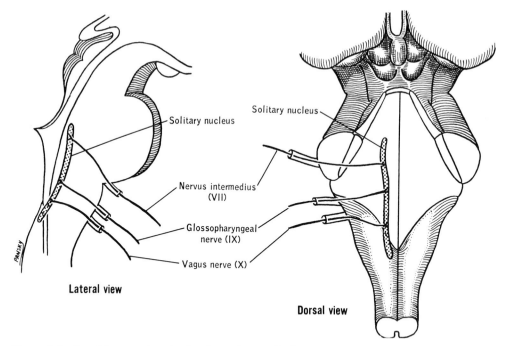

Figure 9-4 Cranial nerves terminating in nucleus solitarius.

medulla in the posterolateral sulcus just caudal to the rootlets of cranial nerve IX (Figs. 1-7, 1-8, 25-4).

After entry, these fibers course dorsomedially to join the tractus solitarius (Fig. 9-3) and descend as a part of the latter. They also terminate in the nucleus of the tractus solitarius (Figs. 9-3, 9-4, 25-2 through 25-5).

First Association Neuron

The cell bodies for all associational neurons related to cranial nerves VII, IX, and X lie in the nucleus of the tractus solitarius. From here, some axons pass through the surrounding reticular formation to go directly to motor nuclei of the brainstem such as the *dorsal motor nucleus of the vagus* (Figs. 1-37, 25-4) or the *salivatory nuclei*. Others may descend into the cord via the reticulospinal tract to end about cells of the intermediolateral or ventral gray columns. The majority, however, probably synapse in various scattered groups of

cells lying in the reticular formation of the medulla, some of which are referred to as *centers* (Chap. 19).

Second Association Neuron

From cells in these and other centers of the medulla, secondary association neurons may pass to the dorsal motor nucleus of the vagus, the nucleus ambiguus, or the hypoglossal nucleus of the brainstem, or may descend into the cord, probably by way of the reticulospinal tract. In the cord, these fibers terminate in the ventral gray columns of the cervical or thoracic regions or in the intermediolateral gray column in the thoracic cord.

Efferent Neuron

From cells in the dorsal motor nucleus of the vagus and from the intermediolateral column of the cord efferent neurons pass by way of the cardiac branches of the vagus and sympathetic trunks, respectively. These reflexively control heart rate and blood pressure (Chap. 14).

From other cells in the dorsal motor nucleus of the vagus, streams of impulses are carried to glands of the digestive tract and to its smooth muscle to bring about secretion of enzymes and to speed up peristalsis.

From the cells of the salivatory nuclei, efferent neurons pass by way of the seventh and ninth cranial nerves to bring the salivary glands under reflex control (Chap. 14).

From the nucleus ambiguus, efferent fibers pass by way of the ninth and tenth cranial nerves to control reflexly the muscles of the pharynx and palate involved in swallowing.

Axons from cells in the hypoglossal nucleus are distributed by way of the twelfth cranial nerve to muscles of the tongue, also concerned with the act of swallowing.

From the cells in the anterior gray column of the lower cervical and thoracic cord, axons pass by way of the phrenic, long thoracic, and intercostal nerves to the diaphragm, serratus anterior, and intercostal muscles, respectively. This pathway controls the rate and depth of respiration.

Conscious Pathways

The conscious pathways associated with the GVA system are not definitely known. It seems probable that the few fibers that do ascend to conscious levels accompany fibers of the somatic afferent system.

COMPARISON OF THE GSA AND GVA SYSTEMS

Structurally, the two systems are similar; they consist of neurons of the monopolar type,

with cells located in ganglia outside the CNS. At cord levels, visceral and somatic fibers run in the dorsal root and join the spinal cord in the same region.

On a structural basis, there are also several differences between the two systems. In the somatic system, sensory fibers are widespread and are contained in all the spinal nerves. Among the cranial nerves, the major portion of the somatic afferents are carried in the trigeminal nerve (V); a few somatic fibers are also present in the vagus nerve (X); some may run in the facial nerve (VII) and glossopharyngeal nerve (IX). Visceral afferents are found in only certain of the spinal nerves, those of the thoracic, upper lumbar, and midsacral levels.

In the spinal nerves, somatic sensations travel through the nerve trunks, following all branches. Visceral fibers of the cord leave the spinal nerve trunk by way of white rami communicantes and accompany the motor fibers of the autonomic system.

The majority of somatic receptors are sensitive to a great variety of environmental changes, whereas the majority of visceral receptors are of the stretch-pressure type, a few being sensitive to chemical changes.

Another difference lies in the fact that ascending secondary pathways within the CNS are well established for somatic sensation but poorly identified for visceral sensation.

CLINICAL CONSIDERATIONS

Since the physiology of this system is so intimately linked to motor activity, no attempt will be made to evaluate the integrity of the GVA system at this time.

Summary
General Visceral Afferent

Trunk	Reflex	Head
1. Free endings or complex tangles Pacinian corpuscles	Receptor	1. Many same as for trunk Chemoreceptors, sensitive to concentrations of O_2 and CO_2
2. Through fibers accompanying visceral efferents, to spinal nerves via white rami, with cells in dorsal root ganglia, entering the cord at thoracic, upper lumbar, and midsacral levels, to terminate in the dorsal gray column	Afferent neuron	2. From receptors deep in face, middle ear, and auditory tube through nerve VII with cells in the geniculate ganglion, into the brainstem, downward in tractus solitarius to end in the nucleus of the tractus solitarius
		From receptors in posterior tongue, tonsil, and pharyngeal wall through nerve IX with cells in the inferior petrosal ganglion, into the brainstem and downward in the tractus solitarius to end in the nucleus of the tractus solitarius
		From chemoreceptors of carotid body and pressure receptors of carotid sinus, through carotid sinus branch of nerve IX, thence as above
		From receptors in the walls of viscera, including heart, great vessels, lungs, and digestive system, through nerve X, with cells in the nodose ganglion, into the brainstem and downward in the tractus solitarius to end in the nucleus of the tractus solitarius
3. From cells in the dorsal gray column directly to ventral gray column at same level, same side; through the fasciculus proprius to the ventral gray at other levels of same side; through the anterior white commissure and fasciculus proprius to the ventral gray at same or other levels of opposite side; or identical with above except for termination, which would be the intermediolateral cell column at any level on either side	Association neuron	3. From cells in the nucleus of the tractus solitarius directly, or through relays in the reticular formation, to superior and inferior salivatory nuclei; dorsal motor nucleus of the vagus; intermediolateral cell column of the cord by way of reticulospinal tract; or
		From cells in the nucleus of the tractus solitarius to the bulbar respiratory and vasomotor centers, which relay to the dorsal motor nucleus of the vagus and, through the reticulospinal tract, to the intermediolateral cell column of the cord
		From cells in the nucleus of the tractus solitarius to the bulbar swallowing center, which relays to the nucleus ambiguus, or
		From the cells in the nucleus of the tractus solitarius to the bulbar respiratory and swallowing centers, which relay to the nucleus of nerve XII and, through the reticulospinal tract, to the ventral gray columns of the cord

4. From the ventral gray column to skeletal muscle of neck, trunk, and extremities or

   From the intermediolateral cell column by way of preganglionics to synapse in autonomic ganglia, thence by postganglionics to heart, smooth muscle, and glands

Efferent neuron

4. From the superior and inferior salivatory nuclei through nerves VII and IX, respectively, to autonomic ganglia and by postganglionics to major salivary glands

   From dorsal motor nucleus of vagus through preganglionics of nerve X to autonomic ganglia and thence, through postganglionics to heart and other viscera or

   From the intermediolateral cell column of the cord, through preganglionics, to autonomic ganglia, thence through postganglionics to heart, blood vessels, and other viscera or

   From cells in nucleus ambiguus through nerves IX and X to the muscles of the pharynx and larynx or

   From nucleus XII to muscles of the tongue; from ventral gray columns to diaphragm and other respiratory muscles

Conscious

5. Same as for reflex

Receptor

6. Same as for reflex except that some fibers ascend in dorsal funiculus to end in nuclei of dorsal funiculus

Neuron I

5-8 Indefinite; probably similar to course and distribution of the trigeminal nerve

7. From cells in the dorsay gray column, through the anterior white commissure, to lateral spinothalamic tract of opposite side, ascending in the latter to terminate in the ventral posterolateral nucleus of the thalamus

Neuron II

   From the nuclei of the dorsal funiculus (gracilis and cuneatus), through internal arcuate fibers, across the midline to the opposite medial lemniscus, in which they ascend to the posterolateral ventral nucleus of the thalamus

8. From the posterolateral ventral nucleus of the thalamus, through the posterior limb of the internal capsule, to be distributed to the postcentral gyrus according to the segmental arrangement of neuron I

Neuron III

Special Visceral Afferent
System (SVA)

OLFACTION

In human beings, smell may not be so important as other special senses. However, the reflex relationships of olfactory impulses are of such fundamental significance in relation to visceral control that their importance should not be overlooked.

Many neuroanatomists describe this system merely as a part of the functional activity of the ancient rhinencephalon. Others describe it as a completely separate system. However, since it is so intimately tied up, either directly or indirectly, with visceral function (location, ingestion, and preparation for digestion of food, or the location and recognition of the opposite sex), it seems logical to place it within the visceral afferent system.

Because of the widespread distribution and separation of parts of the olfactory system, a thorough review of the gross aspects of the brain is essential (Chap. 1). However, certain features of this apparatus require further elucidation.

That portion of the basal region of the hemispheres which extends forward from the anterior commissure and the lamina terminalis to the caudal end of the olfactory tracts is the septal (paraterminal) area. This area includes the subcallosal gyrus, the anterior continuation of the hippocampus, and the subcallosal (parolfactory) area (Figs. 10-1, 10-2).

The cortex around the lateral olfactory stria is known as the *lateral olfactory gyrus (prepyriform area)*. The gyrus curves laterally along the border of the anterior perforated substance and, under cover of the temporal lobe, bends caudomedially toward the inner

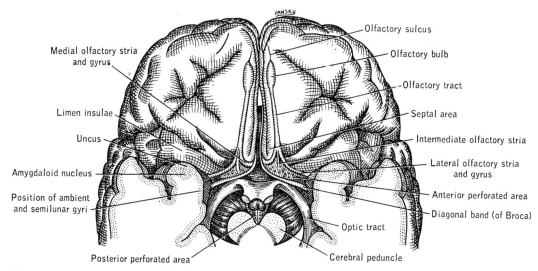

Figure 10-1 Basal aspect of the brain showing the olfactory cortex and adjoining structures.

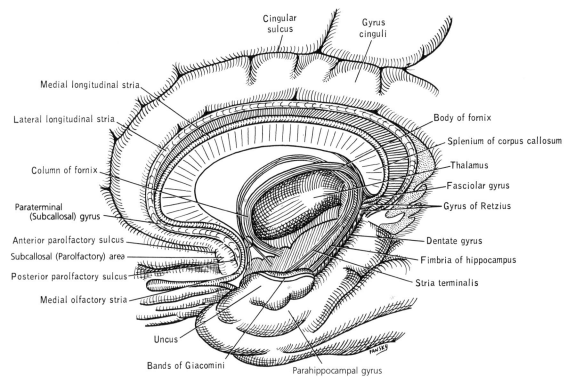

Figure 10-2 Sagittal section of the brain showing the olfactory cortex and associated structures.

surface of the temporal lobe. The region where the bend occurs is the *limen insulae*. The gray matter of this gyrus then spreads out to become continuous with the head of the parahippocampal gyrus. Where this cortical substance spreads out, it forms the *ambient* and *semilunar gyri* (periamygdaloid cortex) which directly overlie the *amygdaloid complex* (Figs. 4-12, 10-1 through 10-3, 25-17, 25-18).

The amygdaloid complex is a large nuclear mass located near the rostral end of the inferior horn of the lateral ventricle, buried in the substance of the temporal lobe (Figs. 10-1 through 10-3). Medially, it is continuous with the cortex of the uncus. Above it lies the lenticular nucleus. Dorsally and rostrally is the anterior perforated substance, and caudally it

appears to be continuous with the tail of the caudate nucleus.

Although originally an important part of the ancient "smell brain," or rhinencephalon, the hippocampal formation and the fornix will not be discussed here but will be described later with the limbic system (Chap. 22).

In addition to the parts mentioned above, there are several fiber bundles which associate this system with other parts of the brain. The first of these are the *medial* and *lateral longitudinal stria*. These bands are embedded in the supracallosal gyrus (induseum griseum) which overlies the external surface of the corpus callosum. Caudally, these fibers become continuous with the hippocampus, while rostrally they unite to form a single fascicle which passes beyond the subcallosal gyrus to enter

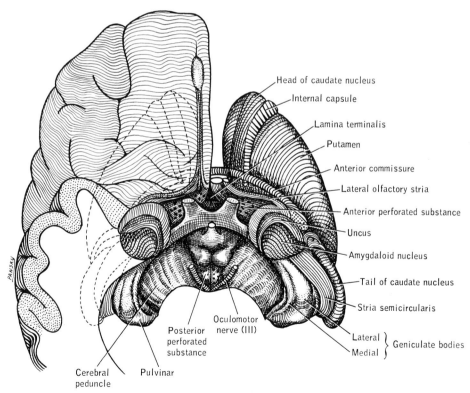

Figure 10-3 Dissection of the brain from the basal surface, showing the relations of the olfactory apparatus, the basal ganglia, and the anterior commissure.

the diagonal band (of Broca). Posteriorly, the dentate gyrus (of the hippocampal formation) also shows continuity with the supracallosal gyrus. A second set of fibers, the *stria terminalis*, runs in a groove separating the dorsal thalamus from the body and tail of the caudate nucleus (Fig. 10-2). These bundles connect the hypothalamus with the amygdala. Still another group of fibers, the *stria medullaris thalami* (Figs. 10-4, 25-14), run rostrally from the habenula along the margin of the roof of the third ventricle. These can be traced toward the region of the medial olfactory gyrus. The last bundle, the *fornix*, will be described later (Chap. 22).

Olfactory Pathways[1]

Receptors

The olfactory receptors lie in a specialized portion of the nasal epithelium occupying the upper part of the nasal chamber, extending about one-third of the way down the nasal septum medially, and over the superior nasal concha, laterally. The olfactory membrane is composed of two types of cells. The first are purely supporting and are of a modified simple columnar type. At the surface, these cells join to form a cuticle which is penetrated by the sensory cells. The latter are very slender cells, the nuclei of which lie in a deeper layer of the membrane than those of the supporting cells. Extending toward the surface from the region of the nucleus is a cytoplasmic process which penetrates the cuticle of the supporting cells. Ten to twelve short hairs arise from the end of the process. These hairs become embedded in the mucus overlying the olfactory surface. The central process of this receptor cell is very fine and pierces the basement membrane of the epithelium. The central processes of

adjoining cells combine to form fascicles of nonmyelinated neural elements. The fascicles pierce the bony roof of the nasal cavity through the cribriform plate of the ethmoid and enter the overlying olfactory bulb, where a synapse is made.

Neuron Chains   (Fig. 10-5)

The bipolar cell described as the receptor also serves as the afferent neuron. These fibers terminate in the olfactory bulb by synapsing with the dendrites of *mitral cells* which lie in the *glomerulus* (Fig. 10-5). The glomerulus also contains processes of both *tufted* and *granule cells*.

Axons of the mitral cells end in a number of places: First, they may synapse with the dendrites of *pyramidal cells* which comprise the *anterior olfactory nucleus* (Fig. 10-5). The latter is a diffuse arrangement of cells occurring throughout the olfactory tract. Axons of other mitral cells, or their collaterals, continue caudally in the *olfactory tract* and may enter either the *lateral* or *medial olfactory stria* (Fig. 10-1). Those running in the lateral stria terminate both in the nuclei of the *amygdaloid complex* and the cortex (area 28) of the uncus region. The latter is the *primary olfactory cortex* (Fig. 10-2, 10-3, 10-5). In addition, some of the collaterals reach the *anterior perforated substance* of the same side. Axons passing through the medial olfactory stria end in the septal region. When present, the *intermediate olfactory stria* also carry fibers to the ipsilateral anterior perforated substance (Fig. 10-1).

The efferent processes of the pyramidal cells also have a variety of projections (Fig. 10-5). Close to its perikaryon, the axon gives rise to a *recurrent collateral* which returns to the ipsilateral bulb to synapse with both tufted and *internal granule cells*. The main axon then continues caudally, sending a collateral via the lateral stria to the ipsilateral amygdala. Most of the pyramidal cell axons course through the medial stria and the *anterior commissure* to

---

[1]Since the neurons of this system are so intimately involved in both reflex and conscious mechanisms, the format as used for other sensory pathways has been altered in this case.

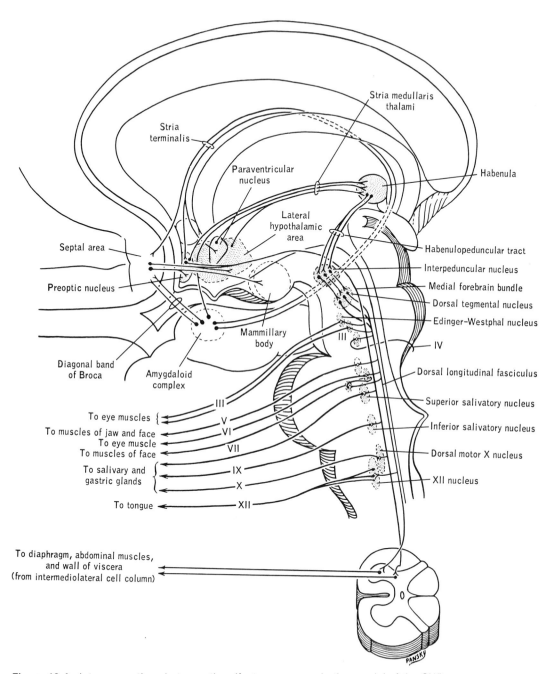

Figure 10-4 Interconnections between the olfactory areas and other nuclei of the CNS.

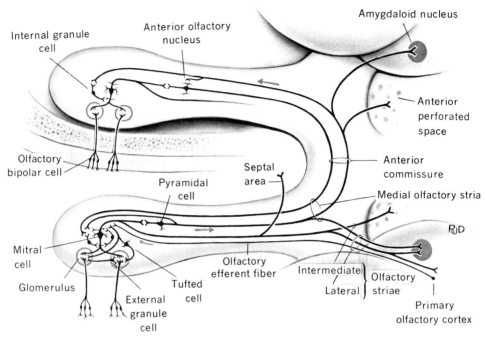

Figure 10-5 Diagram of the olfactory system showing the chief connections from the olfactory mucosa to both cortical and noncortical areas of the CNS. (*From Noback and Demarest, The Human Nervous System, 2d ed., McGraw-Hill Book Company, New York, 1975.*)

reach the contralateral olfactory tract by which they enter the bulb. Here they synapse with internal granule cells. Along their extent these axons give off collaterals which enter the contralateral anterior perforated substance and amygdala.

The granule and tufted cells provide a mechanism for spreading olfactory activation to other parts of this system and also establish reverberating and enhancing circuits. It is possible that some interconnections are inhibitory (corticifugal fibers).

It should be noted that the olfactory system is the only sensory system that sends no fibers to the dorsal thalamus before terminating in primary cortex.

Although it is agreed that human beings are microosmatic creatures in which smell, as a primary sense, is far less important than in

lower animals, the influence of this system on other parts of the CNS is far-reaching (Fig. 10-4). Some of the connections by which these influences may be mediated are indicated below.

From the septal nuclei, fibers descend through the *medial forebrain bundle.* Some of the fibers of this bundle terminate in the *preoptic nuclei,* the *lateral hypothalamic nuclei,* and the *mammillary nuclei* (Figs. 21-1, 21-2). Others from this bundle continue caudally into the tegmentum of the mesencephalon and traverse the brainstem through the reticular formation to synapse around autonomic motor centers of both brain and cord. However, it should be emphasized that the fibers associated with the hypothalamus are probably more important than those continuing directly through the brainstem.

From the amygdaloid complex, fibers pass by way of the *striae terminalis*, which pass caudally along the tail of the caudate nucleus, arch over the dorsal aspect of the thalamus in a sulcus between the latter and the caudate nucleus, to terminate in the *preoptic region*, and the *ventromedial nucleus* of the hypothalamus (Chap. 21). From the preoptic nuclei additional association fibers descend by way of the *medial forebrain bundle* to autonomic centers of the brainstem and cord.

From the septal nuclei, amygdaloid complex, and hypothalamic nuclei, fibers pass by way of the *stria medullaris thalami*. This bundle passes along the lateral edge of the roof of the third ventricle. Most of its fibers end in the habenula (Fig. 25-13) of the same side, while the remainder cross in the habenular commissure to terminate in the habenula of the opposite side.

From the habenula still other association fibers pass ventrocaudally by way of the *habenulopeduncular tract* to terminate in the *interpeduncular nucleus*. This nucleus extends along the interpeduncular fossa from the level of the oculomotor nucleus of the mesencephalon to the pons. From this nucleus still other association fibers run into the reticular nuclei, especially the *dorsal tegmental nucleus*. From this nucleus, fibers pass by way of the *dorsal longitudinal fasciculus* (of Shütz) (Figs. 25-8 through 25-10), to terminate in both somatic and visceral motor nuclei of the brainstem and cord.

It should be indicated at this point that the sensory input, which has been shown to be so widely disseminated throughout the system, could serve as the initiator of several kinds of reflexes.

From cranial nerve nuclei of the brainstem (III, IV, VI, and XII) and the ventral gray columns of the spinal cord, efferent impulses pass by way of certain cranial and any of the spinal nerves. These reflexes may consist of movements of the eyes, tongue, and neck, as well as of the trunk and extremities, in relation to both pleasant and unpleasant odors. Other reflexes of this type involve the nerves to the diaphragm and abdominal musculature used in retching or vomiting in response to highly disagreeable odors.

From the general visceral efferent column of the brainstem, including the superior and inferior salivatory nuclei, together with the dorsal motor nucleus of the vagus, fibers pass by way of cranial nerves VII, IX, and X to initiate reflexes. These consist of the secretion of salivary and gastric glands in response to odors. From the intermediolateral cell column of the cord, as well as others supplied by the vagus, fibers pass through the autonomic system (Chap. 14) to the walls of the viscera, which play a part in the vomiting and retching reflexes.

From nuclei of the special visceral efferent column in the brainstem, fibers pass by way of certain cranial nerves to muscles of the jaws, face, and pharynx. These are especially important in vomiting and retching.

Clinical Considerations

Testing

In the average examination, the measurement of olfactory ability is not considered. Generally, it is enough to test the ability of the patient to recognize test odors when introduced one at a time, into each nostril separately. In addition, quantitative tests have been devised in which a measured amount of test odor is used in one nostril at a time, the patient holding his breath for a moment. The least amount of odor necessary for recognition is called the *minimal identifiable odor* (MIO). When this is determined, a steady stream of test odor is passed through the nostril until fatigue occurs, at which time the patient no longer is aware of the odor. Then each nostril is tested at 30-s intervals with the minimal identifiable odor in order to determine the duration of fatigue.[2]

Pathology

Anosmia (Loss of Smell)   Loss of the sense of smell, especially if bilateral, is ordinarily not of great significance and may be a manifestation of a peripheral defect rather than of one involving the nuclei or tracts of the CNS. Local conditions, such as catarrhal or atrophic rhinitis and polyps, impair the olfactory sense. There are some people who suffer from congenital anosmia. Unilateral anosmia has considerably more significance.

Brain tumors, for example *meningiomas*, in the floor of the anterior cranial fossa may compress the olfactory tract and lead to varying degrees of anosmia. The pressure on the tract will cause an increase in minimal identifiable odor on the diseased side. If the tumor is *intracerebral*, in such a position that no pressure is put upon the olfactory tract, an increase in the duration of fatigue but not in minimal identifiable odor is observed. If the intracerebral tumor lies in the frontal lobe in such a position that compression of the olfactory tract also occurs, there is an increase in minimal identifiable odor as well as an increase in duration of fatigue.

Aneurysms of the internal carotid artery may compress the tracts and lead to anosmia.

Basal skull fractures involving the anterior cranial fossa may also cause anosmia.

GUSTATION

Reflex Pathways

Receptors   (Fig. 10-6)

For the sense of taste, the receptors are *taste buds*, actually a type of chemoreceptor, locat-

ed in the stratified squamous epithelium lining the mouth and oral pharynx. By far the majority are found on the dorsal surface of the tongue; they are particularly numerous on the sides of the *circumvallate papillae* and, to a lesser degree, on the *fungiform papillae*. Taste buds are round or oval in shape, with supporting cells (sustentacular) arched parallel to the outer curvature of the bud. Near the surface, the tips of the sustentacular cells surround a very small opening, the inner taste pore. The latter coincides with a small hiatus in the overlying epithelium, the outer taste pore. From 4 to 20 sensory cells are interspersed in this framework. The sensory cells are slender and rodlike, with a darker nucleus near the middle. The superficial process extends toward a pitlike excavation located in the center of the bud beneath the inner pore. At the end of the process is a small taste hair which projects into the pit. Thus, substances ingested, when in a liquid form, easily enter through the taste pores, to stimulate these cells.

Unlike other special senses, taste receptors are not concentrated in one relatively small area. On the contrary, they have a fairly wide distribution and are associated with cranial nerves VII, IX, and X. For this reason, it is helpful to localize the taste buds into definite zones: anterior two-thirds of the tongue; posterior third of the tongue; inner surface of the lips; lining of the cheeks; soft palate; glossopalatine arch; pharynx; posterior wall of the larynx and epiglottis.

Afferent Neuron   (Fig. 10-7)   All the peripheral processes of the afferent neurons, regardless of the cranial nerve eventually followed, penetrate the basement membrane of the epithelium in the form of nonmyelinated fibrils which end in the taste bud, either diffusely or in some form of intimate contact with the receptor cells.

It is generally easier to describe this circuit by starting with the cranial nerves which are

---

[2]It should be remembered that head colds or local nasal disorders will adversely affect such test results.

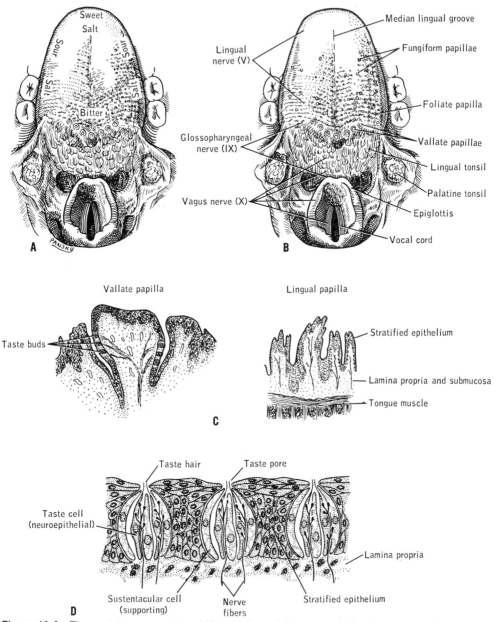

Figure 10-6 The gustatory apparatus. *A.* Dorsal view of the tongue indicating the areas of sensibility to the various modalities of taste. *B.* Dorsal view of the tongue showing the distribution of the different kinds of papillae and the areas supplied by various cranial nerves. *C.* Histologic picture of two types of papillae. *D.* Finer structure of the taste buds.

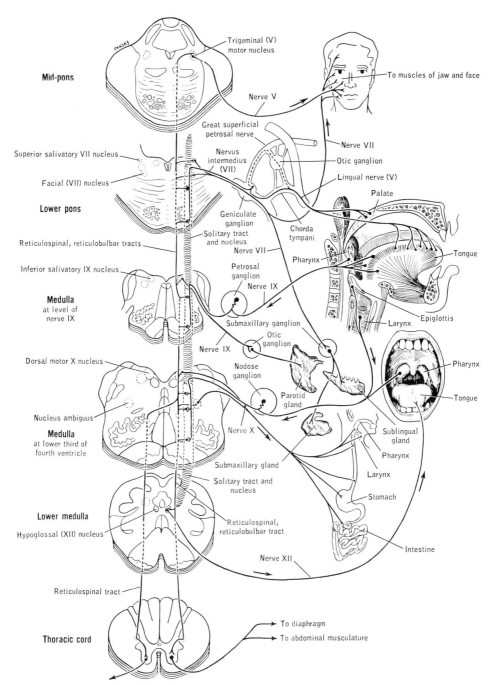

Figure 10-7 Gustatory reflexes, especially those elicited by pleasant tastes.

associated with the taste buds in zones previously described.

Facial Nerve (VII) (Fig. 10-7) From receptors on the anterior two-thirds of the tongue, peripheral processes of the neurons join the branches of the *lingual nerve*, a major branch of the mandibular division of the trigeminal nerve. After following the lingual nerve for some distance, taste fibers diverge to enter the *chorda tympani nerve*. This nerve passes obliquely backward to the petrotympanic fissure, enters the petrous temporal bone, and crosses the lateral wall of the tympanic cavity to join the main trunk of the facial nerve in the facial canal. As an alternate route, some taste fibers from this same portion of the tongue traverse about half the length of the chorda tympani, leave the latter to pass through one of the roots of the *otic ganglion*, which they cross *without* synapse, and enter the *greater petrosal nerve*. They follow the latter to the facial trunk, which they join just below the geniculate ganglion.

From the taste buds of the palate, the peripheral processes of the neurons ascend through the *palatine nerves* into the pterygopalatine ganglion. They pass through this ganglion *without* synapse and leave its dorsal side with the *Vidian nerve*, to become a part of the *greater petrosal nerve*. Through this they join the facial nerve just below the geniculate ganglion.

The cell bodies of all the SVA neurons from the anterior tongue or palate are of the monopolar type and lie in the *geniculate ganglion of the facial nerve* (VII). From here the central processes accumulate in the *nervus intermedius* and continue through this nerve to the brainstem (Figs. 1-7, 1-8). From here they travel dorsomedially through the substance of the medulla, approach the lateral wall of the fourth ventricle, and turn caudally in the *tractus solitarius* (Figs. 10-7, 10-8, 25-5). The taste fibers in this tract then terminate in the *nucle-*

us of the tractus solitarius[3] (Figs. 25-2 through 25-5).

Glossopharyngeal Nerve (IX) (Figs. 10-7, 10-8) From the taste buds on the posterior one-third of the tongue and the anterior pharyngeal wall, the peripheral processes of the afferent neurons run in the *lingual* and *pharyngeal branches*, respectively, of the glossopharyngeal nerve, through which they ascend to the main trunk of that nerve to reach their cell bodies, which lie in the *petrosal ganglion*. The central processes continue their ascent to the superficial attachment of cranial nerve IX (Figs. 1-7, 1-8, 25-5). The intramedullary course is similar to that of nerve VII, in that taste fibers turn caudally in the *tractus solitarius* (Figs. 25-2 through 25-5) to end in the nucleus of that tract.

Vagus Nerve (X) (Figs. 10-7, 10-8) The peripheral processes of afferent neurons whose receptors lie in the posterior pharynx run through the *pharyngeal branch of the vagus nerve*, passing through the pharyngeal plexus, to join the vagus nerve (X) below its nodose ganglion. Fibers from the epiglottis and larynx travel through the *superior laryngeal branch of the vagus*, which joins the main trunk of nerve X. In either case, the monopolar cell bodies for all taste fibers traveling in the vagus lie in the *nodose ganglion*. The central processes ascend with the vagus to its superficial attachment to the brainstem (Figs. 1-7, 1-8, 25-4).

The intramedullary course of these afferent

---

[3]There is a difference of opinion among neuroanatomists as to the termination of the primary taste neurons. The majority favor the belief that the principal synapses are in the nucleus of the tractus solitarius, particularly in the rostral end of it. Others have suggested the presence of a specific cell group called the *gustatory nucleus*, said to lie just medial to the nucleus of the tractus solitarius. In many cases, a definite nuclear mass may be seen, at first squeezed between the dorsal motor nucleus of the vagus and the hypoglossal nucleus. Actually, it may even extend to the medial side of the latter (Fig. 25-4). When it is in this location, the term *nucleus intercalatus* is often applied.

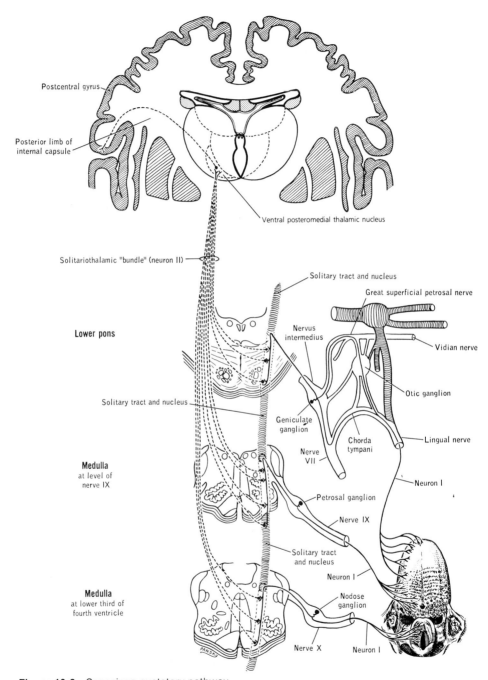

Figure 10-8   Conscious gustatory pathway.

neurons is essentially the same as that described for cranial nerves VII and IX, all eventually bending caudally in the *tractus solitarius* to end in the nucleus of that tract.

Association Neuron (Fig. 10-7)

The direct observation and tracing of such neurons has not been possible. However, reflex reactions which occur in response to taste are so well established that there can be little doubt that such fibers do exist.

The cell bodies for these neurons lie in either the *nucleus of the tractus solitarius* or in the *gustatory nucleus.* Their axons immediately enter the reticular formation, through which they are distributed to the superior and inferior salivatory nuclei; the dorsal motor nucleus of the vagus; the nucleus of the trigeminal and facial nerves; the nucleus ambiguus; and the cells of the ventral gray columns in the cord by way of the reticulospinal tract.

Efferent Neuron (Fig. 10-7)

From cells in the superior and inferior salivatory nuclei and the dorsal motor nucleus of the vagus nerve, efferent neurons, by way of cranial nerves VII, IX, and X, are distributed to the major salivary glands (parotid, submaxillary, and sublingual), the gastric glands, and the muscularis of the alimentary canal. These produce secretion in the glands and peristalsis in the digestive tract in response to food in the mouth.

From cells in the motor nuclei of the trigeminal and facial nerves, axons are distributed to the muscles of the jaws and face which cause changes in facial expression and movements in the jaws in response to food in the mouth.

All the reflexes thus far mentioned are associated predominantly with pleasant tastes. There are also others related to tastes of an unpleasant nature. Among these are reflexes initiated by axons from the dorsal motor nucleus of the vagus, from the nucleus ambiguus, from the hypoglossal nucleus, from the ventral gray column of the cervical cord, and from the ventral gray column of the thoracic cord. These fibers, distributed to the musculature of the digestive tract, pharynx, tongue, diaphragm, and abdomen, are all necessary in the vomiting-retching reflex.

Conscious Pathways (Fig. 10-8)

The pathways followed to cerebral levels have not been definitely established. However, since we do become conscious of many tastes, such pathways must exist.

Receptors

These are the same as described under Reflex Pathways, above.

Neuron I These are identical with the afferent neuron described under Reflex Pathways, above.

Neuron II The cell bodies for these neurons lie either in the rostral end of the *nucleus of the tractus solitarius* or in the *gustatory nucleus.*[3] Most of the axons of these neurons may cross the midline before ascending as the so-called *solitariothalamic bundle* (visceral lemniscus). The course of these fibers is uncertain. However, it appears safe to assume that they would accompany other bundles ascending toward the thalamus, such as the spinothalamic tracts, or the medial lemniscus, or the trigeminothalamic lemnisci. Since the trigeminothalamic bundles are already carrying general somatic impulses arising from receptors of the head, including the mucous membrane of the tongue and mouth, it certainly would not be illogical for the secondary neurons of taste to lie close to them.

There is likewise disagreement as to the exact thalamic nucleus which serves as a terminus for these secondary neurons. Evidence seems to favor the *medial* part of the *ventral posteromedial (VPM) nucleus*, or an *accessory semilunar nucleus* which adjoins the latter on its medial side.

Neuron III The cells of origin of the third neuron lie in either the *VPM* nucleus or an accessory semilunar nucleus. Their axons travel through the posterior limb of the internal capsule. From this point there is further disagreement as to the terminations of these fibers in the cortex. More recent information favors the most ventral part of the postcentral gyrus (opercular part), with extensions deep into the lateral fissure, as the primary gustatory cortex. Since this area is so close to the general sensory cortex for the tongue and also is near the motor areas for movement of the tongue and jaws, such a conclusion seems logical. The older concepts favored either the uncus or the anterior part of the insula as the primary gustatory cortex.

Since the hypothalamus is the highest direct effector center for the visceral efferent mechanism, it would be strange if taste, a special visceral sense, were not connected to some part of the hypothalamus. At least one possibility is suggested by the fact that secondary taste fibers are running in the tegmental reticular formation. These fibers may be carried rostrally to make connections in the reticular formation of the upper pons or lower mesencephalon. From the latter, another set of neurons enters the mammillary peduncle (Chap. 21) to be carried into the mammillary nuclei of the hypothalamus.

Clinical Considerations

Qualities of Taste (Fig. 10-6)

There is some tendency to consider four kinds of taste: sour, sweet, bitter, and salt. These may be thought of as modalities of sensation, just as cold, hot, pain, and temperature are modalities of somatic sensation. This idea is supported by some evidence. First, certain regions of the tongue are more sensitive to one taste than another, and even individual papillae have a fair degree of specificity. Next, the use of certain drugs causes a loss of one kind of taste but not of others. Lastly, one kind of taste elicits one type of response while another initiates another type, as diametrically opposed as swallowing and vomiting. Thus, the tongue is regionally divided on the basis of the taste modality to which it is most sensitive. The tip apparently can distinguish all four modalities, although even here there is a greater sensitivity to sweet and salt. The edges of the tongue are more responsive to sour, while the base is more sensitive to bitter.

Taste sensibilities are described as *ageusia*, a complete absence of taste; *hypogeusia*, diminished taste; and *parageusia*, hallucination or the misinterpretation of taste.

Testing

Since olfaction and gustation are functionally and subjectively so closely allied, an apparent ageusia or hypogeusia may, to a major extent, be due to local conditions of the nose (congestions due to a cold or an obstruction of the passageway). Therefore, as a first step, the examination should begin with an investigation of the nasal chambers.

When the examination of the nose is completed, the various regions of the tongue should be tested with substances possessing the four basic qualities of taste. It is particularly important to note whether a loss of taste is over the entire tongue or over either the right or left halves only. If the anterior two-thirds or the posterior third of the tongue is tested, it could be determined whether the pathologic condition is in the peripheral course of the glossopharyngeal nerve or involves the chorda tympani and facial nerves.

Summary
Smell

Visceral Effects (General)	**Reflex**	*Visceral Effects (General)*

Visceral Effects (General)

1. Hair cells in upper nasal chamber

2. Part of receptor cell, whose central process terminates in the olfactory bulb

3. From olfactory bulb, through olfactory tract, some terminating in anterior olfactory nucleus, others continuing caudally

   From olfactory bulb and from anterior olfactory nucleus, through either medial or lateral olfactory stria

   Fibers of medial stria either end in nuclei of septal area or cross to opposite amygdala

   Fibers of lateral stria either end in nucleus of lateral stria or in amygdala of same side

   From lateral olfactory nucleus to amygdala

4. From amygdala, via diagonal band of Broca, to septal nuclei

   From amygdala, through terminal stria to septal nuclei, preoptic region, and paraventricular nuclei of hypothalamus

   From septal nuclei, through medial forebrain bundle, to preoptic nuclei, lateral hypothalamic area, and mammillary nuclei

   From septal nuclei, amygdala, and hypothalamus through stria medullaris thalami to the habenula

   From habenula through habenulopeduncular tract to the interpeduncular nucleus

   From the interpeduncular nucleus to the dorsal tegmental nucleus

   From septal nuclei through medial forebrain bundle directly to the tegmental reticular nuclei

---

Reflex

Receptor

Afferent neuron

Association neuron to brain centers

Association neuron between centers

Visceral Effects (General)

1. Same as general

2. Same as general

3. Same as general

4. Same as general

5. From septal nuclei and preoptic nuclei through medial forebrain bundle to autonomic nuclei of brainstem and intermediolateral column of cord

   From tegmental reticular nuclei through the reticular formation and reticulospinal tract to autonomic nuclei of brainstem and intermediolateral column of the cord

   From dorsal tegmental nucleus via the dorsal longitudinal fasciculus to autonomic nuclei of the brainstem and the intermediolateral column of the cord

Descending fiber to lower motor nuclei

5. Same as general except for the terminations, the reticular formation, medial forebrain bundle, and dorsal longitudinal fasciculus terminating in nuclei V, VII, IX, and X

6. From the autonomic nuclei of the brainstem (superior and inferior salivatory and dorsal motor nucleus of the vagus) through preganglionics running in nerves VII, IX, and X, to synapse in autonomic ganglia, thence through postganglionics to salivary glands and the muscles and glands of the digestive system

   From the intermediolateral cell column of the cord through preganglionics in the ventral roots of spinal nerves and by white rami, to autonomic ganglia, thence by postganglionics to smooth muscle and glands

Efferent neuron

6. From nucleus V through trigeminal nerve to muscles of mastication

   From nucleus VII through facial nerve to muscles of face

   From nucleus IX and X (ambiguus) through glossopharyngeal and vagus nerves to muscles of pharynx and larynx

Somatic Effects

1–4. Same as above.

1–4 Same as above

5. Same as above except the reticular formation, reticulospinal tract, and dorsal longitudinal fasciculus end around cranial somatic nuclei III, IV, VI, and XII and the ventral gray column of the cord

Descending fiber to lower motor nuclei

6. Efferent neurons from III, IV, and VI pass through their respective nerves to extrinsic ocular muscles

   From nucleus XII, fibers pass to the tongue

   From the ventral column, fibers innervate muscles of neck, trunk, and extremities

Efferent neuron

Conscious

Direct

7. Same as in reflex

Receptor

7. Same as in reflex

8. Same as afferent neuron in reflex

Neuron I

8. Same as afferent neuron in reflex

9. From cells in olfactory bulb through the lateral olfactory stria to end in the prepyriform area, the periamygdaloid area, and the anterior ambient gyrus

Neuron II

9. From cells in the olfactory bulb, ending in anterior olfactory nucleus

   From olfactory nucleus to same areas of cortex as in direct pathway

Indirect

   N.B. Since the thalamus is not involved in this system directly, there is no true neuron III as seen in other afferent systems

Summary
Taste

Somatic Effects

Reflex

Visceral Effects (General)

1. Taste buds

Reflex

1. Same as somatic

2. From receptors on anterior two-thirds of
tongue via lingual, chorda tympani, and
facial nerves, with cell bodies in the geniculate ganglion, into the brainstem bending caudally in the tractus solitarius and
ending in the nucleus of that tract (or
gustatory nucleus)

Afferent
neuron

2. Same as somatic

From receptors on posterior third of
tongue via glossopharyngeal nerve, with
cell bodies in the petrosal ganglion, into
the brainstem, bending caudally in the
tractus solitarius and terminating in the
nucleus of that tract (or gustatory nucleus)

From receptors near epiglottis and the
posterior pharynx via the vagus nerve
with cell bodies in the nodose ganglion,
into the brainstem, bending caudally in
the tractus solitarius and terminating in
the nucleus of that tract (or gustatory
nucleus)

3. From cells in the nucleus of the tractus
solitarius (or gustatory) to the nucleus
of the hypoglossal nerve

Association
neuron

3. From cells in the nucleus of the tractus
solitarius (or gustatory), through the
reticular formation to salivatory nuclei;
dorsal motor nucleus of vagus; through
reticulospinal tract to intermediolateral
column of the cord

From cells in the nucleus of the tractus
solitarius (or gustatory) through the
reticular formation and reticulospinal
tract to the ventral gray column of the
cord

4. From the hypoglossal nucleus through
nerve XII to muscles of tongue

Efferent
neuron

4. From salivatory nuclei by preganglionics
in nerves VII and IX to autonomic
ganglia, thence, through postganglionics,
to the salivary glands

From the ventral gray columns of the
cord through spinal nerves to muscles
of neck, trunk, and extremities

From the dorsal motor nucleus of the
vagus by preganglionics in nerve X, to
terminal autonomic ganglia, thence by
short postganglionics to muscles and
glands of digestive system

From the intermediolateral cell column,
through preganglionics in the ventral
roots of spinal nerves and by white rami
to autonomic ganglia, thence by postganglionics to muscles and glands of digestive system

Visceral Effects (Special)

5. Same as somatic   Receptor

6. Same as somatic   Afferent neuron

7. From cells in the nucleus of the tractus solitarius (or gustatory) through the reticular formation to nuclei V, VII, IX, X, and XI

8. From nucleus V to muscles of mastica-   Efferent
   tion through trigeminal nerve   neuron

   From nucleus VII to muscles of face via facial nerve

   From nucleus ambiguus through nerves IX and X (glossopharyngeal and vagus) to muscles of pharynx and larynx

   From nucleus of XI through accessory nerve to sternocleidomastoid and trapezius muscles

               Summary
               Conscious

1. Same as in reflex   Receptor

2. Same as afferent neuron in reflex   Neuron I

3. From the nucleus of the tractus soli-   Neuron II
   tarius (or gustatory), probably traveling with the trigeminothalamic tracts, to terminate in the medial side of the ventral posteromedial nucleus of the thalamus (sometimes called the accessory arcuate or semilunar necleus)

4. From the accessory arcuate nucleus or Neuron III
   VPM through the posterior limb of the internal capsule to reach the extreme ventral end of the postcentral gyrus (area 43)

Chapter 11

General Proprioception (GP)

By definition, proprioception[1] means receiving stimuli originating in the muscles, tendons, and joints. It is the mechanism involved in the self-regulation of posture and movement. Thus, both position and posture are maintained by a continuous flow of impulses from the musculoskeletal apparatus.

Although the proprioceptive system is of prime importance wherever a complex musculature exists, its activity passes almost unnoticed, for its conscious aspects are less highly developed than those of the exteroceptive senses. However, it does express itself primarily in terms of reflexes.

Since many of the reflexes require great

muscular coordination, another unit of the CNS, the cerebellum, must become involved. Therefore, ascending tracts to that structure are included here. The details of the motor complexes and the descending pathways by which the suprasegmental structures exert their influence upon the motor components will be discussed in other places (Chaps. 13, 17 through 20). The ascending fasciculi to consciousness will be considered briefly.

TRUNK

Simple Reflex Pathways (Figs. 11-1, 11-2)

Receptors

The receptors, located in and among muscles, tendons, and joints, are of several types.

The intramuscular variety are known as

---

[1]Most authors place general proprioception in the GSA system. The latter is then broken down into exteroception, which includes pain, temperature, and touch, and proprioception, as described here.

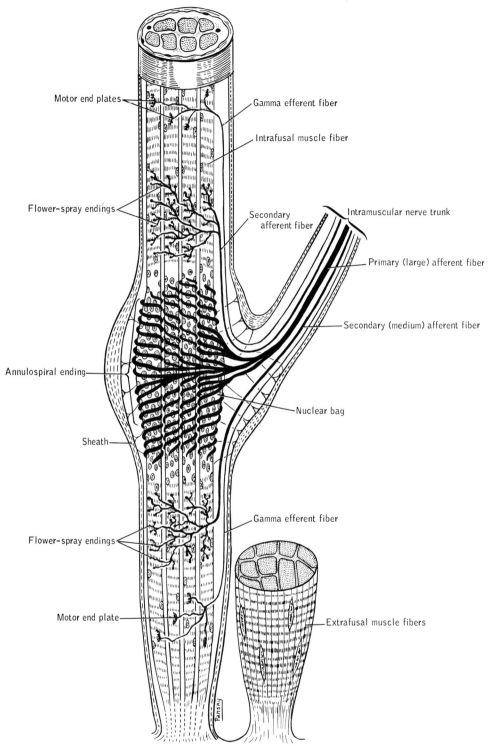

Figure 11-1 Diagram of a muscle spindle showing primary and secondary afferent fibers, gamma efferent fibers, and annulospiral and flower spray endings.

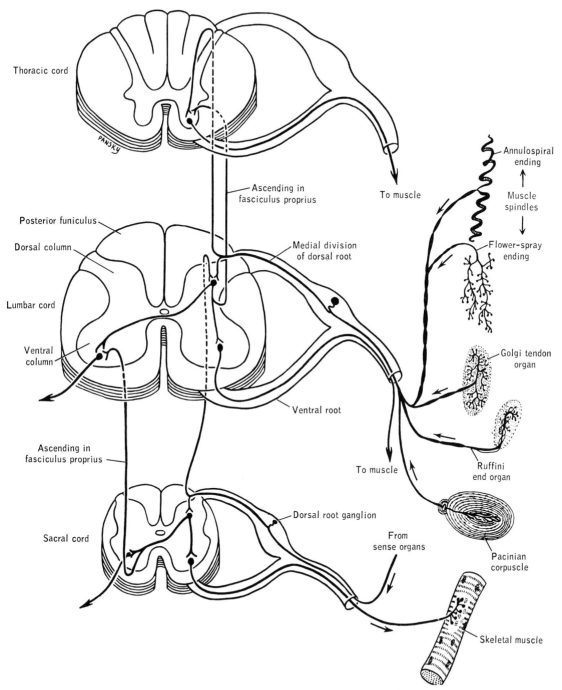

Figure 11-2 Diagram of the general proprioceptive (GP) reflex paths for afferent impulses reaching the CNS through spinal nerves.

muscle spindles. Each spindle is composed of a variable, but usually small, number of atypical, slender skeletal muscle fibers. These are the *intrafusal fibers* and are enclosed in a connective tissue sheath. The latter tissue is attached at the ends of the spindle to the endomysium of the normal skeletal muscle fibers—*the extrafusal fiber.* Toward their ends, the intrafusal fiber is striated and is contractile. The central portion of these fibers is expanded and contains an abnormally large number of nuclei, for which reason it is referred to as the *nuclear bag region.* Between the connective tissue and the sarcolemma of the bag there is a considerable fluid-filled space crossed by connective tissue fibers and nerves. The intrafusal fiber is related to three kinds of neurons (Chaps. 7, 13): (1) small efferents, the *gamma efferents*, which have motor end plates in the polar region of the fiber; (2) primary afferents (A afferents), the largest of the three, which wind around the nuclear bag region as the *annulospiral ending*; (3) secondary afferents (B afferents), which terminate in a group at the periphery of the bag region as the *flower spray endings.* Because the intra- and extrafusal fibers are parallel, they are both stretched when the entire muscle is stretched. The act of stretching stimulates the annulospiral endings. A similar effect is obtained when the polar region of the intrafusal fiber contracts in response to activity in the gamma efferents, for, in such a contraction, the bag region is put under tension (Chap. 13).

The flower spray endings are thought to be activated by a maximum contraction of the muscle fiber.

Within the tendons are Golgi tendon organs similar in basic structure to the muscle spindle except that the modified fibers are collagenous rather than muscular. They are adapted to register stretch of the tendon due to muscle contraction.

Pacinian corpuscles are found in fascia and intermuscular septa and about joint capsules. In the two former locations, they are activated by the swelling of the entire muscle or its larger subdivisions, while those situated within articular capsules record movements at joints.

Afferent Neuron

The neuron related to the annulospiral ending is large and heavily myelinated (A alpha afferent, Table 7-1. Its monopolar cell in the dorsal root ganglion is also large. The fiber associated with the flower spray and tendon endings is intermediate in size (A beta afferents). All central processes are collected in bundles constituting the medial divisions of the dorsal root. As soon as entry into the cord is made, these fibers join the posterior funiculus, those coming in at lower spinal levels lying more medial in the funiculus (Chap. 7). Each individual fiber then bifurcates into long ascending and short descending branches, both of which give off collaterals that end around cells in the gray columns. These terminations may be directly upon efferent neurons or upon the small, numerous interneurons which, in their turn, synapse with the motor neurons.

The A beta afferents are similar to the A alpha afferents in course and termination.

Association Neurons

As noted elsewhere, the central processes of dorsal root ganglion cells synapse directly upon motor neurons without the interposition of a typical association unit, thus establishing a monosynaptic, two-neuron reflex arc. This is the basis for the stretch, or myotatic, reflex (Chap. 13). However, since branches of the afferent neuron also terminate on interneurons, polysynaptic arcs are likewise formed.

Many association neurons, traveling through the fasciculus proprius of the same side, through the anterior white commissure, and through the fasciculus proprius of the opposite side, help to spread the excitation initiated by the afferent neuron to motor cells at all levels of the spinal cord.

Efferent Neuron

Like the efferent limbs of all spinal reflex arcs these too have their cells of origin in the ventral gray columns. Their axons exit from the cord as the ventral roots of spinal nerves.

Coordination (Cerebellar) Pathway (Fig. 11-3)

So many human activities are carried out subconsciously that there is little conception of the tremendous amount of adjustment necessary for proper function. Not only must one set of muscles contract, but the contraction must be to the correct extent while, at the same time, an opposing group must relax to the appropriate degree. Whether in the retention of normal posture or during increased activity due to emergency reactions, a constant flow of impulses from receptors in the trunk musculature must reach the CNS in order to keep the entire body in the proper state of tonus. Consider, for example, the reflex reactions which occur when an attempt is made to regain the normal position after having stumbled or turned an ankle. This requires the rapid contraction of many muscles over a wide area of the body, all demanding regulation and coordination. For both these processes, the cerebellum plays an important role.

Cerebellar Pathway Receptors

These are the same as those of the simple reflex (see Simple Reflex Pathways, above).

Afferent Neuron

The first neuron in the cerebellar circuit is the same as the afferent limb in the simple reflex. However, in this case, the collaterals from the primary fibers synapse not only in the body of the dorsal horn but also in the nucleus dorsalis (of Clarke), a cell column which extends from the eighth cervical through the third lumbar

segments (Fig. 2-5). Because of the limited extent of this nucleus, proprioceptive fibers entering the cord through lower lumbar and sacral nerves must ascend in the fasciculus gracilis to reach the lower portion of this nucleus. Likewise, afferent neurons coming from the upper extremity and neck traveling in spinal nerves cephalic to C8 must run upward in the fasciculus cuneatus to reach the accessory (lateral) cuneate nucleus of the lower medulla.

Ascending (Secondary) Neuron

Axons originating from the body of the dorsal gray column proper at lumbar and sacral levels cross to the opposite side of the cord through the anterior white commissure and pass to the periphery of the cord in the ventral portion of the lateral funiculus. Here, they turn rostrally as the *anterior* or *ventral spinocerebellar tract*. In its upward path, this tract remains lateral and superficial throughout the cord (Fig. 2-7). It takes a position dorsal to the inferior olive and medial to the lateral spinothalamic tract in the medulla (Figs. 25-1 through 25-3). In the pons, it shifts gradually more laterally (Figs. 25-6, 25-7) and then courses dorsally around the external surface of the superior cerebellar peduncle to reach the anterior medullary velum (Fig. 25-9). Through the latter, this tract enters the rostral end of the cerebellar vermis and terminates mainly on the contralateral side.

From Clarke's nucleus most of the axons turn directly laterally on the same side of the cord, where they extend almost to the periphery of the dorsal portion of the lateral funiculus. Here, they turn rostrally as the *dorsal* or *posterior spinocerebellar tract*[2] (Fig. 2-7). Throughout the cord, the dorsal spinocerebellar tract maintains its superficial dorsolateral position. In the medulla it lies just beneath the

[2]Since Clarke's nucleus does not occur below L3, this tract is not found caudal to this level.

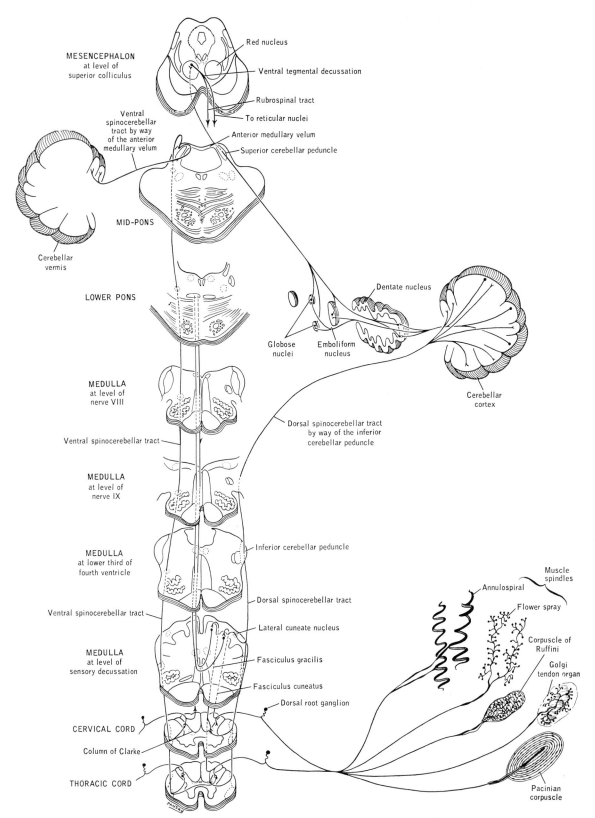

Figure 11-3 The cerebellar circuit as part of the GP reflex mechanism at trunk levels.

surface, overlying the spinal V tract (Figs. 25-1 through 25-3). Gradually it shifts farther dorsally and joins the inferior cerebellar peduncle through which it enters the cerebellum (Chap. 17).

From the accessory cuneate, nucleus fibers ascend rostrally for a short distance before entering the inferior cerebellar peduncle, through which they reach the cerebellum.

Conscious Pathway

Receptors

These are the same as described under Simple Reflex Pathways, above.

Neuron I

This is identical with the afferent neuron described above for simple reflexes.

Neurons II and III

It is believed that the secondary and tertiary neurons follow the same course as indicated for tactile discrimination (Chap. 7).

HEAD

Simple Reflex Pathways

Receptors

These are similar to those of the trunk and are found among the muscles of mastication and facial expression, around the temporomandibular joint, and in the sockets of the teeth.[3]

Afferent Neuron

The peripheral processes from each receptor travel in all three divisions of the trigeminal nerve. From the hard palate and sockets of the upper teeth, some pass via the maxillary branch. However, the vast majority, from the sockets of the lower teeth, the muscles of

[3]Mastication, the adjustment of strength of bite, and at least the first part of deglutition all require some degree of self-regulation.

mastication, and the temperomandibular joint, are found in the mandibular division. Unlike other sensory systems, there is no cell outside the CNS. The peripheral processes merely pass through the ganglion, join the fibers of the motor root, and enter the lateral aspect of the pons. Here these fibers run obliquely dorsomedially and pass between the motor and chief sensory trigeminal nuclei (Fig. 25-9). As they approach the ventrolateral aspect of the fourth ventricle, their course becomes rostral, continuing along the superior portion of the ventricle and into the mesencephalon parallel to the cerebral aqueduct. Thus the term *mesencephalic root* has been given to this fiber bundle (Figs. 1-39, 1-40). From the point where these fibers begin their rostral course until they play out in the midbrain, typical monopolar ganglion cells are associated with each fiber. These cells are collectively known as the *mesencephalic nucleus* (Figs. 25-9, 25-10). The central processes from these cells are difficult to follow. Undoubtedly some of them make direct synapses with cells in the motor nucleus of the trigeminal nerve, thus forming typical two-neuron reflex arcs. Others of these central processes synapse among cells in the reticular formation.

The course of proprioceptive fibers arising in the extrinsic muscle of the eye, tongue, or pharynx is uncertain. Therefore, they will be considered in a very general way.

There is evidence to indicate the presence of proprioceptive fibers associated with spindles in the muscles of the orbit. Some investigators feel that such fibers eventually join the ophthalmic division of the trigeminal nerve and make their way to the mesencephalic nucleus.

The muscles of facial expression are also supplied with proprioceptive afferents. Because of numerous connections between cranial nerves V and VII, some investigators have suggested that the mesencephalic nucleus contains the cell bodies of neurons from the facial nerve as well. The evidence for this contention is poor. Others have suggested that proprioceptive fibers pass through the nervus intermedius, have their cell bodies in the geniculate ganglion, and terminate in the nucleus solitarius.

Because speech requires delicate controls, it is assumed that proprioceptive fibers, running in the vagus and glossopharyngeal nerves, play a vital role in this process. One can only speculate upon the course and connections of such fibers beyond the borders of the medulla, but the nucleus solitarius is a possible terminus.

It is evident that the movements of the tongue are finely controlled. Furthermore, histologic evidence indicates the presence of numerous spindles in the tongue. Although the hypoglossal nerve communicates with both nerve V and nerve IX, there is no good evidence that proprioceptive fibers from the tongue enter either of these nerves.

One school of thought suggests that proprioceptive nuclei may lie in or closely adjacent to the motor nuclei which supply the orbital, facial, lingual, pharyngeal, and laryngeal muscles. However, decisions on this matter must be reserved pending future investigation.

Association Neuron[4]

From cells in the reticular formation of the brainstem, axons spread to all the general somatic and special visceral motor nuclei as parts of polysynaptic reflex arcs.

Efferent Neuron

From the motor nucleus of the trigeminal nerve, axons pass through the portio minor to

---

[4]It should be recalled that certain reflexes, such as some of those involving mastication, are of the two-neuron type, in which the central process of the afferent neuron from the mesencephalic nucleus of the trigeminal nerve substitutes for the association neuron of the typical three-neuron arc.

the muscles of mastication by way of the mandibular division.

From the facial nucleus, axons are distributed to the muscles of facial expression.

From the nucleus ambiguus, fibers are carried to the muscles of the pharynx and larynx by way of the glossopharyngeal and vagus nerves.

From the nuclei of the oculomotor, trochlear, and abducens nerves, axons bring the extrinsic muscles of the eye under reflex control.

Efferent fibers from the hypoglossal nucleus, via cranial nerve XII, bring the muscles of the tongue under reflex control.

Conscious Pathway

Receptors

These are the same as described under Trunk, Simple Reflex Pathways.

Neuron I

This is identical with the afferent neuron described above under Head, Simple Reflex Pathways, except that in this case it is believed that the short central process from the mesencephalic nucleus terminates in the main sensory nucleus of the trigeminal nerve.

Neurons II and III

As far as is known, these neurons may follow the course described for the tactile system of the head (Chap. 7).

CLINICAL CONSIDERATIONS

Testing

A sharp tap is applied to any of several extensor tendons (Fig. 11-4), for example, the triceps, just above the olecranon; the quadriceps tendon, just below the patella; the Achilles tendon, above the calcaneus. If the parts—forearm, leg, or foot as the case may

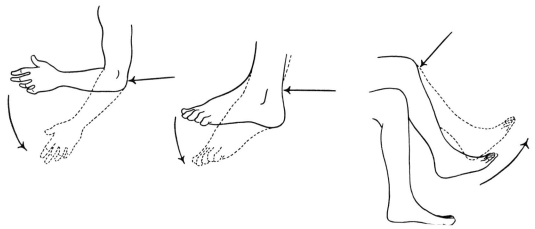

Figure 11-4 Reflex tests. *A.* Extension of the forearm; *B.* Plantar flexion of the foot; *C.* Extension of the leg.

be—are in a state of at least partial flexion at the time the stimulus is applied, the normal response is an extension of the part. By using a variety of testing sites it is possible to more nearly localize a lesion, thus: triceps—C6, C7, (C8?); quadriceps—L2, L3, and L4; ankle—S1 and S2.

With the patient in bed, muscles as relaxed as possible, the different parts of the patient's limbs are moved by the examiner. First, the patient is asked to tell in what position the limbs have been placed and then to tell in what direction the movement has occurred.

The patient is asked to stand with feet together and eyes closed. Is it necessary for the patient to move his or her feet to maintain balance?

The examiner asks the patient to walk and observes the gait. Can the patient walk with eyes closed?

Additional information concerning coordination can be obtained by asking the patient to keep the eyes closed and to touch one finger to the tip of the nose or to place the heel of one foot to the opposite knee, then push it down along the shin.

On examination, lesions involving this system, yield the following findings: *areflexia,* in which no reflexes are elicitable; *astereognosis,*[5] in which the patient, with eyes covered, fails to identify familiar objects placed in the hand; *ataxia,*[6] in which the patient has difficulty in standing without moving the feet, or in walking with eyes closed; *incoordination,* or *asynergia,* in which the various muscles fail to work together or in normal sequence (Chap. 17).

Generally destruction of nerve roots begins near the caudal end of the cord and progresses cranially. Usually the medial division of the dorsal roots of the spinal nerves is attacked and destroyed. Since this is the part carrying the afferent neurons of the proprioceptive reflex arcs, no tendon reflexes in the area of the lesion can be elicited. Likewise, these

[5]It should be recalled that stereognosis is actually a cortical function which depends upon the blending of two or more basic modalities. Thus, loss of proprioception would contribute to the inability to recognize objects.

[6]Since ataxia is also a finding in cases of lesions in other parts of the nervous system, further tests are necessary before a lesion can actually be localized.

patients cannot tell in which position their limbs have been placed or in what direction they have been moved. In order to walk without falling, they must use their eyes to determine where their feet must be placed, because they do not receive the normal impulses from their muscles and joints. They are unable to identify objects placed in their

hands if the disease has spread as far as the lower cervical levels.

Trauma

Any injury which leads to a destruction of the posterior funiculi will result in a loss of the sense of position and movement below the site of the lesion on the same side of the cord.

Summary
General Proprioception

Simple Reflex

Trunk		Head
1. Neuromuscular endings (annulospiral and flower spray) Neurotendinous spindle Tendon–joint corpuscular endings	Receptor	1. Same as for trunk, plus endings in sockets of teeth
2. Through dorsal roots of all spinal nerves, with cell bodies in dorsal root ganglia, into dorsal funiculus (fasciculus gracilis and cuneatus) of the cord to terminate in the dorsal gray columns	Afferent neuron	2. Through the trigeminal nerve and into the brainstem with cell bodies in the mesencephalic nucleus of V, the central processes ending either in reticular formation or directly in the motor nucleus of V
3. From cells in the dorsal gray columns to ventral gray column on same side at same level; through the fasciculus proprius to the ventral gray column at other levels on the same side; through the anterior white commissure and fasciculus proprius to the ventral gray column at the same and other levels on the opposite side of the cord	Association neuron	3. From the reticular formation to other cranial nuclei, especially nuclei VII and XII
4. From the ventral gray columns to skeletal muscle of the neck, trunk, and extremities	Efferent neuron	4. From nucleus V through trigeminal nerve to muscles of mastication From nucleus VII through facial nerve to muscle of face From nucleus XII through the hypoglossal nerve to muscles of the tongue

Conscious

Receptor

Neuron I

Neuron II

Neuron III

See conscious pathways for Tactile Discrimination (Chap. 7).

Cerebellar Circuit

	Receptor	

1. Same as simple reflex, trunk

1. Same as simple reflex, head

2. Same as afferent neuron, simple reflex, trunk terminating in the column of Clarke

Afferent neuron

2. Same as afferent neuron, simple reflex, head, except, in this case, fibers end either in the reticular formation or the chief sensory nucleus of the trigeminal

3. From dorsal gray column to ventral spinocerebellar tract on same side, thence rostrally through the cord and brainstem, through the anterior medullary velum to terminate in the rostral vermis

Afferent cerebellar neuron

3. From the reticular formation through reticulocerebellar fibers which enter the cerebellum through the inferior cerebellar peduncle to end in posterior semilunar lobule

From dorsal gray column, across the cord in the anterior white commissure to ventral spinocerebellar tract of the opposite side, then as above

From chief sensory nucleus through trigeminocerebellar fibers which enter the cerebellum with the ventral spinocerebellar tract through the anterior medullary velum to terminate as above

From Clarke's column, into the dorsal spinocerebellar tract of same side, rostrally through the cord, entering the inferior cerebellar peduncle and terminating in both rostral and caudal portions of the cerebellar cortex

4. From Purkinje cells of cerebellar cortex through the cerebellar medullary core to the central cerebellar nuclei

Corticonuclear neuron

4. From Purkinje cells of the cortex through the white core to reach the central cerebellar nuclei

5. From central nuclei, through the superior cerebellar peduncle to end in the red nucleus

Efferent cerebellar neuron

5. From central nuclei, through the superior cerebellar peduncle to end in the red nucleus

6. From the red nucleus, some fibers decussate in the ventral tegmental decussation and descend through the rubrospinal tract to terminate in the ventral gray column of the cord

Descending neuron

6. From the red nucleus, terminating in the reticular formation and passing through this to reach the motor nucleus of V

From the red nucleus, fibers terminate in the reticular nuclei, and from the latter, fibers pass through the reticulospinal tract to terminate in the ventral gray columns of the cord

7. Same as in simple reflex, trunk

Efferent neuron

7. From nucleus V through the trigeminal nerve to muscles of mastication

Chapter 12

Special Proprioception (SP)

The SP system[1] involves the maintenance of the position of the eyes and body in relation to changes in the orientation of the head. This requires the presence of special receptors located in the *membranous labyrinth* of the vestibular portion of the inner ear.

The vestibular part of the membranous labyrinth consists of several parts (Figs. 8-14, 12-1): the saccule, utricle, and three semicircular canals. These are filled with a fluid called *endolymph*. The semicircular canals are set at right angles to each other and represent all planes of space. They are named according to orientation and their relations: horizontal, anterior, and posterior. The adjoining segments of the anterior and posterior canals fuse to form a single channel to the utricle called the

common crus. The ends of all others empty separately into the utricle. Each of the canals has an enlargement, called the *ampulla*, near the opening. As is the case with general proprioception, the important part of this system concerns reflexes. Here, the reflexes are involved with equilibrium and ocular adjustments. Also included is the coordinating mechanism which is essential for both these complex activities. Conscious pathways will not, and in fact cannot, be discussed in detail due to lack of information.

SIMPLE REFLEX PATHWAYS (Fig. 12-2)

Receptors (Fig. 12-1)

The receptors lie in both the ampullae of the canals and in the utricle and saccule. In the latter two locations they are composed of hair

---

[1]Many authors place this sensory modality in the special somatic afferent (SSA) category.

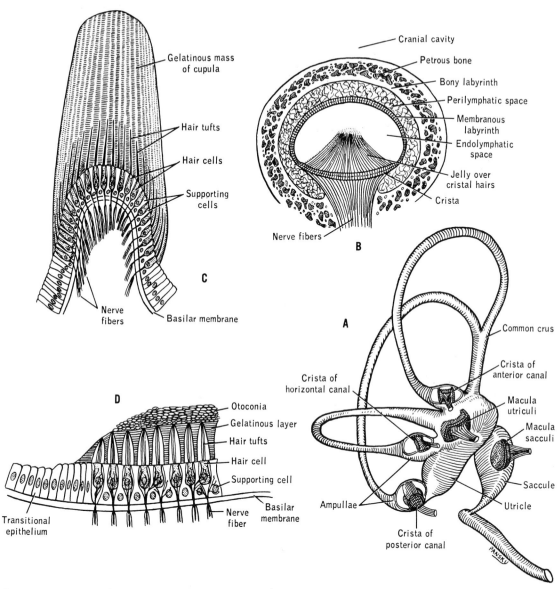

Figure 12-1 Vestibular mechanism. *A.* Lateral view of the membranous labyrinth to illustrate the receptor organs of the ampullae, utricle, and saccule. *B.* Diagrammatic section through the crista of a semicircular canal. *(Adapted from Krieg, Functional Neuroanatomy, 2d ed., McGraw-Hill Book Company, New York, 1953.) C.* Schematic representation (enlarged) of a crista ampullaris as seen in longitudinal section. *D.* Schematic enlargement of a macula.

cells surrounded by supporting elements. Cilia project from the free surface of the sensory cells, while the terminal filaments of the ves-

tibular division of the eighth cranial nerve entwine about their bases. The area of ciliated cells is covered with a cap of jellylike sub-

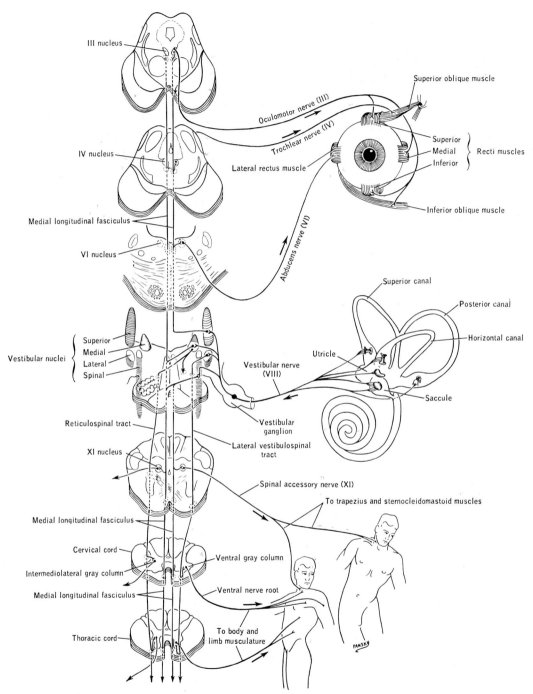

Figure 12-2 Simple vestibular reflex pathways.

stance in which are embedded small crystals of calcium carbonate, the *otoliths (otoconia)*. For this reason the entire cap may be spoken of as the otolithic membrane.

The patch of hair cells in both the utricle and saccule is called the *macula*. In the saccule, the macula is oriented in the sagittal plane with the cilia directed laterally. In the utricle, the macula lies in the horizontal plane (Fig. 12-1) with the cilia directed upward. In both locations, the maculae are prolonged slightly onto the curved surfaces of their respective receptacles, both prolongations being predominantly directed in the frontal plane. Thus, macular surfaces are provided for each of the three planes of space.

Both maculae are thought to be related to posture.[2] In the normal, erect position, the receptors in the utricle are least stimulated. When the head changes position, the maculae are tilted and the otoliths, falling with gravity, exert their influence on the gelatinous cap. This results in a bending or pulling of the cilia, an action sufficient to stimulate the nerve. For example, the right macula of the saccule is maximally stimulated when the individual lies on the right side, while that in the left saccule is least affected.

The groups of hair cells in the ampullae of the semicircular canals are called cristae (Fig. 12-1). Here too there appears to be a gelatinous cap into which the cilia protrude. The latter are displaced by movements of the endolymph contained in the canals, the greatest amount of stimulation arising during rotation, acceleration, and deceleration, all three planes of space being represented. For example, if the head moves clockwise (to the right), pressure is exerted maximally at the anterior end of the right horizontal canal due to the

inertia of the endolymph. Thus, the crista in this location will be activated. However, when rotation to the right stops, the pressure of the moving fluid would be maximal against the crista in the anterior end of the left horizontal canal. Thus, it is evident that these receptors are best adapted to record movement.

Afferent Neuron (Figs. 12-1, 12-3)

The myelinated peripheral processes from the cristae and maculae combine to form the *vestibular portion of the eighth cranial nerve*. They enter the internal auditory meatus, at the base of which is located the *vestibular ganglion*. The cells of this ganglion are of the *bipolar type*. The central processes continue into the cranium to enter the brain at the cerebellopontine angle (Figs. 1-7, 1-8, 25-7). Within the medula they run dorsomedially until they have traversed about two-thirds of the distance to the lateral angle of the fourth ventricle. Here each bifurcates into ascending and descending branches.

These branches terminate in four vestibular nuclei (Figs. 12-3, 12-4, 25-4 through 25-7): *the superior, medial, lateral, and spinal (descending, or inferior)*. The superior (nucleus of Becterew) is triangular in shape, extending rostrally from near the level of nerve entry, along the floor and lateral aspects of the superior recess of the fourth ventricle. The lateral (nucleus of Deiters) is a relatively small, irregular area, containing particularly large cells, lying just ventral to the region where the primary afferent neurons bifurcate. The medial (dorsal or principal nucleus) is the largest of the four and is also triangular in shape, its broadest portion lying at the level of entry of the eighth nerve, tapering to an apex far down the medulla. The spinal, or inferior, nucleus is a long column of cells extending caudally to the level of the nucleus gracilis, the cells being distributed among the fibers of the *spinal,* or *descending, vestibular tract*. All

---

[2]It has been suggested that the macula sacculi is also sensitive to vibrations (vibroreceptor) and that the macula utriculi responds, at least to some extent, to linear acceleration.

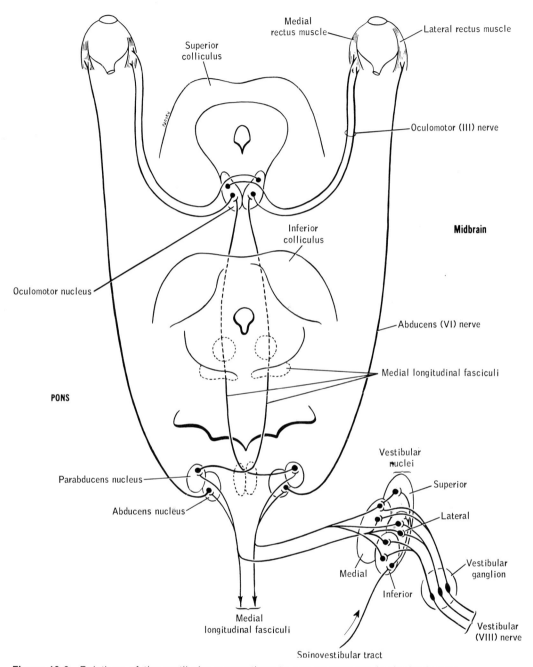

Figure 12-3 Relations of the vestibular connections to eye movements in the horizontal plane.

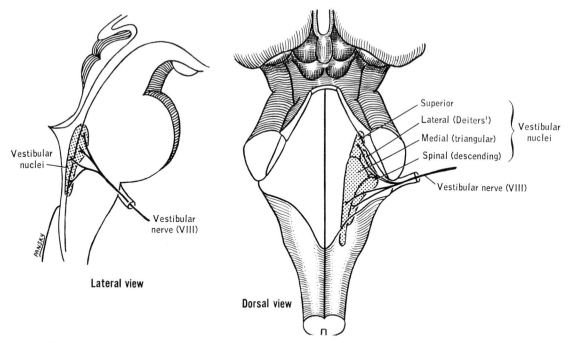

Figure 12-4 Termination of the vestibular nerve in the vestibular nuclei as seen in a lateral and dorsal view.

these nuclei occupy a field in the rhomboid fossa of the fourth ventricle called the *area acoustica* (Figs. 1-32, 12-4).

The ascending branches of the primary fibers pass mainly to the rostral end of the medial nucleus and to the entire superior nucleus. The descending branches unite, forming the *descending, or spinal, vestibular tract.* The latter terminates in the lateral, descending, and possibly the caudal part of the medial nuclei.

Association Neuron

These have their cell bodies in any of the vestibular nuclei.

Fibers from the superior nucleus enter the *medial longitudinal fasciculus* (MLF) (Figs. 12-2, 12-3, 25-1 through 25-11) of the same side and turn rostrally to terminate among the cells of cranial nerves III, IV, and VI.

From the lateral nucleus, the vast majority

of fibers descend on the same side through the brainstem and down the length of the cord in the anterior funiculus as the *vestibulospinal tract* (Fig. 12-2), which terminates among the cells of the ventral columns of the cord.

From the inferior nucleus, fibers pass medially, cross the midline, and descend in the medial longitudinal fasciculus, to terminate in the nucleus of the accessory nerve and the ventral columns of the cervical cord.

From the medial nucleus, axons cross the midline, enter the opposite medial longitudinal fasciculus, and bifurcate into fibers which ascend or descend within that fascicle to terminate as indicated for other fibers traveling in it. Some fibers from this nucleus enter the reticular formation of both sides to be distributed to the motor nuclei belonging to the autonomic system in the brainstem and the intermediolateral column of the cord, by way of the reticulospinal tract.

Efferent Neuron

Axons from the ventral columns of the cord, extending from the lower cervical to the lower sacral levels, are distributed to the skeletal muscles of the trunk and extremities, thus completing a typical somatic reflex. This is very important in relating movements of the body with those of the head and is definitely significant in maintaining balance.

Fibers from the ventral columns of the cord in the cervical region and from the nucleus of the spinal portion of the accessory nerve are distributed to the muscles of the neck, the sternocleidomastoid and trapezius. These muscles are particularly important in maintaining the normal position of the head (Fig. 12-2).

Axons from the somatic efferent columns of the brainstem, particularly the nuclei of the oculomotor, trochlear, and abducens nerves, supply the extrinsic muscles of the eyes, thus coordinating movements of the eyes with those of the head.

Fibers arising from the autonomic centers, especially the dorsal motor nucleus of the vagus and the intermediolateral cell column of the cord, account for the nausea, vomiting, and pallor manifested after overstimulation of the vestibular system.

CEREBELLAR PATHWAY (Fig. 12-5)

Although the details of cerebellar connections will be given later (Chap. 17), it should be emphasized at this point that the cerebellum does exert control over activities initiated by the stimulation of vestibular receptors.

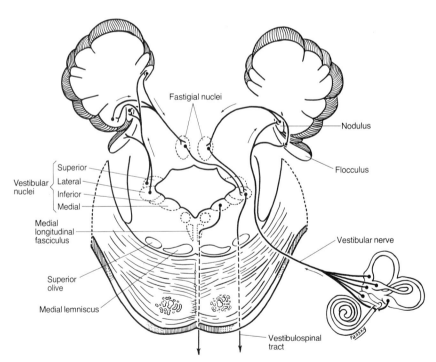

Figure 12-5 Vestibulocerebellar reflex pathway (coordinated reflex). *Left,* indirect path; *right,* direct pathway. The indirect fibers actually arise from the inferior and medial nuclei rather than the superior and lateral as shown here.

Direct Circuit

Receptors

These are the same as described under Simple Reflex Pathways, above.

Afferent Neuron

These are also the same as those indicated under Simple Reflex Pathways. However, cerebellar impulses travel through the ascending branches only and terminate in the nodulus and flocculus of the cerebellum of the same side (Chap. 17).

Descending Neuron

From cells in the cortex of the nodulus and flocculus, fibers descend to terminate in the fastigial nucleus. From this nucleus some axons descend by way of the medial segment of the inferior cerebellar peduncle to end in the vestibular nuclei. Other axons from the fastigial nucleus cross the midline and descend to the vestibular nuclei of the opposite side by way of the *uncinate bundle* (of Russell). Thus, the cerebellum is able to exert influence directly upon the vestibular nuclei. Fibers from these nuclei are then carried by the pathways already described (vestibulospinal tract and medial longitudinal fasciculus) to the same terminations.

Indirect Circuit

Receptors

These are the same as for the direct route, described above.

Afferent Neuron

These are the same as those indicated for the direct route except that they terminate in the inferior and medial vestibular nuclei.

Ascending Neuron

From cells in the inferior and medial nuclei, fibers ascend in the medial segment of the inferior cerebellar peduncle (the juxtarestiform body). They terminate both in the flocculonodular lobe and fastigial nucleus of the cerebellum (Chap. 17).

Descending Neuron (Fig. 12-5)

From cells in the cerebellar cortex of the regions mentioned above, fibers descend to the fastigial nucleus. Arising from the fastigial nucleus, axons descend by the same pathways and have the same terminations as those described for the descending fibers of the direct route.

CONSCIOUS PATHWAY

Little is known about such connections. The receptors certainly would be the same as described for reflexes. The major portion of the primary neuron would also be the same as the afferent neurons of the reflex arcs. However, one group of investigators has suggested that some of these afferent neurons end in the ventral cochlear nucleus and from there follow the auditory pathways to consciousness (Chap. 8).

CLINICAL CONSIDERATIONS

Disease in the vestibular mechanism expresses itself in disturbances of equilibrium, balance, and coordination. Therefore, the simple observation of the patient standing or walking becomes an integral part of the examination. Furthermore, since this system is so intimately tied up with reflex movements of the eyes, such reflexes are important in trying to localize a lesion.

Testing

Tests which apply chiefly to the cerebellar circuits are discussed in Chap. 17.

Before taking up any of the special testing procedures, it is necessary to discuss the relations between the vestibular system and the maintenance of position of the eyes during positional changes of the head. In general, when the head moves slowly in any plane, the eyes do not follow but tend to retain their fixation on the original field. This, in effect, is the same as though they deviated in an opposite direction to that in which the head is turned. (This is true whether the motion is from side to side or up and down.) When the eyes, after a slow movement, reach the limit of deviation in one direction, they move quickly back toward the other extreme. This is called *nystagmus.* The slow movement is a manifestation of activation of the ocular muscle centers through irritation of the vestibular system, whereas the quick movement is regarded as a cerebral reflex, returning the eyeballs to their former position. The *direction of the nystagmus is named in accordance with the direction of the quick, reflex movement.*

Currents in the semicircular canals cause motion of the eyes away from the direction of the movement of the head. Thus, when the head stops moving, the resultant reversal in direction of the flow of the current, due to the inertia of motion, will reverse the direction of the eye movements. This accounts for the dizziness, or vertigo, which is the subjective sensation that the world is revolving. It should be noted, however, that this vertigo occurs only after excessive rotation, which definitely cannot be considered a normal stimulation, since the vestibular system is not adapted to compensate for such excesses.

Rotation (Bárány)   (Fig. 12-6)

The patient is placed in a rotary chair with a headrest which enables the head to be fixed in the desired position to bring one particular pair of semicircular canals into play. In order

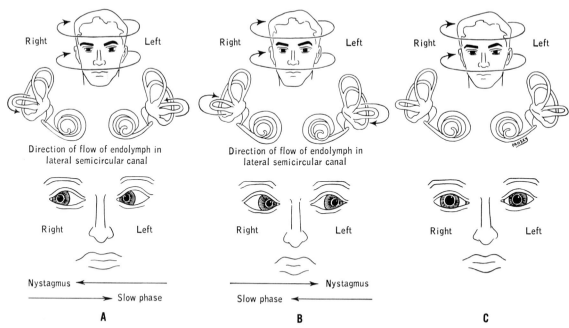

Figure 12-6 Endolymph as related to movements of the eyes. Nystagmus. *A.* Right rotation—acceleration. The endolymph moves from right to left; thus nystagmus is to the right, and the slow phase is to the left. *B.* Right rotation—deceleration. The endolymph moves from left to right; thus nystagmus is to the left, and the slow phase is to the right. *C.* Right rotation—constant velocity. There is no movement of the endolymph and thus no eye movement.

to produce pure horizontal nystagmus, the head is tilted forward about 30°. The chair is then rotated about 10 times quickly in succession. This rotation produces *lymphokinesis*, or motion of the endolymph, in the horizontal canals. At first, the endolymph is displaced in a direction opposite to that in which the canal is moving. This has the effect of causing the eyes to move slowly in a direction opposite to the direction of rotation. When the eyes have reached the limit of movement in this direction, they are quickly snapped back by the cortical fixation reaction. Thus the quick motion, or nystagmus, is in the direction of the rotation. Because the patient is being turned so rapidly, this escapes notice. Gradually, with each successive revolution, the endolymph gathers momentum and begins to move in the direction of the rotation. However, when the chair is suddenly stopped, the momentum of the endolymph causes it to continue to move in the direction of the original movement. Thus, what is seen by the examiner is a horizontal nystagmus in the *direction opposite to the rotation.*

Besides observing nystagmus, one should ask the patient to stand erect, with the eyes closed and the feet together (Romberg position), to note any postural deviations which take the form of falling to one side or the other. Normally, the deviations observed consist of a tendency to fall in a direction opposite to that of the nystagmus. In other words, in *a direction toward the rotation.*

Directional movements of the limbs may also be carried out after the chair has been stopped. The patient is asked to point to the observer's finger, which is held up in front of the patient at such a distance that it can just be reached by the patient's forefinger while the elbow is locked in full extension. The patient is then asked to shut his or her eyes, let the arm fall at the side, and then raise the arm to point at the observer's finger. Deviation *opposite to that of the nystagmus,* in the direction of the rotation, is seen.

Caloric (Fig. 12-7)

In this test, the external auditory meatus is douched with hot (50 to 55°C) or cold (18 to 25°C) water, whereby convection currents are set up in the endolymph. For this purpose, an ordinary ear syringe of 100 ml capacity is sufficient. Three or four syringes in quick succession will generally suffice to elicit a reaction. The great advantage of this test is that it is unilateral; that is, either vestibule can be tested separately, and even one particular semicircular canal can be singled out for examination by placing the head in different positions.

When cold water is introduced into the external meatus, it cools the prominence of the lateral canal, condenses the endolymphatic fluid, and thereby sets up a current downward or toward the back of the head when the patient is lying in the dorsal position (on the back). This flow is thus away from the ampulla of the horizontal canal (ampullofugal), and the eyes are then turned slowly toward the side of the irrigated ear, the movement being alternately interrupted by a quick return movement toward the *contralateral side.* For example, if the cold water is introduced into the right ear, left nystagmus results. With hot water, the prominence is warmed. Thus, the expanding endolymph produces a current toward the ampulla (ampullopetal), which gives rise to a slow turning of the eyes toward the opposite side with a subsequent quick reflex return to the *homolateral side* (Fig. 12-7). For example, with the patient supine, hot water introduced into the right ear causes right nystagmus.[3] It should be noted that the optimal position for eliciting this reaction is the vertical for whatever canal is to be tested. Thus, in order to place the horizontal canal in this plane, the head is inclined backward about 60°,

---

[3]This is according to Ewald's law, which states that the direction of the ocular movements corresponds to the direction of the convection current set up in the semicircular canals.

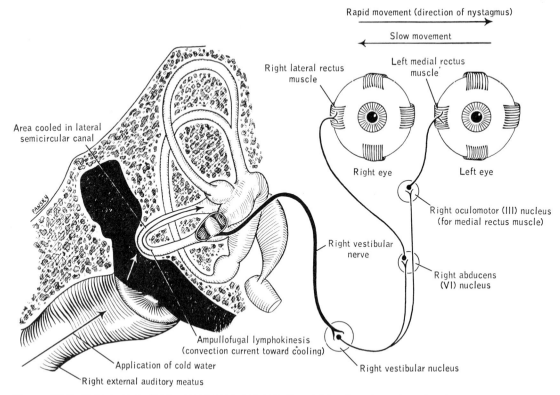

Figure 12-7 Caloric test. Cold water introduced into the right external meatus showing effects opposite to that produced by the introduction of hot water.

which position the head usually assumes when the patient lies on the bed with a small pillow under the back of the head.

If the caloric test is performed in the upright position, the horizontal canal is far removed from the optimal position. For this reason one sees only a faint horizontal nystagmus mixed with a stronger rotatory nystagmus as a result of stimulation of the other two canals, which are now nearly vertical. By changing the position of the head, one can elicit a number of different responses: (1) by introducing cold water into the right ear when the patient is recumbent, one will observe a horizontal nystagmus to the left with past pointing to the right and a slight tendency to fall to the right; (2) by repeating the test with the patient in the sitting position, one will observe a slight nystagmus to the left with much rotatory motion

of the eyes (rotatory nystagmus), a past pointing to the right, and a strong tendency to fall toward the right, due mainly to lymphokinesis in the anterior canal.

Before either of the above-described tests can be applied and before their results can be interpreted, it is necessary to determine whether there is evidence of spontaneous nystagmus, past pointing, or postural deviations. For example, in irritative lesions in the inner ear, along the vestibular nerve, or in certain parts of the cerebellum, all these phenomena may occur, usually with the nystagmus away from the diseased side and the past pointing and tendency to fall toward it. On the other hand, total destruction of the labyrinth on one side may cause the head to decline toward the destroyed vestibule. Furthermore, associated with the spontaneous signs, there may be vertigo, nausea, pallor, and perspiration.

If any of the signs (nystagmus, etc.) appears, it should be ascertained whether any condition exists which could increase the pressure in the middle ear, since vertigo can be caused by such pressure. It is also necessary to be sure that the external auditory meatus is free from obstruction. This is particularly important if the caloric tests are to be used.[4]

It should be obvious that in the rotation tests, both horizontal canals are irritated. However, the canal opposite the side toward which rotation is taking place is being subjected to a more intensive irritation than the other, since it moves through a greater arc. But if one canal is diseased and rotation is set up in the direction toward the diseased side, this side will give a more marked reaction than will the normal side. For example, a spontaneous tendency to fall to the right will be changed to a tendency to fall backward if rotation is toward the right. Of course, in cases where there is a bilateral destruction of the vestibule or its nerve, none of the typical signs appears after rotation.

If the caloric test fails to elicit nystagmus, past pointing, or postural deviations, it can be assumed that a destructive lesion exists on the side being tested.

As a last consideration, an attempt should be made to determine whether the lesion is located peripherally, either in the membranous labyrinth or in the extramedullary course of the vestibular nerve; centrally, within the brainstem; or in the cerebellum.

Concerning the cerebellum, only one point will be made here. The spontaneous nystagmus of cerebellar origin is not altered by changes in position of the head. That of vestibular origin *is* altered by changes in head position.

There are certain definite indications of peripheral lesions. First, because of the close anatomic relations of the auditory and vestibular receptors, together with their afferent neurons, lesions frequently involve hearing, either in the form of buzzing, roaring, or clicking (tinnitus) sounds or by varying degrees of deafness. If the caloric test fails to elicit any response, the lesion is definitely peripheral in location. Lastly, as pointed out previously, peripheral irritative lesions usually produce nystagmus away from the diseased side, together with past pointing and postural deviations toward it. This may be accompanied by episodes of vertigo, nausea, etc.

In case of central lesions, the caloric test elicits past pointing and postural deviations but *no nystagmus.* Further, there is a tendency for the subjective signs, such as vertigo, to be more continuous. However, certain central lesions cause no vertigo and the nystagmus may be coarser and slower, with a tendency to fall toward the normal side. Central disease may also involve other sensory mechanisms or motor apparatus which could not easily be affected by a peripheral lesion.

Specific Pathology

Vertigo is the most characteristic symptom of vestibular disease. Vestibular manifestations may be caused by disease of the labyrinths themselves, the vestibular nerve, the vestibular nuclei, or the supranuclear connections. Vertigo may also, however, be a symptom of general, rather than focal, disease. The labyrinths may be affected by inflammation (Voltolini's disease), hemorrhage, edema, pressure changes, etc. So-called *Ménière's syndrome* is characterized by paroxysmal attacks of vertigo, usually associated with unilateral tinnitus and deafness. It is believed to be due to edema of the labyrinth. Some investigators consider it an inflammatory process or a type of neuralgia affecting the eighth nerve. Other lesions, such as basal or pontine tumors or hemorrhages, can involve either the extra- or intramedullary course of the afferent fibers of the vestibular nerve.

---

[4]Air should be substituted for water if there is evidence of perforated tympanic membranes.

Summary
Special Proprioception

Simple Reflex

Receptor

1. Hair cells in macula of saccule; macula of utricle; cristae of the ampullary region of semicircular canals of inner ear

Afferent neuron

2. Through fibers of vestibular portion of nerve VIII with cells in the vestibular ganglion, into the brainstem to terminate in medial, spinal (descending), superior, or lateral vestibular nuclei

Associaton neuron

3. From medial, spinal, and superior nuclei, fibers ascending and descending on both sides of the brainstem in the MLF, from which terminals are given to cranial nuclei III, IV, and VI and to the ventral gray columns of the spinal cord, in the cervical region

   From the lateral vestibular nucleus, fibers descending via the vestibulospinal tract to the ventral gray columns throughout the cord

Efferent neuron

4. From cranial nuclei III, IV, and VI, fibers passing through their respective nerves to the extrinsic muscles of the eye

   From the ventral gray columns of the cord to skeletal muscles of the neck, trunk, and extremities

Cerebellar Circuit

Direct	Receptor	*Indirect*
1. Same as in simple reflex		1. Same as in simple reflex
2. Same as in simple reflex except that these fibers pass directly to the flocculus and nodulus of the cerebellum (instead of vestibular nuclei)	Afferent neuron	2. Same as in simple reflex except that the termination is in the inferior and medial vestibular nuclei only
3. In this case, the same as above	Ascending cerebellar neuron	3. From the inferior and medial vestibular nuclei, fibers ascending in the juxtarestiform body to end in the flocculus and nodulus
4. From Purkinje cells of the flocculus and nodulus to the fastigial nucleus	Corticonuclear neuron	4. From the cortex (above) to the fastigial nucleus
5. From the fastigial nucleus, through the juxtarestiform body, descending as the fastigiobulbar tract to end in the vestibular nuclei on the same side From the fastigial nucleus, across the midline, to descend in the uncinate fasciculus, terminating in the vestibular nuclei of the opposite side	Descending cerebellar neuron	5. Same as efferent cerebellar neuron in the direct cerebellar circuit

General Somatic Efferent System (GSE)

Early in development, an intimate relation between the primitive nervous system and the premuscle mesoderm (from somites) is established (Chap. 4). This association is maintained throughout development regardless of the distance the muscle tissue may migrate (Fig. 4-14). This is well exemplified by the muscles of the hand or foot, all of which are innervated by nerve fibers whose origins are distant from the muscle. Although it has proved almost impossible to follow the actual course of development, it appears that the muscles of the eye and tongue likewise trace their origins to somites and thus cranial nerves III, IV, VI, and XII can be classified as belonging to the GSE system.

The neurons of this system are multipolar (Chap. 5). The cell bodies of those neurons supplying extrafusal skeletal muscle fibers are large, while those terminating at the polar region of the intrafusal fibers in the muscle spindles (Chap. 11) are much smaller, a fact that is reflected in the size of the axons (Table 13-1). In either case, their many dendrites ramify throughout the gray substance of the ventral horns of the spinal cord or the gray areas of the brainstem. This arrangement makes contacts possible with a variety of other neurons. The single axon of these cells leaves the cord through the ventral roots of spinal nerves or the brainstem through the motor roots of cranial nerves. Their termination is the myoneural junction of skeletal muscle.

When a motor nerve bundle approaches a muscle, it begins to separate into individual

Table 13-1 Classification of Efferent Fibers

Type	Diameter, μm	Conduction, m/s	System
A alpha (α)	12–22	70–120	GS to motor end plates
A gamma (γ)	3–6	15–30	GS to intrafusal fibers
B	<3	3–15	GVE, preganglionic
C	0.3–1.3	0.7–2.3	GVE, postganglionic

fibers. These, in turn, branch repeatedly so that a single nerve fiber may supply many muscle fibers. As each fiber branch nears the muscle, the myelin sheath disappears while the fiber divides into a number of terminal butons (end feet) which are filled with mitochondria and many clear vesicles. The butons fit into a depression of the thickened muscle fiber membrane (sarcolemma) located near the middle of the muscle fiber (Fig. 13-1). This area is the motor end plate. There is a narrow space between the muscle and nerve membranes in this zone. The cleft, which measures 200 to 500 Å in width, is known as the primary synaptic cleft.[1] In addition, the sarcolemma lying beneath the nerve ending is thrown into numerous folds, or palisades, between which are secondary synaptic clefts all opening into the primary space. The side of the buton opposite the end plate is covered by the Schwann cell sheath, as is the distal, unmyelinated portion of the axon. Thus, no part of the nerve is directly exposed to connective tissue. The synaptic clefts contain an electron-dense ground substance which follows the curvature of the palisades. At the periphery of the

[1]So named because it is similar to the cleft found at synapses between neurons.

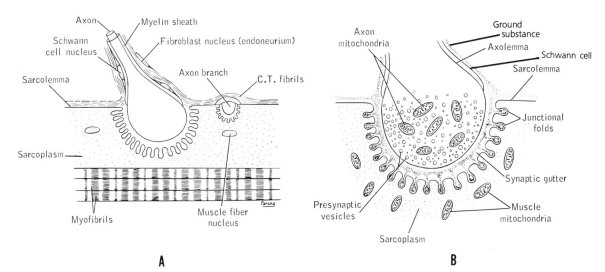

A   B

Figure 13-1 *A.* Diagram of a motor nerve ending on skeletal muscle as observed through the electron microscope. The myelin is seen to end just before the axon reaches the muscle fiber. Schwann cells end at the same point except for "teloglia," which continue onto branches of the axon. Axon branches are seen to lie in invaginations of the sarcolemma known as *synaptic gutters,* or primary synaptic clefts. *B.* Enlarged diagram showing greater details at the synaptic junction. The space between axon and sarcolemma contains an amorphous ground substance.

myoneural junction the ground substance continues upward over the outer surface of the Schwann cells.

The group of muscle fibers which are ultimately supplied by a single nerve fiber through its branchings is called a *motor unit*. There is a considerable difference in the size of these units, depending upon the size of the muscle and especially upon the precision of action of that muscle. Thus, in some of the largest, most powerful muscles, one nerve fiber may supply 200 or more muscle fibers, while in some of the more delicate muscles, the extrinsic ocular group for example, ratios of 1:1 or 1:2 have been reported.

The complete dependence of skeletal muscle upon the integrity of its motor nerve is one of the most striking relationships encountered in the entire human body. Almost immediately upon the loss of its nerve, histologic changes are noted in the muscle. At first, these changes are in the nature of shrinkage, a process which can be reversed when and if new nerve fibers are supplied. Eventually, however, complete atrophy occurs,[2] and the muscle is replaced by connective tissue. In other words, the nerve has a trophic (life-giving) effect upon the muscle. Apparently some substance is transported from the neuron to the muscle fiber. Its exact nature is unknown, but it has been established that it is not the neurotransmitter, for acetylcholine (see below) alone will not sustain a denervated muscle.

Those neurons arising from cells in the brainstem and cord directly supplying the muscles are also known as *lower motor neurons* (for upper motor neuron, see Chaps. 20, 24). Since constant allusion has been made to the synapsing of association neurons from sensory systems with the cell bodies or dendrites of these lower motor or efferent neu-

rons, it should now be clear that impulses arising from many sources can activate this fiber (Fig. 13-2). However, though many systems initiate or modify muscular action in some way, the pathway through which this is accomplished constitutes what is spoken of as a *final common path*.

NEUROMUSCULAR TRANSMISSION

For many years it was believed that the activation of muscle by a nerve was purely an electrical phenomenon. Now, however, it has been shown that stimulation of muscle is basically a matter of chemical transmission, accomplished by the release of acetylcholine (ACh) from the terminal buton of the neuraxon (Chap. 5). As indicated in Chap. 14, this substance is also released at nerve endings in other areas both within and outside the CNS.

It has been observed that there is an active uptake of choline into these motor neurons. Here, the choline, combined with acetyl coenzyme A (acetate) in the presence of the catalyst acetyl transferase (cholineacetylase), forms ACh. Whether this synthesis occurs in the perikaryon and the product is transported down the axon to the end feet or whether the ACh is formed in the buton is not clear. However, regardless of the locus of synthesis, ACh is stored in many clear, electron-lucent vesicles found in the terminals (Figs. 5-25, 13-1).

When an action potential reaches the terminal, there is a coalescence of the vesicles with fusion to the axon membrane. The vesicles then rupture, permitting the release of ACh into the synaptic cleft—the process of exocytosis. It has been shown that Ca^{2+} ions enhance the release of ACh while Mg^{2+} ions tend to suppress the release of this substance.

ACh, free in the cleft, then reacts on the receptor sites of the motor end plate, as described in Chap. 5.

The introduction of the toxic drug *curare*

---

[2]Apparently the rate of atrophy varies in different muscles, and it is thought that the entire process can be reversed at any time up to the point of complete replacement.

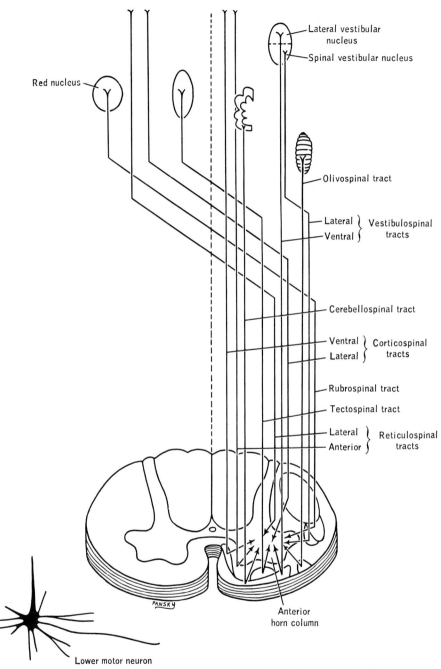

Figure 13-2 Neurons from numerous sources which terminate around, and thus influence, the lower motor neurons of the ventral column of the spinal cord. Illustration of the principle of the final common path.

will produce complete muscle paralysis. This drug either competes for receptor sites with ACh or so combines with these sites as to make a response to ACh impossible.

It should be obvious that normally, after each muscle contraction, there must be a rapid repolarization of the muscle membrane in preparation for subsequent stimulations. Therefore, mechanisms are established to remove ACh (and any excess) once it has produced its effect. These have been indicated elsewhere (Chap. 5). The enzyme needed is acetylcholinesterase (AChE) found in the secondary folds of the motor end plate. It acts through hydrolysis according to the following:

$$ACh + H_2O \xrightarrow{\text{AChE}} choline + acetate$$

The choline thus formed is then reabsorbed into the nerve (Fig. 14-8).

It seems clear from the foregoing that the action of ACh is stimulation. It is, therefore, said to evoke excitatory postsynaptic potential (EPSPs) on the muscle membrane (Chap. 5). Although the action described above occurs in the body musculature, this same substance, together with others, also functions within the CNS as a transmitter from one neuron to another (Chaps. 18, 19).

Certainly no discussion of the motor mechanism would be complete without noting that neurons can be inhibited as well as excited. Thus, many small neurons—interneurons—are found in the gray substance surrounding the motor cells. The axons of these interneurons terminate synaptically on the bodies (soma) of the motor neurons. Such synapses are termed *axosomatic*.[3] These axon terminals release a substance which appears to be the amino acid *glycine* (Fig. 13-3). Another substance released at axon terminals, usually at more cephalic levels in the CNS, is *gamma*

[3]The synapses where EPSPs are evoked are said to occur between the axons of one neuron and the dendrites of another—the *axodendritic type*.

(γ-) *aminobutyrate (GABA)* (Chap. 5). These substances, both glycine and GABA, inhibit the postsynaptic neuron. They evoke inhibitory postsynaptic potentials (IPSPs) (Chap. 5).

SPINAL PATHWAYS

Cell Body

These cells are located in the ventral gray columns of the spinal cord. They tend to be grouped into two major nuclear masses (Fig. 2-5), a *medial mass,* found throughout the length of the cord and thought to supply fibers that go to muscles of the trunk, and a *lateral mass,* found only at the levels of the brachial and lumbosacral plexuses, thus contributing to the girdle musculature and the muscles of the

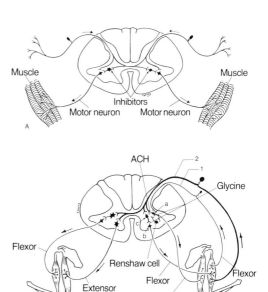

Figure 13-3 *A.* The basic myotatic reflex pattern, showing how the primary afferent neuron activates a motor neuron directly and how, through the intercalated neuron, it may inhibit another motor neuron. *B.* Diagram showing the details of the myotatic apparatus: (1) secondary afferent (B afferent); (2) primary afferent (A afferent); (a) flexor motor neuron; (b) extensor motor neuron; (c) interneuron (intercalary) neuron. Sites for release of ACh and glycine are indicated.

extremities. The medial group is usually sub-divided into ventral and dorsal nuclei. The ventromedial group sends its fibers to the muscles of the back, while the dorsomedial distributes its axons to the intercostal and abdominal muscles. The lateral cell territory is likewise subdivided, the ventrolateral group sending its fibers to the arm or thigh and the dorsolateral to the forearm or leg. At the lower level of each of the plexus enlargements, a third group of cells, called the retrodorsal lateral, is added for the muscles of the hand or foot.

In general, within each of the cell groups of the ventral column at all levels, there is a functional and regional division. The cells in the more ventral portions of the group supply axons to the extensor muscles, while the more dorsally placed cells supply the flexors (Fig. 13-3).

As noted previously, scattered among the larger motor neurons in the ventral gray of the spinal cord (and presumably in cranial GSE nuclei) are the smaller gamma motor neurons. In addition there are the small intercalated neurons—interneurons—whose processes remain within the gray matter on the same side of the CNS. However, their axons pass freely between opposing sets (flexors-extensors) of motor neurons (Fig. 13-3). Among the inter-neurons are the so-called Renshaw cells, whose significance will be discussed later.

Axon

The single axon of the large multipolar motor cells passes in a ventrolateral direction. Be-fore leaving the gray substance of the ventral column, it gives off at least one recurrent collateral which makes a synapse with a neighboring Renshaw cell whose axon, in turn, synapses with the same motor cell which gave origin to the motor axon (Fig. 13-3). The main (chief) axon streams out into the white matter, where it becomes myelinated and emerges from the spinal cord along the ventrolateral

sulcus forming a part of the *ventral root* (Fig. 2-3).

The fine axons from the small motor cells follow the same course but have no collater-als. These are the gamma efferents which terminate on the intrafusal fibers of the muscle spindle (Chap. 11).

At variable distances from the spinal cord all efferent fibers combine with the afferent fibers of the dorsal root to form the spinal nerve trunk (Fig. 13-4). The latter leaves the vertebral column at appropriate levels through intervertebral foramina.

CRANIAL PATHWAYS

In the brainstem, there is also representation of the GSE system. Here, however, the linear continuity of the column is interrupted, the cells being grouped together in four nuclear masses, the axons of which contribute to four different cranial nerves. For this reason, the description which follows will be based upon this division.

Hypoglossal Nerve (XII)

Cell Body

These are aggregated in a nucleus of consider-able length which lies just beneath the floor of the fourth ventricle on either side of the midline. Grossly, location of the nucleus can be distinguished as the hypoglossal trigone (Figs. 1-26, 1-38, 13-5, 25-2 through 25-4). Although the nucleus is slender, it is nearly 2 cm in length, extending rostrally from a little below the olive, nearly to the lower edge of the cochlear nuclei. The cells are similar to those in the ventral gray of the cord.

Axon

The large, single axons of each cell at first stream ventrally through the reticular forma-tion. There is just enough lateral drift so that they bypass the medial lemniscus (Figs. 1-37,

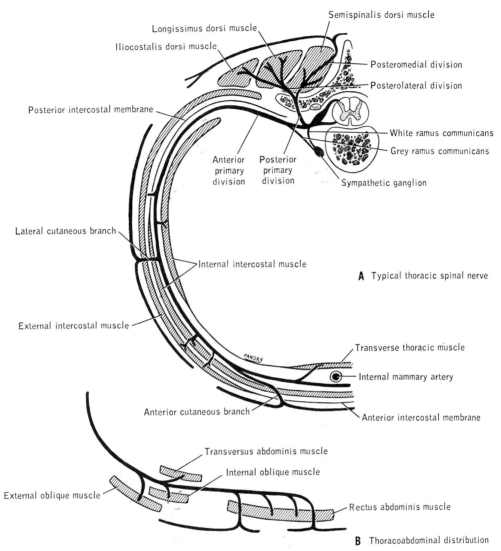

Figure 13-4 Diagram of a typical spinal nerve as demonstrated by a cross section of the body at a midthoracic level.

1-38, 25-2 through 25-4). They turn to pass between the pyramid and the inferior olive, emerging from the side of the medulla in a groove marking the interval between the bulges made by the inferior olivary nucleus and the pyramid (Figs. 1-7, 1-8, 1-37, 1-38, 25-2 through 25-4). The rootlets of the hypoglossal

nerve converge to form the main trunk, the terminations of which lie either in the extrinsic (styloglossus, hyoglossus, and genioglossus) or in the intrinsic muscles of the tongue (Fig. 13-5). Through the action of these muscles, the tongue can be protruded, retracted, or moved from side to side. Such mobility makes the

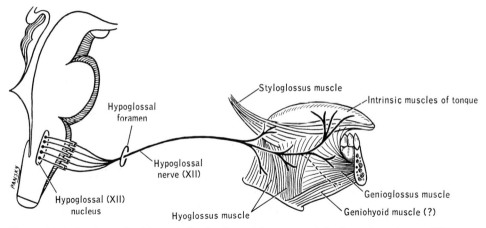

Figure 13-5 Nucleus of origin and distribution of the axons of the hypoglossal nerve (XII).

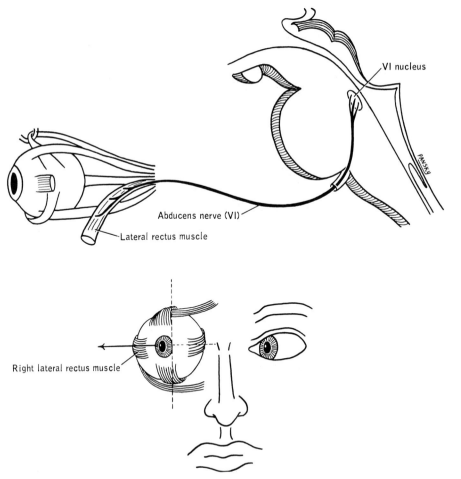

Figure 13-6 Origin and distribution of the abducens nerve (VI).

tongue of inestimable importance in mastication, deglutition, and phonation.

Abducens Nerve (VI) (Fig. 13-6)

Cell Body (Figs. 1-36, 25-7, 25-8)

These are grouped in a small, spherical nucleus located close to the midline in the pons. Because fibers of the facial nerve bend around the nucleus, making a bulge in the floor of the fourth ventricle—the facial colliculus—this nucleus is easily located (Figs. 1-26, 1-27).

Axon (Figs. 1-7, 1-8, 25-8)

The single axons from each cell pass almost directly ventrally near the lateral border of the medial longitudinal fasciculus. At the same time, there is a considerable caudal drift, the fibers emerging from the base of the brainstem in a groove between the pons and the medulla to terminate in the lateral rectus muscle of the eye (Figs. 13-6, 13-7). A contraction of the lateral rectus muscle produces a horizontal turning of the eye toward the side of the head (abduction).

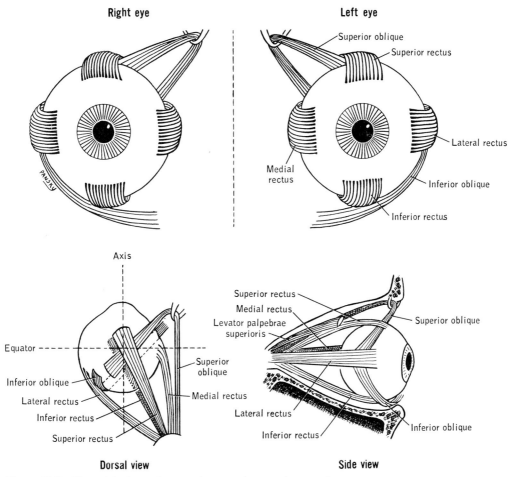

Figure 13-7 The extrinsic ocular muscles seen from various angles.

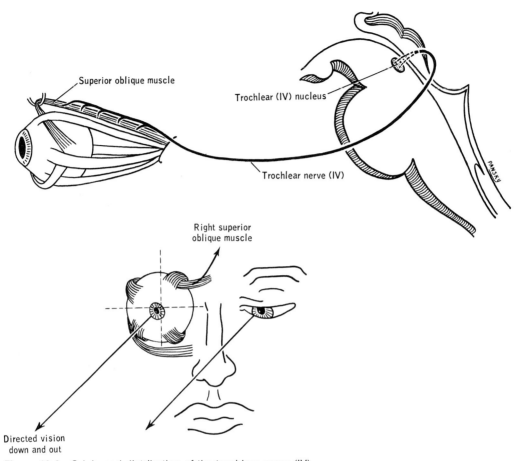

Figure 13-8 Origin and distribution of the trochlear nerve (IV).

Trochlear Nerve (IV) (Fig. 13-8)

Cell Body (Figs. 1-28, 1-34, 25-11)

These cells lie in a small, oval nuclear mass adjoining the midline in the region of the lower mesencephalon, just ventral (anterior) to the cerebral aqueduct at the level of the rostral portion of the inferior colliculus.

Axon (Figs. 25-10, 25-11)

The large single axons from the cells of the nucleus emerge from the dorsolateral aspect of the nucleus and curve dorsally along the border of the central gray substance. At the

same time, there is considerable caudal drift, so that these fibers reach the dorsal side of the brainstem caudal to the inferior colliculus. Here, they enter the anterior medullary velum, decussate, and thus leave the brainstem through its roof (Figs. 1-26, 1-27). These axons, now grouped together as the trochlear nerve (IV), curve ventrally around the lateral aspect of the brainstem and appear at the basal aspect of the brain at the side of the cerebral peduncles. The trochlear nerve terminates in the superior oblique muscle of the eye (Figs. 13-7, 13-8).

Unlike the lateral rectus muscle, which produces movement of the eye in one plane, the superior oblique muscle produces action in more than one plane. It turns the eyeball laterally on its vertical axis (abducts) and downward (depresses) on its horizontal axis.

Oculomotor Nerve (III)

Cell Body   (Figs. 1-28, 13-9, 25-12, 25-13)

These lie in a large nucleus which represents the highest level attained by the GSE column. Since this nerve, unlike nerves IV and VI, supplies five muscles rather than one, its nucleus is large. The oculomotor cell groups lie adjoining the midline and beneath the central gray around the cerebral aqueduct in the rostral mesencephalon. Their lower limits lie near the rostral end of the inferior colliculus. Because of its size and the different muscles it supplies, attempts have been made to divide the nucleus into parts. Roughly, it may be said that the more dorsal cell groups send fibers to the muscles in the superior part of the orbit, the inferior groups innervate the muscles in the floor of the orbit, while the more medial group is concerned with the medial rectus muscle. A part of this group may represent the nucleus of convergence (of Perlia).

Axon   (Figs. 1-7, 1-8, 1-32, 25-12)

They leave the cell bodies in the nucleus and stream almost directly ventrally, cutting through the dorsal tegmental decussation and the medial border of the red nucleus, to emerge from the brainstem along the oculomotor sulcus, into the interpeduncular fossa. Just before reaching the superior orbital fissure through which entry into the orbit is attained, the nerve breaks up into two major branches, a superior, to supply the levator palpebrae and the superior rectus muscles, and an inferior, sending its terminals into the medial rectus, the inferior rectus, and the inferior oblique (Figs. 13-7, 13-9).

Because of the direction of their fibers and the attachments to the eyeball, the superior and inferior recti not only rotate the eye around its horizontal axis, raising (elevating) and lowering (depressing) the bulb, respectively, but they also produce some rotation around the vertical axis. This causes the eye to be turned somewhat inward (adducted). This adductive action (Fig. 13-10) is offset by the superior and inferior obliques, both of which abduct (turn outward) the eyeball in addition to their actions of depression and elevation. Thus the obliques work synergistically with the superior and inferior recti.

STRETCH (MYOTATIC) REFLEX
(Figs. 11-1, 13-3)

This reflex is basic, not only for the maintenance of posture, but also as a background for much of muscular activity. Furthermore, all or parts of the mechanism involved in this reflex are utilized when movement is initiated, controlled, or modified by suprasegmental centers. Thus, a detailed account is essential at this point.

Before considering the actual circuit, several fundamental concepts must be reviewed. First, the maintenance of posture is opposed to gravity. Were it not for a large mass of skeletal muscle referred to as *antigravity*, the body would fall. Second, muscles are arranged around articulations in opposing groups (flexors-extensors; abductors-adductors). When one set of muscles contracts, its opposing set (on the other side of the joint) must relax; otherwise no movement would occur. Third, an afferent neuron from the stretch receptor can directly stimulate a motor neuron. However, branches of this same afferent fiber cannot directly inhibit the neuron of the opposing muscle group since no one afferent neuron can be a stimulator and inhibitor at the same time. This activity must be carried out through an intercalated (interneuron) neuron. Fourth, when tension is placed

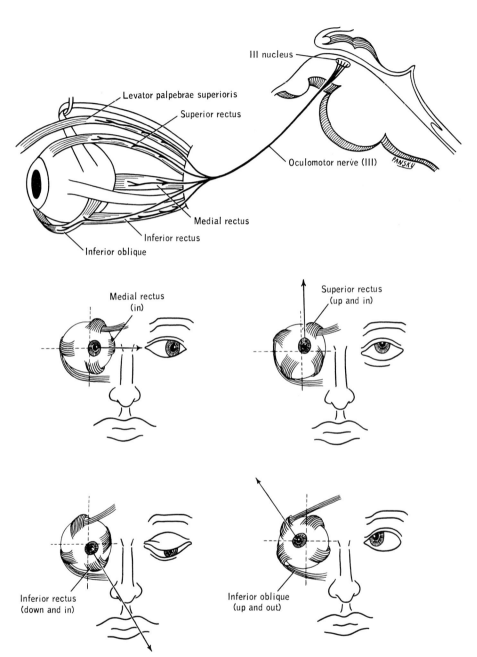

Figure 13-9 Origin and distribution of the oculomotor nerve (III).

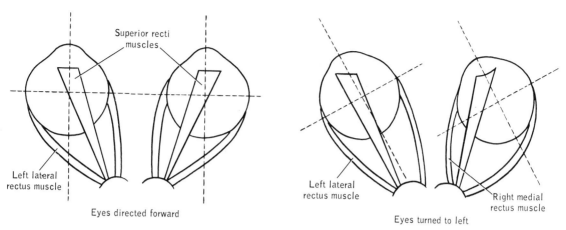

Figure 13-10 Conjugate movement—the synergistic action of the left lateral rectus and right medial rectus muscles.

upon a muscle, usually not all the stretch receptors are fired at the same time. And, fifth, there must be built-in safeguards to prevent the overcontraction of the muscle, as a protection against rupture or evulsion.

With the above facts in mind, let us examine the myotatic reflex as it concerns posture. With the body in the erect position, the force of gravity is trying to pull the body down. Thus, to varying degrees depending upon the location of the antigravity muscle, body weight puts muscle fibers on the stretch. Actually, the pull of but a fraction of an ounce is sufficient to stimulate the annulospiral endings (Chap. 11) which are especially numerous in antigravity muscles. Thus, a volley of impulses passes over the A afferent fibers. Since these make direct synapses on motor cells, a contraction of muscle fibers in the area of the stimulated spindle occurs. When the muscle fiber has contracted, its spindle is no longer stimulated, impulses along the afferent fiber are diminished, and thus the muscle in this area relaxes. Since the set of muscle fibers which has just reacted is refractory, momentarily, to another stimulus, a group of adjoining muscle fibers goes through the same cycle. Thus, an endless series of small group reac-

tions sweeps through the entire muscle. So, in effect, the muscle is in a state of continuous activity, and posture is maintained. However, there is more to it than this, since the opposing muscles must relax. Although the A afferent cannot in itself be activator and suppressor at the same time, it has been shown that some of its telodendria synapse with cells of small intercalated neurons (Fig. 13-3). The axons of the latter travel a short distance to synapse on cells whose axons innervate the flexors. Thus, it is the intercalated neuron which acts as the inhibitor. As a part of this same mechanism, the same afferent neuron sends some of its branches across the cord to come into synaptic relations either directly with motor cells for stimulation or with intercalated neurons for the inhibition of muscular activity on the other side of the body.

It seems obvious that, with an extremely powerful stretch, a muscle might be stimulated into such a powerful contraction that it could be damaged. Theoretically, when a muscle contracts, the annulospiral receptors are no longer activated (stretched), and the muscle should relax from want of an action current. However, there are two other circuits which are involved in the inhibitory mechanism and make possible better control of the extent of muscular contraction. The first of these utilizes the B afferents. These are associated with both the flower spray endings in the muscle spindle and the Golgi tendon endings. The flower sprays are stimulated by a thickening of the intrafusal fiber as the muscle contracts; the tendon receptors are stimulated by the pull of the contracting muscle on its tendon. The central processes of the B afferents terminate directly upon the motor cells responsible for the contraction, thus inhibiting them and leading to relaxation. The second pathway involves the axon collaterals. These arise from the same axons responsible for the muscle contraction. The collaterals synapse with Renshaw cells whose axons terminate upon the same cell which gave rise to the original axon. This depresses the activity of the mother cell (Chap. 5).

Using these same basic patterns, suprasegmental influences can be brought to bear upon the lower motor system. For example, consider the act of picking up some object. This requires the action of the flexors of the forearm (biceps, brachialis, etc.). The descending pathway from the voluntary motor cortex sends terminals into the anterior column to synapse with the cells of the gamma efferents causing a contraction of the polar region of the intrafusal fibers. This, in effect, stretches the bag region of the intrafusal fiber just as though the muscle were being stretched by an extrinsic force. Thus, a stretch reflex is initiated and the flexors contract. However, it is equally important that the extensors (triceps brachii) relax. Therefore, the suprasegmental fiber not only synapses with the neurons for the flexor group but also has connections with interneurons which synapse with the neurons of the extensor group, thus inhibiting the activity of the triceps. The recurrence of the motor axons through the Renshaw cell circuit and the B afferents make possible a modicum of control

over the extent of muscular contraction. Perhaps more important from the point of view of purposeful movement is the fact that the great pool of efferent neurons and interneurons in the ventral horn is open not only to activation by the voluntary cortex but also to other suprasegmental influences which can transform the basic reflex muscle "twitch" into a prolonged action, reinforced, facilitated, or suppressed as the need demands (Chaps. 17 through 20).

POLYSYNAPTIC (WITHDRAWAL) REFLEX

Unlike the monosynaptic reflex, two or more synapses occur between the termination of the afferent neuron and the beginning of the efferent. The number of synapses depends upon the number of interneurons involved.

The stimulus is some noxious substance, most frequently an extreme environmental change leading to tissue destruction (Chap. 7). When such a stimulus is applied, the reaction is one of flexion—a withdrawal of the part involved from the source of the stimulus. Thus, the action potential generated in the afferent neuron evokes EPSPs in one or more interneurons whose axons excite the motor neurons of the flexor muscles. At the same time, the opposing extensors must be relaxed (inhibited). Therefore, the same current in the afferent neuron must stimulate some of the inhibitory interneurons which, in turn, synapse with the extensor motor neurons, thus suppressing their activity.

An event often overlooked concerns what occurs on the side of the body opposite to that receiving the noxious stimulus. If the stimulus is especially strong and, particularly, if applied to the trunk or lower extremity, the contralateral musculature will go into extension to prevent falling to the side or into the source of the stimulus. Thus, the afferent impulse crosses the cord to activate interneurons some of which excite the neurons of the extensors while others inhibit the flexors.

CONJUGATE MOVEMENT

For all animals whose eyes are set in the front of the head, facing forward, it is essential that both eyes move together so that objects under observation can be kept in focus on both retinae at the same time (Fig. 13-10). This is called *conjugate movement.* Such movements are, of course, controlled or influenced by association neurons from many sources in the CNS, at both reflex and voluntary levels. However, the majority of impulses which set off movements of the eye pass to the GSE motor nuclei indirectly through interneurons, the cells of which lie in either the tectum or tegmental reticular formation. Such cell groups are referred to as *centers for conjugate movement,* and it has been suggested that the superior colliculus is concerned with vertical movement, the parabducens nucleus with horizontal movements, and the nucleus of Perlia with convergence.

CLINICAL CONSIDERATIONS

Before one can reasonably expect to understand the clinical examination of this motor system, certain fundamental definitions must be understood.

Definitions

Atrophy

Generally, this means a diminution in size or a wasting away of muscle.

Areflexia

This is a complete absence of all reflexes.

Tone

All muscle, even when in an essentially resting stage, has a certain amount of normal tension, which is actually a constant and extremely low-grade contraction.

Atonia

A condition in which muscle tone is absent.

Spasm

This is almost the exact opposite of atonia, for here there is a strong, involuntary contraction of a muscle or group of muscles. This may be persistent, in which case it is a *tonic spasm,* or it may alternate with periods of relaxation, in which case it is called a *clonic spasm.*

Paralysis

In general, this merely means loss or impairment of motor function because of lesions in the neural or muscular mechanism. This chapter is concerned primarily with the neural part. Usually, two types are dealt with: The first is a *flaccid* paralysis, characterized by atonia, areflexia, and, later, atrophy. The second type is a *spastic* paralysis, characterized by increased tone *(hypertonia),* increased deep-tendon reflexes *(hyperreflexia),* and absent superficial (cremasteric and abdominal) reflexes.

Diplopia

This is double vision, in which a single object appears to be two.

Testing

As in all other diagnoses, it is important to check the case history carefully for evidence of disease or injury. Frequently, important clues are furnished through careful questioning.

A general superficial inspection is made for physical evidence of trauma, either recent, as indicated by a fresh wound, or old, as evidenced by scars. Wasted or shrunken areas should be looked for, since damage to or interruption of lower motor neurons leads to the atrophy of the muscles supplied.

The extremities are bent by the examiner to determine muscle tone and resistance to passive movement (Chap. 17). Tendons are also tapped at certain points to see if reflexes occur (Chap. 11). Both atonia and areflexia are evidence of lower motor neuron defects (flaccid paralysis) and may be apparent long before muscle atrophy is evident. The patient is asked to protrude the tongue. If it deviates toward one side, there is a lesion of the hypoglossal mechanism on the side *toward* which the deviation occurs. This is because of the action of the unopposed muscles, such as the genioglossus, which is normally contracting and which, being the muscle of protrusion, pushes the tongue to the weakened side.

The eye movements must be checked, first by observing the eyes when the patient is directed to look straight ahead, and then by having the patient attempt to follow a slowly moving object, with both eyes open and the head stationary. Since opposing muscles exert a tonic pull, the eye, at rest, will automatically be deviated away from the side of any paralyzed muscle. On the other hand, the eye cannot be turned in the direction of a paralyzed muscle. Usually when attempting to look toward the affected side, the patient experiences diplopia (double vision).

General Pathology

Tumors

These may occur either inside the CNS (intramedullary) or outside at any point along the course of a nerve (extramedullary). Thus, they may destroy a nucleus or the fibers going to or coming from it.

Trauma

This could be of different sorts and might occur in any location. There may be a direct penetrating agent (a knife or bullet) which could damage cells of origin or cut nerve fibers. Damage may also result from traumatized surrounding tissues, such as fragments from broken bones.

Vascular accidents

Spontaneous rupture or occlusions of arterial vessels lead to severe neurologic impairment due to interruptions of vital blood supply. Nervous tissue is especially vulnerable to deficits in circulation.

Pressure

This may be applied to nerves or their nuclei in various ways: (1) increases in intracranial pressure; (2) clots, as from meningeal hemorrhages; (3) displaced parts, as in herniated intervertebral disks; (4) arterial aneurysms (abnormal regional dilatations). In such cases the symptoms are often temporary and will disappear when the cause is removed.

Denervation

Many of the pathologic conditions mentioned in this section involve the destruction of somatic efferent neurons. The structural changes in muscle resulting from denervation have already been mentioned. A physiologic phenomenon, *denervation hypersensitivity,* is also observed. For reasons presently not clear, sites other than the end plate region become reactive to ACh. In fact, the entire muscle membrane may respond. Thus, any ACh present which makes contact with any part of the muscle may cause a muscle contraction. This will even be accentuated by a lack of AChE, since this enzyme is not normally found along the muscle fiber.

Specific Pathology

Poliomyelitis

This is a condition in which a virus attacks nerve cell bodies. A variable number of cells are killed, and this leads to the complete atrophy of all muscle fibers supplied by the axon of the dead cell. At the onset, however, spasticity of the muscles or increased resistance to passive movement is observed. This is probably because of irritation of the anterior gray column cells. However, as the toxic effect of the virus finally overwhelms these cells, flaccidity appears. At this time, many cells are attacked and their axons become nonfunctional. Eventually, some of the cells do recover. Thus, muscles which at first appear to be completely paralyzed may return to partial function.

In the bulbar type of poliomyelitis, the gray matter of the medulla is affected, with the result that vital functions, including respiration, are interfered with.

Myasthenia Gravis

This is a syndrome of fatigue and exhaustion of the muscular system marked by progressive paralysis without sensory disturbance. It can affect any muscle of the body, but the muscles of the face, lips, tongue, throat, and neck are especially selected by this condition.

Normally, ACh is released at the myoneural junction in sufficient quantity to produce a muscle response. Any residue or excess of ACh is destroyed by cholinesterase (AChE). In myesthenia there may be (1) an inadequate amount of ACh, (2) a too rapid hydrolysis of ACh by AChE, (3) a reduction in the number of end plates, (4) some interference with the process by which ACh reaches and acts upon the end plate. Since *prostigmine* and *neostigmine* apparently protect ACh (they are anticholinesterases), these drugs may be used in the treatment of this disease. In fact, prostigmine may be used in the diagnosis of myasthenia. When employed for this purpose, 2 or 3 ml of a 1:2000 solution (with 1/150 gr atropine) is injected intramuscularly. If the muscle weakness improves in $1/2$ to $3/4$ h and actually disappears altogether in 2 h, the indications are that myasthenia gravis is present.

Erb's Palsy

This is sometimes called *upper trunk palsy* and is usually due to injury incurred at birth in which the fifth and usually the sixth cervical nerves are broken as their roots emerge from the cord. This leads to flaccid paralysis and atrophy of all the muscles supplied by these nerves. The condition is particularly evident in such muscles as the upper serratus anterior and rhomboids, innervated by the long thoracic and dorsal scapular nerves, respectively. This leads to winged scapula. The deltoid muscle, innervated by the axillary nerve, will also be affected; this is indicated by the loss of roundness of the shoulder.

Syringomyelia

This condition has already been described (Chap. 7) insofar as it involves the sensory mechanism. However, since it results from a gross enlargement of the central canal of the spinal cord, it can increase in diameter to such an extent that it encroaches upon the ventral horns, thus destroying motor neurons locally in the region of the enlargement. This will lead to bilateral flaccid paralysis of the muscles supplied by the nerves arising from the cord in this area.

Weber's Syndrome (Crossed Oculomotor Paralysis) (Fig. 13-11)

In this case, the lesion occurs along the side of the interpeduncular fossa. In such a position the emerging fibers of the oculomotor nerve (III) together with the medial portion of the cerebral peduncle will be destroyed. This results in the complete paralysis of all muscles supplied by the oculomotor nerve, leaving the superior oblique and lateral rectus muscles (nerves IV and VI) unopposed. Thus, the eye on the affected side will be directed laterally and downward. Since the motor fibers for pupillary constriction, both to light and accommodation, travel in this nerve, there will

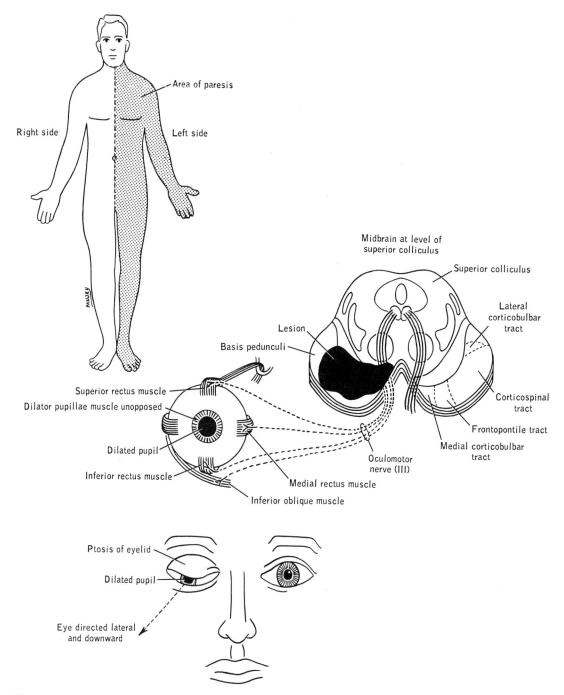

Figure 13-11 Weber's syndrome.

be failure of closure of the pupil. Because of involvement of the basis pedunculi there is also a contralateral paresis of the lower face, tongue, and extremities.

Hemiplegia Alternans Hypoglossica

This condition results from a lesion either at the surface of the medulla, involving the emerging fibers of nerve XII and the pyramids, or within the medulla, catching the hypoglossal fibers in their intramedullary course and the pyramids as well. A paralysis of the tongue occurs on the affected side, since the tongue musculature is deprived of its innervation. When protruded, the tongue points toward the side of the lesion. Because of the inclusion of the pyramid in the lesion, above the decussation, spastic paralysis will occur in the muscles of the opposite side of the body.

Summary
General Somatic Efferent

Spinal		Cranial
1. In the somatic efferent column of the spinal cord Ventral gray column throughout the length of the cord Medial group – throughout the length of the cord Dorsal division Ventral division Lateral group – only in region of brachial and lumbosacral plexuses Retrodorsal division Dorsal division Ventral division Central group – midcervical and sacral levels	Cell body	1. In somatic efferent column of the brainstem Oculomotor nucleus in middle and upper mesencephalon: Dorsal group Ventral group Medial group Trochlear nucleus (IV) in lower mesencephalon Abducens nucleus (VI) in pons Hypoglossal nucleus (XII) in medulla
2. Through the somatic efferent components of all spinal nerves From medical group: Dorsal division – to intercostal and abdominal muscles Ventral division – to axial muscles From lateral group: Retrodorsal division – to muscles of hand and foot Dorsal division – to muscles of forearm and leg Ventral division – to muscles of arm and thigh From central group – to muscles of diaphragm	Efferent fiber	2. Through somatic efferent components of corresponding cranial nerves Through oculomotor nerve (III): From dorsal group to superior rectus muscle of the eye and the levator palpebrae of the upper lid From the ventral group to the inferior rectus and inferior oblique muscles of the eye From the medial group to the medial rectus muscle of the eye Through the trochlear nerve (IV) to the superior oblique muscle of the eye Through the abducens nerve (VI) to the lateral rectus muscle of the eye Through the hypoglossal nerve (XII) to the muscles of the tongue
3. All motor end plates of the muscles of neck, trunk, and extremities derived from somites	Termination	3. All in motor end plates of skeletal muscles, indicated above, derived from somites

Chapter 14

General Visceral Efferent System (GVE) (Autonomic System)[1]

This is the motor system which regulates the organs (viscera) of the body. It includes the control of all smooth (involuntary) muscle, cardiac muscle, and glands.

Certain fundamental features concerning its structure and function must be pointed out. (1) In general, most viscera are supplied by two opposing sets of fibers, one stimulating, the other inhibiting activity. (2) Both the stimulating and inhibiting mechanisms require a two-neuron chain between the nucleus of origin in the CNS and the peripheral organ which is innervated (Fig. 14-1). This necessitates a synapse between the two neurons which occurs in ganglia outside the CNS. Using the ganglion as a point of reference, the fiber lying closest to

the brain or cord is called *preganglionic* (presynaptic might be more appropriate). The second fiber, the cell of origin of which lies in one of the ganglia and which carries impulses to an organ, is called *postganglionic* (or postsynaptic). (3) The cells are of the multipolar type, but they are small. Within the CNS, the cells are located either in the *intermediolateral cell column of the cord* or in nuclei in the brainstem. (4) The termination of the visceral fibers is peculiar. In the organs, fine nerve terminals end in small knobs in contact with a muscle fiber or gland cell, but not all the cells or fibers receive such endings. In fact, the vast majority do not receive any direct nerve terminals. However, it should be noted that, after entering a mass of smooth muscle, the axons of postganglionic fibers develop a series of small beadlike enlargements which come into junctional relation with a number of muscle fibers

[1]The term *autonomic,* freely interpreted, means autonomous—having independent functions, or self-controlling. In other words, it regulates visceral function automatically, without cerebral control.

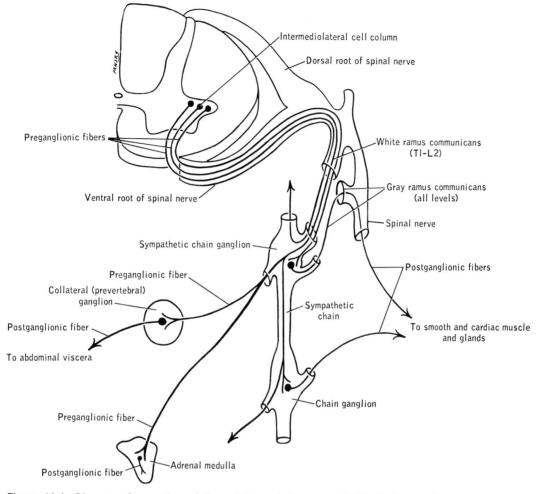

Figure 14-1 Diagram of a section of the spinal cord, two sympathetic chain ganglia, a collateral ganglion, a terminal ganglion, and the connecting nerves to show the distribution of pre- and postganglionic fibers.

located along the course of the nerve. This is the so-called synapse *en passant.*

It has already been suggested (Chaps. 5, 13) that a substance, acetylcholine, is formed at the terminals of somatic efferent fibers and that this substance initiates muscle activity. In the visceral system, such a mechanism is especially necessary, since relatively few cells or fibers actually receive a nerve ending. Thus, large amounts of chemical substances form at the nerve terminals. These pass through the tissue fluids and even through the bloodstream

to reach and thus act upon other cells. Since this is a liquid substance which spreads out from its source, the term *humoral mediation* has been applied to the mechanism.

It is usual to divide the general visceral efferent system into two major portions, based upon the origin of the preganglionic fibers from the CNS. The preganglionic fibers arising from the thoracic and lumbar spinal cord are referred to as the *thoracolumbar* division, or *sympathetic.* The preganglionic fibers originating either in certain cranial nerve nuclei or the sacral cord are referred to as the *craniosacral division,* frequently called *parasympathetic.*

The ganglia of the thoracolumbar (sympathetic) outflow are located opposite each spinal segment[2] lying adjacent to the lateral side of the bodies of the vertebrae. These ganglia are all interconnected by longitudinal fibers, thus forming a continuous chain. The ganglia are termed *chain,* or *paravertebral, ganglia.* The thoracic portion of the chain is continued rostrally into the neck as the cervical sympathetic trunk. Only three ganglia are associated with the latter: the *superior, middle,* and *inferior cervical ganglia.* The lumbar portion of the trunk is continued caudally as far as the coccyx.

TYPES OF VISCERAL CONTROL

1 On-Off This is best illustrated by the control of the caliber of blood vessels in many of the viscera and in the skin. Here, only sympathetic fibers reach the smooth muscle. Thus, the caliber is dependent solely upon the activity of this part of the system. When there is great activity, the vessel decreases in diameter.

2 Reciprocal In this instance there are two separate sets of smooth muscle associated with a particular organ—one set innervated by the sympathetic division and the other by the parasympathetic. This situation is found in the iris of the eye, where the dilator pupillae receives sympathetic fibers while the sphincter pupillae is innervated by the parasympathetic fibers. The former is responsible for the dilation of the pupil, while the latter causes constriction thereof.

3 Antagonistic Here, the same muscle mass receives fibers from both divisions of the

autonomic system, one being excitatory while the other is inhibitory. This situation is found in the heart, where sympathetic fibers excite (increase heart rate) and the parasympathetic inhibit (slow heart rate) cardiac muscle.

THORACOLUMBAR DIVISION

Structure

Preganglionic Neuron

The cell bodies are small and multipolar, located in the intermediolateral column of the thoracic and upper lumbar cord (Fig. 2-5). Axons leave this column, pass ventrally through the gray substance, and cross the anterior funiculus (white matter), where they pick up myelin. They emerge from the cord together with the somatic efferents to become a part of the ventral root. (These preganglionic fibers are type B, myelinated.) They travel in the latter to just beyond the point where the dorsal and ventral roots join to form the spinal nerve trunk. There, the visceral efferents leave the trunk as *white rami communicantes.* After a short distance, the white rami enter the thoracic or lumbar sympathetic trunk. On reaching the sympathetic trunk in the region of the nearest chain ganglion, the fibers in the white ramus may do one of several things: terminate by synapse with a cell or cells in the chain ganglion at the level of entry; pass up or down in the trunk to synapse in one of the chain ganglia above or below the point of entry; pass rostrally through the chain into the cervical sympathetic trunk, many traveling all the way to the superior ganglion before terminating; or pass transversely through the thoracic trunk, forming special nerves which run ventrocaudally to terminate in ganglia which lie in front of the vertebral column. The latter fibers form the *splanchnic nerves* (Figs. 14-2, 14-3), and the ganglia in which they terminate belong to the class of *prevertebral ganglia* (Figs. 14-1 through 14-3). Some of the fibers running in the splanchnic nerves pass on

---

[2]Due to secondary fusions or atypical migrations of neural crest material during development, there may not be a regular 1:1 relationship between ganglia and spinal segments.

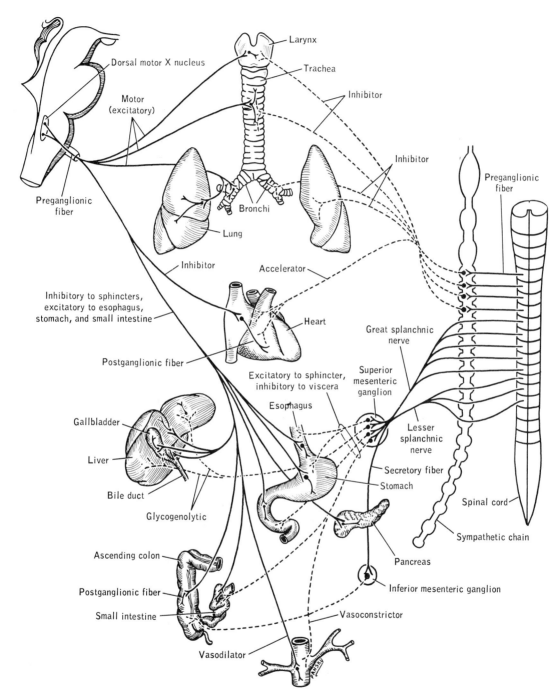

Figure 14-2 Diagram of the autonomic nerve supply to the thoracic and abdominal viscera. Dotted lines, postganglionic fibers of the thoracolumbar outflow. The postganglionic fibers of the craniosacral outflow are represented by short solid lines, usually in or on the walls of the structures innervated. Some functional values have also been assigned to some of the fibers shown.

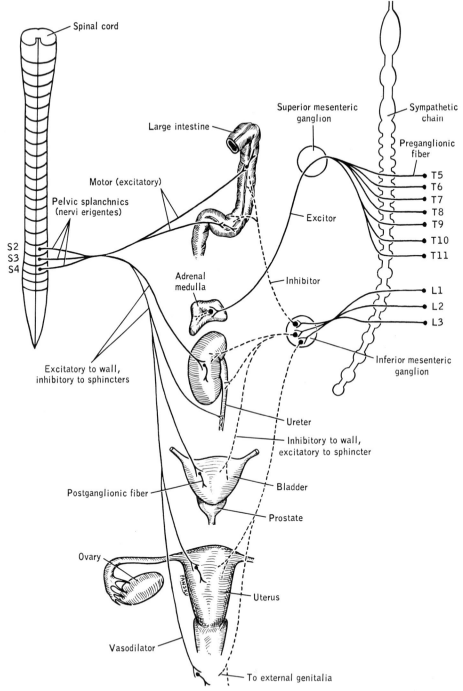

Figure 14-3 Diagram of the autonomic nerve supply to the viscera of the lower abdomen and pelvis. Dotted lines, postganglionic fibers of the thoracolumbar outflow. The postganglionic fibers of the craniosacral outflow are indicated by short solid lines, usually in or on the walls of the structures innervated. Some functional values have been assigned to some of the fibers shown.

through the ganglia to end in the adrenal medulla. It should be emphasized that a fiber may pass through many ganglia but will synapse in only one.

Postganglionic Neuron   (Figs. 14-1 through 14-3)

The small multipolar cells are located in any one of the following ganglia which serve as synaptic stations between pre- and postganglionic fibers: the paravertebrals (including three cervical ganglia, the thoracic or lumbar chain ganglia), or the prevertebrals (including the celiac ganglia and its subdivisions).

Most axons arising from the chain ganglia reenter the spinal nerve trunk by way of *gray rami communicantes* (these are type C, unmyelinated fibers). Such rami leave the sympathetic trunk at all levels to join spinal nerves regardless of whether or not a white ramus is present. These postganglionic fibers then travel with the nerve and follow all its branchings and ramifications to terminate in the walls of peripheral blood vessels, in sweat glands, and in the erector muscles of the hair.

In the upper thorax, some of the postganglionic fibers pass medially to supply the bronchi and lungs.

From the cervical ganglia many descend to form the cardiac nerves to the heart.

From the superior cervical ganglion, most of the postganglionic fibers ascend along the branches of the carotid artery to reach the walls of the vessels of the head, sweat glands of the face, erector muscles of the hair, salivary glands, and dilator muscles of the pupil (Figs. 14-4 through 14-6).

From the celiac or other prevertebral ganglia, the axons follow the branching of the mesenteric blood vessels, sending fibers into their walls and into the muscular coats of all the viscera.

General Function

No hard-and-fast rule can be made regarding the manner in which this division of the autonomic system will act. Its activity is determined by the individuality of the organ supplied. However, two general concepts help in predicting what the reaction is to be: First, the discharge of impulses over this system is associated with expenditure of energy. The second point, closely related to the first, concerns the idea that thoracolumbar outflow is an emergency mechanism.

Since most crises are physical in nature, it is necessary to marshal all possible reactions of the body which would help to meet these forces. First, there must be a release of energy-supplying substances into the bloodstream. This is accomplished by glycogenolysis in the liver. Second, there must then be an increase in blood supply to carry energy materials and oxygen to skeletal muscles and to carry away the increased waste resulting from their activity. The stepped-up circulation is accomplished by heart rate acceleration with accompanying constriction of peripheral and mesenteric blood vessels. Third, an increase in circulating oxygen and a means of disposing of excess carbon dioxide from the blood are necessary; these changes are aided by an increase in the diameter of the air passages.

Concomitant with the above-mentioned reactions it is important to suppress any energy-consuming activity during the time of emergency. Thus, secretion of glands and the contraction of visceral muscles are inhibited.

It is obvious from the foregoing that since the entire body economy is involved, the effects of this system must be widespread. This far-reaching influence is effected in several ways: First, the cells of origin of the system cover a large and physically continuous column. Next, there is usually a ratio of 1 preganglionic fiber to 20 postganglionic. Thus there is a divergence of output from this system. Further, the humors at its axon terminals are readily transmitted through the tissues and even the bloodstream without destruction by enzymatic action. Lastly, impulses flowing through some preganglionic fibers en-

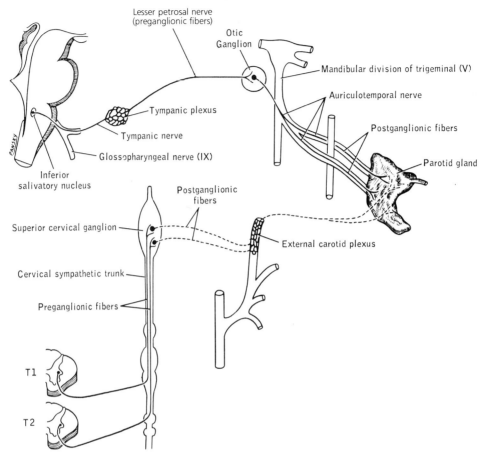

Figure 14-4 Cranial autonomic nerves, with special emphasis on the connections of the otic ganglion, chiefly through cranial nerve IX and the superior cervical sympathetic ganglion. Dotted lines, postganglionic fibers of the thoracolumbar outflow.

ter the adrenal medulla, which secretes a hormone, *epinephrine,* in response to stimulation.

Specific Reactions

In the light of the foregoing discussion of general functions, it seems appropriate to enumerate some of the specific reactions which occur as a result of the activation of the thoracolumbar mechanism.

Pupil of the Eye

The pupils widen because of excitation of the dilator pupillae muscle (Fig. 14-6).

Blood Pressure

This is *elevated* through two methods: (1) constriction of the peripheral (skin) and visceral arteries; (2) cardiac acceleration.

Cardiac Rate

This is greatly *increased* (Fig. 14-2).

Visceral Musculature

Its activity is *inhibited,* accounting in part for "sour stomach" if a crisis occurs immediately after eating (Fig. 14-2).

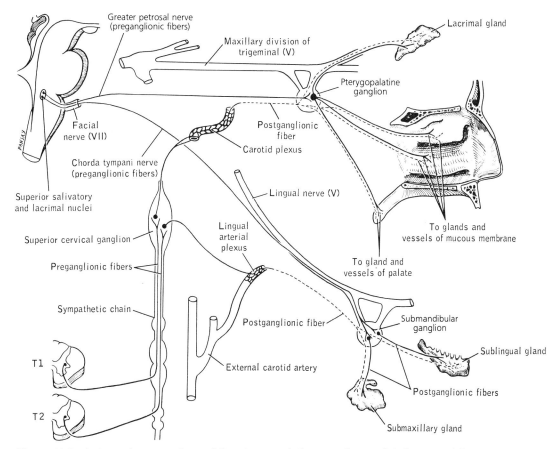

Figure 14-5 Autonomic connections of the pterygopalatine ganglion, mainly from cranial nerve VII and the superior cervical ganglion. Dotted lines, postganglionic fibers of the thoracolumbar outflow.

External Sphincters

Their function is *activated.* Thus, the sphincters are closed more tightly (Figs. 14-2, 14-3).

Salivary and Digestive Glands

Their activity is *inhibited.* This accounts for dryness of the mouth, so often encountered, and also, in part, for indigestion when emergencies arise after eating (Figs. 14-4, 14-5). It is likely that the inhibition of glandular activity is not brought about by a direct influence on the gland cells themselves but through the constriction of blood vessels which supply the glandular alveoli.

Adrenal Medulla

Its cells are *activated.* Epinephrine is poured into the bloodstream, enhancing and reinforcing all the activities just mentioned. In addition, it is responsible for the release of glycogen from the liver, the material necessary to furnish energy for muscle contractions (Fig. 14-3).

CRANIOSACRAL DIVISION

Although cell aggregates (nuclei) of this division occupy a portion typical for the visceral

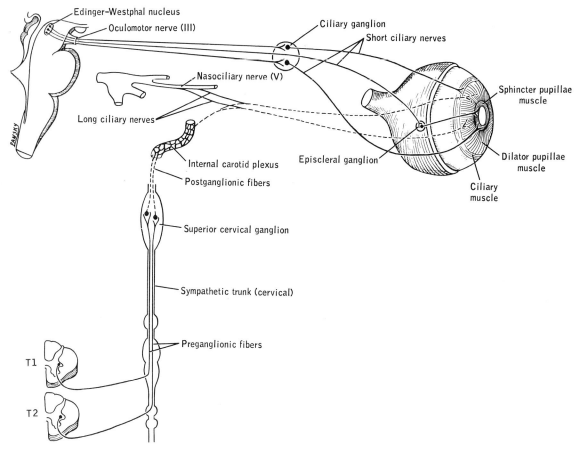

Figure 14-6 Autonomic connections of the ciliary and episcleral ganglia through the oculomotor nerve (III) and the superior cervical ganglion. Dotted lines, postganglion fibers of the thoracolumbar outflow.

efferent system in the CNS, the column is interrupted in many places. Even in the brainstem, where much of the division's concentration occurs, there are considerable gaps between cell groups (Fig. 14-7). For example, the distance between the nucleus of the vagus, the most caudal portion of the cranial outflow, and the second sacral segment of the cord, is enormous. Because of the discontinuity of both nuclei and the nerves in which the fibers run, it is necessary to describe the cranial and sacral parts individually.

Cranial Outflow

Preganglionic Neuron

Edinger-Westphal (EW) Nucleus (Figs. 14-6, 14-7)   The small cells of this group are located in the mesencephalon, where they cap the rostral end of the oculomotor (III) nucleus with some cells lying dorsal and somewhat lateral to the latter nucleus. From the Edinger-Westphal nucleus, axons pass ventrally, join fibers of the GSE system arising from the oculomotor nucleus, and follow their

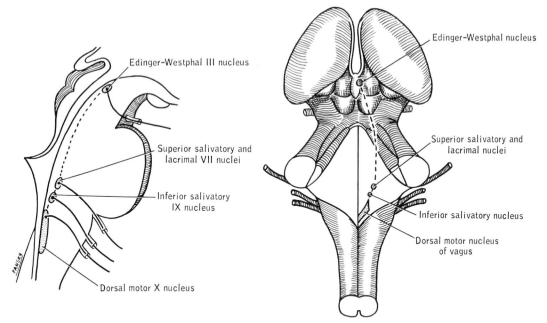

Figure 14-7 Diagram of the cranial nuclear column of the GVE system. *Left,* lateral view; *right,* dorsal view.

course. On entering the orbit, the visceral fibers which are included in the inferior ramus of cranial nerve III, leave that ramus to form the short (motor) root of the ciliary ganglion within which the preganglionic fibers terminate.

Superior Salivatory (and Lacrimal) Nucleus (Figs. 14-5, 14-7)   This is a small group of cells the exact position of which is in some doubt. It apparently lies in the junctional zone between the medulla and pons,[3] in line (longitudinally) with the dorsal motor nucleus of the vagus nerve and a short distance rostral to the latter. Although the presence of a *lacrimal nucleus* has not been definitely established, some of the more rostral neurons of the superior salivatory nucleus may be especially

[3]According to some investigators, it lies in the lateral reticular formation close to the end of the nucleus ambiguus. However, this would seem to be too far lateral.

concerned with the secretion of tears. In any case, axons from this nuclear complex pass ventrocaudally to accompany the SVE fibers of cranial nerve VII with which they travel to the periphery of the brainstem. Here they are joined by incoming afferent fibers. The visceral efferents together with the sensory fibers combine to form the *nervus intermedius,* which lies along the medial side of the large motor root of the facial nerve.

Some of the autonomic fibers, including those from the lacrimal nucleus, leave the facial nerve just beyond the geniculate ganglion and continue rostrally as the *greater petrosal nerve.* The latter emerges from the petrous temporal bone through the hiatus of the facial canal. It crosses the foramen lacerum and is joined by the fibers of the *deep petrosal nerve* to form the *nerve of the pterygoid canal (Vidian).* This nerve then enters the pterygopalatine fossa where the preganglionic parasympathetic fibers enter the pterygopalatine ganglion to synapse with the postganglionic neurons.

The remainder of the autonomic fibers continue in nerve VII throughout most of the facial canal. Then, just above the stylomastoid foramen, visceral efferents leave the facial nerve in company with the SVA fibers to form the *chorda tympani nerve.* The latter curves upward and then forward, crosses the lateral wall of the middle ear, and exits from the temporal bone through the petrotympanic fissure. It then curves downward and forward to unite with the lingual nerve, a branch of the mandibular division of the trigeminal (V). As the lingual nerve bends rostrally just above the submandibular gland, the preganglionic parasympathetic fibers leave that nerve to synapse in the *submandibular ganglion.*

Inferior Salivatory Nucleus   (Figs. 14-4, 14-7)   This is often considered to be the caudal end of the superior salivatory nucleus. Axons from these cells pass ventrocaudally to join the SVE fibers of the glossopharyngeal nerve (IX). They remain in the latter nerve until just below the jugular foramen, where nerve IX exits from the skull. Here the autonomic fibers leave the trunk of the glossopharyngeal to form the *tympanic nerve* (of Jacobson), which then enters the floor of the middle ear. On the medial wall of the middle ear the tympanic nerve breaks up into a plexiform arrangement known as the *tympanic plexus.* Superiorly, the fibers of the plexus recombine into a single nerve known as the *lesser petrosal.* The latter then passes upward and then forward to reach the otic ganglion, where the preganglionic parasympathetic fibers synapse with postganglionic neurons.

Dorsal Motor Nucleus of the Vagus   (Figs. 14-2, 14-7, 25-2 through 25-4)   This large group of cells extends from near the medulla-pons junction caudally to the level of the pyramidal decussation. It lies just beneath the floor of the fourth ventricle, parallel to and

along the lateral side of the hypoglossal nucleus (XII). Axons pass ventrocaudally to accompany the SVE fibers of the vagus. The vagus leaves the skull by way of the jugular foramen and continues caudally through the neck and thorax and into the abdomen. Along the way, preganglionic fibers leave the nerve trunk to synapse in terminal ganglia located in or on the walls of the viscera being innervated.

Postganglionic Neuron

The cell bodies of these neurons lie in the ganglia named above.

Ciliary Ganglion   (Fig. 14-7)   The *short ciliary nerves* pass forward from the ganglion to reach the eyeball. The nerve fibers pierce the sclera and extend rostrally to innervate the *ciliary* and *sphincter pupillae* muscles. The sphincter functions mainly in reflex reactions to light, while the ciliary muscle is concerned with accommodation to near vision.

Pterygopalatine Ganglion   (Fig. 14-6)   From this ganglion some postganglionic fibers join the maxillary division of the trigeminal nerve. They continue in the *zygomatic* branch of the latter and finally diverge from the zygomatic nerve to enter the *lacrimal* branch of the ophthalmic division of the trigeminal. They remain in the lacrimal nerve to the front of the orbit, where they enter the substance of the *lacrimal gland.* These fibers stimulate secretion of the gland. Other postganglionic fibers accompany the *nasal* and *palatine nerves* to supply the *glands* in the *mucous membranes of the nose and palate.*

Submandibular Ganglion   The postganglionic fibers here are short and they almost immediately enter the substance of the submandibular and sublingual glands, where they terminate around some of the serous cells.

Otic Ganglion   (Fig. 14-4)   The postganglionic fibers leave the ganglion by two small twigs which join both roots of the *auriculotemporal branch of the mandibular division of nerve V*. This nerve then carries the autonomic fibers in its upward course. As it passes the parotid gland, the autonomic postganglionic fibers leave the main nerve trunk and enter the parotid gland among the serous acinar cells. It should be recalled that the sympathetic postganglionic fibers terminate around the smooth muscle of the blood vessels and thus inhibit secretion of the gland by vasoconstriction.

Terminal Ganglia From these, the postganglionic fibers tend to be very short. To the sphincter pupillae, they represent axons from *episcleral ganglion* (Fig. 14-6). These are the fibers said to subserve the reflex constriction of the pupil in near vision (accommodation). For the heart and lungs, fibers arise from ganglion cells lying upon the heart wall and bronchi (the cardiac and pulmonary plexuses, respectively) (Fig. 14-2). In the viscera of the alimentary tract, they lie entirely within the walls of the viscera (Fig. 14-2). One group of ganglion cells lies in the connective tissue between the smooth muscle coats. This is called *Auerbach's (myenteric) plexus*. The postganglionic fibers arising here supply the smooth muscles. Another group of ganglion cells lies in the submucous coat. This is *Meissner's (submucosal) plexus*. Its fibers (postganglionic) supply the glands of the tract.

Sacral Outflow

Structure

Cells of the Preganglionic Fibers (Fig. 14-3) The cells of this portion of the system lie in the intermediolateral cell column of the spinal cord at the second, third, and fourth sacral segments.

Axons of the Preganglionic Fibers These fibers pass ventrally to leave the cord with the ventral roots of the second, third, and fourth sacral nerves by *white rami communicantes*, which together are considered *pelvic splanchnic* or *pelvic nerves*. These nerves pass ventrally across the pelvis to end in terminal ganglia about the pelvic viscera and in the wall of the colon, from the region of the splenic flexure downward.

Cells of the Postganglionic Fibers (Fig. 14-4) These cells lie in terminal ganglia in the connective tissue coverings of the pelvic viscera and the lower half of the colon.

Axons of the Postganglionic Fibers (Fig. 14-3) These are relatively short, arising from cells lying in or on the wall of the viscera and passing to the smooth muscle and glands of the pelvic viscera and colon.

General Function

As with the thoracolumbar outflow, there is no set pattern of reaction. This too is determined by the individuality of the organ supplied. However, when the underlying function of this division as a whole is understood, many of its specific reactions can be predicted.

Unlike the sympathetic portion, the craniosacral outflow is a *conservative mechanism*—to save wear and tear and to conserve energy. On this basis, its effects are directly opposed to that of the sympathetic system. It brings visceral function back to a normal level of activity after sympathetic activation. In accomplishing this, there are certain striking differences between these two parts of the autonomic system. In the first place, the parasympathetic system is not anatomically adapted to work as a unit, its regions of origin in the CNS often being widely separated. Furthermore, there is no gland (adrenal medulla) whose hormones act upon the tissues of the entire body. In addition, there is a 1:1 ratio between pre- and postganglionic fibers. This provides for much less divergence than is found in the sympathetic division. In other words, this part of the system can work upon individual organs or organ groups one at a time, as circumstances in those organs demand at a given time. This latter condition is made more certain by the fact that any excess acetylcholine (ACh) produced at the axon terminals of this division is immediately destroyed by cholinesterase (AChE) before it can spread through the tissues or into the bloodstream.

Specific Reactions

Pupil The pupil is *constricted*, thus exhibiting a form of conservation. First, by cutting down the light, visual purple is not broken down so rapidly. Second, it makes the effort put out by the ciliary muscle to accommodate for near vision more efficient by letting in just the correct amount of light.

Blood Pressure Since high blood pressure is more wearing on the walls of the vessels and upon other tissues and organs, as well as on the heart, it is reasonable that the parasympathetic system should *reduce blood pressure.*

Cardiac Rate Logically, the faster the heart works, the more energy must be expended and the greater will be the strain put upon the cardiac muscle fibers. Therefore, the parasympathetic system *slows the heart rate.*

Bronchial Smooth Muscle This is *activated* to constrict the bronchioles. This constriction may occur to protect the delicate pulmonary air sacs from exposure to substances in the inhaled air.

Visceral Smooth Muscle This is *activated.* Intestinal motility is essential for the digestion and absorption of ingested food and is, therefore, conservative.

Glands of the Alimentary Canal These are *stimulated to secrete* enzymes, an action necessary for the utilization of ingested materials.

Certain Sphincters When one understands that the elimination of waste substances is essential for better function of the body and is, therefore, conservative, the *relaxation of certain sphincters* (internal) about the *urethra* and *anal canal,* together with the *contraction of the smooth muscle of the bladder and rectum,* seems perfectly reasonable.

MECHANISM FOR AUTONOMIC CONTROL

The formation, release, and action of the neurotransmitter substance ACh has already been described with the somatic efferent system (Chap. 13). It was also stated earlier that humoral material plays an essential role in the functioning of the visceral efferent system.

It has been demonstrated that there are two neurotransmitters associated with the autonomic system. The first of these is also ACh and thus needs no further comment at this point. The second substance is norepinephrine. It is unclear whether the latter is synthesized in the perikaryon and transported to the axon terminals for storage in presynaptic vesicles or whether the precursors are transported down the axon with synthesis occurring in the terminals. However, regardless of the place of formation, the following represents the chain of synthesis from the precursor L-tyrosine:

$$\text{L-tyrosine} \xrightarrow{\text{tyrosine hydroxylase}} \text{L-dopa}$$
$$\xrightarrow{\text{dopa decarboxylase}} \text{dopamine} \xrightarrow{\text{dopamine-}\beta\text{-hydroxylase}}$$
L-norepinephrine

The end product is subsequently stored in the presynaptic vesicles found both in terminals (Figs. 5-24, 5-25) and axonal varicosities. These vesicles rupture when an action potential passes along the axon, releasing the norepinephrine. This then passes through the axolemma to enter the synaptic cleft.

Electron microscopy has revealed that there are two types of axon endings, and these have been related to the two neurotransmitters stored in the vesicles. The first, or *agranular,* type, contains numerous relatively small, clear vesicles. They are fairly uniform in size, ranging from 400 to 600 Å. In addition, a few large vesicles, in the range of 800 to 1000 Å, may be seen. These may show central cores with variable densities. This agranular type is related to ACh. The second is the *granular* type. The vesicles range in size from 300 to 900 Å. These contain a central core of high electron density. They are associated with norepinephrine.

In the autonomic system, ACh is produced in all preganglionic neurons for both sympathetic and parasympathetic systems. It is the release of this substance into the synaptic clefts that activates the postganglionic neurons. In addition, this same material is produced by and released from all the postganglionic neurons of the parasympathetic division. These are spoken of as *cholinergic fibers,* and sometimes this term is applied to the whole system. In a few locations, ACh is produced in sympathetic postganglionic fibers.

It is said that the ACh molecule has two sides—one muscarinic, the other nicotinic. The receptor sites (loci where synapses or junctions occur) are similarly classified since they are responsive to one side or the other of the molecule.[4] Muscarinic sites are found in smooth muscles and glands. Nicotinic sites are found in the autonomic ganglia.

Perhaps it should be indicated here that there are no true motor end plates on smooth muscle. Apparently the varicosities of the postganglionic axon bulge into shallow depressions in the muscle fiber. Here muscle and nerve membranes are in a close junctional relation with a narrow cleft between.

Norepinephrine is the substance released by most postganglionic sympathetic fibers. Although there is but a single molecule of norepinephrine, it is well known that some structures are excited while others are inhibited by the same substance. This phenomenon is due to the nature of the receptor sites. For want of better terms, one is called *alpha* and is excited by norepinephrine; the other is called *beta* and is inhibited by it. There is one major exception to the latter statement—in cardiac muscle, beta sites are excited rather than inhibited.

A point worthy of note concerns the problem of disposal of excess and unused humors once they have been released from the presynaptic vesicles. This varies depending upon which of the two substances are being considered (Fig. 14-8).

ACh is very rapidly hydrolyzed by the enzyme *cholinesterase* present in the tissues surrounding the receptor sites. This event accounts, in part, for one of the major differences between the sympathetic and parasympathetic divisions of the GVE system. The quick destruction of ACh prevents its diffusion into other areas. Thus the activity of the cholinergic parasympathetic fibers is confined to the particular organ involved.

On the other hand, in the sympathetic division, the removal of norepinephrine is much slower and less efficient, thus permitting the spread of this substance through the tissues to surrounding areas. Much of the excess is taken care of by *reuptake* into the presynaptic terminal. There are also two enzymes which play a part. The first of these is *monoamine oxidase* (MAO). This is believed to work within the neuron by helping to prevent the release of norepinephrine into the synaptic cleft even though the storage vesicles have ruptured. The second enzyme is *catechol-O-methyl transferase* (COMT). This acts outside the nerve terminal by breaking down norepinephrine as it lies in the synaptic cleft.

CHOLINERGIC SYMPATHETIC SITES

Such sites have already been alluded to, but now some of these will be mentioned more specifically:

---

[4]Needless to say these sites respond to the direct application of muscarine or nicotine.

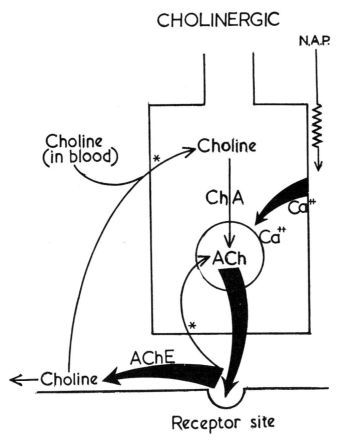

Figure 14-8 Diagram showing the processes involved in the synthesis, release, and disposal of ACh at cholinergic nerve terminals and receptor sites. ACh, acetylcholine; ChA, choline acetyltransferase; AChE, acetylcholinesterase; N.A.P., nerve action potential; * sites of active transport. *(After P. F. Heffron in Samson Wright's Applied Physiology, 12th ed., Oxford University Press, London, 1971.)*

1 Most of the fibers innervating sweat glands are of this type.

2 The vasodilator fibers in skeletal muscle are included in this group. This should not be surprising since ACh is the activator of skeletal muscle.

3 The vasodilator fibers to the blood vessels of the heart are also cholinergic. In this case, since sympathetic adrenergic fibers activate cardiac muscle, it would be disastrous if the smooth muscle in the coronary arteries were also excited by that substance—a situation which would lead to vasoconstriction at a time when the heart needs more circulation, not less.

4 The adrenal medulla is not a true example of cholinergic sympathetic activity. In the three instances cited above, we were dealing with the release of ACh from postganglionic fibers. In the medulla, the postganglionic neurons are actually the secretory cells themselves, acting like postganglionics. In this gland the preganglionic sympathetic fibers which reach this organ through the splanchnic nerves and celiac plexus synapse with the secretory cells. Like all other preganglionic neurons, ACh is released, activating the gland.

CLINICAL CONSIDERATIONS

Thoracolumbar (Sympathetic) System

Testing

There may be many observations which involve parts of this system, but it becomes a problem whether the essential pathologic condition lies in this part of the autonomic system or whether it lies elsewhere but is manifested through this system. Some of the necessary observations include (1) the size and reactions of the pupil; (2) the color and temperature of the skin, especially the distal portions of the upper and lower extremities; (3) cardiac rate and blood pressure under various conditions of rest and exercise; (4) roentgenologic visualization of the blood vessels (angiography). In addition, information should be sought concerning the digestive processes, including salivation and the activities of the lower bowel; lacrimation; temperature control, especially sweating; and the function of the bladder.

Specific Pathology

Horner's Syndrome[5] This syndrome is characterized by miosis, due to paralysis of the dilator of the pupil; a partial ptosis, due to paralysis of the upper tarsal muscle; and enophthalmos, due to paralysis of the orbital or retrobulbar muscle (smooth) of Müller. In addition, in complete Horner's syndrome, there are ipsilateral dilatation of vessels of the face, hand, neck, and conjunctiva, plus ipsilateral anhidrosis. This syndrome may be the result of: the interruption of the descending

sympathetic pathways in the brainstem or spinal cord; lesions in the cord at the level of the ciliospinal center; lesions of the preganglionic fibers in or after they leave the cord; injury to the cervical sympathetic ganglia; or involvement of postganglionic fibers.

Raynaud's Disease This is characterized by pallor or cyanosis of the distal extremities, especially the fingers. Sometimes the nose and ears are involved. This is usually brought on by cold or emotion. When of long standing, cutaneous gangrene, due to lack of adequate circulation, may occur. This condition may be the result of overactivity of the vasoconstrictor fibers of the thoracolumbar outflow.

Buerger's Disease (Thromboangiitis Obliterans) This is said to be an inflammatory and obliterative disease of the blood vessels, particularly of the lower extremities. Reduced circulation here may also lead to gangrene. This condition may have had its inception in, or may be aggravated by, overactivity of the vasoconstrictor fibers.

Erythromelalgia This disease affects the vessels of the extremities, most frequently the hands, in which there is paroxysmal, bilateral vasodilatation, with burning pain and increased skin temperature. It may possibly be due to a lack of activity on the part of the vasoconstrictor fibers.

Hirschsprung's Disease This is characterized by hypertrophic dilatation of the colon. It may have its basis in overactive inhibitor fibers acting upon the colon, allowing dilatation to occur because of the accumulation of fecal material. It may also be due to congenital autonomic aplasia.

Hypertension This term is used here to denote generalized high blood pressure. Because of the importance of this part of the

---

[5]Some of the terms used to describe this syndrome are defined as follows: miosis, an excessive contraction of the pupil; ptosis, drooping of the upper eyelid; enophthalmos, abnormal retraction of the eye into the orbit; and anhidrosis, an abnormal deficiency of sweat.

autonomic system in raising blood pressure, it becomes suspect in the hypertensive patient.

Craniosacral (Parasympathetic) System

Testing

It should be realized that because of the intimate relations of the fibers of this system with others, both motor and sensory, there is little chance that only general visceral efferents will be involved. Therefore, symptoms due to damage of the parasympathetic nerves will be brought out when examination of individual cranial nerves is made. In general, the following items should be kept in mind: (1) The pupils should be checked for constriction in response to light and near objects; (2) the eye can be examined for evidence of the lack of lacrimation; (3) the use of such substances as lemon juice is adequate to test salivary secretion; (4) the usual check of cardiac rate and blood pressure, particularly the time required for both to return to normal, after exercise, may give some clue to the integrity of the system; (5) the digestive processes and the condition of the alimentary canal may give evidence about the parasympathetic nerves; (6) information concerning sexual activity, particularly the ability to erect the penis, should be sought, since engorgement of the genital vessels is a part of the parasympathetic function.

Blocking Agents

It is beyond the scope of this book to become involved in the interesting and medically very important pharmacologic aspects of this system. However, two well-known medicaments should be mentioned. The first of these is *atropine*, which blocks muscarinic sites. When used locally in the eye, for example, the receptor sites in the sphincter pupillae muscle are blocked, thus preventing pupillary constriction. This is very useful to the ophthalmologist when a wide-open pupil is required. The second substance is *curare*. This is used frequently as a skeletal muscle relaxant through its blocking effect at the motor end plates. It can also block all the autonomic ganglia, since these, like the end plates, are nicotinic sites.

Summary
General Visceral Efferent

Thoracolumbar Division	Cell body	Craniosacral Division
1. Intermediolateral gray column of the thoracic and upper lumbar cord		1. Edinger-Westphal (EW) nucleus, in upper mesencephalon
		Superior salivatory nucleus at pons-medulla junction
		Inferior salivatory nucleus, just caudal to the above nucleus
		Dorsal motor nucleus of the vagus, in medulla
		Intermediolateral cell column of the sacral cord at levels S2–S4

2. Through the ventral roots of thoracic and upper lumbar spinal nerves and by white rami communicantes to:

    Synapse in chain (paravertebral) ganglion at level of entry

    Ascend or descend in thoracic and lumbar sympathetic trunk to synapse in chain ganglia above or below level of entry

    Ascend in the cervical sympathetic trunk to synapse in the inferior, middle, or superior cervical ganglia

    Continue transversely through the sympathetic chain, still as preganglionics, especially at levels T6 through T12 (the splanchnic nerves), to synapse in the prevertebral ganglia (i.e., celiac) or the adrenal medulla

Preganglionic fiber and synapse

2. From the EW nucleus via nerve III to terminate by synapse either in ciliary ganglion or episcleral ganglion

    From superior salivatory nucleus via nervus intermedius, facial nerve (VII), great petrosal nerve, and nerve of the pterygoid canal to terminate in the pterygopalatine ganglion

    From superior salivatory nucleus via nervus intermedius, facial nerve (VII), great petrosal nerve, and nerve of the pterygoid canal to terminate in the pterygopalatine ganglion

    From the superior salivatory nucleus via nervus intermedius, facial (VII), chorda tympani, and lingual nerves to the submandibular ganglion

    From the dorsal motor nucleus of the vagus via the vagus nerve (X) to terminal ganglia lying near, in, or on the walls of the viscera

    Through the ventral roots of the corresponding sacral nerves (S2–S4), as the pelvic splanchnic nerves, to terminate in the terminal ganglia in or on the walls of the lower colon and pelvic viscera

3. From chain ganglia, through gray rami communicantes to spinal nerves for distribution to peripheral blood vessels; smooth muscle (arrector pili); and glands of the skin

    From certain chain ganglia, especially upper thoracic, to bronchi and lungs

    From all cervical ganglia as cardiac nerves to the heart

    From the superior cervical ganglion, mainly through the carotid plexus and by fibers along the branches of the carotid to: the blood vessels of the head; the glands of the head; the smooth muscles and glands in the skin of the head; and the dilator pupillae, together with the smooth muscle of the lids and orbit, of the eye. The heart receives fibers from this ganglion via cardiac nerves

Postganglionic fiber and termination

3. From ciliary ganglion to ciliary muscle and sphincter pupillae muscles, for light

    From the episcleral ganglion to muscles as above, for accomodation

    From pterygopalatine ganglion, to maxillary division of trigeminal (V), through zygomatic branch, to the lacrimal branch of the ophthalmic division of the trigeminal (V), to the lacrimal gland

    From the pterygopalatine ganglion, through nasal and palatine nerves, to glands of nose and palate

    From submandibular ganglion to submandibular and sublingual glands

    From otic ganglion through the auriculotemporal branch of the mandibular division of the trigeminal nerve (V) to the parotid gland

    From terminal ganglia of:
    Cardiac plexus — to heart
    Pulmonary plexus — to bronchi
    Auerbach's plexus — to smooth muscle of viscera (digestive system)
    Meissner's plexus — to glands of viscera (digestive system)

    From terminal ganglia of pelvis to smooth muscles and glands of pelvic viscera including lower colon

Innervation of the Viscera

Organ	Sympathetic		
	Preganglionic	Postganglionic	Action
Arrector pili	All levels	All ganglia of trunk and chain	Erects hair
Bladder muscle	TII–L2	Hypogastric gang. and plexus	Relaxes
Cavernous tissue	L2	Hypogastric gang. and plexus	Deturgescence
Ciliary muscle	C8–T2	Sup. cervical gang.	Relaxes
Colon	T6–T10	Sup. and inf. mesenteric gang. and plexuses	Inhibits peristalsis
Coronary vessels	T1–T5	Cervical and thoracic gang.	Dilates
Heart muscle	T1–T5	Cervical and thoracic gang.	Accelerates rate
Iris of eye	C8–T3	Sup. cervical gang.	Dilates pupil
Kidney	T10–T11	Renal gang. and plexus	Constricts pelvis and vessels
Lacrimal gland	T1–T3	Sup. cervical gang.	Vasoconstricts to reduce secretion
Liver	T5–T6	Celiac gang. and plexus	Glycogenolysis
Lung	T2–5	Thoracic gang.	Relaxes bronchial mm.
Mammary gland	T2–T6	Thoracic gang.	Constricts ducts
Nasal and oral glands	T1–T3	Sup. cervical gang.	Vasoconstr. to reduce secretion
Pancreas	T5–T6	Celiac gang. and plexus	Vasoconstr. to reduce secretion
Parotid gland	T1–T3	Sup. cervical gang.	Vasoconstr. to reduce secretion
Stomach	T6–T10	Celiac gang. and plexus	Inhibits peristalsis, vasoconstr., inhibits secretion
Small intestine	T6–T10	Celiac and sup. mesenteric gang. and plexus	Inhibits peristalsis, inhibits secretion, vasoconstr.
Sphincters			
Anal	L2	Hypogastric gang. and plexus	Constricts
Pyloric	T6–T10	Celiac gang. and plexus	Constricts
Urethral	L2	Hypogastric gang. and plexus	Constricts
Sublingual and submandibular glands	T1–T3	Sup. cervical gang.	Vasoconstr. to reduce secretion
Sweat glands	All levels	All trunk and chain ganglia	Stimulates secretion

Innervation of the Viscera (cont.)

Parasympathetic		
Preganglionic	**Postganglionic**	**Action**
Not proved to be present		
S2–S4	Intrinsic ganglia	Contracts
S2–S4	Vesical plexus	Turgescence
EW nucleus	Episcleral gang.	Contracts
Dorsal motor X	Myenteric and submucosal plexuses	Excites peristalsis
Dorsal motor X	Cardiac plexus and ganglia	Constricts
Dorsal motor X R. vagus, SA node L. vagus, AV node	Cardiac plexus and ganglia	Decelerates rate
EW nucleus	Ciliary gang.	Constricts pupil
Not proved to be present		
Lacrimal or superior salivatory	Pterygopalatine gang.	Stimulates secretion
Dorsal motor X	Unknown	Contracts gall bladder
Dorsal motor X	Pulmonary plexus	Constricts bronchi
Not proved to be present		
Lacrimal or sup. salivatory nuclei	Pterygopalatine gang.	Stimulates secretion
Dorsal motor X	Intrinsic ganglia	Increases secretion
Inf. salivat. nucleus	Otic ganglion	Stimulates secretion
Dorsal motor X	Myenteric and submucosal plexi	Stimulates peristalsis and secretions
Dorsal motor X	Myenteric and submucosal plexi	Stimulates peristalsis secretion
S2–S4	Intrinsic gang.	Relaxes
Dorsal motor X	Myenteric gang.	Relaxes
S2–S4	Intrinsic gang. and plexus	Relaxes
Inf. salivat. nucleus	Pterygopalatine and submandibular ganglia	Stimulates secretion
Not proved to be present		

Special Visceral Efferent System (SVE)

This is the motor system which supplies striated, skeletal muscle derived from the embryonic branchial arches. In the latter respect, it is different from the somatic efferent system which innervates muscle derived from somites (Chap. 13).

Early in development, the mesoderm surrounding the foregut becomes divided into four complete segments and one incomplete segment by the appearance of pharyngeal pouches and clefts (Figs. 4-13, 4-14). These divisions are called *branchial arches* and are usually designated by numbers arranged consecutively from rostral to caudal. One cranial nerve enters each of the first three arches: the trigeminal (V) into the first; the facial (VII) into the second; and the glossopharyngeal (IX) into the third. Branches from the vagus nerve (X) supply both the complete fourth and partial fifth arches.

Almost from the beginning, the nerves in each arch establish a close relationship with the premuscle masses which differentiate in the arch. This relationship persists throughout future development, regardless of the distance a muscle must migrate from its site of origin. On this basis, all the special visceral musculature can be arranged in groups, together with the nerve supply, according to the branchial arch from which the muscles came.

From the first branchial arch arise the *muscles of mastication,* all innervated by the *trigeminal nerve* (V). In addition to these are the *mylohyoid, anterior belly of the digastric, tensor veli palatini,* and the *tensor tympani* muscles, also supplied by the fifth cranial nerve.

All the muscles of *facial expression,* including the *occipitalis, frontalis, muscles of the auricle,* and the *platysma,* develop from the second branchial arch and are innervated by the *facial nerve* (VII). The *posterior belly of the digastric muscle,* as well as the *stapedius muscle,* also comes from this arch and is similarly innervated.

The *stylopharyngeus* is the only muscle which has been proved to arise from the third arch. It is probable, however, that some of the *pharyngeal constrictors* also arise here. These muscles are innervated by the *glossopharyngeal nerve* (IX).

Most of the muscles of the *pharynx* and all the muscles of the *larynx,* innervated by the *vagus nerve* (X), arise from the fourth and fifth arches. The *glossopharyngeus, palatoglossus,* and *levator veli palatini* muscles are also believed to be derived from the fourth arch, since they are likewise supplied by the vagus nerve.

Like the somatic motor column of the head, this nuclear column is discontinuous along its rostrocaudal extent (Fig. 15-1). The special visceral efferent nuclei assume an intermediate position between the somatic and general visceral columns in a transverse plane but lie ventral to both.[1]

PATHWAYS

Since this system is made up of fibers running in several cranial nerves, it is advantageous to describe each nerve individually.

Trigeminal Nerve (V)

Cell Body   (Figs. 1-35, 15-2, 25-9)

These are of the multipolar type, perhaps a little smaller than those in the somatic system.

[1]Actually, some of these nuclei may be drawn somewhat out of line because of the tendency for cell masses to migrate in the direction from which most of their stimuli arrive. This is the theory of *neurobiotaxis.*

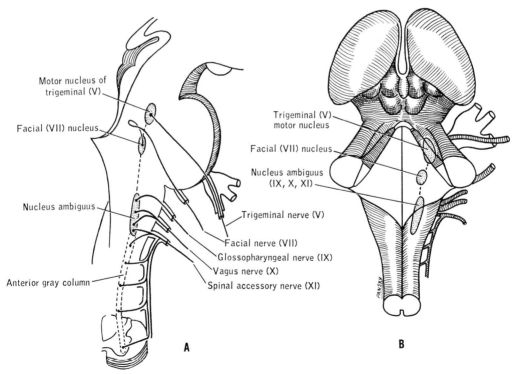

Figure 15-1 Diagram of the special visceral efferent (SVE) nuclear column of the brainstem. *A.* Lateral view. *B.* Dorsal view.

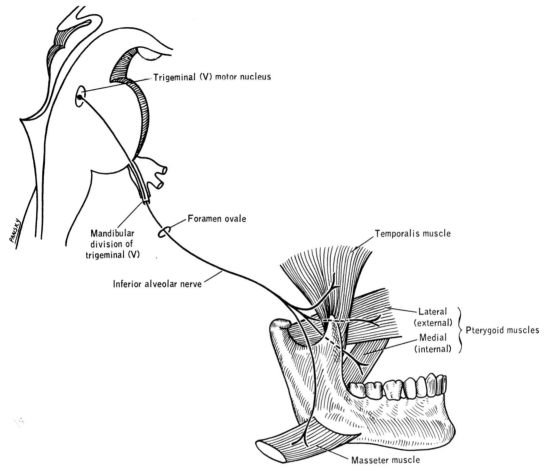

Figure 15-2 Origin and distribution of the trigeminal nerve (V) fibers to the muscles of mastication.

They are aggregated in the motor nucleus of the trigeminal nerve, located in the upper pons.

Axon (Figs. 1-35, 25-9)

The single axons from each cell pass to the lateral aspect of the nucleus, where they encounter afferent fibers belonging to the trigeminal nerve. The motor fibers accompany the afferent fibers ventrolaterally across the pons to become superficial on its ventrolateral surface (Figs. 1-7, 1-8). Here, the motor fibers are collected in a bundle which is attached to the pons slightly rostral and medial to the larger mass of afferent fibers. The latter are spoken of as the *sensory root* or, since there are so many of them, the *portio major.* The efferents are collectively known as the *motor root,* or *portio minor.*

After leaving the brainstem, the motor root lies along the medial side of the sensory root but is not fused with it. It crosses the medial aspect of the posterior portion of the semilunar ganglion and continues downward along the mandibular division, to exit from the middle cranial fossa through the foramen ovale.

Just below the skull, the motor fibers actually become part of the mandibular root.

In response to the excitation of these fibers, a variety of activities ensues. The masseter and the pterygoid internus muscles close the jaw; the temporalis muscle closes the jaw and in part retracts the mandible; the pterygoid externus muscle is important in the grinding action, protruding the mandible and moving it from side to side. The anterior belly of the digastric muscle—and to a lesser degree the mylohyoid (when the hyoid bone is fixed)—depresses the mandible. The tensor tympani muscle increases tension on the tympanic membrane, while the tensor veli palatini muscle has a similar effect on the soft palate (Fig. 15-2).

Facial Nerve (VII)

Cell Body (Figs. 1-36, 15-3, 25-8)

These multipolar cells are grouped into a nucleus located in the ventrolateral portion of the pontine reticular formation not far from the caudal limit of the pons.

Axon (Figs. 1-36, 15-3, 25-7, 25-8)

The axons from these cells pass dorsomedially from the nucleus in widely scattered bundles, the first part of the root of the facial nerve. These bundles approach the midline just beneath the floor of the fourth ventricle. Here they come together in a solid fascicle, the fibers now being directed rostrally along the medial side of the abducens nucleus, just

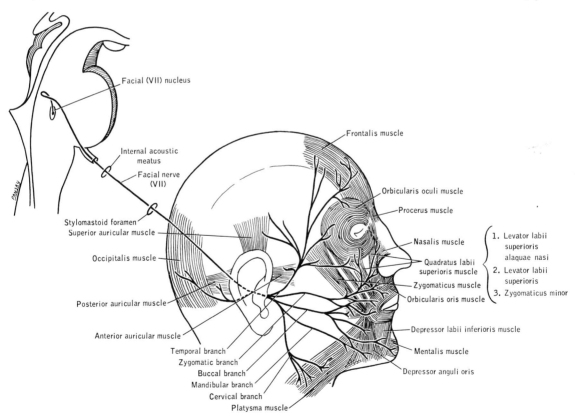

Figure 15-3 Origin and distribution of the facial nerve (VII) to the muscles of facial expression.

dorsal to the medial longitudinal fasciculus. This portion is sometimes called the ascending part of the facial nerve. Near the rostral end of nucleus VI, the facial fibers turn abruptly over the dorsal side of the abducens nucleus. This portion is known as the internal genu.[2] After crossing the abducens nucleus, the facial fibers are directed ventrolaterally with considerable caudal drift so that this group, called the second part of the root of the facial nerve, passes near the lateral side of the facial nucleus to exit from the lateral aspect of the caudal pons medial to the superficial attachment of the acoustic nerve (Figs. 1-7, 1-8). After leaving the brainstem, facial fibers run in close proximity to the acoustic nerve, the nervus intermedius lying between them. They continue laterally and enter the internal acoustic meatus.

The ability of the face to change expression, in response to impulses carried through the facial nerve, is well known. The arrangement of the muscle fibers around the eyes and mouth has useful and important functions, especially in closing the eyelids (for protection), in moving the lips, in speaking, and in retaining food in the mouth while it is being masticated. The stapedius muscle puts tension on the stapes and, through it, on the membrane which supports it. This is an adjunct to hearing. The posterior belly of the digastric muscle helps to elevate and retract the hyoid, as in swallowing.

Glossopharyngeal Nerve (IX)

Cell Body   (Figs. 15-4, 25-5)

The multipolar cells for this sytem are located in the nucleus ambiguus. This cell group is poorly circumscribed but has a considerable longitudinal extent (Fig. 15-1), located in the

___

[2]This is at least partially responsible for the elevation in the floor of the fourth ventricle called the *facial colliculus* (Figs. 1-26, 1-27).

reticular formation throughout the length of the medulla oblongata. The cells of this nucleus are usually found scattered among the network of fibers in the lateral reticular formation between the inferior olive and the spinal trigeminal tract.

Axon   (Figs. 15-4, 25-5)

These are from cells at the rostral end of the nucleus ambiguus. At first, they are directed dorsally. After a short distance they curve laterally and then pass ventrolaterally with some rostral drift to accompany afferents and general visceral efferents of nerve IX. On reaching the lateral aspect of the medulla, in company with the vagus nerve, they emerge along the posterolateral sulcus, dorsal to the olive (Figs. 1-7, 1-8). In company with the vagus and accessory nerves, the glossopharyngeal nerve courses caudally to leave the posterior cranial fossa through the jugular foramen.

The action of the stylopharyngeus muscle in helping to elevate the pharynx and to increase the transverse diameter of the latter to receive the bolus of food from the mouth in the first part of deglutition, is of great importance (Fig. 15-4). Since it is not certain whether the glossopharyngeal nerve contributes to the innervation of the pharyngeal constrictors, their action will be discussed with the vagus nerve.

Vagus Nerve (X)

For the sake of convenience, the vagus nerve is considered as having two parts, a chief, or rostral, segment and a vagal accessory portion, not to be confused with cranial nerve XI.

Chief or Rostral Portions of the Vagus Nerve

Cell Body   (Figs. 1-37, 15-1, 15-5, 25-4)   The cells of this part of the vagus nerve lie in the lower rostral and intermediate portions of the nucleus ambiguus, its more rostral limit

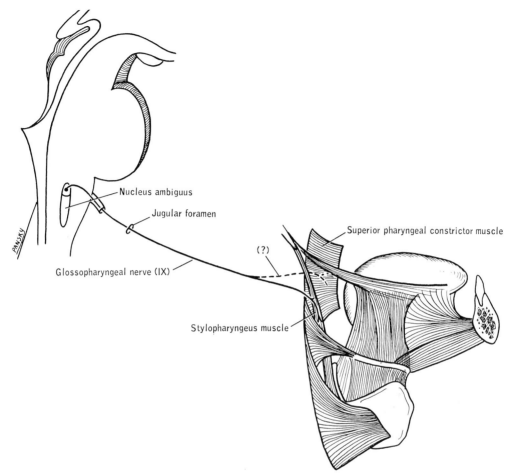

Figure 15-4　Origin and distribution of the glossopharyngeal nerve (IX) to the muscles of the pharynx.

nearly overlapping the cells of the glossopharyngeal nerve.

Axon　(Figs. 1-7, 1-8, 15-5, 25-4)

The direction, course, and relations of these fibers, both within and outside the medulla, are similar to those already described for the glossopharyngeal nerve and need not be repeated.

　The fibers of this part of the vagus nerve terminate in the pharyngeal constrictors, the

levator veli palatini, the palatoglossus, and the palatopharyngeus muscles, which are essential for swallowing (Fig. 15-5). As the food mass moves from the tongue to glide over the epiglottis, the palatoglossus muscles, which act as constrictors of the fauces, contract behind the bolus, helping it move down and also preventing its return. At the same time, the levators of the palate raise the velum of the palate, both to accommodate the bolus and to prevent its passage into the nasopharynx.

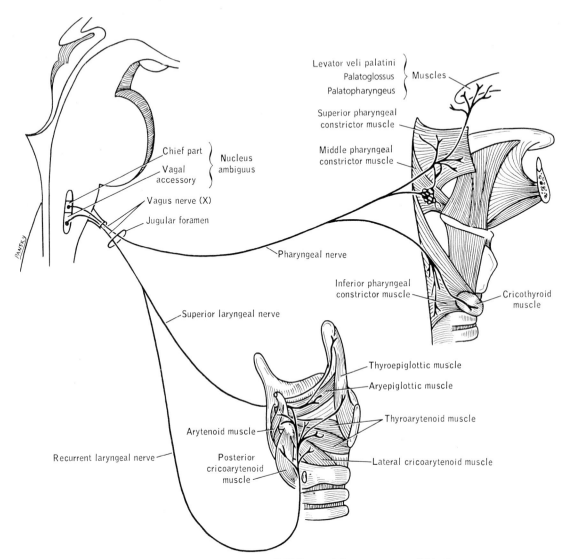

Figure 15-5 Nucleus of origin and distribution of the SVE fibers of the vagus nerve (X) to the muscles of the palate, pharynx, and larynx.

At the same time, the palatopharyngeus muscles are contracting to raise the pharynx over the bolus.

Accessory Portion of the Vagus Nerve

Cell Body (Fig. 15-5)

The cells of this portion also lie in the nucleus ambiguus, but in its caudal portion only. No

further comment need be made concerning this nucleus.

Axon (Figs. 1-7, 1-8, 15-5)

Their course within the brainstem is so similar to that described for the glossopharyngeal nerve and chief vagus nerve segment that no repetition is necessary. The extramedullary course is also similar to that of the nerves mentioned above, although a short distance below the exit from the brainstem they are joined by the ascending spinal accessory nerve fibers, with which they exit from the skull through the jugular foramen. Just below the skull, the vagal accessory joins the rostral or chief segment to form a common trunk.

All the vagal accessory fibers terminate around the muscles of the larynx and either change the tension on the vocal cords or regulate the size of the aperture between them. Thus, the posterior cricoarytenoid, the lateral cricoarytenoid, and the lateral and oblique arytenoid muscles open or close the glottis, while the cricothyroid and the thyroarytenoid muscles regulate the tension (Fig. 15-5).

Accessory (Spinal Accessory) Nerve (XI)

This nerve, if it is to be considered an entity in itself and thus classified as one of the 12 cranial nerves, holds an equivocal position. There is no positive agreement as to whether the muscles it supplies come from the branchial arch mesoderm or from cervical somites. From the position of its nucleus, the point of emergence from the CNS, and its intimate relationship with a branchial motor nerve (X), it is likely that the upper part of both the trapezius and sternocleidomastoid muscles is derived from branchial arches below the fifth, arches which have disappeared long since in the process of evolution.

Cell Body   (Figs. 1-39, 15-1, 15-6, 25-1)

Most of the cells lie in the lateral part of the anterior gray column in the upper five seg-

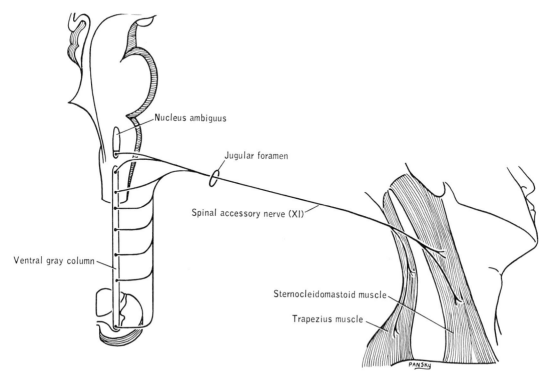

Figure 15-6   Origin and distribution of the spinal accessory nerve (XI) to the muscles of the neck.

ments of the cervical cord and persist in the lower medulla as far as the rostral limit of the pyramidal decussation.

Axon   (Figs. 1-39, 15-1, 15-6)

These are at first directed dorsolaterally, then laterally with rostral inclination, to emerge on the surface of the cord between the attachments of the dorsal and ventral roots of the upper cervical nerves. A short distance lateral to the edge of the cord these axons unite into a fascicle which runs rostrally beside the spinal cord (Figs. 1-7, 1-8, 15-1, 15-6) and enters the posterior cranial fossa through the foramen magnum (Fig. 16-11) to join the caudal fibers of the vagal accessory. Here the spinal accessory fibers swing laterally and then caudally to leave the skull with the vagal accessory through the jugular foramen.

When the nerve is active, the upper part of the trapezius muscle draws the head to the same side and turns the face to the opposite side. It also draws the scapula upward and braces the shoulders. The two sides acting together bend the head back. The sternocleidomastoid muscle, acting on one side alone, bends the cervical vertebral column to that side, so that the head approaches the shoulder. At the same time, the head is rotated, pointing the chin upward and to the opposite side.

CLINICAL CONSIDERATIONS

Testing

There are few actual tests to determine the integrity of the various parts of this system. However, several observations can be made.

The examiner notes whether there is any deviation of the mandible. If the motor root of nerve V is damaged, the jaw may tend to deviate toward the side of the lesion.

The ability to move the mandible is tested by asking the patient to chew.

Since these muscles are also subject to atrophy when motor fibers are interrupted, the examiner looks for wasting in the masseteric

area. Long-standing lesions in the trigeminal motor pathway would result in obvious shrinking in this region.

The examiner notes whether there is asymmetry of the face. In facial nerve paralysis, the affected side will sag because the weight of the facial tissue will drag against the atonic and atrophying facial muscles. A smoothing out of the nasolabial fold may also be noted.

In this same connection, it should be noted whether the corner of the mouth droops.

Since the facial muscles are important in keeping substances in the mouth, one should look for evidence of, or inquire about, dribbling of saliva from the corners of the mouth. This would occur on the paralyzed side.

It should be determined whether the eye can be blinked. Since the orbicularis oculi is the muscle performing eye closure, the eye cannot be closed on the affected side in cases of interruption or destruction of the facial nerve.

It is important to observe whether facial paralysis, when present, is total, i.e., whether the muscles above the eye (corrugator and frontalis), as well as those below, are affected. Total paralysis is indicative of disease either of the facial nucleus or along the course of its fibers. If the supraorbital muscles still contract, the lesion usually lies in the pathway of the upper motor neuron (Chap. 20).

One should notice whether there is difficulty in swallowing. Since nerves IX and X are responsible for the innervation of the palate and pharyngeal musculature, involvement of these nuclei would be extremely serious in this connection. Naturally, because of their much greater distribution, interruption of the vagal pathways is clinically more significant.

The physician should examine the pharynx and note whether there is deviation of the uvula (Fig. 15-8). When the muscles on one side of the palate are paralyzed, the unopposed action of the normal muscles on the other side draws the uvula off center, away from the affected side. The palate droops on the paralyzed side, and gag reflexes on that

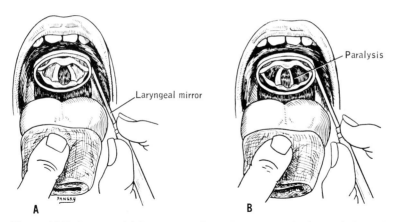

Figure 15-7 Laryngeal inlet as seen through a laryngeal mirror. *A.* Normal vocal folds. *B.* Paralysis of the left vocal fold, such as might occur with damage to the left recurrent nerve.

side are diminished or absent. The examiner should also inquire about any tendency toward regurgitation from the mouth or pharynx into the nasal cavities.

One should listen to the voice. Since the vagus nerve supplies muscles of the larynx, lesions in this system lead to abnormalities in phonation. A laryngeal mirror or laryngoscope will show the vocal fold on the normal side to have a greater dorsolateral divergence from the midline (Fig. 15-7).

General Pathology

The same conditions which adversely affect the somatic efferent system—tumors, either intra- or extramedullary; vascular accidents; or trauma—can also destroy or damage portions of the SVE mechanism. It is very rare, however, for such lesions to select isolated parts of this system without involving neighboring portions of other systems, some of which would present even more striking defects than are noticed in examinations just for SVE nerves. This is especially true when the pathologic condition lies within the CNS. Therefore, no attempt will be made to list all possible lesions or their locations in which the SVE fibers are included as a part of a much more generalized involvement. However, lesions including the facial and vagus nerves

produce striking symptoms, the former because of the obvious differences between the two sides of the face; the latter because of the difficulties in swallowing and speaking.

Specific Pathology

Bell's Palsy

This is a general term applied to a facial paralysis, usually due to injury or disease in the peripheral part of nerve VII. Sometimes this results from an irritation, in which case,

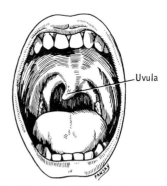

Figure 15-8 Sagging of the left palate and pharyngeal wall, together with deviation of the uvula to the right, such as may occur with a lesion of the left vagus nerve. If the lesion occurs in the vagus nerve proximal to the origin of the recurrent nerve, this sign will be seen in conjunction with that shown in Fig. 15-7B. The muscles involved in this paralysis include levator veli palatini, palatoglossus, palatopharyngeus.

the paralysis may be only temporary. In disease and in surgery around the parotid gland, this nerve may be permanently damaged. Occasionally, in extensive disease of the middle ear followed by radical surgery on the middle ear, the facial nerve may be involved. This palsy is characterized by a lack of expression on the diseased side; the nasolabial groove is indistinct on that side; the palpebral fissure is larger on the diseased side; in chewing, food particles accumulate on the paralyzed side and the saliva may drip from the corner of the mouth. Depending on the location of the disease, certain autonomic reflexes, such as lacrimation and salivation, may be absent.

Trauma

In *surgery on the sensory root of the trigeminal (V) nerve* for the relief of trigeminal neuralgia (tic douloureux), the motor root, which adjoins the sensory root, on its medial side, may be inadvertently cut. This leads to paralysis of

muscles of mastication with deviation of the jaw toward the paralyzed side and wasting away of the masseteric area on the side that has been operated upon.

In *surgery on the thyroid gland* for goiter, occasionally the recurrent laryngeal branch of the vagus nerve is destroyed. This leads to the paralysis of all the laryngeal muscles except the cricothyroid (Fig. 15-7). Abnormalities in the voice result. Should this occur bilaterally, normal phonation is impossible. There may also be difficulties in respiration because the rima glottidis cannot be altered.

Destruction of the nucleus ambiguus or emerging fibers of the vagus (X) nerve due to vascular thrombosis will lead to paralysis of the palatine and pharyngeal muscles on the side of the lesion. This results in difficulty in swallowing. On examination of the pharynx, the pharyngeal wall will be seen to sag on the side of the lesion and the uvula to deviate to the contralateral side (Fig. 15-8).

Summary
Special Visceral Efferent

1. In the special visceral efferent column
of the brainstem

<u>Cell body</u>

Motor nucleus of the trigeminal (V) in
the upper pons

Facial nucleus (VII) in the lower pons

Nucleus ambiguus (nucleus for nerves
IX and X):
  Rostral end
  Intermediate part
  Caudal end

Accessory nucleus (XI) in lateral part of
ventral gray column of the upper five
cervical segments, and lower medulla,
extending rostrally from this (as high as
pyramidal decussation)

2. From motor V, leaving brainstem
through the portio minor into the
mandibular division of the trigeminal
(V) for distribution to masseter,
temporalis, pterygoids, mylohyoid,
anterior belly of the digastric, tensor
veli palatini, and tenor tympani muscles

<u>Efferent fiber</u>

From motor VII through the facial nerve
(VII) to all muscles of facial expression,
including the occipitalis and auricular
group, plus the platysma, posterior belly
of digastric, and the stapedius muscles

From nucleus ambiguus:
  Rostral end, by way of the glossopharyngeal nerve (IX), to the stylopharyngeus (and superior pharyngeal
  constrictor?)

  Intermediate part, through the chief
  part of the vagus nerve (X), to the
  pharyngeal constrictors, the levator
  veli palatini, the palatoglossus, and
  palatopharyngeus muscles

  Caudal end, through the vagal accessory fibers (part of vagus nerve), to
  the muscles of the larynx

From accessory nucleus through spinal
accessory nerve (XI) to sternocleidomastoid and trapezius muscles

3. All in motor end plates in the skeletal
muscle derived from mesoderm of
branchial arch origin

<u>Termination</u>

Chapter 16

Summary of Functional Components of Peripheral Nerves

SPINAL NERVES

Although each spinal nerve may differ as to the number of fibers belonging to each of the functional components, they all contain at least some representatives of the GSA, GVA, GP, GSE, and GVE systems. Some of the information is so general that it will be given only once, under General Considerations, and will not be repeated for individual spinal nerves. The distribution of the receptors of the GSA system will be shown on the figures illustrating dermatomes (Figs. 16-1 through 16-3). The receptors for the GP system are distributed with the terminals of the GSE fibers and will, therefore, not be considered separately. In many cases, the fibers of the GVA system are sparse, their distribution is not definite, and their terminations are not

clear. Therefore, it is not considered necessary (or even always possible) to list all components of each nerve. *Their presence is implied.* Only occasional mention will be made of some of these components when a point is to be emphasized.

FUNCTIONAL COMPONENTS OF SPINAL NERVES

General Considerations

   I Afferent components
     A GSA (Chap. 7)
       1 Receptors
         a Types
           (1) Free endings—for pain
           (2) Bulbs of Krause and Ruffini—possibly for temperature

(3) Corpuscles of Meissner and Merkel—for touch

(4) Peritricheal arborizations—for touch

b Location

(1) Epidermis

(2) Dermis

(3) Around hair follicles

c Distribution—see dermatomes (Figs. 16-1 through 16-3)

2 Cell bodies—in dorsal root ganglion of each nerve

3 Terminations

a Substantia gelatinosa—for pain and temperature

b Body of dorsal column—for touch

4 Symptoms of disease—anesthesia in area of distribution

B GP (Chap. 11)

1 Receptors

a Types

(1) Muscle spindles

(2) Tendon spindles

(3) Pacinian corpuscles

b Location

(1) Among muscle fibers

(2) In fascia

(3) Along tendons

(4) In joint capsules

c Distribution

(1) In same muscles supplied by GSE fibers of the nerve

(2) In articulations crossed by the nerve

2 Cell bodies—in dorsal root ganglion of each nerve

3 Terminations

a Body of dorsal column

b Clarke's column, T1 through L3

c Lateral cuneate nucleus, for neck

d Nucleus cuneatus, for upper half of body

e Nucleus gracilis, for lower half of body

4 Symptoms of disease

a Loss of tendon reflexes

b Ataxia in muscles supplied

C GVA (Chap. 9)

1 Receptors

a Types

(1) Free

(2) Nets or tangles

(3) Pacinian corpuscles (?)

b Location

(1) On mucous surfaces

(2) On serous surfaces

(3) Among muscle fibers

c Distribution

(1) In walls of all viscera

(2) In supporting tissue, like mesenteries

(3) In body wall

2 Cell bodies—in dorsal root ganglia of each nerve

3 Termination—dorsal gray column of cord

4 Symptoms of disease—not clear-cut but perhaps some loss of proper reflex adjustments of the viscera

II Efferent components

A GSE (Chap. 13)

1 Origin—from the ventral gray columns of the cord

2 Terminations—in the motor end plates of all skeletal muscle derived from somites

3 Distribution—in general, given with each nerve under Specific Considerations

4 Symptoms of disease

a Flaccid paralysis in muscles supplied

b Atrophy of muscles supplied

B GVE—Sympathetic (Chap. 14)

1 Preganglionic

a Origin—intermediolateral gray column, T1 through L2

b Terminations

(1) Ganglia of cervical sympathetic

(2) Chain ganglia

(3) Celiac ganglia

(4) Adrenal medulla

2 Postganglionic

a Origin—any of ganglia listed under *B, b,* above

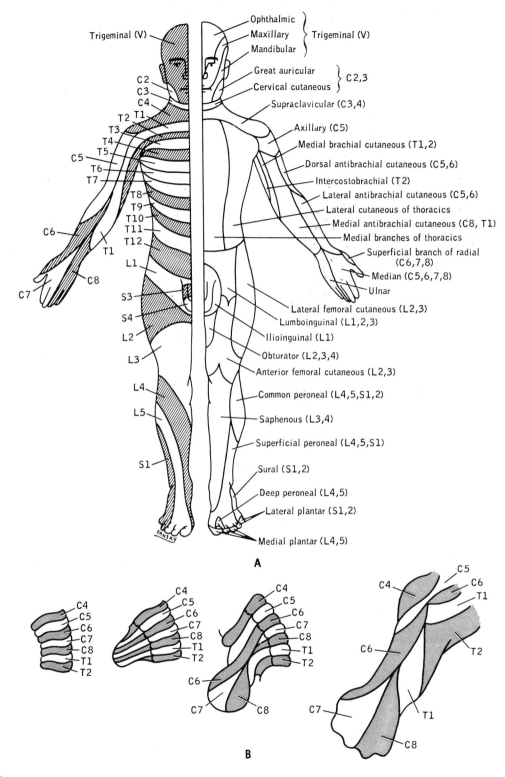

Trigeminal (V)

Ophthalmic
Maxillary } Trigeminal (V)
Mandibular

Great auricular } C2,3
Cervical cutaneous

Supraclavicular (C3,4)

C2
C3
C4

T2 T1
T3
T4
T5
C5
T6
T7

Axillary (C5)
Medial brachial cutaneous (T1,2)
Dorsal antibrachial cutaneous (C5,6)
Intercostobrachial (T2)
Lateral antibrachial cutaneous (C5,6)
Lateral cutaneous of thoracics
Medial antibrachial cutaneous (C8, T1)
Medial branches of thoracics
Superficial branch of radial (C6,7,8)
Median (C5,6,7,8)
Ulnar

T8
T9
T10
T11
T12

C6

T1

C8

C7

L1

S3
S4
L2

L3

L4

L5

S1

Lateral femoral cutaneous (L2,3)
Lumboinguinal (L1,2,3)
Ilioinguinal (L1)
Obturator (L2,3,4)
Anterior femoral cutaneous (L2,3)
Common peroneal (L4,5,S1,2)
Saphenous (L3,4)
Superficial peroneal (L4,5,S1)
Sural (S1,2)
Deep peroneal (L4,5)
Lateral plantar (S1,2)
Medial plantar (L4,5)

PANSKY

A

C4
C5
C6
C7
C8
T1
T2

C4
C5
C6
C7
C8
T1
T2

C4
C5
C6
C7
C8
T1
T2

C6
C7
C8

C5
C4
C6
T1

C6
T2

C7
T1
C8

B

b Terminations

    (1) Smooth muscles and glands of head and trunk

    (2) Heart

    (3) Smooth muscle and glands of abdominal and thoracic viscera

3 Symptoms of disease: signs of hyperactivity or of hypoactivity, depending upon the specific characteristics of the organ innervated and upon the nature of the pathologic condition

C GVE—Parasympathetic (Chap. 14)

  1 Preganglionic

    a Origin — intermediolateral cell column, S2 through S4

    b Terminations

      (1) Ganglia in or on walls of pelvic viscera

      (2) Ganglia in walls of lower half of colon

  2 Postganglionic

    a Origin—in any of ganglia listed under *C, b,* above

    b Terminations

      (1) Smooth muscle of pelvic viscera

      (2) Glands of pelvis

      (3) Muscle and glands of lower colon

3 Symptoms of disease—similar to those under *B,* 3, above but mainly referable to the pelvic viscera or genital apparatus

Specific Considerations

I Cervical

  A GSE (Figs. 16-1, 16-2; Chap. 13)

    1 Distribution

    a Muscles of occipital triangle

    b Through the *superior limb of the ansa cervicalis* to genio- and thyrohyoid muscles

II Cervicals 2 through 4—*cervical plexus*

  A GSE (Chap. 13)

    1 Distribution

    a From C2 and C3 through the *ansa cervicalis* to infrahyoid muscles

    b To longus and recti capitis

    c From C3 and C4 to trapezius and sternocleidomastoid muscles

    d From C4 through *phrenic nerve* to diaphragm

III Cervicals 5 through 8 and T1—*brachial plexus*

  A GVA (Chap. 9)

    1 Distribution

    a Blood vessels of upper extremity and neck

 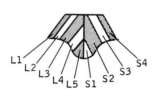 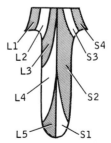

C

Figure 16-1 Peripheral distribution of sensory nerve fibers. *A.* Anterior view: *right,* distribution of cutaneous nerves; *left,* dermatomes, or segemental distribution of the cutaneous nerves; *B.* Diagram of development of the upper limb illustrating the derivation of its segmental (dermatome) innervation. *C.* Diagram of developmental stages of the lower limb illustrating the derivation of its segmental (dermatome) innervation.

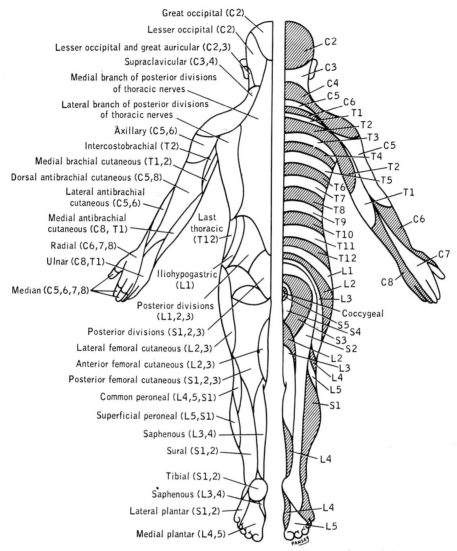

Figure 16-2 Peripheral distribution of sensory nerve fibers showing the same features as in Fig. 16-1*A*, but from the dorsal side: dermatomes on the right, cutaneous nerves on the left.

b Heart
B GSE (Chap. 13)
  1 Distribution
    a From C5 through *dorsal scapular nerve* to rhomboid muscles
    b From C5 and C6 through *suprascapular nerve* to supra- and infraspinatus muscles
    c From C5 and C6 through *sub-*

scapular nerves to subscapularis and teres major muscles
d From C5, C6, and C7 through the *long thoracic nerve* to serratus anterior
e From C5, C6, and C7 through the *lateral pectoral nerve* to the pectoralis major muscle
f From C8 and T1 through the

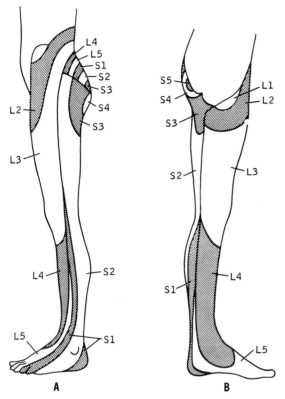

Figure 16-3 Lower extremity showing the distribution of the dermatomes. *A.* Lateral view. *B.* Medial view.

medial pectoral nerve to the pectoralis major and minor

g From C5, C6, and C7 through the *thoracodorsal nerve* to the latissimus dorsi

h From C5, C6, and C7 through the *musculocutaneous nerve* to biceps brachii, coracobrachialis, and brachialis muscles

i From C6, C7, C8, and T1 through the *median nerve* to most of flexors of wrist and fingers (see ulnar nerve); to the flexors, the short abductor, and opponens of the thumb; to the first and second lumbrical muscles

j From C8 and T1 through the *ulnar nerve* to flexor carpi ulnaris, ulnar half of flexor digitorum profundus, muscles of fifth finger, adductor and part of short flexor of thumb, all the interossei, and the third and fourth lumbrical muscles

k From C5 and C6 through the *axillary nerve* to the deltoid and teres minor muscles

l From C5, C6, C7, C8, and T1 through the *radial nerve* to the brachioradialis, triceps brachii, extensor carpi radialis, and all the extensors of wrist and fingers on the dorsal side of the forearm

C GVE (Chap. 14)
 1 Preganglionic
  a Origin — intermediolateral cell column of level T1

    b Terminations
        (1) First thoracic chain ganglion
        (2) Cervical ganglia of cervical sympathetic
    2 Postganglionic
        a Origin—any of ganglia under *C, b,* above
        b Terminations
            (1) Vessels, glands, and smooth muscle of head and neck
            (2) Vessels in upper extremity
            (3) Heart
IV Thoracics 2 through 6
    A GVA (Chap. 9)
        1 Distribution—thoracic viscera, including the heart
    B GSE (Chap. 13; Figs. 16-1, 16-2)
        1 Distribution
            a From each of these levels through *intercostal nerves* to intercostal muscles, serratus posterior superior, and upper external abdominal oblique
    C GVE (Chap. 14)
        1 Preganglionic
            a Origin — intermediolateral cell column
            b Terminations
                (1) Upper thoracic chain ganglia
                (2) Cervical sympathetic ganglia
        2 Postganglionic
            a Origin—any of ganglia under *C, b,* above
            b Terminations
                (1) Dilator pupillae
                (2) Glands of head and neck
                (3) Walls of blood vessels of head, neck, upper extremity, and body walls (thorax)
                (4) Heart
                (5) Lungs
V Thoracics 7 through 12
    A GVA (Chap. 9)
        1 Distribution—abdominal viscera
    B GSE (Chap. 13; Figs. 16-1, 16-2)
        1 Distribution—to all abdominal muscles
    C GVE (Chap. 14)

    1 Preganglionic
        a Origin—intermediolateral cell column
        b Terminations
            (1) Lower thoracic chain ganglia
            (2) Through the *splanchnic nerves* to celiac ganglia
            (3) Adrenal medulla
    2 Postganglionic
        a Origin—under *b,* (1), (2), above
        b Terminations
            (1) Blood vessels of abdominal wall
            (2) All blood vessels of abdominal viscera
            (3) Walls of all abdominal viscera
VI Lumbar 1 through 4—*lumbar plexus*
    A GVA (Chap. 9)
        1 Distribution
            a Abdominal and pelvic viscera
            b Vessels of thigh
    B GSE (Chap. 13)
        1 Distribution
            a From L1 through *ilioinguinal nerve* to the internal oblique
            b From L1 and L2 through the *genitofemoral nerve* to the cremaster muscle
            c From L2, L3, and L4 through the *obturator nerve* to the gracilis, obturator externus, and all adductor muscles of thigh
            d From L2, L3, and L4 through the *femoral nerve* to the iliacus, pectineus, sartorius, and all the quadriceps femoris (extensors of leg)
            e From L3 and L4 to iliacus and psoas
            f From L4 to form *lumbosacral trunk* with L5 (see VII, below)
    C GVE (Chap. 14)
        1 Preganglionic
            a Origin—intermediolateral cell column, at levels L1 and L2 (possibly L3)
            b Terminations

(1) Ganglia of lumbar chain
(2) Celiac and inferior mesenteric ganglia
(3) Ganglia of pelvic plexus (?)
2 Postganglionic
a Origin—any of ganglia under *C, b,* above
b Terminations
(1) Blood vessels of thigh
(2) Blood vessels of abdominal and pelvic viscera
(3) Walls of abdominal and pelvic viscera
VII Lumbar 5 and sacrals 1 through 3—*sacral plexus*
A GVA (Chap. 9)
1 Distribution
a Vessels of back of thigh; leg; foot
b All pelvic viscera, mainly in S2 and S3 (also S4)
B GSE (Chap. 13)
1 Distribution
a From L4, L5, and S1 to quadratus femoris and gemellus inferior muscles
b From L5, S1, and S2 to obturator internus and gemellus superior muscles
c From S2 to piriformis muscle
d From L4, L5, and S1 through the *superior gluteal* nerve to gluteus medius and minimus muscles
e From L5, S1, and S2 through the *inferior gluteal* nerve to the gluteus maximus muscle
f From L4, L5, S1, and S2 through the *common peroneal division* of the *sciatic nerve* to short head of biceps femoris, all peroneal muscles, extensors of the ankle, extensors of the toes, extensor of the large toe, and first two dorsal interosseous muscles
g From L4, L5, S1, S2, and S3, through the *tibial division* of the *sciatic nerve* to all the hamstring muscles except short head of the biceps femoris (under *f,* above);

all flexors of the ankle; all flexors of the toes, including the short muscles in the sole of the foot
C GVE (Chap. 14)
1 Preganglionic
a Origin—intermediolateral cell column at levels S2 and S3 (and usually S4)
b Termination, through the pelvic splanchnic nerves, to
(1) Ganglia in or on walls of pelvic viscera
(2) Ganglia in wall of lower colon
2 Postganglionic
a Origin—in any of ganglia under *C, b,* above
b Terminations
(1) Pelvic viscera
(2) Colon, lower half
(3) Genitalia
VIII Sacrals 4 and 5, with contributions from sacrals 2 and 3
A GVA (Chap. 9)
1 Distribution
a Genitalia
b External sphincters
B GSE (Chap. 13)
1 Distribution
a From S4 (and also S3 and S5) to
(1) Muscles of pelvic diaphragm
(2) External anal sphincter
b From S2, S3, and S4 through the *pudendal nerve* to all perineal muscles, including the external sphincters of anus and urethra
C GVE (Chap. 14)
1 Preganglionic—none
2 Postganglionic
a Origin
(1) For sympathetic outflow from inferior mesenteric and lumbar ganglia
(2) For parasympathetic outflow from ganglia of pelvic plexus
b Termination—external genitalia

CRANIAL NERVES

Since the cranial nerves differ considerably in the representation of the various systems, and particularly because the special categories have been included, each nerve will be considered separately. However, in certain general respects they are similar to the spinal nerves, and these items will not be repeated in each case. For example, the distribution of the GSA receptors will be shown on a figure; the GSA receptors for pain, temperature, and touch are the same type as those associated with the spinal nerves; the GP receptors are the same as those for the muscles of the limbs and trunk and have the same general distribution as the motor fibers supplying the cranial musculature; the symptoms of disease will be referable to the areas of distribution; and the receptors for the GVA are the same type

except that with certain of the cranial nerves chemoreceptors are utilized.

FUNCTIONAL COMPONENTS OF CRANIAL NERVES (Figs. 16-4, 16-5)

Specific Considerations

    I Olfactory
      A SVA (Chap. 10)
        1 Receptors
          a Type—hair cells
          b Location—nasal mucous membrane
          c Distribution upper third of nasal cavity
        2 Cell bodies—in membrane
        3 Termination—olfactory bulb
        4 Symptoms of disease—anosmia
   II Optic
      A SSA (Chap. 8)

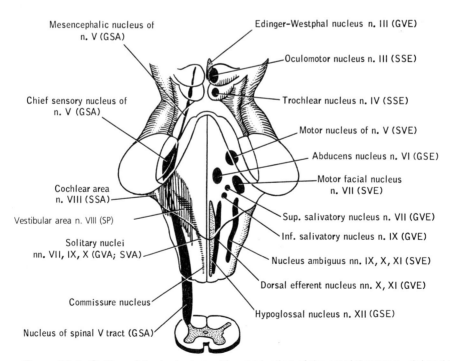

Figure 16-4 Outline of the brainstem with a projection of the cranial nerve nuclei and their components. Afferents are shown on the left, efferents on the right.

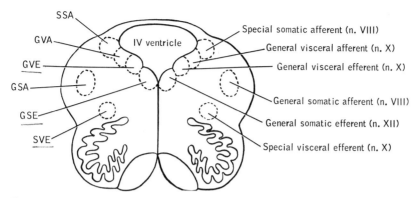

Figure 16-5 A schematic diagram of a section of the medulla illustrating the position of the cranial nerve nuclei according to function.

1 Receptors
  a Types
    (1) Rods
    (2) Cones
  b Location—retina of eye, layers 2, 3, 4, and 5
  c Distribution—in sensory part of retina
2 Cell bodies—bipolar cells of retina
3 Termination—ganglion layer of retina
4 Symptoms of disease—anopsia

III Oculomotor
  A GP (Chap. 11)
    1 Receptors
      a Distribution—extrinsic eye muscles except lateral rectus and superior oblique
    2 Cell bodies—mesencephalic nucleus of trigeminal
    3 Termination—through mesencephalic nucleus to reticular formation of brainstem
  B GSE (Chap. 13)
    1 Origin—oculomotor nucleus
    2 Termination—all extrinsic ocular muscles except the lateral rectus and superior oblique
    3 Symptoms of disease—eye looks downward and outward with no convergence

C GVE (Chap. 14)
  1 Preganglionic
    a Origin—Edinger-Westphal nucleus
    b Termination—ciliary and episcleral ganglia
  2 Postganglionic
    a Origin—under C, b, above
    b Termination—sphincter pupillae and ciliary muscle
  3 Symptoms of disease—pupils do not constrict to light or for accommodation

IV Trochlear
  A GP (Chap. 11)
    1 Receptors
      a Distribution—superior oblique
    2 Cell bodies—mesencephalic nucleus of trigeminal
    3 Termination—through mesencephalic nucleus to reticular formation of brainstem
  B GSE (Chap. 13)
    1 Origin—trochlear nucleus
    2 Termination — superior oblique muscle of eye
    3 Symptoms of disease—eye tends to look slightly upward

V Trigeminal (Fig. 16-6)
  A GSA (Fig. 16-1A) (Chap. 7)
    1 Receptors

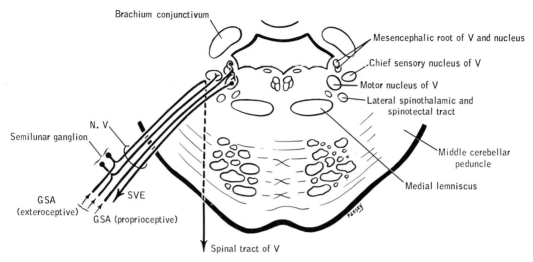

Figure 16-6 Diagram of the functional components of the trigeminal (V) nerve.

a Distribution—skin of face, conjunctiva and mucous membrane of nose and mouth
2 Cell bodies—semilunar (Gasserian) ganglion
3 Terminations
  a Pain and temperature—spinal V nucleus
  b Touch—chief sensory nucleus
4 Symptoms of disease—anesthesia in area of distribution
B GP (Chap. 11)
  1 Receptors
    a Distribution
      (1) Muscles of mastication
      (2) Temporomandibular joint
      (3) Sockets of teeth
  2 Cell bodies—mesencephalic nucleus
  3 Termination—through mesencephalic nucleus to reticular formation of the brainstem
C SVE (Chap. 15)
  1 Origin—motor nucleus of trigeminal
  2 Terminations
    a Muscles of mastication
    b Anterior belly digastric
    c Tensor tympani

    d Tensor veli palatini
    e Mylohyoid
  3 Symptoms of disease—paralysis of jaws
VI Abducens (Fig. 16-7)
  A GP (Chap. 11)
    1 Receptors
      a Distribution—lateral rectus muscle of eye
    2 Cell bodies—mesencephalic nucleus of trigeminal
    3 Termination—through mesencephalic nucleus to reticular formation of brainstem
  B GSE (Chap. 14)
    1 Origin—abducens nucleus
    2 Termination—lateral rectus muscle of eye
    3 Symptoms of disease—eye turns inward
VII Facial (Fig. 16-7)
  A GP (Chap. 11)
    1 Receptors
      a Muscles of facial expression
    2 Cell bodies—mesencephalic nucleus of trigeminal
    3 Termination—reticular formation of brainstem by way of the mesencephalic nucleus

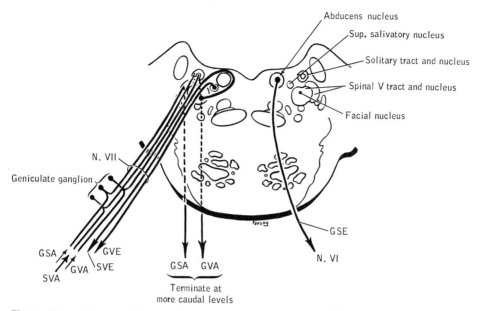

Figure 16-7 Diagram of the functional components of the facial (VII) nerve.

B GVA (Chap. 9)
  1 Receptors
    a Distribution—deep tissues of face
  2 Cell bodies—geniculate ganglion
  3 Termination—nucleus of tractus solitarius
C SVA (Chap. 10)
  1 Receptors
    a Type—taste buds
    b Location—in epithelium of tongue
    c Distribution—anterior two-thirds of the tongue
  2 Cell bodies—geniculate ganglion
  3 Termination—nucleus of tractus solitarius (or gustatory nucleus)
  4 Symptoms of disease—ageusia on anterior two-thirds of tongue
D SVE (Chap. 15)
  1 Origin—facial nucleus
  2 Terminations
    a Muscles of facial expression, including the platysma
    b Posterior belly of digastric
    c Stylohyoid

  d Stapedius
  3 Symptoms of disease—facial paralysis (Bell's palsy)
E GVE (Chap. 14)
  1 Preganglionic
    a Origin
      (1) Superior salivatory nucleus
      (2) Lacrimal nucleus
    b Terminations
      (1) Submandibular ganglion
      (2) Pterygopalatine ganglion
  2 Postganglionic
    a Origin, under *b*, (1) and (2), above
    b Terminations
      (1) Submandibular and sublingual salivary glands—under *b*, (1), above
      (2) Lacrimal gland—under *b*,(2), above
  3 Symptoms of disease—poor secretion from glands of termination
VIII Acoustic (Fig. 16-8)
  A SSA (Chap. 8)
    1 Receptors
      a Type—hair cells
      b Location—organ of Corti

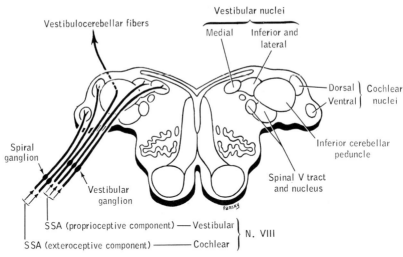

Figure 16-8 Diagram of the functional components of the acoustic (VIII) nerve.

c Distribution—cochlear duct of inner ear

2 Cell bodies—spiral ganglion

3 Terminations

a Dorsal cochlear nucleus

b Ventral cochlear nucleus

4 Symptoms of disease—deafness

B SP (Chap. 12)

1 Receptors

a Type—hair cells

b Location

(1) Cristae

(2) Maculae

c Distribution

(1) Ampullae of semicircular canals of inner ear, under *b*, (1), above

(2) Utriculus of inner ear, under *b*, (2), above

(3) Sacculus of inner ear, under *b*, (2), above

2 Cell bodies—vestibular ganglion

3 Terminations

a Vestibular nuclei (superior, medial, lateral, and spinal)

b Cerebellum

IX Glossopharyngeal (Fig. 16-9)

A GVA (Chap. 9)

1 Receptors

a Types

(1) General

(2) Chemoreceptors

b Distribution

(1) Pharynx

(2) Posterior third of tongue

(3) Carotid sinus

2 Cell bodies—petrosal ganglion

3 Termination—nucleus of tractus solitarius

4 Symptoms of disease—interference with the afferent limb of the swallowing reflex

B SVA (Chap 10)

1 Receptors

a Type—taste buds

b Location—epithelium of tongue

c Distribution—posterior third of tongue

2 Cell bodies—petrosal ganglion

3 Termination—nucleus of tractus solitarius (or the gustatory nucleus?)

4 Symptoms of disease—ageusia on posterior third of tongue

C GVE (Chap. 14)

1 Preganglionic

a Origin—inferior salivatory nucleus

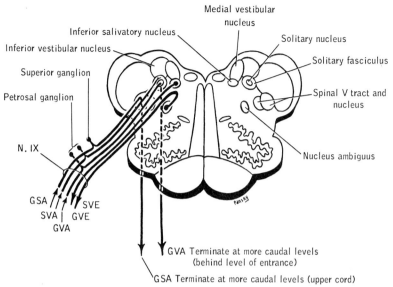

Figure 16-9 Diagram of the functional components of the glossopharyngeal (IX) nerve.

b Termination—otic ganglion

2 Postganglionic

  a Origin—under *C, b,* above

  b Termination—parotid salivary gland

3 Symptoms of disease—decreased secretion of the parotid

D SVE (Chap. 15)

  1 Origin—nucleus ambiguus

  2 Terminations

    a Stylopharyngeus muscle

    b Superior pharyngeal constrictor (?)

  3 Symptoms of disease—some difficulty in swallowing

X Vagus (Fig. 16-10)

  A GSA (Chap. 7)

    1 Receptors

      a Distribution—external auditory meatus

    2 Cell bodies—jugular ganglion

    3 Termination—spinal V nucleus

    4· Symptoms of disease—anesthesia in area of distribution

  B GVA (Chap. 9)

    1 Receptors

      a Distribution

        (1) Pharynx

        (2) Respiratory system including larynx, trachea, bronchi

        (3) Digestive system, esophagus through the middle of colon, inclusive

        (4) Circulatory system including the heart, arch of the aorta, and carotid sinus

    2 Cell bodies—nodose ganglion

    3 Termination—nucleus of the tractus solitarius

    4 Symptoms of disease

      a Loss of reflex control of circulation (heart rate, etc.)

      b Disturbances in depth of respiration

      c Poor digestion

  C SVA (Chap. 10)

    1 Receptors

      a Type—taste buds

      b Location—in epithelium

      c Distribution

        (1) Epiglottis

        (2) Tongue adjacent to epiglottis

        (3) Lower pharynx (?)

    2 Cell bodies—nodose ganglion

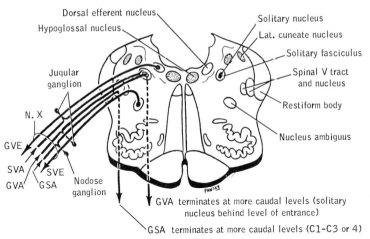

Figure 16-10 Diagram of the functional components of the vagus (X) nerve.

3 Termination—nucleus of tractus solitarius (or gustatory nucleus?)

4 Symptoms of disease—ageusia in area of distribution

D GVE (Chap. 14)

1 Preganglionic

  a Origin—dorsal motor nucleus of the vagus

  b Termination—in terminal ganglia

    (1) Of cardiac plexuses

    (2) Of pulmonary plexuses

    (3) Of esophageal plexuses

    (4) In Auerbach's plexus in alimentary canal

    (5) In Meissner's plexus

2 Postganglionic

  a Origin—in any of ganglia under *D, 1, b,* above

  b Terminations

    (1) Heart

    (2) Smooth muscle and glands of trachea and bronchi

    (3) Muscle of esophagus

    (4) From Auerbach's plexus to smooth muscle of alimentary canal to midcolon

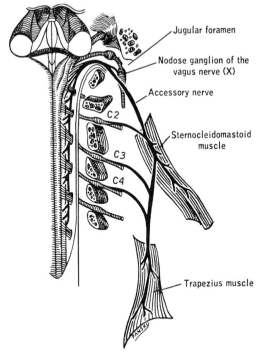

Figure 16-11 Course, distribution, and relations of the spinal accessory nerve (XI).

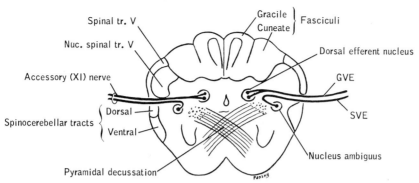

Figure 16-12 Diagram of a section of the lower medulla at the level of the pyramidal decussation showing the components of the accessory (XI) nerve.

(5) From Meissner's plexus to glands of walls of alimentary canal to midcolon
3 Symptoms of disease
  a Loss of reflex control of circulatory system, as heart rate and blood pressure
  b Poor digestion due to decreased secretion of digestive enzymes and slowing of peristalsis
E SVE (Chap. 15)
  1 Origin—nucleus ambiguus
  2 Terminations
    a Pharyngeal constrictors
    b Muscles of larynx
    c Muscles of palate
  3 Symptoms of disease
    a Difficulty in swallowing
    b Difficulty in speaking
XI Accessory (Figs. 16-11, 16-12)
  A GP (?) (Chap. 11)
    1 Receptors
      a Distribution—in muscles supplied by SVE
  B SVE (Chap. 15)
    1 Origin

      a Nucleus ambiguus
      b Lateral aspect of ventral horns of upper cervical cord
      c Remnants of ventral horn in lower medulla
    2 Terminations
      a From *B, 1, a,* above, to larynx and pharynx with vagus
      b From *B,* 1, *b* and *B,* 1, *c,* above, to the sternocleidomastoid and trapezius muscles
    3 Symptoms of disease—difficulty in turning the head and possibly in swallowing
XII Hypoglossal
  A GP (Chap. 11)
    1 Receptors
      a Distribution—muscles of tongue
    2 Cell bodies—location uncertain
    3 Termination—uncertain
  B GSE (Chap. 13)
    1 Origin—hypoglossal nucleus
    2 Termination—all muscles of tongue
    3 Symptoms of disease—paralysis of tongue

C5 | C6 | C7 | C8 | T1

Biceps brachii .... Musculocutaneous n.
Brachialis .... Musculocutaneous and radial nn.
Brachioradialis .... Radial n.
Coracobrachialis ..... Musculocutaneous n.
Deltoid........... Axillary n.
Infraspinatous .... Suprascapular n.
Subscapularis .... Upper and lower subscapular n.
Supraspinatus....... Suprascapular n.
Teres major......... Lower subscapular n.
Teres minor .... Axillary n.

Abd. pollicis longus .... Deep radial n.
Ext. carpi radialis brevis ..... Deep radial n.
Ext. carpi radialis longus .... Radial n.
Ext. pollicis brevis .... Deep radial n.
Flex. carpi radialis .... Median n.
Palmaris longus .... Median n.
Pronator teres .... Median n.
Supinator .... Deep radial n.
Ext. carpi ulnaris .... Deep radial n.
Ext. digitorum .... Deep radial n.
Ext. indicis............ Deep radial n.
Ext. pollicis longus .... Deep radial n.
Triceps brachii........ Radial n.

Anconeus .... Radial n.
Ext. digiti minimi .... Deep radial n.
Flex. digitorum profundus ..... Median and ulnar nn.
Flex. digitorum superficialis ..... Median n.

Abd. digiti minimi .... Deep ulnar n.
Abd pollicis brevis .... Median n.
Add. pollicis .... Deep ulnar n.
Flex. carpi ulnaris .... Ulnar n.
Flex. digiti minimi .... Deep ulnar n.
Flex. pollicis brevis......... Median n.
Flex. pollicis longus .... Median n.
Interossei .... Deep ulnar n.
Lumbricales .... Deep ulnar and median nn.
Opponens digiti minimi ..... Deep ulnar n.
Opponens pollicis .... Deep ulnar n.
Palmaris brevis......... Superficial ulnar n.
Pronator quadratus .... Median n.

Add. brevis . . .	Obturator n.
Add. longus . . .	Obturator n.
Gracilis	Obturator n.
Sartorius	Femoral n.

Iliacus	Femoral n.
Psoas major . . .	Nn. to psoas

Obturator externus . .	Obturator n.
Pectineus	Femoral n.
Quadriceps femoris . . .	Femoral n.

Add. magnus . . . . Obturator and sciatic nn.

Tibialis anterior . . . . . Deep peroneal n.

Gluteus medius	Superior gluteal n.
Gluteus minimus	Superior gluteal n.
Inf. gemellus	N. to quadratus femoris
Lumbricales	Medial and lateral plantar nn.
Plantaris	Tibial n.
Popliteus	Tibial n.
Quadratus femoris . . .	N. to quadratus femoris
Tensor fascia latae . . .	Superior gluteal n.

Semimembranosus	Sciatic n.
Semitendinosus	Sciatic n.

Ext. digitorum longus . . .	Deep peroneal n.
Ext. hallucis longus	Deep peroneal n.
Peroneus brevis	Superficial peroneal n.
Peroneus longus	Superficial peroneal n.
Tibialis posterior	Tibia n.

Gluteus maximus	Inferior gluteal n.
Obturator internus	N. to obt. internus
Soleus	Tibial n.
Sup. gemellus	N. to obt. internus
Biceps femoris	Sciatic n.

Abd. digiti minimi	Lat. plantar n.
Abd. hallucis	Med. plantar n.
Add. hallucis	Lat. plantar n.
Ext. digit. brevis	Deep peroneal n.
Ext. hallucis brevis	Deep peroneal n.
Flex. digiti minimi	Lat. plantar n.
Flex. digit brevis	Med plantar n.
Flex. digit. longus	Tibial n.
Flex. hallucis brevis	Med. plantar n.
Flex. hallucis longus	Tibial n.
Gastrocnemius	Tibial n.
Interossei	Lateral plantar n.
Piriformis	N. to piriformis
Quadratus plantae	Lat. plantar n.

The Cerebellum

The chief concerns of the cerebellum include synergy, which is defined as "the facility by which movements are properly grouped for the performance of acts requiring special adjustments"; the establishment and maintenance of equilibrium; and the regulation of muscle tone. To appreciate what this means, it is necessary to analyze, in terms of muscular performance, the mechanics of movement. (1) The initiation of movement requires the contraction of a muscle or a group of muscles. Simultaneously, however, an opposing set of muscles must relax. (2) For the proper performance of a movement, a definite amount of muscular contraction is required. This can be controlled only by the adjustment of the number of muscle fibers[1] involved in the reaction, which, in turn, is a function of the number of nerve fibers activated. (3) The proper duration of the nerve impulses for the completion of an act is important. (4) Especially when the action requires movement at several joints, it is essential for muscles to contract and relax in the proper sequence.

In order to accomplish these things, the cerebellum must function as a computer for the integration of sensory and motor signals. Accordingly, the cerebellum receives continuous information from the muscular system concerning the tension states and the length of individual as well as groups of muscles. Streams of impulses set up by movements must also reach the cerebellum from the joints. Furthermore, information from the vestibular receptors in the inner ear must reach the cerebellum. In order to function as a computer the cerebellum must, at the same time, also receive signals from all other parts of the CNS which participate in the regulation of motor activity. These structures include

---

[1]According to the all-or-none law, a muscle fiber receiving a stimulus strong enough to cause a contraction at all will contract to its fullest. Therefore, the strength of the contraction of a muscle as a whole depends upon the number of contracting fibers, the latter being a function of the number of nerves carrying activating impulses.

portions of the brainstem reticular formation, the red nucleus, the vestibular nuclei, and the cerebral cortex. Following receipt of signals from these sites, the cerebellum must possess an internal organization capable of processing this information. The region where such processing occurs is the cerebellar cortex. Finally, the computer mechanism within the cerebellum must possess an output with which it could feed back signals to all the structures which provide input to the cerebellum and which participate in the regulation and control of motor activities. Figure 17-1 is a schematic diagram of the reciprocal interrelations between the cerebellum and other components of the motor system(s).

STRUCTURE OF THE CEREBELLUM

Gross (Fig. 17-2)

The major structural features have already been given (Figs. 1-29 through 1-32). However, since reference is often made to divisions based upon evolutionary and developmental concepts, a description of the cerebellum would be incomplete without considering these aspects.

Early in phylogenesis, the cerebellum appears as lateral elevations of the ancient hindbrain which are almost a part of the primordial vestibular apparatus. Later, a median unpaired portion appears. This condition persists in animal forms without limbs. With the ap-

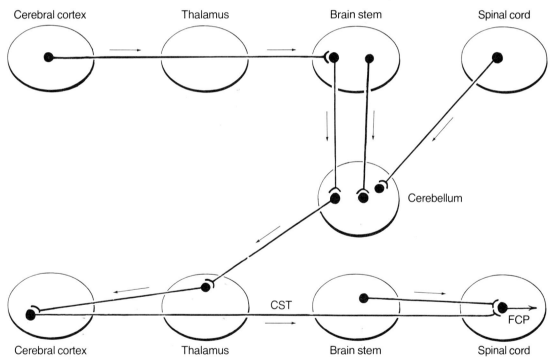

Figure 17-1 Schematic diagram illustrating some of the relations between the cerebellum and other structures which constitute the motor systems including the axons arising from the ventral horn cells identified as the final common path (FCP). Within this scheme the FCP is acted upon by neurons in the brainstem (BS) such as the reticulospinal tract, rubrospinal tract, vestibulospinal tract, and corticospinal tract (CST) arising from the sensorimotor cortex. In turn, each of the regions which modulate the ventral horns of the spinal cord appear to maintain either direct or indirect reciprocal connections with the cerebellum. Such reciprocal connections provide an essential ingredient to the computer functions of the cerebellum.

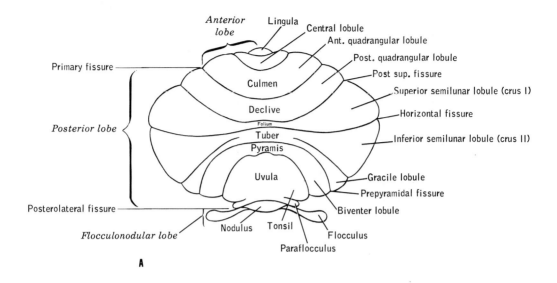

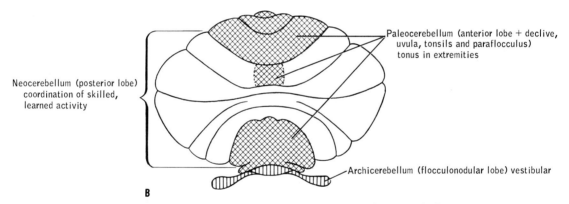

Figure 17-2 *A.* Diagram of the major fissures, lobes, and lobules of the cerebellum. *(Modified after Larsell, 1951; Jansen and Brodal, 1958.) B.* Diagram of the cerebellum divided on the basis of phylogenesis and function.

pearance of appendages, the median cerebellar body expands laterally. This expansion is the progenitor of the body of the cerebellum (hemispheres). At about the same stage of evolution, the two lateral parts of the original vestibular cerebellum join across the midline, forming the *flocculonodular lobe,* separated from the body by the posterolateral fissure (Figs. 1-32, 17-2). Because of its early phylo-

genetic appearance, the flocculonodular lobe is often referred to as the *archicerebellum.*[2]

Early in development, the body of the cerebellum lying rostral to the posterolateral fissure is divided into an anterior and posterior lobe by the appearance of the primary fissure (Figs. 1-29, 1-31, 1-32, 4-6, 17-2, 17-3). Since

[2]The prefix *archi-* denotes first, or original.

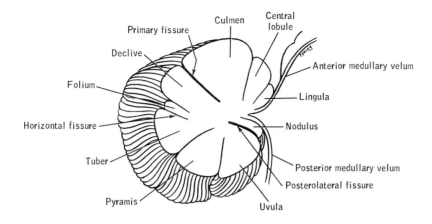

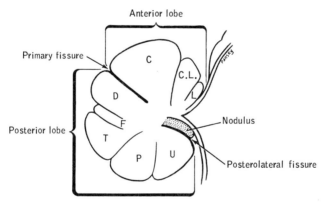

Figure 17-3 Diagram of a sagittal section through the midline of the cerebellum showing the principal fissures and divisions of the vermis.

the small median portions of both these lobes of the body are also very old, appearing almost at the same time as the flocculonodular lobe, they are included as part of the archicerebellum. However, the lateral expansion of these parts, developing later, is referred to as the *paleocerebellum* [3] (Fig. 17-2).

Phylogenetically, the appearance of the cerebral hemispheres makes possible a tremendous range of voluntary actions. Therefore, there is an enlargement of the cerebellum,

proportionate in extent to the size of the voluntary motor centers of the cerebrum. This is the *neocerebellum* [4] (Fig. 17-2), which accounts for the great size of the human cerebellum.

According to some authorities, the neocerebellum is the major and most rostral part of the posterior lobe of the cerebellum. According to others, the neocerebellum is represented by the middle lobe. Using the latter designation, that portion lying in front of the

[3] *Paleo-* means old but neither original nor as old as *archi-*.

[4] *Neo-* means new or recent.

primary fissure, including the lingula, central lobule, culmen, and anterior quadrangular lobule, belongs to the anterior lobe (Figs. 1-29, 1-31, 1-32). The middle lobe, the rostral boundary of which is the primary fissure, includes (from front to back) the declive, with the posterior quadrangular lobule; the folium, with its lateral portion, the superior semilunar lobule; the tuber, and its extension, the inferior semilunar lobule. Just behind the tuber of the vermis, the prepyramidal fissure usually can be seen. This is the line dividing the middle from the posterior lobe. The latter is made up, from front to back, of the pyramis

and its biventer lobule, and the uvula, with its lateral extension, the tonsil.

Internal Structure and Central Nuclei (Fig. 17-4)

Long, narrow folds of cortex (folia) cover a central core of white substance which is continuous from one hemisphere to the other through the vermis. Embedded in the medullary core are groups of gray substance, the cerebellar nuclei. The largest and most lateral is an irregular lamina of cells which resembles a crumpled sac with an open mouth, the hilus, directed medially. This is the *dentate nucleus*.

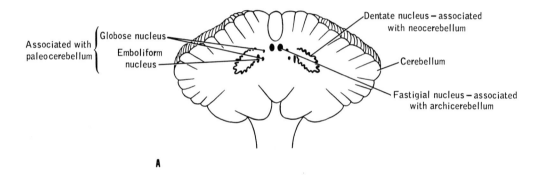

A

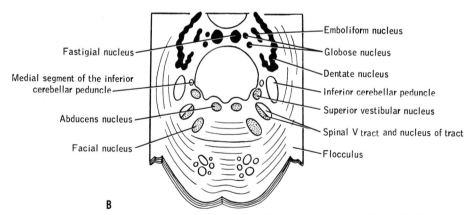

B

Figure 17-4 *A.* Transverse section of the adult cerebellum illustrating the cerebellar nuclei. *B.* Vertical section through the adult cerebellum and brainstem at the level of the nuclei of the abducens (VI) and facial (VII) nerves. The fourth ventricle, inferior cerebellar peduncle, and the cerebellar nuclei are also shown.

Close to the hilus lies a narrow plate of cells called the *emboliform nucleus*. Medial to the inferior portion of the latter lie one or more rounded gray areas called the *globose nuclei*. Closely adjoining the midline, in the core of the vermis, are the *fastigial nuclei*.

Afferent Connections of the Cerebellum

As previously indicated, the cerebellum must be capable of receiving inputs from all portions of the CNS which relate to the control of motor activity if it is to maintain its computer-like regulatory function. Therefore, in this section we shall consider the organization of the afferent supply to the cerebellum.

Characteristics of Cerebellar Afferent Fibers

There are two types of fibers which carry impulses to the cerebellum. They are identified morphologically as *mossy* and *climbing fibers* (Fig. 17-5). The *mossy fibers* are found in all parts of the cerebellum. They course through and give rise to many branches within the granular layer. These branches terminate by forming *mossy fiber rosettes* which are held in clawlike dendrites of the granule cells. Impulses pass through the granule cells to come into synaptic relations with the dendrites of the Purkinje cells, many of which can be activated by an impulse traveling in but one afferent fiber. It is significant that a single mossy fiber rosette forms the focus of a *cerebellar glomerulus*, the site of synaptic relations between mossy fiber axons and both granule cell dendrites and Golgi cell axon terminals. The cerebellar glomerulus (Fig. 17-6) is situated in the granule cell layer and consists of (1) a mossy fiber rosette, (2) the dendrites of many granule cells, (3) the proximal aspect of Golgi cell dendrites, and (4) the terminals of Golgi cell axons. The mossy fibers presumably issue from all parts of the CNS associated with the cerebellar afferent supply. The climbing fibers are long and slender. They issue principally from the inferior olivary nucleus. Other structures also giving rise to climbing fibers include the deep pontine nuclei and the reticular formation. They ascend through the granule and Purkinje cell layers to enter the molecular layer. Here, they climb, like a vine on a trellis, among the dendritic branches of the Purkinje cells.

Spinocerebellar Fibers   (Fig. 17-7)

These fibers are important in bringing into the cerebellum information concerning the tension state of muscles and the orientation of articulations. They travel in several different pathways from various points of origin.

The *dorsal (posterior) spinocerebellar tract* arises from the nucleus dorsalis of Clarke (C8 to L3). Fibers from this nucleus pass laterally into the white matter of the spinal cord and ascend without interruption to the cerebellar cortex via the inferior cerebellar peduncle. These fibers terminate within the medial part of the anterior lobe, the pyramis, and the paramedian lobule. They are activated following stimulation of muscle spindles or Golgi tendon organs of the lower limbs. Thus, the second-order neurons in this pathway which possesses a rapid conduction velocity (30 to 110 m/s), may be driven by A alpha, A beta, or possibly even group II afferents (Chap. 7), all of whose cell bodies lie in dorsal root ganglia and whose axons terminate in the nucleus dorsalis. In addition, the dorsal spinocerebellar tract is believed to transmit exteroceptive impulses from pressure or touch receptors in the skin. In general, it has been suggested that this tract is concerned with the status of individual limb muscles (Fig. 17-7).

The *anterior spinocerebellar tract* arises from diffuse sites in the anterior and lateral spinal gray matter at lumbar and sacral levels. Axons of this tract cross to the opposite side and ascend in the lateral aspect of the lateral funiculus immediately ventral to the dorsal

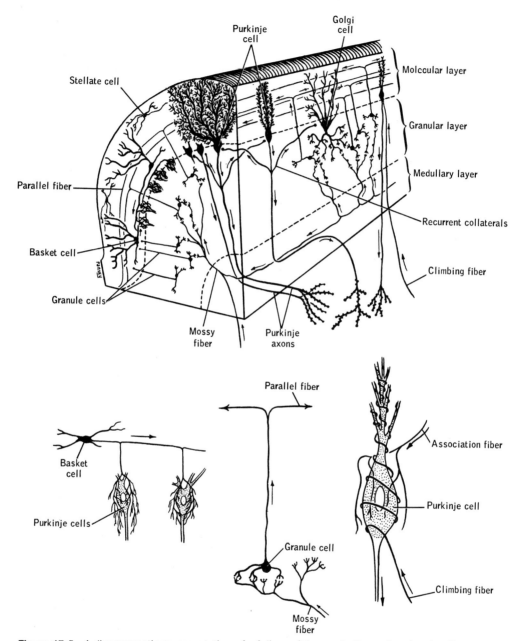

Figure 17-5 A diagrammatic representation of a folium of the cerebellar cortex showing the arrangement of cells and fibers as seen in both longitudinal and transverse sections. The relations between fiber types and cells are also illustrated.

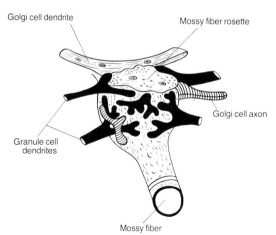

Golgi cell dendrite

Mossy fiber rosette

Golgi cell axon

Granule cell dendrites

Mossy fiber

Figure 17-6 Reconstruction of a cerebellar glomerulus. One mossy fiber rosette is shown having synaptic contacts with several granule cell dendrites plus the dendrite and axons of Golgi cells. *(After Eccles, Ito, and Szentagothai, in Sir John Eccles, The Cerebellum as a Neuronal Machine, Springer-Verlag New York Inc., New York, 1967.)*

spinocerebellar tract. In contrast to the course of the posterior spinocerebellar tract, the anterior tract follows a circuitous route into the cerebellum via the superior cerebellar peduncle. Fibers which enter this peduncle pass to the contralateral cerebellum and terminate principally in the vermal region of the anterior lobe. Although some of the fibers do terminate bilaterally, the majority are distributed to the contralateral side. Fibers in this tract have conduction velocities between 70 and 120 m/s and convey impulses from Golgi tendon organs (A beta fibers) and flexor reflex afferents of the lower limb. It has been suggested that fibers in this tract transmit information concerning posture and movements of muscle groups or of an entire limb (Fig. 17-7).

The *rostral spinocerebellar tract* has recently been described in the cat and corresponds to the forelimb equivalent of the anterior spinocerebellar tract. This bundle arises from the cervical cord and ascends, uncrossed, in the anterolateral white matter of the cord to the anterior lobe of the cerebellum through both inferior and superior cerebellar peduncles. Similar to the anterior spinocerebellar tract, it conveys information concerning flexor reflex afferents and tendon organs.

Cuneocerebellar Fibers

The *cuneocerebellar tract* arises from the accessory cuneate nucleus situated in the dorsolateral part of the lower medulla. Impulses reaching this nucleus originate from muscle spindles associated with the upper limb and travel via A alpha afferents. These fibers enter the spinal cord at cervical levels and ascend through the fasciculus cuneatus. Cuneocerebellar fibers enter the cerebellum through the inferior peduncle and terminate in the forelimb region of the anterior lobe, pyramis, and paramedian lobule (Fig. 17-7).

Vestibulocerebellar Fibers

Fibers from the vestibular apparatus (Figs. 12-5, 17-8) may enter the cerebellum by two general routes: (1) a direct ascending branch of the vestibular nerve which courses upward along the medial side of the inferior cerebellar peduncle to enter the homolateral flocculonodular lobe and (2) an indirect path arising in the inferior and medial vestibular nuclei (Chap. 12). These fibers enter the cerebellum mainly through the juxtarestiform body, which lies just medial to the inferior cerebellar peduncle. They terminate bilaterally within the flocculonodular lobe and the fastigial nucleus (Fig. 17-8).

Trigeminocerebellar Fibers

Secondary proprioceptive fibers, arising in the mesencephalic nucleus and terminating in the dentate and emboliform nuclei, have been reported. Other sensory modalities, especially touch, have secondary fibers arising in the chief sensory nucleus of the trigeminal and ending in the anterior quadrangular lobule and tonsil. It is also possible that both crossed and uncrossed fibers may arise in the spinal nucle-

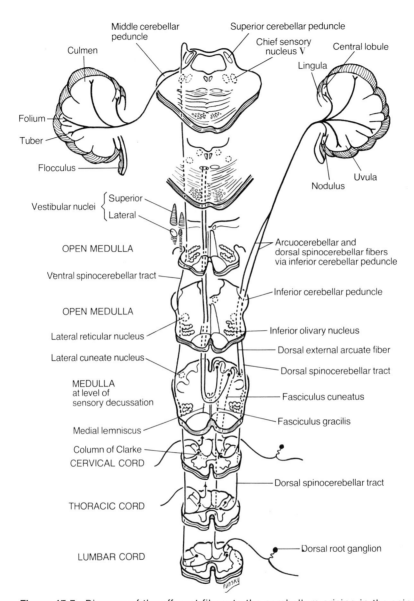

Figure 17-7 Diagram of the afferent fibers to the cerebellum arising in the spinal cord.

us of the trigeminal and ascend to these same areas of the cerebellum.

Reticulocerebellar Fibers

These fibers arise predominantly from two regions of the medulla and one site in the pons. Fibers from the lateral and paramedian reticular nuclei remain uncrossed as they join the inferior cerebellar peduncle to be distributed chiefly to the vermis of the anterior lobe. Other fibers appear to terminate in the pyramis and uvula of the posterior lobe as well. Although much of the transmission within the reticular formation is modality-nonspecific, it is believed that the lateral reticular nucleus receives tactile impulses conveyed from the

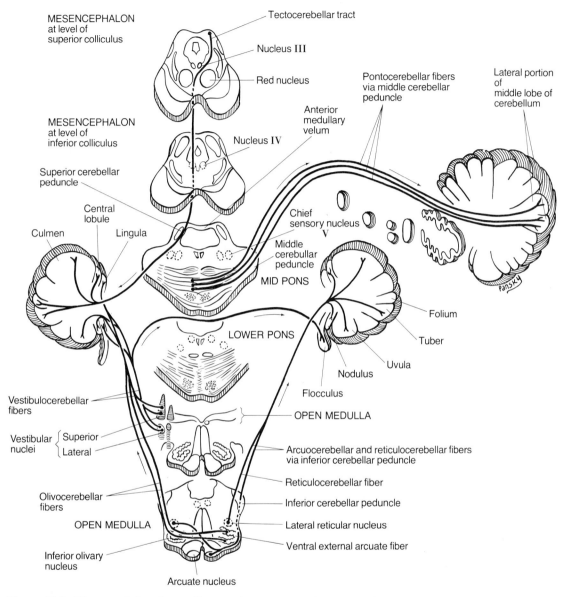

Figure 17-8 Diagram of the afferent fibers to the cerebellum from the brainstem.

spinal cord within the anterolateral funiculus. Thus, this system of fibers may be responsible for the transmission of somatic impulses to various sites within the cerebellar cortex (Figs. 17-8, 17-9).

The cerebellar cortex also receives input from the pontine reticular formation. Fibers arising from the reticulotegmental nucleus travel via the middle cerebellar peduncle and are distributed mainly to the vermal regions of the anterior and posterior lobes. It is of interest to point out that some of the nuclei which supply the cerebellum also receive a substantial input from sensorimotor cortex and thus

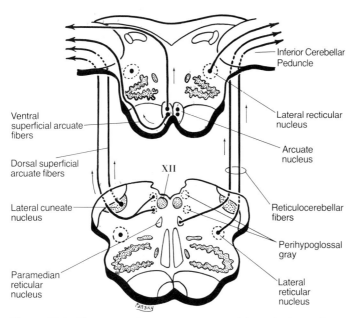

Figure 17-9 Diagram to demonstrate some of the reticulo- and arcuatocerebellar fibers of the brainstem. *(After Crosby, Humphrey, and Lauer, Correlative Anatomy of the Nervous System. The Macmillan Company, New York, 1962.)*

provide an anatomic basis for a selected feedback circuit.

Olivocerebellar Fibers

The inferior olivary complex is composed of a principal (chief) olivary nucleus, a dorsal accessory nucleus, and a medial accessory nucleus. The principal nucleus consists of a dorsal and a ventral lamella with a laterally placed interlamellar band connecting the two. Because of the descending fibers from the red nucleus, which pass in the central tegmental tract, and others from the sensorimotor cortex, both of which end here, the olivocerebellar circuit may be under both direct and indirect cortical control.

The inferior olive is related to most of the spinal afferent systems by fibers ascending in the spinoolivary tract. The latter arises from cells in the dorsal horn of the spinal cord on the side opposite to the tract. In this way, olivocerebellar fibers transmit impulses from cutaneous afferents, joint afferents, and some

muscle afferents as well. Olivocerebellar fibers arise from the entire complex, cross the midline, usually passing through the olive of the other side, and ascend into the cerebellum by way of the inferior cerebellar peduncle. It should be noted that these fibers contribute the largest single component of this peduncle. Those fibers which have their origin in the chief nucleus have a wide distribution to the hemispheres of both the anterior and posterior lobes. From the medial accessory olive, fibers terminate in the flocculonodular lobe, the pyramis, uvula, declive, and fastigial nucleus. The dorsal accessory olive sends most of its fibers to the vermal portions of the anterior lobe and to the declive and folium of the posterior lobe (Fig. 17-10). From what has been described above it is possible to view the inferior olivary complex as an important focal relay station for the modulation and transmission of signals to large segments of the cerebellar cortex from the spinal cord, red nucleus, and sensorimotor cortex (Fig. 17-11).

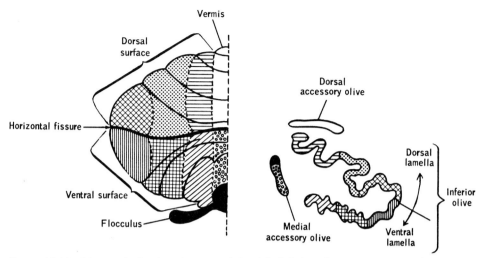

Figure 17-10 Diagram indicating the parts of the right inferior olivary complex showing the projection of its parts via the olivocerebellar fibers to specific areas of the left half of the cerebellum. *(Modified after Huber, 1899; Hamby and Gardner, 1935; Szentagothai, 1942.)*

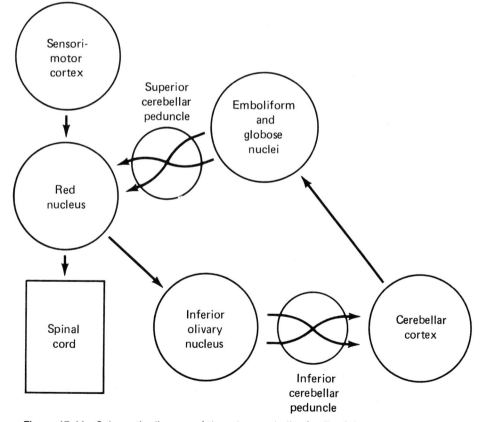

Figure 17-11 Schematic diagram of the rubrocerebellar feedback loop.

Tectocerebellar Fibers   (Fig. 17-8)

The *tectocerebellar tract* probably arises both in the superior and inferior colliculi (tectum). From the caudal limits of the latter, fibers enter the anterior medullary velum, where they are believed to undergo a partial decussation. In the cerebellum they terminate in the anterior lobe, especially in the caudal part of the anterior quadrangular lobule; in the posterior lobe, including the folium, tuber, and pyramis; and in the most medial portion of the hemispheres adjoining these vermal regions. The tectum of the mesencephalon has been shown to be centers for visual and auditory reflexes; thus this pathway has to do with the coordination of the motor portion of these reflexes. It has been suggested that the tectocerebellar route is the most important pathway linking auditory impulses to the cerebellum. Visual impulses may have other routes such as tectopontine-pontocerebellar or occipitopontine-pontocerebellar pathways.

Pontocerebellar Fibers   (Figs. 17-8, 17-12, 25-6 through 25-9)

The mass of *pontocerebellar fibers* is concerned with the coordination of movements initiated in the sensorimotor cortex of the cerebrum. Descending fibers from the frontal, parietotemperooccipital, and temporal association areas as well as collaterals of the pyramidal fibers arising in the precentral gyrus terminate among the pontine nuclei. The latter are scattered among the fascicles of the basal pons. Attempts have been made to subdivide the pontine gray into nuclear groups, i.e., dorsolateral, lateral, medial, and ventral, but they are so poorly circumscribed that only a general division will be made here—lateral and medial. From cells in these groups, fibers arise, most of which cross to ascend into the cerebellum by way of the middle cerebellar peduncle. The vast majority of these terminate in the neocerebellar cortex, both of the hemispheres and the vermis. This includes

most of the posterior lobe. There is also an overlap into the paleocerebellum of the anterior lobe, especially in the anterior quadrangular lobule and the culmen.

Arcuatocerebellar Fibers   (Figs. 17-8, 17-9, 25-5)

The arcuate nuclei from which these fibers arise are found on the ventral and medial surfaces of the pyramids of the medulla. Since it is believed that these nuclei have the same origin as those of the pontine gray and actually represent displaced pontine nuclei, this circuit acts as a supplement to the corticopontocerebellar pathway. Collaterals from the descending corticospinal tracts terminate among cells of the arcuate nuclei. Fibers arising in these nuclei leave in two streams: (1) the ventral external arcuates, (2) the arcuatocerebellar fibers. The former pass along the external ventral and lateral surfaces of the medulla, join the inferior cerebellar peduncle, and enter the cerebellum. The latter run dorsally near the midline, to the floor of the fourth ventricle, whence they stream laterally as the striae medullares to enter the cerebellum by way of the inferior cerebellar peduncle. In general, it has been said that these fibers end in the flocculus. However, it seems likely that they may overlap the fibers in the pontocerebellar system.

ORGANIZATION OF THE CEREBELLAR CORTEX

Microscopic Anatomy

The superficial gray matter of the cerebellum is thrown into folds (folia), the long axes of which are arranged transversely from one hemisphere to the other. The center of each folium is composed of medullary substance through which all fibers enter or leave the cortex.

The arrangement of the cells and fibers within the cortex is an adaptation to functional requirements. First, the cerebellum must be

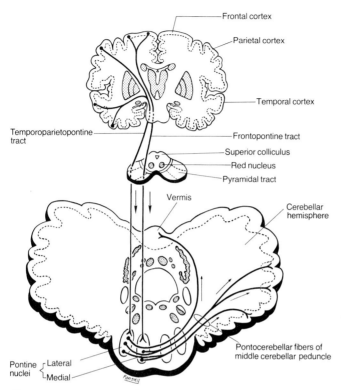

Figure 17-12 Diagram of the cerebropontocerebellar circuit showing the origin of the fibers from the cerebrum, their position in the cerebral peduncle, the pontine nuclei, and the distribution to the cerebellar vermis and hemispheres.

able to disseminate its influence over the entire body musculature. To accomplish this, it must be possible for a single impulse to spread over, and thus activate, large areas of the cortex. Second, the influence of the cerebellum, in many instances, is reinforcing, enhancing, and perpetuating. For this to be possible, impulses leaving the cortex must be able to reactivate the same areas in the cortex from which they originally arose.

The cortex is composed of three layers (Fig. 17-5): the inner, or *granular* layer; the middle, or *Purkinje cell layer*; and the outer, or *molecular layer*.

Granular (Inner) Layer

Two types of cells are found here. The predominant type is a small neuron called the *granule cell.* Its three to five dendrites spray out through this layer and terminate in small clawlike arrangements for the reception of afferent fibers entering the cerebellar cortex. The single axon passes outward through the Purkinje layer to enter the molecular layer, where it terminates in a T-shaped bifurcation. These branches are so arranged as to extend in the long axis of the folium. Thus, in their course, synaptic relations with dendrites of many Purkinje cells are facilitated. In addition to the granule cells, some larger cells *(stellate)* are found, particularly in that portion of the granule layer nearest the Purkinje cells. These cells have dendrites extending into the molecular layer. The axons are short and branch repeatedly into a plexiform arrangement within the granular layer itself.

Purkinje (Middle) Layer

This layer is one cell in thickness and contains one cell type, the Purkinje cell. The body of the cell is flask-shaped, the neck of the flask being directed superficially toward the surface of the cortex. From the neck arise one or two thick dendrites which enter the outer molecular layer. Within the molecular layer, the dendrites branch repeatedly, the branching taking place at right angles to the long axis of the folium. From the large end of the cell body, opposite the neck, a single axon extends across the inner granular layer, enters the white core of the folium, and terminates in one of the central nuclei. Within the granular layer, the axon gives rise to collaterals which pass backward through the layer to end in synaptic relations with adjoining Purkinje cells. This facilitates spreading of the stimulation over wider cortical areas and adds strength and persistence to the total effect.

Molecular (Outer) Layer

It contains the dendrites of Purkinje cells, the axons of granule cells, and the fine dendrites of some of the larger cells of the granular layer. In addition there are also three cell types: One is a small neuron of the Golgi type II class, the processes of which apparently ramify in the more superficial part of this layer and in the granular layer. Another type is the *basket cell*. This has several branching dendrites which extend into the outer portion of this layer, and a single axon which runs at right angles to the long axis of the folium. Each axon gives off several collaterals which bend inward toward the Purkinje cells, around which they form a network and axosomatic synapses. A third type is called the *stellate cell*. It is found in the outer molecular layer and is similar to the basket cell but smaller in size. It is activated by the parallel fiber, and, in turn, its axons form axodendritic contacts with Purkinje cells. The organization of cere-bellar cortex as demonstrated by the Golgi method is shown in Fig. 17-5.

Physiology of the Cerebellar Cortex

As a result of the work of Eccles and his colleagues, information processing within the cerebellar cortex has become better understood. A schematic diagram of the organization is shown in Fig. 17-13. It is now clear that stimulation of either of the input pathways to the cerebellar cortex produces excitatory effects upon their target neurons. Specifically, the mossy fibers will concurrently activate a number of granule cells, while a climbing fiber will activate an individual Purkinje cell. Consider first the processing of information along the mossy fiber–granule cell pathway. Following activation of this pathway, parallel fibers will have excitatory effects upon the dendrites of basket cells, Purkinje cells, stellate cells, and Golgi cells. The Golgi cells can be excited by either mossy fibers or by parallel fibers. In any event, Golgi cell activation results in granule cell inhibition. Thus, the Golgi cell is involved in both feedback and "feedforward" inhibition. The feedback circuit includes mossy fiber → granule cell → Golgi cell → granule cell, while the "feedforward" circuit includes mossy fiber → Golgi cell → granule cell. It should be noted that when a given group of parallel fibers is activated, these axons appear as a beam which activates a number of Purkinje cells along a particular folium through which the parallel fibers pass. Basket and stellate cells serve to inhibit Purkinje cells, the basket cell providing the most effective inhibition by virtue of its numerous axosomatic contacts with the Purkinje cell (Fig. 17-13).

In viewing the relation between the mossy fiber and the Purkinje cell, it appears that the mossy fiber can directly excite the Purkinje cell and indirectly inhibit it. In this way, Purkinje cells directly affected by an active beam of parallel fibers will display an

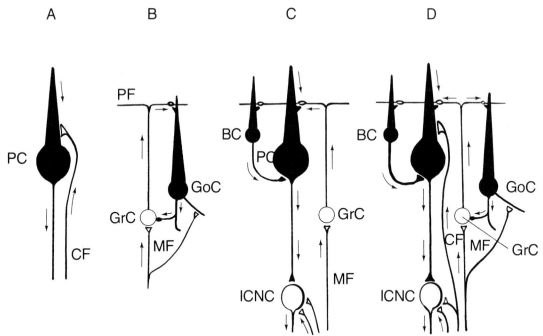

Figure 17-13 *A through D.* Diagram of the most significant neuronal connections in the cerebellum. All cells in black are inhibitory. BC, basket cell; CF, climbing fiber; GrC, granule cell; GoC, Golgi cell; ICNC, deep cerebellar nuclei; MF, mossy fiber; PC, Purkinje cell; PF, parallel fiber. *(From Eccles, Ito, and Szentagothai in Sir John Eccles, The Cerebellum as a Neuronal Machine, Springer-Verlag New York Inc., New York, 1967.)*

excitatory-inhibitory sequence, while off-beam Purkinje cells will merely be inhibited by diffusely activated basket and stellate cells.

The exclusive output of the cerebellar cortex arises from the Purkinje cell axons. These axons make synaptic contact with the deep cerebellar nuclei and the lateral vestibular (Deiters') nucleus. Strangely enough, Purkinje cells uniformly inhibit each of their target neurons. Accordingly, such an observation would seem to suggest that the total output of the cerebellum is inhibitory. However, it has been shown that the deep cerebellar nuclei are continuously excited by collaterals of both mossy and climbing fibers (Fig. 17-13). Therefore, the function of the Purkinje cells is to provide inhibitory modulation of the deep cerebellar nuclei. The latter, in turn, appear to have excitatory effects upon their target neurons in the brainstem and thalamus.

Efferent Connections of the Cerebellum (Figs. 17-14 through 17-17)

The efferent fibers are arranged in two major groups: (1) those which arise in the cortex and, since they carry impulses away from the cortex, are called *corticofugal* and (2) those which arise in the central nuclei and leave the cerebellum proper *(nucleofugal).*

Corticofugal

These are of two varieties: (1) the direct pass from the cortex into the brainstem and (2) the corticonuclear run from the cortex to the central nuclei.

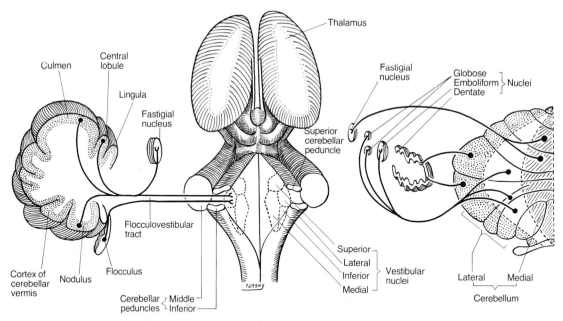

Figure 17-14   Corticonuclear fibers of the cerebellum.

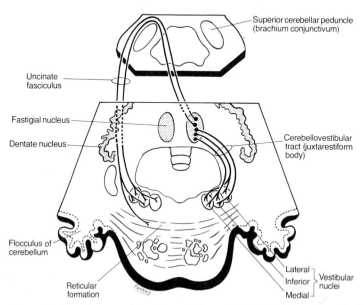

Figure 17-15   Diagram of the efferent fibers of the fastigial nucleus illustrating the descending pathways. *(Based on Walberg et al., 1962, after Wallenberg-Klimoff and Gerebtzoff, 1941.)*

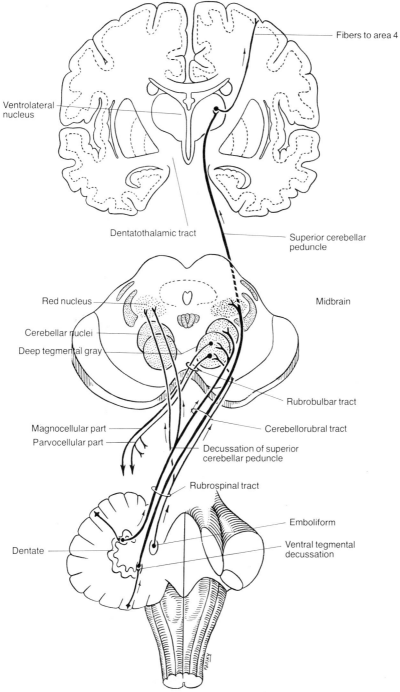

Figure 17-16 Diagrammatic representation of the projection fibers from the cerebellum to the midbrain, thalamus, and cerebrum.

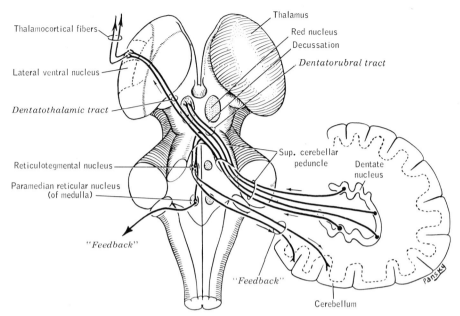

Figure 17-17 Diagram of the dentatothalamocortical pathways via the superior cerebellar peduncle. The feedback circuit via the reticular nuclei and the reticulocerebellar fibers is also shown.

Direct (Fig. 17-14) These fibers are relatively few. They arise in the flocculus and pass to the superior and lateral vestibular nuclei as the *flocculovestibular tract,* or they ascend in the superior cerebellar peduncle as the *flocculooculomotor tract.* In addition to these, fibers arising in the nodulus and uvula of the posterior lobe and in the lingula, central lobule, and culmen of the anterior lobe have been traced to the vestibular nuclei. Direct fibers from the nodulus to the reticular formation of the medulla have also been described.

Corticonuclear One group of these fibers has the same cortical origin as described for the direct fibers but terminates in the fastigial nuclei (Figs. 1-33, 17-14, 17-15, 25-7). Another group arises in the biventer lobule, tonsil, medial part of the ansiform lobule, and lateral part of the anterior lobe to terminate in the

emboliform and globose nuclei[5] (Figs. 17-14, 25-7, 25-8). The lateral part of the ansiform lobule and perhaps the paraflocculus send their fibers to the dentate nucleus. According to a general rule, it may be said that the vermis sends its fibers to the fastigial and globose nuclei; the cortex of the hemispheres adjacent to the vermis sends its fibers to the globose and emboliform nuclei; the lateral portion of the hemispheres send their fibers to the dentate nucleus.

Efferents from the Medial Nuclei

Fastigial Fibers (Fig. 17-15) The *fastigiobulbar tract,* also known as the *cerebellovestibular tract,* arises in the fastigial nucleus. Some of its fibers cross while others remain on

[5]For practical purposes these two nuclei may be grouped together as the nucleus interpositus.

the same side. In either case, they descend to the brainstem in the medial segment of the inferior cerebellar peduncle to terminate in the vestibular nuclei. The corticonuclear projection to the fastigial nucleus as well as the fastigial projection to the lateral vestibular nucleus are somatotopically arranged (Fig. 17-14).

The *uncinate bundle (of Russell)* (Fig. 17-15), also known as the *cerebellospinal tract,* arises from the fastigial nucleus also. The majority of its fibers cross in the so-called inferior cerebellar commissure and ascend for a very short distance with the fibers of the superior cerebellar peduncle. They then curve around over the peduncle (hook over it; thus the name *uncinate)* and descend from the cerebellum in the medial segment of the inferior cerebellar peduncle. Both crossed and uncrossed fibers of this bundle extend into the vestibular nuclei, while the reticular formation of the medulla and pons receive fibers from the contralateral side.

Dentate Fibers   *Dentatorubral* and *dentatothalamic fibers* (Figs. 17-16, 17-17) arise almost exclusively in the dentate nucleus. However, both emboliform and globose nuclei contribute some fibers to these groups. These bundles make up the bulk of the superior cerebellar peduncle, the major efferent pathway from the cerebellum. The fibers from the dentate nucleus project to the ventrolateral thalamic nucleus, while those from the emboliform and globose nuclei project chiefly to the contralateral red nucleus. The peduncles pass rostrally out of the cerebellum and form the lateral walls of the superior portion of the fourth ventricle (Figs. 1-26, 1-27, 1-30). In their forward course, the peduncles gradually sink into the pontine tegmentum and pass into the tegmental area of the midbrain. In the caudal part of the mesencephalon most of the fibers in the peduncles decussate. A few of the uncrossed fibers may end in the tegmental gray of the pons or in reticular nuclei lying farther caudally. After decussating, the peduncle breaks up into fascicles, the majority of which ascend. The descending fibers run for at least part of their course either in or closely adjacent to the central tegmental tract. Most of them terminate in the reticulotegmental nucleus.

There are two major groups of ascending fibers: the *cerebellorubral,* which arise chiefly in the globose and emboliform nuclei, and the *dentatothalamic* fibers, which arise in the dentate nucleus. Rostral to the decussation, the former terminate topographically in both the large and small-celled portions of the red nucleus, terminations among the large cells being more numerous. The dentatothalamic fascicles bypass the red nucleus and continue into the diencephalon where they end in the ventrolateral nucleus of the thalamus. From the latter, fibers ascend through the internal capsule to the motor cortex. Fibers arising in the red nucleus and descending to the dentate nucleus of the cerebellum have also been described.

Circuits to Motor Centers

It has just been shown that efferent cerebellar fibers carry streams of impulses to the vestibular nuclei, the reticular nuclei, the red nucleus, and the ventrolateral nucleus of the thalamus but that none of these fibers reach motor neurons directly. It is therefore necessary to describe the pathways by which the cerebellum eventually influences motor nuclei.

Vestibular Pathway

In an earlier chapter (Chap. 12) it was demonstrated how the vestibular nuclei are related to the body musculature; the musculature of the trunk through the *lateral vestibulospinal tract;* the motor centers of the neck musculature through the *medial longitudinal fasciculus;* and the motor centers of the brainstem, including those for the ocular muscles, through ascending and descending fibers of the medial longitudinal fasciculus.

Reticular Pathway

From cells in the various nuclei of the bulbar reticular formation, fibers may reach the motor nuclei of the brainstem and, through the *reticulospinal tract,* make contact with the cells in the ventral columns of the spinal cord.

Rubrospinal Pathway   (Chap. 18)

In human beings, the rubrospinal tract is a small group of fibers arising in the red nucleus. They leave the nucleus, decussate in the ventral tegmental decussation, and descend through the brainstem and upper spinal cord, sending collaterals into the ventral gray columns.

Thalamocortical Pathway

Through this pathway, fibers arising in the ventrolateral nuclei may be distributed to the primary sensorimotor area of the cortex (Chaps. 18, 20, 23, 24).

Feedback Circuits of the Cerebellum

The previous section has indicated that certain sites which both supply the cerebellum and receive fibers from it play a significant role in the organization of motor activity. In addition, there are other sites which reciprocally communicate with the cerebellum about the status of individual and groups of muscles as well as about other sensory information such as sensation from cutaneous receptors. That the cerebellum is capable of receiving such sensory and motor signals from all relevant regions of the CNS and, at the same time, is capable of sending back signals to these sites reflects the single most important feature of its organization as a computer of sensorimotor

integration. This characteristic is schematized in a series of figures (Figs. 17-11, 17-18 through 17-21) which indicate the important feedback pathways associated with the cerebellum.

EVALUATION OF THE CEREBELLAR CIRCUITS

Before attempting to understand how the cerebellum or any other suprasegmental center is able to effect or modify activity, it is essential to review the basic motor pattern (Chap. 13) and to recall the numerous descending fiber tracts which terminate within the anterior column of the spinal cord and the cranial motor nuclei. In addition, it is necessary to know that (1) due to an inherent quality in the descending fibers themselves, some will cause stimulation while others will inhibit these same cells; (2) the same descending fiber cannot act directly as an activator and suppressor at the same time but, through a synapse with an interneuron, a suppressor effect may be produced on another cell. Thus, a descending fiber may terminate directly on a motor fiber causing the related muscle to contract while at the same time this same fiber may synapse on an interneuron. The axon of the interneuron ends on a cell in another part of the cell group which supplies the antagonistic muscle. This leads to a relaxation of the antagonist.

At this point, it might be useful to demonstrate the action of the cerebellar circuit using conjugate deviation of the eyes (Chap. 13) in response to a vestibular stimulus as an example. Thus, a particular movement of the head, due to the inertia of the endolymph in the semicircular canal (Chap. 11), stimulates the cristae of the left vestibule. As a result, volleys of afferent impulses stream through the left vestibular nerve to terminate in several of the vestibular nuclei (medial, spinal, and lateral). From here, association neurons cross the

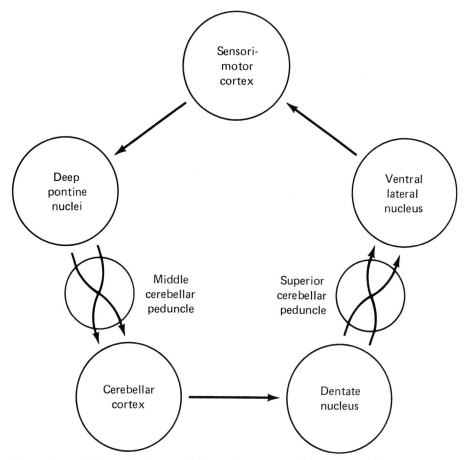

Figure 17-18 Schematic diagram of the corticocerebellar feedback circuit.

midline and enter the medial longitudinal fasciculus (MLF). As the latter bundle passes the right abducens nucleus, either collaterals or terminals enter that nucleus. Typical somatic motor axons leave this nucleus, pass by way of the abducens nerve (VI) to the right lateral rectus muscle, causing its contraction. However, as a part of this total action, the left medial rectus must also contract so that the left eye moves in the same direction as the right. Thus, fibers from the left vestibular nuclei terminate in the paraabducens nucleus from which fibers reenter the MLF of the left side and run to the medial part of the oculo-

motor nucleus (III). Thence, fibers pass by way of the oculomotor nerve to the left medial rectus. However, this is only part of the story for, at the same time, there must be a compensatory relaxation of the right medial rectus and the left lateral rectus muscles. Now, it should be recalled that the same impulses set up in the left vestibular nerve which produced the activity described above are also carried both to the cerebellar cortex and to the left fastigial nucleus. From the latter, impulses are carried back to the vestibular nuclei via the fastigiobulbar tract. These cerebellar impulses apparently enhance and reinforce the nerve

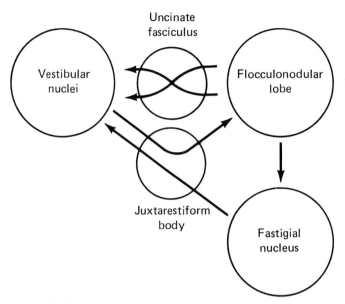

Figure 17-19 Schematic diagram of the vestibulocerebellar feedback circuit.

flow from the latter to the right lateral rectus and left medial rectus. At the same time, fibers from the left fastigial nucleus pass to the right vestibular nuclei either through the crossed fibers in the fastigiobulbar tract or in the uncinate bundle. These fibers tend to suppress the activity of the right vestibular nuclei which, in turn, leads to a diminution of tone in the left lateral and right medial rectus muscles. Thus, conjugate movement is facilitated.

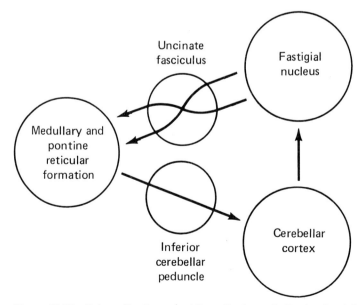

Figure 17-20 Schematic diagram of the reticulocerebellar feedback loop.

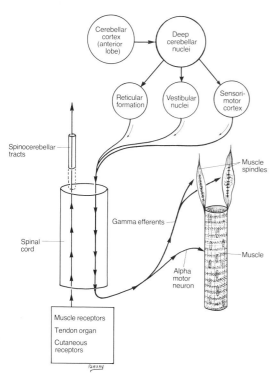

Figure 17-21 Schematic diagram of the spinocerebellar feedback circuit.

Although the circuit described above demonstrates only a part of the vestibuloocular mechanisms, similar connections involving the motor nerves controlling the musculature of the neck and trunk which are important in maintaining balance are also present. In this case, cerebellar influences reach the vestibular nuclei through the fastigiobulbar tract and the uncinate bundle, whence impulses are relayed caudalward both in the MLF and the vestibulospinal tract.

Reflexes initiated through the activity of the SSA system (both auditory and visual) apparently require cerebellar integration. For this reason, the tectocerebellar fibers link the reflex association centers of the mesencephalon with the cortex of the cerebellum. The latter then acts upon the motor centers by the pathways described through either the fas-

tigial nucleus or nucleus interpositus, through reticular formation or possibly the dentate and red nuclei, and finally through the rubroreticular or rubrospinal route.

Since all the skilled, voluntary movements initiated in the motor cortex of the cerebral hemispheres require the highest degree of synergy, massive fiber pathways link the cerebrum and cerebellum. Thus, one could visualize muscular activity as being initiated by impulses descending from the cerebral cortex instead of being initiated as a part of a reflex arc. Except for the use of different pathways, the modifying influences of the cerebellum would be the same. Descending from cerebral motor centers are the corticopontine fibers. These pass downward through the internal capsule (Fig. 1-13; Chap. 24) and the basis pedunculi to terminate in the homolateral pontine nuclei. Axons from the latter cross the midline, curve dorsally in the contralateral middle cerebellar peduncle and end chiefly in the neocerebellar cortex. The cerebellum then could influence voluntary muscular activity in several ways: (1) through the red nucleus and then directly to motor centers via the rubrospinal tract or from the red nucleus indirectly, through the reticular formation and reticulospinal tract, and (2) through the thalamus, by way of the dentatothalamic, thalamocortical circuit to the sensorimotor cortex which contributes to the corticospinal system. It should be noted that, in either case, the action of motor cells could be facilitated or suppressed.

CLINICAL CONSIDERATIONS

Since the cerebellum is so intimately related to action and movements of all sorts, it is necessary to use examinations which help localize the lesion as being distinctly in the cerebellum and not, for example, in the posterior funiculi of the cord; in the inner ear; in the vestibular nerve or its nuclei; or in the pyramidal system somewhere along its course.

Before the procedure for examination is described, it is necessary to understand the terms used in connection with lesions of the motor systems. *Hypotonia, areflexia, ataxia,* and *nystagmus* have already been defined (Chap. 13). Other important terms are *hyporeflexia,* a weakening of reflexes, usually associated with hypotonia; *asynergia,* a loss of the facility to coordinate more or less complex movements which have a special function;[6] *asthenia,* a lack or diminution of muscular strength; *atelokinesia,* a term sometimes used for the intention or action tremor seen near the termination of a voluntary movement; *adiadochokinesia,* the inability to perform rapid, alternating movements; *dysmetria,* the improper measuring of distance in muscular acts. The latter is a disturbance in the power to control the range of movement, as in past pointing.

Testing

In this system, an attempt is made to localize the lesion in a very general way. For this purpose, it is most convenient to classify the defects or disturbances under four categories: *defective postural fixation, disturbances of skilled or voluntary acts, disturbed equilibrium, disturbances in gait* and *postural reflexes.*

Postural Fixation

The muscles are palpated to see whether they are firm or flabby, flabbiness indicating hypotonia.

It is noted whether the extremity at rest appears to lie in an awkward position.

The examiner notes whether there is any loss in resistance to passive movement when attempting to bend an extremity.

The examiner notes whether the upper extremity flops about aimlessly when the shoulder is shaken.

When the patient is asked to keep eyes closed and extend both arms in front, the arm on the side of the lesion frequently is lower and less fully extended and tends to drift laterally. When the arms are abducted to the side, the affected side tends to drift medially.

The patient is asked to sit on the edge of a table so that his or her legs hang down freely. If the examiner extends the patient's leg, then releases it, the leg on the diseased side will show an increase in the number of pendular swings (Fig. 17-22).

The rebound phenomenon is checked by having the patient flex the arm against resistance which the examiner suddenly releases. In cerebellar disease, the arm often rebounds markedly before it is checked (Fig. 17-22).

The patient is asked to sit on the bed, legs extended and heels down on the bed. When the patient is instructed to lie down quickly, the patient's feet fly into the air if cerebellar lesions are present.

Disturbances in Voluntary Skills [7]

Such disturbances involve abnormalities in the rate, range, direction, or force of movement, frequently referred to as *ataxia.* These errors are sometimes accompanied by action or intention tremors. Thus, the examiner in the course of the tests given below will be watching to see whether a movement is slow in starting; whether the force and speed during movement are uneven; whether movement is slow in stopping and whether it stops at the desired spot, without overreaching; whether there is slowness in starting successive components of more complex movements, i.e., whether the complex movement is decomposed into parts by a series of jerks; and whether there is any tremor present which becomes more marked near the end of a given movement.

---

[6]In some patients, the different components of an act may not follow in the proper sequence, come at the proper time, or be of the proper strength.

[7]Disturbances in voluntary skills and often in postural fixation indicate a lesion in the lateral part of the hemispheres.

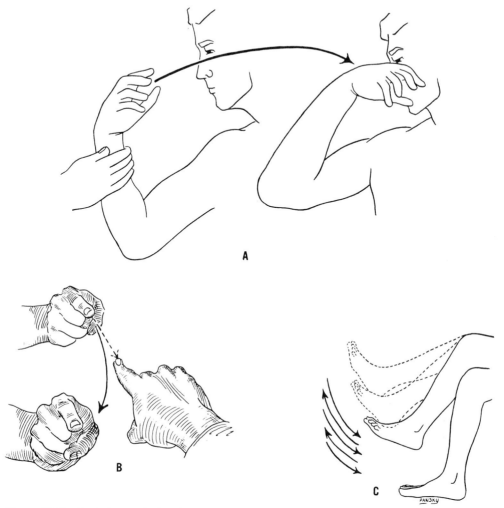

Figure 17-22 Tests for cerebellar disease. *A.* Rebound phenomenon—in disease there is no reciprocal antagonistic reaction to check the hand. *B.* Past pointing—deviation to the side of the lesion in unilateral cerebellar disease. *C.* Pendulumlike response—to-and-fro movement.

The patient is asked to touch the tip of his or her nose with the index finger of either hand, starting with the extremity extended. This should be done simultaneously with both extremities.

The patient is instructed to touch the tip of his or her nose and the examiner's finger alternately, with the examiner's finger changing position from time to time. The patient later is asked to follow with the patient's own finger the moving finger of the examiner (Fig. 17-22).

The patient is asked to place the heel of one foot to the knee of the other extremity.

The patient is asked to follow with the great toe the moving finger of the examiner, particularly in such a way that both thigh and leg will be flexed.

The patient is asked to perform certain tasks requiring alternation of movement, such as wiggling fingers, tapping the foot, or pronating and supinating the forearm. When certain cerebellar lesions are present, these acts are slow, the rhythm is poor, and the alternating action is clumsy, irregular, and variable in force.

Disturbed Equilibrium

In this category, no particular tests are necessary. Observation of the patient is usually sufficient. The examiner merely sees whether the patient can stand or sit, unsupported. Usually, if a cerebellar lesion is present, the patient tends to fall and the head wobbles and oscillates. If walking is possible at all, the gait is *reeling* and *drunken.* When equilibrium is disturbed, the lesions are usually basal, involving either the archicerebellar cortex of the flocculonodular lobe or the medial part of the posterior lobe.

Disturbed Gait and Posture

Certain types of abnormality should be described. First, in a unilateral cerebellar lesion with the gait deviating toward the side of the lesion, the leg on the affected side shows incoordination of movement. The second type has been indicated under Disturbed Equilibrium as the reeling, drunken gait.

The third variety may sometimes be observed when there is a lesion of the anterior lobe, which is considered to control the synergies of walking.[8] The gait is wide-based, with bilateral deviation, and is often stiff-legged. These observations of gait should be made during the following tests:

The patient is asked to stand up, walk, stop quickly, turn quickly, and return.

---

[8]As should be understood, in standing there has to be an excess tone in the extensor muscles. This is the positive supporting reaction. In walking, the legs must alternate in having and not having this extensor tone.

The patient is asked to walk a line, heel to toe.

The patient is asked to lie recumbent in bed, and firm pressure is applied to the sole of the foot so that the examiner may feel for tonal increase in the muscles of the thigh.

Nystagmus

Various clinical signs are often associated with cerebellar diseases but are not necessarily primary for lesions of the cerebellum. One of these is *nystagmus*. However, one of the three types of nystagmus is referable to the cerebellum alone. This is *deviation nystagmus,* characterized by four signs: (1) With the eyes in the midline position, there is a fine nystagmus with the quick component toward the side of the lesion. (2) When the eyes are fixed 10 to 30° to the side away from the lesion, there is no nystagmus. (3) When the eyes are shifted beyond 30° away from the lesion, nystagmus again occurs, with the quick component away from the lesion. (4) When the eyes are shifted well beyond the midline toward the side of the lesion, a very coarse nystagmus, with the quick portion toward the lesion side, occurs.

Specific Pathology

In addition to trauma, which may destroy parts of the cerebellum through externally applied force, certain other conditions may produce some or all of the above symptoms. These include certain congenital defects in which there is either agenesis or abnormal development; abscesses and tumors, either of the cerebellum or of surrounding parts which encroach upon the cerebellum; hemorrhage in one of its vessels or occlusions thereof; and cortical atrophy.

CORTEX OF CEREBELLUM

  I Layers
    A Granule (inner)
      1 Granule—dendrites receive affer-

ent cerebellar fibers; axons pass to molecular layer and synapse with Purkinje cell dendrites and with Golgi cells

    2 Stellate—dendrites spray out in molecular layer; axons branch in granular layer

B Purkinje (middle)—dendrites spread out in molecular layer to synapse with axons of granule cells; axon leaves cortex and passes through the granular layer to reach the medullary core of the cerebellum to end in the deep nuclei and the lateral vestibular nucleus

C Molecular (outer)

    1 Basket—dendrites branch in outer part of layer; axon branches to synapse with rows of Purkinje cells

    2 Golgi type II—short dendrites and axon extending horizontally in superficial part of layer to synapse with granule cell dendrites

II Fibers (morphologic types)

A Mossy—afferent cerebellar fibers, ending with synapses among dendrites of granule cells in all parts of the cerebellum

B Climbing—afferents from inferior olivary nucleus which synapse with Purkinje cell dendrites directly

SUMMARY OF CONNECTIONS

Cerebellar Afferents

I Through inferior peduncle (restiform body)

A Dorsal spinocerebellar tract

    1 Origin: column of Clarke in dorsal gray of spinal cord

    2 Termination: central lobule, culmen, and posterior semilunar lobule

B Dorsal external arcuate fibers

    1 Origin: accessory cuneate nucleus

    2 Termination: same as *A*, 2, above

C Reticulocerebellar fibers

    1 Origin: lateral reticular nucleus, reticulotegmental nucleus, and paramedian reticular nucleus

    2 Termination: same as *A*, 2, above

D Olivocerebellar fibers

    1 Origin: inferior olivary nucleus

    2 Termination: all cerebellar cortex of the opposite side except the flocculus

E Arcuocerebellar fibers

    1 Origin: arcuate nuclei via ventral external arcuate fibers

    2 Termination: opposite hemispheres of middle lobe

II Through middle peduncle (brachium pontis)

A Pontocerebellar fibers

    1 Origin: pontine nuclei

    2 Termination: mainly in cortex of middle lobe on opposite side; to lesser extent, the vermis of middle lobe

III Through juxtarestiform body (medial segment of inferior peduncle)

A Direct vestibulocerebellar fibers

    1 Origin: vestibular ganglion

    2 Termination: flocculus, nodulus, and lingula

B Indirect vestibulocerebellar fibers

    1 Origin: inferior and medial vestibular nuclei

    2 Termination: flocculus of both sides, nodulus, uvula, and lingula

IV Through anterior medullary velum

A Ventral spinocerebellar tract

    1 Origin: body of dorsal, central, and possibly ventral gray column of the cord

    2 Termination: central lobule, culmen, and posterior semilunar lobule

B Trigeminocerebellar fibers

    1 Origin: mesencephalic nucleus of the trigeminal nerve (V)

    2 Termination: mainly in posterior semilunar lobule

C Tectocerebellar fibers

    1 Origin: corpora quadrigemina

    2 Termination: tuber, folium, and posterior semilunar lobule

Cerebellar Efferents

I Corticofugal
  A Direct: cortex to brainstem nuclei
    1 Origin: flocculus and nodulus
    2 Termination: lateral vestibular nucleus
  B Corticonuclear (indirect): cortex to deep cerebellar nuclei
    1 Origin: from same area as I, A, 1, above
    2 Termination: fastigial nucleus
    3 Origin: intermediolateral aspect of hemispheres
    4 Termination: emboliform and globose (interposed) nuclei
    5 Origin: lateral aspect of hemispheres
    6 Termination: dentate nucleus
II Nuclear efferents
  A Through juxtarestiform body
    1 Fastigiobulbar tract
      a Origin: fastigial nucleus
      b Termination: crossed and uncrossed to vestibular nuclei
  B Through anterior medullary velum and peripeduncular route
    1 Uncinate bundle (of Russell)
      a Origin: fastigial nucleus
      b Termination: crossed fibers to reticular formation and possibly vestibular nuclei
  C Through superior peduncle (brachium conjunctivum)
    1 Dentatorubral
      a Origin: dentate and interposed nuclei
      b Termination: crossed to opposite red nucleus
    2 Dentatothalamic fibers
      a Origin: dentate nucleus
      b Termination: crossed, to opposite ventrolateral nucleus of thalamus

Summary

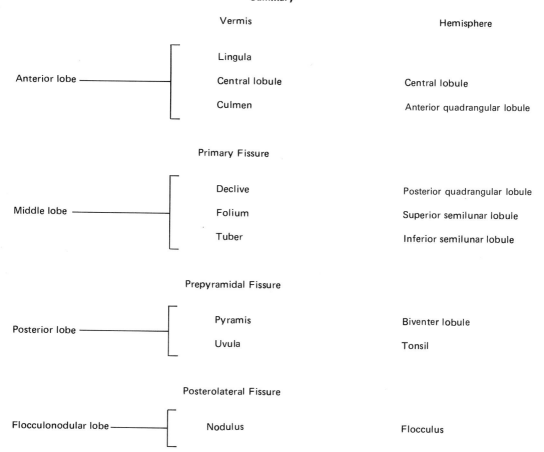

Vermis | Hemisphere

Anterior lobe
- Lingula
- Central lobule — Central lobule
- Culmen — Anterior quadrangular lobule

Primary Fissure

Middle lobe
- Declive — Posterior quadrangular lobule
- Folium — Superior semilunar lobule
- Tuber — Inferior semilunar lobule

Prepyramidal Fissure

Posterior lobe
- Pyramis — Biventer lobule
- Uvula — Tonsil

Posterolateral Fissure

Flocculonodular lobe
- Nodulus — Flocculus

The Basal Ganglia and Related Structures

In several chapters we attempt to conceptualize the motor systems according to the following scheme: There exists a primary sensorimotor cortex from which voluntary movement is initiated through the corticospinal and corticobulbar tracts. Fibers contained in this pathway are frequently referred to as *upper motor neurons*. They make synapse with *lower motor neurons* situated in either the ventral horn of the spinal cord or motor components of cranial nerves situated in the brainstem which innervate skeletal muscle. Activation of the final common path is then directly related to and immediately precedes the initiation of a motor response. We shall note that certain nuclear regions of the brainstem give rise to pathways which directly modulate the activity of alpha and gamma motor neurons. These pathways include the reticulospinal tracts, (Chaps. 17, 19, 20), the vestibulospinal tracts,

and the rubrospinal tract. Superimposed upon these brainstem supraspinal mechanisms is the cerebellum (Chap. 17), which seems to orchestrate much of the activity of those structures which provide sensory input from muscles, tendons, and cutaneous receptors as well as many parts of the CNS which modulate the anterior horn of the spinal cord. Still another component of the motor systems involves the basal ganglia. Their principal responsibility is to modulate the activity of the sensorimotor cortex. Fig. 18-1 is a schematic diagram of the organization of each of the components of this system.

COMPONENTS OF THE BASAL GANGLIA

The basal ganglia consist of the *caudate nucleus, putamen,* and *globus pallidus.* Phylogenetically, the amygdala is included with the

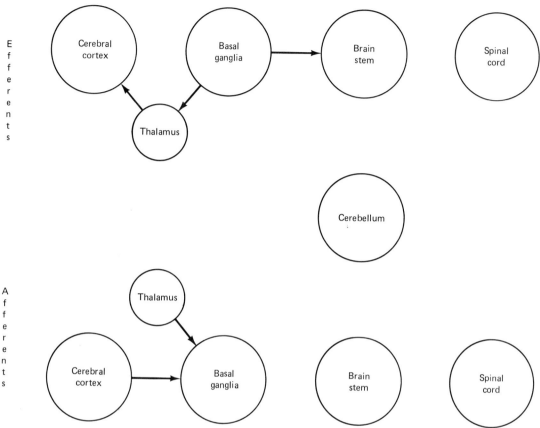

Figure 18-1 Schematic diagram of the primary input/output relation of the basal ganglia.

basal ganglia and is identified as the archistriatum—the oldest part of the basal ganglia. However, from a functional point of view, the amygdala is much more closely related to the limbic system. For this reason it will be considered with that system in another chapter (Chap. 22). The claustrum is also sometimes considered as one of the basal ganglia. However, it arises from the deep cortical layers of the insular region. Although its functions remain unclear, it is probably more closely related to the cortex than the basal ganglia. Accordingly, no discussion of the claustrum will be attempted here. In addition to the basic components of the basal ganglia, several other nuclear groups, critical

to its organization, should be considered. They include the *substantia nigra* and *subthalamic nucleus.*

Corpus Striatum[1] (Figs. 1-11 through 1-14, 1-15, 1-21, 25-15 through 25-20)

The term *corpus striatum* is applied to the combined *caudate* and *lenticular nuclei.* The lenticular nucleus is given its name by its similarity to the shape of a lens. It consists of the putamen and globus pallidus. Both the caudate nucleus and putamen represent phy-

---

[1]The striated appearance is due to the intermingling of gray matter connecting the ventral part of the head of the caudate and putamen with the fibers of the internal capsule.

logenetically newer structures and are collectively referred to as the *neostriatum*. The globus pallidus, consisting of a larger lateral and smaller medial segment, is referred to as the *paleostriatum*.

CONNECTIONS OF THE BASAL GANGLIA

In our attempt to conceptualize the functional organization of the basal ganglia, it is important to identify the principal afferent sources, internal connections, efferent pathways, and their target structures. A schematic diagram illustrating the direction of flow of information through this complex is shown in Fig. 18-2.

As a general principle, the caudate and putamen (neostriatum) serve as major receiving areas for the afferent fibers. Information from the neostriatum is then directly transmitted to the globus pallidus (paleostriatum) which serves as the major source of outflow pathways of the basal ganglia.

Afferent Connections

As indicated above, the caudate nucleus and putamen (neostriatum) serve as primary sites for the reception of impulses which arise mainly from the cerebral cortex. A number of investigators have analyzed the afferent connections of the neostriatum arising from the cerebral cortex. The results of such studies indicate that the neostriatum is supplied by much of the cerebral cortex in a topographic manner. For example, it has been shown that the dorsal aspect of the caudate nucleus receives fibers from the dorsomedial margin of the hemisphere while the ventromedial aspect of the head of the caudate nucleus receives fibers from more lateral (temporal) regions of the cortex (Fig. 18-3). In a similar manner, other areas of the cortex project to separate sites within the neostriatum. The greatest number of fibers arise from the frontal lobe. In addition, it has been shown that in some species the sensorimotor cortex provides bi-

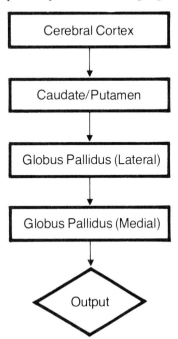

Figure 18-2 Outline of information flow through the basal ganglia.

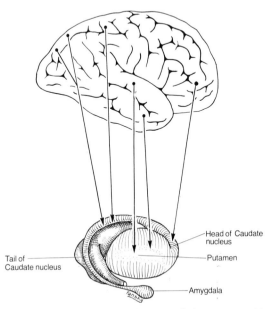

Figure 18-3 Schematic diagram of the topographic organization of the massive cortical input to the neostriatum.

lateral projection to the caudate nucleus. Recently, it has been shown that when two distinct regions on the cerebral cortex are interconnected by cortical fibers, each region provides a converging input to the same site in the caudate nucleus (Fig. 18-4). This finding, in addition to the results of other studies already noted, suggest that the functions of the basal ganglia are strongly dependent upon the input from the cerebral cortex. In other words, the neostriatum is endowed with inputs from sensory, motor, and association areas of the cerebral cortex.

A second identifiable projection to the neostriatum arises from the centromedian nucleus (CN) of the thalamus and is distributed to the putamen (Fig. 18-5). It is sometimes referred to as the *thalamostriate pathway.* Since the centromedian is a nonspecific thalamic nucleus which receives modality-nonspecific inputs from the brainstem reticular formation, this projection may enable the reticular system to indirectly modulate the activity of neostriatal neurons.

Efferent Connections

As noted above, information from both the caudate nucleus and putamen are transmitted primarily to the lateral pallidal segment which subsequently transmits to the medial segment (Fig. 18-2). Of significance is the fact that the principal output of the entire basal ganglia arises from the medial segment of the pallidum. From this segment, two major pathways have been described. One of these, the *ansa lenticularis,* arises mainly from lateral cell groups in this segment. Axons initially sweep ventromedially around the ventral surface of the pallidum and pass caudally and somewhat dorsally through the region of the prerubral field.[2] At this level the fibers sweep in a lateral and more dorsal direction joining the *thalamic fasciculus.*[3] These fibers ultimately terminate

[2]The prerubral field represents a group of scattered cells and fiber tracts which lie immediately rostral to the red nucleus and is sometimes referred to as the H field of Forel.

[3]The thalamic fasciculus consists of fibers of the ansa lenticularis, lenticular fasciculus, and dentatothalamic fibers and is sometimes referred to the H_1 field of Forel.

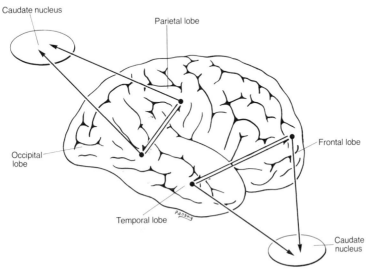

Figure 18-4 Schematic diagram of the fundamental principal that two cortical sites which are reciprocally connected provide converging input to the same site on the caudate nucleus.

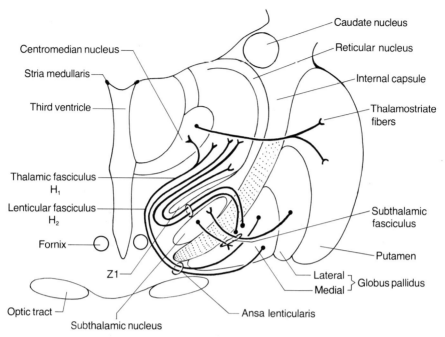

Figure 18-5 Schematic diagram of pallidofugal fiber systems in a transverse plane. Fibers of the ansa lenticularis arise from the outer portion of the medial pallidal segment, pass ventrally, medially, and rostrally around the internal capsule, and enter the prerubral field. Fibers of the lenticular fasiculus (H_2) issue from the dorsal surface of the inner part of the medial pallidal segment, traverse the posterior limb of the internal capsule, and pass medially dorsal to the subthalamic nucleus to enter the prerubral field. The ansa lenticularis and the lenticular fasciculus merge in the prerubral field (field H of Forel, not labeled here) and project dorsolaterally as components of the thalamic fasciculus (H_1). Fibers of the thalamic fasciculus (H_1) pass dorsal to the zona incerta (ZI). The subthalamic fasciculus consists of pallidosubthalamic fibers arising from the lateral pallidal segment, and subthalamopallidal fibers that terminate largely in the medial pallidal segment. Both components of the subthalamic fasciculus traverse the internal capsule. Thalamostriate fibers from the centromedian nucleus project to the putamen, as part of a feedback system. *(Modified after Carpenter, Human Neuroanatomy, 7th ed., The Williams & Wilkins Company, Baltimore, 1976.)*

in the ventral lateral (VL), ventral anterior (VA), and centromedian thalamic nuclei (Figs. 18-5, 18-6).

The second pathway, known as the *lenticular fasciculus,*[4] arises, in general, from medial cell groups in the medial pallidal segment and traverses the internal capsule. It passes first ventrally between the subthalamic nucleus and zona incerta. The fibers then make a C-shaped turn around the dorsal surface of the

zona incerta to join the thalamic fasciculus at the level of the prerubral field. The ultimate destination of this pathway includes the same target sites as the ansa lenticularis—VL, VA, and CM (Figs. 18-5, 18-6).

Collectively, the ansa lenticularis and lenticular fasciculus provide a critical anatomic mechanism by which the basal ganglia can modify neuronal activity in sensorimotor cortex, since it is well established that VL projects topographically to area 4 (primary motor cortex) (Fig. 18-7) while VA projects to area 6 (premotor area) (Fig. 18-8).

---

[4]The lenticular fasciculus is sometimes referred to as the H_2 field of Forel.

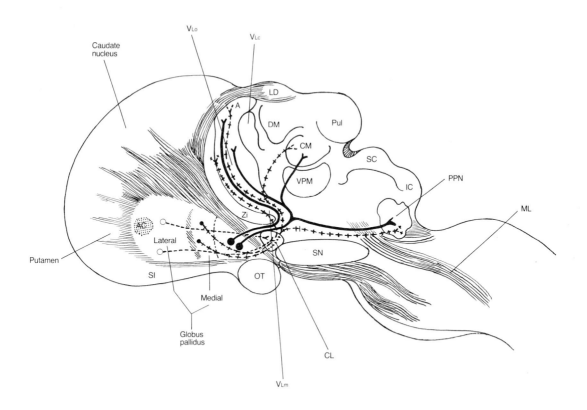

NOTE: Solid Line [—] = Lenticular fasciculus
Dotted Line [-----------------] = Subthalamic fasciculus
Cross Lines [+ + + + + + + + +] = Ansa lenticularis

Figure 18-6 Schematic diagram of the efferent connections and terminations of pallidofugal fibers arising from the medial and lateral pallidal segments shown in a sagittal plane. Fibers of the ansa lenticularis and lenticular fasciculus merge in field H of Forel. The bulk of these fibers passes in the thalamic fasciculus to the ventral lateral (VLo and VLm) and ventral anterior (VA) thalamic nuclei. Some fibers separate from the thalamic fasciculus and pass to the centromedian (CM) nucleus. Descending pallidofugal fibers from the medial pallidal segment form the pallidotegmental bundle; these fibers terminate upon cells of the pedunculopontine nucleus (PPN). Pallidosubthalamic fibers arising from the lateral pallidal segment project to the subthalamic nucleus (CL). AC, anterior commissure; DM, dorsomedial nucleus; H, Forel's field H; IC, inferior colliculus; LD, lateral dorsal nucleus; ML, medial lemniscus; OT, optic tract; Pul., pulvinar; SC, superior colliculus; SI, substantia innominata; SN, substantia nigra; VLc, ventral lateral nucleus, pars caudalis; VPM, ventral posteromedial nucleus; ZI, zona incerta. *(Modified after Carpenter, Human Neuroanatomy, 7th ed., The Williams & Wilkins Company, Baltimore, 1976.)*

Although it is clear from the foregoing discussion that the principal objective of the basal ganglia is to modulate the sensorimotor cortex, there exists a second possible way by which it can modulate motor activity. This anatomic mechanism involves fibers which also arise from the medial pallidal segment but pass in a caudal direction to the dorsolateral tegmentum, terminating in the pedunculopontine nucleus of the brainstem reticular formation (Fig. 18-6). Since it has been shown that electrical stimulation of this region of the reticular formation can facilitate motor activity, presumably via the reticulospinal pathways

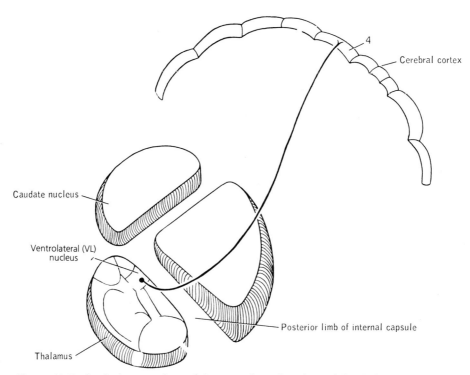

Figure 18-7 Cortical connections of the ventrolateral nucleus of the thalamus.

(Chap. 19), it is plausible to conceive of this pallidotegmental bundle as an anatomic template by which the basal ganglia can modulate brainstem mechanisms which, in turn, regulate motor activity at the level of the spinal cord.

CONNECTIONS OF THE SUBTHALAMIC NUCLEUS AND SUBSTANTIA NIGRA

In addition to the afferent and efferent connections of the basal ganglia described above, there exists a separate set of relationships which significantly link both the subthalamic nucleus and substantia nigra with the basal ganglia. As will be shown below, both these structures play important roles in the regulation of motor activity.

Consider first the anatomic relation between the subthalamic nucleus and the basal ganglia.

In brief, the subthalamic nucleus is reciprocally connected with the pallidum. Specifically, fibers from the lateral segment of the globus pallidus supply the subthalamic nucleus, while fibers which issue from the subthalamic nucleus cross through the internal capsule and terminate in the medial pallidal segment. Collectively, both afferent and efferent fibers of the subthalamic nucleus are referred to as the *subthalamic fasciculus* (Fig. 18-5). Functionally, it appears that the subthalamic nucleus serves to provide an inhibitory brake upon the pallidus. This conclusion is based, in part, upon studies by Carpenter and Strominger, who noted that lesions of the subthalamic nucleus in the monkey result in (1) the appearance of degenerating axon terminals in the medial pallidal segment and, at the same time, (2) the appearance of a contralateral hemiballism (see page 360 for a description of this

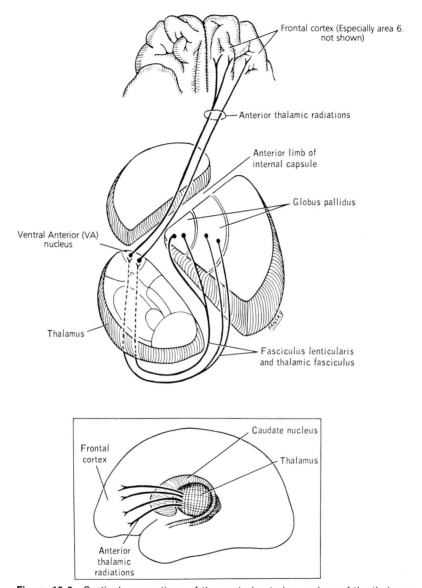

Figure 18-8 Cortical connections of the ventral anterior nucleus of the thalamus.

form of dyskinesia[5]), which has also been observed in human beings following lesions in this same structure. That this syndrome can be

[5] *Dyskinesia* is a general term which refers to various kinds of abnormal, involuntary movements described at the end of this chapter.

ameliorated by lesions of the medial pallidal segment, its output pathway, or the ventrolateral thalamic nucleus implies that the globus pallidus normally exerts a potent excitatory effect upon motor activity. Such activity must also be subjected to inhibitory control by the subthalamic nucleus in order for normal motor responses to occur which are free of abnormal, involuntary movements.

The connections of the substantia nigra are of equal significance. With regard to the afferent connections of the substantia nigra, it is now well established that the caudate nucleus and putamen project topographically to the substantia nigra in such a way that the medial portions of the caudate project to the medial parts of the nigra while the lateral portions of the caudate project to the lateral parts of the nigra. In general, fibers from caudal (caudate body) parts of the caudate nucleus and putamen project to caudal parts of the nigra, and fibers from the rostral (head) parts of the caudate supply the rostral nigra. Thus, the neostriatum provides the largest contribution to the nigra. This bundle is sometimes referred to as *strionigral fibers.* Recent studies suggest that other regions may also supply the nigra. These include the globus pallidus and the brainstem raphe nuclei. Of particular interest is the fact that raphe neurons produce 5-hydroxytryptamine (serotonin) (Chap. 19). Therefore, it is possible that this pathway provides a basis for chemical interactions between serotonin and dopamine,[6] which is synthesized in the nigra.

Efferent fibers from the nigra are distributed to the neostriatum and to VL and VA of the thalamus (Fig. 18-9). Cells which are situated in the compact division of the substantia nigra synthesize dopamine, and this transmitter substance reaches the neostriatum via axoplasmic transport in *nigrostriatal neurons.* In this way, the connections between nigra and striatum are reciprocal. This projection is particularly important in that its disruption and related reduction in striatal dopamine content are linked to *paralysis agitans* (Parkinson's disease). The evidence for this conclusion is

as follows: (1) there is an absence of striatal and nigral dopamine in patients with paralysis agitans; (2) lesions of the substantia nigra have been associated with the presence of this disease; and (3) the use of L-dopa (L-dihydroxyphenylalanine), a dopamine precursor, has been remarkably successful as replacement therapy in alleviating symptoms of this disease. *Nigrothalamic fibers* arise from the reticular division of the substantia nigra and appear to follow the *mammillothalamic tract* to innervate the ventrolateral and ventral anterior nuclei. It is possible that this pathway enables the substantia nigra to regulate motor functions by a second mechanism—by modulating the thalamic relay neurons which supply the primary motor and premotor cortices.

CLINICAL CONSIDERATIONS

It is clear that certain components of the basal ganglia can serve to either facilitate or inhibit motor activity. For example, electrical stimulation of the caudate nucleus has been known to suppress motor activity. A suppressor function was also implied for the subthalamic nucleus as a result of behavioral analysis of lesion experiments. On the other hand, stimulation of either the globus pallidus or its outflow pathways facilitate the occurrence of such movement patterns as contraversive turning and postural changes. As a result of alterations in the delicate balance between facilitating and suppressing mechanisms, abnormalities in motor function appear. In practice, three general types of abnormality are seen: loss of certain movements; involuntary movements; aberrations in states of muscle tone, i.e., hypotonia, spasticity, or rigidity.

Abnormalities of Motor Function

Tone

Abnormalities in tone may take one of two directions: exaggerated, as in hypertonicity (rigidity), or decreased, as in hypotonia. The

---

[6]The biosynthesis of dopamine involves the following steps: L-tyrosine is converted to L-dopa (dihydroxyphenylalanine) by the enzyme tyrosine hydroxylase; L-dopa is then decarboxylated into dopamine.

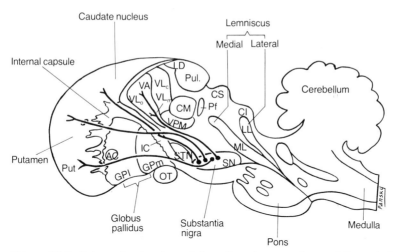

Figure 18-9 Schematic drawing of the efferent connections of the substantia nigra in sagittal section. Ascending fibers from the substantia nigra (SN) pass rostrally into Forel's field H and divide into a small medial bundle which projects to the thalamus and a larger lateral bundle which courses through the internal capsule. Medially projecting nigral efferent fibers pass to the medial part of the ventral lateral (VLm) and the magnocellular part of the ventral anterior (VAmc) thalamic nuclei. These fibers parallel the course of the mammillothalamic tract. Nigrostriatal fibers pass laterally, mainly dorsal to the subthalamic nucleus (STN), cross through the internal capsule, and enter the putamen and caudate nucleus via the globus pallidus and posterior limb of the internal capsule. AC, anterior commissure; CI, inferior colliculus; CM, centromedian thalamic nucleus; CS, superior colliculus; GPl and GPm, lateral and medial segments of the globus pallidus; LD, lateral dorsal thalamic nucleus; OT, optic tract; paracentral thalamic nucleus; Pf, parafascicular nucleus; Pul, pulvinar; VA, ventral anterior thalamic nucleus; VLc and VLo, ventral lateral thalamic nucleus (caudal and oral parts); VPM, ventral posteromedial thalamic nucleus; ZI, zona incerta. *(Modified after Carpenter, Human Neuroanatomy, 7th ed., The Williams & Wilkins Company, Baltimore, 1976.)*

disorder of tone most frequently encountered is one of increase. Sometimes the degree of hypertonia is so great that volitional and emotional movements are almost completely suppressed. Patients may appear paralyzed, but tests will prove that they are not. The face is masklike, the expression is changed infrequently and then only with difficulty, and these patients do not blink their eyes. They do not swing their arms in walking. Part of their difficulty is due to actual increased tone and part to the suppression of accompanying voluntary movements of the limb. In spasticity the increase in tone is observed for the most part in the antigravity muscles. When there is widespread pathologic change over much of the frontal lobe or in a large segment of the basal ganglia, increased tone is seen in virtually all muscle groups. In contrast to the picture seen in spasticity, the tendon reflexes are usually not found to be increased. When the hypertonia is so general, the condition is usually called *rigidity*. Rigidity is classified as *plastic* or *cogwheel*.

Plastic Rigidity In such cases, the hypertonia is constant, and the examiner can feel a constant, continuous, and smooth resistance to passive stretching.

Cogwheel Rigidity In this case an examiner will find that the resistance to passive stretch is not smooth but is discontinuous; there is an alternation of resistance and lack of resistance. This condition may actually be due to a milder form of the same pathologic changes responsible for the plastic type of rigidity, but in this case not so much of the suppressor mechanism is interrupted.

Involuntary Movements

Several of these movements are encountered. Among them are *tremors, choreiform movements, athetosis, hemiballism,* and *dystonia.* The underlying cause is unknown.

Tremors Tremors are of various sorts, depending upon when they occur. When they appear while the body is at rest, they are called *postural (static,* or *alternating).* This tremor consists of the alternating contraction of opposing muscle groups—flexors and extensors, abductors and adductors. In the hands this tremor is characterized by thumb opposing fingers in the "pill-rolling" maneuver. In most cases this type of tremor is suppressed during voluntary acts and may disappear in sleep. It is more severe in emotional states. *Action,* or *intention tremors* always appear during voluntary acts, increasing in severity near the end of the action. They are not seen at rest.

Choreiform Movements These movements are rapid, dancing, and jerky. They appear somewhat purposeful. There may be a rapid flexion of a finger, abduction of the arm, elevation of a shoulder, a grimace around the mouth, or a twitching of the facial muscles. They may occur at rest and may also accompany voluntary acts.

Athetosis This is a slow pattern of movement rather than an isolated act. It may occur either at rest or in the course of voluntary action. The movement begins slowly and is often seen in the distal part of the upper extremity, where there are alternating hyperextension and flexion of the fingers, usually with abduction (Fig. 18-10). The wrist may

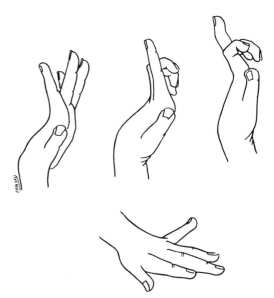

Figure 18-10 Athetoid movements of the hand.

slowly flex and pronate. The arm is often retracted. This is referred to as *serpentine movement.* Grimaces of the face frequently occur simultaneously with the limb action. The muscles are hypertonic during the active phase of the movement but are hypotonic at rest. Most frequently the corpus striatum and cortex are involved. However, lesions have been seen in the globus pallidus and thalamus. The site of the lesion is usually contralateral to that of the abnormal movement.

Dystonic Movements These movements are slow, writhing, and involuntary, with bizarre, grotesque tortions and twistings of the shoulder and pelvic girdle as well as of the trunk. There are spasmodic alterations of muscle tone, first hypertonus, then hypotonus predominating. There may be rigidity, scoliosis, and lordosis.[7]

Ballism This is characterized by involuntary movements of the entire limb, beginning in the proximal portions and passing in waves

[7]Scoliosis is an abnormal lateral curvature of the spinal column. Lordosis is a curvature of the lumbar spinal column with a forward convexity.

down the extremity. There may be wild swinging of the arms. Rolling, wavelike patterns seem to flow down the arm from time to time. When both limbs of the same side are involved, this is called *hemiballism;* when only one is involved, it is *monoballism.* Like chorea and athetosis, this is thought to be a release phenomenon. In other words, lesions in one center or pathway have removed the regulating influences which the diseased structure normally has upon related, normal portions of the system. Thus, with the regulatory influence gone or diminished, overactivity of the normal part results.

It seems probable that, in the case of choreiform and choreoathetoid movements where degeneration in the caudate nucleus and putamen is observed, the lesion may also involve the sensorimotor cortex and adjacent structures.

Testing

Few specific tests need to be made for this system. Much depends on merely observing the patient to see whether there is evidence of any of the abnormal movements of the types given above. Facial expression should be noted, to see if there are changes under different conditions. Patients should be watched while they are walking to see if the normal associative movements, such as swinging of the arms, occur in a normal way.

However, one specific type of test should be performed. It involves the manipulation of the extremities to get an impression of the muscle tone and of resistance to passive movement. At this time, the presence or absence of rigidity can be determined, and if it is present, its type—plastic or cogwheel—can be ascertained. The type may sometimes best be brought out by alternately pronating and supinating the forearm.

Specific Pathology

Although the various nuclear groups and their interconnections have been described in some

detail, it is difficult to localize the particular portion involved on the basis of symptoms seen among patients. It might be said that any successful skillful motor performance is the result of the integration of the entire motor mechanism. This represents not only a balance between facilitatory and inhibitory effects but a balance which can be subject to rapid alterations with the initiation of a specific action. Thus, if any part is destroyed or otherwise blocked, the resulting movement will represent the product of the parts still capable of function. For example, a pathologic process may involve the facilitatory mechanism. This, therefore, leads to a lack of influx of activating influences, together with an unchecked suppressor system. Conversely, disease in the inhibitory system removes the inhibitor impulses and leaves unchecked the facilitatory apparatus. However, since many of the nuclear masses and their interconnections are close together or even intermingled, it is obvious that lesions of the CNS will inevitably damage parts of both the facilitatory and inhibitory apparatuses simultaneously. Thus, the resulting motor performance will be the product of the undamaged parts of both systems. In the specific considerations listed below, an attempt has been made, where possible, to correlate the physical signs with the pathologic changes of the CNS as determined after postmortem examination.

Hemiballism

The movement pattern has already been discussed. It is the only one of the "diseases" of the "basal ganglia" the onset of which may be sudden. It is frequently the result of destruction of the contralateral subthalamic nucleus from vascular or other disorders. Lesions involving the pallidosubthalamic fibers may also produce these symptoms.

Paralysis Agitans (Parkinsonism)

In these cases, extensive degeneration of the globus pallidus and substantia nigra and cortex is seen. The putamen and caudate are involved to a lesser degree. By some, the substantia nigra is considered to be most important. The cause is unknown. This disease is characterized by rigidity of both the plastic and cogwheel types. The trunk may be especially affected, and this may lead to the assumption of a flexed posture (Fig. 18-11). Postural tremor is present and is especially marked in the distal extremities, with a rate of about five tremors per second. These occur at rest and disappear with voluntary movement.

Encephalitis

While parkinsonism usually occurs later in life, encephalitis may lead to the appearance of these signs at any age. There may be trunk flexion, and the tremor in these cases occurs at the rate of about eight per second. It has been found that when rigidity is the most striking feature, the most severe damage is in the

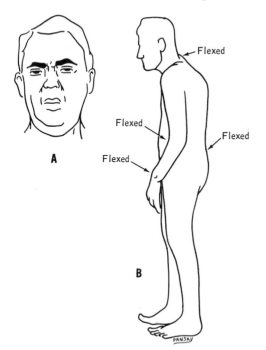

Figure 18-11 Paralysis agitans. Anxious smoothed-out facies with little mobility.

globus pallidus and the reticular portion of the substantia nigra. If tremor is the dominant sign, the compact zone of the substantia nigra shows more extensive pathologic change, while the pallidum exhibits less.

Hepatolenticular Disease (Wilson's Disease)

This is a rare, familial disease, usually fatal, occurring in young people. It is characterized clinically by an intention tremor, athetoid movements, rigidity, dysarthria, dysphagia, contractures, muscle weakness, progressive dementia, and emaciation.[8] In many cases, a peculiar golden-brown pigmented ring (Kayser-Fleischer ring) is seen at the outer margins of the cornea. The neuropathologic process is essentially limited to the corpus striatum. It consists of bilateral, symmetric, and visible cavitation, with degeneration of the putamen. Pathologic changes have also been found in other widely scattered areas of the brain, including the ventral lateral nucleus of the thalamus, the midbrain tegmentum, and the substantia nigra. Like parkinsonism, the tremor disappears with sleep.

Sydenham's Chorea

This is a disease of children or adolescents, often associated with rheumatic fever. There are quick, irregular, involuntary, asymmetric, purposeless movements, increased by emotional or other stimuli. The pathologic changes have never been adequately studied, but petechial lesions in the corpus striatum and cortex have been described.

Huntington's Chorea

This is an adult disease, onset of which occurs between the ages of 35 and 40 (sometimes earlier). Moderate to severe choreiform movements are coupled with progressive mental deterioration. There is degeneration in both

[8]Dysarthria is imperfect articulation in speech. Dysphagia is difficulty in swallowing. Dementia is a mental deterioration.

the cortex and the basal ganglia (caudate nucleus and putamen). The disease is definitely hereditary.

Dystonia Musculorum Deformans (Torsion Spasm) (Fig. 18-12)

Dystonic movements have been observed frequently as a sequel to epidemic encephalitis. In these cases, however, other signs and symptoms betray the acute, inflammatory origin of the disease. In the syndrome as described by one group of neurologists, these dystonic movements constitute virtually the whole clinical picture. It is a chronic, progressive disease, usually beginning between the ages of 8 and 15. It appears to occur most commonly among Russian Jews. In typical cases, the diagnosis can be made at a glance. Slow, patternlike movements, twisting of the pelvis, spasmodic torticollis, scoliosis, and contractures of the feet (striatal foot) point to the nature of the condition. The few cases which have come to autopsy have shown degenerative changes in midbrain, pons, and cerebellum in addition to the striatum and cerebral cortex, where the damage is principally observed.

As pointed out earlier, diseases of the basal ganglia destroy only portions of the system so that an imbalance exists between excitation and inhibition. Since it is patently impossible to restore the damaged part, most therapy attempts to destroy a portion of the normal or overactive region as a counterbalance. For example, it has been found that destruction of parts of the globus pallidus relieves contralateral rigidity, while destruction of parts of the thalamus helps to relieve contralateral tremor. Lesions placed in these same areas tend to ameliorate dystonic symptoms. It might also be noted that intention tremors encountered in certain cerebellar diseases may be relieved by placing lesions in the ventral lateral nucleus of the thalamus.

SUMMARY

I Parts
    A Cortex: areas 4, 6
    B Basal nuclei
       1 Corpus striatum
          a Caudate nucleus
          b Putamen (outer segment of the lenticular nucleus)
       2 Globus pallidus (inner portion of the lenticular nucleus)
          a Outer segment
          b Inner segment
    C Subthalamus
       1 Subthalamic nucleus
    D Mesencephalon
       1 Substantia nigra
       2 Deep tegmental nucleus
II Connections
    A Corpus striatum (caudate nucleus and putamen)
       1 Receives afferents from
          a Wide areas of the cerebral cortex
          b Centrum medianum of the thalamus
       2 Sends efferents to
          a Outer segment of globus pallidus
          b Inner segment of globus pallidus (few)
          c Substantia nigra
    B Globus pallidus
       1 Receives afferents from

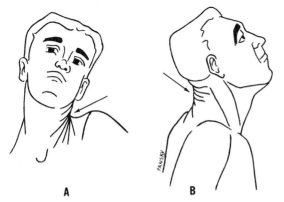

Figure 18-12 Basal ganglia disease. *A.* Spasmodic dystonia. *B.* Dystonia—postencephalitic.

      a Striatum (chiefly to the outer segment)

2 Sends efferents by three streams

      a Ansa lenticularis, from inner segment, to join

      b Fasciculus lenticularis, from both segments; the combined streams give

          (1) Thalamic fasciculus (pallido-thalamic) fibers to the ventral lateral and ventral anterior nuclei of the thalamus

      c Pallidosubthalamic fibers to

          (1) Subthalamic nucleus

          (2) Substantia nigra

      d Pallidotegmental fibers to the pedunculopontine nucleus

C Substantia nigra

  1 Receives afferents from

      a Striatum

      b Pallidum

  2 Sends efferents to

      a Neostriatum

      b Ventral lateral nucleus of thalamus

      c Ventral anterior nucleus of the thalamus

      d Deep tegmental nucleus of the mesencephalon

D Subthalamic nucleus

  1 Receives afferents from

      a Pallidum (outer segment)

  2 Sends efferents to

      a Pallidum (inner segment)

The Reticular Formation

In previous chapters we have attempted to analyze, in general, the functions of separate groups of anatomically related structures whose functions appear to be primarily either sensory or motor. In this chapter we will consider the anatomic organization and functional characteristics of a group of structures linked together under the general rubric of *reticular formation.* One of the unique and remarkable features of these structures is that they do not partake in the elaboration of a single function but, instead, participate in the organization of a variety of processes. These include the modulation and transmission of sensory information to higher centers, modulation of motor activity, control of autonomic responses, regulation of the sleep-wakefulness cycle, and the cortical EEG as well as the site of origin of most, if not all, of the monoamines distributed through the CNS.

ANATOMIC CONSIDERATIONS

The reticular formation is generally considered to represent a phylogenetically old part of the brain (since it constitutes a prominent portion of the brainstem of lower forms) and is situated in the medulla, pons, and midbrain. It consists of a large number of cell groups and many fiber systems which travel around or through these nuclear groups, creating a reticular appearance and thus providing the basis for the name reticular formation.

A general feature of the organization of the reticular formation is that it can be subdivided in the following way: The medial two-thirds contains many large cells and constitutes the principal effector region; the lateral one-third is made up of small cells and represents, in most instances, the affector region; and the midline (raphe) constitutes the region where cells produce serotonin for distribution to the rest of the brain and spinal cord (Figs. 19-1 through 19-4). Cranial nerve nuclei and secondary sensory pathways form an outer shell which surrounds the reticular formation both dorsally and laterally. Ventrally, the reticular formation is surrounded by the medial lemniscus and descending motor pathways. Thus, the reticular formation is strategically positioned so that many different systems can easily provide significant input into it and, in this way, establish a basis by which it can modulate a wide variety of functions.

Afferent Connections

The reticular formation receives its afferent supply from the spinal cord, cerebellum, hypothalamus, pallidum, and cerebral cortex.

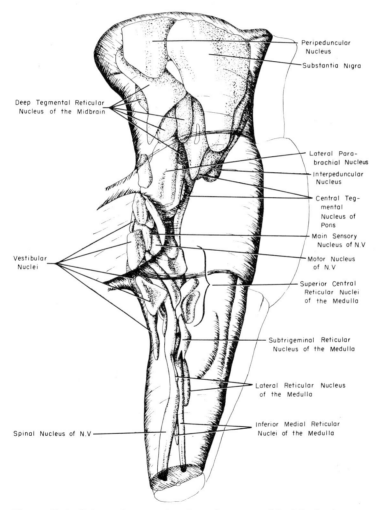

Figure 19-1 Schematic reconstruction of some nuclei of the brainstem reticular formation as seen from the lateral aspect. Several cranial nerve nuclei are also shown. *(From Peele, The Neuroanatomic Basis for Clinical Neurology, 3d. ed., McGraw-Hill Book Company, New York, 1977.)*

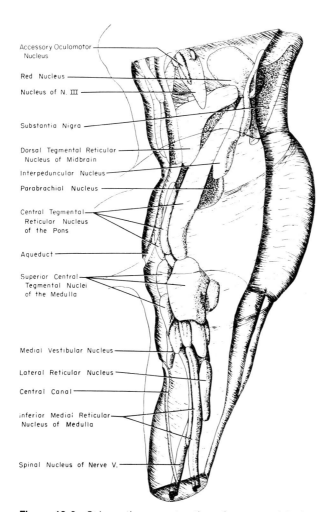

Accessory Oculomotor
Nucleus

Red Nucleus

Nucleus of N. III

Substantia Nigra

Dorsal Tegmental Reticular
Nucleus of Midbrain

Interpeduncular Nucleus

Parabrachial Nucleus

Central Tegmental
Reticular Nucleus
of the Pons

Aqueduct

Superior Central
Tegmental Nuclei
of the Medulla

Medial Vestibular Nucleus

Lateral Reticular Nucleus

Central Canal

Inferior Medial Reticular
Nucleus of Medulla

Spinal Nucleus of Nerve V.

Figure 19-2 Schematic reconstruction of some nuclei of the brainstem reticular formation as seen from a parasagittal plane near the midline. Several cranial nerve nuclei are also shown. *(From Peele, The Neuroanatomic Basis for Clinical Neurology, 3d ed., McGraw-Hill Book Company, New York, 1977.)*

Collaterals of secondary auditory, trigeminal, and vestibular fibers also provide important inputs.

From the Spinal Cord

Fibers in the *spinoreticular tract* appear to arise from the posterior horn at all levels of the spinal cord and ascend in the anterolateral funiculus in association with the lateral spinothalamic tract (Fig. 19-5). They terminate

mainly within selected levels of the medial two-thirds of the medulla and pons with only a few reaching the midbrain. These fibers make synapse ipsilaterally at medullary levels in the nucleus gigantocellularis and lateral reticular nucleus. At pontine levels the fibers terminate bilaterally in the nucleus reticularis pontis caudalis and oralis (Fig. 19-5). As will be shown, the principal sites in the medulla and pons where spinoreticular fibers terminate

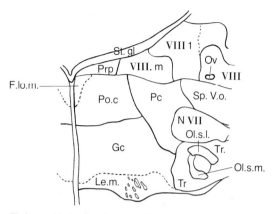

Figure 19-3 Semischematic representation of a Nissl-stained section through the brainstem at a low pontine level. The facial nucleus (N.VII), the rostral part of the spinal trigeminal nucleus (SP. V.o), parts of the vestibular nuclei (VIII L. and VIII m), the nucleus praepositus (Prp), the medial longitudinal fasciculus (Fl.o.m.), and the medial lemniscus (Le.m) surround the reticular formation. Within this, three subdivisions can be separated at this level, the nuclei gigantocellularis (Gc), pontis caudalis (Po.c), and parvicellularis (Pc). *(From Brodal, Neurological Anatomy, 2d ed., Oxford University Press, London, 1969.)*

give rise to long ascending and descending fibers. In this way spinoreticular fibers constitute the first part of a chain of neurons which ultimately innervate the thalamus and cerebral cortex. This multisynaptic pathway constitutes the anatomic basis of the *reticular activating system* (RAS). The latter plays a major role in the modulation of cortical neurons which is manifested in altered levels of states of consciousness.

From the Cerebellum

In Chap. 17, the reciprocal connections between the cerebellum and reticular formation were described. Briefly, the afferents to the reticular formation from the cerebellum arise from the fastigial nucleus. They are both crossed and uncrossed as they pass through the *uncinate fasciculus* to terminate in the reticular formation of the medulla and pons. This pathway forms part of a feedback circuit between the cerebellum and reticular forma-

tion which probably relates to the regulation of motor activities by each of these structures.

From the Sensory Systems (Secondary Sensory Fibers)

It is now commonly accepted that a number of different sensory systems provide inputs to the reticular formation. Spinoreticular fibers associated with the spinothalamic system have already been described. Other systems include collaterals of ascending auditory fibers and axons from the vestibular and trigeminal nuclei as well. It is also possible that a number of optic fibers destined for the superior colliculus send collaterals into the midbrain reticular formation. Further, it is plausible that some tertiary olfactory fibers supply the reticular formation. Such connections may involve certain limbic structures such as the hippocampal formation and septal area which are known to have some projections that reach the midbrain reticular formation (Chaps. 21, 22). Perhaps the most significant feature concerning the presence of multiple sensory input into the reticular formation is that upstream reticulofugal transmission of these signals is of a nonspecific nature in contrast to the specificity characteristic of other lines of transmission such as the dorsal column–medial lemniscus pathway. Presumably, and as noted above, the main function of any of these sensory signals which reach the reticular formation is to cause the reticular activating system to alter excitability levels of its target neurons.

From the Hypothalamus and Limbic System

Both lateral and medial regions of the hypothalamus supply descending fibers which reach the reticular formation. Fibers which issue from the lateral hypothalamus pass via the medial forebrain bundle to the ventral tegmental area. Fibers which issue from the medial hypothalamus follow the periventricu-

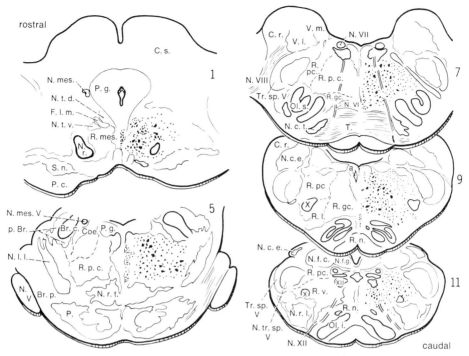

Figure 19-4 A cytoarchitectonic map of the reticular formation of the cat. In a series of transverse sections are plotted the various cell groups and their composition of small, medium-sized, and large cells. Coe, nucleus subceruleus; F.l.m., medial longitudinal fasciculus; M.c.e., external cuneate nucleus; N.f.c., nucleus cuneatus; N.f.g., nucleus gracilis; N.r., red nucleus; M.r.l., lateral reticular nucleus (nucleus of lateral funiculus); N.r.t., nucleus reticularis tegmenti pontis; N.tr.sp.V., spinal nucleus of trigeminal nerve; P., pontine nuclei; P.g., periaqueductal gray; R.gc., nucleus reticularis gigantocellularis; R.mes., reticular formation of the mesencephalon; R.n., nuclei of the raphe; R.p.c., nucleus reticularis pontis caudalis; R.pc., nucleus reticularis parvicellularis; R.v., nucleus reticularis ventralis. *(From Brodal, Neurological Anatomy, 2d ed., Oxford University Press, London, 1969.)*

lar system downstream to dorsal portions of the tegmentum and to the central gray region mainly of the midbrain and pons. Other groups of fibers arise from the mammillary bodies and are distributed to the dorsal and ventral tegmental nuclei (Chap. 21). Still additional fibers from the hippocampal formation, septal area, and nucleus accumbens project to the ventral and central tegmental areas. The descending connections from the hypothalamus to the reticular formation provide a basis by which central autonomic effects elicited by the hypothalamus can be generated via a multisynaptic pathway to the spinal cord.

From the Cerebral Cortex

Fibers mainly from sensorimotor cortex are distributed principally to the medial two-thirds of the reticular formation in a unique manner. The fibers terminate in the nucleus gigantocellularis of the medulla and in the region of the nucleus reticularis pontis caudalis and oralis (Fig. 19-6). As noted above, these regions give rise to long ascending and descending reticulofugal fibers.

From the Globus Pallidus

As noted in Chap. 18, in addition to the overwhelming majority of fibers which are

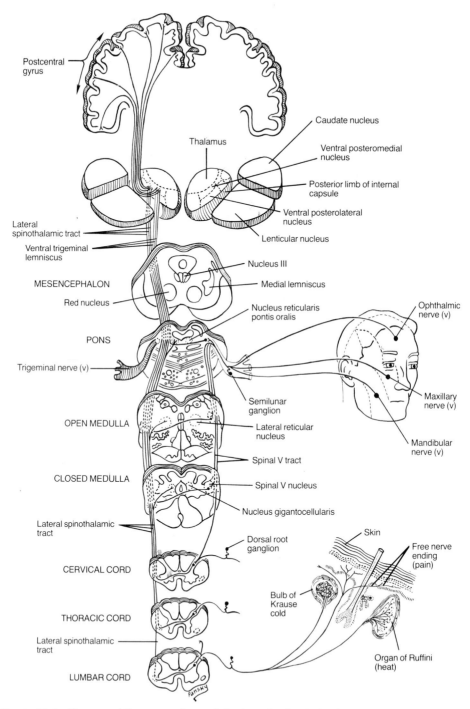

Figure 19-5 Diagram of the connections of the lateral spinothalamic tract to the reticular formation.

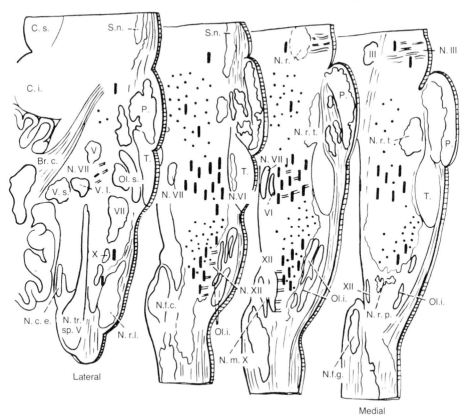

Figure 19-6 In parasagittal sections through the cat's brainstem are plotted the regions of the medial two-thirds of the reticular formation, which receive the maximum of fibers from the cerebral cortex (dots), and the regions from which the majority of long ascending fibers take origin (vertical bars). Note overlap in the region dorsal to the middle part of the inferior olive. Br.c, brachium conjunctivum; N.f.c. and N.f.g., nucleus cuneatus and nucleus gracilis; N.VII, facial nerve; V, VI, VII, X, and XII, motor nuclei of cranial nerves. *(From Brodal, Neurological Anatomy, 2d ed., Oxford University Press, London, 1969.)*

distributed to the thalamus, some fibers from the medial pallidal segment project downstream, terminating in the pedunculopontine nucleus of the reticular formation. It is possible that this group of fibers may enable the basal ganglia to modulate motor activity via descending reticulospinal fibers.

ORGANIZATION AND DISTRIBUTION OF RETICULOFUGAL FIBERS

Organizational Features

It is generally agreed that the long ascending and descending fiber systems of the reticular

formation arise from the medial two-thirds of this structure while the lateral third contains neurons which travel only short distances and serve mainly as interneurons. With regard to the organization of the long ascending and descending fibers, several principles of organization are evident: (1) the main dendritic branches of neurons are oriented in a plane perpendicular to the long axis of the brainstem (Fig. 19-7). This particular feature increases the likelihood that ascending and descending fiber systems from other parts of the CNS can make synaptic contact with these neurons; (2) many cells of the medial two-thirds of the

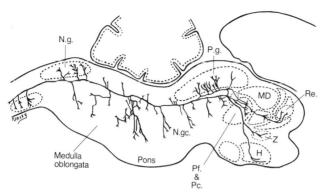

Figure 19-7 Drawing of a sagittal Golgi section from the brainstem of a 2-day-old rat, showing a single large cell in the magnocellular nucleus. It emits an axon which bifurcates into an ascending and a descending branch. The latter gives off collaterals to the adjacent reticular formation (N.gc., nucleus reticularis gigantocellularis), to the nucleus gracilis (N.g.), and to the ventral horn in the spinal cord. The ascending branch gives off collaterals to the reticular formation and the periaqueductal gray (P.g.) and then appears to supply several thalamic nuclei (Pf. and Pc., parafascicularis and paracentralis; Re., reuniens; and others), the hypothalamus (H), and the so-called zone incerta (Z). MD, dorsomedial thalamic nucleus. *(From Brodal, Neurological Anatomy, 2d ed., Oxford University Press, London, 1969, based on Scheibel & Scheibel, 1958.)*

reticular formation give rise to bifurcating axons which can travel for long distances in both directions (Fig. 19-8); (3) there is reason to believe that neurons which project primarily in an upstream direction are situated ventral to those which pass primarily in a downstream direction. However, each of these neurons can make synaptic contact with the other by virtue of its axon collaterals (Fig. 19-8). As shown in Fig. 19-8, these latter two organizational features provide an inherent integrating mechanism by which the reticular formation can synchronously signal upstream as well as downstream targets.

Efferent Connections

The efferent fibers of the reticular formation are distributed to the spinal cord, cerebellum, hypothalamus, and thalamus. In addition, an important group of monoamine fibers have also been shown to be distributed to wide areas of both the spinal cord and forebrain.

To the Spinal Cord

Reticulospinal fibers have their origin both in the pons and medulla. Fibers from the pons issue from the nucleus reticularis pontis caudalis and oralis and descend ipsilaterally in the medial part of the anterior funiculus to all levels of the spinal cord. These fibers terminate in the ventral and intermediate gray matter—laminae 7 and 8—of the spinal cord which corresponds to the termination sites of descending vestibulospinal and tectospinal fibers. The medullary reticulospinal system arises from the nucleus reticularis gigantocellularis and descends bilaterally in the anterior funiculus. These fibers terminate at all levels of the cord but slightly more dorsally than do the pontine fibers (Fig. 19-9).

It is now well established that the reticular formation plays a significant role in a number of different functions. For example, electrical stimulation of the reticular formation can modulate a variety of motor responses. Stimulation of the ventromedial part of the medul-

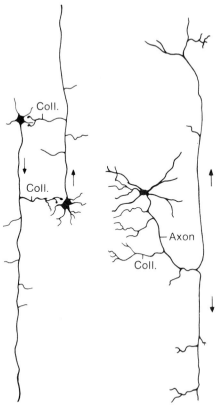

Figure 19-8 Diagram of two anatomic features which make possible a close correlation of caudally and rostrally directed influences of the reticular formation. To the right a simplified drawing of a typical cell in the medial reticular formation. Its axon gives off a long ascending and a long descending branch provided with collaterals. To the left a diagram showing how cells giving off ascending and descending axons, respectively, may influence each other by way of collaterals. *(From Brodal, Neurological Anatomy, 2d ed., Oxford University Press, London, 1969.)*

closely related to the pontine reticulospinal tract. Although it is possible for the reticular formation to modulate both alpha and gamma motor neurons, it is likely that the primary action of the reticulospinal tracts is directly upon the gamma system. Since the alpha motor neurons are influenced by the gamma loop, it is possible for the reticular formation to indirectly modulate the alpha motor neurons as well.

Another process that may be modulated by the reticulospinal system is respiration. Electrical stimulation of the ventral and medial portions of the medulla produce inspiratory responses, while more lateral and rostral levels produce expiratory responses. It has also been demonstrated that several other regions of the brainstem reticular formation take part in the central control of respiration. One such region includes the lower pons and is referred to as an *apneustic center.* Under experimental conditions in which the vagus nerve is cut and the input to this region from the upper pons is removed, the apneustic center can produce prolonged periods of inspiration. A second region, referred to as the *pneumotaxic center,* is situated in the upper pons and is associated with increases in the rate of respiration. Although the exact relation between the apneustic and pneumotaxic centers remains unknown, it is believed that the pneumotaxic center may inhibit the action of the apneustic center (Fig. 19-10). Neuronal populations which are thought to be situated in the medulla and which are sensitive to changes in carbon dioxide or pH can produce changes in the rates of respiration when appropriately activated. Such central receptors appear to parallel the functions of other, peripheral chemoreceptors located in the carotid arteries and aortic arch which also sense changes in carbon dioxide tension or altered pH. Fibers associated with these receptors enter the CNS via the glossopharyngeal and vagus nerves and thus constitute the afferent limb of a central reflex

lary reticular formation inhibits cortically elicited movement, decerebrate rigidity, as well as myotatic reflexes and muscle tone. In contrast, stimulation of more lateral and rostral sites, such as the pons and midbrain, produces facilitatory effects upon these motor responses. It is likely that the inhibitory zones are associated with the medullary reticulospinal tract while the facilitatory regions are more

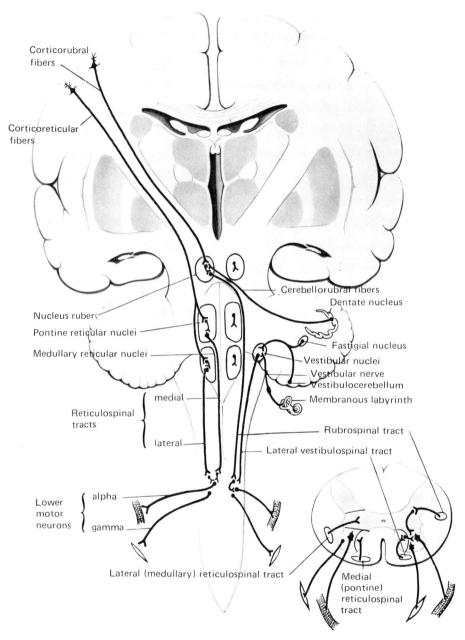

Figure 19-9 Descending motor pathways to the spinal cord, including the reticulospinal tracts (corticoreticulospinal pathways), rubrospinal tracts (corticorubrospinal pathway), and vestibulospinal tracts. *(From Noback and Demarest, The Human Nervous System, 2d ed., McGraw-Hill Book Company, New York, 1975.)*

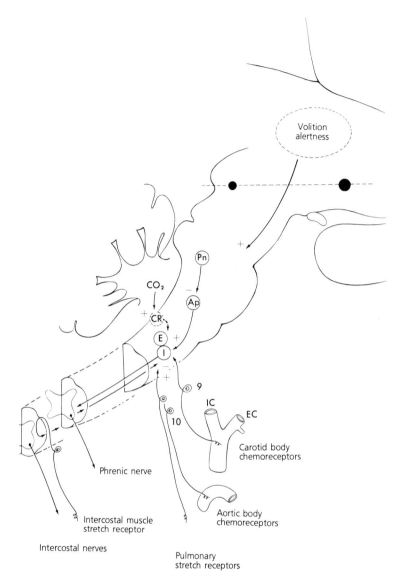

Figure 19-10 Central areas and peripheral structures involved in control of respiration. Sites where stimulation or activation of projections produces an increase in rate and depth of inspiration are shown with a plus sign; sites where stimulation produces a decrease are shown with a minus sign. E,I, expiratory and inspiratory portions of the medullary respiratory center; CR, presumed central chemoreceptors for CO_2; Ap, apneustic center; Pn, pneumotaxic center. *(From Willis and Grossman, Medical Neurobiology, The C. V. Mosby Company, St. Louis, 1974.)*

whose efferent limb is believed to be regulated by the reticulospinal tracts.

Cardiovascular responses are also associated with these portions of the medulla and pons. Stimulation of the medial part of the medulla—the region which is associated with motor inhibition and inspiratory responses—can also produce a depression in blood pressure and a decrease in heart rate, while the opposite reactions can occur following stimulation of more lateral and rostral sites—the same regions associated with facilitation of motor responses and expiration.

Several other features regarding central regulation of cardiovascular responses ought to be noted. First, both pressor and depressor responses apparently involve the pontine and medullary reticulospinal tracts, respectively. Second, pontine and medullary neurons associated with pressor and depressor reactions can be controlled directly or indirectly by the hypothalamus, limbic system, and prefrontal cortex. Third, the reticular pressor neurons are probably inhibited directly following activation of the afferent limb of the carotid sinus reflex. In this reflex, an increase in blood pressure within the carotid sinus results in a discharge of neurons in the afferent fibers of the glossopharyngeal nerve, which then ultimately activates the vagus nerve to produce a decrease in heart rate. Therefore, the inhibitory effects of carotid sinus activation upon pressor neurons help to ensure the success of the homeostatic reflex mechanism.

To the Cerebellum

As noted above and in Chap. 17, the cerebellum and reticular formation are reciprocally connected. This anatomic feature provides the afferent limb of a feedback mechanism to the cerebellum by which it can modulate the activity of an important region of the CNS associated with the motor regulation of the spinal cord. The cerebellar afferents arise from the lateral and paramedian reticular nu-

clei of the medulla and the reticular tegmental nucleus of the pons. The fibers are distributed to wide areas of the anterior and posterior lobes of the cerebellum.

To the Hypothalamus and Limbic System

Afferents to the hypothalamus and limbic system arise mainly from a number of different sites in the midbrain reticular formation and probably play important roles in the regulation of complex autonomic, endocrine, and behavioral processes associated with these structures. One such site includes the dorsal and deep tegmental nuclei whose fibers pass through the mammillary peduncle to the lateral mammillary nucleus. A second site is the ventral tegmental area whose axons ascend through the medial forebrain bundle and are distributed to the lateral hypothalamus, septal area, and nucleus accumbens (Fig. 19-11). Another bundle arising from the periaqueductal gray substance forms an ascending component of the periventricular system of fibers which passes adjacent to the third ventricle and cerebral aqueduct and terminates in the medial regions of the hypothalamus (Fig. 19-11). Lesions of the midbrain central gray and ventral tegmental area significantly interfere with selected forms of aggressive reactions associated with the medial and lateral hypothalamic areas, respectively. This fact indicates that these sites in the midbrain form essential links in the organization of selected behaviors normally identified with functions of the hypothalamus. Other fiber systems which supply the hypothalamus and limbic system represent the monoamine distribution from the brainstem and will be considered separately at the end of this chapter.

To the Thalamus

An important function of the reticular formation concerns its role as a cortical activating system. It is generally accepted that fibers arising from wide areas of the brainstem retic-

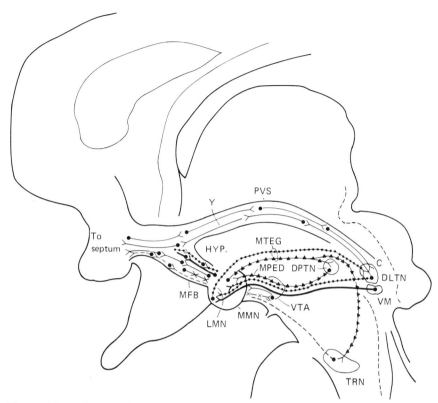

Figure 19-11 Schematic reconstruction to show some interconnections between the hypothalamus and brainstem tegmental regions. DLTN, dorsal tegmental nucleus with central (C) and ventromedial (VM) parts; DPTN, deep tegmental nucleus; HYP, hypothalamus; LMN, lateral mammillary nucleus; MFG, medial forebrain bundle; MMN, medial mammillary nucleus; MPed, mammillary peduncle; MTeg, mammillotegmental tract; PVS, periventricular system; TRN, tegmental reticular nucleus; VTA, ventral tegmental area. *(From Peele, The Neuroanatomic Basis for Clinical Neurology, 3d ed., McGraw-Hill Book Company, New York, 1977.)*

ular formation supply nonspecific thalamic nuclei and the ventral anterior nucleus, thus constituting an essential link in this functional pathway (Fig. 19-12). Fibers arising from such nonspecific thalamic nuclei as the intralaminar and midline cell groups have a wide distribution to much of the cerebral cortex, while the ventral anterior nucleus diffusely supplies the frontal lobe. Stimulation of any of these nuclear groups at low frequencies produces a distinctive cortical electrical pattern identified as a *recruiting response*. This response is characterized by a surface negative cortical

wave which rapidly reaches a maximum and then slowly decreases. Additional stimulation produces a waxing and waning effect upon the cortical wave. It also should be noted that low-frequency stimulation of the nonspecific thalamus produces a behavioral drowsy pattern. Electrical stimulation of the brainstem reticular formation can suppress or inhibit the recruiting response and, at the same time, produce a block of the alpha rhythm (that which constitutes an electroencephalographic component of a behavioral arousal reaction). Therefore, it may be concluded that the brain-

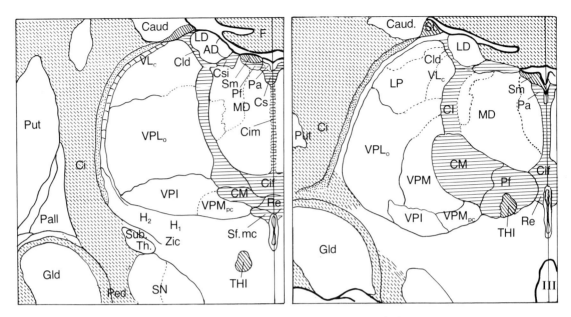

Figure 19-12 Drawings of transverse sections through the thalamus of the macaque monkey, showing the arrangement and subdivisions of the "nonspecific" thalamic nuclei. The reticular nucleus is indicated by dots, the intralaminar and midline nuclei by horizontal hatchings. The section to the left is placed most rostrally. Ci, internal capsule; Cif, nucleus centralis inferior; Cim, nucleus centralis intermedialis; Cl, nucleus centralis lateralis; CM, centromedian nucleus; Cs, nucleus centralis superior; Csl, nucleus centralis superior lateralis; Gld, nucleus geniculatus dorsalis; LP, nucleus lateralis posterior; MD, dorsomedial nucleus; Pa, nucleus paraventricularis; Pf, nucleus parafascicularis; R, nucleus reticularis; Re, nucleus reuniens; Sf.mc, nucleus subfascicularis pars magnocellularis; Sm, stria medullaris; SN, substantia nigra; St, stria terminalis; THI, tractus habenulointerpeduncularis; VLc, nucleus ventralis lateralis, pars caudalis; VPI, nucleus ventralis inferior; VPLo, nucleus ventralis posterior lateralis, pars oralis; VPM, nucleus ventralis posterior medialis; VPMpc, nucleus ventralis posterior medialis, pars parvocellularis. *(From Brodal, Neurological Anatomy, 2d ed., Oxford University Press, London, 1969.)*

stem reticular formation projections to the nonspecific thalamus serve as the initial link in a pathway which can produce activation of the cortex and behavioral arousal. The second component of this system would correspond to the nonspecific thalamic distribution to the cortex.

That the reticular activating system is dependent upon a variety of sensory input is suggested from the observation that a high spinal transection (i.e., *encéphale isolé*) does not eliminate a cortical EEG arousal pattern while a transection rostral to N.V (i.e., *cerveau isolé*) produces an EEG pattern characteristic

of an animal which is asleep (Fig. 19-13). With the spinal transection, sensory inputs to the reticular formation remain chiefly intact, whereas with a midcollicular cut the overwhelming sensory inputs to the midbrain reticular formation, especially from the trigeminal and auditory systems, are completely eliminated.

Monoamine Pathways and the Sleep-Wakefulness Cycle

In recent years it has been shown by histofluorescence techniques that the entire monoamine distribution in the CNS originates from selected cell clusters located in the brainstem. These transmitters include dopamine, norepinephrine,[1] and serotonin[2] (5-hydroxytryptamine). The dopamine fibers associated with the brainstem have their origin in the substantia nigra (Chap. 18) and ventral tegmental area. Fibers from the substantia nigra to the corpus striatum are referred to as the *nigrostriatal* dopamine system, while fibers which arise from the ventral tegmentum constitute the *mesolimbic* dopamine system. Mesolimbic fibers are distributed through the medial forebrain bundle to parts of the limbic system such as the septal area, nucleus accumbens, and olfactory tubercle (Fig. 19-14). Additional fibers also innervate the prefrontal cortex and adjacent portions of the anterior cingulate gyrus.

The norepinephrine-containing cell bodies are found in both the pons and medulla. They give rise to several groups of collecting bundles which ascend to innervate the hypothalamus, limbic system, and prefrontal cortex. Other fibers from the lower medulla innervate the spinal cord as well. Of unique interest is a group of norepinephrine neurons situated in the locus ceruleus which have a very extensive distribution to the hippocampal formation, entorhinal cortex, and cerebellar cortex (Figs. 19-15 through 19-17). The norepinephrine pathways appear to play an important role in states of sleep and wakefulness. In particular, the nucleus locus ceruleus has been linked to the regulation of paradoxical sleep, a sleep characterized by an alert EEG pattern which

is similar to that occurring in the waking state. Lesions of the locus ceruleus or the administration of alpha methyldopa (which synthesizes the false transmitter alpha methylnorepinephrine) can suppress paradoxical sleep. In addition, long-lasting arousal is produced following increases in cerebral catecholamines. These findings provide considerable support for the role of the nucleus locus ceruleus in paradoxical sleep.

The serotonin pathway arises from cell bodies located in the dorsal and median raphe nuclei. The axons pass rostrally through the lateral hypothalamus to reach the amygdala, septal area, frontal cortex, cingulate gyrus, and hippocampal formation (Figs. 19-16, 19-17). This system also plays an important role in the regulation of the sleep-wakefulness cycle. Some of the evidence which supports this conclusion is as follows: Lesions of the raphe system as well as the administration of such drugs as *p*-chlorophenylalanine, which blocks serotonin synthesis at the tryptophane hydroxylase step, produces states of prolonged wakefulness (insomnia); replacement treatment with the serotonin precursor 5-hydroxytryptophan will restore normal states of both slow-wave and paradoxical sleep.

The opposing effects of the norepinephrine and serotonin systems upon the sleep states indicate that sleep reflects, at least in part, a dynamic process involving an interaction between these two populations of monoamine neurons rather than a mere "turning off" of the reticular activating system, as was once believed.

Other functions associated with the monoamine pathways presumably relate to their interactions with the hypothalamus and limbic system. There appears to be a growing body of evidence which suggests that these transmitters play a significant role in the elaboration and control of rage reactions which are generally associated with the hypothalamus and limbic system. The exact manner by which the

---

[1]The biosynthesis of norepinephrine involves the following steps: tyrosine is converted to L-dihydroxyphenylalanine (L-dopa) by the enzyme tyrosine hydroxylase; L-dopa is then decarboxylated by the enzyme amino acid decarboxylase into dopamine; dopamine is converted into norepinephrine by the enzyme dopamine-β-oxidase.

[2]The biosynthesis of serotonin (5-hydroxytryptamine) involves the following steps: tryptophan is converted into 5-hydroxytryptophan by the enzyme tryptophan hydroxylase; 5-hydroxytryptophan is converted into serotonin by the enzyme amino acid decarboxylase.

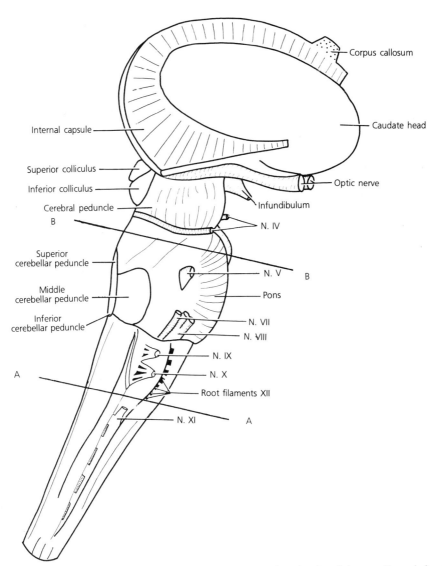

Figure 19-13 Lateral view of the brainstem showing levels of transection. A-A, near cord-medulla junction; B-B, at the upper pons, rostral to the trigeminal nerve. *(Based on Curtis, Jacobson, and Marcus, W. B. Saunders Company, Philadelphia, 1972.)*

monoamines control emotional behavior, including their sites of action, remains unclear. Nevertheless, it is presently believed that major tranquilizers help to produce changes in mood by acting upon the neuronal systems associated with the monoamine pathways.

Finally, from a clinical viewpoint, it has been shown that lesions of the brainstem are associated with disturbances of consciousness. Damage to the reticular formation at the level of the pons or midbrain, usually the result of a cerebrovascular accident, produces

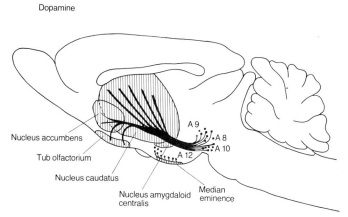

Figure 19-14 Sagittal projection of the dopamine (DA) pathways. The stripes indicate nerve terminal areas. A-8-A-10, dopamine cell groups of the brainstem. A-12, the median eminence. *(From Ungerstedt, Acta Physiol. Scand.* [*Suppl.*] *367, 82:1–48, 1971.)*

coma in most cases. There appears to be some variation in the EEG patterns following lesions of different parts of the reticular formation. For example, slow waves of large amplitude are seen with damage to the midbrain reticular formation. In contrast, pontine lesions are more closely related to an EEG characteristic of the awake, drowsy state (alpha rhythm) of the normal individual. With some brainstem lesions the patient may exhib-

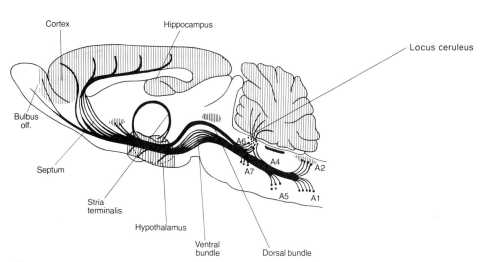

Figure 19-15 Sagittal projection of the ascending NA (norepinephrine, or noradrenaline) pathways. The stripes indicate the major nerve terminal areas. A-1–A-7, brainstem norepinephrine (noradrenaline) cell groups. *(From Ungerstedt, Acta Physiol. Scand.* [*Suppl.*] *367, 82:1–48, 1971.)*

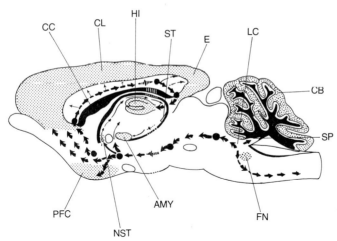

Figure 19-16 Schematic representation on a sagittal plane of the efferent pathways of the locus ceruleus. Note that the stria terminalis, amygdala, and pyriform cortex are lateral to the plane of the figure. Arrows indicate fiber bundles running longitudinally. Shaded region, terminal areas; CC, corpus callosum; CL, claustrum; HI, hippocampus; ST, stria terminalis; E, entorhinal cortex; FN, facial nucleus; AMY, amygdala; PFC, pyriform cortex; NST, bed nucleus of the stria terminalis. *(From Pickel, Segal, and Bloom, J. Comp. Neurol., 155:15–42, 1974.)*

it an EEG pattern similar to that characteristic of slow-wave sleep. However, in this instance the patient lies quietly but can display a variety of autonomic and somatomotor reflexes as

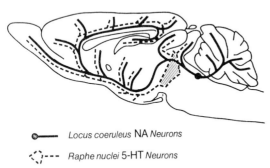

●— *Locus coeruleus* NA *Neurons*

◁--- *Raphe nuclei* 5-HT *Neurons*

Figure 19-17 Schematic illustration of the monosynaptic norepinephrine, or noradrenaline, (NA) and 5-hydroxytryptamine (5-HT) connections to the cortices of the brain. The cerulocortical neurons (solid line) and the ascending mesencephalic neurons (broken line) are illustrated with their diffuse innervation of the cerebellar and cerebral cortex (neocortex, paleocortex, archicortex). The collaterals given off to the colliculi, thalamus, and the septal region are also indicated. *(Based on Fuxe, Lidbrink, and Olson, in The Sleeping Brain, Perspect. Brain Sci., 1:122–127, 1972.)*

well as normal eye movements. This form of hypersomnia is referred to as *coma vigil*, or *akinetic mutism.* Lesions of the lower brainstem also result in loss of consciousness. Frequently, however, there are accompanying respiratory and cardiovascular disturbances which become fatal.

SUMMARY

  I Afferents from:
    A Spinal Cord
      1 Spinoreticular fibers follow spinothalamic tracts to terminate mainly in medulla and pons.
    B Cerebellum
      1 From fastigeal nucleus fibers pass crossed and uncrossed via uncinate fasciculus to end in medulla and pons.
    C Cranial nerve nuclei—secondary fibers from:
      1 Auditory system
      2 Visual system
      3 Somatosensory system

    D Hypothalamus by way of the following pathways which pass mainly to the midbrain and pons:
      1 Descending components of the medial forebrain bundle
      2 Mammillary peduncle
      3 Periventricular system
    E Cerebral cortex
      1 From sensorimotor cortex via corticoreticular fibers to the large-celled regions of the pons and medulla
    F Pallidum
      1 From medial pallidal segment fibers project to the pedunculopontine nucleus.
II Efferent to:
    A Spinal Cord
      1 Lateral reticulospinal tract from large-celled region of the medulla to all levels of the spinal cord
      2 Medial reticulospinal tract from large-celled regions of the pons to all levels of the spinal cord
    B Cerebellum
      1 Anterior and posterior lobes from:
        a Lateral nucleus of medulla
        b Paramedian nucleus of medulla
        c Reticulotegmental nucleus of pons

    C Hypothalamus and Limbic System
      1 Lateral mammillary nucleus from deep tegmental nucleus
      2 Lateral hypothalamus, nucleus accumbens, septal area, anterior cingulate gyrus, and hippocampal formation from ventral tegmental area
      3 Medial hypothalamus from the periaqueductal gray
    D Thalamus
      1 Nonspecific thalamic nuclei from widespread regions of the reticular formation
    E Monoamine pathways
      1 Dopamine pathway from ventral tegmental area via medial forebrain bundle to lateral hypothalamus, limbic system, and prefrontal cortex
      2 Norepinephrine pathway from a number of cell groups in the medulla and pons to the hypothalamus, limbic system, and prefrontal cortex
      3 Serotonin pathway from the raphe neurons of the pons and midbrain through the lateral hypothalamus to much of the limbic system and frontal cortex

Chapter 20

Suprasegmental Pathways for the Control of Muscular Activity

Muscular activity is controlled and/or modified from several levels of the CNS (Chaps. 13, 17 through 19, 24). The first of these lies in the ventral horns of the spinal cord or in the cranial motor nuclei of the brainstem. Neurons with such origins are the lower motor neurons, or final common path, as previously described (Chap. 13). The others are located in many different places and exert their influences on the final common path by way of neurons descending in a number of tracts which, collectively, are spoken of as upper motor neurons. The suprasegmental levels which participate in this massive integrative mechanism include the cerebellum (Chap. 17); the basal ganglia with their associated nuclei (Chap. 18); the reticular formation (Chap. 19); and the cerebral cortex (Chap. 24).

It is still common practice to divide the descending motor pathways into two major groups, the pyramidal and extrapyramidal. The former refers only to that portion arising from specific areas of the cerebral cortex and descending through the pyramids of the brainstem to terminate on or around alpha motor neurons. The extrapyramidal includes all other descending tracts, even those which may arise in the cortex and run in parallel with the pyramidal system (corticorubral, rubrospinal, etc.).

Functionally and anatomically, it is difficult to define a "true pyramidal system" since long projection fibers of both pyramidal and extrapyramidal systems often travel in close association with each other. It has been shown that the extrapyramidal system sets up approximate positions of gross adjustment, is the background of the motor system, is related to tonic control, and may be either activator or inhibitor. The pyramidal system, on the other hand, stimulates muscular activity and is responsible for the precise and specific movements necessary for all fine and skillful activities. Thus, extrapyramidal and pyramidal systems combine their influences upon the lower motor neurons so that volitional impulses are modified and amplified to result in an orderly muscular response.

The pyramidal system will be described in some detail below. Since the sources of the other suprasegmental pathways have already been discussed, these descending tracts will be only summarized in this chapter.

PYRAMIDAL SYSTEM

Parts and Connections

As already noted, this system is concerned with precise and skilled movements, especially those of the distal extremities (hand or foot). It is concerned with the contraction of individual muscles and is the pathway by which one selects the "prime mover" for any activity. However, it appears that whole movement patterns originally evolve in other areas of the CNS (basal ganglia, etc.) and that these are then modulated in the cerebral hemispheres through sensory input coming to the cortex from the thalamus. The latter, in turn, receives afferent impulses from the periphery by way of such ascending systems as the lateral spinothalamic tract. Thus, since the pyramidal tracts are the only direct pathway from the cortex to the spinal cord, this descending system serves as a final channel by which the movement patterns are conveyed to the spinal motor mechanism.

Pathways

From wide cortical origins in the sensorimotor cortex (areas 4 and 6 of the frontal lobe and areas 3, 1, and 2 of the parietal lobe) efferent (corticofugal) fibers descend by way of corticospinal and corticobulbar pathways to reach the ventral gray columns of the cord and the cranial motor nuclei of the brainstem.

Corticospinal This is a long pathway which may measure a meter or so in length. It consists of about 1 million fibers, 60 percent of which originate from frontal areas and 40 percent from parietal cortex. The vast majority of these fibers (90 percent) are small, with diameters ranging from 1 to 4 nm. Somewhat less than 9 percent have diameters of 5 to 10 nm, while the other have diameters in the range of 10 to 22 nm. The latter probably are the axons of Betz cells.

All the corticofugal fibers pass through the corona radiata into the posterior limb of the internal capsule, where those fibers destined for the upper extremity lie in the rostral portion, nearest the genu, while those of the lower limb lie more caudally (Fig. 1-13). At the rostral border of the mesencephalon they join other descending cortical fibers in the formation of the cerebral peduncles (basis pedunculi or pes pedunculi) and occupy the middle three-fifths of the peduncles (Figs. 1-28, 25-12). The descending cortical fibers enter the rostral end of the pons, through which they descend in irregular bundles lying in the ventral portion of the pons (Figs. 1-34 through 1-36, 25-10). At the caudal end of the pons, these fiber bundles recombine to form the medullary pyramids, which extend throughout much of the length of the medulla (Figs. 1-37, 1-38, 20-1, 25-4, 25-5). Just above the cord-medulla junction, 85 to 90 percent of the fibers leave each pyramid and cross the ventral fissure. This is known as the motor decussation (pyramidal decussation) (Figs. 1-39, 20-1, 25-1). Thus both crossed and uncrossed fibers continue into the spinal cord.

Crossed Fibers From the region of the decussation these fibers continue in the con-

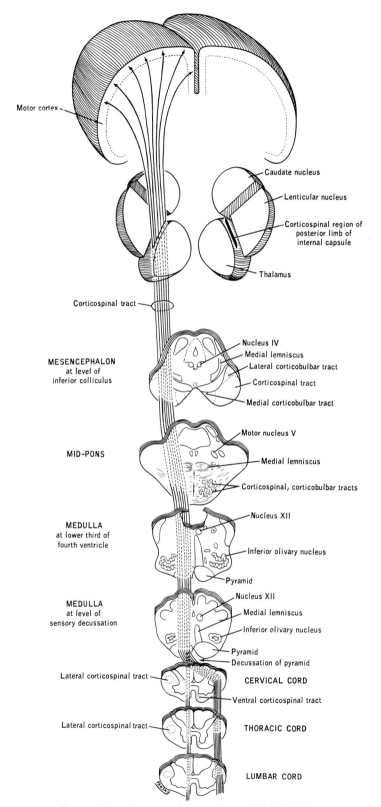

Figure 20-1 Diagram of the corticospinal pathway.

tralateral lateral funiculus of the cord in a circular bundle which lies between the fasciculus proprius and the dorsal spinocerebellar tract (Fig. 2-7). This is designated as the *lateral corticospinal tract.* Although this tract gradually becomes smaller as it descends, because of the continuous terminations of its fibers at higher levels, it may be traced to the caudal limits of the cord. Fifty percent of this tract ends in the cervical cord, twenty percent at thoracic levels, while thirty percent continues to the lower portions of the cord. In the lower lumbar and sacral regions it lies superficially along the lateral edge of the lateral funiculus because of the absence of the dorsal spinocerebellar tract at these levels. Only a small number (about 10 percent) end directly on alpha motor neurons of lamina 9 of the ventral horns. All of the remainder terminate upon interneurons of laminae 4 through 7.[1] These, in their turn, end among motor cells and produce the same effects as described under the somatic efferent system (Chap. 13).

Uncrossed Fibers Many of the uncrossed fibers continue downward into the cord in a direct line with the pyramids, entering the anterior funiculus and occupying a small area adjoining the anterior fissure of the cord (Fig. 2-7). This is the *ventral (anterior) corticospinal tract.* Although some of its fibers are said to continue throughout the cord, it is difficult to trace this tract below thoracic levels. Before the fibers terminate, they cross through the anterior white commissure to end among motor cells or upon interneurons of laminae 7 and 8. A few uncrossed fibers run caudally in the lateral corticospinal tract of the same side. This may be the same group of fibers once described as the *ventrolateral corticospinal tract (Barne's Tract).* Little is known about their terminations or their significance.

Corticobulbar Fibers[2] (Fig. 20-2) The cells of origin lie predominantly in the lower part of the motor cortex. All fibers converge as they pass through the corona radiata and come to lie in the genu of the internal capsule. Continuing downward, they enter the cerebral peduncle, where they lie medial and dorsal to the corticospinal fibers.

Just caudal to the subthalamus, corticobulbar fibers separate into two main groups. One of these accompanies the corticospinal fibers through the pons and medullary pyramids, giving off fibers to motor nuclei at successively lower levels. Some may actually continue beyond the motor decussation into the upper cervical cord to control neck muscles associated with movement of the head. The other group, often referred to as aberrant fibers, separates from the main mass as small bundles passing into the reticular formation. Of these, some course dorsomedially and cross the midline to reach motor nuclei of the opposite side; others go to nuclei of the same side. Some detach from the main pyramidal bundle quite a distance above the nucleus for which they are destined and descend in the region of the medial lemniscus. They usually do not cross until they reach the level of the nucleus to be supplied. Several groups of aberrant fibers have been described. Some of these diverge from their descending course at various levels: subthalamus, rostral mesencephalon, upper pons, and pons-medulla junction. It is thought that most of the corticobulbar fibers end in nuclei of the reticular formation—these serving as interneurons. The axons of the latter use the reticular formation, the medial longitudinal fasciculus (MLF), or the medial lemniscus to reach cranial motor nuclei.

In general, most of the cranial motor nuclei receive both crossed and uncrossed cortical

---

[1] Axons arising from areas 3, 1, and 2 of the parietal cortex appear to be those which terminate in laminae 4, 5, and 6.

[2] Although the term *bulb* usually refers only to the pons and medulla, these fibers also terminate in the mesencephalon.

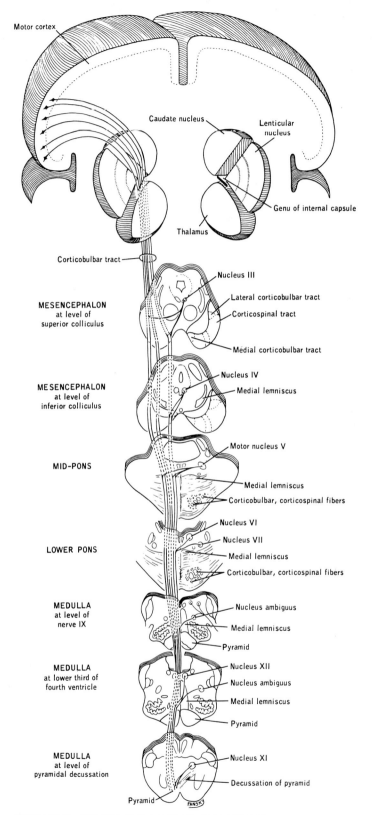

Figure 20-2 Diagram of the corticobulbar pathway.

fibers. However, though the rostral part of the facial nucleus, which supplies the muscles of the face above the eyes, receives both crossed and uncrossed fibers, the caudal part of the nucleus receives crossed fibers only (Fig. 20-3). The abducens nucleus is also said to receive only the crossed variety.

CLINICAL CONSIDERATIONS

In cases of lesions involving the pyramidal system, certain findings are commonly encountered: (1) All the cortical types of conditioned reflex are eliminated, loss being most apparent in the hands and in the speech apparatus; (2) since the motor nerves (lower motor neurons) are intact, there is no degeneration of muscle, although some diminution of muscle size occurs owing to disuse.

One chief difficulty is the problem of whether flaccid (Chap. 13) or spastic paralysis is most commonly found when a lesion involves the pyramidal system. Spastic paralysis is characterized by hypertonia, increased resistance to passive movement, and exaggerated reflexes. It seems probable that since the pyramidal fibers are mainly excitatory, a lesion affecting only the true pyramidal neurons would lead to the flaccid type of paralysis. This has been demonstrated under strictly

Brain stem at level of facial nucleus

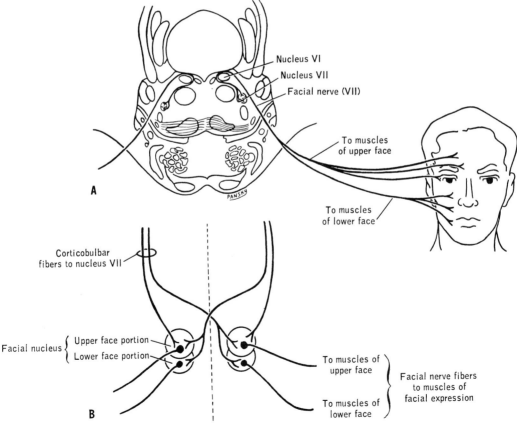

Figure 20-3 The corticobulbar fibers to the facial (VII) nucleus.

experimental conditions. However, in clinical practice, the pyramidal and extrapyramidal systems are so closely associated that lesions involving one will invariably encompass both. Thus, it is usual to observe, at least in the early stages (whether the condition occurs from a vascular accident or trauma), a state of flaccidity, due both to loss of pyramidal excitation and to shock. Days and perhaps even weeks later, this early condition is superseded by a permanent spasticity, apparently owing to the loss of the inhibitor fibers normally part of the extrapyramidal system. With these inhibitors removed, the lower motor neurons are exposed directly to the innumerable impulses traveling to them via the many association neurons derived from afferent systems; thus hyperreflexia and hypertonia result.

Testing

The examiner checks for the ability to perform voluntary, skilled activities as directed.

The deep reflexes are examined as described in the chapter on proprioception (Chap. 11). In upper motor lesions, these reflexes are exaggerated.

Superficial reflexes, particularly on the abdomen, are checked by stroking the skin lightly. Both the abdominal and cremasteric reflexes are abolished at first. Later they return but are difficult to elicit and then tend to be slow and weak.

The plantar surface of the foot is stroked in the heel-to-toe direction. In upper motor neuron lesions, the toes are spread apart and the great toe is dorsiflexed (Babinski sign). It is possible that this reaction represents a reversion to the more primitive reaction which actually may be dorsiflexion, since it is seen in infants before cortical control is established.

Although the foregoing tests will suffice to indicate whether pathologic change involves the upper motor neurons of the pyramidal system, they are not adequate to localize the lesions within the CNS. Lesions of only one pyramidal tract produce the same symptoms irrespective of the level at which the damage occurs, whether in the cortex, internal capsule, midbrain, pons, or medulla. Criteria other than pyramidal tract signs are thus needed to determine the level of the lesion. In the brainstem such supplementary information can be gained by noting disturbances in the function of cranial nerves III through XII. Such disturbances may be upper motor neuron in nature and are significant in localizing the lesion because of the differences in level at which corticobulbar fibers diverge from the corticospinal tract. They may also be lower motor neuron in type, involving either the nucleus or origin or emerging fibers of the cranial nerves. This is particularly important since sites of cranial nerve nuclei have been well established. Furthermore, since it should be clear that within the brainstem and cord focal lesions in the corticospinal pathways are virtually impossible, sensory tracts may also be involved, and examinations of these systems may also contribute to the localization of the lesion (Fig. 20-4).

Specific Pathology

Specific pathologic changes may be the result of direct trauma either from wounds about the head involving the motor cortex directly or from damage to the spinal cord (resulting from fracture of the spine, gunshot wounds, etc.) which interrupts the upper motor neuron pathway in its descent. Other changes are due to some form of vascular accident in which the blood supply is cut off, either from cell bodies or from their long processes.

Before discussing particular conditions, it is necessary to define certain terms. *Monoplegia* refers to paralysis of one part (upper or lower extremity). *Hemiplegia* is the paralysis of both the upper and lower extremities on the same side. *Quadriplegia (tetraplegia)* is the paralysis of all four extremities. *Paraplegia* signifies the paralysis of both lower extremities.

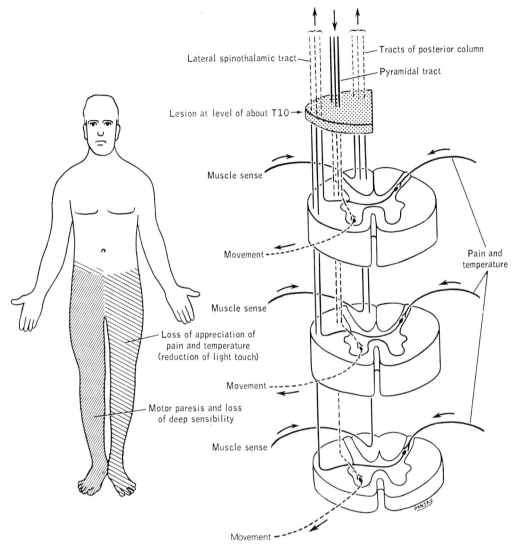

Figure 20-4 The Brown-Séquard syndrome, resulting from a lesion on the right half of the spinal cord in the region of T10. *Note:* motor paralysis is on the same side, deep anesthesia and cutaneous hyperesthesia on the same side, cutaneous anesthesia on the opposite side.

Hemiplegia

Lesions which produce this condition may occur in several locations. When the lesion is in the motor cortex, sensory involvement may or may not appear, the size of the lesion determining the extent of the paralysis. When the lesion is in the internal capsule, general sensibilities are always involved, and if the lesion is large enough, vision and hearing may be affected. Lesions of the central portion of the cerebral peduncles may give pure hemiplegia without interruption of the sensory system and may or may not involve the cranial nerves. Lesions in the basal portion of the pons may give very few symptoms unless the area of pathologic change is extremely large, since the corticospinal fibers are here split up into scattered bundles.

Hemiplegia Cruciata (Fig. 20-5) This is due to a lesion involving the lateral aspect of the pyramidal decussation where crossed fibers to the lower extremities and uncrossed fibers to the upper extremities are passing. It results in paralysis of the homolateral arm and contralateral leg.

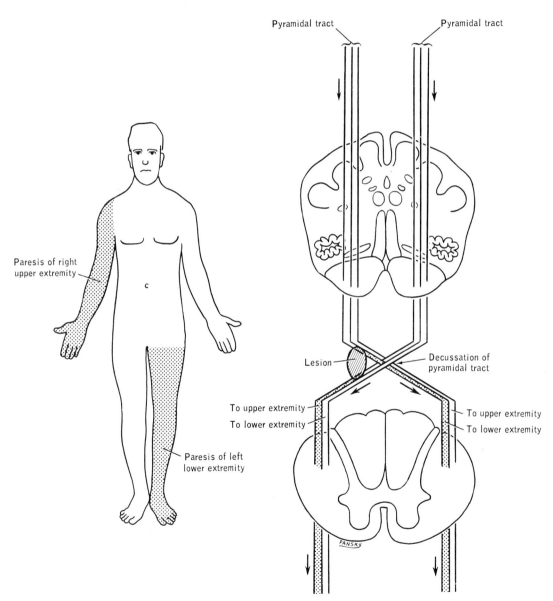

Figure 20-5 Hemiplegia cruciata due to a lesion on the right side of the pyramidal decussation.

Hemiplegia Alternata (Alternating Hemiplegia) (Fig. 20-6) This is a symptom complex in which there is an altered function of cranial nerves of the same side and an altered function of one of the long pathways connected with the opposite side. There are several patterns of this type, depending on the location of the lesion.

When the lesion is in the cerebral peduncle, there is an oculomotor paralysis of the homolateral side, owing to an interruption of the emerging fibers of the third cranial nerve, and a contralateral paralysis of the lower face, tongue, and extremities, owing to interruption of the corticospinal and corticobulbar fibers. This condition is called *crossed oculomotor paralysis*, or *Weber's syndrome*.

Lesions of the caudal portion of the pons may produce a *hemiplegia alternata facialis*, or *crossed facial paralysis (Millard-Gubler syndrome)*, which results in a homolateral facial paralysis plus contralateral paralysis of tongue and extremities.

Lesions in the medulla may lead to paralysis of the homolateral half of the tongue and a paralysis of the contralateral extremities, *hemiplegia alternata hypoglossica*, or *crossed hypoglossal paralysis*.

Jacksonian Epilepsy

This condition appears as involuntary muscular reactions which may begin with the involvement of relatively few muscles or muscle groups but eventually may spread to include most of them on one side of the body. This condition arises as a result of an irritative lesion at some point on or near the motor cortex. A clue to its exact location is given by noticing which muscles react at the beginning of the attack.

OTHER SUPRASEGMENTAL PATHWAYS

Vestibulospinal Tract (Chap. 12)

This arises from the lateral vestibular nucleus. It descends as an uncrossed pathway through the lateral part of the medullary tegmentum and extends throughout the spinal cord in the anterior part of the lateral funiculus (Chap. 2). It is sometimes referred to as the *lateral vestibulospinal tract*. The fibers from this tract terminate among the interneurons in the medial part of lamina 7 and in lamina 8 of the spinal gray matter. Its influences are facilitatory on the extensor musculature, especially that part concerned with posture and the maintenance of equilibrium. It should also be recalled that cerebellar influences on the lower motor apparatus are mediated through this tract.

Medial Longitudinal Fasciculus (MLF) (Chap. 12)

Although most of the fibers of this bundle remain in and ascend through the brainstem to integrate eye movement with changes in position of the head, other fibers arising in vestibular nuclei descend through the medial part of the medullary tegmentum and enter the anterior funiculus of the spinal cord. Here, the bundle is frequently referred to as the *medial vestibulospinal tract*. It extends only through the cervical cord, where its fibers terminate in the ventral horn around neurons supplying the neck musculature. Thus, it is important in helping to maintain the normal orientation of the head.

Reticulospinal Tracts (Chap. 19)

The *pontine,* or *medial reticulospinal tract* arises from the nuclei reticularis oralis and caudalis in the pons. It descends basically uncrossed, its fibers lying adjacent to or even within the MLF; it runs throughout the spinal cord in the anterior funiculus. Its fibers enter lamina 8 and part of lamina 7 to terminate on interneurons. The latter, in their turn, synapse chiefly on gamma efferents. The activity of this pathway is facilitatory on the spinal motor mechanism, especially the extensor neurons. (It is possible that they may have an inhibitory influence on the flexor apparatus.)

The *medullary,* or *lateral, reticulospinal*

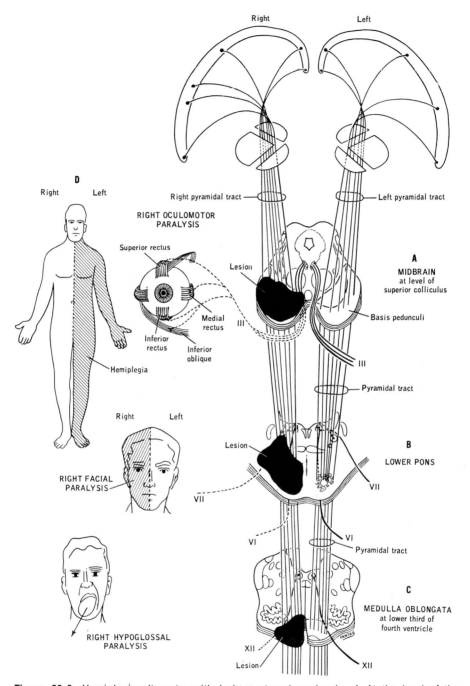

Figure 20-6 Hemiplegia alternata, with lesions at various levels. *A.* At the level of the emerging fibers of nerve III, involving this nerve and a portion of the adjoining cerebral peduncle. *B.* At the level of nerve VII. *C.* At the level of nerve XII, involving emerging fibers of the hypoglossal nerve and the adjoining pyramid. *D.* Area of body paralysis with lesions at levels *A, B,* or *C.*

tract arises from the nucleus gigantocellularis of the medulla. It descends mainly uncrossed in the lateral medullary tegmentum and extends throughout the cord in the anterior part of the lateral funiculus. Its fibers terminate among interneurons chiefly in lamina 7. The interneurons again play upon gamma efferents. The influence of this tract is basically inhibitory, especially on the extensor muscle tone. Stimulation of this system can actually suppress the myotatic stretch reflex and can eliminate decerebrate rigidity.

Both medullary and pontine nuclei receive descending fibers from the frontal cortex, areas 4 and 6, and the parietal cortex, areas 3, 1, and 2.

It should be obvious from the foregoing that the two reticulospinal tracts have antagonistic effects upon the motor apparatus. Therefore, there must be a proper balance between the two if normal activity is to occur.

Rubrospinal Tract (Chap. 18)

Before describing the tract, a word should be said about the structure from which it originates.

The red nucleus was so named because of its pinkish appearance in fresh specimens. The color is probably related to its vascularity rather than to the presence of any form of pigment, although it is supposedly rich in iron. Although it appears round in a given cross section, it is actually oval with a transverse diameter of about 0.5 cm. It attains its greatest prominence in the rostral mesencephalon but extends from the caudal level of the superior colliculus into the lower diencephalon. In typical cross sections of the brainstem, it is seen to occupy the medial portion of the midbrain tegmenta (Figs. 1-28, 25-12, 25-15). With myelin or fiber stains it appears to have a "capsule." This effect is due to the presence of the fibers of the superior cerebellar peduncle which sends fiber terminals both into and around the nucleus. The nucleus is usually divided into two parts based upon the size of the cells located therein. The caudal portion is called *magnocellular* because large cells predominate here, while the rostral part of the nucleus contains small cells and is referred to as the *parvocellular* portion.

The fibers comprising the rubrospinal tract apparently originate from both large and small cells of the red nucleus, although it is still held by many that the magnocellular component predominates. On leaving the nucleus all fibers cross immediately to the other side in the *ventral tegmental decussation*, descend through the brainstem tegmentum, and continue caudally throughout the cord in the lateral funiculus immediately adjacent to the lateral corticospinal tract. Like the latter, the rubrospinal tract is concerned with the appendicular musculature, in particular with the more proximal parts of each limb. Within the tract, fibers lying in the dorsomedial portion are distributed to the upper extremity, while the ventral group is concerned with the lower limb. Again, like the corticospinal fibers, their chief influence is facilitatory on the flexor musculature. Although some fibers may synapse directly on alpha motor neurons, the vast majority terminate first upon interneurons in the area.

It should be noted that the rubral system receives much input both from the cerebellum (Chap. 17) and the cerebral cortex. Thus, the cerebellum may be able to modify lower motor activity through this pathway. Cortical fibers from the sensorimotor cortex descend through the posterior limb of the internal capsule to terminate in a somatotopic manner upon the red nucleus. Specifically, fibers from the cortex to the upper limb project to the dorsal part of the nucleus, while fibers originating from the cortical region associated with the lower limb project to the ventral part of the nucleus. Therefore this tract becomes part of a backup system for the corticospinal pathway. It may be referred to as the *corticorubrospinal system*.

Tectospinal Tract   (Chap. 8)

This small tract arises from the deep portions of the superior colliculus. Its fibers cross to the opposite side in the *dorsal tegmental decussation*. After crossing, the fibers descend through the brainstem in close proximity to, or even as a part of, the MLF. The tract continues into the anterior funiculus of the spinal cord but usually cannot be traced below cervical levels. It is mainly concerned with movements initiated within the visual system.

DECEREBRATE RIGIDITY

It has been known for many years that an animal with the brainstem transected through the mesencephalon exhibits extreme hyperextension of its limbs. There are several factors working together which produce this phenomenon: First, as indicated elsewhere (Chap. 8), there are fibers descending in the corticospinal pathways from cortical areas 3, 1, and 2 of the parietal lobe which end among the sensory transmission nuclei of the dorsal horn. These have an inhibitory effect on afferent impulses entering the cord through the dorsal roots of spinal nerves. Lacking this kind of inhibition, muscle tone is increased by way of the spinal reflex circuits. Second, the lateral reticulospinal tract is a strong inhibitor of the extensor musculature. However, to provide this inhibition, descending fibers from the cortex are required to activate the medullary reticular nuclei. Apparently, these nuclei are incapable of intrinsic activity. Thus, in transecting the brainstem cephalic to the medulla the necessary cortical influence is lost. Third, the medial reticulospinal tract, which tends to be facilitatory in nature and requires no descending cerebral influences for its activity, is still capable of function. Fourth, it has been noted that the vestibulospinal pathway is highly facilitatory on extensor muscle tone. This system needs no descending cortical influences and is dependent only upon afferent impulses from the vestibular receptors. Thus, this system can act upon a totally uninhibited extensor mechanism with resulting rigidity.

**Summary
Pyramidal System**

Trunk		Head
Trunk		**Head**
1. Sensorimotor cortex	Cell type	1. Same as for trunk.
2. Paracentral lobule and upper two-thirds of precentral gyrus (area 4).	Location	2. Lower third of the precentral gyrus.
3. In order: corona radiata, posterior limb of the internal capsule, middle three-fifths of cerebral peduncle, scattered fascicles in the pons, pyramids in upper medulla. In the lower medulla, 80 to 90 percent cross to the opposite side of the brainstem through the decussation of the pyramids to become the lateral corticospinal tracts which descend through the spinal cord in the lateral funiculus. In the lower medulla, 10 to 20 percent remain uncrossed, descending on the same side of the brainstem and passing through the spinal cord in the anterior funiculus as the ventral corticospinal tract.	Course	3. In order: corona radiata; genu of the internal capsule; cerebral peduncles, dorsal and medial to the corticospinals. From here, fibers may either continue caudally with the corticospinal fibers or form aberrant bundles at various levels in the subthalamus, mesencephalon, pons, or medulla.
4. From the lateral corticospinal tract fibers may terminate either directly around motor cells in the ventral gray columns of the cord or around cells of intercalary neurons in the dorsal gray columns, which, in turn, send their axons to synapse with motor cells in the ventral gray columns. From the ventral corticospinal tract, fibers pass medially and cross to the opposite side of the cord through the anterior white commissure, just before terminating around motor cells of the ventral gray column.	Termination	4. Those running with corticospinals end in ventral gray columns of upper cervical cord. Subthalamic aberrants go to the rostral end of nucleus III. Peduncular aberrants pass to nuclei III, IV, V, and XI. Pontine aberrants pass to contralateral V and nucleus ambiguous, for nerves IX and X. Medullary aberrants pass to nuclei VII and XII.

The Hypothalamus

The hypothalamus constitutes only a very small volume of the forebrain, yet it plays an extremely important part in the organization of a variety of behavioral and autonomic processes. It is essential for temperature regulation, water metabolism, and general metabolism. It is critical for the elaboration of aggressive and defensive reactions, feeding, drinking, and sexual behavior. Further, it modulates and controls both sympathetic and parasympathetic responses. It is also true that certain of these processes involve interactions between hypothalamic neurons and the pituitary gland. Thus, control of endocrine function is still another vital function of the hypothalamus.

STRUCTURE OF THE HYPOTHALAMUS

Gross

The gross structure and relations have been described elsewhere (Chap. 1).

Hypothalamic Nuclei (Figs. 21-1, 21-2)

The hypothalamus is broken up into several nuclear groups. Among the most definite of these are the *preoptic*, the *supraoptic*, the *paraventricular*, the *ventromedial*, the *tuberal*, the *dorsomedial*, and the *mammillary*. In addition, there are four other regional divisions, designated merely as *anterior, lateral, dorsal*, and *posterior areas*.

CONNECTIONS

Afferent Pathways

Fornix (Figs. 1-16, 1-21, 10-2, 21-3, 25-1 through 25-19)

The origin of these fibers from the hippocampal formation has been indicated in the special visceral afferent system, and their course is described in Chap. 22. Fibers arising from the subicular cortex constitute the entirety of the postcommissural fornix and terminate

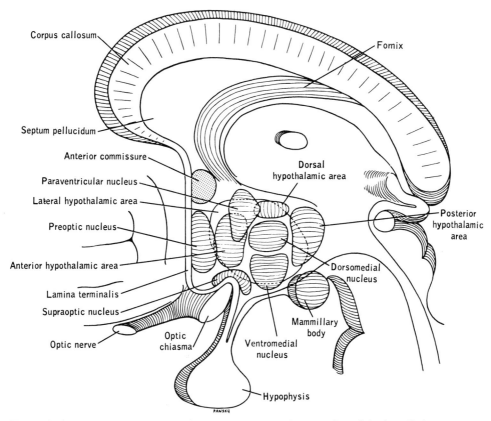

Figure 21-1 Hypothalamic nuclei. Three dimensional reconstruction of the hypothalamus.

in the ventromedial hypothalamic nucleus and the mammillary bodies.

Medial Forebrain Bundle (Figs. 10-4, 21-3)

At least a portion of its fibers arise in the olfactory brain, particularly the ventromedial part in the vicinity of the olfactory stria and perhaps other parts of the adjoining basal forebrain. The overwhelming majority of fibers, however, arise from the septal area, and these fibers terminate throughout the preoptic area. Other components of this bundle pass on through the lateral hypothalamic area, some fibers apparently ending there while others descend to terminate in the lateral portion of the mammillary body. What is left of the bundle continues caudally into the tegmentum of the mesencephalon. A number of fibers

which arise in the ventral and central tegmental fields of the midbrain and in the median raphe of both pons and midbrain pass rostrally through the lateral hypothalamus within the medial forebrain bundle. These fibers represent, to a large extent, the monoamine-containing fibers of the brainstem. Some of them may terminate in the hypothalamus, but most of them appear to be distributed to the limbic system and frontal lobe (Chap. 22).

Thalamohypothalamic Fibers (Fig. 21-4)

These fibers arise in the dorsomedial nucleus of the thalamus and are distributed to the midline thalamic nuclei. From the posterior midline thalamus, a multisynaptic chain of fibers passes in a rostral direction through the midline thalamus. Neurons arising at the level

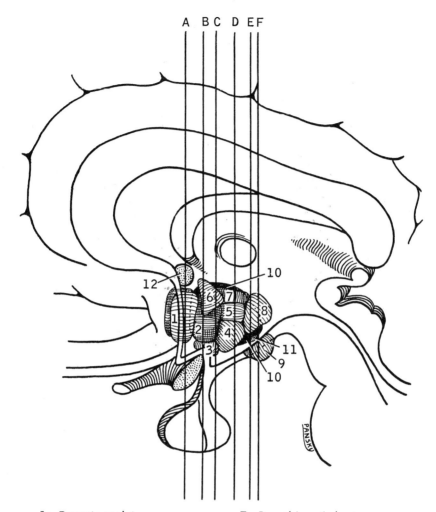

A B C D E F

12 10

6 7 10
5 8
1
2
4
3 11
9
10

PANSKY

1. Preoptic nuclei
2. Anterior hypothalamic area
3. Supraoptic nucleus
4. Ventromedial nucleus
5. Dorsomedial nucleus
6. Paraventricular nucleus
7. Dorsal hypothalamic area
8. Posterior hypothalamic area
9. Mammillary body
10. Lateral hypothalamic area
11. Intercalated nucleus
12. Anterior commissure

Figure 21-2 General topography of the hypothalamus, the first part indicating the planes for the vertical sections shown in parts *A* through *F. (After Netter, Ciba Clinical Symposia.)*

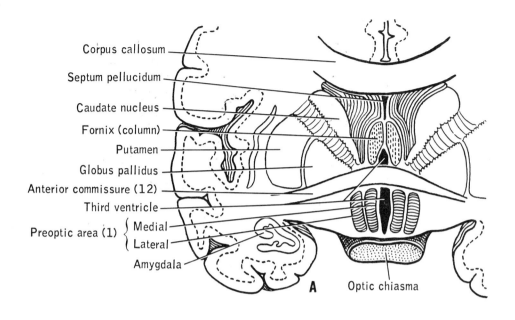

Corpus callosum

Septum pellucidum

Caudate nucleus

Fornix (column)

Putamen

Globus pallidus

Anterior commissure (12)

Third ventricle

Preoptic area (1) { Medial
                  { Lateral

Amygdala

Optic chiasma

A

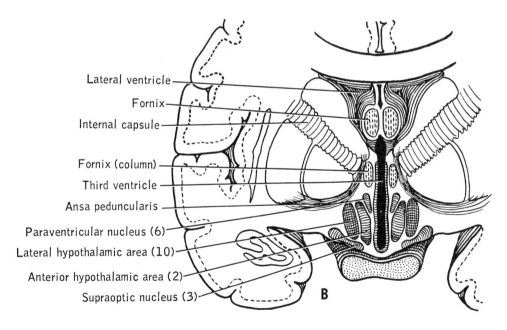

Lateral ventricle

Fornix

Internal capsule

Fornix (column)

Third ventricle

Ansa peduncularis

Paraventricular nucleus (6)

Lateral hypothalamic area (10)

Anterior hypothalamic area (2)

Supraoptic nucleus (3)

B

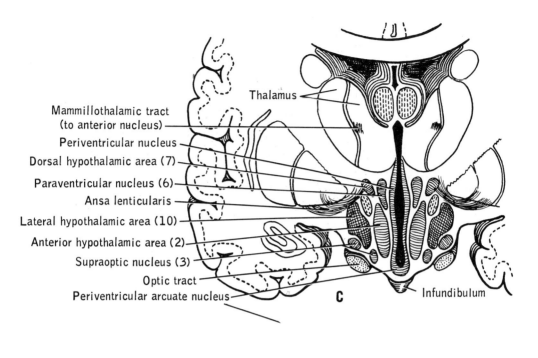

Mammillothalamic tract (to anterior nucleus)
Periventricular nucleus
Dorsal hypothalamic area (7)
Paraventricular nucleus (6)
Ansa lenticularis
Lateral hypothalamic area (10)
Anterior hypothalamic area (2)
Supraoptic nucleus (3)
Optic tract
Periventricular arcuate nucleus

Thalamus

Infundibulum

C

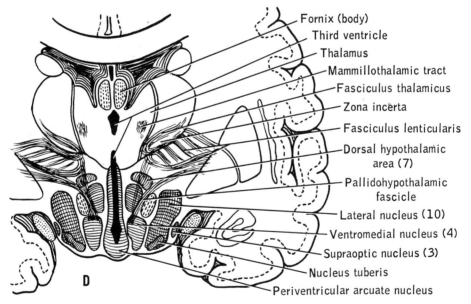

Fornix (body)
Third ventricle
Thalamus
Mammillothalamic tract
Fasciculus thalamicus
Zona incerta
Fasciculus lenticularis
Dorsal hypothalamic area (7)
Pallidohypothalamic fascicle
Lateral nucleus (10)
Ventromedial nucleus (4)
Supraoptic nucleus (3)
Nucleus tuberis
Periventricular arcuate nucleus

D

Fig. 21-2. C, D.

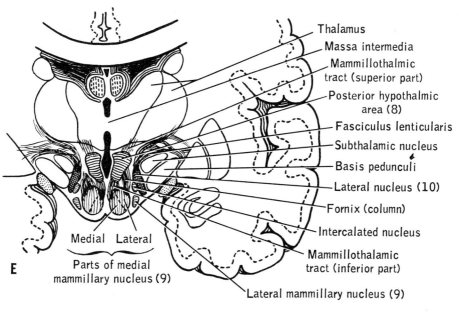

Thalamus
Massa intermedia
Mammillothalmic tract (superior part)
Posterior hypothalmic area (8)
Fasciculus lenticularis
Subthalamic nucleus
Basis pedunculi
Lateral nucleus (10)
Fornix (column)
Intercalated nucleus
Mammillothalamic tract (inferior part)
Lateral mammillary nucleus (9)

Medial   Lateral
Parts of medial mammillary nucleus (9)

E

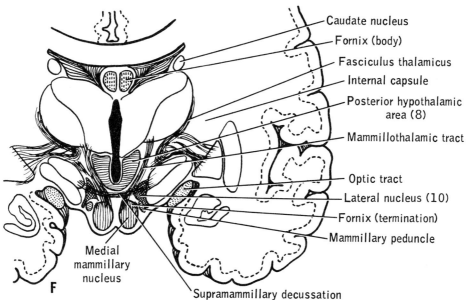

Caudate nucleus
Fornix (body)
Fasciculus thalamicus
Internal capsule
Posterior hypothalamic area (8)
Mammillothalamic tract
Optic tract
Lateral nucleus (10)
Fornix (termination)
Mammillary peduncle

Medial mammillary nucleus

F

Supramammillary decussation

Fig. 21-2. E, F.

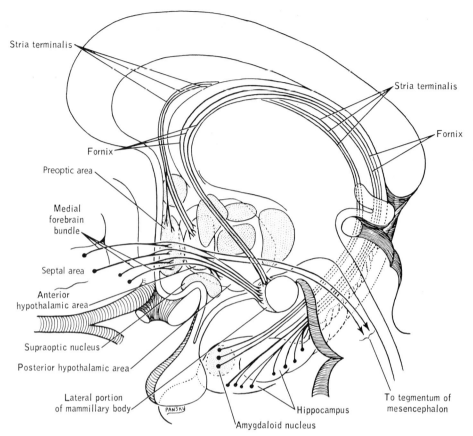

Figure 21-3 Some of the afferent pathways to the hypothalamus, showing in particular the fornix, the medial forebrain bundle, and the stria terminalis.

of the rostral part of the nucleus reuniens are distributed to the perifornical lateral hypothalamus.

Stria Terminalis (Figs. 10-2, 10-4, 21-3)

The position and course of these fibers have already been described (Chap. 10). They begin in the amygdaloid complex and terminate in the medial preoptic area, bed nucleus of the stria terminalis, and ventromedial hypothalamic nucleus.

Ventral Amygdaloid Pathway

This fiber bundle arises chiefly from the basolateral amygdala and adjoining pyriform cor-

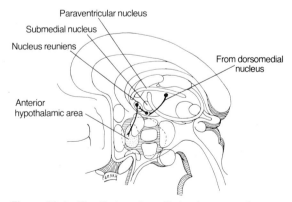

Figure 21-4 The thalamohypothalamic connections.

tex. Axons are distributed via the medial forebrain bundle to the lateral hypothalamic area (Chap. 22).

Mammillary Peduncle   (Figs. 21-2*F*, 21-5)

This tract arises in the midbrain tegmentum (ventral and dorsal tegmental nuclei) and possibly acts as a relay center for impulses arising in various lower brainstem centers. Fibers principally from the dorsal tegmental nuclei terminate in the mammillary bodies, while fibers from the ventral tegmentum pass in a rostral direction through the medial forebrain bundle (see above).

Periventricular Fiber System

A number of fiber systems ascend and descend near the walls of the third ventricle and cerebral aqueduct of the brainstem. Most of these fibers constitute hypothalamic efferents. Nevertheless, a number of fibers pass rostrally into the medial hypothalamic zone from the periaqueductal gray of the midbrain and represent another link between these two regions.

Retinohypothalamic Fibers

Most retinal fibers terminate in the lateral geniculate bodies or visual-related structures of the midbrain. However, it has been report-

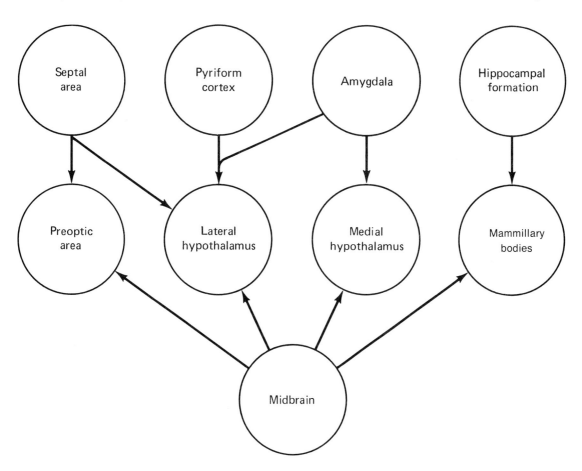

Figure 21-5   Summary diagram of the principal sources of afferent fibers to the hypothalamus.

ed that some optic fibers terminate in the region of the supraoptic (suprachiasmatic) nucleus. This bundle might play a role in the way light affects the mammalian reproductive cycle.

Efferent Pathways

Mammillothalamic Tract (Bundle of Vicq d'Azyr)   (Figs. 21-6, 25-16, 25-17)

Most of these fibers take origin in the medial portion of the mammillary body. The aggregate forms a prominent bundle which courses cephalically, with rostral inclination, to reach the anterior nucleus of the thalamus. This, in turn, gives rise to ascending thalamocortical fibers to the gyrus cinguli. Thus, it can be seen

that a circular circuit—hypothalamus, thalamus, cortex, thalamus, hypothalamus—is established.

Mammillotegmental Tract   (Figs. 21-6, 21-7)

The fibers of this tract also take origin in the medial portion of the mammillary bodies. Coursing caudally through the mesencephalon, some crossing to the opposite side, they terminate in the lateral and central reticular nuclei of the tegmentum. From here, by way of relays in the reticular formation, the cranial autonomic nuclei are activated. This influence is continued to the intermediolateral column of the spinal cord through the reticulospinal tract.

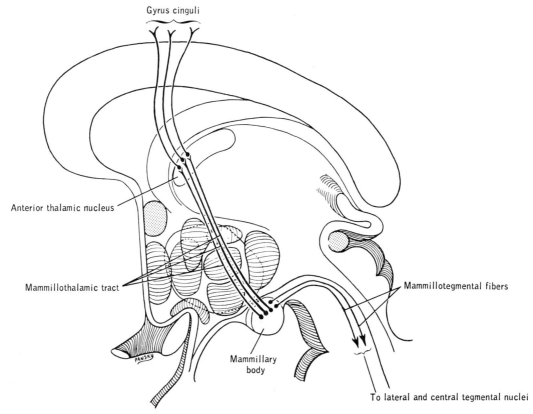

Figure 21-6   The mammillothalamic tract and the mammillotegmental connections.

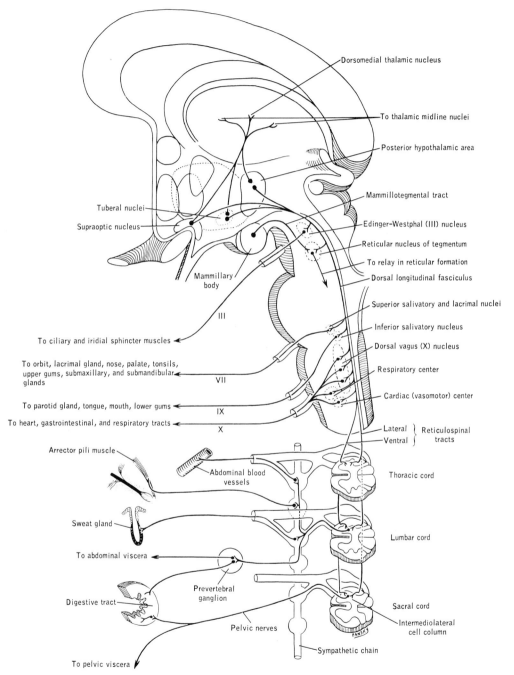

Figure 21-7 The periventricular fibers of the hypothalamus. *Note:* The dorsal longitudinal fasciculus is probably a multisynaptic chain rather than a continuous band as shown in the figure.

Hypothalamicohypophyseal Fibers
(Fig. 21-8)

Most of the fibers of this system terminate in the neurohypophysis.[1] Many fibers arise in the supraoptic and paraventricular nucleus, traverse the infundibular stem, and terminate in the neural lobe. It appears that many of those fibers arising in the paraventricular nuclei terminate in the supraoptic nucleus and the tuber cinereum, only a few going all the way to the neural lobe. There are also some fibers running in the lateral and posterior portions of the infundibular stalk which arise from tuberal nuclei—the *tuberohypophyseal fibers*. It is im-

[1]This includes the neural lobe of the pituitary and the infundibulum, which consists of an infundibular stem running cephalically from the neural lobe and the median eminence of the tuber cinereum to which the stem attaches.

probable that any of the fibers from the hypothalamus pass into the anterior lobe of the pituitary.

The fibers descending from the hypothalamus to the neural hypophysis strongly indicate the importance of the hypothalamus in the activation of the posterior lobe of the pituitary. Evidence also indicates that the hypothalamus can influence (if not control) the secretion of the adenohypophysis. However, since there are few, if any, descending fibers from the hypothalamus to the anterior lobe and since the fibers brought to the anterior lobe through the autonomic nervous system do not appear significant enough to control secretion, some other mechanism must be found to account for these influences. Experience supports the contention that the functional interrelation between the adenohypo-

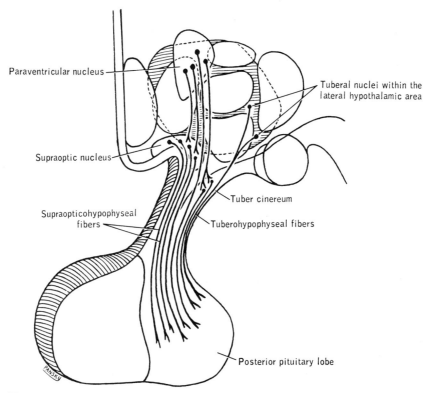

Figure 21-8   The hypothalamicohypophyseal paths.

physis and the hypothalamus is a neurovascular linkage. The acceptance of this tenet, however, is dependent upon the acceptance of the theory of neural secretion. Certainly there is much to support this concept. Further, it has been established that the hormones attributed to the posterior pituitary are the products of the nervous tissue which make up the neural hypophysis, with the possibility that such secretions may even be produced in the hypothalamus itself. The actual manner by which hypothalamic secretions are brought to bear on the cells of the anterior lobe is best indicated diagrammatically (Fig. 21-9).

Medial Forebrain Bundle   (Fig. 10-4, 21-3)

Fibers from all levels of the lateral hypothalamus and preoptic area give rise to axons which enter the medial forebrain bundle. Ascending fibers in this bundle supply the septal area, preoptic region, and diagonal band nuclei. It has been shown that some fibers from the lateral hypothalamus may ascend (probably in the medial forebrain bundle) to innervate portions of the frontal and parietal lobes. This newly discovered pathway may serve as a means by which the cerebral cortex can receive information concerning the internal milieu of the organism and also synchronize cortical activity with hypothalamic function. Cells from all levels of the lateral hypothalamus give rise to axons which descend in the medial forebrain bundle to the ventral tegmental area of the midbrain.

Stria Medullaris

From the anterior third of the lateral hypothalamus a group of fibers enter the stria medullaris and are distributed to the lateral habenular nucleus.

Hypothalamoamygdaloid Fibers

Although the stria terminalis is chiefly identified as a hypothalamic afferent system, some fibers contained in the bundle have been traced from the ventromedial hypothalamic nucleus back into the amygdaloid complex. Thus, the amygdala and ventromedial hypothalamus are reciprocally connected.

FUNCTIONS OF THE HYPOTHALAMUS (Fig. 21-10)

Emotion   (Figs. 21-11, 21-12)

Although it is in no way implied that the hypothalamus is the emotional center, it can be said that it does take part in the activities of the autonomic system which accompany emotion. There is good evidence that certain areas of the cerebral cortex and limbic system act as inhibitors for these activities. Through cortical destruction (bilateral frontal lobe lesions of the septal area or amygdala) animals can easily be induced to demonstrate behavior usually seen in rage, provided the posterior hypothalamus is intact. The reactions include dilation of the pupil; erection of the hair; increase in cardiac rate and blood pressure; increase in salivation.

Different forms of emotional states can be elicited following electrical stimulation of the hypothalamus. Stimulation of the lateral hypothalamus in the cat produces a form of aggressive reaction known as *quiet biting attack.* In this form of aggression, the cat, which normally does not spontaneously attack either an anesthetized or an awake rat, will stalk and then bite the back of the neck of the rat and/or strike it with its forepaw. This form of aggression resembles the natural predatory response of a cat upon a prey object and, in general, is accompanied by few autonomic signs other than some pupillary dilation and some increase in heart rate. Electrical stimulation of the ventromedial hypothalamus produces a different form of aggressive reaction. Upon stimulation of this region, a cat will display a marked sympathetic response. It will strike at any moving object within its visual field and will display marked vocalization, retraction of

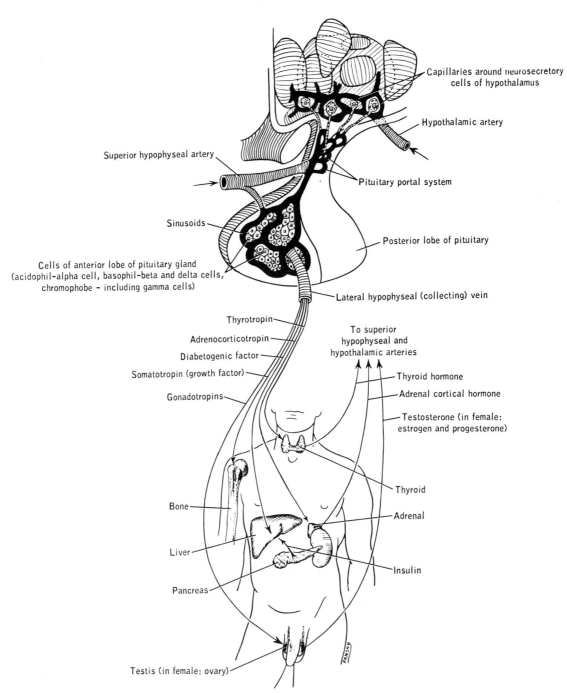

Figure 21-9 The relation of the hypothalamus to the anterior pituitary and thus to the other endocrines, liver, and bone marrow. *(After Netter, Ciba Clinical Symposia.)*

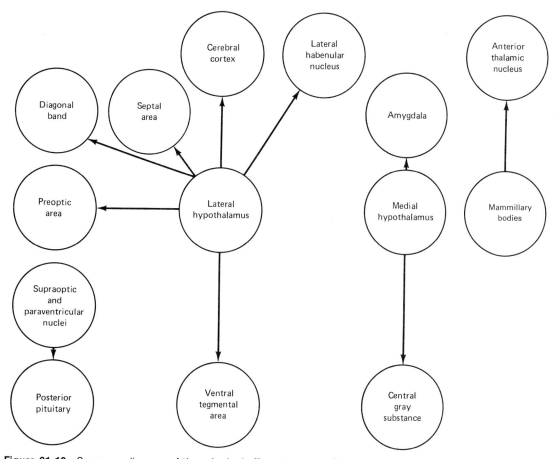

Figure 21-10 Summary diagram of the principal efferent targets of the hypothalamus.

the ears, arching of the back, and piloerection. This constellation of response characteristics is very similar to the type of defensive reaction noted in a cat which is attacked by another animal. For this reason, this response pattern is frequently referred to as *affective defense,* or *affective display.*

It is somewhat of a paradox that lesions of the ventromedial hypothalamus can produce similar defense reactions. An adequate explanation of why stimulation and destruction of a single site in the hypothalamus can produce the same behavioral response has not yet been advanced. A third type of response elicited from the hypothalamus is referred to as a *flight reaction.* Following electrical stimulation of wide regions within the hypothalamus, the animal immediately attempts to escape from its cage. Feeding responses in cats and both feeding and drinking behavior in rats can be elicited following stimulation of lateral regions of the hypothalamus. The effects of lesions of the hypothalamus upon feeding behavior are considered later in this chapter.

Renal Outflow (Water Excretion)
(Fig. 21-13)

Some years ago it was shown that among the substances secreted by the posterior pituitary is the *antidiuretic hormone.* The absence of

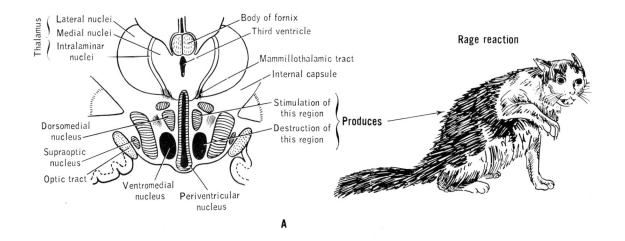

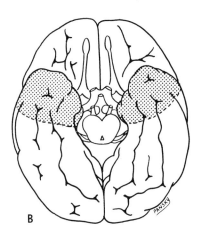

Figure 21-11 *A.* Hypothalamic mechanism in emotional behavior. *B.* Lesions in amygdaloid nuclei and adjacent rhinencephalon (dotted area) may produce in some species (rat, cat, monkey) gentle, tame, fearless animals with the males in a sexually hyperactive state. *(After Netter, Ciba Clinical Symposia.)*

this secretion leads to a clinical condition known as *diabetes insipidus*, characterized by the excretion of excessive amounts of low-specific-gravity urine. The antidiuretic hormone, which apparently keeps water excretion within physiologic limits, passes into the capillaries of the infundibular stalk. Most recent evidence indicates that this hormone is a neurosecretion, produced by the cells of the supraoptic nucleus of the hypothalamus. The

secretion migrates along the axons of this tract, to be discharged into the capillaries of the posterior lobe. The amount of secretion may be regulated in two ways: (1) Nervous influences are carried to the nucleus by way of afferent hypothalamic fiber systems, which may account for variations in urine output in different emotional states; (2) the cells of the supraoptic nucleus respond to changes in blood and tissue fluids surrounding them. In

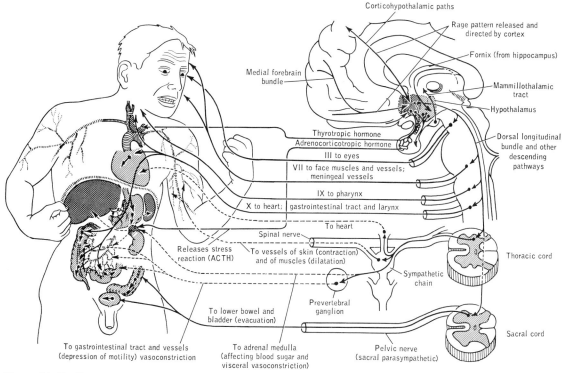

Figure 21-12 Neurogenic and hormonal pathways in the rage reaction. (See note for Fig. 21-7.) *(After Netter, Ciba Clinical Symposia.)*

other words, if tissue fluid is in excess in the hypothalamus (which would be a reflection of the condition over the entire body), less antidiuretic hormone would be indicated so that the overabundance of intercellular fluid could be drained off through the kidneys. In this connection it has been shown that there are receptors, probably within the supraoptic nucleus, capable of detecting changes in osmotic pressure (osmoreceptors), since the injection of hypertonic saline solution into the internal carotid artery leads to antidiuresis.

It is believed that the target of the antidiuretic hormone is the distal convoluted tubule of the kidney. The target is reached through regulation of the amount of water resorbed into the bloodstream from the glomerular filtrate. For example, when hypertonic saline

solution is injected into the internal carotid artery, the blood in the hypothalamic arterial branches becomes hyperosmotic, stimulating a condition of dehydration seen in patients after hemorrhage or hyperemesis. This causes an increase of production and release of the antidiuretic factor into the capillaries of the infundibular stalk. The factor is then carried through the systemic circulation to the kidneys, the distal convoluted tubules of which respond by resorbing more water in order to help reestablish isotonicity in the blood.

Temperature Regulation (Fig. 21-14)

The maintenance of a constant body temperature (the homothermic state) depends upon a balance between heat loss and heat production and/or conservation. This balance is apparent-

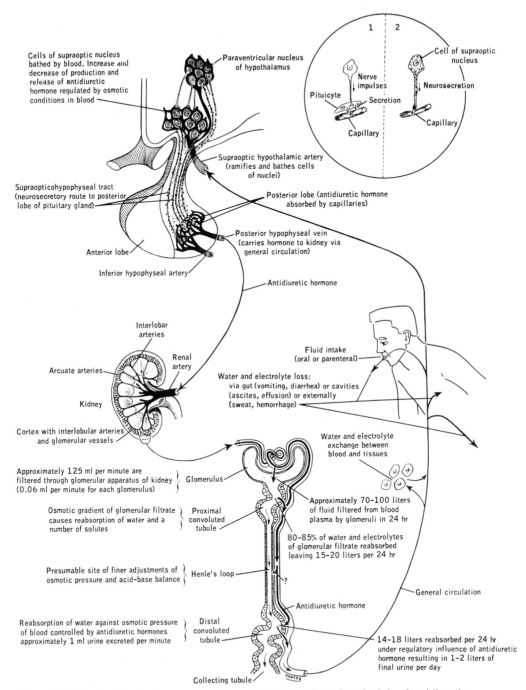

Figure 21-13 Control of water excretion and water balance. Theories of origin of antidiuretic hormone: (1) Pituicytes release hormone under nervous influence. (2) Hormone produced as neurosecretion by cells in the supraoptic nucleus are conducted by nerve fibers to posterior lobe for storage or absorption. *(After Netter, Ciba Clinical Symposia.)*

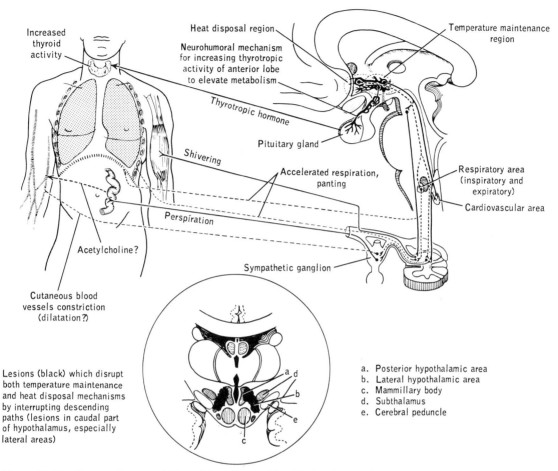

Figure 21-14 Temperature regulation. *(After Netter, Ciba Clinical Symposia.)*

ly brought about through the activity of two different neuron groups. One of these groups is affected by a rise in temperature of the blood, the other by a decline in temperature. Since the neurons having similar sensitivities to temperature change are grouped together in specific areas, one set is regarded as the *heat-loss* or *heat-dissipation center*, the other as the *heat-production* or *heat-conservation center*.

The heat-loss center is a relatively small area in the anterior hypothalamus, about 4 mm from the midsagittal line between the anterior commissure and the optic chiasma; it extends rostrally into the preoptic area. When the blood temperature rises, the cells of this center discharge over descending hypothalamic efferents to the respiratory and cardiovascular centers of the brainstem and spinal cord. These centers respond by initiating vasodilation and perspiration.

The neurons which compose the heat-production center are located mainly in the caudal portion of the lateral hypothalamus. When the temperature of the blood declines, these neurons discharge caudally over the same descending pathways utilized by those of the heat-loss center. This results in vaso-constriction, piloerection, increased cardiac rate, and elevated basal metabolic rate. Shivering is definitely a part of this process, since the rapid, involuntary contraction of the somatic musculature produces heat.[2]

Blood Pressure Regulation (Fig. 21-15)

The reflex control of blood pressure has already been discussed in the chapters on the GVA and GVE systems and the reticular formation. However, it should be indicated here that when generalized blood pressure changes are required, especially if the need is prolonged, the hypothalamus is activated and, through the same descending efferents, exerts influence upon the vasopressor and depressor centers of the reticular formation of the medulla. When the blood pressure change is initiated by emotional factors, it is certain that the hypothalamus is involved (Fig. 21-11). This is an important factor in the consideration of neurogenic or emotional hypertension in which the descending fibers from the hypothalamus activate the medullary vasopressor center. This, in turn, through the reticulospinal tracts, accelerates the heart and produces mesenteric vasoconstriction directly through nerve fibers and indirectly through epinephrine secreted by the adrenal medulla under the activating influence of the thoracolumbar autonomic fibers.

Appetite Control (Fig. 21-16)

As noted above, there is good supportive evidence that the hypothalamus is important in regard to appetite and thus is directly involved in the problems of obesity and malnutrition. These subjects will be discussed further under Clinical Considerations.

---

[2]This is further proof that the somatic efferent columns of the cord can be activated through the descending hypothalamic fibers.

Sleeping-Waking Mechanism (Chap. 19)

It has been shown that if normal, nonfatigued persons receive a certain amount of stimulation, from whatever source, they will remain awake and conscious of their surroundings. This means that when sufficient ascending impulses reach the cortex, it is activated. Normally the great sensory pathways, passing through thalamic nuclei to the cortex, are important in this connection. However, it has been shown experimentally that with these pathways intact, somnolence will occur with bilateral lesions placed in the posterior hypothalamus. These lesions, nevertheless, may reflect damage to ascending fibers from the reticular formation which are destined for nonspecific thalamic nuclei and represent a component of the brainstem reticular activating system. The question of whether the hypothalamus is inactive during sleep has been raised. Evidence points to the likelihood that it is active. For example, changes in growth hormone and adrenocorticotropic hormone (ACTH) secretion occur during sleep. Such observations suggest that the hypothalamus may effect augmentation of growth hormone —and corticotropin-releasing factors during such quiescent periods.

CLINICAL CONSIDERATIONS
Testing

There are no specific tests to be performed. However, certain symptoms commonly appear as a result of disease in this region. They include obesity, amenorrhea, diabetes insipidus, and disorders of sleep and of thermal regulation. In addition, emaciation, ulcerations of the alimentary tract, premature sexual development, and emotional disturbances are also attributable to hypothalamic disease. Frequently, certain of these symptoms appear together in a complex known as a hypothalamic syndrome, the diabetes insipidus and emaci-

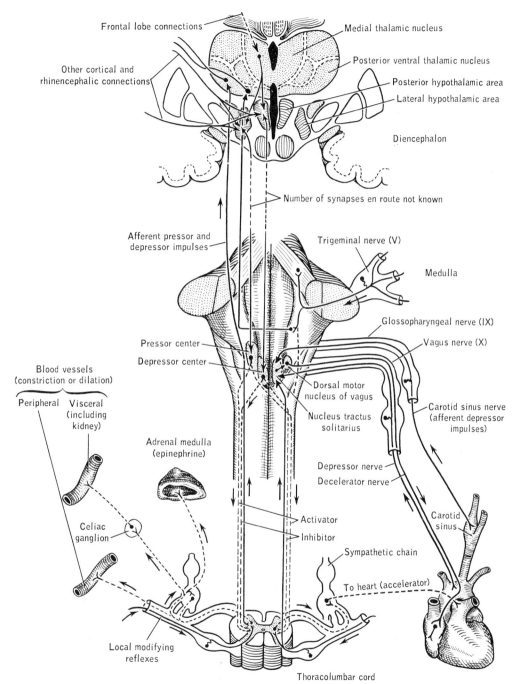

Figure 21-15 Blood pressure regulation. *(After Netter, Ciba Clinical Symposia.) Note:* The connection between the medial thalamic nucleus and the lateral hypothalamic area is probably a multisynaptic chain rather than a continuous band as shown in the figure.

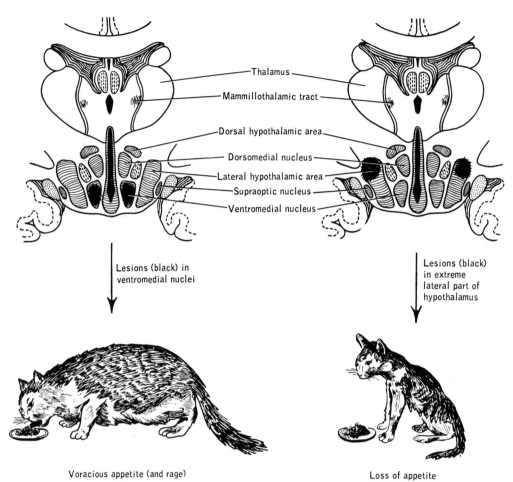

Thalamus

Mammillothalamic tract

Dorsal hypothalamic area

Dorsomedial nucleus

Lateral hypothalamic area

Supraoptic nucleus

Ventromedial nucleus

Lesions (black) in ventromedial nuclei

Lesions (black) in extreme lateral part of hypothalamus

Voracious appetite (and rage)

Loss of appetite

Figure 21-16 Hypothalamic control of appetite. *(After Netter, Ciba Clinical Symposia.)*

ation syndrome, the adiposogenital dystrophy complex, and a syndrome characterized by somnolence and disorders of temperature control.

Specific Pathology

The hypothalamus is subject to the same types of pathologic change found in other parts of the CNS. These changes may be precipitated by *trauma* resulting from surgery about the pituitary; by *injury* to the bones at the base of the skull; by *degenerative processes* caused by

disturbances of vascularity; by *inflammatory lesions,* either primary within the nervous tissue or in the meninges; and by several types of *tumors,* arising in the posterolateral walls or floor of the third ventricle or in the hypophysis.

Hyperthermia

This condition is characterized by a very high temperature, sometimes terminating fatally. It has been encountered in human beings particularly after surgery in or about the hypophysis, and is thought to be related to a destruction of the heat-loss center in the anterior hypothalamus. This may be coupled with a simultaneous irritation of the heat-production center located more posteriorly.

Poikilothermia

Bilateral lesions in the posterior hypothalamus, behind the heat-production center, may cut off the temperature-control mechanism entirely from lower centers. This will leave body temperature completely at the mercy of the environment.

Diabetes Insipidus

This condition is characterized by great thirst with excessive water intake (polydypsia) and an unbelievably high urine production (polyuria). Although both these symptoms may be found in diabetes mellitus, the urine in diabetes insipidus is of low specific gravity and does not contain glucose. Lesions may occur in the supraoptic nucleus or in its projection through the infundibular stalk to the posterior pituitary. This cuts off the production of the antidiuretic hormone, leaving the diuretic substance[3] of the adenohypophysis unopposed.

Adiposogenital Dystrophy (Froehlich's Syndrome)

The two symptoms, adiposity and genital dystrophy, may occur together or separately. Most characteristically, fat tends to accumulate in the lower abdomen and around the hips, the so-called feminine type of distribution. The genitalia are underdeveloped, and there are changes in secondary sex characteristics. The exact site of the lesion in human beings is not known, but it appears from clinical experience that the anterior and lateral areas of the

---

[3]The production of the diuretic substance also appears to be in some way regulated by the hypothalamus; it has been noted that extensive hypothalamic lesions lead to oliguria (low urine production).

tuber cinereum and the ventromedial nucleus are involved. Recently, newer techniques have shown that lesions in the region of the ventromedial nucleus will cause marked increase in appetite, frequently associated with rage states. The aberration is so intense that an animal will eat heavily and wolfishly although it is already well fed. Since animals with destructive lesions in this region are somewhat less active than normal, they easily become obese. There is some feeling that the obesity is the result of changes in fat and carbohydrate metabolism resulting from the suppression of certain anterior lobe secretions. This theory is supported by the fact that in some experimental animals with lesions in this area, there is a tendency toward hypogonadism. In others, there seems to be a lack in the somatotropic hormone.

When lesions are placed in the lateral hypothalamic regions, appetite is almost completely lost both in normal animals and in those with already existing ventromedial nuclei lesions.

There is further evidence that the hypothalamus exerts regulatory influences on the anterior lobe, chiefly through humoral substances in the hypothalamiconeurohypophyseal portal system of veins. These influences include lesions of the median eminence, causing loss of sexual activity and atrophy of the genitalia.

Hypertension (Fig. 21-17)

Although hypertension usually subsides when the emotional episode passes, the periods of hypertension may be long in the so-called chronic worrier. When prolonged, the high pressure may permanently alter the kidney in such a way that it secretes abnormal amounts of renin (a renal vasopressor substance) which can lead to a continuous hypertension, even in the absence of stress. It is also felt that the same factors which overstimulate the hypothalamus in the manner just described may

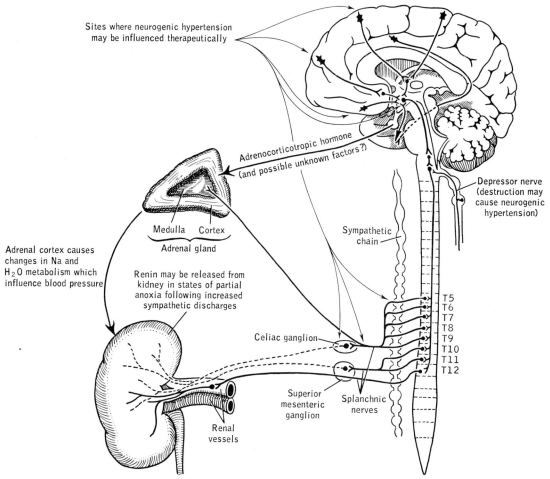

Sites where neurogenic hypertension
may be influenced therapeutically

Depressor nerve
(destruction may
cause neurogenic
hypertension)

Adrenocorticotropic hormone
(and possible unknown factors?)

Medulla   Cortex
Adrenal gland

Sympathetic
chain

Adrenal cortex causes
changes in Na and
H_2O metabolism which
influence blood pressure

Renin may be released from
kidney in states of partial
anoxia following increased
sympathetic discharges

Celiac ganglion

T5
T6
T7
T8
T9
T10
T11
T12

Superior
mesenteric
ganglion

Splanchnic
nerves

Renal
vessels

Figure 21-17 Neurogenic and humoral hypertension. Emotional tension, anxiety states, and
other mental stresses induce hypothalamic stimulation which in turn influences peripheral
circulation. *(After Netter, Ciba Clinical Symposia.)*

also cause it to secrete a substance into the
bloodstream (a neurosecretion[4]) which is car-

[4]These secretions are referred to as *hypothalamic
releasing factors,* or *hypophysiotrophic hormones.* The
neurons which produce such secretions are called hypophysiotrophic neurons. Illustrations of the hypophysiotrophic hormones include the *thyrotropin-releasing hormone* (TRH), *corticotropin-releasing factor* (CRF), *luteini-
zing hormone-releasing hormone* (LHRH), *growth hormone release–inhibiting hormone* (somatostic, GIH), *pro-
lactin release–inhibiting factor* (PIF), *prolactin-releasing
factor* (PRF), and *melanocyte-stimulating hormone-
releasing* and *inhibiting factors* (MRF and MIF).

ried to the anterior pituitary. This, in turn, is
stimulated to secrete ACTH. An oversecre-
tion of the adrenal cortex may also be concerned with hypertension.

Amenorrhea, Impotence, and Sexual Infantilism

This symptom complex may arise as a result
of disorders in either the hypothalamus or the
hypophysis. With destruction of the anterior
and tuberal portions of the hypothalamus,

there is loss of the regulatory secretions which govern the production of gonadotropic hormones. The exact nature of the sexual disorders will depend upon the patient's sex and age when the lesion occurs. In children, development of sexual organs and the sexual functions are retarded. If the lesion occurs after puberty, there may be a regression of sexual function and a reversal of secondary sexual characteristics that is especially noticeable in males. An opposite effect is the so-called *pubertas precox,* the premature development of the genitalia and sexual function. In this condition the hypothalamic control mechanism is in some way blocked, permitting an unchecked secretion of gonadotropin. It is sometimes associated with internal hydrocephalus. More frequently, however, especially when the signs appear very early, it may be related to a hematoma. When the signs occur later, they are often caused by tumors, encephalitis, or meningitis.

Disorders of Sleep

These may occur as a result of encephalitis. They may consist of the occurrence of short periods of sleep during normal waking hours or of prolonged periods of sleep. The latter condition can result from destruction of the caudal hypothalamus or from damage in the transition zone between diencephalon and mesencephalon, perhaps as far down as the central tegmental area in the mesencephalon. Insomnia has also been described in cases of encephalitis. Again, as noted above, involvement of the hypothalamus may be secondary to damage to the ascending reticular activating system.

Disorders of Emotions

Inflammations, vascular disturbances, and neoplasms in or about the hypothalamus have led to many aberrant activities. Sometimes these take the form of impaired memory with lesions of the mammillary bodies or of mania-cal outbursts with excitement and destructiveness when lesions are located in the ventromedial nucleus.

Recently, surgical lesions have been placed in the posteromedial regions of the hypothalamus (referred to as the *ergotropic triangle)* as a means of reducing or eliminating aggressive and hostile behavior in schizophrenic and other severely emotionally disturbed patients. Reports of such lesions, in general, show a reduction both in aggressive behavior and in sympathetic reactions. It is reasonable to conclude here that such lesions disrupt the major descending outflow of the hypothalamus into the brainstem as well as some of the ascending monoamine and other brainstem fibers which supply the forebrain.

Miscellaneous Effects

Through animal experimentation, it has also been shown that stimulation of the hypothalamus produces ovulation (in rabbits); lesions in the central area result in a fall of metabolic rate; stimulation and inhibition of certain regions speed up or slow down the production of thyrotropic hormones; hyperglycemia has resulted from stimulation of the hypothalamus and if prolonged in the tuberal region will cause a decrease in sensitivity to insulin. Hypothalamic lesions have been shown in some animals to cause an increase in sensitivity to insulin. In pancreatectomized cats, this has led to a reduction in insulin requirements.

SUMMARY

   I Parts
     A Definite nuclei: preoptic, supraoptic, paraventricular, posterior, dorsomedial, ventromedial, tuberal, and mammillary
     B Regional divisions: anterior, lateral, dorsal and posterior
  II Afferent connections
     A Fornix

1 Origin—hippocampal formation (subicular cortex)

2 Termination—ventromedial hypothalamus and mammillary nuclei

3 Function—one of chief paths from cortex to hypothalamus; may be involved in emotions and memory

B Medial forebrain bundle

1 Origin—septal nuclei, basal forebrain, amygdala, ventral tegmentum, monoamine neurons

2 Termination—mammillary nuclei, lateral hypothalamic area, and ventral tegmentum

3 Function—ascending fibers from midbrain tegmentum to hypothalamus; descending fibers to lateral hypothalamus and midbrain tegmentum; olfactovisceral and olfactoviscerosomatic correlation in hypothalamus and hemispheres

C Periventricular fibers

1 Origin—periaqueductal gray of brainstem

2 Termination—anterior, tuberal, and posterior areas and periaqueductal portions of the brainstem

3 Function—cerebral influences on visceral function

D Stria terminalis

1 Origin—amygdaloid complex

2 Termination—preoptic nucleus and anterior area

3 Function—part of the olfactovisceral reflex relay system

E Mammillary peduncle

1 Origin—tegmentum of mesencephalon

2 Termination—mammillary nuclei

3 Function—possible activation of hypothalamus through ascending reticular fibers; correlation of gustatory and visceral sense with somatic afferents from the mucous membranes of nose and mouth

III Efferent connections

A Mammillothalamic tract (bundle of Vicq d'Azyr)

1 Origin—medial mammillary nucleus

2 Termination—anterior nucleus of thalamus (and via relays to gyrus cinguli)

3 Function—part of hypothalamic activation of cortex by way of anterior thalamic nucleus; reciprocal circuit through gyrus cinguli; thalamocortical impulses from hypothalamus resulting from correlation of gustatory and olfactory impulses

B Mammillotegmental tract

1 Origin—medial mammillary nucleus

2 Termination—central reticular nucleus of the mesencephalic tegmentum

3 Function—part of descending control mechanism of autonomic centers in brainstem and spinal cord

C Periventricular fibers

1 Origin—posterior nuclei, medial nuclei

2 Termination—dorsal tegmental nuclei of the mesencephalon; parasympathetic nuclei of the brainstem; the vital centers in the medullary reticular formation (i.e., cardiac and respiratory); the intermediolateral column of the cord —all these through the dorsal longitudinal fasciculus (of Schütz) and through the reticulospinal tracts

3 Function—probably supplemental, carrying hypothalamic control to brainstem parasympathetic nuclei and vital centers

D Hypothalamohypophyseal fibers

1 Origin—supraoptic and paraventricular nuclei

2 Termination—neurohypophysis

3 Origin—tuberal nuclei

4 Termination—neurohypophysis

5 Function—activation of posterior lobe of pituitary with influence on secretion of adenohypophysis

The Limbic System

The term *limbic system* was first used to describe a series of structures which form a margin about the cerebral cortex. These structures include the *hippocampal formation, septal area, amygdala,* and *cingulate gyrus.* More recent definitions of the limbic system include the concept that a limbic structure is one which is in some way, either directly or indirectly, in communication with the hypothalamus. Within this framework, the limbic system may be expanded to include such other structures as the *pyriform* and *entorhinal cortices, olfactory cortex,* and the *prefrontal cortex.*

The various functions of the limbic system that have been described are exceedingly complex. Others remain unknown. Nevertheless, the thesis advanced in this chapter and the principal point upon which our attention will be focused is that the primary role of the limbic system is to modulate or regulate the activity of the hypothalamus. Accordingly, the limbic inputs into the hypothalamus can, in general, be divided into two systems: a *hippocampal-septal circuit* and a second system which involves the *mediodorsal thalamic nucleus.* In the following section the anatomic organization of each of these systems will be considered separately.

ANATOMY OF THE HIPPOCAMPAL FORMATION AND SEPTAL AREA

Hippocampal Formation

Histology and Local Circuitry

The hippocampal formation consists of the *cornu Ammonis, dentate gyrus,* and *subicular complex* (Figs. 22-1 through 22-7). The princi-

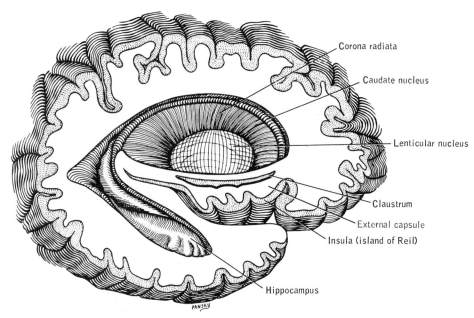

Figure 22-1 Lateral aspect of a dissection of a human cerebral hemisphere after removal of both opercula, the insula, the external capsule, and part of the temporal lobe. The hippocampus has been exposed.

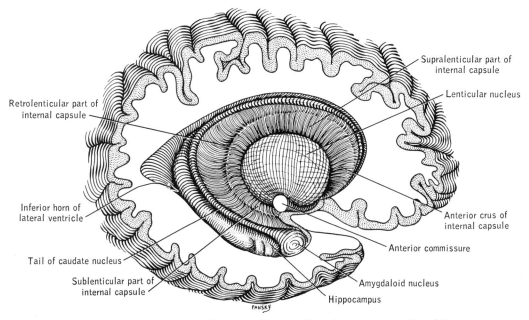

Figure 22-2 This is an extension of the dissection shown in Fig. 22-1, a larger portion of the temporal lobe having been removed to give greater exposure of the hippocampus and amygdala.

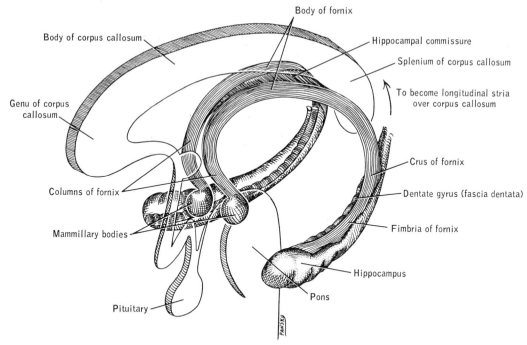

Figure 22-3 A diagrammatic representation of a reconstruction of the fornix.

pal cell type of the cornu Ammonis is the pyramidal cell. Its basal dendrites extend out laterally and somewhat superficially toward the ventricular surface. The apical dendrite extends away from the ventricular surface in the direction of the dentate gyrus. The axon of the pyramidal cell passes directly into the most superficial layer of cortex called the *alveus* and constitutes the efferent channel of the hippocampus. A second cell type, identified as the basket cell, lies proximal to the pyramidal cell and makes axosomatic contact with the pyramidal cell. The structure of the cornu Ammonis can then be said to have the following layers: an external *plexiform layer* situated adjacent to the ventricular surface which contains the axons of pyramidal cells as well as axons from regions afferent to the hippocampal formation; a layer containing basal dendrites and basket cells called the *stratum oriens;* a layer of pyramidal cells appropriately called the *pyramidal cell layer;*

the innermost two layers referred to as the *stratum radiatum* and *stratum lacunosummoleculare* which contain the apical dendrites of the pyramidal cells as well as certain afferents to the cornu Ammonis from the entorhinal cortex.

The pyramidal cells of the cornu Ammonis are arranged in a C-shaped formation interlocking it with the C-shaped arrangement of the dentate gyrus (Fig. 22-6). The cornu Ammonis itself has been divided into a number of different fields. The pyramidal cells situated closest to the subicular cortex and farthest from the dentate gyrus are referred to as the *CA1 field,* while the *CA4 field* is located within the hilus of the dentate gyrus. The *CA2* and *CA3 fields* are interposed between the other two CA fields. The CA1 field contains the smallest pyramidal cells, while the CA3-CA4 region contains the largest cells. The CA3 field is connected with the CA1 field by a group of axon collaterals known as *Schäffer collaterals.*

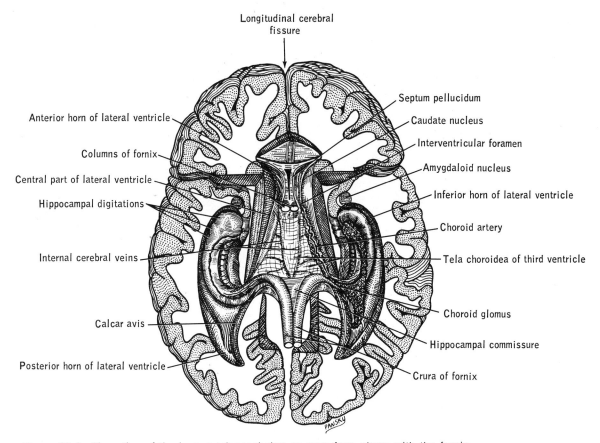

Longitudinal cerebral
fissure

Anterior horn of lateral ventricle

Columns of fornix

Central part of lateral ventricle

Hippocampal digitations

Internal cerebral veins

Calcar avis

Posterior horn of lateral ventricle

Septum pellucidum

Caudate nucleus

Interventricular foramen

Amygdaloid nucleus

Inferior horn of lateral ventricle

Choroid artery

Tela choroidea of third ventricle

Choroid glomus

Hippocampal commissure

Crura of fornix

Figure 22-4 Dissection of the human telencephalon as seen from above with the fornix reflected to expose the hippocampal commissure.

The CA1 field is somewhat unique in that it is very susceptible to anoxia, especially during temporal lobe epilepsy. This region is known as *Sommer's sector.*

The dentate gyrus has also been described as a multilayered cortical structure. The principal cell type is the *granule cell.* It contains an axon called the *mossy fiber* which makes synaptic contact with CA3 pyramidal cells. Deep to the granule cell layer lies the *polymorphic cell layer,* which is composed of modified pyramidal cells. External to the granule cell layer lies a *molecular cell layer,* which is apposed to the molecular cell layer of the cornu Ammonis. It is composed mainly of axons of hippocampal afferents.

The third component of the hippocampal formation is the subicular complex and constitutes a transitional region between the cornu Ammonis and adjacent entorhinal and retrosplenial cortices. This region can be distinguished from the cornu Ammonis by a marked thickening of the pyramidal cell layer (Figs. 22-6, 22-7). The subicular complex has also been divided into a number of subareas. That portion closest to the CA1 field is referred to as the *prosubiculum,* the region which is closest to the entorhinal cortex and which displays the greatest cell thickening is called the *presubiculum,* and the area which is centrally located between these two area is called the *subiculum* proper.

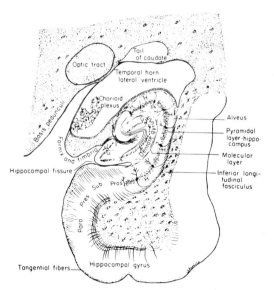

Figure 22-5 Diagram for the orientation of hippocampus and dentate gyrus. H., hippocampus; PARA., parasubiculum; PRES.; presubiculum; PROS., prosubiculum; SUB., subiculum. *(From Peele, The Neuroanatomic Basis for Clinical Neurology, 3d ed., McGraw-Hill Book Company, New York, 1977.)*

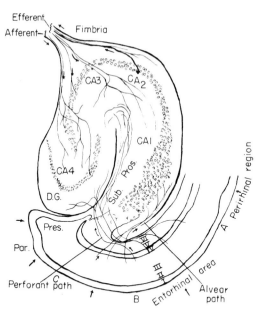

Figure 22-6 The alvear and perforant paths entering the hippocampus. The fibers entering and leaving via the fimbria and hippocampal commissure are also included. The arrows outside the figure serve to divide the entorhinal area into three parts, A, B, C. The arrows inside the figure indicate the direction of impulses. The four regions of the hippocampus are indicated as CA1 to CA4. D.G., dentate gyrus; PAR., parasubiculum; PRES., presubiculum; PROS., prosubiculum; SUB., subiculum. *(From Peele, The Neuroanatomic Basis for Clinical Neurology, 3d ed., McGraw-Hill Book Company, New York, 1977.)*

Afferent Connections

The afferent supply to the hippocampal formation is derived from a number of sources. One primary site is the *entorhinal cortex.* This area gives rise to a series of pathways that course through the molecular layers of the dentate gyrus and cornu Ammonis or alveus to innervate much of the hippocampal formation. A second important afferent source of the hippocampal formation arises from the diagonal band component of the septal area (see Septal Area, below). The fibers from this region enter the hippocampal formation via the fornix bundle and are distributed in a diffuse manner to all cell fields of the cornu Ammonis and subicular cortex. A third source of hippocampal afferents includes several cortical regions such as the pyriform cortex and prefrontal cortex. Other sites, which include the cingulate gyrus and anterior thalamic nucleus, project to the presubicular component

of the hippocampal formation, while the visual, auditory, somatosensory, and gustatory regions of neocortex indirectly supply the hippocampal formation via synaptic contacts with the entorhinal area. Thus, the hippocampal formation is endowed with a rich and complex afferent supply which probably relates to the processing of information associated with a variety of sensory qualities as well as with the status of other components of the limbic system.

Efferent Connections

The output of the hippocampal formation arises from the axons of pyramidal cells of both the cornu Ammonis and subicular complex

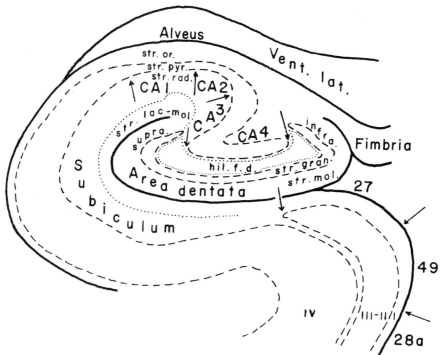

Figure 22-7 Hippocampal region in the rhesus monkey in horizontal section showing the respective layers of the hippocampal and dentate gyrus. The layers are drawn and the sections of the hippocampal formation are indicated. 28-A, entorhinal area; HILF.d., hilus fasciae dentatae; 49, parasubiculum; 27, presubiculum; STR.GRA., stratum granulosum; STR.LAC.-mol., stratum lacunosum moleculare; STR.PYR., stratum pyramidale; STR.RAD., stratum radiatum; SUPRA and INFRA, supra- and infrapyramidal limbs of the stratum granulosum. Roman numerals refer to the layers of cortical areas 17, 28-A, and 49. *(From Carpenter, Human Neuroanatomy, 7th ed., The Williams & Wilkins Company, Baltimore, 1977.)*

and form the overwhelming majority of axons found in the fornix system. The fornix system, itself, has two components: One passes rostral to the anterior commissure and supplies the septal area and is referred to as the *precommissural fornix* (Fig. 22-8); a second passes just caudal to the anterior commissure and descends through the hypothalamus to supply the mammillary bodies, adjacent parts of the hypothalamus, and anterior thalamic nucleus (*postcommissural fornix*). Additional fibers within the postcommissural fornix are believed to reach the midbrain as well. The fibers which pass through the precommissural fornix arise from the CA fields of the cornu Ammonis and the subicular complex with the

exception of the presubiculum. This projection is topographically organized in that fibers situated near the anterior pole of the hippocampal formation project to the most lateral region of the dorsal septal area while neurons situated progressively more caudally in the hippocampal formation project to progressively more medial portions of the dorsal septum (Fig. 22-8). The postcommissural fornix arises exclusively from the subicular complex and apparently does not involve the pyramidal cells of the cornu Ammonis (Fig. 22-9). In addition to supplying the postcommissural fornix, subicular cells innervate adjacent regions of entorhinal and posterior cingulate cortices (Figs. 22-10, 22-11). In

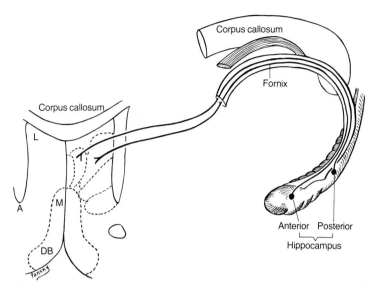

Figure 22-8 Schematic diagram of the topographic organization of the precommissural fornix. A., nucleus accumbens; DB., nucleus of the diagonal band; L., lateral septum; M., medial septum.

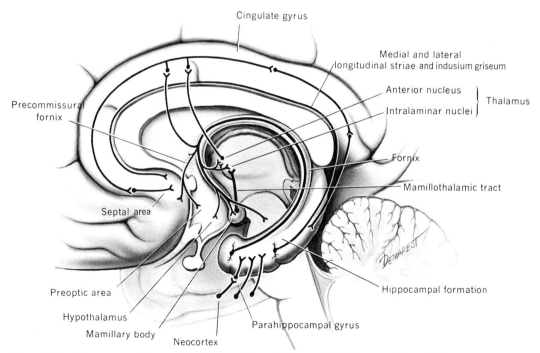

Figure 22-9 Some connections of the limbic system. Note especially the projections of the postcommissural fornix to the anterior thalamic nucleus and mammillary bodies. *(From Noback and Demarest, The Human Nervous System, 2d ed., McGraw-Hill Book Company, New York, 1975.)*

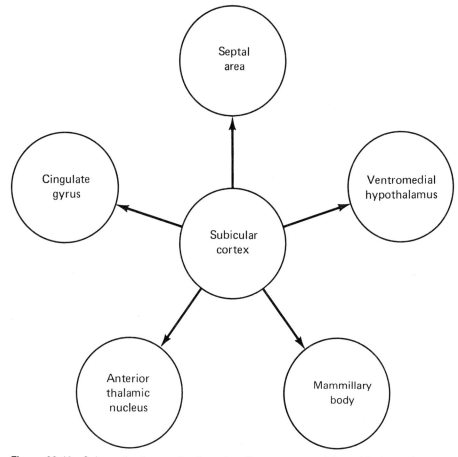

Figure 22-10 Schematic diagram to show the efferent targets of the subicular cortex.

this fashion, the subicular complex is quite unique in that it can be viewed as a nodal point for possible activation of much of the limbic system.

Commissural Connections

The ventral aspect of the fornix contains fibers which are commissural in nature and thus serve to connect the two hippocampi. The fibers which pass through the commissure of the fornix appear to arise primarily, if not exclusively, from the CA3-CA4 areas of the hippocampus and terminate in most instances in the homotypical region of the contralateral hippocampus (Fig. 22-11).

Functions

Numerous experiments by a large number of investigators have suggested that the hippocampal formation takes part in a wide variety of functions. Perhaps, the most significant of these relate to its effects upon hypothalamic activities. Several such important functions include aggressive behavior and autonomic and endocrine responses. Experimental animal studies and human clinical investigations strongly implicate a significant role for the hippocampal formation in the control of aggressive reactions. In animals, electrical stimulation of the hippocampal formation at current intensities below those necessary to

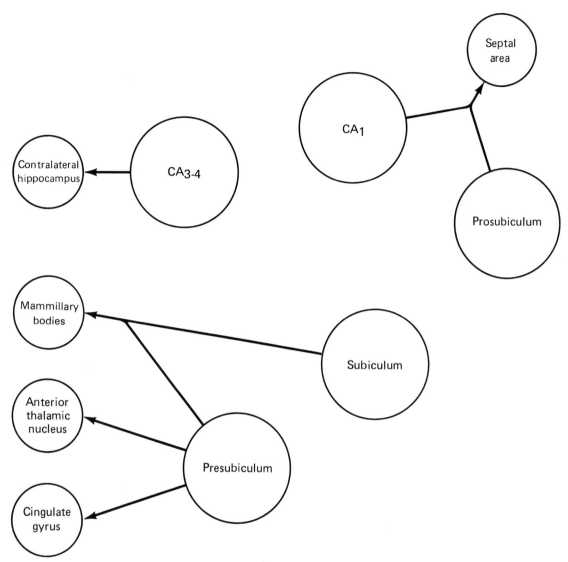

Figure 22-11   Schematic diagram illustrating the efferent targets of the components of the hippocampal formation.

initiate seizure activity does not generate any behavioral responses that can be clearly observed. Instead, electrical stimulation (in the cat) modulates aggressive reactions initiated elsewhere in the CNS such as noted in the hypothalamus. Regarding the nature of the modulating response, experiments have shown that the hippocampal formation is not uniform in its effects upon aggression. Stimulation of regions close to the amygdala (i.e., temporal pole of the hippocampal formation) tend to facilitate the occurrence of aggressive reactions, while stimulation of regions situated closer to the septal area (i.e., septal pole of the hippocampal formation) tend to suppress aggressive reactions. Since both regions of the hippocampal formation project their axons to different areas of the septum, it is likely that the hippocampal formation generates its effects upon hypothalamic aggression via its differential synaptic linkages in the septal area. In this way, the septal area may be viewed, in part, as a relay nucleus to the hypothalamus for information transmitted to it from the hippocampal formation.

Aggressive reactions and rage behavior also have been reported in human beings in association with lesions, tumors, or seizure activity involving the temporal lobe in general and the hippocampal formation in particular. Although it is extremely difficult to state unequivocally whether such trauma to the hippocampal formation corresponds more closely to an effect characteristic of an experimental lesion or of electrical stimulation, the conclusion that the sum total of the effects generated by these injuries upon the hippocampal formation is mediated through the septal area upon the hypothalamus remains a most likely possibility.

Over the past few years there has been an increasing amount of evidence which suggests a role of the hippocampal formation, as well as other limbic structures, in the regulation of endocrine function. For example, it has been shown that estradiol-concentrating neurons are densely packed in the ventral regions of the hippocampal formation and that corticosterone is localized in very heavy concentrations in that structure as well. Further, injections of corticosterone have a general inhibitory effect upon hippocampal neurons. Lesions of the hippocampus or section of the fornix disrupt the diurnal rhythm of ACTH release, and stimulation of this structure inhibits ovulation in spontaneously ovulating rats.

Such findings suggest that the hippocampal formation may be selectively sensitive to the levels of different hormones in the blood and thus serves as a component of a feedback system upon the pituitary via the hypothalamus. It should be further noted that in the rat—the animal most commonly utilized for neuroendocrine studies—there exists a unique pathway that arises from the subiculum near the temporal pole of the hippocampus called the *medial corticohypothalamic tract.* This pathway projects directly into the ventromedial region of the hypothalamus which is generally believed to contain the hypophysiotrophic hormones that control pituitary function.

The role of the hippocampal formation in the regulation of aggressive and endocrine functions through its control of the hypothalamus has been stressed. However, there are a variety of other functions attributed to the hippocampal formation for which no clear-cut anatomic mechanism can be identified. These include learning, memory, and seizure activity. Evidence that the hippocampal formation participates in learning processes is suggested from EEG and ablation experiments. EEG recordings from the hippocampal formation indicate that under certain conditions a rhythmic slow wave of 4 to 7 per s, called the *theta rhythm,* appears. It can be initiated in response to selective sensory stimuli. It has been shown to occur as the animal is approaching a goal as well as during different phases of classic or operant conditioning. It also seems somewhat correlated with the neocortical alpha block and the onset of the beta rhythm. It is present during periods of paradoxical sleep.

A large number of experimental ablation experiments have been conducted in lower animals. Several different kinds of behavioral dysfunctions resulting from this experimental procedure are worthy of note. Although no sensory or motor deficits can be readily observed, hippocampectomized animals appear to be more active than normal animals, exhibit more exploratory behavior in a novel environment, show a heightened startle reaction to a sudden loud stimulus, and seem to display a perseveration of their responses in a learning situation regardless of whether they are correct or incorrect. Related to this last phenomenon is the observation that when animals are required to delay their responses for a fixed period of time (such as bar pressing only at fixed temporal intervals) or during passive avoidance testing, rats subjected to lesions of the hippocampus routinely respond during the period when no response should be made. Another characteristic of hippocampectomized animals that has recently been described relates to the phenomenon of spatial learning, or spatial memory. Normal rats can easily learn to enter the correct arm of either a simple Y maze or a series of correct arms in a more complicated radial maze. Apparently, animals with lesions of the hippocampus consistently fail at this task, as they characteristically and repeatedly return to make the same error.

Lesions of the hippocampus in human beings have also been associated with disturbances of learning and memory. One such disturbance is known as *Korsakoff's syndrome.* It results from the toxic effects of alcohol or from vitamin B deficiency which damages either the hippocampus or several of its target neurons such as in the mammillary bodies or thalamus. It is characterized by the presence of both retrograde and anterograde amnesia. Specifically, patients have a great deal of difficulty in recalling events in the recent past as well as handling and retaining newly acquired information. Like the rat, these patients also display a marked perseverative response pattern. Patients who have undergone temporal lobectomies (which involve the hippocampus) for treatment of psychomotor epilepsy also exhibit a defect known as *short-term memory disorder.* In these instances, patients display a severe anterograde amnesia and a much less severe retrograde amnesia with little diminution of intellectual abilities. They can recall events in the remote past and those prior to surgery with little difficulty. However, they are unable to learn new facts such as the names and addresses of friends. On specific short-term-memory diagnostic tests, patients generally perform quite poorly. For instance, a control population can easily select the correct geometric form from a pool of objects which matches one shown 40 to 60 s earlier, while patients with bilateral damage to the hippocampus cannot perform such a task. Lesions restricted to the anterior aspect of the temporal lobe and which may involve the amygdala but which spare the hippocampus do not result in this defect.

An adequate account of the anatomic and functional mechanisms underlying the role of the hippocampal formation in learning and memory has yet to be elaborated. Many hypotheses remain tenable. For example, it is plausible to consider that the hippocampal formation normally receives and processes tertiary sensory information during the learning process which results in its orderly categorization and storage. Thus, lesions of the hippocampus may result in the loss of the appropriate attentional mechanisms necessary for conditioning of the sensory cues critical to learning and recall. Such a loss might also be reflected in the failure of patients with hippocampal lesions to appropriately encode (i.e., abstract and categorize) relevant information.

That the hippocampal formation has a very low threshold for seizures is yet another characteristic of this structure. However, this is not unique within the limbic system. In fact, one of the most obvious features of limbic system physiology is that most of its components maintain very low thresholds for the initiation of seizure activity. Seizure discharges recorded from the hippocampal formation have very high amplitudes and frequencies and reflect the synchronous discharge of large assemblies of cells that appear to become self-sustaining. Frequently, hippocampal seizures have no behavioral concomitants and can be detected by EEG recordings, especially if the seizure is limited to the temporal lobe. However, when the seizure spreads to other limbic and related structures such as the amygdala, overt behavioral manifestations become apparent such as smacking the lips, swallowing, and chewing movements. Seizures of the temporal lobe which involve the hippocampus (called temporal lobe seizures or partial seizures) also make the patient appear confused and may produce hallucinations involving auditory, vertiginous, and gustatory sensations. As noted above, temporal lobe seizures may be accompanied by aggressive reactions, especially when an attempt is made

to move or give direction to the patient. It has been suggested that vascularization, glial formation, and fibrosis constitute factors which may lead to the onset of epilepsy although they are also found in nonepileptogenic foci.

Septal Area

Histology

The septal area in the human being is situated rostral to the lamina terminalis and anterior commissure, ventral to the corpus callosum and septum pellucidum, and medial to the lateral ventricles and striatum (Fig. 22-12). It corresponds to the cortical regions referred to as the *paraolfactory area* and *subcallosal*

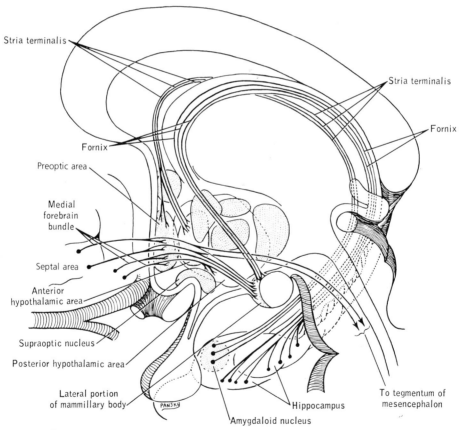

Figure 22-12 Some of the afferent pathways to the hypothalamus showing in particular the fornix, the medial forebrain bundle, and the stria terminalis.

gyrus (Figs 1-4, 1-5). In lower forms, the septal area also includes the region occupied by the septum pellucidum in the human being and thus constitutes a greater relative volume of tissue. The septal tissue itself includes a number of different cell types as well as a variety of different fiber systems related to it. Although as many as 20 (or more) different cell types have been identified in the septum, it is convenient in the present text to characterize the septal nuclei in the following way: much of the area dorsal to the level of the anterior commissure is occupied by the *lateral septal nucleus*; the narrow area bordering the midline can be distinguished from the lateral nucleus since it contains large-sized cells. This area is called the *medial septal nucleus* and becomes continuous with another cell group ventral to it and situated below the level of the anterior commissure called the *nucleus of the diagonal band (of Broca)* (Fig. 22-8). Two other cell groups frequently associated with the septal area include the *bed nucleus of the stria terminalis,* which lies adjacent to the anterior commissure and ventral aspect of the lateral ventricle, and the *nucleus accumbens,* which lies immediately rostral to the bed nucleus of the stria terminalis and separates the ventral aspect of the caudate head from the ventral septum.

Afferent Connections

The septal area receives a major afferent supply from the hippocampal formation and for this reason (as discussed above) can be viewed as a relay nucleus of that structure (Fig. 22-8). As previously noted, hippocampal fibers are distributed in a topographic manner principally to the entire lateral septal nucleus. Other sources of afferents to the septal area include the lateral hypothalamus and ventral tegmental area. It is of interest to point out that the input to the lateral septum and nucleus accumbens from the ventral tegmental area is primarily dopaminergic in nature. Addition-

al efferent sources include amygdaloid fibers contained in the stria terminalis which terminate in its bed nucleus and a number of secondary olfactory fibers which appear to reach the diagonal band and medial septum.

Efferent Connections

The major efferent pathways link the septum with the hippocampal formation, hypothalamus, midbrain, and dorsal thalamus (Fig. 22-12). It is now well established that the hippocampal formation and septal area are reciprocally connected. Septal fibers project topographically to the hippocampal formation and arise mainly from the nucleus of the diagonal band and adjacent tissue. Like the topographic pattern described for hippocampal efferents to the septum, the cells of origin in the ventral septum which project to the hippocampal formation are organized in a medial-to-lateral sequence so that neurons situated most medially project to dorsal regions of the hippocampal formation located near its septal pole while progressively more laterally situated neurons project to more ventral and anterior regions approaching its temporal pole (Fig. 22-13).

The distribution of fibers to the hippocampal formation represents but one of the projections arising from the nucleus of the diagonal band. In fact, the diagonal band is similar to the connections of the subicular cortex in that it makes contact with much of the limbic system (Fig. 22-14). These additional projections of the diagonal band include the olfactory, prefrontal, and anterior cingulate cortices; amygdala; mammillary bodies; habenular complex; and nucleus medialis dorsalis of the thalamus. Thus, the subicular cortex and nucleus of the diagonal band can be viewed as two poles of the limbic system which are endowed with the capacity to modulate most (if not all) of the components of the limbic system.

Another significant projection of the septal

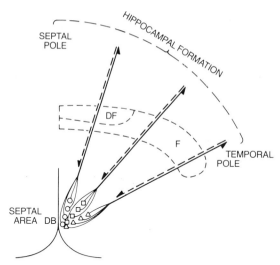

Figure 22-13 Schematic diagram illustrating the topographical organization of the diagonal band efferents to the hippocampal formation. Dotted lines indicate parallel projections of hippocampal efferents terminating in the dorsal septum. DB., diagonal band; DF., dorsal fornix; F., fimbria. *(Courtesy of Dr. Richard Meibach.)*

area arises from the region dorsal to the anterior commissure, the same region which constitutes the receiving area for hippocampal afferents. Cells from this region give rise to axons that join the medial forebrain bundle and represent the largest single component of that bundle. These fibers are distributed to the lateral and medial preoptic areas, lateral hypothalamus, and ventral tegmentum. In this way, the septal area is capable of receiving information from the hippocampal formation and relaying it to the preopticohypothalamic network as a disynaptic pathway. Said otherwise, the septohypothalamic pathway provides the anatomic mechanism which enables the hippocampal formation to modulate the hypothalamus.

It should also be noted that the medial forebrain bundle represents a key element in the circuit linking the limbic system with the midbrain and hypothalamus. Both the nucleus accumbens and bed nucleus of the stria terminalis also supply fibers to the midbrain that pass through the medial forebrain bundle.

Since this pathway reciprocally connects the midbrain with the septal area and hypothalamus, the septal area can be viewed as a central relay or nodal point not only for the transmission of hippocampal inputs to the hypothalamus and midbrain but for all other inputs from the midbrain and hypothalamus to the rest of the limbic system.

Functions

Inasmuch as the septal area is so closely linked to the hippocampal formation, it is not at all surprising that many of the functions attributed to the latter are also identified with the former. For instance, the septal area has been strongly implicated in the regulation of aggressive and rage behavior. Lesions of the septal area in rats produce a behavioral pattern sometimes known as the *septal syndrome.* It is characterized by a hyperemotionality, a marked increase in aggressive behavior, a heightened startle reaction, and a general difficulty in handling (by the experimenter). Electrical stimulation of the septal area, interestingly enough, produces a suppression of aggressive reactions in cats. Electrical stimulation also suppresses or facilitates (in some instances) cardiovascular responses as well as single-unit activity in the hypothalamus. It has also been demonstrated that electrical stimulation of the septal area modulates self-stimulation and drinking behavior produced from sites in the lateral hypothalamus.

These findings clearly point to the conclusion that the septal area exerts a powerful modulatory effect upon aggressive behavior and other responses associated with the hypothalamus. This relationship also applies to the regulation of the hypothalamic-pituitary axis. Indeed, stimulation of the septum suppresses adrenal activity and ACTH secretion in the rat. Lesions of the septal area or the pathway from the septum to the hypothalamus facilitate ACTH release and can result in a state of constant estrus.

Concerning other functions associated with

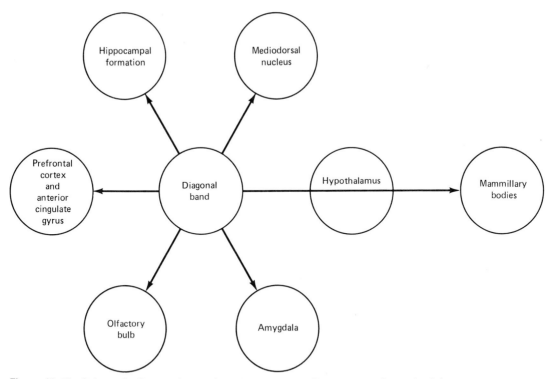

Figure 22-14 Schematic diagram illustrating diagonal band efferent targets in much of the limbic system.

the septal area, it has been shown that lesions of this region can facilitate the acquisition of a conditioned avoidance response in a shuttle box, impair learning of a passive avoidance response, and facilitate exploratory behavior both in a maze and in the open field. Recent evidence has also suggested that the neurons situated in the diagonal band function as the generator and origin of the theta rhythm recorded in the hippocampus and elsewhere.

LIMBIC STRUCTURES RELATED TO THE NUCLEUS MEDIALIS DORSALIS OF THE THALAMUS (Figs. 22-15 through 22-17)

Amygdala

Histology

The amygdala consists of a number of subnuclear groups plus a cortical mantle that includes much of the pyriform lobe. Individual nuclear groups can be identified fairly easily, and they include *lateral, basal, medial, anterior, central,* and *cortical nuclei.* However, it is quite common to divide the entire complex into two components: a *corticomedial group,* which includes those structures which lie in the dorsal and medial aspect of the complex, and a *basolateral group,* which includes the remaining components. The amygdala is also intimately related to the adjacent cortex, which is referred to as the *prepyriform area* at rostral levels and as the *periamygdaloid cortex* at somewhat more posterior levels.

Afferent Connections

The amygdala receives its afferent supply from several different sources. Perhaps to a greater extent than the limbic structures considered above, the amygdala is closely linked

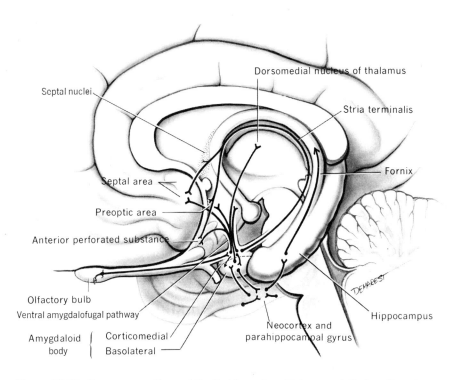

Figure 22-15   Some connections of the limbic system. Note especially the efferent connections of the amygdala. *(From Noback and Demarest, The Human Nervous System, 2d ed., McGraw-Hill Book Company, New York, 1975.)*

with cortical tissue. The corticomedial nuclear group receives direct inputs from the olfactory bulb, while the basolateral group receives indirect olfactory information from the prepyriform and pyriform cortices. The lateral aspect of the amygdala receives a direct input

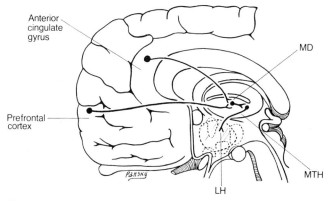

Figure 22-16   Schematic diagram illustrating the indirect connections between the prefrontal cortex and anterior cingulate gyrus to the lateral hypothalamus by way of the medialis dorsalis and the midline thalamic nuclei. LH., lateral hypothalamus; MD., medialis dorsalis; MTH., midline thalamic nuclei. *(Courtesy of Dr. Henry Edinger and Dr. Alan Siegel.)*

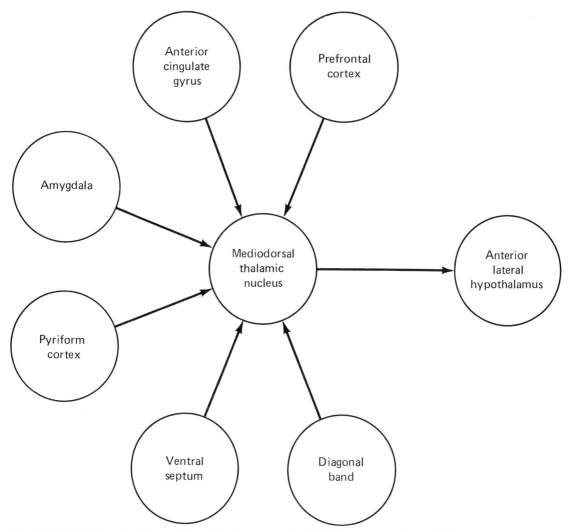

Figure 22-17 Schematic diagram illustrating the converging limbic inputs upon the medialis dorsalis (mediodorsal) and the pathway to the lateral hypothalamus.

from the adjacent inferior temporal gyrus. Further, the basolateral group also receives a direct input from the nucleus of the diagonal band and is reciprocally connected with the orbitofrontal cortex. Other inputs to the amygdala include projections from the medial thalamus to the anterior amygdala, from ventromedial hypothalamus via the stria terminalis diffusely to the amygdala, and from brainstem dopaminergic neurons to the central nucleus.

Efferent Connections

As indicated at the beginning of this chapter, a primary functional characteristic of the limbic system is to modulate the hypothalamus. In the case of the amygdala, it can achieve this effect by both direct and indirect pathways. There exist two direct routes—the stria terminalis and the ventral amygdalofugal pathways. The stria terminalis appears to arise principally from the corticomedial group and the adjacent pyriform cortex and is distributed to the bed nucleus of the stria terminalis, the medial preoptic area, anterior medial hypothalamus, and ventromedial hypothalamic nucleus. The ventral amygdalofugal pathway arises mainly from the basolateral amygdala, pyriform, and periamygdaloid cortices. The fibers course in a medial direction beneath the pallidum and enter the lateral preoptic area and lateral hypothalamus (Fig. 22-15). Other fibers appear to descend in the medial forebrain bundle in the hypothalamus and terminate throughout the brainstem reticular formation. Thus, the amygdala can directly control the activity of neurons in both the lateral and medial regions of the hypothalamus. In addition, an indirect route by which the amygdala can modulate the hypothalamus involves the medialis dorsalis. Fibers from both basolateral and corticomedial groups project directly to the medialis dorsalis. As noted in Chap. 21, second-order fibers from the nucleus medialis dorsalis pass into nearby midline thalamic nuclei, and through a multisynaptic chain which extends in a rostral direction through the midline thalamus. Finally, fibers enter the perifornical lateral hypothalamus from the rostral aspect of the midline thalamus.

Functions

The most salient features regarding the functions of the limbic structures considered thus far include their role in aggression and rage, autonomic and endocrine functions, and other manifestations of emotionality. These functional characteristics are of equal, if not greater, significance with regard to the amygdala. Many studies have clearly implicated the amygdala in the regulation of different forms of emotional behavior. However, not all of them have produced uniform results. One group of studies has indicated that following lesions of the amygdala complex in rats, cats, or monkeys, a taming effect ensues. Another group of studies has indicated just the reverse—that following such lesions animals become hyperemotional, are difficult to han-

dle, and display heightened aggressive and defensive postures. The application of electrical stimulation experiments have somewhat clarified these opposite findings. It appears that different regions of the amygdala exert opposing effects upon aggressive behavior. Stimulation of the corticomedial group produces the most pronounced inhibitory effects upon aggressive behavior, while activation of the lateral nucleus seems to facilitate the occurrence of this response. Thus, it seems that the amygdala exerts dynamic and opposing effects upon the hypothalamic rage mechanism although it would appear from the experimental evidence that the inhibitory functions are more pronounced. Nevertheless, several lesion and ablation studies in monkeys and human beings which have been classically described and replicated by several investigators and which emphasize their taming effects will be noted here.

One such effect of amygdaloid lesions is referred to as the *Kluver-Bucy syndrome.* This syndrome is characterized by hypersexuality, a change in dietary habits, a decrease in fear toward normally fear-producing objects (including human beings), a tendency to explore and contact orally inedible objects, and a visual agnosia. This constellation of behaviors has also been reproduced with lesions restricted to the pyriform cortex and inferior temporal gyrus—regions which project fibers directly to the amygdala. In view of the findings based upon electrical stimulation studies and the results of more restrictive lesions of the amygdala, it appears that the Kluver-Bucy syndrome results when the sites in the basolateral complex which normally facilitate the occurrence of aggressive tendencies are destroyed or when the main input to this region is eliminated (i.e., inferior temporal lobe lesion).

Similarly, the results of surgical removal of portions of the amygdala in aggressive human patients, especially in connection with temporal lobe epilepsy, have been reported. Some of the findings include a general decrease in aggressive and explosive behavior, an increase in IQ, and a decrease in hyperactivity. In the light of the above discussion, it is reasonable to suggest that the lesions in these cases may have involved the basolateral complex.

It has also been reported that while electrical stimulation of much of the amygdala does not produce any overt behaviors, activation of the basal complex or the stria terminalis can directly initiate an affective defense reaction similar to that elicited from the ventromedial hypothalamus. The results of electrical stimulation in the human being have been noted. In general, stimulation evoked different kinds of emotional feelings and moods. Some of these include feelings of relief, relaxation, detachment, a need to be by oneself, and a pleasant sensation.

The effects of electrical stimulation upon autonomic responses have also been reported. In general, pressor responses tend to be dominant, especially in regions which give rise to defense reactions. However, a bradycardia could be identified following stimulation mainly from the medial division of the amygdala. It has also been reported that stimulation can evoke or modulate respiratory movements (acceleration of breathing, lowering of amplitude, or inhibiting breathing) associated with pupillary dilation and micturition.

The amygdala is also known to modulate food and water intake (functions normally associated with the hypothalamus). It appears from stimulation experiments that anterior and medial components exert a facilitatory effect while the basolateral component plays an inhibitory role. Ablation experiments have, in general, supported this division of function. Aphagia results following lesions of the medial component, while hyperphagia can be observed when lesions are placed in the basolateral complex.

That the amygdala plays a role in endocrine function has been demonstrated by the following observations: Estrogen-concentrating neurons are known to be present in high densities in the amygdala. Stimulation of the corticomedial division can induce ovulation, while transection of the stria terminalis can abolish this response. The basolateral amygdala facilitates growth hormone release, whereas the corticomedial division exerts an inhibitory effect upon growth hormone release. ACTH release is facilitated by amygdaloid stimulation, especially from the basolateral division, or by lesions in the corticomedial division. Thus, the two major anatomic components of the amygdala appear to maintain a differential influence upon a variety of functions associated with the hypothalamus.

Cortical Components of the Limbic Lobe
Prefrontal Cortex and Anterior Cingulate Gyrus

Anatomic Considerations The prefrontal cortex receives fibers from all parts of the cerebral cortex. It receives its subcortical afferent supply from the brainstem monoamine neurons, hypothalamus, nucleus medialis dorsalis, nucleus of the diagonal band, and basolateral amygdala. Cortical association fibers from the prefrontal cortex supply the temporal lobe and the underlying limbic structures (amygdala, subicular complex, and possibly hippocampus). Other association fibers may also supply other regions of cortex. The principal subcortical projection of the prefrontal cortex is the nucleus medialis dorsalis (Fig. 22-16).

The anterior cingulate gyrus receives its principal subcortical afferent supply from the anteromedial thalamic nucleus, the ventral tegmental area, which transports dopamine to this region, and the nucleus of the diagonal band. The major subcortical projection of the anterior cingulate gyrus is to the nucleus medialis dorsalis (Fig. 22-16) and to the presubiculum. Thus, it should be noted that these two limbic cortical regions appear not to have any direct input into the hypothalamus. Instead, any modulation of hypothalamic processes that may be attributed to them can most likely be achieved via their inputs into the nucleus medialis dorsalis (Figs. 22-16, 22-17). Accordingly, possible modulation effects upon the hypothalamus must follow an indirect route.

Functional Considerations *Prefrontal Cortex* The evolution and development of the frontal lobe in general and the prefrontal cortex in particular can be easily detected in a comparison of their relative sizes in several species such as rat, cat, monkey, and the human being. The prefrontal cortex reaches its greatest size and complexity in human beings. It is nevertheless present in a rudimentary form in the rat and to a slightly greater extent in the cat.

The prefrontal cortex has been linked functionally with both emotional and intellectual processes. Concerning emotional behavior, lesions of the frontal lobe have been shown to produce an increase in intraspecific aggression in monkeys but not in male cats. Lesions in female cats have been reported to result in a decrease in the frequency of aggressive acts committed. Electrical stimulation, on the other hand, has tended to yield a more consistent pattern of results. Stimulation of either the medial or orbital aspect of the prefrontal cortex powerfully inhibits hypothalamically elicited aggression in cats that do not spontaneously attack rats as well as aggression in cats that do spontaneously attack rats. It is significant to note that the functional pathway mediating this inhibitory effect has recently been examined and strongly implicates the nucleus medialis dorsalis in the organization of this cortically elicited process. The findings indicate that the inhibitory effect generated from the prefrontal cortex can be eliminated following lesions of the nucleus medialis dorsalis. In addition, it should be noted that the nucleus medialis dorsalis is further implicated

in the pathway for regulation of aggressive reactions. This conclusion is based on the observation that electrical stimulation of this structure can produce powerful modulation of hypothalamic responses.

The importance of the prefrontal cortex in the regulation of human emotional behavior has been recognized by neurosurgeons for many years. In 1936 a technique was devised which included an undercutting of the afferent and efferent connections of the prefrontal cortex and has been referred to as *prefrontal lobotomy*. This procedure was designed initially to alleviate some of the aggressive and related behavioral manifestations of psychotic patients and, later on, as a relief for patients suffering from intractible pain. This procedure has met with some limited success in that mild personality changes have been reported from time to time. However, consistent agreement concerning the overall effects of this procedure has been lacking in the literature. More recently, the development of tranquilizing drugs have provided a noninvasive alternative to the use of prefrontal lobotomy. Accordingly, this surgical procedure is rarely performed at the present time.

Other behavioral, autonomic, and visceral functions frequently associated with the hypothalamus can be influenced by the prefrontal cortex. Specifically, lesions of the prefrontal cortex have been shown to produce an increase in feeding behavior, while stimulation tends to have an inhibitory effect. Electrical stimulation can also produce an inhibition of respiratory movements, alter blood pressure, inhibit gastric motility, and raise the temperature of the extremities.

Regarding other functions of the prefrontal cortex, it has been demonstrated that lesions in the monkey can produce hypermotility and hyperreactivity to external stimuli. Perhaps the most clear-cut dysfunction associated with lesions of the prefrontal cortex involves the performance of cats, dogs, and monkeys in the delayed-response test. In this paradigm, the animal is shown briefly in which of two places food has been placed but is required to postpone its retrieval for a given length of time. Normal animals master this task quite easily, but animals with prefrontal lesions commit many errors. Similarly, if an animal is required to discriminate between two auditory or visual signals and in addition delay its response, animals with prefrontal lesions will commit many more errors than normal animals.

In human patients who have sustained lesions of the frontal lobe as a result of tumors or gunshot wounds, both a perceptual and intellectual deficit appear to be present. Such patients have difficulty in accurately identifying the perceived vertical when the body is tilted. When patients with prefrontal lesions are given a group of cards that can be sorted on the basis of color, shape, or number of figures on each card, they can easily master this task until they are requested to shift their criteria for categorization (e.g., from numbers to shape). Under these circumstances they tend to perseverate on the original strategy employed. It has been suggested that the frontal lobe disorder can be characterized as a "derangement in behavioral programming." These individuals seem to lose sight of the purpose of their actions and their intended goals. It is plausible that the disruption of the connections between the frontal lobe with parietal and temporal cortices play important roles in the generation of such deficits.

Anterior Cingulate Gyrus A number of different studies have suggested that the anterior aspect of the cingulate cortex plays a potent role in the regulation of hypothalamic processes. Electrical stimulation of this region suppresses hypothalamically elicited attack behavior in the cat, while lesions have resulted in facilitation of the occurrence of this response in several species. In human beings, tumors of this region have sometimes been associated with a heightened aggressive re-sponse. Electrical stimulation has also been reported to produce respiratory arrest, a fall in blood pressure, cardiac slowing, and attention (or orienting) responses.

SUMMARY

I Hippocampal formation
  A Afferents from:
    1 Entorhinal cortex
    2 Nucleus of the diagonal band
    3 Contralateral hippocampus
    4 Brainstem raphe
    5 Anterior cingulate cortex
    6 Prefrontal cortex
  B Efferents to:
    1 Septal area via precommissural fornix
    2 Mammillary bodies and adjacent parts of hypothalamus
    3 Anterior thalamic nucleus via postcommissural fornix
    4 Entorhinal cortex
    5 Posterior cingulate cortex
II Septal area
  A Afferents from:
    1 Hippocampal formation
    2 Ventral tegmental area
    3 Lateral hypothalamus
    4 Olfactory cortex
    5 Amygdala
  B Efferents arising in nucleus accumbens and dorsal septum to:
    1 Preoptic area
    2 Lateral hypothalamus
    3 Tegmentum
  C Efferents arising in nucleus of the diagonal band to:
    1 Hippocampal formation
    2 Amygdala
    3 Prefrontal cortex
    4 Anterior cingulate cortex
    5 Olfactory bulb
    6 Mammillary bodies
III Amygdala
  A Afferents from:
    1 Olfactory cortex
    2 Pyriform cortex
    3 Temporal neocortex

    4 Prefrontal cortex
    5 Ventromedial hypothalamus
    6 Ventral tegmentum
    7 Medialis dorsalis (of thalamus)
  B Efferents via the stria terminalis to:
    1 Medial preoptic area
    2 Bed nucleus of the stria terminalis
    3 Ventromedial hypothalamus
  C Efferents via ventral amygdalofugal
    pathway to:
    1 Lateral hypothalamus
    2 Ventral tegmentum
  D Efferents to:
    1 Nucleus medialis dorsalis
    2 Prefrontal cortex
IV Prefrontal cortex
  A Afferents from:
    1 Neocortical area—temporal and pa-
      rietal
    2 Limbic structures
      a Hypothalamus
      b Amygdala
      c Nucleus of the diagonal band
    3 Brainstem monoamine pathways
    4 Nucleus medialis dorsalis of thala-
      mus
  B Efferents to:
    1 Nucleus medialis dorsalis

    2 Limbic structures
      a Amygdala
      b Hippocampal formation
      c Temporal lobe
V Anterior cingulate gyrus
  A Afferents from:
    1 Anteromedial nucleus of thalamus
    2 Nucleus of the diagonal band
    3 Ventral tegmental dopamine area
  B Efferents to:
    1 Nucleus medialis dorsalis of thala-
      mus
    2 Presubiculum
VI Relay components
  A Septal area—principal relay neurons
    for transmission of impulses to hypo-
    thalamus from hippocampal forma-
    tion
  B Nucleus medialis dorsalis of thal-
    amus—principal relay nucleus for
    transmission of impulses to hypothal-
    amus (via multisynaptic pathway)
    from:
    1 Prefrontal cortex
    2 Anterior cingulate gyrus
    3 Nucleus of the diagonal band
    4 Olfactory cortex
    5 Amygdala

The Thalamus

STRUCTURE

Gross

The thalamus is the largest portion of the diencephalon. Its gross relationships to the mesencephalon, internal capsule, and basal nuclei of the telencephalon have already been described (Chap. 1).

Thalamic Nuclei (Figs. 23-1 through 23-3)

The thalamus is divided into two parts by a sheet of myelinated fibers called the *internal medullary lamina*. This divides the thalamus into a medial and a lateral area. Each of these major areas is further subdivided into specific nuclear masses. The medial portion consists of the dorsomedial (Fig. 25-15) and anterior nuclei (Figs. 25-15 through 25-17); the latter is enclosed within the medullary lamina. The

lateral portion is divided into a dorsal and ventral tier of nuclei. The caudal aspect of the ventral tier is often referred to as the *metathalamus* and includes the medial and lateral geniculate nuclei (Figs. 25-13, 25-14). Further subdivisions into still smaller areas become enormously complicated, especially since certain of these nuclei remain unclassified.

Closely related to these structures is the *epithalamus*, which consists of the lateral and medial habenular nuclei, the pineal gland, stria medullaris, and roof of the third ventricle. The lateral habenular nucleus receives fibers passing in the stria medullaris from the anterior lateral hypothalamus, preoptic area, diagonal band nucleus, medial pallidal segment, and substantia innominata. The medial habenular nucleus receives fibers from the posterior part of the dorsal septum, the nucleus of the diago-

445

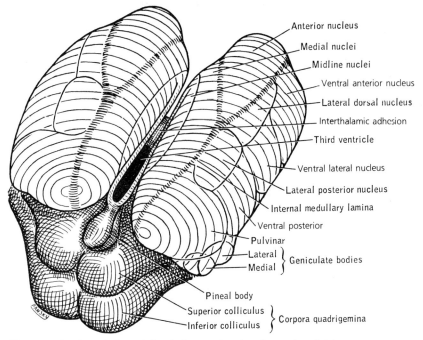

Figure 23-1 Dorsal view of the thalamus showing the major divisions.

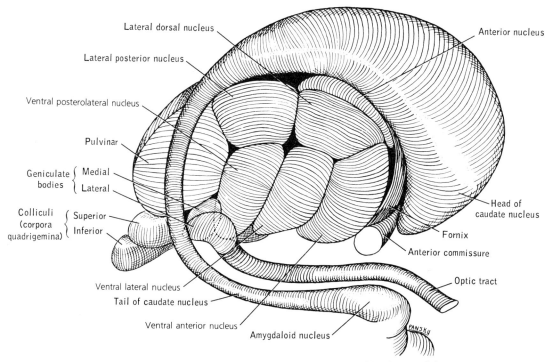

Figure 23-2 Reconstruction of the thalamic nuclei seen from the lateral side. Some of the related structures also are shown.

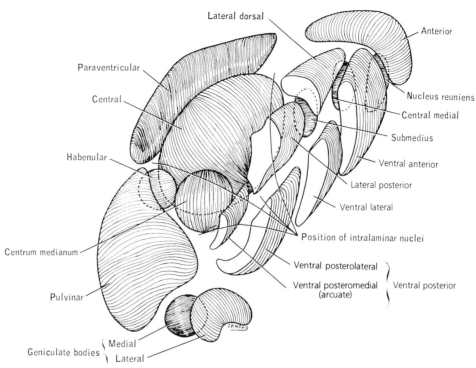

Figure 23-3 Three-dimensional reconstruction of the important thalamic nuclei as seen from above, showing their relationships to each other.

nal band, and the basal nucleus of the substantia innominata. The major output of the habenular complex passes from the medial nucleus through the habenulopeduncular tract (sometimes called the fasciculus retroflexus) to the interpeduncular nucleus of the midbrain. Other fibers from the habenular complex are believed to project to the brainstem raphe complex and possibly to other brainstem monoamine-containing neurons such as the locus ceruleus.

The pineal gland has been shown to be related to endocrine function. In fact, the presence of melatonin appears to act upon the anterior pituitary to suppress the female gonads. It also contains enzymes necessary for the synthesis of serotonin. In addition, it contains approximately 50 times as much serotonin (per gram) as the whole brain. The pineal gland is controlled through the release of norepinephrine originating in the superior cervical ganglion.

The dorsal portion of the lateral nucleus is divided from front to back into the *lateral dorsal* (Fig. 25-14), *lateral posterior* (Fig. 25-14), and *pulvinar* (Fig. 25-13); the ventral portion of the lateral thalamic mass consists of the *ventral anterior, ventral lateral* (Figs. 25-15, 25-16), and *ventral posterior nuclei.* The ventral posterior nucleus is usually described as consisting of the *ventral posteromedial* (arcuate or semilunar) nucleus, adjacent to which a separate *accessory arcuate* may be found, and the *ventral posterolateral nucleus.*

In addition to the above, more obvious divisions, there are three other scattered sets of nuclei: (1) *nuclei of the midline,* which make up the lamina of gray substance lining the third ventricle and are particularly prominent in its dorsal half as well as in the interthalamic adhesion (when the latter is present); (2) nuclei scattered in the internal medullary lamina, the so-called *intralaminar nuclei*, which include the *paracentral, central lateral, centrum medianum* (Fig. 25-14), and the *parafascicular*[1]; (3) the *thalamic reticular nucleus,* which is embedded in the external medullary lamina.

FUNCTIONAL CLASSIFICATION OF THE THALAMIC NUCLEI

Three general nuclear groups are considered. The first, and probably oldest, is the *midline, intralaminar nuclei* and *thalamic reticular nucleus,* the fibers of which are primarily related to the rhinencephalon, the hypothalamus, and possibly the striatum. The second group is made up of the nuclei in the ventral tier of the lateral thalamus, including the metathalamus. These nuclei are primarily *cortical relay (extrinsic)* in nature, receiving terminals from all the great ascending systems of the body and sending efferents to the neocortex. The third group is composed of *association (intrinsic) nuclei.* They receive few, if any, ascending sensory fibers, their afferents being mainly from other parts of the brain while their efferents are distributed particularly to association areas of the cortex. The anterior and medial nuclei, together with the nuclei in the dorsal part of the lateral nucleus, make up this group.

CONNECTIONS OF THE NUCLEI

Nuclei of the Midline

These nuclei receive terminals and many collaterals from the spinothalamic tracts, the

trigeminothalamic tracts, and the medial lemniscus. It also appears that some of the fibers from the tectal region and certain thalamic nuclei also reach the midline complex. Some efferents descend into the hypothalamus and into the entorhinal cortex; others appear to reach portions in both the medial and lateral thalamic areas. It is said that these nuclei are important for impulses arising in the viscera, and it has been suggested that integration here permits some appreciation of pain.

Cortical Relay Nuclei[2]

Sensory Systems

Ventral Posteromedial Nucleus (Fig. 23-4) This nucleus serves the GSA and GP systems. The afferents enter by way of the trigeminothalamic tract. The efferents pass through the posterior limb of the internal capsule to areas 1, 2, and 3 on the postcentral gyrus.

Ventral Posterolateral Nucleus (Fig. 23-4) This area is also a relay center in the GSA and GP systems. The afferents are the lateral and ventral spinothalamic tracts and the medial lemniscus. The efferents pass through the posterior limb of the internal capsule to areas 1, 2, and 3 of the postcentral gyrus (Fig. 24-9).

Medial Geniculate Body (Nucleus) (Fig. 8-16) This is an SSA relay area for hearing. The afferents travel from the cochlear nuclei via the lateral lemniscus and brachium of the inferior colliculus, plus possible relays from nuclei of the trapezoid body, lateral lemniscus, superior olive, and inferior colliculus. The efferents (auditory radiations) pass through the sublenticular part of the internal capsule as the geniculotemporal fibers to the transverse temporal gyrus (Fig. 8-16).

---

[1]It is now quite common to group the centrum medianum and the parafascicular nucleus together with the nucleus medialis dorsalis and midline thalamic nuclei in a unit referred to as the *medial nuclei*—probably a more logical arrangement when these nuclei are considered on a functional basis.

[2]Any nucleus whose efferents project upon the cerebral cortex may receive reciprocal (descending) fibers from the same cortical area.

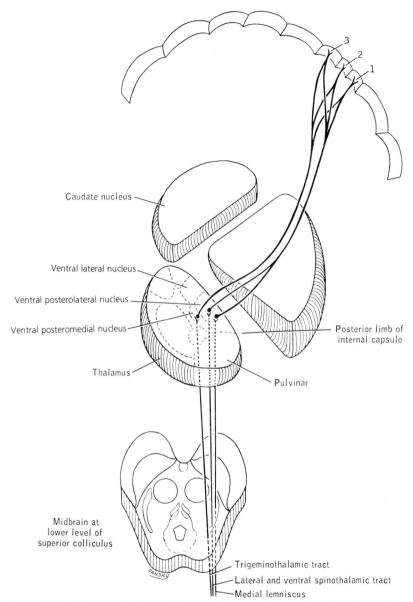

Figure 23-4 Afferent and efferent fibers of the ventral posterolateral and ventral posteromedial nuclei of the thalamus.

Lateral Geniculate Body (Nucleus) (Fig. 8-5) This is a special somatic relay area for vision. The afferents enter through the optic tract and possibly relays from the nucleus of the superior colliculus via the brachium of the superior colliculus. The efferents (optic radiations) travel through the retrolenticular part of the internal capsule as the geniculocalcarine tract to the cortex along the banks of the calcarine fissure (Figs. 8-4, 8-7, 24-8).

Motor System

Ventral Anterior Nucleus (Fig. 23-5) The afferents arise mainly from the medial segment of the globus pallidus and ascend in the ansa and fasciculus lenticularis. There are also ascending connections from the substantia nigra and from such thalamic groups as the midline and intralaminar nuclei. The efferents pass through the internal capsule to area 6 of the frontal cortex.

Ventral Lateral Nucleus (Fig. 23-6) The afferents are chiefly dentatothalamic fibers which travel by way of the superior cerebellar peduncle. Other afferents come from the substantia nigra and from the medial pallidal

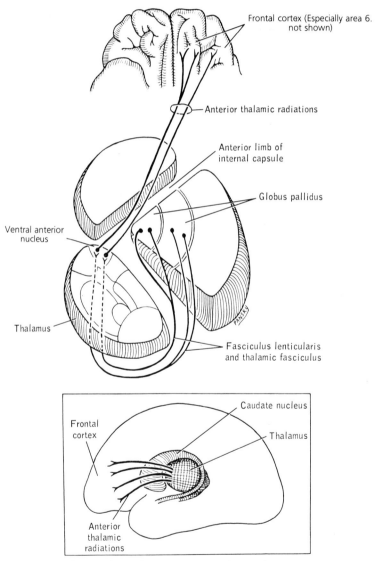

Figure 23-5 Connections of the ventral anterior nucleus.

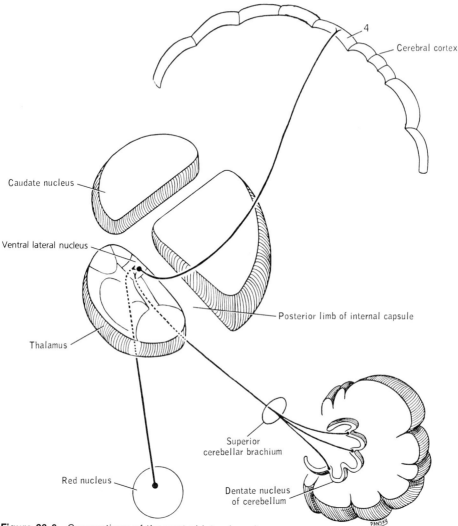

Figure 23-6 Connections of the ventral lateral nucleus.

segment by way of the thalamic fasciculus. The efferents travel through the posterior limb of the internal capsule to area 4 of the frontal motor cortex.

ASSOCIATION NUCLEI

Anterior Nucleus

The afferents are chiefly fibers of the mammillothalamic tract plus some others which appear to branch out of the fornix. The efferent fibers have a wide distribution to the cortex. They ascend through the anterior limb of the internal capsule to reach the posterior half of the gyrus cinguli (area 23) and the presubiculum.

Dorsomedial Nucleus

The afferents come from a variety of sources, among them the prefrontal cortex, anterior cingulate gyrus, amygdala, pyriform and pre-pyriform cortices, nucleus of the diagonal band, midline thalamus, centrum medianum, and reticular thalamic nucleus. Its efferents are also widespread, passing indirectly to the hypothalamus via the midline thalamus and directly to the reticular thalamic nucleus, mid-brain central gray, amygdala, and to a large expanse of the frontal cortex (areas 8, 9, 11, 12, 19, and 45 through 47; Fig. 24-6). Because the medialis dorsalis receives considerable input from the limbic system and limbic system–related structures and also indirectly innervates the hypothalamus, this structure may be viewed as an integration center for visceral impulses and as a relay nucleus for the transmission of limbic impulses to the hypothalamus.

Centromedian Nucleus (Centrum Medianum)

Although this rather large nucleus is actually one of the intralaminar nuclei, it is usually functionally grouped with the dorsomedial nucleus. The sources and the pathways for its afferent fibers are not altogether clear, but the following seem fairly certain: the brainstem reticular formation, the spinothalamic tracts, and the cerebellum, the last as offshoots from the dentatorubrothalamic system. In addition, the globus pallidus and area 4 of the cerebral cortex contribute fibers to this nucleus. Its efferents project to the ventral anterior nucleus, to others of the intralaminar group, and to the cortical relay nuclei.

Lateral Dorsal and Lateral Posterior Nuclei (Fig. 23-7)

These two nuclei forming the more rostral part of the dorsal tier of the lateral thalamic mass are both considered association nuclei. The *lateral dorsal* is actually a caudal extension of the anterior nucleus. It has primary reciprocal connections with the gyrus cinguli and with certain parts of the parietal lobe (precuneus). The *lateral posterior nucleus* receives affer-

ents largely from the ventral posterior nuclei and also from several other thalamic nuclear groups. There are also reciprocal connections with cortical areas 5 and 7 (Chap. 24).

Pulvinar (Fig. 23-7)

This, the largest of the thalamic nuclei, is said to be "polysensory" because of the wide variety of systems which send fibers into it by way of other thalamic nuclei. First, it receives afferents from both the geniculate bodies. Second, fibers come into it from the intralaminar group. Third, it is believed to receive fibers from the superior colliculus. There are many reciprocal connections with cortical association areas in the temporal, parietal, and occipital lobes (area 18, 19, 39, 40; Chap. 24).

Thalamic Reticular System

Up to this point, the thalamus has been considered as an integrating mechanism, both with and without cortical projections. When the latter are present, the cortical projection areas are specific. More recently, through electrical stimulation experiments, a far more extensive relation between thalamus and cortex has been shown. The nuclei which exert this widespread influence belong to a "diffuse" thalamocortical mechanism, sometimes designated as the *thalamic reticular system.* This system is difficult to define anatomically, partially because many of its nuclei have been listed in other groups. Those nuclei, often classified as *midline,* are considered *reticular.* They are the *rhomboid, central medial,* and *reuniens.* To these are added four nuclei usually listed with medial group nuclei by most authors: the *centrum medianum, paracentral, central lateral,* and *parafascicular.* In addition, other authors place a portion of the anterior nucleus and the ventral anterior on the list of thalamic reticular nuclei. The *reticular nucleus proper,* often classified with the *lateral thalamic nuclei,* since it does, in part, separate the external medullary lamina from

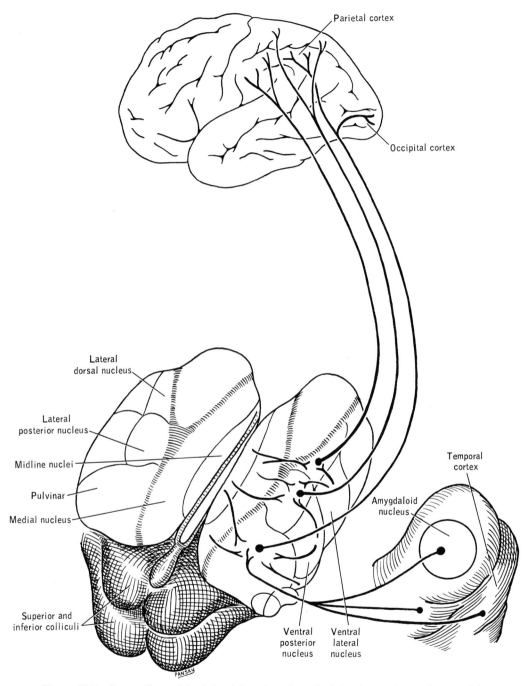

Figure 23-7 Connections of the lateral dorsal nucleus, the lateral posterior nucleus, and the pulvinar.

the internal capsule laterally, is also a member of this system. The evidence indicates that all these nuclei of the system are interconnected; the stimulation of one activates others.

It is not necessary to repeat afferent connections of this system since they have been given under the midline and medial group nuclei.

The efferents of this reticular mechanism may influence the cortex by way of other thalamic nuclei: the lateral dorsal, lateral posterior, and pulvinar, belonging to the dorsal tier of the lateral division; and the anterior thalamic nucleus, submedial nucleus, and possibly others of the medial group (See Chap. 24).

EVALUATION OF THALAMIC FUNCTION

In lower forms in which a cortex has not yet developed, the thalamus is the highest sensory correlation center. Here, there is an integration of visceral and somatic afferents, and appropriate motor responses are initiated through thalamic connections to the basal nuclei for somatic activity and to the hypothalamus for visceral activity. The human thalamus still maintains a measure of its original function in the correlation of motor and sensory activities, indicated by the fact that the ventral lateral and the ventral anterior nuclei lie in the neural stream between the cerebellum and cortex and the striatum and cortex, respectively. Nor are other functions, particularly in regard to visceral sense, pain, temperature, and simple touch, completely lost in human beings, even though the thalamus has been overshadowed by the evolution of the cerebral cortex. Since the cortex is the supreme sensory integration center, afferent impulses, originally fed into the thalamus, must be passed on to the cortex. Thus, the thalamus is now a relay center to the cerebrum, the ventral posterior nuclei, and the metathalamus being important in this regard, all projecting to specific primary cortical ar-

eas: the gyri bounding the central fissure, including areas 1, 2, and 3 (the somatosensory zones); the occipital pole region, area 17 (for vision); and the superior temporal gyrus, area 41 (for hearing). These cortical areas, therefore, depend, for their activation, on sensory material already processed by the integration mechanism of the thalamus (Fig. 24-8).

The facilitation of thalamic integration is doubtless the underlying reason why the relay nuclei give rise to many efferent fibers destined for the associative (elaborative) nuclei of the thalamus: the lateral dorsal, lateral posterior, dorsomedial, and pulvinar. These nuclei likewise emit thalamocortical fibers directed not toward the primary sensory areas but to the so-called association cortex. Thus, general somatic impulses are carried to portions anterior and posterior to the pre- and postcentral gyri, the prefrontal and posterior parietal cortex, respectively. The more complex visual impulses reach the cortex rostral to the occipital pole in areas 18 and 19, while the more integrated auditory impulses reach area 22, which adjoins the primary auditory cortex in the temporal lobe (Fig. 24-9).

Intimately related to thalamic function are the two other aspects of sensation: affective and discriminative. On the one hand, *affective* sensation, which pertains to a feeling of mental strain, forms the basis of general bodily well-being or malaise. Included in this category are pain, temperature, agreeableness, disagreeableness, and some tactile sensations. The evidence seems clear that the thalamus itself is related to consciousness and simple recognition of touch, pain, temperature, and pleasant or unpleasant "affect" qualities. Thus, the reactions mediated through the medial thalamic efferents to the hypothalamus are primarily affective, the resulting reactions being immediate, excessive, and accompanied by general secretory, vasomotor, or other visceral changes.

The second aspect of sensation is *discriminative,* permitting stimuli to be compared as to intensity, locality, and relationships in time or space. On these discriminations the perception of form, size, and texture is based. Movements are also compared as to extent, direction, and sequence. However, although impulses carrying the information necessary for such discernment reach the thalamus and are relayed through and integrated by the thalamus, the cortex is essential in all matters of discrimination. This is amply borne out by the fact that in widespread cortical lesions, discrimination, including sense of position, is lost, while simple recognition of pain or touch, without localization, is retained. So, in contrast to affective sensation, discriminative sensations are precise, not excessive, and often delayed.

It is believed that the dorsomedial nucleus, which receives impulses from the limbic system, is the site for appreciation of the "affect" qualities of somatic sensation. Furthermore, these qualities are integrated with visceral sensation, the resulting synthesis then being transmitted to the cortex. Hence, the cortex receives a blending of the somatic impulses which underlie cortical discrimination together with the so-called feeling tone produced through visceral activities. Therefore, the prefrontal cortex, the recipient of this thalamic discharge, is thought to be the area where discriminative cortical activities reach their greatest refinement.

Another aspect of thalamic function involves the thalamic reticular system. It is possible that this diffuse system may govern both local and general states of cortical response to incoming sensory stimuli. It has been suggested that specific thalamic relay nuclei permit the almost limitless diversified and intricate neural patterns which form the foundation for memory, thought, or complex behavior, while the force and the stimulus necessary to activate and sustain these cerebral circuits may be provided by the thalamic reticular system.

A functional evaluation of the thalamus would be incomplete without some consideration of the corticothalamic fibers. It has been established that any thalamic nucleus which sends its efferents to the cerebral cortex, receives, in turn, fibers coming down from the same cortical area. There are at least two possible reasons for this: (1) the cortex exerts a kind of inhibitory influence on the thalamus, and (2) the cortex is a mechanism to make the thalamus more susceptible at certain times to afferent impulses of a particular sort, which in its turn will better influence this same cortical area. It has been suggested that this may be a mechanism for sensory attention. It is also obvious that the connection of the thalamus to the cortex and of the cortex to the thalamus forms a typical reverberating circuit, a mechanism which helps to maintain and amplify stimuli to ensure proper response.

CLINICAL CONSIDERATIONS

Testing

Little specific testing can be done. Because of the nature of the thalamus, with all the sensory and motor fibers passing through it, testing involves examination of the various sensory components over the body, including the special senses, observation of motor activity, and inquiry about the "feeling tone" of the patient.

Types of Pathologic Change

The position of the thalamus more or less protects it from trauma. However, like other portions of the nervous system, its function may be destroyed by tumor, inflammatory disease, or degenerative changes as a sequel to a primary vascular condition (thrombosis, embolism, or hemorrhage).

Specific Pathology

Clinically, there is described a symptom complex known as the *thalamic syndrome,* almost invariably due to thrombosis, in either the posterior cerebral artery or its thalamogeniculate branch. This syndrome is characterized by several findings. First, there is usually a contralateral hemiparesis, often associated with a transitory blockade, resulting from edema of the corticospinal tracts as they descend in the posterior limb of the internal capsule. Second, at the onset there is complete contralateral hemianesthesia and hemianalgesia. Gradually some of the superficial sensibility, such as that to pain, temperature, and gross touch, returns. However, the loss of position sense and stereognosis is usually permanent. There may or may not be sensory disturbances in the face, since the ventral posteromedial nucleus may be far enough medial to escape damage. The lateral geniculate body or its connecting fibers may also be involved in this lesion, which leads to a homonymous hemianopsia. A third and not uncommon finding is hyperaffectivity to superficial stimuli— the sensation of a pin, the movement of a brush, tickling, or touching being very unpleasant or even painful. In some instances there is severe contralateral intractable pain, either spontaneous or related to an ordinarily innocuous superficial cutaneous stimulus such as a movement or an emotional state. Concerning intractable pain, lesions placed in the medialis dorsalis or in its cortical target, the prefrontal cortex, have been effective in the treatment of this disorder. In these instances, the patients typically report that they feel pain but that it doesn't bother them. Another frequent occurrence is ataxia, characterized by the loss of deep sensibility and the appreciation of movement. In addition, certain involuntary movements may be encountered. The first of these is intention tremor, usually related to damage of the ventral lateral nucleus or its afferents (the dentatothalamic fibers from the cerebellum). When choreoathetoid movements are also seen, it is believed that the pallidothalamic fibers are involved in the lesion. Lastly, sometimes encountered in diseases of this region is the "thalamic hand," found on the contralateral side. In this condi-

tion, the fingers are flexed at the metacarpophalangeal joints, while the distal phalanges are extended. The wrist is flexed and pronated. However, in these cases, the muscle tone is actually reduced, and the position of the extremity usually can be altered quite easily. Many neurologists feel that "thalamic hand" is due not to damage in the thalamus but rather to lesions in adjacent, nonthalamic structures.

SUMMARY

I Functional classification
  A Nuclei of the thalamic reticular system, consisting of reticular nucleus proper plus nuclei of midline and the intralaminar nuclei. Primarily related to the rhinencephalon, hypothalamus, and corpus striatum.
  B Cortical relay nuclei (extrinsic), consisting of the nuclei in the ventral tier of the lateral division of the thalamus, including the metathalamus. These receive terminals of all great afferent systems, except the olfactory, and send projection fibers to the neocortex.
  C Association nuclei (intrinsic), consisting of the anterior nucleus, the medial nuclei, and the nuclei of the dorsal tier of the lateral division of the thalamus, including the pulvinar. These receive terminals from other parts of the brain and send efferents to association areas of the cortex.
II Connections
  A Nuclei of midline, taken as a nonspecific group
    1 Afferents from spinothalamics, trigeminothalamics, medial lemniscus, visceral systems, corpora quadrigemina, and other thalamic nuclei
    2 Efferents to hypothalamus, basal ganglia, and other parts of thalamus
    3 Function: cortical activation, hypothalamic stimulation, appreciation of pain (?)
  B Cortical relay nuclei

1 Sensory systems
  a Ventral posteromedial nucleus
    (1) Afferents from the trigeminothalamic tracts serving the GSA and GP systems of the head
    (2) Efferents to specific primary sensory cortex of the postcentral gyrus (area 1, 2, 3)
    (3) Function: relay of general somatic (and proprioceptive) impulses from head to areas 3, 1, 2 on postcentral gyrus
  b Ventral posterolateral nucleus
    (1) Afferents from the lateral and ventral spinothalamic tracts and the medial lemniscus serving the GSA and GP systems of the trunk and extremities; the solitariothalamic tract serving the SVA system for taste
    (2) Efferents to specific primary sensory cortex of the postcentral gyrus, areas 3, 1, 2 (somesthetic); area 43 (gustatory)
    (3) Function: relay of general somatic and proprioceptive impulses from the trunk and limbs to areas 3, 1, 2 on the postcentral gyrus; relay of special visceral impulses from the mouth and tongue to the gustatory cortex, area 43
  c Medial geniculate body
    (1) Afferents from the lateral lemniscus and brachium of the inferior colliculus, serving the SSA system for hearing
    (2) Efferents to specific primary sensory cortex of the superior temporal gyrus (area 41)
    (3) Function: relay of auditory (special somatic) impulses to cortical area 41 on superior temporal gyrus
  d Lateral geniculate body
    (1) Afferents from the optic tract (and perhaps brachium of superior colliculus) serving the SSA system for vision
    (2) Efferents to specific primary sensory cortex along the calcarine fissure and at the occipital pole (area 17)
    (3) Function: relay of optic (special somatic) impulses to cortical area 17 along calcarine fissure of occipital lobe
2 Motor systems
  a Ventral anterior nucleus
    (1) Afferents from globus pallidus via fasciculus lenticularis and ansa lenticularis; substantia nigra; midline and intralaminar thalamic nuclei
    (2) Efferents to frontal motor area
    (3) Function: relay of influence of globus pallidus on cortical area 6 and perhaps others for stabilization of voluntary and automatic action
  b Ventral lateral nucleus
    (1) Afferents from dentate nucleus of the cerebellum via the superior cerebellar peduncle (some direct, others relayed through the red nucleus); substantia nigra; globus pallidus via the thalamic fasciculus
    (2) Efferents to motor and premotor cortex (area 4, 6)
    (3) Function: relay of cerebellar influence directly to motor cortex, area 4; stabilization of voluntary action
C Association nuclei
  1 Anterior nucleus
    a Afferents from mammillary nucleus via mammillothalamic tract; presubiculum via the fornix; retrosplenial cortex via the internal capsule

b Efferents to gyrus cinguli and retrosplenial cortex (area 23)

c Function: relay of impulses from the hypothalamus to gyrus cinguli; part of the "emotion circuit"

2 Dorsomedial nucleus

  a Afferents from prefrontal cortex and anterior cingulate gyrus (area 24); amygdala; pyriform and prepyriform cortices; nucleus of the diagonal band; other thalamic nuclei such as midline, reticular nucleus and centrum medianum

  b Efferents to the hypothalamus, indirectly; corpus striatum; frontal lobe cortex (areas 8, 9, 11, 12, 19, 24, 25, 45 through 47)

  c Function: integration of somatic and visceral function; influences on hypothalamic activity

3 Centrum medianum

  a Afferents from spinothalamic tracts; brainstem reticular formation; globus pallidus

  b Efferents to caudate nucleus; putamen; dorsomedial, ventral anterior, and cortical relay nuclei

  c Function: relay in the reticular activating system; modulation of specific and association relay nuclei

4 Lateral dorsal and lateral posterior

  a Afferents from gyrus cinguli and parietal lobe; ventral posterior and other thalamic nuclei

  b Efferents to superior parietal cortex except postcentral gyrus (especially area 5, 7); gyrus cinguli

  c Function: relay from other thalamic nuclei to association areas of cortex

5 Pulvinar

  a Afferents from intralaminar nuclei; parietal and occipital cortices; superior colliculus (?)

  b Efferents to cortical association areas of parietal, temporal, and occipital lobes (area 18, 19, 39, 40)

  c Function: relay of acousticovisual integration to associative areas of cortex in parietal and occipital lobes

D Reticular thalamic nucleus

  1 Afferents: See nuclei of midline and medial group.

  2 Efferents to other thalamic nuclei, i.e., lateral dorsal; lateral posterior; medialis dorsalis; pulvinar; anterior. In this way it influences the cortex and the cortical inputs to the thalamic nuclei.

  3 Function: possible relay in the reticular activating system; modulation of thalamic and cortical neurons.

Divisions and Major Nuclear Groups of the Thalamus

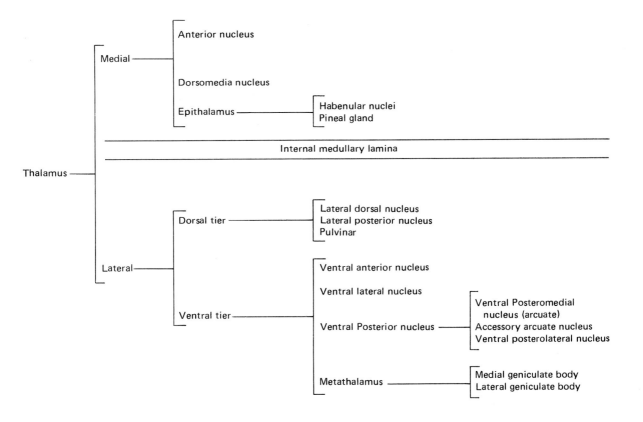

Minor Thalamic Nuclei and Functional Regrouping

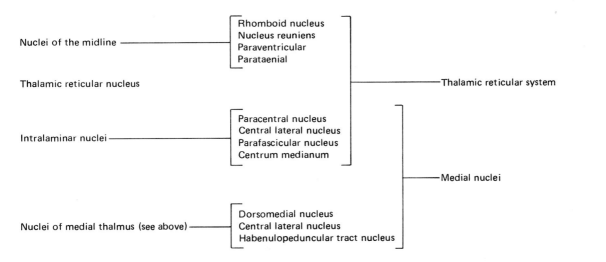

The Cerebrum

STRUCTURE

Gross

The position and relations of the principal sulci and gyri, together with the divisions into lobes, have already been discussed (Chap. 1).

Microscopic

Cortex (Gray Matter)

Cell Types (Fig. 24-1) *Pyramidal Cells* These are the most characteristic cells found in the cortex and are one of the two most numerous. As the name implies, they have the shape of pyramids, the apices of which are directed toward the brain surface as apical dendrites. Other, finer dendrites may sprout from any part of the surface of the cell. The latter usually extend horizontally with branching in the vicinity of the parent cell. The single axon, springing from the base of the cell, is directed internally toward the white matter. In some cases, the axons actually enter the white substance; in others, they terminate in deeper layers of the cortex. Each cell has a large, round, vesicular nucleus and contains distinct Nissl bodies. The size of the cells varies considerably. They are classified as small when their height is 10 to 12 μm; medium, from 20 to 30 μm; large, from 45 to 50 μm; and giant, when the height exceeds 100 μm. These last are the pyramidal cells of Betz.

Stellate Cells (Granule Cells) These are small polygonal or triangular cells with a dark nucleus and a small amount of cytoplasm. They measure 4 to 8 μm at their widest point. Each cell has numerous small dendrites coursing in all directions and a short axon which branches in the vicinity of the cell body. Some of the larger of these cells resemble the pyramidal cells although they are not so large.

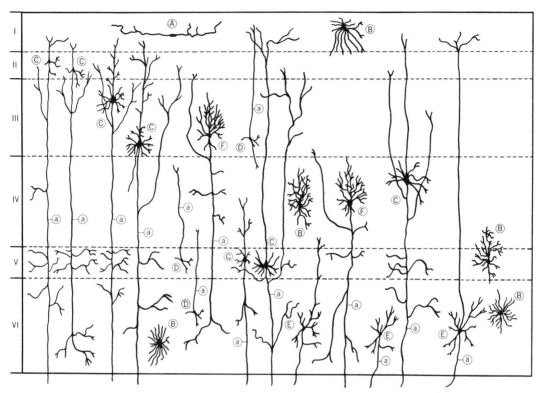

Figure 24-1 Nerve cells and neuroglia of the cerebral cortex. *A.* Horizontal cells of Cajal. *B.* Neuroglia. *C.* Pyramidal cells, medium and large. *D.* Cell of Martinotti. *E.* Fusiform cell (spindle cell). *F.* Stellate cell (granule cell). Cells are placed according to the layer of the cortex in which they are usually found. Axons are indicated by (a).

Their apical dendrites also extend toward the surface, while the single axon may enter the white matter.

Fusiform Cells (Spindle) In these, the long axis of the spindle-shaped cell is perpendicular to the surface. A dendrite is attached to each end of the cell. The deeper one ramifies within the same cortical layer containing the cell body; the superficial one, running toward the surface, often reaches the most external layer. The axon springs from the middle or lower part of the cell and runs into the white matter.

Horizontal Cells (of Cajal) These are small spindle- or pear-shaped cells with their axons extending horizontally, parallel to the surface, and remaining, throughout their length, within the cortical layer containing the cell body. The dendrites are short and also remain in this same layer.

Ascending Axon Cells (of Martinotti) These cells are small and polygonal in shape, with short dendrites arborizing in the vicinity of the cell body. Their axons are directed toward the surface, each giving off collaterals to all cortical layers through which they pass.

Intracortical Fibers (Fig. 24-2) These may be classified according to their direction as either *radial* or *tangential*. The former run in fine bundles at right angles to the brain surface and include the axons of the pyramidal, fusiform, large stellate, and Martinotti cells as well as ascending afferent and associa-

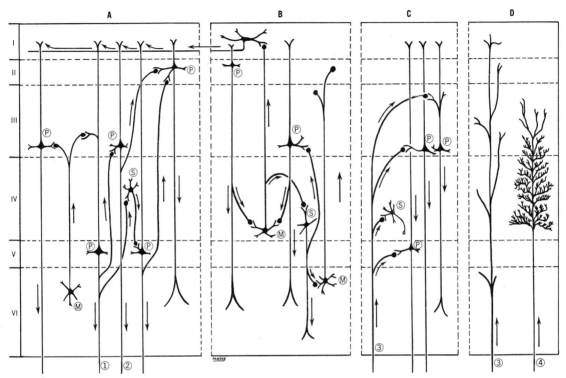

Figure 24-2 Diagram of cortical fibers. The black spheres represent points of synapse. *A.* Connections of efferent cortical neurons. *B.* Connections of intracortical neurons. *C.* Connections of afferent (thalamocortical) neurons. *D.* Mode of termination of afferent cortical fibers. P, pyramidal cell; M. Martinotti cell; S, spindle cell; (1) projection efferent; (2) association efferent; (3) specific afferent; (4) association afferent. *(Based on data by de No', in Peele, The Neuroanatomic Basis for Clinical Neurology, 3d ed., McGraw-Hill Book Company, New York, 1977.)*

tion fibers which terminate in the cortex. The tangential fibers run horizontally, parallel to the surface, and often are found in distinct bands. They are of several types: the terminal branches of afferent projection or association fibers, the axons of which usually reach a certain cortical depth and then bifurcate into horizontal branches; the axons of horizontal and granule cells; and the collaterals of the pyramidal and fusiform cells.

Layers (Fig. 24-3) The six basic cortical layers usually described are indicated below, starting with the most external.

Molecular or Plexiform (I) This layer contains few cells, those present being the small

stellate and horizontal types. There is a fairly dense layer of tangential fibers composed of axons of these cells, the dendrites of deeper-lying pyramidal and fusiform cells, and the axon terminals of Martinotti cells.

Outer Granular Layer (II) This layer is made up of many closely packed, small stellate cells. Their apical dendrites all enter the molecular layer. Their axons pass deep, many ending within the cortex, others entering the white substance. Terminating within this layer are some axons from the deeper Martinotti cells. Dendrites from fusiform cells and still deeper-lying pyramidal cells pass through this layer to reach the molecular layer.

Outer Pyramidal Layer (III) This is made

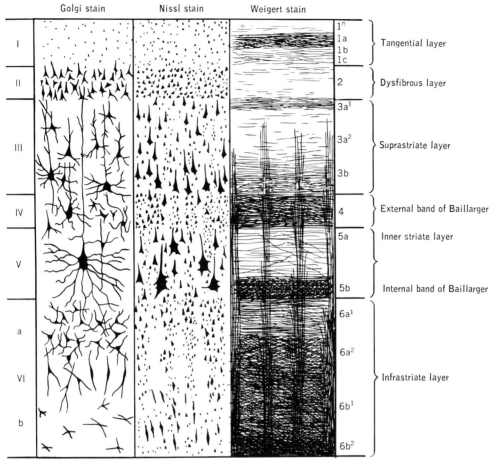

Figure 24-3 Diagram of the basic cytoarchitecture of the cerebral cortex. (I) molecular layer; (II) outer granular layer; (III) outer pyramidal layer; (IV) inner granular layer; (V) inner pyramidal layer; (VI) fusiform layer. Certain subdivisions are also indicated: (3a′) band of Bechterew; (4) external band of Baillarger; (5b) internal band of Baillarger. *(After Brodmann, in Peele, The Neuroanatomic Basis for Clinical Neurology, 3d ed. McGraw-Hill Book Company, New York, 1977.)*

up of pyramidal cells, among which are scattered stellate and Martinotti cells. Sometimes this layer is subdivided into an outer zone, in which lie medium pyramidal cells, and an inner zone, composed of large pyramidal cells. The apical dendrites of both sizes run superficially to reach the molecular layer. Most of the axons run internally, leave the cortex, and enter the white substance. Some, however, remain in the cortex. A band of horizontal fibers, the band of Kaes-Bechterew, may also be seen in the outer portion of this layer.

Inner Granular Layer (IV) The majority of cells are of the small stellate variety. They are numerous and closely packed. The axons of many are short and remain within this layer. Some of the larger cells have axons running to deeper cortical layers. The entire layer contains a large number of horizontal fibers, the so-called *external band of Baillarger*. These are mainly the terminal ramifications of the thalamocortical radiations, since this is the receiving layer for most impulses arising in subcortical levels.

Inner Pyramidal Layer (V) This layer is composed chiefly of medium and large pyramidal cells, among which are also scattered stellate and Martinotti cells. The apical dendrites of the large cells penetrate all the way to the outermost layer of the cortex, those of the small ones apparently ramifying mainly in layer IV. All axons of these cells enter the white substance. In the deeper part of this layer is a considerable band of horizontal fibers, the *internal band of Baillarger.*

Fusiform Layer (VI) The predominant cell type here is the fusiform cell, the long axis of which is perpendicular to the surface. Interspersed among the fusiform cells are cells of Martinotti, stellate cells, and small pyramidal cells. The dendrites of the larger fusiform cells reach the outer plexiform layer, but those of the smaller ones reach layer IV only, while a few may even remain in layer VI. The axons of the fusiform cells enter the white substance. The sixth layer is sometimes further subdivided into an outer portion, containing closely packed, large cells, and an inner portion, containing smaller, more loosely arranged cells.

Types of Cortex There is considerable variation in thickness and cellular development in the cortical layers. In addition, there are differences in the total thickness of the cortex, in the number of afferent and efferent fibers, and in the number, distinctness, and position of the horizontal bands (band of Kaes-Bechterew; internal and external bands of Baillarger). On the basis of these variations, several types of cortex have been described. For this classification, the reader is referred to the work of von Economo.

FIBERS OF THE CORTEX

Afferent Fibers (Corticopedal)

In any area of the cortex, two types of afferent fibers are recognized: specific and nonspecific.

Specific

These fibers arise in nuclei outside the hemispheres and belong chiefly to the somesthetic, optic, and auditory systems. They terminate in the primary sensory areas.[1]

Somesthetic (Chap. 7) These fibers arise in the ventral posteromedial and ventral posterolateral nuclei of the thalamus, relaying sensation of pain, temperature, and light touch upward from the trunk and head. This group of thalamocortical projections is found in the posterior part of the lenticulothalamic portion of the internal capsule (Figs. 1-13, 24-4). *General proprioception* from the same body areas probably follows this same course.

Optic (Chap. 8) All the optic radiations arise in the lateral geniculate nucleus. Those arising more dorsally in this nucleus, destined to terminate in that part of the occipital lobe above the calcarine fissure, travel in the retrolenticular part of the internal capsule. The remainder of the optic fibers, arising in the lateral and ventral portions of the lateral geniculate body, which terminate in the occipital lobe, caudal to the calcarine fissure, first pass horizontally in the sublenticular part of the posterior limb of the internal capsule before turning posteriorly toward the visual cortex.

Auditory (Chap. 8) These fibers arise in the medial geniculate body and, in their course to the superior temporal gyrus, pass horizontally in the sublenticular part of the internal capsule.

Vestibular and General Visceral (Chaps. 9, 12) Ascending fibers belonging to these systems (special proprioception and general visceral afferent, respectively) are known to exist. Even though vague, there is conscious recognition of position and balance and there is an awareness of the viscera. From what is known of the cortical areas which receive

[1] Most of them end in cortical layer IV.

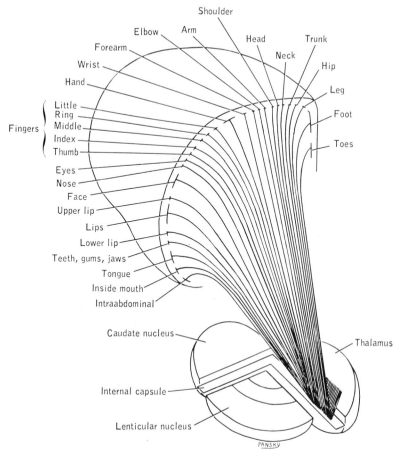

Figure 24-4 Sensory sequence in the postcentral cortex and internal capsule. *(Adapted from Penfield and Jasper, Epilepsy and the Functional Anatomy of the Human Brain, Little, Brown and Company, Boston, 1954.)*

these fibers, it seems certain that they must travel in the lenticulothalamic part of the internal capsule. *The special visceral afferent* fibers for taste probably follow this same course, and are distributed to the opercular part of the postcentral gyrus.

Nonspecific

These are the thalamocortical radiations arising in the elaborative or associational thalamic nuclei. They end in cortical[2] areas adjacent to the primary sensory cortex.

[2]They terminate chiefly in layer IV.

From the dorsomedial nucleus, definitely, and perhaps from some of the lateral nuclei, fibers destined for the frontal lobe ascend through the anterior limb of the internal capsule.

The ventral lateral thalamic nucleus sends its fibers into the rostral part of the lenticulothalamic part of the internal capsule for distribution to the frontal lobe (area 4).

Fibers associated with the ventral anterior nucleus are diffusely distributed to area 6 and other parts of the frontal lobe.

The lateral and posterior nuclei project mainly to the parietal and occipital lobes through the retrolenticular part of the internal capsule.

The anterior thalamic nucleus appears to project through the posterior limb of the internal capsule and terminate in the posterior cingulate gyrus, retrosplenial cortex, and presubiculum.

Association Fibers

These fibers arise in one cortical area to terminate in other cortical areas of the same side. They give off branches to several cortical layers.[3] Association fibers may be short, running from one gyrus to its next nearest neighbor (arcuate fibers), or they may be long, extending from the most remote portions of the hemisphere. These bundles have been indicated (Figs. 1-17, 1-18) and the specific ipsilateral cortical connections have already been discussed (Chap. 1).

Commissural Fibers (Figs. 1-6, 1-14, 1-16, 1-17, 1-20, 1-21)

These neurons arise in the cortex of one hemisphere, cross the midline, and are distributed to similar cortical areas of the opposite hemisphere. Their endings are comparable to those of the association fibers.

There are three major pathways by which the two halves of the cerebrum are united across the midline. Two of these, the anterior and hippocampal, interconnect parts of the archipallium. The third, the corpus callosum, by far the largest, unites the two neopallial hemispheres (Chap. 1).

Anterior Commissure

The position of this bundle has been noted elsewhere (Chap. 1; Fig. 25-10). It crosses through the lamina terminalis. After crossing, the fibers are found to be arranged in two groups: The rostral group is smaller and consists of fibers uniting the two olfactory bulbs. The caudal group interconnects the pyriform

and amygdaloid regions[4] and possibly the temporal neocortex of both sides.

Hippocampal Commissure

Its position and relations have been indicated in the sections on gross anatomy (Chap. 1) and the special visceral afferent (olfactory) system (Chap. 10). The fibers unite the two hippocampi and the dentate gyri. At first, these commissural fibers accompany those of the fornix, going through its fimbria and posterior pillars. As the latter converge beneath the splenium of the corpus callosum, the commissural fibers diverge medially, cross the midline and penetrate the fornix of the opposite side to reach the hippocampus and dentate gyrus.

Corpus Callosum

Its position and important relations have already been indicated in the gross (Chap. 1; Figs. 25-13 through 25-20). With the possible exception of a few fibers from the middle and inferior temporal gyri which may cross in the anterior commissure, all the other neocortical areas are connected through this commissure.

Those fibers from the prefrontal cortices traverse the most anterior part of the corpus and arch rostrally as soon as the crossing occurs. In the posterior part of the corpus, the fibers interconnecting the occipital lobes bend posteriorly immediately after crossing the midline. The fibers in the middle part run transversely, but after crossing, they sweep superiorly and inferiorly within the hemisphere to reach the appropriate regions of the opposite cortex. The superior fibers, in particular, intermingle with the fibers of the internal capsule in a region known as the *corona radiata*. It should be recalled that the occipital radiations of the corpus callosum form the roof and lateral wall of the posterior horn of

---

[3]The chief arborization is in layers II and III.

[4]Some investigators now feel that parts of the middle and inferior temporal gyri, which are neocortical, are also united by fibers in the posterior part of the anterior commissure.

the lateral ventricle. The term *tapetum* is often applied to the callosal fibers in this position.

Although the complete distribution of all the fibers in the human corpus callosum is not known, there is evidence for some very specific interconnections. For the sake of completeness, these are given in the footnote below.[5]

Intracortical Fibers (Fig. 24-2)

The cortex contains many neurons the axons of which remain entirely within the cortical layers. These are chiefly small cells with ascending. horizontal, or short axons. Even the pyramidal, fusiform, and large stellate cells with axons leaving the cortex contribute to the intracortical mechanism by giving collaterals to other cortical layers.[6] This arrangement makes possible a direct synaptic relation between the cells of layer VI and the great afferent systems terminating in layer IV. The pyramidal, fusiform, and large stellate cells in the deeper layers of the cortex send their

---

[5]The precentral gyrus is believed to receive fibers from areas 4, 6, 1, 5, and 7 of the other side (area 4 from the opposite 4, 5, and 6, while area 6 receives from the contralateral 6 only). Area 4s transmits to the opposite area 32, and area 6 sends callosal fibers to contralateral 6, 4, 1, 5, and 39. Areas 1, 5, and 39 of the parietal lobe receives fibers from the frontal lobe areas 4 and 6. The parietal cortex appears to transmit callosal fibers from areas 1 and 2 to areas 1, 2, 3, and 4; from area 5 to opposite 5, 3, 2, 1, and 4; from area 7 to the contralateral 7, 5, 2, and 1. The chief known interconnections between the occipital lobes run through the occipital radiations of the corpus callosum, uniting areas 18 and 19, the visual association areas, on either side. The chief commissural fibers of the temporal lobe, which pass by way of the corpus callosum, unite areas 41 and 42, the auditory receptive zone.

[6]The pyramidal cells found in layers II through IV have some dendrites in their respective layers of origin, but their apical dendrites extend outward to the molecular layer (I). As their axons descend, they give off some recurrent collaterals to their own layer, but mainly horizontal collaterals are distributed to layers V and VI. However, some of the pyramidal cells in layer V have short apical dendrites which reach only to layer IV, while the basal dendrites ramify in layer V. The fusiform cells in layer VI show a similar distribution: the superficial dendrites reach layers I through IV; the deep dendrite ramifies within layer VI.

axons out of the cortex but have the horizontal type of collateral that runs at right angles to the stem axon into any layer. In addition, recurrent collaterals ascend and ramify in more superficial layers.[7] In this way, any activating impulse reaching a neuron in the efferent layers can spread laterally through this layer or be returned to the superficial layers in the same territory, setting up short, reverberating circuits.

It is obvious that the stellate cells with short axons, the horizontal cells, and the cells with ascending axons (Martinotti) make possible almost limitless intracortical connections: locally, within the same layer; from layer to layer, vertically; and horizontally, from one region to another. Because of this arrangement, it has been suggested that a given vertical strip of cortex is a basic, physiologic unit—a complete intracortical arc, composed of afferent, associational, and efferent connections. Within each strip, afferent impulses are constantly being shifted from superficial to deeper layers and back again to the superficial, finally leaving the cortex through efferent channels. Since all the vertical chains are interconnected horizontally, a cortical excitation induced at a specific point, by the incidence of an afferent impulse, may spread to adjoining units.

Efferent Fibers (Corticofugal)

These are of three sorts: projection, to subcortical centers; association, to other parts of the same hemisphere; and commissural, to the cortex of the contralateral hemisphere.

Projection Fibers

These are axons of pyramidal cells lying mainly in layer V and VI (possibly in other layers). Axons of fusiform cells, especially in layer VI, also contribute to the mass of projection fibers. Among the fibers belonging to this group

---

[7]Most of these ramifications are in layers II and III.

are corticothalamic, corticospinal, corticobulbar, corticorubral, corticostriate, and corticopontine. The *corticothalamic fibers* will not be described specifically. In general, the same areas of the cortex receiving projection fibers from a particular thalamic nucleus will give rise to descending fibers, which follow the same course to terminate in that nucleus. *Corticospinal fibers* occupy an intermediate position in the rostral region of the lenticulothalamic part of the internal capsule. The fibers are arranged so that those destined for

the cervical region lie nearest to the genu while those for the foot are farther posterior (Figs. 1-13, 24-5). The *corticobulbar fibers* descend, from the motor areas of the cortex, in the genu and extreme rostral edge of the lenticulothalamic portion of the internal capsule (Fig. 1-13). *Corticorubral fibers,* arising in the frontal lobe, descend in the lenticulothalamic part of the internal capsule, close to the corticospinal group, but lie perhaps slightly farther laterally. *Corticostriate fibers* arise from wide areas of the cerebral cortex, the

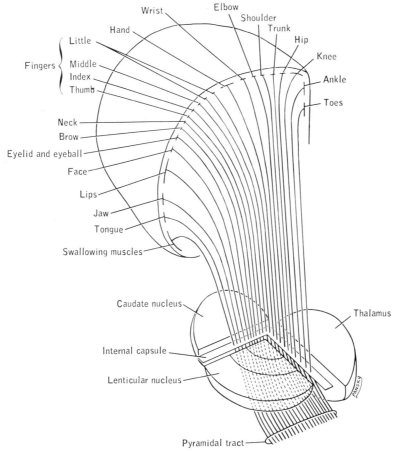

Figure 24-5 Motor sequence in the precentral cortex and internal capsule. *(Adapted from Penfield and Jasper, Epilepsy and the Functional Anatomy of the Human Brain, Little, Brown and Company, Boston, 1954.)*

frontal lobe supplying the largest number. A few fibers from the frontal and temporal cortices appear to innervate the substantia nigra as *corticonigral fibers*. It seems likely that they lie in the lenticulothalamic part of the capsule, accompanying corticospinal and corticorubral fibers. The corticopontine fibers are usually designated according to their lobe of origin. *Frontopontine* fibers arise in the frontal lobe and descend in the anterior limb of the internal capsule. *Temporopontine* and *occipitopontine* fibers apparently traverse the sublenticular portion of the internal capsule.

At the rostral border of the midbrain, the corticospinal, corticobulbar, and corticopontine fibers from the internal capsule converge into massive bundles called the *cerebral peduncles* (Figs. 1-8, 1-28). Although widely separated just below the diencephalon, the penduncles converge and lie close together at the rostral border of the pons. The fibers running through the basis pedunculi are somewhat segregated, depending on their origin and destination. For convenience, the peduncle can be divided into fifths. In the most medial fifth lie the frontopontine fibers, while the temporopontine fibers lie at the other extreme in the lateral fifth. Between these two, and occupying the intermediate three-fifths, are the corticospinal fibers. In the medial and extreme lateral portions of the latter zone are many corticobulbar fibers destined for cranial nerve nuclei lying farther caudally in the brainstem.

Association Fibers

These arise chiefly from the small or medium-sized pyramidal cells.[8] The fusiform cells of the deepest layer, VI, also contribute association fibers. The large, stellate cells of this same layer may give rise to the very short association fibers, the arcuates, running from one gyrus to the next, by curving beneath the intervening sulci.

Commissural Fibers

These are mainly from small and medium-sized pyramidal cells.[9]

CORTICAL AREAS

Over the past 50 years, several investigators have mapped the cortex according to variations in structural characteristics. Although the original maps indicated some 20 areas, more recent work has subdivided many of these into a grand total of 200 or more zones. Experimental and pathologic research has demonstrated specific functional differences among a large number of these zones. Since many of these functional areas will be frequently referred to, the cortical maps, based upon the investigation of Brodmann (Figs. 24-6, 24-7), have been included.

Primary Sensory Areas   (Fig. 24-8)

Somesthetic

This is the region of the postcentral gyrus, including its medial extension into the paracentral lobule. It receives fibers from both the ventral posteromedial and ventral posterolateral nuclei of the thalamus, which, in turn, act as relays for fibers of the spinothalamic tracts, the medial lemniscus, and the trigeminothalamic bundles. Thus, this cortical zone subserves all general somatic sensibility both superficial and deep. Each small part on the opposite side of the body has a point-for-point representation on the cortex. According to the cortical maps, the primary somesthetic region includes areas 3, 1, and 2. It should be emphasized that this sensory cortex is not primarily concerned with the recognition of sensory modalities, which is a thalamic function, but is

---

[8]Particularly from those cells in layers II and III.

[9]Mainly in layers III and V.

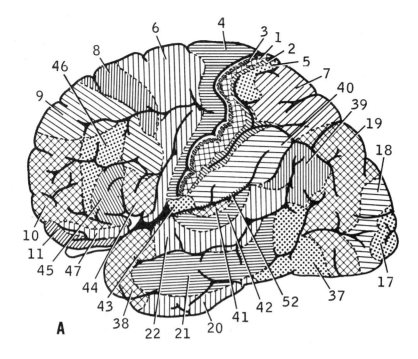

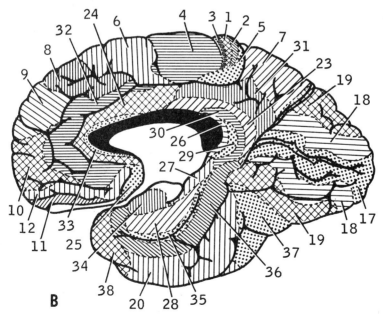

Figure 24-6 Cytoarchitectural maps of the human cerebral cortex. *A. Lateral surface. B. Medial surface. (Adapted from Brodmann in Peele, The Neuroanatomic Basis for Clinical Neurology, 3d ed., McGraw-Hill Book Company, New York 1977.)*

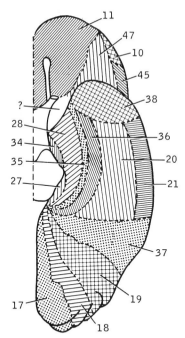

Figure 24-7 Cytoarchitecutral maps of the human cerebral cortex as seen on the basal surface. *(Adapted from Brodmann, in Peele, The Neuroanatomic Basis for Clinical Neurology, 3d ed., McGraw-Hill Book Company, New York, 1977.)*

important in discrimination, particularly in the recognition of spatial relations, the appreciation of similarities or differences between objects, and the recognition of stimuli of different intensities. Although some pain impulses are believed to terminate in the primary somesthetic area, a more likely region would be somatic area II (the area just caudal to the opercular part of the parietal cortex).

Visual

This zone, located chiefly on the medial side of the hemisphere, in the walls of the calcarine fissure, includes portions of the cuneus and the lingual gyrus. A variable amount (usually small) of visual cortex extends over onto the lateral aspect of the occipital lobe. This entire visual region is indicated on the maps as area 17. It receives its fibers from the lateral genic-

ulate nucleus via the retrolenticular part of the internal capsule, as the geniculocalcarine tract. The macular portion of the retina is represented on the caudal third of the area. The paracentral retina is represented in the middle portion, while the peripheral retina is represented on the most rostral portion of this area. The upper retina projects to the cuneate portion of area 17, while the lower retina projects to the part belonging to the lingual gyrus. In area 17, the separate impulses from the two retinae are blended into a single image. There are several other prime functions for this area. Among them are the perception of color; the localization of objects in space, related to the optic axis; the recognition of shape; and the discrimination of shape. The final recognition of objects seen, however, depends upon integration in other regions of the hemisphere.

Auditory

This region lies on the upper surface of the superior temporal gyrus, most of it facing the lateral (Sylvian) fissure. Here are one or two small gyri, known as the *transverse gyri* (of Heschl), which run transversely across the main gyrus. The more rostral of these is believed to be the primary auditory receptive area, designated on the map as area 41. Immediately surrounding the latter, except for its medial side, is a narrow strip of cortex numbered area 42, which, according to some investigators, should be included as a part of the primary receptive zone. Others consider area 42 to be associative in nature. The auditory receptive cortex receives from the medial geniculate body projection fibers which travel as auditory radiations or geniculotemporal fibers through the sub- and retrolenticular parts of the internal capsule. There is some evidence that specific parts of the geniculate body project to specific parts of the auditory cortex so that impulses resulting from high tones are relayed through the dorsal and ante-

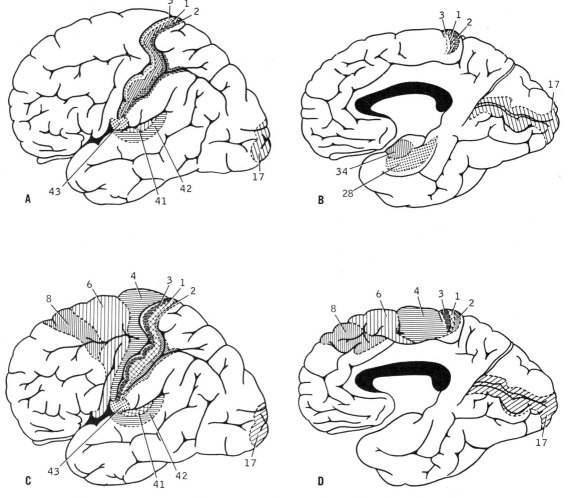

Figure 24-8 Primary sensory areas of the cortex. *A.* Lateral surface. *B.* Medial surface. *C.* Primary sensory areas of the cortex as related to the thalamic relay nuclei, lateral view. *D.* Primary sensory areas of the cortex as related to the thalamic nuclei, medial view. VPL, ventral posterolateral nucleus to areas 3, 2, 1; VPM, ventral posteromedial nucleus to areas 3, 2, 1; medial geniculate body to areas 41 (and 42); lateral geniculate body to area 17; accessory arcuate nucleus to area 43; ventral lateral nucleus to areas 4, 6, 8. *(Adapted from Brodmann, in Peele, The Neuroanatomic Basis for Clinical Neurology, 3d ed., McGraw-Hill Book Company, New York, 1977.)*

rior parts of the geniculate body to the posterior region of the cortical area, while impulses produced by lower tones, passing through the ventral and posterior parts of the geniculate body, reach the rostral part of the auditory cortex.

Olfactory

Since the cortical areas concerned with smell were completely discussed in connection with the special visceral afferent system (Chap. 10), they will only be reviewed here. The primary cortical receptive zones seem to be the prepyriform and periamygdaloid regions, the latter including the semilunar and ambient gyri. In other words, this is the lateral olfactory gyrus (prepyriform) as it lies along the rostro-lateral border of the anterior perforated substance and the gray mass that has covered the amygdaloid complex (periamygdaloid). Both of these represent the most rostral portions of the pyriform lobe.

Gustatory

As pointed out elsewhere (Chap. 10), there is a difference of opinion as to where this area lies. Among the suggested locations are the uncus, or a part of the neighboring temporal lobe; the anterior part of the insula; and the opercular part of the postcentral gyrus. The insular position seems to have the least support. The intimate relation between taste and smell gives some logic to the uncus, since it is so close to the primary olfactory cortex. More recent evidence indicates that the opercular region, at the foot of the postcentral gyrus, in the region adjacent to the insula, is the primary gustatory cortex, designated as area 43 on the map. In this position, the primary taste cortex lies close to the somatic representation of the tongue and to the motor centers controlling jaw and tongue movements.

Secondary Sensory Areas   (Fig. 24-9.)

Heretofore, this discussion has dealt with only a relatively small portion of the cortex and in the light of a specific function, i.e., as the center of sensory reception. Each area of the cortex receives specific sensory impulses from peripheral receptors. On reaching the cortex, these impulses produce sharply defined sensations (vision, touch, etc.). Sensations of position and movements are also accurate. However, although awareness of sensation has now been brought to its highest level, the perceptive level required for the recognition of an object has not yet been attained. This requires the association of the primary stimuli into progressively more complex sensory combinations, which, naturally, necessitates a spreading over a somewhat wider field. Thus, there are regions closely adjoining the primary receptive centers, sometimes called *parasensory areas* or *sensory psychic areas,* which serve to elaborate primary sensory impulses into unisensory perception.

Somesthetic Perception

The secondary cortex for this system has been described as lying around the inferior end of the central fissure and a part of the rostral area 40. In addition to its obvious connections to the associative cortex, the primary sensory cortex is strongly connected to other cortical zones.[10] The underlying reasons for the connections of the sensory areas with the motor cortex are obvious, for it is through such interrelations that sensory recognition may initiate voluntary action. However, it may not be clear why there are connections to the more posterior portions of the parietal lobe. This may be explained by the fact that although the primary, together with its adjacent secondary, cortex is capable of integrating, localizing, and comparing afferent impulses of the GSA and GP systems, in order to gain the concept of form, size, or texture, it is necessary to blend tactile, proprioceptive and pressure impulses. This requires further integration, which occurs in the posterior parietal lobe, probably with the assistance of the nonspecific thalamic nuclei and their projections.

Visual Perception

On the maps, the visual perceptive areas are indicated as 18 and 19. It has been shown that the primary visual cortex, area 17, has short

---

[10]Thus, area 1 receives fibers from areas 4, 6, 39, 40, 5, and 7, while at the same time it gives efferents to 4, 5, 7, and 39. Although afferents to area 2 have not been proved, efferents from area 2 appear to reach areas 31 and 32. Because of its location, the interconnections of area 3 have not been established.

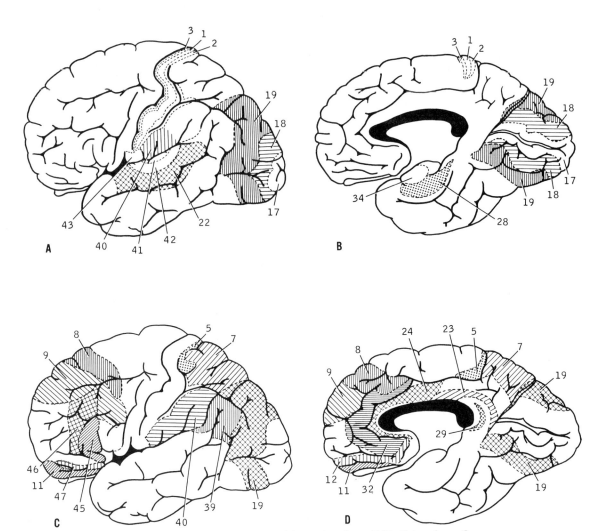

Figure 24-9 Secondary sensory areas of the cortex. *A.* Lateral surface. *B.* Medial surface. *C.* Cortex related to associative thalamic nuclei, lateral view. *D.* Cortex related to associative thalamic nuclei, medial view. Anterior nucleus to areas 23, 24, 32; dorsal medial nucleus to areas 8, 9, 11, 12, 19, 45, 46, 47; submedial nucleus to areas 8 and 46; lateral dorsal and lateral posterior nuclei to gyrus cinguli and areas 5, 7, 19, 39, 40; pulvinar to areas 18, 19, 39, 40. *(Adapted from Brodmann, in Peele, The Neuroanatomic Basis for Clinical Neurology, 3d ed., McGraw-Hill Book Company, New York, 1977.)*

association fibers leading into area 18 and, through the latter, to area 19. Both areas 18 and 19 send fibers back into 17, thus forming reverberating circuits.[11] Area 18 is of particu-

[11]In addition, areas 18 and 19 are interconnected to area 37 and appear to receive fibers from auditory areas 41, 42, and 22.

lar importance, at least as far as the purely visual impulses are concerned. The interpretation of the printed word is thought to be a function of this cortical zone as well as in the region of the left angular gyrus, including parts of the rostral portion of the occipital lobe and the posterior part of the parietal lobe.

The positive spatial localization of an object in relation to self also seems to be a function of this same general region. The visual cortical areas also give rise to various projection fibers, some going to the pons (corticopontine), some to the tectum of the mesencephalon (corticotectal), and still others to the tegmentum (corticotegmental), including the oculomotor complex and possibly the parabducens and abducens nuclei. It is through such circuits as these to the lower centers that the involuntary or automatic movements of the eyes are initiated. Fixation on objects, whether moving or stationary, can be maintained through these cortical connections. Included in this mechanism, too, are the accommodation reflexes involving the pupillary and ciliary muscles in the adjustment to near and far vision (Chaps. 8 and 13).

Auditory Perception

The larger part of the superior temporal gyrus surrounding areas 41 and 42 is definitely auditory associative cortex. It is given number 22 on the map and is, of course, strongly interconnected with both areas 41 and 42.[12] The primary auditory cortex perceives simple auditory impulses. However, the integrative mechanism of the associative cortex is required for the appreciation of intricate sounds. The blending of auditory impulses necessary for the interpretation of sounds, such as speech, occurs in this same general region, especially in the dominant hemisphere (the left, for right-handed individuals). There are few projection fibers to lower centers. Corticogeniculate (to the medial geniculate body) and corticotectal fibers (to the roof of the mesencephalon) have been described. Such projection fibers are probably important in the

[12]In addition to these connections, fibers leave the primary auditory cortex to reach area 8 (the eye field); areas 18 and 19; areas 6, 44, 43, and 1 of the frontal and parietal lobes, respectively; and areas 21 and 37, mainly in the inferior and posterior parts of the temporal lobe. The auditory associative cortex also has connections to areas 45 and 10.

conscious effort to "listen," which involves tension changes on the part of the tensor tympani and stapedius muscles. Also the turning of the head and eyes to follow the source of sound, during conscious and attentive states, uses such cortical circuits originating in areas 41 and 42. That the auditory cortex is in corticocortical relation to the motor speech area should not be surprising. The connections posteriorly to the visual association areas are logical, when one considers the relation between sight and sound.

Olfactory Perception

The chief associative olfactory region seems to be the entorhinal area, which includes most of the rostral portion of the parahippocampal gyrus and is designated on the map as area 28. This area shows many associative connections to the neocortex of the temporal lobe, for the most part through the perirhinal cortex, area 35 (in the rhinal fissure), and perhaps through the caudally located retrosubicular area 48, which lies behind area 35. These olfactory centers are important in associating smell with both visceral and somatic activities. The connections with the neocortical regions bring smell into a position to initiate voluntary action and bring it also into association with other afferent systems, relating it to the learning and memory complex.

Motor Areas (Figs. 24-10, 24-11)

Pyramidal

Impulses which initiate muscular activity may arise in the cortex. It was once thought that this system began on a relatively narrow strip of cortex on the precentral gyrus and that the tracts originating here consisted of the axons of the giant pyramidal cells (of Betz) in Brodmann's area 4.[13] It now is known that as few as 2 percent of the fibers have such origins. It is

[13]It should be noted that there are also fibers arising in area 4 which are said to belong to the extrapyramidal system.

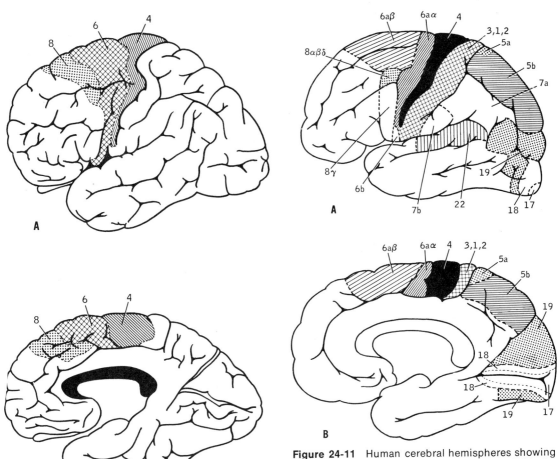

Figure 24-10 Motor areas of the cortex. *A.* Lateral surface. *B.* Medial surface. *(Adapted from Brodmann, in Peele, The Neuroanatomic Basis for Clinical Neurology, 3d ed., McGraw-Hill Book Company, New York, 1977.)*

Figure 24-11 Human cerebral hemispheres showing areas of excitable cortex. *A.* Lateral surface. *B.* Medial surface. *(Adapted from Foerster, in Peele, The Neuroanatomic Basis for Clinical Neurology, 3d ed., McGraw-Hill Book Company, New York, 1977).*

well established that widespread cortical regions are involved. Roughly, these include a part of the frontal lobe anterior to the central sulcus commonly referred to as *motor cortex* and part of the parietal lobe just posterior to this sulcus, a region once believed to be exclusively the receiving area for somatic afferent pathways. These two regions are known as *sensorimotor cortex* and include Brodmann's areas 8, 6, and 4 of the frontal

cortex and areas 3, 1, 2, and 5 (7?) of the parietal lobe.[14] Although most of the *sensorimotor cortex* lies on the lateral aspect of the hemispheres, this complex extends onto the medial aspect, facing the sagittal fissure.

Experimental evidence indicates that the entire body musculature has a specific point-for-point orientation within the motor area (Fig. 24-5). Of interest, however, is the great disparity in size or extent of the various

[14] Areas 3, 1, 2, 5, and possibly 7 give rise to pyramidal fibers in lower animals.

muscle areas within the motor cortex. By far the largest area is that representing the hand, and within this division the thumb occupies the largest portion. Although not so large as that of the hand, the foot area is larger than that for the thigh, while areas for the mouth (jaw, tongue, and lips) and face are proportionately larger than those for the arm, leg, or foot. Thus, it becomes apparent that cortical extent is not proportional to the total muscle mass but rather to the elaborateness and delicacy of movements of the parts. This is essential since greater skill is required for the use of the hand and in speaking than for other types of movement.

The numerous corticocortical interconnections of area 4 are given in the footnote below.[15]

Since further experimentation has been done using various sorts of electrical stimuli applied directly to the cortex, some of the cortical areas shown above have been further subdivided. These divisions are well demonstrated on the maps of Foerster (Fig. 24-11). The type of movement elicited by such stimulation varies. Some movements are characterized by contractions of small muscle groups or even of individual muscles. Such responses are referred to as *isolated,* or *discrete.* When the muscular contractions are more widespread, they are called *mass movements,* which are further classified as either *adversive,* involving turning of the head, eyes, or limbs to one side, or *synergic,* involving flexion or extension. When area 4 is stimulated, isolated movements occur. When areas 6aα, 3, 1, and 2 are excited, isolated movements also occur, provided area 4 is intact; when area 4 is

ablated, stimulation of these regions results in mass movements. If the stimulus is applied to areas 6aβ, 5a, 5b, and 22, head, eyes, and trunk rotate to the opposite side (adversion), together with synergic flexion or extension of the contralateral extremities. The presence or absence of area 4 does not affect this activity. Stimulation of areas 8α, 8β, and 19 results in turning of the head and eyes to the opposite side. The stimulus applied to 6aβ produces rhythmic coordinated movements by muscles controlled by cranial nerves V, VII, IX, X, and XII. The most common flexor synergy pattern is the flexion and abduction of the arm and flexion of the forearm, with the hand pronated and the fist either open or closed. Extension is less commonly seen but is also associated with the pronated hand. With this action in the upper extremity, there is a corresponding flexion pattern in the lower extremity which involves a flexion at the hip and knee with dorsal flexion of the foot and toes. When the extensor pattern occurs, all these movements are exactly opposite in the corresponding joint. As a result of these experiments and other considerations, it was concluded that only that part of the cortex through which isolated movements could be elicited should be considered pyramidal. All the other areas, stimulation of which produces mass movements, are to be considered extrapyramidal.

In concluding the study of this portion of the motor apparatus, the function of the pyramidal system may now be summarized: (1) It is the only initiator of isolated voluntary movements. (2) It facilitates the mechanisms fundamental to the maintenance of muscle tone. (3) It maintains the deep reflexes at low threshold.

Extrapyramidal (Fig. 24-12)

As defined in Chap. 20, all descending systems except the pyramidal are considered extrapyramidal. In the present context we will discuss only those impulses initiating muscular activity which arise in the cortex but

---

[15]It receives fibers from areas 6, 8, 9, and 10 of the frontal lobe, from areas 3, 1, 2, 5, and 7 (possibly 39 and 40) of the parietal lobe, and from areas 21 and 22 of the temporal lobe. From the opposite hemisphere, it receives fibers from areas 4, 6, 1, 5, and 7. Area 4 sends efferent association fibers to areas 1, 5, 6, 7, and 39. It should also be recalled that both areas 4 and 6 receive thalamocortical fibers from the anterior and ventral lateral nuclei of the thalamus.

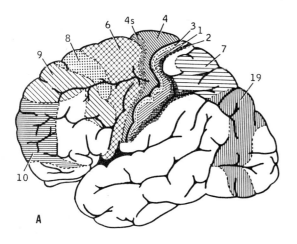

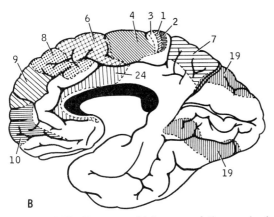

Figure 24-12 Extrapyramidal areas of the cerebral cortex. *A.* Lateral surface. *B.* Medial Surface.

descend in pathways parallel to, but not included in, the pyramidal route. In a sense, it is a backup system. More complex in structure than the very recently evolved pyramidal pathway, it owes its complexity to the evolution of the motor mechanism itself wherein each new rostrally developed structure maintains connections with the older, more caudal parts.

Any performance which requires precision or dexterity involves the activity of large numbers of muscles. Generally, those muscles

located toward the distal ends of the extremities may be considered the "prime movers" in the act. As they contract, regardless of what the action is, the muscles opposing them must either undergo complete inhibition or must at least be relaxed to a certain degree. However, if the finger muscles are to have a solid base against which to work, the wrist must be fixed. This requires the correct amount of tension exerted by the muscles acting on the wrist, in this case called the *synergists*. Other synergists necessarily must act upon the elbow and shoulder, fixing them or permitting the proper amount of movement. For some feats of skill, the muscles of the trunk, both lower extremities, and the opposite upper limb may be involved. This often calls for rapid changes in posture and alterations in the degree of contraction of all the muscles performing the act. The pyramidal system makes possible the selection for use of an individual muscle and coordinates its contraction with the activity of the opposing muscles (antagonists) and the synergists. An entire series of these prime movers can rapidly be thrown into action, and just as rapidly, the necessary alterations are made in antagonists and synergists. The extrapyramidal system makes possible the essential postural adjustments for the activity of the active limbs and maintains the proper tone, so important for easy muscular action.

There appear to be many areas of the cortex which contribute fibers to this parallel pathway. It is believed that areas 4, 4s, and 6 are especially involved, with lesser contributions from areas 8, 9, 19, 24, 3, 1, 2, and 7. From such divergent zones, cortical fibers descend to the basal ganglia and their associated nuclei[16] (Chap. 18).

Under our present definition of *extrapyra-*

[16]Areas 4s, 8, 9, 24, 2, and 19 discharge to the caudate nucleus; area 6 and part of 4 project to the putamen; areas 4 and 6 are also believed to be connected to the red nucleus; area 19 discharges to the putamen; and areas 4s, 8, 24, 2, and 19 have efferents leading to the medullary reticular nuclei, especially to the inhibitor center.

midal, corticofugal fibers which terminate in pontine nuclei, as a part of the corticoponto-cerebellar circuit, must be included in this system. The frontopontocerebellar fibers arise in areas 4, 6, and 10. They enter the anterior limb of the internal capsule, traverse the cerebral peduncle in its medial one-fifth, and terminate in the ipsilateral pontine nuclei. From the ipsilateral pontine nuclei, fibers cross the midline in the contralateral middle cerebellar peduncle to the cerebellum. Temporoponto-cerebellar fibers arise from the caudal parts of the middle and inferior temporal gyri, enter the posterior limb of the internal capsule through the sublenticular portion, and descend in the lateral one-fifth of the cerebral peduncle. On entering the pons, the disposition is the same as that of the frontopontine group.[17] It is the corticopontocerebellar circuit that brings the influence of the cerebellum to bear upon voluntary action.

It has been shown by some investigators that electrical stimulation of certain cortical areas, in the absence of large portions of the pyramidal system, will produce mass movements. However, stimulation of certain other portions has quite the opposite effect. Such zones have been referred to as *suppressor strips.* No attempt will be made here to detail these phenomena,[18] since the concept of a specific cortical suppressor area has been challenged in recent years.

In general one might summarize the extra-pyramidal system as one which activates large muscle groups and simultaneously suppresses the activity of others in the production of stereotyped movement patterns; suppresses mechanisms underlying tone; and elevates the

threshold of deep reflexes. Its function, however, is adapted to the performance of the pyramidal system, for it should be understood that any complex movement involving skill depends upon the proper cooperation between these two portions of the motor apparatus.

CORTICAL ASSOCIATION

Just as the afferent and efferent systems at the lowest levels of the CNS are related through association neurons, so they are related in the cerebrum. It seems likely that the vast majority of the estimated 14 billion cortical neurons is of the association type. The ever-increasing number of these neurons, keeping pace with the evolutionary changes, has increased the possibilities of reaction enormously by opening many more pathways between the sensory and motor areas.

In general, the sensory areas lie posterior to the central fissure. However, it should be obvious that the conscious recognition of many things is far more involved than the possibilities encompassed within the boundaries of unisensory perception. Thus, it is necessary for associations to be made linking the various parasensory areas into complex neural patterns by which their impulses are blended into multisensory perceptions. For example, tactile and kinesthetic stimuli are combined into perceptions of form, size, and texture. However, the final recognition of an object may require visual or auditory impressions as well. For these final intricate associations the logical location is the large cortical territory lying among the unisensory perceptive zones.[19]

Even as this receptive-preceptive mechanism is described, it is necessary to consider another large and perhaps most important

---

[17]There are also believed to be occipitopontocerebellar fibers arising in area 19 which accompany the temporopontine fibers and parietopontocerebellar fibers arising in the superior parietal lobule.

[18]The reader is referred to the work of Bucy as presented in Ranson and Clark, *The Anatomy of the Nervous System,* 10th ed., W. B. Saunders Company, Philadelphia, 1959.

[19]This includes all the cortex bounded superiorly and rostrally by areas 5 and 7 (the somesthetic psychic area), posteriorly by area 18 (the visual psychic zone), and caudally by area 22 (the auditory psychic area).

function of the cortex, *associative memory.* The ability to recall past sensory experiences and to correlate them with traces of former reactions is the basis of learning. The exact mechanism underlying memory is open to speculation. One theory is based upon the knowledge that external influences can modify the structure of various tissues; it is also known that such processes occur in other parts of the nervous system below the cortex. Thus, it is possible that neurons of the cortex represent the ultimate in modifiability. Hence, changes in the cortex, because of its tremendous capacity for modification by the receipt of external stimuli, alter the action of stimuli reaching the cortex at a later time and furnish the basis of conscious and unconscious memory. Others prefer to explain memory on more structural considerations, based upon cerebral architecture. Thus, memory depends upon the setting up by nerve impulses, resulting from externally applied stimuli, of perpetually reverberating circuits through neural side chains. Then, when some facilitating impulse, which may take any form, lowers the threshold of the side chain, a memory circuit is allowed to enter consciousness. Such circuits as these occur in the large associative areas of the cortex and quite probably within some of the other regions, the specific functions of which are not definitely established. That such might be the case has been demonstrated in human beings, in whom the stimulation of certain regions on the temporal lobe brought out a definite re-creation of past events, or the memory of persons long gone, or the recollection of words of a poem or song. Actually, these memories were complete, would persist as long as the stimulus was applied, and could be repeated if the same stimulus were applied to the same spot. Interestingly enough, the same emotional pattern which was associated with the original event accompanied the recollection, particularly if the emotion were fear. As a matter of fact, cortical stimulation some-

times elicited the emotion alone and not the complete memory picture.

It now should be clear that any object, regardless of its nature, is ultimately represented by a fabric of memories woven together, in a set pattern, from the fibers of the sensory systems which once had been activated by stimuli. Then, at a later time, an impulse, initiated by something seen, heard, or felt, "pulls upon the proper string" and releases the pattern from the intricate maze within the fabric. At this point, the object is recognized or remembered as having been seen or felt or heard before.

Although this discussion has mentioned somesthetic, visual, or auditory perceptions, it should be clear that there are many times when olfactory impulses are also woven into the pattern.

It now becomes necessary to consider another aspect of cortical function. Heretofore, the receptive-perceptive (appreciative) portions have been described. The extensive areas lying rostral to the central fissure must now be discussed.

Within the frontal lobe, primary motor centers have been demonstrated. Thus, in area 4, there are points the activity of which leads to the contraction of individual muscles or small groups of muscles required for special movements of the limbs or face. Superimposed on the primary motor centers are intricate association zones related to the action phase of cortical function. These are the premotor (paramotor) areas essential for complicated activities such as locomotion, mastication, swallowing, and, perhaps most complex of all, speaking.

The responses appropriate for meeting the overall situation in which the individual finds himself are initiated, it is true, in the cerebral cortex. They probably begin in specific primary sensory areas of the cortex, passing via internuncial neurons into association areas adjoining the primary centers, and finally, after traversing a myriad of association fibers involving widespread regions of the cortex, terminate about the cells in area 4. This area, then, far from being the center of origin for voluntary action, serves merely as a tool by which the whole cortex exerts its influence over lower motor neurons.[20] In this way, the manner of response to various combinations of stimuli is immeasurably influenced by sensory impressions built up and stored in association regions over an entire lifetime.

Many reactions which pass as voluntary are actually in the nature of cortical reflexes, completely automatic, and apparently occurring without thought as to how they arose. In other words, motor responses follow a regular pattern created by innumerable repetitions of a given stimulus. For example, the driver of a car stops suddenly when a traffic light changes or a pedestrian suddenly appears in the road ahead. In these instances, stimuli applied to the retina initiate impulses which traverse the optic pathway to its primary center in the calcarine cortex. From here, through association fibers, other impulses pass to adjoining areas of the occipital lobe (parasensory) and continue forward through portions of the parietal cortex to end, finally, among the neurons of the frontal motor areas. From here fibers descend to the lumbosacral cord, causing the lower limb to apply the brake. The same sort of reaction can be initiated through the auditory system. Thus, it should be obvious that much of motor activity is initially reflex in character and that its patterns are established through repeated sensory associations (practice) in the cortex.

It is possible that the hippocampal forma-

tion plays a role in motor functions, since stimulation appears to inhibit certain motor patterns while lesions in this region tend to facilitate their occurrence. Fibers from the subicular cortex innervate the posterior cingulate gyrus (area 23) either directly or indirectly via the anterior thalamic nucleus. It is likely that the posterior cingulate gyrus in turn makes synaptic connections with parts of the frontal cortex which relate to the organization of motor behavior. Therefore, it is reasonable to speculate that the hippocampal formation modulates motor activity via this indirect route.

Thus, it can be seen that the cortex influences action in several ways which set it apart from the purely reflex mechanism from which it evolved. Among these ways are the following: It allows for a delay in response to external influences, permits a variety of responses to external influences, and aids in the interpretation of responses.

Lying rostral to the premotor area is an extensive region known as the prefrontal cortex; it is especially highly developed in human beings. It is known that this region receives strong thalamic projections from the dorsomedial nucleus, which, likewise, is at its developmental peak in human beings. Here, the cortex is related to autonomic centers through its indirect pathway to the hypothalamus, involving the medialis dorsalis and midline thalamus, and, via the uncinate fasciculus and cingulum, to the rostral portions of the temporal lobe, to which has been ascribed the function of storage of specific memory. There are also direct and indirect connections with the parietal and occipital association areas. Thus, any or all of the complex and intricate memory patterns developed in other portions of the brain can be assembled here in even more complex pictures. It is these patterns which make possible the higher mental faculties, namely, abstract thinking, judgment, development of ethical standards, and the con-

---

[20]Recent electrophysiologic data has suggested that, immediately prior to a voluntary movement, neurons in both the cerebellum and basal ganglia discharge ahead of those situated in area 4. This observation suggests that the neural process underlying the initiation of movement involves neurons in the cerebellum and basal ganglia which serve to assist the programming of the pyramidal tract neurons.

trol of emotional behavior. Thus, on a purely speculative basis, one might consider the possibility that the prefrontal cortex is concerned not primarily with memory or general intelligence but with foresight. Inherent here is the ability not only to recognize a problem as a current incident but to relate it to the past and to anticipate its future possibilities. It is said that the prefrontal regions are responsible for giving direction to, and initiative for, mental processes. Here too lies the capacity to make personal adjustments. The influence of this part of the cortex on the control of emotional reactions is probably exerted, together with that of the limbic lobe, by way of the hypothalamus and the autonomic nervous system.

The authors do not wish to leave the impression that there are distinctly functional divisions of the cortex—one receptive-perceptive, another expressive, etc. What must be constantly kept in mind is that the divisions represent highly integrated phases of a constant, uninterrupted process and that every action which grows out of it depends upon the working together of all portions of the brain. A destruction of any part of this total mechanism will cause defects in function of the whole cortex, and the severity of the defects will be proportional to the extent of the destruction. However, because of this functional and anatomic division, the symptoms will be more a reflection of defects in *understanding,* when the lesions are in the caudal half of the hemisphere; they will reflect defects in *doing,* when the lesions lie in the rostral half of the cortex.

CONSCIOUSNESS

Without responsiveness to impressions made by the senses, without awareness of one's own thoughts and actions, none of what has been said of cortical function would have significance. From time to time, the site of consciousness has been variously placed. It is difficult to localize it sharply, but there seems little doubt that it is chiefly the result of cortical activity. However, the diencephalon seems to be a prime prerequisite if consciousness is to exist. Destruction at that level often leads to somnolence, while stimulation of the thalamic reticular formation or the reticular formation of the brainstem, transmitted through the thalamus, alters cortical electrical activity. Therefore, no discussion of consciousness would be complete without mention of the reticular activating system (RAS).[21] The parts of this system have already been enumerated (see Chaps. 19 and 23).

It has been shown that arousal to a waking state can be accomplished in the absence of the specific ascending sensory fiber tracts. In other words, there is an extralemniscal system which receives impulses from all sensory systems and carries them upward through a series of relays to influence widespread cortical areas in an alerting reaction. It extends the length of the CNS from spinal cord through the lower medulla, pons, midbrain, subthalamus, hypothalamus, and ventromedial thalamus. Direct stimulation of selected regions of the reticular formation in the brainstem produces changes in the EEG which are identical to those seen in awaking from sleep.

Functions ascribed to the reticular system are general arousal, the regulation of sleep-wakefulness cycles and general alerting of attentiveness. The relation of the RAS to consciousness is difficult to establish. Consciousness has been defined as an "awareness of environment and of self." It is perhaps alertness that characterizes the waking state, the level of consciousness which is affected overall by the RAS.

Some investigators have gone so far as to state that RAS integrates corticofugal impuls-

---

[21]Part of the discussion of the reticular activating systems has been adapted from the *Visceral Brain* and *Reticular Activating System* through the courtesy of the Schering Corporation.

es into memory patterns and thus is related to the learning process.

It has also been postulated that there are descending corticoreticular pathways from specific cortical areas. Through such pathways the degree of consciousness may be controlled by the cortex, thus setting up a selective mechanism for conscious responsiveness.

Because of its direct relation to the hypothalamus and also through the influence of the latter on the pituitary gland, the RAS is also implicated in emotions.

CLINICAL CONSIDERATIONS

Testing

Since the cortex represents the ultimate receptive center for the afferent systems and the highest level of control for the voluntary motor apparatus, and since the internal capsule is the great fiber pathway connecting the cortex with lower levels, tests already described for the integrity of each of the systems help in localizing lesions. However, because of the nature of cortical function, most of the tests for cerebral disease must necessarily be designed to show defects in association or integration. Thus, one must determine several facts about the receptive-appreciative areas. Recognition (*gnosis*) should be tested, the patient being asked to identify various common objects by handling them without actually seeing them. Tests for recognition of objects by sight should also be included. The ability to understand common words, both spoken and written, should be investigated. Simple memory tests and tests for normal associations should be given.

The expressive side of cortical function is also examined. Tasks requiring the use of the extremities, particularly the fingers and, to a lesser degree, the toes, should be given the patient. The examiner should listen to the patient's speech, giving attention not only to sound formation, but to the words and to the order in which they are spoken. The ability to write must also be ascertained. The presence or absence of muscle paralysis and its nature and location are determined. The examiner inquires about the possible occurrence of seizures which may involve voluntary muscles, and whether such involuntary contractions are seen over a wide area of the body. If this is the case, it is helpful to find out which sets of muscles contract first. Emotional reactions should be observed, and information concerning social behavior should be sought. It also is logical to investigate the state of activity of the autonomic nervous system.

Several other tools available to the physician are helpful in localizing cortical lesions. The first is the x-ray, particularly the ventriculogram and pneumoencephalogram (Chap. 3), through which the ventricular system and subarachnoid space are visualized. Angiography has also become an important aid in the diagnosis and localization of intracranial lesions. A radiopaque substance, such as Diodrast, is injected into the internal carotid artery just above its origin, outlining the cerebral arteries. Films taken a few seconds later show the venous system (venogram). A second diagnostic tool is the electroencephalogram (EEG), a valuable addition to the neurologist's armamentarium (Fig. 24-13). The basis of electroencephalography is that the human brain generates electrical potentials which can be measured, amplified, and recorded by placing electrodes on the scalp. Changes in amplitude and frequency of the brain waves occur in various disease processes. The EEG is especially valuable in the diagnosis of the convulsive disorders and in the localization of various intracranial lesions such as neoplasms, trauma, abscesses, or hematomas. It has likewise been shown that various conditions, actions, and substances such as: drowsiness, sleep, age, hypoxia, acapnia, hypoglycemia, opening and closing of the eye, and

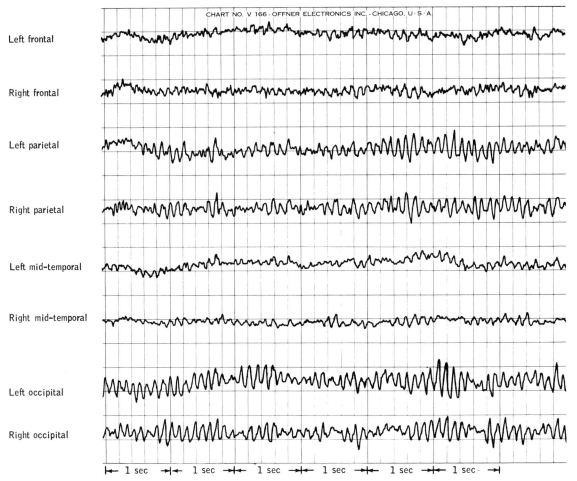

Left frontal

Right frontal

Left parietal

Right parietal

Left mid-temporal

Right mid-temporal

Left occipital

Right occipital

|← 1 sec →|← 1 sec →|← 1 sec →|← 1 sec →|← 1 sec →|← 1 sec →|

Figure 24-13 Normal electroencephalogram showing typical patterns from the frontal, parietal, temporal, and occipital areas of both hemispheres.

attention drugs may alter the brain wave pattern. The EEG has its limitations, however, and normal-appearing records may be obtained in spite of clinical evidence of severe organic brain disease.

Another means of detecting the presence of tumors in the cerebrum is the echogram (Fig. 24-14). In this procedure, a series of ultrasonic waves is beamed across the head, and the echo is recorded. A shift in the midline peak toward the left, for example, would indicate a lesion in the right hemisphere.

Manifestation of Cortical Lesions

Paralysis

In this section, this term is used to apply only to loss or impairment of motor function.

Flaccid This type of paralysis, together with muscular atrophy, has been discussed in another chapter (Chap. 13).

Spastic As the name implies, there is an increase in muscle tone, as well as an exag-

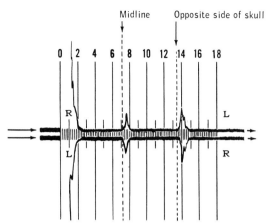

Figure 24-14 Normal echogram. A tumor would result in a shift in the midline peak toward one side or the other.

geration of deep tendon reflexes. It is probably more clinically sound, in dealing with this symptom as related to cortical lesions, to include it as a manifestation encompassed within the complex upper motor neuron syndrome. It seems pointless to become involved in an academic discussion of the effects of lesions purely within the pyramidal or extrapyramidal parts, for even under ideal experimental conditions, it is virtually impossible to separate the two. There is little doubt that most lesions seen in clinical practice involve both parts of the upper motor apparatus. In summary, damage to the pyramidal portion is responsible for lack of voluntary motor response. Hypertonia, hyperreflexia, and clonus are due to loss of the extrapyramidal part. The former is a sign of deficit of the initiating forces normally supplied by the pyramidal appartus; the latter is a sign of release from the normal control exerted over lower centers by the extrapyramidal connections.

Apraxia

In a general way, this is a condition in which there is loss of ability to perform purposeful movements although there is no paralysis. Three varieties have been described: ideational, motor, and ideomotor. *Ideational* apraxia is believed to be due to loss of the ideational concept of the act and is often manifested in diffuse brain disorders such as cerebral arteriosclerois. *Motor* apraxia is thought to represent a loss of the kinesthetic memory of an act. The purpose of the intended act is usually apparent but the execution remains defective. It is usually associated with lesions on or near the precentral gyrus. *Ideomotor* apraxia refers to a state in which the patient cannot perform an act correctly although old habitual motor acts can be accomplished spontaneously or regularly and often with perserveration. It is associated with lesions of the dominant cerebral hemisphere, frequently involving the supramarginal gyrus.

Agnosia

This term means the loss of ability to recognize the import of sensory stimuli. In an extensive cortical lesion, the individual may not recognize an object by using all the great afferent routes because of the damage to the major association regions. However it is not uncommon for only one of the sensory systems to be involved, in which case the term applied to this condition is referable to that particular aspect. For example, *astereognosis* is the inability to recognize the form and nature of objects by touch, while *visual agnosia* is the loss of ability to recognize that which is seen. When used in this specific sense, the lesion is usually located in the association area of that system.

Autotopagnosia (Body Image Agnosia)

This deals with the inability to localize or orient correctly the different parts of the body. Lesions in the posterior portion of the parietal lobe, especially in the dominant hemisphere, may lead to this condition.

Aphasia   (Fig. 24-15)

In general, this may be defined as the loss of power of expression by speech or writing, or it

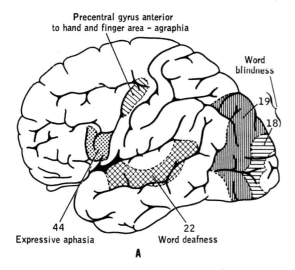

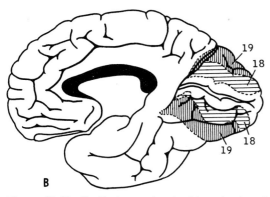

Figure 24-15 Cortical areas involved in aphasias. *A.* Lateral surface. *B.* Medial surface.

deafness. In such conditions, spoken words are not understood although hearing is normal. Lesions are usually in the superior or posterior part of the superior temporal gyrus of the dominant hemisphere. The other type of receptive aphasia is *alexia,* or *word blindness.* In these cases, the patient cannot interpret the written word although vision is normal. The lesion is usually in the transition area between the occipital and parietal lobes, in areas 18 and 19. The angular gyrus is often mentioned in this connection.

Expressive (Ataxic Aphasia) Within this class, two motor complexes are involved also. One, usually called simply *motor aphasia,* denotes the loss of ability to carry out the coordinated movements of lips, tongue, palate, and larynx necessary for speaking although there is no paralysis of any of the muscles in the parts mentioned. Lesions causing this condition are found in Broca's speech area 44, which includes the triangular and opercular portions of the inferior frontal gyrus. The term *agraphia* is usually applied to the instances in which the patient cannot write although there is no paralysis of the muscles of the fingers, forearm, or arm. The lesion is probably located in the frontal lobe, just rostral to the hand and finger areas of the precentral gyrus.

Two other aphasias are often mentioned: (1) *amnestic (nominal) aphasia,* the defective use of words, the inability to name objects, colors, etc., often coupled with a loss of memory for words; (2) *semantic aphasia,* the inability to understand words and phrases or the significance and relations of things in the environment. The latter, in particular, occurs with extensive lesions in the inferior parietal lobule and parts adjacent to it.

Anesthesia

This has been discussed under the GSA system. In cortical lesions, particularly involving areas 3, 1, and 2, there is loss of localization of

may be a loss of the powers of comprehending spoken or written words. Hence, there are two major types of aphasia, one concerned with the receptive mechanism, *receptive aphasia,* and the other with the expressive part of cortical function, *expressive aphasia.* Actually, most aphasias are not pure but are mixtures of both types (*mixed aphasia*).

Receptive In this class are usually included two subdivisions, although the term *sensory aphasia* is often used to cover both. In order to distinguish between the two, the term sensory aphasia will be used in the sense of *word*

peripheral stimuli although awareness, especially of pain, and, to a lesser degree, of temperature, is possible at the thalamic level.

Anopsia

In the sense used here it means a lack of vision due to a cortical lesion in area 17 of the occipital lobe.

Anosmia

In this defect, in which there is a loss of smell, a lesion occurs in such a way as to interrupt the olfactory tracts or to involve the semilunar or ambient gyri or the rostral end of the parahippocampal gyrus. In complete anosmia, both sides are affected.

Ageusia

This is inability to taste. A central lesion leading to such a deficit would undoubtedly lie in the parietal opercular region. To be complete, it would have to be bilateral.

Anesthesia, Anopsia, Spastic Paralysis

Because of the representation of nearly all the systems, a lesion in the posterior limb of the internal capsule can produce symptoms referable to the somesthetic senses, vision, hearing to a lesser degree, as well as the voluntary motor system. Nowhere else in the CNS could a relatively small lesion produce such widespread effects in so many systems. This is the outstanding characteristic of capsular lesions.

Types of Pathology

The same types of pathologic change noted elsewhere in the nervous system may be encountered here, viz., tumors, congenital malformations, inflammatory disease, degenerative or vascular disease, or trauma.

Symptoms of Specific Pathology

Jacksonian Epilepsy

The signs seen in this condition are motor. It usually begins with clonic convulsive movements of a small muscle or a small group of muscles. These movements, then, may spread, eventually involving most of the muscles on one side of the body. At least in the beginning, the lesion is irritative in nature. It may be due to a tumor, a scar, or gummas of various sorts located within or enroaching upon the precentral gyrus. However, this condition can also be found in the absence of apparent pathologic alterations. Since surgery may be of value in the treatment of this condition, it is important to notice which sets of muscles are first to contract during the seizure, because this usually indicates the focal point of the lesion. Since each of the muscle groups has a constant representation on the precentral gyrus, this observation helps the surgeon determine the site for exploration.

Hemiplegia

Spastic paralysis of muscles of the opposite side of the body, due to an upper motor neuron lesion, has been discussed elsewhere (Chap. 20). In connection with the cortex, a lesion would have to involve a major portion of the precentral gyrus to produce this condition.

Severe Anxiety States or Depression

Thus far, in considering clinical cases, the concern in this book has been primarily with organic disease which has led to a destruction of, or encroachment upon, nuclei or fiber pathways. In a book of this kind, it is not possible even to speculate upon the innumerable functional states which lie in the field of psychiatry or psychology. However, certain surgical procedures, sometimes lumped under the heading of prefrontal lobotomy, deserve some attention. They affect the connections between the frontal lobe and the thalamus. In general, they have been employed to deal with severe obsessive-compulsive and paranoid states, anxiety and aggressive states, schizophrenic psychoses, and intractable pain. In frontal leukotomy or lobotomy, the cortical-subcortical connections in the frontal lobe (usually about the level of the anterior part of the lateral ventricle) are severed. Topectomy refers to the bilateral removal of cortical areas, usually 9 and 10, of the brain. In cortical undercutting operations, performed relatively less frequently, the connections are interrupted at a level just below the cortex. In the operation of thalamotomy, a lesion is made in the dorsomedial nucleus of the thalamus by means of stereotaxic devices. Actually, bilateral leukotomy has received some success in the treatment of intractable pain (Chap. 22), while anxiety and states of depression are treated more successfully by Valium and lithium, respectively, which represent noninvasive (drug) forms of therapy.

SUMMARY

I Primary sensory—sensory receptive
  A Somesthetic: postcentral gyrus; termination for GSA system; areas 1, 2, and 3
  B Visual: on both sides of the calcarine fissure, on medial side of occipital lobe, and at the occipital pole, area 17
  C Auditory: upper part of the superior temporal gyrus, areas 41 and 42
  D Olfactory: the prepyriform and periamygdaloid cortex, areas 34 and anterior 28
  E Gustatory: most ventral end of postcentral gyrus, area 43
II Secondary sensory—sensory perceptive
  A Somesthetic: area 40 (and 43?)
  B Visual: areas 18 and 19
  C Auditory: area 22
  D Olfactory: posterior 28 (and 35?)
  E Gustatory: opercular part of parietal cortex
III Motor
  A Pyramidal: predominantly area 4, but also area 6; sends fibers by way of corticobulbar and corticospinal tracts to terminate about lower motor neurons
  B Extrapyramidal: much of cerebral cortex; sends fibers to caudate nucleus and putamen
    1 Areas 4 and 6 to red nucleus
    2 Arcas 4 and 6 to medullary, pontine, and midbrain reticular nuclei
    3 Corticothalamic fibers form reciprocal connections with specific relay and association thalamic nuclei
  C Corticopontine circuit
    1 Areas 4 and 6 (and 10?) to pontile nuclei as part of the frontopontine fibers in the corticopontocerebellar pathway
    2 Parts of the middle and inferior temporal gyri as a part of the temporopontine fibers in the corticopontocerebellar pathway
    3 Occipital and parietal fibers as part of the occipitopontine and parietopontine pathways
IV Fibers
  A Afferents
    1 Specific
      a Somesthetic: from the ventral posteromedial and ventral posterolateral nuclei of the thalamus through the posterior limb of the internal capsule to primary cortical areas on the postcentral gyrus (areas 1, 2, and 3); for pain, temperature, and touch from the head, neck, trunk, and extremities. A second somatic area II is also believed to receive pain impulses.
      b Proprioceptive: essentially the same as under Somesthetic.
      c Visual: from the lateral geniculate body of the thalamus via geniculocalcarine fibers in the sub- and retrolenticular parts of the internal capsule to the primary visual cortex (area 17).
      d Auditory: from the medial geniculate body of the thalamus via geniculotemporal fibers in the sublenticular part of the internal capsule to the primary auditory cortex (areas 41, and 42?).

f Gustatory: from the accessory arcuate nucleus of the thalamus through the posterior limb of the internal capsule to the most ventral end of the postcentral gyrus (area 43).

2 Nonspecific

  a From the dorsomedial nucleus, and perhaps some of the lateral nuclei, through the anterior limb of the internal capsule to the frontal lobe (areas 8, 9, 11, 12, 19, 45, 46, and 47)

  b From the anterior nucleus, through the anterior limb of the internal capsule to the gyrus cinguli (area 23) retrosplenial cortex, and presubiculum

  c From the lateral dorsal and lateral posterior nuclei, through the posterior limb of the internal capsule to all parietal cortex, except the postcentral gyrus

  d From midline and other nonspecific thalamic nuclei to wide regions of the cerebral cortex

B Association fibers: see Chap. 1

C Commissural fibers

  1 Anterior commissure

    a Rostral part: unites the olfactory bulbs

    b Caudal part: joins the pyriform and amygdaloid regions as well as the middle and inferior temporal gyri of the two hemispheres

  2 Hippocampal: unites the two hippocampi and dentate gyri

  3 Corpus callosum: unites all areas of the neocortex in the two hemispheres except the middle and inferior temporal gyri

D Efferents (descending projection)

  1 Corticothalamic: to same thalamic areas that contribute thalamocortical fibers (afferents) to the cortex

  2 Corticobulbar

  3 Corticospinal

  4 Corticostriate

  5 Corticorubral

  6 Corticonigral

  7 Corticotegmental

  8 Corticopontine

Atlas of Sections
of the Brain

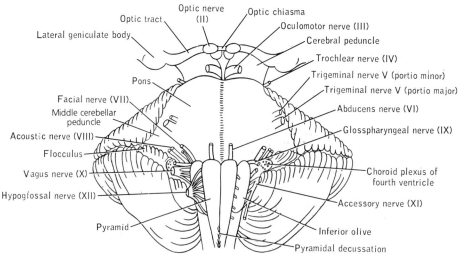

Reference Figure An outline of the basal aspect of the brainstem showing the superficial
structures cut in making the transverse sections illustrated in Figs. 25-1 through 25-12.

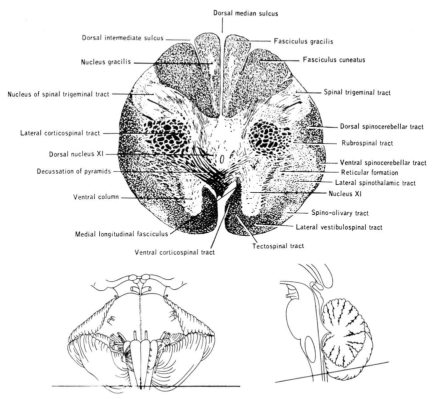

Figure 25-1 Section through the medulla near the middle of the pyramidal decussation.

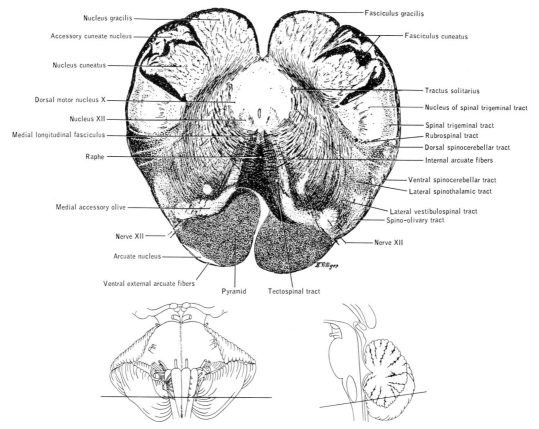

Nucleus gracilis

Accessory cuneate nucleus

Nucleus cuneatus

Dorsal motor nucleus X

Nucleus XII

Medial longitudinal fasciculus

Raphe

Medial accessory olive

Nerve XII

Arcuate nucleus

Ventral external arcuate fibers

Pyramid

Tectospinal tract

Fasciculus gracilis

Fasciculus cuneatus

Tractus solitarius

Nucleus of spinal trigeminal tract

Spinal trigeminal tract

Rubrospinal tract

Dorsal spinocerebellar tract

Internal arcuate fibers

Ventral spinocerebellar tract

Lateral spinothalamic tract

Lateral vestibulospinal tract

Spino-olivary tract

Nerve XII

Figure 25-2 Section through the medulla at the rostral end of the pyramidal decussation showing the internal arcuate fibers at the caudal level of the sensory decussation.

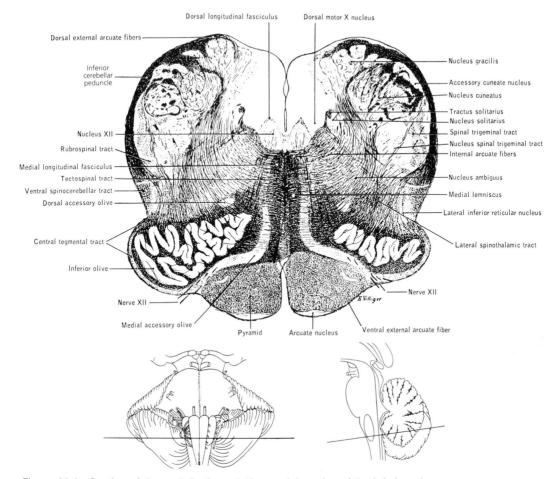

Figure 25-3 Section of the medulla through the caudal portion of the inferior olive.

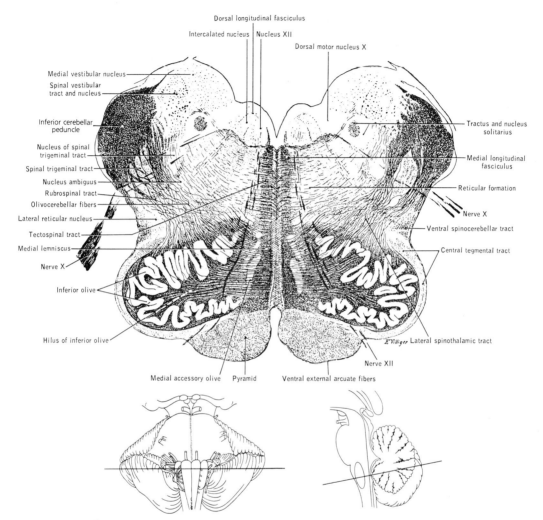

Figure 25-4   Section of the medulla at the level of the emerging fibers of the vagus nerve (X).

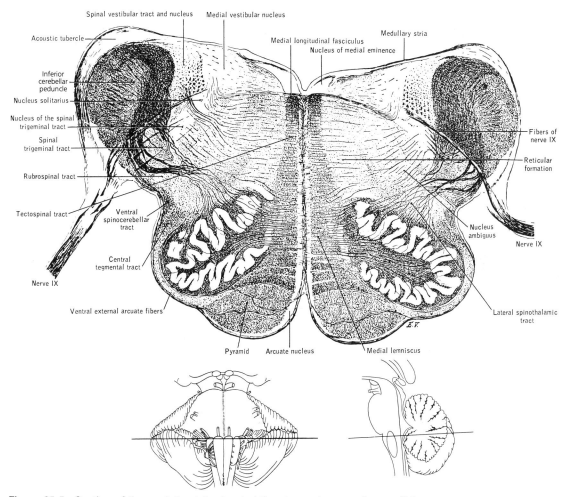

Figure 25-5 Section of the medulla at the level of the glossopharyngeal nerve (IX).

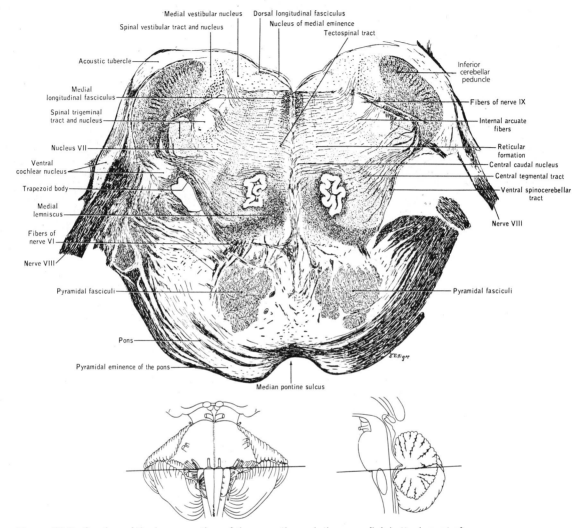

Figure 25-6 Section of the lower portion of the pons through the superficial attachment of the acoustic nerve (VIII).

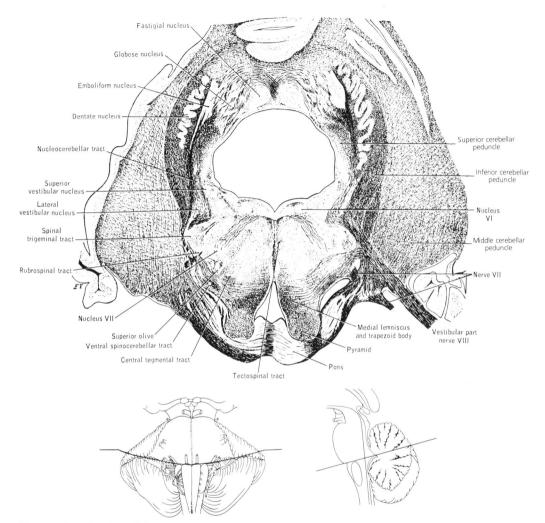

Fastigial nucleus

Globose nucleus

Emboliform nucleus

Dentate nucleus

Nucleocerebellar tract

Superior vestibular nucleus

Lateral vestibular nucleus

Spinal trigeminal tract

Rubrospinal tract

Nucleus VII

Superior olive

Ventral spinocerebellar tract

Central tegmental tract

Tectospinal tract

Superior cerebellar peduncle

Inferior cerebellar peduncle

Nucleus VI

Middle cerebellar peduncle

Nerve VII

Vestibular part nerve VIII

Medial lemniscus and trapezoid body

Pyramid

Pons

Figure 25-7 Section of the pons at the level of the superficial attachment of nerve VIII and the nucleus of the facial nerve (VII).

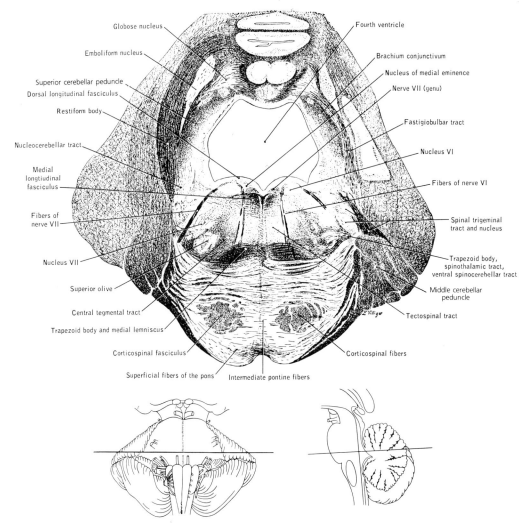

Figure 25-8 Section of the pons through the level of the internal genu of nerve VII and the nucleus of the abducens nerve (VI).

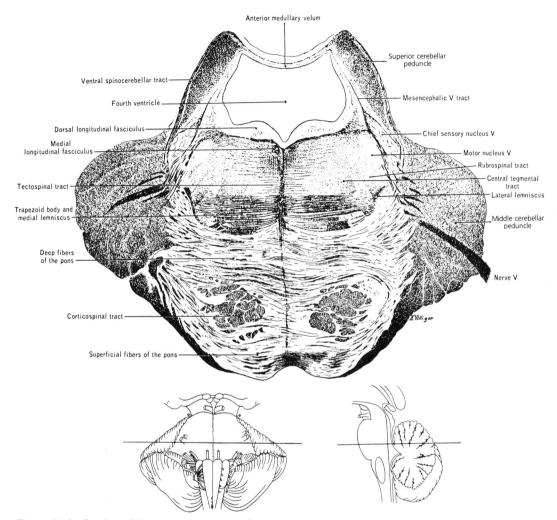

Figure 25-9 Section of the pons at the level of the superficial attachment of the trigeminal nerve (V) together with the chief sensory and motor nuclei of nerve V.

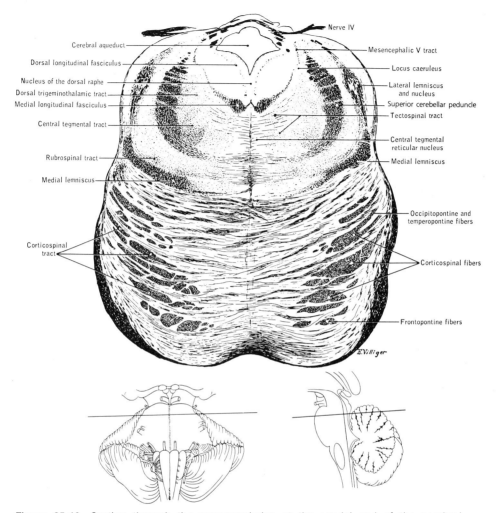

Figure 25-10 Section through the mesencephalon at the caudal end of the cerebral aqueduct, showing the emerging fibers of the trochlear nerve (IV).

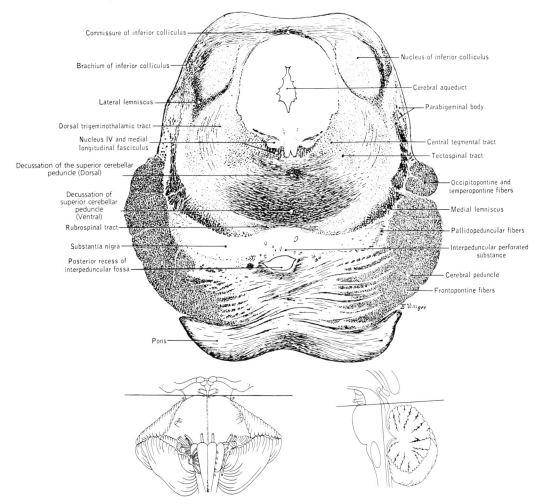

Commissure of inferior colliculus

Brachium of inferior colliculus

Lateral lemniscus

Dorsal trigeminothalamic tract

Nucleus IV and medial
longitudinal fasciculus

Decussation of the superior cerebellar
peduncle (Dorsal)

Decussation of
superior cerebellar
peduncle
(Ventral)

Rubrospinal tract

Substantia nigra

Posterior recess of
interpeduncular fossa

Pons

Nucleus of inferior colliculus

Cerebral aqueduct

Parabigeminal body

Central tegmental tract

Tectospinal tract

Occipitopontine and
temperopontine fibers

Medial lemniscus

Pallidopeduncular fibers

Interpeduncular perforated
substance

Cerebral peduncle

Frontopontine fibers

Figure 25-11 Section of the mesencephalon at the level of the inferior colliculus, showing the nucleus of nerve IV.

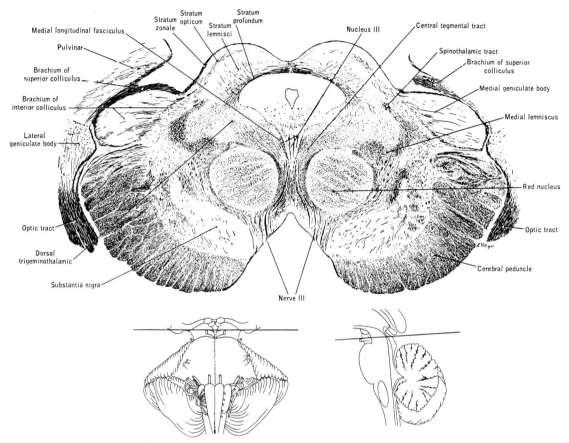

Figure 25-12 Section of the mesencephalon showing the superficial attachment of nerve III as well as the caudal projection of the thalamus.

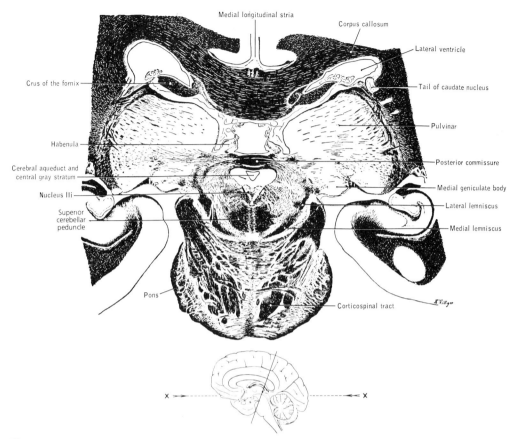

Medial longitudinal stria

Corpus callosum

Lateral ventricle

Crus of the fornix

Tail of caudate nucleus

Pulvinar

Habenula

Posterior commissure

Cerebral aqueduct and central gray stratum

Medial geniculate body

Nucleus IIi

Lateral lemniscus

Superior cerebellar peduncle

Medial lemniscus

Pons

Corticospinal tract

X

X

Figure 25-13 Oblique section of the brain showing the pons mesencephalon, and posterior commissure.

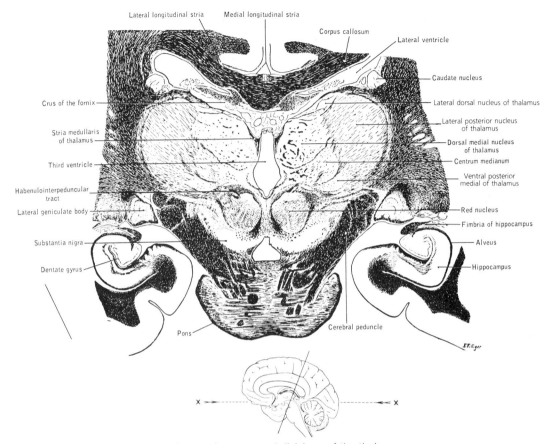

Figure 25-14 Section of the brain showing some subdivisions of the thalamus.

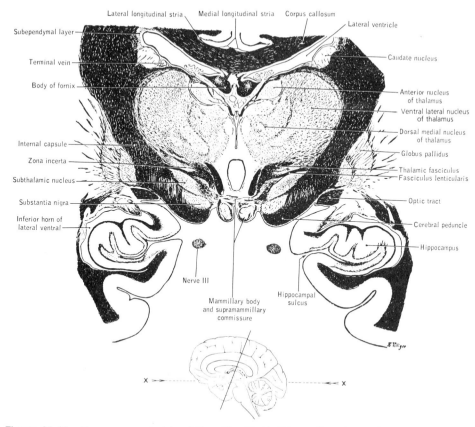

Figure 25-15 At a more rostral level than Fig. 25-14, this section shows the subthalamic nucleus, the zona incerta, and the caudal end of the anterior nucleus of the thalamus.

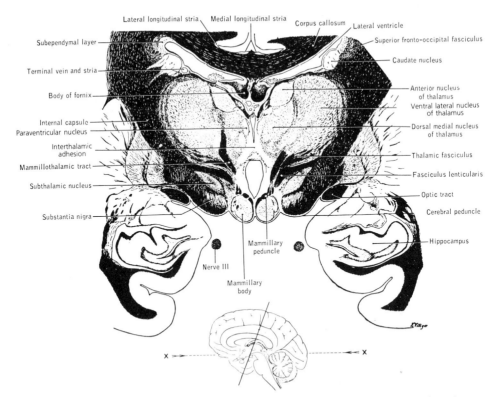

Figure 25-16 This section is still farther rostral than that in Fig. 25-15, cutting the hypothalamus at the level of the lower portion of the mammillary bodies and the thalamus at the level of its anterior nucleus.

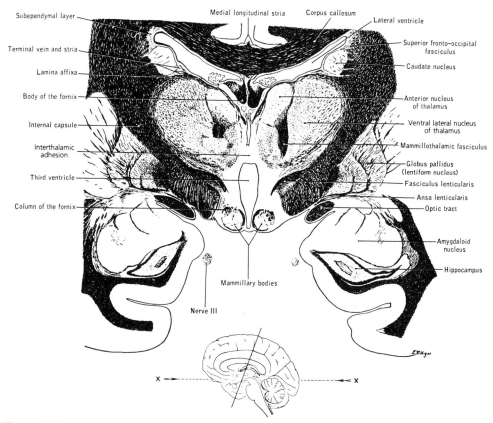

Subependymal layer

Medial longitudinal stria

Corpus callosum

Lateral ventricle

Terminal vein and stria

Superior fronto-occipital fasciculus

Lamina affixa

Caudate nucleus

Body of the fornix

Anterior nucleus of thalamus

Internal capsule

Ventral lateral nucleus of thalamus

Interthalamic adhesion

Mammillothalamic fasciculus

Globus pallidus (lentiform nucleus)

Third ventricle

Fasciculus lenticularis

Ansa lenticularis

Column of the fornix

Optic tract

Amygdaloid nucleus

Hippocampus

Mammillary bodies

Nerve III

X

X

Figure 25-17 This section passes through the rostral end of the mammillary bodies.

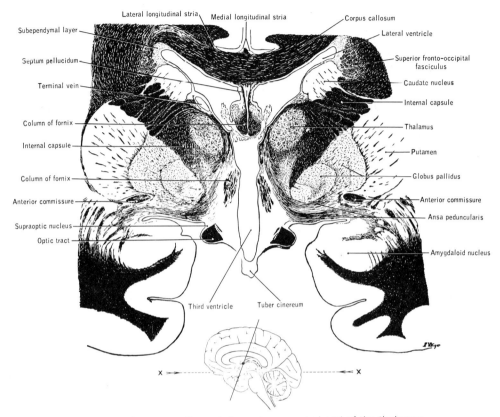

Figure 25-18 This section passes through the extreme rostral end of the thalamus.

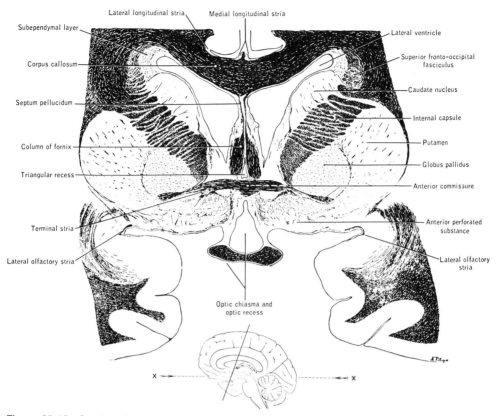

Figure 25-19 Section of the brain at the level of the optic chiasma and the central portion of the anterior commissure.

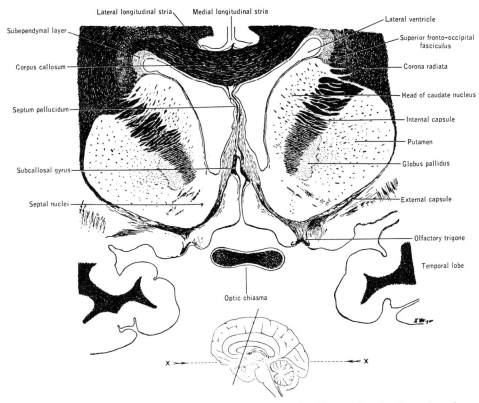

Figure 25-20 Section through the rostral portion of the optic chiasma showing the union of the head of the caudate nucleus with the lenticular nucleus.

Clinical Cases

Case 1

A woman, aged 38, came to her physician complaining that for the past several months she had noticed an increasing weakness, first in her right hand, and later in her left. When questioned, she revealed that actually, before she had noticed the onset of the weakness, she had injured her right hand, on two occasions, separated by several weeks. Once she had burned herself with the iron, the other time she had cut herself with a knife, but in neither case did she suffer pain. Even superficial examination indicated that the metacarpal bones of both hands stood out clearly, suggesting atrophy of the intrinsic muscles of the hand. When asked to abduct or adduct the fingers, adduct the thumb, or oppose the fifth digit, she could not do so. It was also discovered that there was a bilateral analgesia over

the medial side of the hand, extending about to midpalm, including the ring finger and part of the middle finger. The area of analgesia extended up the forearm, involving the medial half of the volar surface and nearly half of the dorsal side. Up the arm, on the anterior surface, the region involved was the medial two-thirds of that surface to near the level of the axilla. The entire medial aspect of the arm was also insensitive to pain. On the dorsal side, less than the medial half was affected. There was a slight drooping of the eyelids, particularly marked on the right, with pupillary constriction also noticeable on this side. The right eyeball appeared to be more deeply set in the orbit. There was some weakness in both flexion and extension of the wrist, with a slight amount of atrophy of the muscles of the forearm.

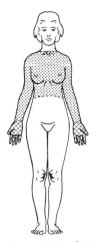
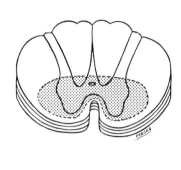

Figure 26-1 Case 1.

Diagnosis (Fig. 26-1) This is a case of *syringomyelia*. The pathologic process soon breaks the commissures carrying fibers from the dorsal gray columns to the lateral spinothalamic tracts. Since these fibers cross almost immediately, there is a bilateral loss of pain and temperature sense corresponding roughly to the area of the lesion but not extending elsewhere, since the spinothalamic tracts themselves are undamaged. As the cavity enlarges, it encroaches on the ventral gray columns and destroys them in an area corresponding to the maximum area of the lesion. This is the reason for the flaccid paralysis with atrophy. The dermatomes involved in the analgesia indicate that the pathologic change lies at levels C8 and T1. This is further confirmed by the atrophy of the intrinsic muscles of the hand. There is also indication, from the position of the spread of analgesia, that C7 is becoming involved. The appearance of ptosis, miosis, and enophthalmos, all signs of Horner's syndrome, indicates that the intermediolateral cell column, giving rise to white rami of the thoracolumbar autonomic nerves, has been destroyed, at least to the level of T1 on the right side. Apparently, the cavity had not pushed so far toward the left.

Case 2

A 21-year-old male construction worker complained that he was somewhat indisposed and inclined to feel chilly. He also complained of headache and of a slight stiffness of the neck. He became worse during the following day and his temperature rose to 100.2°F. He passed a restless night and the following morning showed signs of weakness in both upper extremities; the weakness was more marked on the right. During the day, there was a progressive increase in the paralysis, and toward night there seemed to be a speech defect. That evening a physician was called, and the following was disclosed: There was no impairment in function of cranial motor nerves III, IV, V, VI, VII, or XII; pupillary reflexes were normal; there was a noticeable speech defect; respiration was shallow; the patient yawned continuously and complained that the room was stuffy; except for a slight movement of the hand, the right upper extremity was completely paralyzed, the left was very weak; stiffness in the neck was marked, particularly in flexion and extension; there were no abnormalities in muscular action or reflexes in the lower extremities. The respiratory difficulty became rapidly worse, and com-

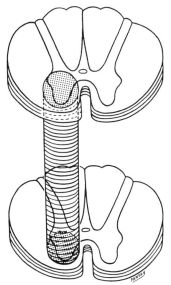

Figure 26-2 Case 2.

plete failure occurred early the following morning. There were no signs of circulatory involvement.

Diagnosis (Fig. 26-2) This is a case of *poliomyelitis* involving the cervical cord, extending at least as far caudally as C7. The disease process encompassed the origin of the phrenic nerve as well as the nerves to the accessory respiratory muscles. The motor cells in the ventral gray columns at all these levels were destroyed.

Case 3

A man, aged 45, reported to his physician that for the past 4 years he had experienced sharp pains in his lower extremities and, to a lesser extent, around the axilla. The episodes of pain became more frequent and sometimes were so severe that sedation was required. Within the past year he had begun to experience difficulty in walking. Examination revealed that his gait was unsteady and broad-based, with a flinging or flapping of legs and feet. A positive Romberg sign was present. Cranial nerves were intact except that pupils were unequal, irregular, and miotic and did not react to light but constricted on accommodation convergence (typical *Argyll Robertson pupil*). Motor power was intact. Deep tendon reflexes were absent in both lower extremities. Position and vibratory sensations were absent in both lower extremities and slightly impaired in the upper extremities.

Diagnosis (Fig. 26-3) All the symptoms indicate *tabes dorsalis*. The patient later admitted to exposure to syphilis but showed no external manifestations. The disease process first attacked the dorsal roots of the lower spinal nerves. This irritation was the cause of the pain experienced earlier. Later, most of the medial divisions of the dorsal roots were destroyed and, of course, the dorsal funiculus from these levels degenerated. It was the loss of these fibers that accounted for the loss of

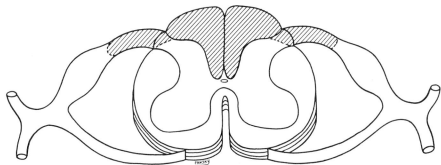

Figure 26-3 Case 3.

reflexes and the appearance of the Romberg sign. The Argyll Robertson pupil indicated that the disease had destroyed the pretectal zone, which is essential in the light reflex but is not involved in accommodation.

Case 4

A 40-year-old man gave the following history when admitted to the neurologic service: About a year previously, he had noted definite diminution of strength in his right hand. Three or four months later, shrinkage of the muscles in that hand became apparent. About the same time, the onset of the same symptoms was noted in the left hand. Approximately 1 year after his difficulties began, he found some trouble in walking, his legs seemed weak, and there was evidence of wasting of the musculature of the lower extremities, more noticeable on the right than on the left. Recently he had been forced to remain in bed as he could no longer get about. Examination revealed weakness of both upper extremities (especially distally in both hands) and of both lower extremities, which were also spastic. Atrophy and fasciculations of the musculature of both upper extremities and of the right lower extremity were present. Deep tendon reflexes were absent in both upper extremities and hyperactive in both lower extremities. Abdominal reflexes were absent bilaterally, and there were bilateral Babinski reflexes.

Diagnosis (Fig. 26-4) The loss of volitional movement, plus hyperreflexia, abnormal

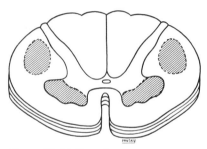

Figure 26-4 Case 4.

reflexes, and spasticity in certain areas, is indicative of an upper motor neuron lesion. The loss of deep reflexes, with atrophy and degeneration, is typical of a lower motor neuron defect. This condition, called *amyotrophic lateral sclerosis*, selectively attacks the motor system, causing degeneration not only of the corticospinal tracts but also of the ventral gray columns.

Case 5

A 40-year-old woman was first seen by the neurologic service 2 years after an accident concerning which she gave the following information: She had fallen backwards down the stairs; on recovering consciousness some 30 minutes later, she was completely paralyzed in all extremities and had no feeling in her arms; she was hospitalized, and surgery was suggested. This she refused and shortly thereafter she was sent home, with her condition essentially unchanged. Gradually, she regained use of her upper limbs, but her legs were still paralyzed. Within a few weeks, sensation returned to both upper extremities. Later, the paralysis began to disappear from the left lower limb but it still felt "numb." Examination revealed the following: All the cranial motor nerves responded normally; light and accommodation reflexes were normal; voluntary movement and reflexes were normal in both upper extremities; there was no voluntary movement in the right lower extremity, but the knee jerk was exaggerated and there was slight rigidity; position sense was also lost in this limb; sensations of pain and temperature were normal on the right side; the left lower extremity showed normal voluntary movement, reflexes, and position sense; the loss of pain and temperature sense was complete over the entire left lower limb, and this condition extended onto the trunk to just above the inguinal ligament. A later follow-up proved that the conditions enumerated above persisted for the remainder of her life.

Diagnosis The loss of voluntary movement in the right lower limb, with spasticity and hyperreflexia, indicates an upper motor neuron lesion on the right side, somewhere between the brachial and lumbosacral plexuses. This is further supported by loss of position sense on the same side caused by damage to the posterior funiculus of that side. The loss of pain and temperature sensation on the left also points to a lesion on the right side, since these modalities cross to the opposite lateral spinothalamic tract within two segments of the level of entry into the cord. This fact helps to localize the damaged area to about the tenth thoracic level, on the right. This is the typical *Brown-Séquard syndrome,* due to a degeneration caused by a permanent vascular insufficiency resulting from trauma to the vessels in this area.[1]

Case 6

A 65-year-old man suddenly lapsed into unconsciousness for several hours. When he regained consciousness, he found that he could neither speak nor move his right arm or leg. In a few days, he was able to talk, although he still was unable to use his tongue properly. A few weeks later he was examined by a physician who made the following observations: There was a definite spastic paralysis of the right upper and lower extremities, with increased reflexes, absent abdominal reflexes, and a positive Babinski reflex; no atrophy was noted; the protruded tongue deviated to the left and definite atrophy was observed on the left side of the tongue; no paralysis could be detected in larynx, pharynx, or palate, nor were the jaws, face, or eyes involved; pain and temperature reception were normal over the entire trunk and head; there was almost complete loss of position and vibratory sense

and of two-point discrimination over the right half of the body, exclusive of the face.

Diagnosis (Chap. 20) The left-sided deviation of the tongue with atrophy indicated a lesion involving the nucleus or fibers of the left hypoglossal nerve. Since both extremities on the right showed spastic paralysis, typical of an upper motor neuron lesion, the pyramidal tract on the left, above the decussation, was involved. In this case, *hemiplegia alternata hypoglossi,* there was also loss of position and vibratory sense and tactile discrimination on the right. Since the medial lemniscus lies just dorsal to the pyramid, it was included in the lesion and, since it is rostral to the sensory decussation, caused symptoms referred to the right side of the body.

Case 7

A 55-year-old woman complained of dizziness and fell down before help could reach her. She did not lose consciousness. It was noted at the time that both eyes turned toward the right and that her speech was not normal. However, she was not given a complete examination for over 2 months. At this time, it was found that both muscle tone and reflexes were normal and equal in all four extremities. However, there was some incoordination in both the right limbs. There was no detectable paralysis of the jaws, facial muscles, or tongue, but an inspection of the pharynx showed that the uvula was directed toward the left, indicating a right-sided paralysis of the palate. Laryngoscopic investigation also suggested paralysis of the right vocal cord. When standing with her feet together and eyes closed, the patient tended to fall to the right. There was loss of pain and temperature sensations on the right side of the face and left side of the entire trunk. Tactile sensation was normal.

Diagnosis (Fig. 26-5; Chap. 15) The initial dizziness and conjugate deviation to the right indicate a disturbance of an irritative nature

---

[1] In the case here presented, the symptoms resulted primarily from vascular damage to one side of the cord. This syndrome is more commonly encountered when the cord is actually cut by bone fragments, bullets, knives, etc.

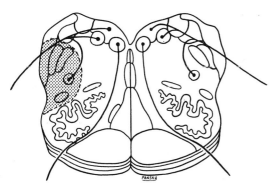

Figure 26-5 Case 7.

involving the right vestibular nuclei. With time, degeneration involving some of the right vestibular nerve fibers had occurred, as indicated by the patient's tendency to fall to the right. Loss of pain and temperature sensation on the left side of the body is conclusive proof of interruption of the lateral spinothalamic tract on the right; loss of these senses on the right side of the face suggests involvement of the spinal V tract and its nucleus. The paralysis of the palate and the vocal cord on the right indicates damage to the nucleus ambiguus and emerging vagal fibers on the right. The slight incoordination is suggestive of some involvement of the cerebellum or its connections. In this case, a *thrombus* had developed in the *posterior inferior cerebellar artery,* which led to the destruction of the dorsolateral portion of the right side of the medulla, including the inferior portion of the restiform body containing the dorsal spinocerebellar tract; the ventral spinocerebellar tract; the lateral spinothalamic tract; the spinal V tract and its nucleus; part of the nucleus ambiguus; emerging fibers of the vagus; and the caudal group of vestibular nuclei.

Case 8

A young boy, aged 8, was admitted to the neurologic service. There was no history of birth injury, nor had there been any unusual childhood diseases. His growth and develop-

ment were normal. About 6 months previously, however, he had screamed with severe pain in the back of his neck and had vomited, these events occurring when he first got out of bed in the morning. Similar attacks of pain and vomiting recurred at varying intervals. His mother also noted that he carried his head tilted to the right and walked unsteadily. Recently, these episodes had become very frequent and the boy was unable to play. Examination in the clinic indicated the following: On percussion, the head gave a "cracked-pot" sound; the head was tilted to the right; there was a slight stiffness of the neck; both optic disks were swollen but the visual fields were normal; there was a course nystagmus on looking to the left, with a quicker, finer nystagmus on looking to the right; the pupils were equal and the light reflexes were normal; the eye movements were normal; the remainder of the cranial nerves were intact; the extremities, especially on the left, were hypotonic; there was bilateral heel-to-knee and finger-to-nose ataxia and intention tremor, again more marked on the left; gait was wide-based and unsteady with a tendency to reel toward the left; there were no sensory or reflex changes and no pathologic reflexes.

Diagnosis The boy was taken to surgery, where it was found that a large growth had developed in the *left cerebellar hemisphere.* It was removed and was found to be an *astrocytoma* of the hemisphere. Convalescence was uneventful.

Case 9

A young girl, aged 14, was admitted to the hospital for diagnosis. According to the history, her birth had been normal and uncomplicated. There had been no unusual illness or accidents during her childhood and her growth and development were normal. About a year before this admission, the girl began to complain of "ringing or buzzing" in her right ear, a condition which had persisted since. Shortly thereafter, the school physician reported that the girl was "hard of hearing" in the right ear. As time went on, there was some dizziness and she complained of difficulty in seeing. Later, weakness and awkwardness of the right upper extremity appeared. Although her appetite was good, she was experiencing difficulty in swallowing solid foods. Examination revealed the following: Nystagmus to the left; the patient was unable to follow the examiner's finger when moved to her right, and when this was tried with both eyes open, she complained of double vision; at rest, the right eye tended to turn inward; the pupils were regular, equal, and responded normally to light, the visual fields were normal, but there was some papilledema bilaterally; the right side of her face, including the muscles above the eye, showed evidence of paralysis; an inspection of the pharynx showed that the uvula was directed toward the left and the right side of the palate drooped; tests revealed that there was almost 100 percent loss of hearing in the right ear, in both air-conducted and bone-conducted sound; the caloric tests in the right ear produced no eye responses, while on the left, nearly normal responses were induced; there were weakness and an intention tremor of the right upper extremity.

Diagnosis The findings given above suggested a tumor of the posterior fossa on the right side, and surgery was recommended. At operation, a tumor was found in the *right cerebellopontine angle*, involving the following cranial nerves: VI, VII, VIII, IX, and X. There was also some pressure on the inferior part of the cerebellum. This is a typical *acoustic neurinoma*.

Case 10

A woman, aged 44, told the examining physician that beginning several months before, she had experienced rather severe headaches in the frontal region, which she had attributed to sinusitis. Somewhat later, she noticed weakness in her right upper extremity and clumsiness of the fingers of that hand. There was also weakness of the right lower extremity. With the onset of the muscular weakness, speech difficulties appeared, and there was trouble with vision. Questions about the ocular disturbance showed it to be double vision (diplopia). Examination revealed that the left pupil was larger than the right, and that when seen from in front, the left eye turned outward and somewhat downward. There was no convergence in this eye, nor could light or accommodation reflexes be elicited. There was ptosis of the left lid. There was no voluntary action in either extremity on the right. The Achilles and patellar reflexes were both exaggerated, and a positive Babinski reflex was found, all on the right side. There was paralysis of the facial muscles below the eye on the right, and the tongue, when protruded, deviated to the right, but there was no sign of atrophy.

Diagnosis (Chap. 20) The eye signs, characterized by a dilated pupil, with no response to light or accommodation; ptosis of the lid; lack of convergence with a lateral downward deviation, owing to the unopposed action of the lateral rectus and superior oblique muscles, all point to the destruction of the third nerve or nucleus, including the autonomic component for pupillary constriction. The spastic paralysis, with hyperreflexia on the opposite side of the body, suggests an upper motor neuron lesion including the corticobulbar fibers to the muscles of the face and tongue. The only place where the third nerve on one side lies close to the upper motor neurons for the other side is in the midbrain, where the emerging fibers of the oculomotor nerve are next to the medial side of the basis pedunculi. Thus, a tumor here would account for all the signs, including the headache. This is a case of *hemiplegia alternata oculomotoria,* or *Weber's syndrome.*

Case 11

A young girl, aged 13, was admitted to the medical clinic for observation. The family history was negative. Her birth was normal and uncomplicated. There was no record of serious illness during infancy or early childhood. During her first years of life, growth and development had been normal. Recently, there had been little growth, and she remained slender and underweight. Her mental development was normal. When she was about 8 years old, she had developed a persistent polyuria, accompanied by polydipsia. At that time she was given Pitressin, with striking results. Examination revealed that she was undersized, underweight, and undernourished with no evidence of pigmentation or cutaneous tumors; her genitalia were infantile; her optic nerve heads showed slight pallor; her vision was normal, but there was complete bitemporal hemianopsia; her blood sugar level was low.

Diagnosis　The findings suggested a tumor in or near the anterior hypothalamus, and surgery was recommended. At operation, a *growth* was discovered which had disrupted the *optic chiasma* and encroached upon the hypothalamus in the region of the *infundibulum* and *tuber cinereum.*

Case 12

A man, aged 62, fainted while attending a hotly contested ball game. He was unconscious for nearly 48 hours. When he regained consciousness, he was paralyzed in both extremities on the right. Seven weeks later he was given a thorough examination. At this time, there was hyperreflexia and spasticity in both the right upper and lower extremities. When protruded, the tongue deviated toward the right, but there was no atrophy. Paralysis of the facial muscles, on the right side, below

the eye, was noted. There was impairment of all modalities of sensation over the entire right side of the body and face, but the various sensory modalities were affected to different degrees. The sensations of position, vibration, and two-point touch were lost completely. There was some loss of temperature sense, but pain appeared little affected in the same area. The pupils responded normally to light, but it was found that the patient suffered from right homonymous hemianopsia.

Diagnosis　The spastic paralysis on the right indicated an upper motor neuron lesion. Since there was paralysis of the tongue, without atrophy, and since only the facial muscles below the eye were involved, proof of destruction of both corticospinal and corticobulbar fibers was complete. The sensory disturbances were of major importance. Position and vibratory sense and tactile discrimination require cortical connections. There was impairment of thermal sense, but pain was recognized. This indicated that the lesion was high, above thalamic levels, since the thalamus may be the conscious center for pain. The visual defect is characteristic of lesions in either the optic or geniculocalcarine tracts. A single lesion which involves the upper motor neurons and, at the same time, encompasses the general and special somatic systems, together with proprioception, would have to lie in the *posterior limb of the internal capsule.* The manner of onset of the symptoms suggested a *hemorrhage* in that region of the capsule (Fig. 26-6).

Case 13

A young man, aged 20, was referred to a neurologist with the following history: At the age of 18 he had suffered an attack of subacute bacterial endocarditis, which had been treated with heavy doses of penicillin over a period of 6 weeks. One day, about 8 months previous to the present visit, he had suddenly fainted and

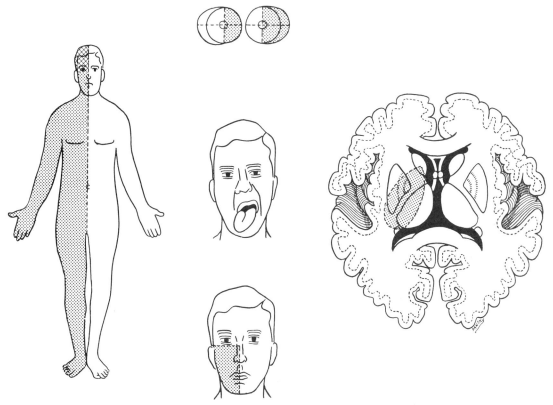

Figure 26-6   Case 12.

had been unconscious for several hours. Although consciousness returned, his mind was "hazy" for 5 or 6 days and he was not able to speak. Examination revealed spasticity in the right upper extremity, with loss of voluntary movement but no atrophy. There were no disturbances in the right lower or in either of the left extremities. The protruded tongue deviated to the right, but there was no atrophy. The facial muscles, below the eye, on the right were paralyzed. There were no visual defects nor somesthetic disturbances.

Diagnosis   Spastic paralysis in the right upper extremity means upper motor neuron involvement. The paralysis of the facial muscles below the eye also indicates upper motor rather than lower motor neuron lesions. The

paralysis of the tongue, without atrophy, also supports this view. Because of the inclusion of the cranial motor defects, the lesion could lie in the cortex, subcortical white matter, internal capsule, or basis pedunculi. However, in the latter two locations, a lesion would almost certainly cause a paralysis in the lower extremity as well. A capsular lesion would also show severe sensory disturbances. By elimination, the cortex remains. This location is confirmed by the presence of motor aphasia, the loss of speech resulting from an involvement of Broca's area in the frontal opercular area of the dominant hemisphere. Since this is a right-handed individual, the lesion is on the *left side*, including *the lower part of the precentral gyrus* and the *frontal operculum*. This is doubtless the result of an *embolism* in the

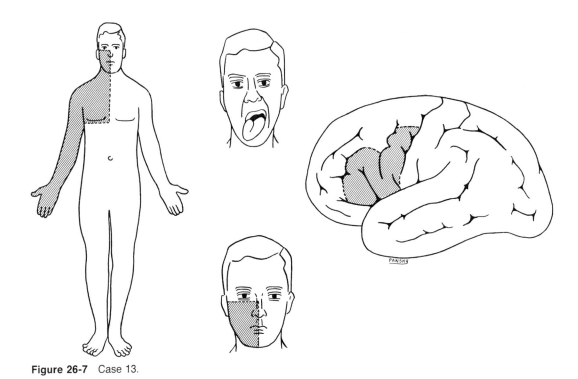

Figure 26-7 Case 13.

branch of the *middle cerebral artery* supplying this region. The medical history contributes the evidence of endocarditis, in which emboli are not uncommon (Fig. 26-7).

Case 14

A man, aged 52, came to the clinic complaining of pains and weakness in his legs. Over the past few weeks the pain had become more severe; his legs were so sensitive that even the touch of a bed sheet was almost intolerable, and it was now very difficult for him to walk. His family history was negative, and there was no report of any recent severe illness or injury. He did say, however, that he had been a consistently heavy drinker for years and in the past few months his alcohol consumption had increased. Examination revealed that the patient was undernourished, to the point of emaciation. There was a bilateral loss of the deep reflexes at both knee and ankle. The muscles were atonic and flaccid, and there was

indication of some atrophy. Although the patient could walk, he showed the peculiar "stepping gait" (need to raise feet to keep from tripping) characteristic of bilateral foot drop. Sensory impairment of the "stocking" variety was observed on both extremities. In this case, all forms of sensation, especially touch and position sense, were greatly impaired, but there was hypersensitivity to a pinprick. The skin of the lower extremities was somewhat reddened, and there was edema. Except for a tremor in the upper limbs, no other signs were observed. The cranial nerves were normal.

Diagnosis The severe and progressive symptoms, with flaccidity and atrophy, are characteristic of lower motor neuron lesions. The coloration of the skin and edema are suggestive of involvement of the autonomic fibers to the blood vessels of the lower extremity. The gradual loss of sensations of touch with an early hypersensitivity to pain are often indicative of an inflammatory process with progressive degeneration of peripheral nerves. These signs, together with the history of heavy drinking, lead to the diagnosis of a *peripheral neuritis (neuropathy)* due to alcohol (alcohol polyneuropathy).

Case 15

A man, aged 64, was admitted to the clinic. He said that perhaps 2 years previously he had been bothered by a shaking in his left arm, beginning in the fingers. Since that time the shaking had spread to his neck and right arm. At this time, a tentative diagnosis of paralysis agitans was made, and the case was followed for several years. During the next 2 years the condition spread to involve his lower limbs. When last examined, the following positive signs were seen: A fine-to-moderate rhythmic tremor was seen in his upper extremities; when the patient was standing, the head sagged forward and the shoulders were stooped with ventral flexion of the trunk; the arms were somewhat extended and adducted and flexed except for the distal phalanges, which were extended; the gait was slow and deliberate, and there was no associated swinging of the arms while walking; there had been a definite increase in muscular rigidity since the previous examination; the face was mask-like and without change of expression. On the negative side, no true paralysis was found, although voluntary motor action was slowed; the deep reflexes were intact; the abdominal reflexes were present and somewhat hyperactive; there was no Babinski sign; there were no abnormalities in pupillary reaction; there were no sensory disturbances over the trunk, and both motor and sensory cranial components were normal.

Diagnosis (Fig. 18-11) A diagnosis of *paralysis agitans (Parkinson's disease)* could be based on several outstanding features. Among these, the most important are lack of associ-

ated movements, marked changes in posture, expressionless face, increased muscular tonus, and tremor. These signs, linked with the absence of evidence for pyramidal tract lesions, cranial nerve palsies, or sensory disturbances, make the diagnosis conclusive.

Case 16

A young man, aged 22, was referred to a neurologist by a physician representing the state athletic commission. The following history was obtained: The patient was a professional boxer. One night, several weeks previously, he had been knocked out in the last round of a preliminary event. He was unconscious for about 10 minutes. On regaining consciousness, he got up, and although still a bit hazy, he dressed, with some help, and was taken home by one of his handlers. On arrival, he appeared to have recovered completely. The following day he took it easy and there were no signs of any trouble. The second day, he began to feel dizzy and to experience a dull headache, which became progressively worse during the following several days. The dizziness was more severe, and there was occasional vomiting. However, all these signs disappeared by the end of a week, and for the next month or so he was free of symptoms. About 5 weeks after the initial knockout, he began training again. Two days later the headache, dizziness, and vomiting returned, accompanied by slight paralysis and weakness on the left side. His manager immediately took him to the commission doctor, who made the referral. On examination it was found that the pupil of the right eye was wider than the left, with a slight ptosis of the lid on the right; the optic disks were choked; there was a left-sided hemiplegia (spastic paralysis) especially marked in the upper extremity, with a considerable loss of voluntary movement in the fingers on that side; both Rinne's and Weber's tests indicated impairment of hearing of the central type, in both ears; there was some degree of mental confusion. At the same time, it was found that the temperature was normal but the pulse was slow. The cerebrospinal fluid pressure was elevated but was otherwise normal and showed no traces of blood.

Diagnosis The history of trauma, followed by an asymptomatic (lucid) interval, which, in turn, was followed by headache, vertigo, and unilateral muscular weakness with signs of increased intracranial pressure, all point toward a *chronic* type of *subdural hemorrhage* (hematoma) resulting from trauma. The dilatation of the right pupil, ptosis of the right lid, and spastic paralysis on the left indicated that the hematoma was on the right side. The greater severity of the paralysis in the upper extremity, plus the auditory defects, suggests that the hematoma lies over the lower part of the frontal and parietal lobes and the upper temporal lobe, centered close to the central sulcus.

Case 17

A young girl, aged 13, was brought to a neurologist at the suggestion of her family physician. She had a history of frequent sore throat. Three years previously, during an attack of sore throat, she had complained of soreness in her joints. At that time, her family was told that she had rheumatic fever. Early in the present year she had an especially severe attack of tonsillitis. During the girl's recuperation from this illness, her mother first noticed involuntary, sudden, abrupt, and jerking movements in her daughter's right arm. Sometimes the movements involved the shoulder, sometimes the forearm and hand. More recently, involuntary tossing of the head had begun. The mother stated that these movements became exaggerated when the girl was excited, were less noticeable when she was resting quietly, and that she had never observed them at all while the girl was sleeping. The examination confirmed the mother's observations. A hypotonia was noted but the

reflexes were quite normal. Although the patient at first appeared to be suffering from muscular weakness, as evidenced by dropping objects held in the hand, this was found to be because of the involuntary movements. There was some incoordination and awkwardness, especially when reaching for objects. With the arms outstretched, the hands were flexed at the wrist with overextension at the metacarpophalangeal joints. When the arms were stretched over the head, the palm, particularly of the right hand, turned outward with overpronation at the elbow. The face was more or less serene, the expression rather blank. There was evidence of irritability and emotional instability. There were no abnormal disturbances of sensation.

Diagnosis The history of rheumatic fever, the recent sore throats, the choreiform movements, the choreic hand and "pronator sign" in a female of this age all contribute to the diagnosis of *Sydenham's chorea (St. Vitus' dance)*.

Case 18

A woman, aged 65, consulted her physician because of persistent headache of several weeks' duration on the right side of the face, especially around the eye. She also complained of occasional double vision. At this time she was treated for sinusitis and was sent home. Several weeks later she returned, complaining that the pain was growing steadily worse. On examination it was found that the sinuses were clear and that there were no marked visual defects, either in acuity or fields. Test results for glaucoma were also negative. However, it was noted that there was exophthalmos, with pulsation, in the right eye; with both eyes open, the patient complained of double vision when the examiner's finger was moved toward the patient's right, and with the left eye covered, the right eye did not follow a moving object to the right; although other movements of the right eye were possible, they were definitely weaker and more difficult than on the left; all movements of the left eye were normal. Ophthalmoscopic examination indicated a right papilledema. When pressure was applied to the right carotid in the neck, the pulsations in the right eye disappeared. Spinal fluid pressure and contents were normal. All other test results were negative.

Diagnosis (Fig. 26-8) The head pain, localized in the area of distribution of the ophthalmic division of the trigeminal nerve, in the absence of disease of the sinuses or primary disease of the eye, suggests an irritation along the course of the nerve. Paralysis of the lateral rectus muscle indicates a definite involvement of the abducens nerve, while weakness of the other extrinsic ocular muscles on the right suggests a progressive involvement of both the oculomotor and trochlear nerves. The disk sign and exophthalmos in the right eye indicate increased retroocular pressure, while the pulsations give evidence of an arterial involvement on that side. This was confirmed when the carotid artery in the neck was momentarily closed by pressure. Localization was made somewhat more exact by the fact that there is a place where an arterial enlargement could affect not only the sensory nerves but also the motor nerves to the extrinsic ocular muscles. The diagnosis was of an *aneurysm of the internal carotid artery* in the middle-to-anterior portion of the right cavernous sinus.

Case 19

A young boy, aged 5, was brought into the hospital during a summer hot spell complaining of a generalized intense headache. His parents indicated that he had vomited, had complained of a stiff neck, and seemed to be delirious, apathetic, and almost in a stupor. When asked whether the boy had had any

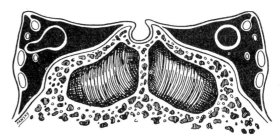

Figure 26-8 Case 18.

fever, the parents said that there had been a very slight fever and that there might even have been some chills. Upon examination, the headache still persisted, and neck stiffness was evident, with the neck muscles sore to the touch and an almost absolute inability to flex the neck muscles. On attempting to flex the head, there was flexion of the legs at the knees (Brudzinski sign), and from a flexed thigh it was exceedingly difficult to extend the leg completely due to pain in the back (Kernig's sign). There was some mental confusion, and the boy's temperature was 103°F.

Diagnosis The history of headache, fever, mental confusion, and the obvious meningeal signs of neck stiffness, Brudzinski sign, and Kernig sign all indicate a diagnosis of *meningitis*. In meningococcic, pneumococcic, and streptococcic, or staphylococcic infections the temperature is usually over 102°F. In TB meningitis, the temperature is usually between 100 and 101°F, and in syphilitic meningitis the temperature is usally normal. There may be associated chills, rapid pulse, and rapid respiration. Meningitis is most typically found in males and in children under 6, and occurs most frequently in the summer.

Case 20

A young man, aged 25, was referred to a neurologist by his family physician for diagnostic verification. The history concerned predominantly a condition of lower back pain which was first initiated when the patient bent over, several months earlier, in an attempt to lift a very heavy object. He said he felt a "snap in the back," and could hardly straighten out. Since then, there have been recurring episodes of back pain localized in the lower portion which at times have been brief, but now the pain has persisted for almost a week. The pain apparently is relieved somewhat by standing or lying down and is aggravated by bending, standing straight up, or even by coughing and sneezing. Recently, too, there has been leg pain in the left leg which seems to radiate along the back and side of the thigh. The leg pain is severe and it, too, seems to be aggravated by posture, coughing, sneezing, bowel movements, walking, and exertion in general. On examination, the neurologist found some loss of lumbar lordosis and spasm of the paravertebral muscles; manipulation of the leg was painful, lumbar spine movement was limited, extension of spine was painful, and lateral flexion of the spine was restricted. Walking was painful, and the patient seemed to favor his left leg by limping slightly. Lasègue's test was positive, and there was a decrease in the Achilles reflex.

Diagnosis The recurrent history, lower back pain following an attempt to lift a heavy object, limited lumbar spine movements, painful extension of the spine, pain relief and exaggeration by position change, pain on the straight leg-raising test, positive Lasègue's test, and leg pain following the sciatic nerve distribution all point to a diagnosis of a *herniated disk* in the lumbar region impinging on the roots of the left sciatic nerve.

Case 21

A young man, aged 35, was brought to a neurologist on the advice of his family physician. Although the onset of the symptoms was a bit uncertain since they apparently began gradually and slowly, these were the facts as

presented to the neurologist: There had been a gradual, slowly developing stiffness in the patient's back, which also involved his shoulder and hip joints. The stiffness of the "spine" had developed over many months. Initially there had been no pain, but soon pain occurred in the thorax, neck, and lower back, and on both sides. On examination, the neurologist noted that there was no kyphosis, some muscular atrophy, and a stiff, rigid, "poker" spine; the head was thrust forward and the trunk held rigid in walking; the spine muscles were in spasm; and there was hyperesthesia in pain zones. X-ray examination revealed some decalcification of the joints, blurring of joint faces, and a narrowing and obliteration of affective intervertebral disks.

Diagnosis The diagnosis is based on the stiff spine, back pain, root pain, involvement of the hip and shoulder, lack of kyphosis, and atrophy of spine muscles with no cord involvement. The disease is referred to as *spondylarthritis ankylopoietica,* or *Marie-Strümpell's disease,* or even *spondylitis deformans.* The cause is unknown, and the process is probably an infectious disease of the vertebral column and adjacent structures. Involvement of the hip and shoulder classifies this as Marie-Strümpell's disease.

Case 22

A woman, aged 45, was admitted to the hospital by her physician. Following fever and malaise, there had developed an acute inflammatory skin lesion, unilaterally in a girdle-like location in the middle of her right chest and back. There had also been a unilateral girdle-like eruption of vesicles on a red, inflamed base with severe pain. The vesicles were distributed along an area innervated by spinal roots 8 to 10. There was also an accompanying paresthesia. The pain was sharp, knifelike, and there later developed a decreased sensitivity to touch. Following the patient's brief stay in the hospital, the eruption and the pain disappeared within 7 to 10 days.

Diagnosis The unilateral involvement following distribution in the areas of spinal roots with anatomic precision, the typically radicular pain and vesicles all indicate a diagnosis of *Herpes zoster* (posterior poliomyelitis), an infectious disease of the dorsal spinal root, spinal root ganglion, and posterior horn of the spinal cord.

Case 23

A man, aged 50, noticed that his voice was suddenly getting hoarse and that he was having difficulty in swallowing. His physician referred him to a neurologist. The patient further developed dysarthria (a structural defect of speech; stuttering), and it was noticed that his shoulder and neck muscles, the trapezius, as well as the sternocleidomastoid, were paralyzed on the right side. On closer examination, there was found to be an ipsilateral paralysis of the right palate, an ipsilateral paralysis of the larynx on the right side, and an ipsilateral paralysis of the right tongue.

Diagnosis This is a syndrome known as *Jackson's syndrome,* in which there is an ipsilateral paralysis of the palate, larynx, tongue, and sternocleidomastoid and trapezius muscles due to a lesion which causes softening of the XIIth nucleus (hypoglossal), nucleus ambiguus, and the XIth nucleus (accessory). Such a lesion is obviously located in the lower medulla.

Case 24

A 35-year-old woman developed hemiplegia of her left side (paralysis of one side of the body) and was admitted to the hospital where she was seen by a neurologist. On physical examination it was noted that besides the hemiplegia there was diplopia and internal strabismus of the right eye. There was also a loss of power to rotate the right eyeball outward. The external rectus muscle of the right eye was found to be paralyzed. There was no other cranial nerve involvement.

Diagnosis The condition is diagnosed by the right external rectus muscle paralysis and the left hemiplegia (contralateral). This syndrome is known as the *Millard-Gubler syndrome,* or *pontile syndrome,* and involves a vascular lesion or tumor located in the pons (in this case in the right pons) where it can effectively destroy the VIth nerve and the pyramidal tract prior to its decussation, thus giving an ipsilateral cranial nerve involvement and a contralateral hemiplegia.

Examination
of the Nervous System

The examination of the nervous system depends largely on inspection and palpation, occasionally upon percussion, and if vascular lesions are suspected, auscultation may be of value. The *history* is of great importance, and the actual neurologic examination is the observation of the patient's neurophysiology under a series of tests. The major testing categories are presented below.

A Mental State

Consider the patient's state of awareness and degree of cooperation, and if there is any abnormality, evaluate the condition in terms of a toxic confusional state, a psychosis, dementia, or a word or thought disorder secondary to a cerebral disease.

B Motor system

Determine whether all muscles are involved or whether specific muscle groups are involved. Check the muscles for fatigability, tenderness, atrophy, degree of re-

sistance to passive movement, strength of the muscles, and their ability to perform coordinated movements quickly. Tendon reflexes should be evaluated, keeping in mind the level of the CNS being tested. Some of the more common tests are:

1 Direct light reflex

Light shone into eye causes pupil to constrict.

2 Consensual light reflex

Light shone into one eye also causes opposite pupil to constrict.

3 Pupillary accommodation reflex

On near vision eyes converge and pupils constrict; on distant vision pupils dilate. (In an Argyll Robertson pupil there is light response but no accommodation.)

4 Corneal reflex

Touch edge of cornea with cotton wisp and get closure of eyes.

5 Deep reflexes (actually stretching reflexes)
  a Biceps (C5-C6)
  b Brachioradialis (C5-C6)
  c Scapulohumeral (C5-T1)
  d Triceps (C7-C8)
  e Upper abdominal (T8-T9)
  f Middle abdominal (T9-T10)
  g Lower abdominal (T11-T12)
  h Quadriceps (L2-L4), knee jerk or patellar
  i Adductor (L2-L4)
  j Hamstring (L4-S2)
  k Achilles (L5-S2) ankle jerk
6 Superficial reflexes (receptors in skin and not in muscle)
  a Upper abdominal (T5-T8)
  b Midabdominal (T9-T11)
  c Lower abdominal (T11-T12)
  d Cremasteric (L1-L2)
  e Plantar (L4-S2)
  f Superficial anal (L1-L2)
7 Abnormal reflexes in pyramidal tract disease
  a Clonus (an abnormal response of the stretch reflex from release of central inhibition)
    (1) Ankle
    (2) Patellar
    (3) Wrist
  b Babinski sign (hallucal dorsiflexion reflex)
  c Oppenheim's sign (hallucal dorsiflexion reflex)
  d Grasp reflex
  e Hoffman's sign
  f Mayer's reflex
  g Palm-chin reflex (Radovici's sign)
8 Meningeal irritation
  a Kernig's sign
  b Brudzinski's sign
  c Nuchal rigidity
  d Spinal rigidity
9 Coordination
  a Ataxia
  b Romberg's sign
  c Check stance in standing, walking, with eyes closed, and direction of falling.

10 Testing diadochokinesia (ability to arrest one motor system and substitute another)
  a Test with alternating movements
  b Stewart-Holmes rebound sign
11 Test for dyssynergia
  a Finger-to-nose test
  b Heel-to-knee test
12 The gait
  a Ataxia (in cerebellar disease)
  b Ataxia (in posterior column disease)
  c Steppage gait: top drop
  d Spastic gait: hemiplegia
  e Spastic gait: scissors gait (paraplegia)
  f Propulsive gait: parkinsonian gait
  g Clownish gait: Huntington's chorea
  h Waddling gait: muscular dystrophy
  i Bizarre gait: hysteria (use Hoover's sign)
C Sensory system
Several types of sensation should be studied including pain (pinprick), light touch, temperature, vibratory, and position sense.
  1 Superficial pain
    Use pinprick and compare symmetric zones with same degree of pressure.
  2 Deep pain
    Can use pressure on eyeballs, testes, nerve trunks, and tendons.
  3 Temperature
    Use both hot and cold, but not extremes.
  4 Tactile sense
    Test with eyes closed.
  5 Proprioceptive sense
    a Position
    b Pressure
    c Vibratory
  6 Testing higher integrative functions
    a Stereognosis (ability to distinguish forms)
    b Two-point discrimination
    c Perception of figures on skin (graphesthesia)
D Autonomic nervous system
  1 Temperature regulation
  2 Vasomotor disorders

Vasospasm; vasodilatation; dermatographia

3 Perspiration
Localized areas of sweating may occur in syringomyelia, peripheral nerve disease, or neuropathy. Anhidrosis is a component of Horner's syndrome.
4 Trophic
5 Pilomotor reactions

E Cranial Nerves
1 Olfactory
Ask the patient to identify familiar odors such as tobacco, coffee, peppermint.
2 Optic
Use suitable tests for vision, depending on patient's acuity and ability to cooperate.
Examine the fundi with an ophthalmoscope.
Test visual fields by the confrontation method.
3 Oculomotor
Check abnormalities of the eyelids.
Check action of all eye muscles except the external rectus, superior oblique, and dilator muscles of pupil.
4 Trochlear
Test the superior oblique muscle.
5 Trigeminal
a Motor division
Look for tremor of the lips, involuntary chewing movements, and trismus (spasm of the masticatory muscles).
Test the pairs of temporal and masseter muscles, and compare muscle tension on both sides.
Have patient open mouth, and note any mandible deviation.
b Sensory division
Test tactile perception of facial skin.
Test sense of touch in oral mucosa.
Test pain sensibility of skin and mucosa.
Test corneal reflex.
6 Abducens
Test the external rectus muscle.
7 Facial

a Motor
Inspect the face in repose for flaccid paralysis.
Check for upper or lower motor neuron lesion (UMN or LMN).
UMN lesions do not affect the upper lid or forehead.
(1) Face in repose
Shallow nasolabial folds in both UMN and LMN.
Palpebral fissure widened in LMN.
(2) Elevation of eyebrow
Elevation and wrinkling of forehead absent in LMN, present in UMN.
(3) Frowning
Lowering of eyebrows absent in LMN, present in UMN.
(4) Tight eye closure
Absent in LMN, lid closed normally in UMN.
(5) Showing teeth
The mouth does not elevate in either LMN or UMN.
(6) Whistling
Absent in both LMN and UMN.
(7) Puffing cheeks
Absent in both LMN and UMN.
(8) Smiling
The mouth does not elevate in LMN.
b Sensory (taste)
Test anterior two-thirds of tongue with sugar, vinegar, quinine, and salt.
8 Acoustic
a Cochlear
Rough quantitative test for hearing loss (whispered word, spoken word, ticking watch).
Weber's test: Place tuning fork against forehead and note in which ear sound is heard best.
Rinne's test: Tests both bone and air conduction.
b Vestibular
Barany's test.
Caloric test: Note nystagmus after

applying hot and cold water in external ear.

Pointing test.

Labyrinthine tests for falling, positional nystagmus, past pointing.

9 Glossopharyngeal

Also has both motor and sensory fibers and is usually tested along with the vagus nerve.

Test swallowing.

Test for anesthesia of upper part of pharynx and soft palate.

Test taste sensation of posterior third of tongue.

10 Vagus

Have patient say "ah" and note uvula deviation.

Note convergence of faucial pillars.

Test gag reflex.

Test areas of pharyngeal mucosa for areas of anesthesia.

a Larynx

Watch laryngeal contours in neck to see if they elevate in swallowing. Note hoarseness, dyspnea, and inspiratory distress.

Check vocal cords.

11 Accessory

Palpate the upper borders of the trapezius muscles while patient raises his shoulders against the resistance.

Test the sternocleidomastoid muscle.

12 Hypoglossal

When the tongue protrudes, look for tremors and other involuntary movements.

Note any atrophy or tongue deviation.

Test muscle strength by having patient push tongue against cheek while your hand resists from outside.

Test lingual speech.

Common Vascular Brain Syndromes[1]

The importance of the proper management of patients with cerebral vascular damage is recognized and accepted. As a guide to prognosis and to future therapy, it is often essential to establish the site and extent of the damaged area.

[1]Given through the courtesy of Drs. Alfred Ebel, Nicholas Panin, Milton Holtzman, and Jose Cibeira, Veterans Administration Hospitals, Bronx, New York, and East Orange, New Jersey.

Symptoms resulting from the occlusion of the middle cerebral artery are well known and usually present no diagnostic problems. Pathology in other cerebral vessels or in the vascular supply of the brainstem frequently present difficulties in localization.

The schema given below is designed to show the relation between lesion and syndrome.

Symptom or finding	Structure involved
Occlusions of cerebral arteries	
Anterior cerebral artery:	
Contralateral: Monoplegia (leg)	Medial superior area of paracentral lobule
Loss of sensation	Thalamocortical radiation
When dominant hemisphere is affected:	
Mental confusion	Frontal lobe ischemia
Apraxia	Corpus callosum
Aphasia	Cortical speech area

Symptom or finding	Structure involved
Occlusions of cerebral arteries	
Anterior choroidal artery:	
Homonymous hemianopia	Geniculocalcarine tract (visual radiation)
Contralateral: Hemiplegia	Internal capsule and basis pedunculi (corticospinal tract)
Hemianesthesia	Internal capsule, posterior limb
Middle cerebral artery:	
Homonymous hemianopia	Optic tract
Contralateral: Hemiplegia	Internal capsule, anterior area
Hemianesthesia	Internal capsule, posterior limb
When dominant hemisphere is affected:	
Global aphasia	Cortical damage, motor and sensory speech centers
Posterior cerebral artery:	
Homonymous hemianopia	Visual radiation
Dejerine-Roussy syndrome:	
Contralateral: Hemiparesis or hemiplegia	Internal capsule
Impaired superficial sensation	Posterolateral nucleus of thalamus (pulvinar)
Loss of sensation	Posterolateral nucleus of thalamus
Agonizing burning pain	Dorsal nucleus of thalamus
Choreoathetoid movements	Red nucleus
Ataxia	Spinocerebellar tract
Tremor	Midbrain—tegmental area
Internal carotid artery:	
Transient or permanent:	
Homonymous hemianopia	Optic tract or visual radiation
Contralateral:	
Hemiplegia	Internal capsule
Hemianesthesia	Thalamocortical radiation or posterior limb of internal capsule
Homolateral:	
Amaurosis	Ophthalmic artery thrombosis
When dominant hemisphere is affected:	
Aphasia	Cortical damage, motor and sensory speech centers
Occlusions of brainstem arteries	
Superior cerebellar artery:	
Homolateral:	
Cerebellar ataxia	Spinocerebellar tract
Choreiform movements	Red nucleus
Horner's syndrome	Reticular formation
Contralateral:	
Loss of pain and temperature sensation over face and body	Sensory nucleus V; lateral and medial lemniscus
Central facial weakness	Tracts above the nucleus VII
Partial deafness	Lateral lemniscus

Symptom or finding	Structure involved
Occlusions of brainstem arteries	

Anterior inferior cerebellar artery:
Homolateral:

Symptom or finding	Structure involved
Cerebellar ataxia	Spinocerebellar tract
Horner's syndrome	Reticular formation
Deafness	Cochlear nuclei (VIII)
Facial paralysis	Nucleus VII
Loss of sensation to face	Nucleus and spinal tract of V

Contralateral:

Symptom or finding	Structure involved
Loss of pain and temperature sensation over the body	Lateral spinothalamic tract

Posterior inferior cerebellar artery:
Homolateral:

Symptom or finding	Structure involved
Cerebellar ataxia	Spinocerebellar tract
Horner's syndrome	Reticular formation
Loss of sensation to face	Nucleus of spinal tract V
Dysphagia	Nucleus ambiguus (glossopharyngeal nerve)
Dysphonia	Nucleus ambiguus (vagus nerve)
Nystagmus	Spinocerebellar tract

Contralateral:

Symptom or finding	Structure involved
Loss of pain and temperature sensation over the body	Lateral spinothalamic tract

Basilar artery:
Unilateral, bilateral, or crossed involvement of the elements in the paramedian and lateral areas, complete or partial, according to the site of the occlusion and the efficiency of the collateral circulation.

Vertebral artery:
The symptoms and signs are chiefly those of occlusion of the posterior inferior cerebellar artery.

Weber's syndrome (midbrain:
paramedian area and nucleus III):
Homolateral:

Symptom or finding	Structure involved
Ptosis	Oculomotor nucleus (III)
External squint	Oculomotor nucleus (III)
Fixed mydriasis	Oculomotor nucleus (III)

Contralateral:

Symptom or finding	Structure involved
Hemiplegia	Pyramidal tract

Benedikt's syndrome (midbrain):
Same as Weber's syndrome, plus:
Contralateral:

Symptom or finding	Structure involved
Hemianesthesia	Medial lemniscus
Choreiform movements	Rubrospinal tract

Millard-Gubler's syndrome (pons):
Homolateral:

Symptom or finding	Structure involved
Inward deviation of the eye	Abducens nucleus (VI)
Facial paralysis	Facial nerve (VII)

Symptom or finding	Structure involved
Occlusions of brainstem arteries	

Contralateral:
   Hemiplegia — Pyramidal tract

Foville's syndrome (pons):
   Same as Millard-Gubler's syndrome, plus:
   Paralysis of conjugate gaze to the
     side of the lesion — Medial longitudinal fasciculus

Wallenberg's syndrome (same as posterior
   cerebellar artery):
Homolateral:
   Cerebellar ataxia — Spinocerebellar tract
   Horner's syndrome — Reticular formation
   Loss of sensation to face — Nucleus of spinal V tract
   Dysphagia — Nucleus ambiguus (glossopharyngeal nerve)
   Dysphonia — Nucleus ambiguus (vagus nerve)
   Nystagmus — Spinocerebellar tract
Contralateral:
   Loss of pain and temperature sensation
     over the body — Lateral spinothalamic tract

Note: Lesions in the paramedian areas (pontine or basilar arteries) produce contralateral hemiplegia and loss of proprioception. All lesions in the lateral areas *above* the pons result in contralateral sensory loss to face and body. All lesions in the lateral areas *below* the midbrain produce homolateral sensory loss to the face, and contralateral sensory loss to the body.

Bibliography

Adams, R. D., and M. Victor: *Principles of Neurology,* McGraw-Hill, New York, 1977.

Adelmann, H. B.: The problem of cyclopia, *Q. Rev. Biol.,* p. I, **2**:161; p. II, **2**:284, 1936.

Ades, H. W., and J. M. Brookhart: The central auditory pathway, *J. Neurophysiol.,* **13**:189, 1950.

Ades, H. W., and D. Raab: Recovery of motor function after two-stage extirpation of area 4 in monkeys, *J. Neurophysiol.,* **9**:55, 1946.

Adrian, E. D.: *The Basis of Sensation: The Action of Sense Organs,* Norton, New York, 1928.

Adrian, E. D.: Afferent areas in the cerebellum connected with the limbs, *Brain,* **66**:289, 1943.

Adrian, E. D., and B. H. C. Matthews: The Berger rhythm: Potential changes from the occipital lobes in man, *Brain,* **57**:355, 1934.

Aidley, D. J.: *The Physiology of Excitable Cells,* Cambridge, London, 1971.

Alpers, B. J.: *Clinical Neurology,* Davis, Philadelphia, 1947.

Anderson, F. D., and C. M. Berry: Degeneration studies of long ascending fiber systems in the cat brain stem, *J. Comp. Neurol.,* **111**:195, 1959.

Andy, O. J., and H. Stephan: *The Septum of the Cat,* Charles C Thomas, Springfield, Ill., 1964.

Anson, B. J., and W. G. Maddock: *Callander's Surgical Anatomy,* 3d ed., Saunders, Philadelphia, 1952.

Anthony, C. P.: *Textbook of Anatomy and Physiology,* 4th ed., Mosby, St. Louis, 1955.

Arey, L. B.: *Developmental Anatomy,* 7th ed., Saunders, Philadelphia, 1965.

Bach, L. M. N., and H. W. Magoun: The vestibular nuclei as an excitatory mechanism for the cord, *J. Neurophysiol.,* **10**:331, 1947.

Bailey, F. R., in W. M. Copenhaver and D. D. Johnson (eds.), *Textbook of Histology,* 14th ed., Williams & Wilkins, Baltimore, 1958.

Bailey, P.: *Intracranial Tumors,* Charles C Thomas, Springfield, Ill., 1948.

Bailey, P., and G. von Bonin: *The Isocortex of Man,* University of Illinois Press, Urbana, 1951.

Bailey, P., G. von Bonin, E. W. Davis, H. W. Garol, and W. S. McCulloch: Further observations on associational pathways in the brain of *Macaca mulatta, J. Neuropathol. Exp. Neurol.,* 3:413, 1944.

Bailey, P., H. W. Garol, and W. S. McCulloch: Cortical origin and distribution of corpus callosum and anterior commissure in the chimpanzee, *J. Neurophysiol.,* 4:564, 1941.

Baker, A. B., H. A. Matzke, and J. R. Brown: Poliomyelitis. III. Bulbar poliomyelitis: A study of medullary function. *AMA Arch. Neurol. Psychiatry,* 63:257, 1950.

Bard, P.: A diencephalic mechanism for the expression of rage with special reference to the sympathetic nervous system, *Am. J. Physiol.,* 84:490, 1928.

Bard, P., and V. B. Mountcastle: Some forebrain mechanisms involved in expression of rage with special reference to suppression of angry behavior, *Assoc. Res. Nerv. Ment. Dis. Proc.,* 27:361, 1948.

Barker, D.: The innervation of the muscle spindle, *Q. J. Microsc. Sci.,* 89:143, 1948.

Barnes, S.: Degeneration in hemiplegia: With special reference to a ventrolateral pyramidal tract, the accessory fillet and Pick's bundle, *Brain,* 24:463, 1901.

Barnes, W. T., H. W. Magoun, and S. W. Ranson: The ascending auditory pathway in the brain stem of the monkey, *J. Comp. Neurol.,* 79:129, 1943.

Beattie, J., G. R. Brow, and C. N. Long: Physiological and anatomical evidence for the existence of nerve tracts connecting the hypothalamus and spinal sympathetic centers, *Proc. Ry. Soc. Lond.* [Biol.], 106:253, 1930.

Beck, E.: The origin, course and termination of the prefrontopontine tract in the human brain, *Brain,* 73:368, 1950.

Benda, C. E., and S. Cobb: On the pathogenesis of paralysis agitans, *Medicine,* 21:95, 1942.

Berger, H.: Über das Elektrenkepathalogramm des Menschen, *Arch. Psychiatr. Nervenkr.,* 87:527, 1929.

Berman, A. L.: *The Brain Stem of the Cat: A Cytoarchitectonic Atlas with Stereotaxic Coordinates,* University of Wisconsin Press, Madison, 1968.

Bing, R., and W. Haymaker: *Regional Diagnosis in Lesions of the Brain and Spinal Cord,* 11th ed., Mosby, St. Louis, 1940.

Bloom, W., and D. W. Fawcett: *A Textbook of Histology,* 10th ed., Saunders, Philadelphia, 1975.

Bonin, G. von: Architecture of the precentral motor cortex and some adjacent areas, in P. C. Bucy (ed.), *The Precentral Motor Cortex,* 2d ed., University of Illinois Press, Urbana, 1949.

Bornstein, W. S.: Cortical representation of taste in man and monkey, *Yale J. Biol. Med.,* 12:719, 1940.

Bosma, J. F., and E. Gellhorn: Electromyographic studies of muscular coordination on stimulation of the motor cortex, *J. Neurophysiol.,* 9:263, 1946.

Botterell, E. H., and J. F. Fulton: Functional localization in the cerebellum of primates, *J. Comp. Neurol.,* 69:31, 1938.

Boynton, E. P., and M. Hines: On the question of threshold in stimulation of the motor cortex, *Am. J. Physiol.,* 106:175, 1933.

Brady, J. V., and W. J. H. Nauta: Subcortical mechanisms in emotional behavior: affective changes following septal forebrain lesions in the albino rat, *J. Comp. Physiol. Psychol.,* 46:339, 1953.

Brock, S.: *Basis of Clinical Neurology,* Williams & Wilkins, Baltimore, 1945.

Brodal, A.: Experimentelle Untersuchen über die olivo-cerebellare Lokalisation, *Z. Gesamte Neurol. Psychiatr.,* 169:1, 1940.

Brodal, A.: Central course of afferent fibers for pain in facial, glossopharyngeal and vagus nerves. Clinical observations, *Arch. Neurol. Psychiatry,* 57:292, 1947.

Brodal, A.: The hippocampus and the sense of smell: A review, *Brain,* 70:179, 1947.

Brodal, A.: *Neurological Anatomy,* Oxford University Press, New York, 1948.

Brodmann, K.: Vergleichende Lokalisationslehre der Grosshirnrinde in ihren Prinzipien dargestellt auf Grund des Zellenbaues, Barth, Munich, 1909.

Brodmann, K.: *Die allgemeine Chirurgie der Gehirnkrankheiten: Neue Deutsch Chirurgie,* Bd. 11, Ferd. Enke Verlag, Stuttgart, 1914.

Brouwer, B.: Projection of the retina on the cortex in man, *Res. Publ. Assoc. Res. Nerv. Ment. Dis.,* 13:529, 1934.

Buchanan, A. R.: *Functional Neuroanatomy,* 3d ed., Lea & Febiger, Philadelphia, 1957.

Bucy, P. C.: Cortical extirpation in the treatment of involuntary movements, *Res. Publ. Assoc. Res. Nerv. Ment. Dis.,* 21:551, 1942.

Bucy, P. C.: Effects of extirpation in man, in P. C. Bucy (ed.), *The Precentral Motor Cortex,* 2d ed., University of Illinois Press, Urbana, 1949.

Bucy, P. C.: Relation to abnormal involuntary movements, in P. C. Bucy (ed.), *The Precentral Motor Cortex,* 2d ed., University of Illinois Press, Urbana, 1949.

Bucy, P. C., in S. W. Ranson and S. L. Clark, *The Anatomy of the Nervous System,* 10th ed., Saunders, Philadelphia, 1959.

Bucy, P. C., and J. F. Fulton: Ipsilateral representation in the motor and premotor cortex in monkeys, *Brain,* 56:318, 1933.

Bumke, O., and O. Foerster: *Handbuch der Neurologie,* Bd. 5, Springer-Verlag, Berlin, 1936.

Burnstock, G., and M. E. Holman: Smooth muscle: Autonomic nerve transmission, *Annu. Rev. Physiol.,* 25:61, 1963.

Burnstock, G.: Structure of smooth muscle and its innervation, in E. Bulbring, A. F. Brading, W. A. Jones, and T. Torrela (eds.), *Smooth Muscle,* Williams & Wilkins, Baltimore, 1970.

Cajal, Ramon Y. S.: *Histologie de systeme nerveux de l'homme et des vertébrés,* 2 vols., Maloine, Paris, 1909.

Cameron, D. E., and M. D. Pradas: Bilateral frontal gyrectomy: Psychiatric results, *Res. Publ. Assoc. Res. Nerv. Ment. Dis.,* 27:534, 1948.

Campbell, A. W.: *Histological Studies on the Localization of Cerebral Function,* Cambridge, New York, 1905.

Carmel, P. W.: Efferent projections of the ventral anterior nucleus of the thalamus in the monkey, *Am. J. Anat.,* 128:159, 1970.

Carpenter, M. B.: Ventral tier thalamic nuclei, in D. Williams (ed.), *Modern Trends in Neurology,* vol. 4, Butterworth, London, 1967.

Carpenter, M. B.: *Human Neuroanatomy,* 7th ed., Williams & Wilkins, Baltimore, 1976.

Carpenter, M. B., and P. Peter: Nigrostriatal and nigrothalamic fibers in the rhesus monkey, *J. Comp. Neurol.,* 144:93, 1972.

Carpenter, M. B., and N. L. Strominger: Efferent fibers of the subthalamic nucleus in the monkey:

A comparison of the efferent projections of the subthalamic nucleus, substantia nigra and globus pallidus, *Am. J. Anat.,* 121:41, 1967.

Caton, R.: The electric current of the brain, *Br. Med. J.,* 2:278, 1875.

Chang, H.-T., T. R. Rugh, and A. A. Ward, Jr.: Topographical representation of muscles in motor cortex of monkeys, *J. Neurophysiol.,* 10:39, 1947.

Chi, C. C., and J. P. Flynn: Neuroanatomic projections related to biting attack elicited from hypothalamus in cats, *Brain Res.,* 35:49, 1971.

Clark, G.: The mode of representation in the motor cortex, *Brain,* 71:320, 1948.

Clark, G.: Suppression and facilitation: A review, *Q. Chicago Med. School,* 10:14, 1949.

Clark, G., and J. W. Ward: Responses elicited from the cortex of monkeys by electrical stimulation through fixed electrodes, *Brain,* 71:332, 1948.

Clark, W. E. L.: The mammalian oculomotor nucleus, *J. Anat.,* 60:426, 1926.

Clark, W. E. L.: The topography and homologies of the hypothalamic nuclei in man, *J. Anat.,* 70:203, 1935.

Clark, W. E. L.: The visual centers of the brain and their connexions, *Physiol. Rev.,* 22:205, 1942.

Clark, W. E. L.: The connexions of the frontal lobes in the brain, *Lancet,* 1:353, 1948.

Clark, W. E. L., J. Beattie, G. Riddogh, and N. M. Dott: *The Hypothalamus,* Oliver & Boyd, Edinburgh, 1938.

Clark, W. E. L., and R. H. Boggan: On the connections of the anterior nucleus of the thalamus, *J. Anat.,* 67:215, 1933.

Clemente, C. D., and M. H. Chase: Neurological substrates of aggressive behavior, *Annu. Rev. Physiol.,* 35:329, 1973.

Cobb, S.: *Foundations of Neuropsychiatry,* Williams & Wilkins, Baltimore, 1941.

Cobb, S.: *Borderlands of Psychiatry,* Harvard, Cambridge, Mass., 1943.

Cobb, S.: *Emotions and Clinical Medicine,* Norton, New York, 1950.

Conrad, L. C. A., C. M. Leonard, and P. N. Pfaff: Connections of the median and dorsal raphe nuclei in the rat: An autoradiographic and degeneration study, *J. Comp. Neurol.,* 156:179, 1974.

Cooper, J. R., F. E. Bloom, and R. H. Roth: The

Biochemical Basis of Neuropharmacology, 2d ed., Oxford, New York, 1974.

Corning, H. K.: *Lehrbuch der topographischen Anatomie,* Auf. 14 u. 15, Verlag Bergman, Munich, 1923.

Corning, H. K.: *Lehrbuch der Entwicklungsgeschichte des Menschen,* Auf. 14 u. 15, Verlag Bergman, Munich, 1925.

Courville, C. B.: *Pathology of the Central Nervous System,* Pacific, Mountain View, Calif., 1950.

Courville, J.: Somatotopical organization of the projection from the nucleus interpositus anterior of the cerebellum to the red nucleus: An experimental study in the cat with silver impregnation methods, *Exp. Brain Res.,* **2**:191, 1966.

Courville, J., N. Diakiw, and A. Brodal: Cerebellar corticonuclear projection in the cat: The paramedian lobule: An experimental study with silver methods, *Brain Res.,* **50**:25, 1973.

Crosby, E. C., and J. W. Henderson: The mammalian midbrain and isthmus regions. II. Fiber connections of the superior colliculus, *J. Comp. Neurol.,* **88**:53, 1948.

Crosby, E. C., and T. Humphrey: Studies on the vertebrate telencephalon. II. The nuclear pattern of the anterior olfactory nucleus, tuberculum olfactorum and the amygdaloid complex in adult man, *J. Comp. Neurol.,* **74**:309, 1941.

Crosby, E. C., T. Humphrey and E. W. Lauer: *Correlative Anatomy of the Nervous System.* Macmillan, New York, 1962.

Cunningham, D. J., in J. C. Brash and E. B. Jamieson (eds.), *Textbook of Anatomy,* 8th ed., Oxford, New York, 1947.

Curtis, H. J.: The intercortical connections of the corpus callosum as indicated by evoked potentials, *J. Neurophysiol.,* **3**:407, 1940.

Davis, H.: Physiology of hearing, in E. P. Fowler (ed.), *Loose Leaf Medicine of the Ear,* Nelson, New York, 1939.

Davison, C.: The role of the globus pallidus and substantia nigra in the production of rigidity and tremor, *Res. Publ. Assoc. Res. Nerv. Ment. Dis.,* **21**:261, 1942.

Deecke, L., D. W. F. Schwarz, and J. M. Fredrickson: Nucleus ventroposterior inferior (VPI) as the vestibular thalamic relay in the Rhesus monkey. I. Field potential investigation, *Exp. Brain Res.,* **20**:88, 1974.

DeFrance, J. (ed.): *The Septal Nuclei,* Plenum, New York, 1976.

DeJong, R. N.: *The Neurological Examination,* Hoeber-Harper, Hagerstown, Md., 1950.

Denny-Brown, D.: *The Cerebral Control of Movement,* Liverpool University Press, Liverpool, 1966.

Denny-Brown, D., and E. H. Botterell: The motor functions of the agranular frontal cortex, *Res. Publ. Assoc. Res. Nerv. Ment. Dis.,* **27**:235, 1948.

Domesick, V. B.: Projection from the cingulate cortex in the rat, *Brain Res.,* **12**:296, 1969.

Dow, R. S.: The evolution and anatomy of the cerebellum, *Biol. Rev.,* **17**:179, 1942.

Dow, R. S., and G. Moruzzi: *The Physiology and Pathology of the Cerebellum,* University of Minnesota Press, Minneapolis, 1958.

Dusser de Barenne, J. G.: Origin of the motor reactions produced by electrical stimulation of the cerebral cortex, *Arch. Neurol. Psychiatry,* **31**:1129, 1934.

Dusser de Barenne, J. G., H. W. Garol, and W. S. McCulloch: Physiological neuronography of the corticostriatal connections, *Res. Publ. Assoc. Res. Nerv. Ment. Dis.,* **21**:246, 1942.

Dusser de Barenne, J. G., and W. S. McCulloch: Sensorimotor cortex, nucleus caudatus and thalamus opticus, *J. Neurophysiol.,* **1**:364, 1938.

Dusser de Barenne, J. G., and W. S. McCulloch: Suppression of motor response obtained from area 4 by stimulation of area 4s, *J. Neurophysiol.,* **4**:311, 1941.

Eager, R.: Efferent cortico-nuclear pathways in the cerebellum of the cat, *J. Comp. Neurol.,* **120**:81, 1963.

Eccles, J. C.: An electrical hypothesis of synaptic and neuromuscular transmission. *Nature,* **156**:680, 1945.

Eccles, J. C.: Acetylcholine and synaptic transmission in the spinal cord, *J. Neurophysiol.,* **10**:197, 1947.

Eccles, J. C., M. Ito, and J. Szentagothai: *The Cerebellum as a Neuronal Machine,* Springer-Verlag, New York, 1967.

Economo, C. von: *The Cytoarchitectonics of the Human Cerebral Cortex,* Oxford, New York, 1929.

Economo, C. von, and G. Koskinas: Die Cytoarchitektonik der Hirnrinde der erwachsenen Menschen, Springer-Verlag, Vienna, 1925.

Egger, M. D., and J. P. Flynn: Effects of electrical stimulation of the amygdala on hypothalamically elicited attack behavior in cats, *J. Neurophysiol.,* **26**:705, 1963.

Eleftheriou, E. (ed.): *The Neurobiology of the Amygdala,* Plenum, New York, 1972.

Elliott, H. C.: *Textbook of Neuroanatomy,* Lippincott, Philadelphia, 1963.

Elsberg, C. A., and E. D. Brewer: The sense of smell. X. A detailed description of the technique of two olfactory tests used for the localization of supratentorial tumors of the brain, *Bull. Neurol. Inst. N.Y.,* **4**:501, 1935.

Emmers, R.: Separate relays of tactile, thermal and gustatory modalities in the cat thalamus. *Proc. Soc. Exp. Biol. Med.,* **121**:527, 1966.

Evarts, E. V.: Brain mechanisms in movement, *Sci. Amr.,* **229**:96, 1973.

Eyzaguirre, C.: *Physiology of the Nervous System,* Year Book, 1969.

Favill, J.: The relationship of eye muscles to semicircular canal currents in rotationally induced nystagmus, *Res. Publ. Assoc. Res. Nerv. Ment. Dis.,* **6**:530, 1929.

Fernandez de Molina, A., and R. W. Hunsperger: Organization of the subcortical system governing defense and flight reactions in the cat, *J. Physiol. (Lond.),* **160**:200, 1962.

Fields, W. S., R. Guilleman, and C. A. Carton: Hypothalamic-hypophyseal interrelationships, *Proc. Houston Neurol. Soc.,* vol. 3, 1955.

Flynn, J. P., H. Vanegas, W. Foote, and S. Edwards: Neural mechanisms involved in a cat's attack on a rat, in R. E. Whalen (ed.), *The Neural Control of Behavior,* Academic, New York, 1970.

Foerster, O.: The cerebral cortex in man, *Lancet,* **2**:309, 1931.

Foerster, O.: The dermatomes in man, *Brain,* **56**:1, 1933.

Foerster, O.: Motorische Felder und Bahnen, in O. Bumke and O. Foerster (eds.), *Handbuch der Neurologie,* Springer-Verlag, Berlin, 1936.

Foerster, O.: Sensible corticale Felder, in O. Bumke and O. Foerster (eds.), *Handbuch der Neurologie,* Springer-Verlag, Berlin, 1936.

Ford, F. R.: *Diseases of the Nervous System in Infancy, Childhood and Adolescence,* Charles C Thomas, Springfield, Ill., 1937.

Freeman, W., and J. W. Watts: Interpretation of function of frontal lobes based upon observations in 48 cases of prefrontal lobotomy, *Yale J. Biol. Med.,* **11**:527, 1939.

Freeman, W., and J. W. Watts: Retrograde degeneration of the thalamus following prefrontal lobotomy, *J. Comp. Neurol.,* **86**:65, 1947.

Freeman, W., and J. W. Watts: Psychosurgery, in *The Treatment of Mental Disorders and Intractable Pain,* Charles C Thomas, Springfield, Ill., 1950.

French, J. D., O. Sugar, and J. G. Chusid: Corticocortical connections of the superior bank of the sylvian fissure in the monkey, *J. Neurophysiol.,* **11**:185, 1948.

Frigyesi, T. L., E. Rinvik, and M. D. Yahr (eds.): *Corticothalamic Projections and Sensorimotor Activities,* Raven, Hewlett, N.Y., 1972.

Fulton, J. F.: *Physiology of the Nervous System,* 2d ed., Oxford, New York, 1943.

Fulton, J. F., E. G. T. Liddell, and D. M. Rioch: The influence of unilateral destruction of the vestibular nuclei upon posture and the knee jerk, *Brain,* **53**:327, 1930.

Fulton, J. F., and D. Sheehan: The uncrossed lateral pyramidal tract in higher primates, *J. Anat.,* **69**:181, 1935.

Galambos, R.: Suppression of auditory nerve activity by stimulation of efferent fibers to the cochlea, *J. Neurophysiol.,* **19**:424, 1956.

Ganong, W. F.: *Review of Medical Physiology,* 6th ed., Lange, Los Altos, Calif., 1973.

Ganong, W. F., and L. Martini (eds.): *Frontiers in Neuroendocrinology,* Oxford, New York, 1973.

Gardner, E.: *Fundamentals of Neurology,* 3d ed., Saunders, Philadelphia, 1958.

Gardner, E., and H. M. Cuneo: Lateral spinothalamic tract and associated tracts in man, *Arch. Neurol. Psychiatry,* **53**:423, 1945.

Garol, H. W., and P. C. Bucy: Suppression of motor response in man, *Arch. Neurol. Psychiatry,* **51**:528, 1944.

Gellhorn, E.: The influence of alterations in posture of the limbs on cortically induced movements, *Brain,* **71**:26, 1948.

Gellhorn, E., and L. Thompson: The influence of muscle pain on cortically induced movements, *Am. J. Physiol.,* **142**:231, 1944.

Gibbs, F. A., and E. L. Gibbs: *Atlas of Encephalography,* Addison-Wesley, Cambridge, Mass., 1950.

Gibbs, F. A., E. L. Gibbs, and W. G. Lennox: Cerebral dysrhythmias of epilepsy, *Arch. Neurol. Psychiatry,* **39**:298, 1938.

Gilbert, M. S.: Early development of the human diencephalon, *J. Comp. Neurol.,* **62**:81, 1935.

Givner, I.: Episcleral ganglion cells, *Arch. Ophthalmol.,* N.S., **22**:82, 1939.

Glees, P.: The anatomical basis for corticostriate connexions, *J. Anat.,* **78**:47, 1944.

Glees, P., and P. D. Wall: Fiber connections of the subthalamic region and the centromedian nucleus of the thalamus, *Brain,* **69**:195, 1946.

Globus, J. H.: *Practical Neuroanatomy,* Wood, Baltimore, 1937.

Grant, F. C., and L. M. Weinberger: Experiences with intramedullary tractotomy. I. Relief of facial pain and summary of operative results, *Arch. Surg.,* **42**:681, 1941.

Grant, J. C. B.: *An Atlas of Human Anatomy,* 6th ed., Williams & Wilkins, Baltimore, 1972.

Gray, H., in C. M. Goss (ed.), *Anatomy of the Human Body,* 29th ed., Lea & Febiger, Philadelphia, 1973.

Greep, R., and L. Weiss (eds.): *Histology,* 3d ed., McGraw-Hill, New York, 1973.

Greischeimer, E. M.: *Physiology and Anatomy,* 7th ed., Lippincott, Philadelphia, 1955.

Grundfest, H., and B. Campbell: Origin, conduction and termination of the spino-cerebellar tract in cats, *J. Neurophysiol.,* **5**:275, 1942.

Ham, A. W.: *Histology,* 7th ed., Lippincott, Philadelphia, 1974.

Hamilton, W. J., J. B. Boyd, and H. W. Mossman: *Human Embryology,* 3d ed., Williams & Wilkins, Baltimore, 1962.

Hammond, W. S., and C. L. Yntema: Depletion of the thoraco-lumbar sympathetic system following removal of neural crest in the chick, *J. Comp. Neurol.,* **86**:237, 1947.

Hardesty, I.: On the development and nature of neuroglia, *Am. J. Anat.,* **3**:229, 1904.

Hardesty, I.: On the occurrence of the sheath cells and nature of axon sheaths in the central nervous system, *Am. J. Anat.,* **4**:329, 1905.

Harris, G. W.: Neural control of the pituitary gland, *Physiol. Rev.,* **28**:139, 1948.

Harrison, F.: The hypothalamus and sleep, *Res. Publ. Assoc. Res. Nerv. Ment. Dis.,* **20**:635, 1940.

Hartridge, H.: *Recent Advances in the Physiology of Vision,* McGraw-Hill, New York, 1950.

Hausman, L.: Pure flaccid hemiplegia uncomplicated by sensory defect, *Trans. Am. Neurol. Assoc.,* **65**:217, 1939.

Haymaker, W.: *Bing's Local Diagnosis in Neurological Diseases,* 14th ed., Mosby, St. Louis, 1956.

Haymaker, W., E. Anderson, and W. J. H. Nauta: *The Hypothalamus,* Charles C. Thomas, Springfield, Ill., 1969.

Haymaker, W. E., and M. B. Woodhall: *Peripheral Nerve Injuries: Principals of Diagnosis,* Saunders, Philadelphia, 1953.

Head, H.: *Studies in Neurology,* Oxford, New York, 1920.

Hebb, D. O., and W. Penfield: Human behavior after extensive bilateral removal from the frontal lobes, *Arch. Neurol. Psychiatry,* **44**:421, 1940.

Heimer, L., and W. J. H. Nauta: The hypothalamic distribution of the stria terminalis in the rat, *Brain Res.,* **13**:284, 1969.

Herrick, C. J.: The functions of the olfactory parts of the cerebral cortex, *Proc. Natl. Acad. Sci. U.S.A.,* **19**:7, 1933.

Herter, C. A., and L. P. Clarke: *Diagnosis of Organic Nervous Diseases,* Putnam, New York, 1907.

Hertwig, R.: *A Manual of Zoology,* Holt, New York, 1905.

Hess, W. R.: *The Functional Organization of the Diencephalon,* Grune & Stratton, New York, 1958.

Hilton, J.: *On Rest and Pain: A Course of Lectures,* Wood, Baltimore, 1879.

Hines, M.: The anterior border of the monkey's motor cortex and the production of spasticity, *Am. J. Physiol.,* **116**:76, 1936.

Hines, M.: The motor cortex, *Bull. Johns Hopkins Hosp.,* **60**:313, 1937.

Hines, M.: Control of movements by the cerebral cortex in primates, *Biol. Rev.,* **18**:1, 1943.

Hines, M.: Significance of the precentral motor cortex, in P. C. Bucy (ed.), *The Precentral Motor Cortex,* 2d ed., University of Illinois Press, Urbana, 1949.

His, W., Jr.: Über die Entwickelung des Bauchsympathikus beim Hünchen und Menschen, *Arch. Anat. Physiol. Anat. Ab. Suppl.* S, p. 137, 1897.

His, W., Jr.: *Die Entwickelung des menschlichen Gehirns wahrend der ersten Monate,* vol. 4, p. 176, S. Hirzel Verlag, Leipzig, 1904.

Hochstetter, F.: *Beitrage zur Entwickelungs-geschichte des menschlichen Gehirns,* Teil I, S.1, and Teil II, S.1, Deuticke, Vienna, 1929.

Holmes, G.: The cerebellum of man, *Brain,* **62**:1, 1939.

Holmes, G.: The organization of the visual cortex in man, *Proc. Ry. Soc. Lond. [Biol.],* **132**:348, 1944.

Holmes, G., and W. P. May: On the exact origin of the pyramidal tracts in man and other mammals, *Brain,* **32**:1, 1909.

Hornykiewicz, O.: Dopamine (3-hydroxytyramine) and brain function, *Pharmacol. Rev.,* **18**:925, 1966.

Huber, G. C.: The reptilian optic tectum, *J. Comp. Neurol.,* **57**:57, 1933.

Huber, G. C., E. C. Crosby, R. T. Woodburne, L. A. Gillilan, J. O. Brown, and B. Tamthai: The mammalian midbrain and isthmus region. I. The nuclear pattern, *J. Comp. Neurol.,* **78**:129, 1943.

Ingram, W. R.: Nuclear organization and chief connections of the primate hypothalamus, *Res. Publ. Assoc. Res. Nerv. Ment. Dis.,* **20**:195, 1940.

Ingvar, S.: Studies in neurology. I. The phylogenetic continuity of the central nervous system. II. On cerebellar function, *Bull. Johns Hopkins Hosp.,* **43**:315, 1928.

Isaacson, R. L., and K. H. Pribram (eds.): *The Hippocampus,* 2 vols., Plenum, New York, 1975.

Jacobsen, C. F.: Influence of motor and premotor area lesions upon the retention of skilled movements in monkeys and chimpanzees, *Res. Publ. Assoc. Res. Nerv. Ment. Dis.,* **13**:225, 1934.

Jasper, H. H.: Diffuse projection systems: The integrative action of the thalamic reticular system, *Electroencephalogr. Clin. Neurophysiol.,* **1**:405, 1949.

Jasper, H. H.: *Reticular Formation of the Brain,* Little, Brown, Boston, 1958.

Jones, E. G., and R. Y. Leavitt: Retrograde axonal transport and the demonstration of non-specific projections to the cerebral cortex and striatum from thalamic intralaminar nuclei in the cat, rat and monkey, *J. Comp. Neurol.,* **154**:349, 1974.

Jones, E. G., and T. P. S. Powell: The ipsilateral cortical connexions of the somatic sensory areas in the cat, *Brain Res.,* **9**:71, 1968.

Jones, E. G., and T. P. S. Powell: Connexions of the somatic sensory cortex of the rhesus monkey. I.

Ipsilateral cortical connexions, *Brain,* **92**:477, 1969.

Jones, E. G., and T. P. S. Powell: Connexions of the somatic sensory cortex of the rhesus monkey. II. Contralateral cortical connexions, *Brain,* **92**:717, 1969.

Jones, E. G., and T. P. S. Powell: Connexions of the somatic sensory cortex in the rhesus monkey. III. Thalamic connexions. *Brain,* **93**:37, 1970.

Jones, I. H.: Vestibular experiences, *Laryngoscope,* **59**:354, 1949.

Jones, T., and W. C. Shepard: *A Manual of Surgical Anatomy,* Saunders, Philadelphia, 1945.

Jordan, H. E.: *A Textbook of Histology,* 9th ed., Appleton-Century-Crofts, New York, 1952.

Jouvet, M.: Neurophysiology of the states of sleep, *Physiol. Rev.,* **47**:117, 1967.

Jordan, H. E., and J. E. Kindred: *Textbook of Embryology,* 5th ed., Appleton-Century-Crofts, New York, 1948.

Judovich, B. D., and W. Bates: *Segmental Neuralgia in Painful Syndromes,* Davis, Philadelphia, 1944.

Kappers, C. V. A., G. C. Huber, and E. C. Crosby: *The Comparative Anatomy of the Nervous System of Vertebrates,* Macmillan, New York, 1936.

Keibel, F., and F. P. Mall: *Manual of Human Embryology,* Lippincott, Philadelphia, 1910.

Keiller, W.: *Nerve Tracts of the Brain Stem and Cord,* Macmillan, New York, 1927.

Kemp, J. M., and T. P. S. Powell: The corticostriate projection in the monkey, *Brain,* **93**:525, 1970.

Kievit, J., and H. G. J. M. Kuypers: Basal forebrain and hypothalamic connections to frontal and parietal cortex in the rhesus monkey, *Science,* **187**:660, 1975.

Kimber, D. C., C. E. Gray, C. E. Stackpole, and L. C. Leavell: *Textbook of Anatomy and Physiology,* 13th ed., Macmillan, New York, 1957.

Kingsbury, B. F.: The fundamental plan of the vertebrate brain, *J. Comp. Neurol.,* **34**:461, 1922.

Kluver, H., and P. C. Bucy: "Psychic blindness" and other symptoms following bilateral temporal lobectomy in rhesus monkeys, *Am. J. Physiol.,* **119**:352, 1937.

Kodama, S.: Über die sogenannten Basalganglien, *Schweiz, Arch. Neurol. Psychiatr.,* **18**:179, 1926.

Kremer, W. F.: Autonomic and somatic reactions

induced by stimulation of the cingular gyrus in dogs, *J. Neurophysiol.,* **10**:371, 1947.

Krieg, W. J. S.: *Functional Neuroanatomy,* McGraw-Hill, New York, 1953.

Krieg, W. J. S.: Connections of the cerebral cortex of the monkey, *Symp. Biol. Hung.,* **5**:177, 1965.

Kuntz, A.: *The Neuroanatomic Basis of Surgery of the Autonomic Nervous System,* Charles C. Thomas, Springfield, Ill., 1949.

Kuntz, A.: *A Textbook of Neuroanatomy,* 5th ed., Lea & Febiger, Philadelphia, 1950.

Kurtz, S. M.: *Electron Microscopic Anatomy,* Academic, New York, 1964.

Kuypers, H. G. J. M., and D. G. Lawrence: Cortical projections to the red nucleus and the brain stem in the rhesus monkey, *Brain Res.,* **4**:151, 1967.

Langley, L. L., I. R. Telford, and J. B. Christenson: *Dynamic Anatomy and Physiology,* 4th ed., McGraw-Hill, New York, 1974.

Langworthy, O. R.: Development of behavior patterns and myelinization of the human fetus and infant, *Carnegie Contrib. Embryol.,* **34**(228):145, 1933.

Lanz, T., von, and W. Wachsmith: *Praktische Anatomie,* Springer-Verlag, Berlin, 1935.

Larsell, O.: The cerebellum: A review and interpretation, *Arch. Neurol. Psychiatry,* **38**:580, 1937.

Larsell, O.: *Anatomy of the Nervous System,* 2d ed., Appleton-Century-Crofts, New York, 1951.

Lassek, A. M.: The human pyramidal tract. II. A numerical investigation of the Betz cells of the motor area, *Arch. Neurol. Psychiatry,* **44**:718, 1940.

Lassek, A. M.: The pyramidal tract: Basic considerations of corticospinal neurons, *Res. Publ. Assoc. Res. Nerv. Ment. Dis.* **27**:106, 1947.

Levin, P. M.: Efferent fibers, in P. C. Bucy (ed.), *The Premotor Cortex,* 2d ed., University of Illinois Press, Urbana, 1949.

Levin, P. M., and F. K. Bradford: The exact origin of the corticospinal tract in the monkey, *J. Comp. Neurol.,* **68**:411, 1938.

Lewis, D., and W. E. Dandy: The course of the nerve fibers transmitting the sensation of taste, *Arch. Surg.,* **21**:249, 1930.

Lewis, T.: *Pain,* Macmillan, New York, 1942.

Lindsley, D. B.: Brainstem influences on spinal motor activity, *Res. Publ. Assoc. Res. Nerv. Ment. Dis.,* **30**:174, 1952.

List, C. F.: Intraspinal epidermoids, dermoids and dermal sinuses, *Surg. Gynecol. Obstet.,* **73**:525, 1941.

Livingston, W. K.: *The Clinical Aspects of Visceral Neurology,* Charles C Thomas, Springfield, Ill., 1935.

Livingston, W. K.: *Pain Mechanisms,* Macmillan, New York, 1943.

Lloyd, D. P. C.: Functional organization of the spinal cord, *Physiol. Rev.,* **24**:1, 1944.

Lloyd, D. P. C.: Facilitation and inhibition of spinal motor neurons, *J. Neurophysiol.,* **9**:421, 1946.

Lloyd, D. P. C., and H.-T. Chang: Afferent fibers in muscle nerves, *J. Neurophysiol.,* **11**:199, 1948.

Lorente de Nó, R.: Studies on the structure of the cerebral cortex. I. The area entorhinalis, *J. Psychol. Neurol.,* **45**:381, 1933.

Lorente de Nó, R.: Studies on the structure of the cerebral cortex: Continuation of study of ammonic system, *J. Psychol. Neurol.,* **46**:113, 1934.

Lorente de Nó, R.: Cerebral cortex: Architecture, intracortical connections, motor projections, in J. F. Fulton (ed.), *Physiology of the Nervous System,* 3d ed., Oxford, New York, 1949.

McCulloch, W. S.: The functional organization of the cerebral cortex, *Physiol. Rev.,* **24**:390, 1944.

McCulloch, W. S.: Modes of functional organization of the cerebral cortex, *Fed. Proc.,* **6**:448, 1947.

McCulloch, W. S.: Some connections of the frontal lobe established by physiological neuronography, *Res. Publ. Assoc. Res. Nerv. Ment. Dis.,* **27**:95, 1948.

McCulloch, W. S.: Cortico-cortical connections, in P. C. Bucy (ed.), *The Precentral Motor Cortex,* 2d ed., University of Illinois Press, Urbana, 1949.

McCulloch, W. S., and H. W. Garol: Cortical origin and distribution of corpus callosum and anterior commissure in the monkey, *J. Neurophysiol.,* **4**:555, 1941.

McCulloch, W. S., C. Graf, and H. W. Magoun: A cortico-bulbo-reticular pathway from area 4s, *J. Neurophysiol.,* **9**:127, 1946.

McCulloch, W. S., and E. Henneman: The projection of area 19 to the reticular formation, *Fed. Proc.,* **7**:79, 1948.

MacDonnell, M. F., and J. P. Flynn: Attack elicited by stimulation of the thalamus and adjacent structures of cats, *Behaviour,* **31**:185, 1968.

McLardy, T.: The thalamic projection to frontal cortex in man, *J. Neurol. Neurosurg. Psychiatry,* N.S., **13**:198, 1950.

MacLean, P. D.: Psychosomatic disease and the "visceral brain": Recent developments bearing on the Papez theory of emotion, *Psychosom. Med.,* **11**:338, 1949.

MacLean, P. D.: Limbic system and emotional behavior, *AMA Arch. Neurol. Psychol.,* **73**:130, 1955.

Magoun, H. W.: Descending connections from the hypothalamus, *Res. Publ. Assoc. Res. Nerv. Ment. Dis.,* **20**:270, 1940.

Magoun, H. W.: Bulbar inhibition and facilitation of motor activity, *Science,* **100**:549, 1949.

Magoun, H. W.: Caudal and cephalic influences of the brainstem reticular formation, *Physiol. Rev.,* **30**:459, 1950.

Magoun, H. W., D. Atlas, W. K. Hare, and S. W. Ranson: The afferent path of the pupillary light reflex in the monkey, *Brain,* **59**:234, 1936.

Magoun, H. W., and L. E. Beaton: The salivatory motor nucleus in the monkey, *Am. J. Physiol.,* **136**:720, 1942.

Magoun, H. W., and R. Rhines: An inhibitory mechanism in the bulbar reticular formation, *J. Neurophysiol.,* **9**:165, 1946.

Magoun, H. W., and R. Rhines: *Spasticity: The Stretch-reflex and Extrapyramidal Systems,* Charles C Thomas, Springfield, Ill., 1947.

Marburg, O.: *Mikroskopisch-topographischer Atlas des menschlichen Zentralnervensystems,* Deuticke, Leipzig, 1910.

Marburg, O.: Modern views regarding the anatomy and physiology of the vestibular tracts, Laryngoscope, **49**:631, 1939.

Marburg, O.: The structure and fiber connections of the human habenula, *J. Comp. Neurol.,* **80**:211, 1944.

Massion, J.: The mammalian red nucleus, *Physiol. Rev.,* **47**:383, 1967.

Maximow, A. A., and W. Bloom: *A Textbook of Histology,* 7th ed., Saunders, Philadelphia, 1957.

Meibach, R. C., and A. Siegel: Efferent connections of the septal nuclei in the rat: An analysis utilizing retrograde and anterograde transport methods, *Brain Res.,* **119**:1, 1977.

Meibach, R. C., and A. Siegel: Efferent connection of the hippocampal formation in the rat, *Brain Res.,* **124**:197, 1977.

Melzack, R., and P. D. Wall: Pain mechanism: A new theory, *Science,* **150**:971, 1965.

Merrillees, N. C. K., G. Burnstock, and M. E. Holman: Correlation of fine structure and physiology of the innervation of smooth muscle in the guinea pig vas deferens, *J. Cell Biol.,* **19**:529, 1963.

Merzenich, M. M., P. L. Knight, and G. L. Roth: Cochleotopic organization of the primary auditory cortex in the cat, *Brain Res.,* **63**:343, 1973.

Mettler, F. A.: Relation between pyramidal and extrapyramidal function, *Res. Publ. Assoc. Res. Nerv. Ment. Dis.,* **21**:150, 1942.

Mettler, F. A.: Fiber connections of the corpus striatum of the monkey and baboon, *J. Comp. Neurol.,* **82**:169, 1945.

Mettler, F. A.: *Neuroanatomy,* 2d ed., Mosby, St. Louis, 1948.

Mettler, F. A.: The nonpyramidal motor projections from the frontal cerebral cortex, *Res. Publ. Assoc. Res. Nerv. Ment. Dis.,* **27**:162, 1948.

Mettler, F. A., and C. C. Mettler: Role of the neostriatum, *Am. J. Physiol.,* **133**:594, 1941.

Meyer, A., E. Beck, and T. McLardy: Prefrontal leucotomy: A neuroanatomical report, *Brain,* **70**:18, 1947.

Meyer, M.: Study of efferent connexions of the frontal lobe in the human brain after leucotomy, *Brain,* **72**:265, 1949.

Meyers, R., D. B. Sweeney, and J. T. Schwidde: Hemiballismus: Etiology and surgical treatment, *J. Neurol. Neurosurg. Psychiatry,* N.S., **13**:115, 1950.

Millhouse, O. E.: A golgi study of the descending medial forebrain bundle, *Brain Res.,* **15**:341, 1969.

Monakow, C. von: Biologisches und Morphogenetisches über die Mikrocephalia vera, *Schweiz. Arch. Neurol. Psychiatr.,* **18**:191, 1926.

Moniz, E.: Tentatives operatoire dans le traitement de certaines psychoses, Masson, Paris, 1936.

Monrad-Krohn, G. H.: *Clinical Examination of the Nervous System,* 7th ed., Hoeber-Harper, Hagerstown, Md., 1938.

Morgane, P. J., and J. Panksepp (eds.): *Handbook of the Hypothalamus,* Dekker, New York, 1978.

Moruzzi, G., and H. W. Magoun: Brain stem reticular formation and activation of the EEG, *Electro-encephalogr. Clin. Neurophysiol.,* **1**:455, 1949.

Mountcastle, V. B.: *Medical Physiology,* 13th ed., Mosby, St. Louis, 1974.

Murphy, J. P., and E. Gellhorn: The influence of hypothalamic stimulation on cortically induced movements and on action potentials of the cortex, *J. Neurophysiol.,* **8**:341, 1945.

Murphy, J. P., and E. Gellhorn: Further investigations on diencephalic-cortical relations and their significance for the problem of emotion, *J. Neurophysiol.,* **8**:431, 1945.

Nathan, P. W., and J. W. A. Turner: Efferent pathway for pupillary contraction, *Brain,* **65**:343, 1942.

Nauta, W. J. H.: Hippocampal projections and related neural pathways to the midbrain in the cat, *Brain,* **81**:319, 1958.

Nauta, W. J. H.: Neural associations of the amygdaloid complex in the monkey, *Brain,* **85**:505, 1962.

Nauta, W. J. H.: The problem of the frontal lobe: A reinterpretation, *J. Psychiatr. Res.,* **8**:167, 1971.

Nauta, W. J. H., and H. G. J. M. Kuypers: Some ascending pathways in the brainstem reticular formation, in H. Jasper et al., *Reticular Formation of the Brain: Henry Ford Hospital Symposium,* Little, Brown, Boston, 1958.

Nauta, W. J. H., and W. R. Mehler: Projections from the lentiform nucleus in the monkey, *Brain Res.,* **1**:3, 1966.

Neilson, J. M.: *Memory and Amnesia,* San Lucas Press, Los Angeles, Calif., 1958.

Netter, F. H.: *The Central Nervous System,* Ciba, Summit, N.J., 1950.

Newman, H. H.: *Vertebrate Zoology,* Macmillan, New York, 1921.

Niemer, W. T., and H. W. Magoun: Reticulospinal tracts influencing motor activity, *J. Comp. Neurol.,* **87**:367,1947.

Noback, C. R. and R. J. Demarest: *The Human Nervous System: Basic Principles of Neurology,* 2d ed., McGraw-Hill, New York, 1975.

Noback, C. R. and R. J. Demarest: *The Nervous System: Introduction and Review,* 2d ed., McGraw-Hill, New York, 1977.

Noback, C. R., and L. K. Laemle: Structural and functional aspects of the visual pathways of primates, in C. R. Noback and W. Montagna (eds.), *The Primate Brain: Advances in Primatol-ogy,* vol. I, Appleton-Century-Crofts, New York, 1970.

Nulsen, F. E., S. P. W. Black, and C. G. Drake: Inhibition and facilitation of motor activity by the anterior cerebellum, *Fed. Proc.,* **7**:86, 1948.

Nyberg-Hansen, R.: Sites and mode of termination of reticulospinal fibers in the cat, *J. Comp. Neurol.,* **124**:71, 1965.

Olszewski, J.: The cytoarchitecture of the human reticular formation, in J. F. Delafresnaye (ed.): *Brain Mechanisms and Consciousness,* Blackwell Scientific, Oxford, 1954.

Oscarsson, O.: Functional organization of the spino- and cuneocerebellar tracts, *Physiol. Rev.,* **45**:495, 1965.

Palay, S. L., and Chan-Palay, V.: *Cerebellar Cortex: Cytology and Organization,* Springer-Verlag, Berlin, 1974.

Papez, J. W.: Reticulospinal tracts in the cat: Marchi method, *J. Comp. Neurol.,* **41**:365, 1926.

Papez, J. W.: *Comparative Neurology,* Crowell-Collier, New York, 1929.

Papez, J. W.: A proposed mechanism of emotion, *Arch. Neurol. Psychiatry,* **38**:725, 1937.

Papez, J. W.: A summary of fiber connections of the basal ganglia with each other and with other portions of the brain, *Res. Publ. Assoc. Res. Nerv. Ment. Dis.,* **21**:21, 1942.

Papez, J. W., and W. A. Stotler: Connections of the red nucleus, *Arch. Neurol. Psychiatry,* **44**:776, 1940.

Parker, H. L.: *Clinical Studies in Neurology,* Charles C Thomas, Springfield, Ill., 1956.

Patten, B. M.: *Human Embryology,* 3d ed., McGraw-Hill, New York, 1968.

Patton, H. D., and T. C. Rugh: The relation of the foot of the pre- and postcentral gyrus to taste in the monkey and chimpanzee, *Fed. Proc.,* **5**:79, 1946.

Peck, S. R.: *Atlas of Human Anatomy for the Artist,* Oxford, New York, 1956.

Peele, T. L.: Cytoarchitecture of individual parietal areas in the monkey and the distribution of efferent fibers, *J. Comp. Neurol.,* **77**:693, 1942.

Peele, T. L.: *The Neuroanatomic Basis for Clinical Neurology,* 3d ed., McGraw-Hill, New York, 1977.

Penfield, W.: The cerebral cortex and consciousness, *Harvey Lect.,* **32**:35, 1936.

Penfield, W.: Some observations on the cerebral

cortex of man, *Proc. Ry. Soc. Lond. [Biol.]*, **134**:329, 1947.

Penfield, W.: Symposium on gyrectomy. I. Bilateral frontal gyrectomy and postoperative intelligence, *Res. Publ. Assoc. Res. Nerv. Ment. Dis.*, **27**:519, 1948.

Penfield, W., and E. Boldrey: Somatic motor and sensory representation in the cerebral cortex of man as studied by electrical stimulation, *Brain*, **60**:389, 1937.

Penfield, W., and T. C. Erickson: *Epilepsy and Cerebral Localization: A study of the Mechanism, Treatment and Prevention of Epileptic Seizures*, Charles C Thomas, Springfield, Ill., 1941.

Penfield, W., and J. P. Evans: Functional defects produced by cerebral lobectomies, *Res. Publ. Assoc. Res. Nerv. Ment. Dis.*, **13**:352, 1934.

Penfield, W., and B. Milner: Memory deficit produced by bilateral lesions in the hippocampal zone, *Arch. Neurol. Psychiatry*, **79**:475, 1958.

Penfield, W., and T. Rasmussen: Vocalization and arrest of speech, *Arch. Neurol. Psychiatry*, **61**:21, 1949.

Penfield, W., and T. Rasmussen: *The Cerebral Cortex of Man: A Clinical Study of Localization of Function*, Macmillan, New York, 1950.

Peters, A., S. L. Palay, and H. deF. Webster: *The Fine Structure of the Nervous System*, Saunders, Philadelphia, 1976.

Petr, R., L. B. Holden, and J. Jirout: The efferent intercortical connections of the superficial cortex of the temporal lobe, *J. Neuropathol. Exp. Neurol.*, **8**:100, 1949.

Petras, J. M.: Some efferent connections of the motor and somatosensory cortex of simian primates and Felid, Canid and Procyonid carnivores, *Ann. N.Y. Acad. Sci.*, **167**:469, 1969.

Pfaff, D., and M. Keiner: Atlas of estradiol-concentrating cells in the central nervous system of the female rat, *J. Comp. Neurol.*, **151**:121, 1973.

Pickel, V. M., M. Segal, and F. E. Bloom: A radiographic study of the efferent pathways of the nucleus locus ceruleus, *J. Comp. Neurol.*, **155**:15, 1974.

Pitts, R. F.: The respiratory center and its descending pathways, *J. Comp. Neurol.*, **72**:605, 1940.

Polyac, S. L.: *The Retina*, University of Chicago Press, Chicago, 1941.

Purpura, D. P., and M. D. Yahr: *The Thalamus*, Columbia, New York, 1966.

Putnam, T. J.: Studies on the central visual system. IV. The details of the organization of the geniculostriate system in man, *Arch. Neurol. Psychiatry*, **16**:638, 1926.

Raisman, G.:The connexions of the septum, *Brain*, **89**:317, 1966.

Raisman, G.: Neural connexions of hypothalamus, *Br. Med. Bull.*, **22**:197, 1966.

Ramon-Moliner, E., and W. J. H. Nauta: The isodendritic core of the brainstem, *J. Comp. Neurol.*, **126**:311, 1966.

Ranson, S. W.: Regulation of body temperature, *Res. Publ. Assoc. Res. Nerv. Ment. Dis.*, **20**:342, 1940.

Ranson, S. W., and P. R. Billingsley: Afferent spinal paths and the vasomotor reflexes: Studies in the vasomotor reflex arcs IV, *Am. J. Physiol.*, **42**:16, 1916.

Ranson, S. W., and S. L. Clark: *The Anatomy of the Nervous System*, 10th ed., Saunders, Philadelphia, 1959.

Ranson, S. W., and H. W. Magoun: The hypothalamus, *Ergeb. Physiol.*, **41**:56, 1939.

Ranson, S. W., and S. W. Ranson, Jr.: Efferent fibers of the corpus striatum, *Res. Publ. Assoc. Res. Nerv. Ment. Dis.*, **21**:69, 1942.

Rasmussen, A. T.: *The Principal Nervous Pathways*, 4th ed., Macmillan, New York, 1952.

Rasmussen, A. T., and W. T. Peyton: The location of the lateral spinothalamic tract in the brain stem of man, *Surgery*, **10**:699, 1941.

Rasmussen, A. T., and W. T. Peyton: The course and termination of the medial lemniscus in man, *J. Comp. Neurol.*, **88**:411, 1948.

Rasmussen, G. L.: The olivary peduncle and other projections of the superior olivary complex, *J. Comp. Neurol.*, **84**:141, 1946.

Rasmussen, G. L.: Further observations on the termination of the efferent cochlear bundle, *Anat. Rec.*, **106**:69, 1950.

Rasmussen, G. L.: Further observations of the efferent cochlear bundle, *J. Comp. Neurol.*, **99**:61, 1953.

Ray, B. S., J. C. Hinsey, and W. A. Geohegan: Observations on the distribution of the sympathetic nerves to the pupil and upper extremity as determined by stimulation of anterior roots in man, *Ann. Surg.*, **118**:647, 1943.

Reeves, A. G., and F. Plum: Hyperphagia, rage and dementia accompanying a ventromedial hypothalamic neoplasm, *Arch. Neurol.*, **20**:616, 1969.

Rhines, R., and H. W. Magoun: Brain stem facilitation of cortical motor response, *J. Neurophysiol.*, **9**:219, 1946.

Richardson, K. C.: The fine structure of the nerve endings in smooth muscle of the rat vas deferens, *J. Anat.*, **96**:427, 1962.

Richardson, K. C.: The fine structure of the albino rabbit iris with special reference to the identification of adrenergic and cholinergic nerves and nerve endings in its intrinsic muscles, *Am. J. Anat.*, **114**:173, 1964.

Riley, H. A.: *An Atlas of the Basal Ganglia, Brain Stem and Spinal Cord*, Williams & Wilkins, Baltimore, 1943.

Rinvik, E., and F. Walberg: Demonstration of a somatotopically arranged cortico-rubral projection in the cat: An experimental study with silver methods, *J. Comp. Neurol.*, **120**:393, 1963.

Robinson, M. F., W. Freeman, and J. W. Watts: Personality changes after psychosurgery, *Dig. Neurol. Psychiatry Inst. Living*, **17**:558, 1949.

Rose, J. E., and C. N. Woolsey: Organization of the mammalian thalamus and its relationship to the cerebral cortex, *Electroencephalogr. Clin. Neurophysiol.*, **1**:391, 1949.

Rossi, G. F., and A. Zanchetti: The brain stem reticular formation: Anatomy and physiology, *Arch. Ital. Biol.*, **95**:239, 1957.

Rouvière, H.: *Atlas aide-mémoire d'anatomie*, Masson, Paris, 1947.

Ruch, T. C., and H. D. Patton: *Physiology and Biophysics*, 19th ed., Saunders, Philadelphia, 1965.

Rylander, G.: Personality analysis before and after frontal lobotomy, *Res. Publ. Assoc. Res. Nerv. Ment. Dis.*, **27**:691, 1948.

Sachs, E., J., S. J. Brendler, and J. F. Fulton: The orbital gyri, *Brain*, **72**:227, 1949.

Saunders, R. L. de C. H., W. H. Feindel, and V. R. Carvalho: X-ray microscopy of the blood vessels of the human brain, pt. I, *Med. Biol. Illus.*, **15**:108, 1965.

Saunders, R. L. de C. H., W. H. Feindel, and V. R. Carvalho: X-ray microscopy of the blood vessels of the human brain, pt. II, *Med. Biol. Illus.*, **15**:234, 1965.

Scarff, J. F.: Primary cortical centers for movements of upper and lower extremity in man: Observations based on electrical stimulation, *Arch. Neurol. Psychiatry*, **44**:243, 1940.

Schaeffer, J. P., (ed.): *Morris' Human Anatomy*, 11th ed., McGraw-Hill, New York, 1953.

Scheibel, M. E., and A. B. Scheibel: Structural substrates for integrative patterns in the brainstem reticular core, in *The Reticular Formation of the Brain*, Henry Ford Hospital International Symposium, Little, Brown, Boston, 1958.

Scheibel, M. E., and A. B. Scheibel: The organization of the ventral anterior nucleus of the thalamus: A Golgi study, *Brain Res.*, **1**:250, 1966.

Scheibel, M. E., and A. B. Scheibel: Anatomical basis of attention mechanisms in vertebrate brains, in G. C. Quarton et al. (eds.), *The Neurosciences*, Rockefeller University Press, New York, 1967.

Schreiner, L. H., and A. Kling: Effects of castration on hypersexual behavior induced by rhinencephalic injury in the cat, *Arch. Neurol. Psychiatry*, **72**:180, 1954.

Schreiner, L. H., D. B. Lindsey, and H. W. Magoun: Role of the brain stem facilitatory systems in the maintenance of spasticity, *J. Neurophysiol.*, **12**:207, 1949.

Schwartz, H. G., and G. Weddell: Observations on the pathways transmitting the sensation of taste, *Brain*, **61**:99, 1938.

Seddon, H. J., P. B. Medawar, and H. Smith: Rate of regeneration of peripheral nerves in man, *J. Physiol. (Lond.)*, **102**:191, 1943.

Seletz, E.: *Surgery of Peripheral Nerves*, Charles C Thomas, Springfield, Ill., 1951.

Shapiro, H. H.: *Maxillofacial Anatomy*, Lippincott, Philadelphia, 1954.

Sheehan, D.: The autonomic nervous system, *Ann. Rev. Physiol.*, **3**:399, 1941.

Sheps, J. G.: The nuclear configuration and cortical connections of the human thalamus, *J. Comp. Neurol.*, **83**:1, 1945.

Sherrington, L. H.: *The Integrative Action of the Nervous System*, Yale, New Haven, Conn., 1906.

Siegel, A., and J. Chabora: Effects of electrical stimulation of the cingulate gyrus upon attack behavior elicited from the hypothalamus in the cat, *Brain Res.*, **32**:169, 1971.

Siegel, A., and H. Edinger: Hypothalamic control

of aggression and rage, in P. J. Morgane and J. Panksepp (eds.), *Handbook of the Hypothalamus,* Dekker, New York, 1978.

Siegel, A., H. Edinger, and H. Lowenthal: Effects of electrical stimulation of the medial aspect of the prefrontal cortex upon attack behavior in cats, *Brain Res.,* **66**:467, 1974.

Siegel, A., H. Edinger, and S. Ohgami: The topographical organization of the hippocampal projection to the septal area: A comparative neuroanatomical analysis in the gerbil, rat, rabbit, and cat, *J. Comp. Neurol.,* **157**:359, 1974.

Siegel, A., and J. P. Flynn: Differential effects of stimulation and lesions of the hippocampus and adjacent regions upon attack behavior in cats, *Brain Res.,* **7**:252, 1968.

Siegel, A., and D. Skog: Effects of electrical stimulation of the septum upon attack behavior elicited from the hypothalamus in the cat, *Brain Res.,* **23**:371, 1970.

Siegel, A., R. Troiano, and H. Edinger: The pathway from the mediodorsal nucleus to the hypothalamus in the cat, *Exp. Neurol.,* **41**:569, 1973.

Siegel, A., R. Troiano, and A. Royce: Differential efferent projections of the anterior and posterior cingulate gyrus to the thalamus in the cat, *Exp. Neurol.,* **38**:192, 1973.

Sloan, N., and H. Jasper: Studies on the regulatory functions of the anterior limbic cortex, *Electroencephalogr. Clin. Neurophysiol.,* **2**:317, 1950.

Smith, W. K.: The functional significance of the rostral cingular cortex as revealed by its responses to electrical excitation, *J. Neurophysiol.,* **8**:241, 1945.

Smyth, G. E.: The systematization and central connections of the spinal tract and nucleus of the trigeminal nerve, *Brain,* **62**:41, 1939.

Snider, R. S.: Recent contributions to the anatomy and physiology of the cerebellum, *Arch. Neurol. Psychiatry,* **64**:196, 1950.

Snider, R. S., W. S. McCulloch, and H. W. Magoun: A cerebello-bulboreticular pathway for suppression, *J. Neurophysiol.,* **12**:325, 1949.

Snider, R. S., H. W. Magoun, and W. S. McCulloch: A suppressor cerebello-bulbo-reticular pathway from the anterior lobe and paramedian lobules, *Fed. Proc.,* **6**:207, 1947.

Snider, R. S., and A. Stowell: Receiving areas of the tactile, auditory, and visual systems in the cerebellum, *J. Neurophysiol.,* **7**:331, 1944.

Spalteholz, W.: *Hand-Atlas of Human Anatomy,* 7th ed., vol. 3, Lippincott, Philadelphia, 1955.

Spiegel, E. A.: Labyrinth and cortex: Electroencephalogram in stimulation of the labyrinth, *Arch. Neurol. Psychiatry,* **31**:469, 1934.

Spiegel, E. A., and I. Sommer: *Neurology of the Eye, Ear, Nose and Throat,* Grune & Stratton, New York, 1944.

Spofford, W. R.: *Neuroanatomy,* Oxford, New York, 1942.

Starzl, T. E., and H. W. Magoun: Organization of the diffuse thalamic projection system, *J. Neurophysiol.,* **14**:133, 1951.

Streeter, G. L.: Factors involved in the formation of the filum terminale, *Am. J. Anat.,* **25**:1, 1919.

Strong, O. S., and A. Elwyn: *Human Neuroanatomy,* 5th ed., Williams & Wilkins, Baltimore, 1964.

Sugar, O., L. V. Amador, and B. Griponissiotes: Corticocortical connections of the cortex buried in intraparietal and principal sulci of monkey, *J. Neuropathol. Exp. Neurol.,* **9**:430, 1950.

Sugar, O., J. D. French, and J. G. Chusid: Corticocortical connections of the superior surface of the temporal operculum in the monkey, *J. Neurophysiol.,* **11**:175, 1948.

Sugar, O., R. Petr, L. V. Amador, and B. Griponis: Corticocortical connections of the walls of the superior temporal sulcus of the monkey, *J. Neuropathol. Exp. Neurol.,* **9**:179, 1950.

Sunderland, S.: The projection of the cerebral cortex on the pons and cerebellum in the macaque monkey, *J. Anat.,* **74**:201, 1940.

Sutin, J.: The periventicular stratum of the hypothalamus, *Int. Rev. Neurobiol.,* **9**:263, 1966.

Szabo, J.: Topical distribution of the striatal efferents in the monkey, *Exp. Neurol.,* **5**:21, 1962.

Szentagothai, J., B. Flerko, B. Mess, and B. Halasz: *Hypothalamic Control of the Anterior Pituitary,* Akademiai Kiado, Budapest, 1968.

Taylor, E. W.: *Case Histories in Neurology,* Leonard, Boston, 1912.

Teitelbaum, P., and A. N. Epstein: The lateral hypothalamic syndrome: Recovery of feeding and drinking after lateral hypothalamic lesions, *Psychol. Rev.,* **69**:74, 1962.

Testut, L., and A. Latarjet: *Traité d'anatomie humaine,* vols. II, III, Doin, Paris, 1948, 1949.

Thorek, P.: *Anatomy in Surgery,* Lippincott, Philadelphia, 1956.

Tilney, F.: *The Brain, from Ape to Man,* Hoeber-Harper, Hagerstown, Md., 1928.

Tilney, F., and L. F. Warren: A contribution to the study of the epiphysis cerebri with an interpretation of the morphological, physiological and clinical evidence, *Am. J. Anat. Memoirs* no. 9, p. 7, 1919.

Toldt, C.: *An Atlas of Human Anatomy,* 2d ed., Macmillan, New York, 1928.

Tongray, J. E., and W. J. S. Kreig: The nuclei of the human thalamus: A comparative approach, *J. Comp. Neurol.,* 85:421, 1946.

Tower, S. S.: The dissociation of cortical excitation from cortical inhibition by pyramidal section and the syndrome of that lesion in the cat, *Brain,* 58:238, 1935.

Tower, S. S.: Pyramidal lesions in the monkey, *Brain,* 63:36, 1940.

Tower, S. S.: The pyramidal tract, in P. C. Bucy (ed.), *The Precentral Motor Cortex,* 2d ed., University of Illinois Press, Urbana, 1949.

Troiano, R., and A. Siegel: The ascending and descending connections of the hypothalamus in the cat, *Exp. Neurol.,* 49:161, 1975.

Ungerstedt, V.: Stereotaxic mapping of the monoamine pathways in the rat brain, *Acta Physiol. Scand. [Suppl.],* 82:1, 1971.

Velasco, M., and D. B. Lindsley: Role of the orbital cortex in the regulation of thalamo-cortical electrical activity, *Science,* 149:1375, 1965.

Villiger, E.: *Brain and Spinal Cord,* McGraw-Hill, New York, 1918.

Vonderahe, A. R.: Anatomic basis of emotion, *Ohio State Med. J.,* 39:325, 1943.

Walberg, F., O. Pompciano, A. Brodal, and J. Jansen: Fastigiovestibular projection in the cat: An experimental study with silver impregnation methods, *J. Comp. Neurol.,* 118:49, 1962.

Wald, G.: Molecular basis of visual excitation, *Science,* 162:230, 1968.

Walker, A. E.: *The Primate Thalamus,* University of Chicago Press, Chicago, 1938.

Walker, A. E.: The spinothalamic tract in man, *Arch. Neurol. Exp. Psychiatry,* 43:284, 1940.

Walshe, F. M. R.: The giant cells of Betz, the motor cortex and the pyramidal tract: A critical review, *Brain,* 65:409, 1942.

Walzl, E. M., and V. Mountcastle: Projection of vestibular nerve to cerebral cortex of the cat, *Am. J. Physiol.,* 159:595, 1949.

Ward, A. A., Jr.: The cingular gyrus: Area 24, *J. Neurophysiol.,* 11:13, 1948.

Ward, A. A., Jr.: The cingulate gyrus and personality, *Res. Publ. Assoc. Res. Nerv. Ment. Dis.,* 27:438, 1948.

Ward, A. A., Jr., and W. S. McCulloch: The projection of the frontal lobe on the hypothalamus, *J. Neurophysiol.,* 10:309, 1947.

Ward, A. A., Jr., J. K. Peden, and O. Sugar: Corticocortical connections in the monkey with special reference to area 6, *J. Neurophysiol.,* 9:453, 1946.

Ward, J. W., and V. LeQuire: Responses elicited by electrical stimulation of the gyrus cinguli in unanaesthetized cats, *Anat. Rec.,* 106:91, 1950.

Warren, J. M., and K. Akert: *Frontal Granular Cortex and Behavior,* McGraw-Hill, New York, 1964.

Wasman, M., and J. P. Flynn: Directed attack elicited from hypothalamus, *Arch. Neurol.,* 6:220, 1962.

Wechsler, I. S.: *A Textbook of Clinical Neurology,* 6th ed., Saunders, Philadelphia, 1947.

Weddell, G., J. A. Harpman, D. G. Lambley, and L. Young: The innervation of the musculature of the tongue, *J. Anat.,* 74:255, 1940.

Wheatley, M. D.: The hypothalamus and affective behavior in cats, *Arch. Neurol. Psychiatry,* 52:296, 1944.

White, J. C., R. H. Smithwick, and F. A. Simeone: *The Autonomic Nervous System,* 3d ed., Macmillan, New York, 1952.

Whitfield, I. C.: *The Auditory Pathway,* Williams & Wilkins, Baltimore, 1967.

Whittier, J. R., and F. A. Mettler: Studies on the subthalamus of the Rhesus monkey. I. Anatomy and fiber connections of the subthalamic nucleus of Luys, *J. Comp. Neurol.,* 90:281, 1949.

Whittier, J. R., and F. A. Mettler: Studies on the subthalamus of the Rhesus monkey. II. Hyperkinesia and other physiologic effects of subthalamic lesions, with special reference to the subthalamic nucleus of Luys, *J. Comp. Neurol.,* 90:319, 1949.

Williams, J. F.: *A Textbook of Anatomy and Physiology,* 2d ed., Saunders, Philadelphia, 1928.

Willis, W. D., and R. G. Grossman: *Medical Neurobiology,* 2d ed., Mosby, St. Louis, 1976.

Woerdeman, M. W.: *Atlas of Human Anatomy,* McGraw-Hill, New York, 1950.

Wolff, H. G.: *Headache and Other Head Pain,* Oxford, New York, 1948.

Woodburne, R. T., E. C. Crosby, and R. E. McCotter: The mammalian midbrain and isthmus regions. II. The fiber connections. A. The relations of the tegmentum of the midbrain with the basal ganglia in *Macaca mulatta, J. Comp. Neurol.,* **85**:67, 1946.

Yacorzynski, G. K., and L. Davis: An experimental study of the functions of the frontal lobes in man, *Psychosom. Med.,* **7**:97, 1945.

Yahr, M. D., and D. P. Purpura (eds.): *Neurophysiological Basis of Normal and Abnormal Motor Activities,* Raven Press, Hewlett, N.Y., 1967.

Yeterian, E. H., and G. W. Van Hoesen: Corticostriate projections in the rhesus monkey. I. The organization of certain cortico-caudate connections, *Brain Res.,* **139**:43, 1978.

Index

Index